Lecture Notes in Computer Science 11623

Commenced Publication in 1973
Founding and Former Series Editors:
Gerhard Goos, Juris Hartmanis, and Jan van Leeuwen

Editorial Board Members

More information about this series at http://www.springer.com/series/7407

Sanjay Misra · Osvaldo Gervasi ·
Beniamino Murgante · Elena Stankova ·
Vladimir Korkhov · Carmelo Torre ·
Ana Maria A. C. Rocha ·
David Taniar · Bernady O. Apduhan ·
Eufemia Tarantino (Eds.)

Computational Science and Its Applications – ICCSA 2019

19th International Conference
Saint Petersburg, Russia, July 1–4, 2019
Proceedings, Part V

 Springer

Editors
Sanjay Misra (iD)
Covenant University
Ota, Nigeria

Beniamino Murgante (iD)
University of Basilicata
Potenza, Italy

Vladimir Korkhov (iD)
Saint Petersburg State University
Saint Petersburg, Russia

Ana Maria A. C. Rocha (iD)
University of Minho
Braga, Portugal

Bernady O. Apduhan
Kyushu Sangyo University
Fukuoka, Japan

Osvaldo Gervasi (iD)
University of Perugia
Perugia, Italy

Elena Stankova (iD)
Saint Petersburg State University
Saint Petersburg, Russia

Carmelo Torre (iD)
Polytechnic University of Bari
Bari, Italy

David Taniar (iD)
Monash University
Clayton, VIC, Australia

Eufemia Tarantino (iD)
Polytechnic University of Bari
Bari, Italy

ISSN 0302-9743   ISSN 1611-3349 (electronic)
Lecture Notes in Computer Science
ISBN 978-3-030-24307-4   ISBN 978-3-030-24308-1 (eBook)
https://doi.org/10.1007/978-3-030-24308-1

LNCS Sublibrary: SL1 – Theoretical Computer Science and General Issues

This Springer imprint is published by the registered company Springer Nature Switzerland AG
The registered company address is: Gewerbestrasse 11, 6330 Cham, Switzerland

Preface

These six volumes (LNCS volumes 11619–11624) consist of the peer-reviewed papers from the 2019 International Conference on Computational Science and Its Applications (ICCSA 2019) held in St. Petersburg, Russia during July 1–4, 2019, in collaboration with the St. Petersburg University, St. Petersburg, Russia.

ICCSA 2019 was a successful event in the International Conferences on Computational Science and Its Applications (ICCSA) series, previously held in Melbourne, Australia (2018), Trieste, Italy (2017), Beijing, China (2016), Banff, Canada (2015), Guimaraes, Portugal (2014), Ho Chi Minh City, Vietnam (2013), Salvador, Brazil (2012), Santander, Spain (2011), Fukuoka, Japan (2010), Suwon, South Korea (2009), Perugia, Italy (2008), Kuala Lumpur, Malaysia (2007), Glasgow, UK (2006), Singapore (2005), Assisi, Italy (2004), Montreal, Canada (2003), and (as ICCS) Amsterdam, The Netherlands (2002) and San Francisco, USA (2001).

Computational science is a main pillar of most of the current research, industrial and commercial activities, and plays a unique role in exploiting ICT innovative technologies. The ICCSA conference series have been providing a venue to researchers and industry practitioners to discuss new ideas, to share complex problems and their solutions, and to shape new trends in computational science.

Apart from the general track, ICCSA 2019 also included 33 workshops, in various areas of computational sciences, ranging from computational science technologies, to specific areas of computational sciences, such as software engineering, security, artificial intelligence, and blockchain technologies. We accepted 64 papers distributed in the five general tracks, 259 in workshops and ten short papers. We would like to show our appreciations to the workshop chairs and co-chairs.

The success of the ICCSA conference series, in general, and ICCSA 2019, in particular, is due to the support of many people: authors, presenters, participants, keynote speakers, workshop chairs, Organizing Committee members, student volunteers, Program Committee members, Advisory Committee members, international liaison chairs, reviewers and people in other various roles. We would like to thank them all.

We also thank our publisher, Springer, for accepting to publish the proceedings, for sponsoring part of the best papers awards and for their kind assistance and cooperation during the editing process.

We cordially invite you to visit the ICCSA website http://www.iccsa.org where you can find all relevant information about this interesting and exciting event.

July 2019

Osvaldo Gervasi
Beniamino Murgante
Sanjay Misra

Welcome to St. Petersburg

Welcome to St. Petersburg, the Venice of the North, the city of three revolutions, creation of czar Peter the Great, the most European city in Russia. ICCSA 2019 was hosted by St. Petersburg State University, during July 1–4, 2019.

St. Petersburg is the second largest city in Russia after Moscow. It is the former capital of Russia and has a lot of attractions related to this role in the past: imperial palaces and parks both in the city center and suburbs, respectable buildings of nobles and state institutions, multitude of rivers and canals with more than 300 bridges of various forms and sizes. Extraordinary history and rich cultural traditions of both imperial Russia and the Soviet Union attracted and inspired many examples of world's greatest architecture, literature, music, and visual art, some of which can be found in the famous Hermitage and State Russian Museum located in the heart of the city. Late June and early July is the season of white nights where the sun sets only for a few hours, and the nighttime is covered with mysterious twilight.

What to do in the city:

- Enjoy the white nights, see the open bridges during the night and cargo ships passing by from Ladoga Lake to the Gulf of Finland and back. Dvortsovy bridge is open at about 1am. Be sure to stay on the correct side of the river when the bridges open!
- Visit Hermitage (Winter palace) and State Russian Museum to see great examples of international and Russian art, and the Kunstkammer, the oldest museum of St. Petersburg founded by Peter the Great.
- Travel to St. Petersburg suburbs Peterhof and Tsarskoe Selo to see imperial palaces and splendid parks, famous Peterhof fountains.
- Eat Russian food: borsch (beetroot soup), pelmeni and vareniki (meat and sweet dumplings), bliny (pancakes), vinegret (beetroot salad), drink kvas and maybe some vodka.
- Walk around and inside the Peter and Paul Fortress, the place where the city began in 1703.
- Visit the Mariinsky Theater for famous Russian ballet and opera.
- Have a boat tour along the Neva River and canals to look at the city from the water.
- Walk along Nevsky Prospect, the main street of the city.
- Climb St. Isaac's Cathedral colonnade to enjoy great city views.
- Go down to the Metro, the city's underground train network with some Soviet-style museum-like stations.
- Pay a visit to the recently renovated Summer Garden, the oldest park of St. Petersburg.
- Visit a new modern open space on the New Holland Island to see modern art exhibitions, performances and just to relax and enjoy sitting on the grass with an ice cream or lemonade during a hot summer day.

St. Petersburg State University is the oldest university in Russia, an actively developing, world-class center of research and education. The university dates back to 1724, when Peter the Great founded the Academy of Sciences and Arts as well as the first Academic University and the university preparatory school in Russia. At present there are over 5,000 academic staff members and more than 30,000 students, receiving education in more than 400 educational programs at 25 faculties and institutes.

The venue of ICCSA is the Faculty of Economics located on Tavricheskaya Street, other faculties and university buildings are distributed all over the city with the main campus located on Vasilievsky Island and the natural science faculties (Mathematics and Mechanics, Applied Mathematics and Control Processes, Physics, Chemistry) located on the campus about 40 kilometers away from the city center in Peterhof.

Elena Stankova
Vladimir Korkhov
Nataliia Kulabukhova

Organization

ICCSA 2019 was organized by St. Petersburg University (Russia), University of Perugia (Italy), University of Basilicata (Italy), Monash University (Australia), Kyushu Sangyo University (Japan), University of Minho, (Portugal).

Honorary General Chairs

Antonio Laganà	University of Perugia, Italy
Norio Shiratori	Tohoku University, Japan
Kenneth C. J. Tan	Sardina Systems, Estonia

General Chairs

Osvaldo Gervasi	University of Perugia, Italy
Elena Stankova	St. Petersburg University, Russia
Bernady O. Apduhan	Kyushu Sangyo University, Japan

Program Committee Chairs

Beniamino Murgante	University of Basilicata, Italy
David Taniar	Monash University, Australia
Vladimir Korkov	St. Petersburg University, Russia
Ana Maria A. C. Rocha	University of Minho, Portugal

International Advisory Committee

Jemal Abawajy	Deakin University, Australia
Dharma P. Agarwal	University of Cincinnati, USA
Rajkumar Buyya	Melbourne University, Australia
Claudia Bauzer Medeiros	University of Campinas, Brazil
Manfred M. Fisher	Vienna University of Economics and Business, Austria
Marina L. Gavrilova	University of Calgary, Canada
Yee Leung	Chinese University of Hong Kong, SAR China

International Liaison Chairs

Ana Carla P. Bitencourt	Universidade Federal do Reconcavo da Bahia, Brazil
Giuseppe Borruso	University of Trieste, Italy
Alfredo Cuzzocrea	ICAR-CNR and University of Calabria, Italy
Maria Irene Falcão	University of Minho, Portugal
Robert C. H. Hsu	Chung Hua University, Taiwan
Tai-Hoon Kim	Hannam University, South Korea
Sanjay Misra	Covenant University, Nigeria

Takashi Naka   Kyushu Sangyo University, Japan
Rafael D. C. Santos   National Institute for Space Research, Brazil
Maribel Yasmina Santos   University of Minho, Portugal

Workshop and Session Organizing Chairs

Beniamino Murgante   University of Basilicata, Italy
Sanjay Misra   Covenant University, Nigeria
Jorge Gustavo Rocha   University of Minho, Portugal

Award Chair

Wenny Rahayu   La Trobe University, Australia

Publicity Committee Chairs

Elmer Dadios   De La Salle University, Philippines
Hong Quang Nguyen   International University (VNU-HCM), Vietnam
Daisuke Takahashi   Tsukuba University, Japan
Shangwang Wang   Beijing University of Posts and Telecommunications,
                                China

Workshop Organizers

Advanced Transport Tools and Methods (A2TM 2019)

Massimiliano Petri   University of Pisa, Italy
Antonio Pratelli   University of Pisa, Italy

Advanced Computational Approaches in Fractals, Wavelet, Entropy and Data Mining Applications (AAFTWTETDT 2019)

Yeliz Karaca   University of Massachusetts Medical School, USA
Yu-Dong Zhang   University of Leicester, UK
Majaz Moonis   University of Massachusettes Medical School, USA

Advances in Artificial Intelligence Learning Technologies: Blended Learning, STEM, Computational Thinking and Coding (AAILT 2019)

Alfredo Milani   University of Perugia, Italy
Sergio Tasso   University of Perugia, Italy
Valentina Poggioni   University of Perugia, Italy

Affective Computing and Emotion Recognition (ACER-EMORE 2019)

Alfredo Milani   University of Perugia, Italy
Valentina Franzoni   University of Perugia, Italy
Giulio Biondi   University of Florence, Itay

Advances in Information Systems and Technologies for Emergency Management, Risk Assessment and Mitigation Based on the Resilience Concepts (ASTER 2019)

Maurizio Pollino	ENEA, Italy
Marco Vona	University of Basilicata, Italy
Beniamino Murgante	University of Basilicata, Italy

Blockchain and Distributed Ledgers: Technologies and Application (BDLTA 2019)

Vladimir Korkhov	St. Petersburg State University, Russia
Elena Stankova	St. Petersburg State University, Russia

Bio and Neuro-inspired Computing and Applications (BIONCA 2019)

Nadia Nedjah	State University of Rio de Janeiro, Brazil
Luiza de Macedo Mourell	State University of Rio de Janeiro, Brazil

Computer Aided Modeling, Simulation, and Analysis (CAMSA 2018)

Jie Shen	University of Michigan, USA
Hao Chen	Shanghai University of Engineering Science, China
Youguo He	Jiangsu University, China

Computational and Applied Statistics (CAS 2019)

Ana Cristina Braga	University of Minho, Portugal

Computational Mathematics, Statistics, and Information Management (CMSIM 2019)

M. Filomena Teodoro	Portuguese Naval Academy and Lisbon University, Portugal

Computational Optimization and Applications (COA 2019)

Ana Maria Rocha	University of Minho, Portugal
Humberto Rocha	University of Coimbra, Portugal

Computational Astrochemistry (CompAstro 2019)

Marzio Rosi	University of Perugia, Italy
Dimitrios Skouteris	Master-up, Perugia, Italy
Fanny Vazart	Université Grenoble Alpes, France
Albert Rimola	Universitat Autònoma de Barcelona, Spain

Cities, Technologies, and Planning (CTP 2019)

Beniamino Murgante	University of Basilicata, Italy
Giuseppe Borruso	University of Trieste, Italy

Econometrics and Multidimensional Evaluation in the Urban Environment (EMEUE 2019)

Carmelo M. Torre	Polytechnic of Bari, Italy
Pierluigi Morano	Polytechnic of Bari, Italy
Maria Cerreta	University of Naples Federico II, Italy
Paola Perchinunno	University of Bari, Italy
Francesco Tajani	University of Rome La Sapienza, Italy

Future Computing System Technologies and Applications (FISTA 2019)

Bernady O. Apduhan	Kyushu Sangyo University, Japan
Rafael Santos	National Institute for Space Research, Brazil

Geographical Analysis, Urban Modeling, Spatial Statistics (GEO-AND-MOD 2019)

Beniamino Murgante	University of Basilicata, Italy
Giuseppe Borruso	University of Trieste, Italy
Hartmut Asche	University of Potsdam, Germany

Geomatics for Resource Monitoring and Control (GRMC 2019)

Eufemia Tarantino	Polytechnic of Bari, Italy
Rosa Lasaponara	Italian Research Council, IMAA-CNR, Italy
Benedetto Figorito	ARPA Puglia, Italy
Umberto Fratino	Polytechnic of Bari, Italy

International Symposium on Software Quality (ISSQ 2019)

Sanjay Misra	Covenant University, Nigeria

Land Use Monitoring for Sustainability (LUMS 2019)

Carmelo M. Torre	Polytechnic of Bari, Italy
Alessandro Bonifazi	Polytechnic of Bari, Italy
Pasquale Balena	Polytechnic of Bari, Italy
Beniamino Murgante	University of Basilicata, Italy
Eric Gielen	Polytechnic University of Valencia, Spain

Machine Learning for Space and Earth Observation Data (ML-SEOD 2019)

Rafael Santos	Brazilian National Institute for Space Research, Brazil
Karine Reis Ferreira	National Institute for Space Research, Brazil

Mobile-Computing, Sensing, and Actuation in Cyber Physical Systems (MSA4CPS 2019)

Saad Qaisar	National University of Sciences and Technology, Pakistan
Moonseong Kim	Seoul Theological University, South Korea

Quantum Chemical Modeling of Solids with Computers: From Plane Waves to Local Structures (QuaCheSol 2019)

Andrei Tchougréeff   Russia Academy of Sciences, Russia
Richard Dronskowski   RWTH Aachen University, Germany
Taku Onishi   Mie University and Tromsoe University, Japan

Scientific Computing Infrastructure (SCI 2019)

Vladimir Korkhov   St. Petersburg State University, Russia
Elena Stankova   St. Petersburg State University, Russia
Nataliia Kulabukhova   St. Petersburg State University, Russia

Computational Studies for Energy and Comfort in Building (SECoB 2019)

Senhorinha Teixeira   University of Minho, Portugal
Angela Silva   Viana do Castelo Polytechnic Institute, Portugal
Ana Maria Rocha   University of Minho, Portugal

Software Engineering Processes and Applications (SEPA 2019)

Sanjay Misra   Covenant University, Nigeria

Smart Factory Convergence (SFC 2019)

Jongpil Jeong   Sungkyunkwan University, South Korea

Smart City and Water. Resource and Risk (Smart_Water 2019)

Giuseppe Borruso   University of Trieste, Italy
Ginevra Balletto   University of Cagliari, Italy
Gianfranco Becciu   Polytechnic University of Milan, Italy
Chiara Garau   University of Cagliari, Italy
Beniamino Murgante   University of Basilicata, Italy
Francesco Viola   University of Cagliari, Italy

Sustainability Performance Assessment: Models, Approaches, and Applications Toward Interdisciplinary and Integrated Solutions (SPA 2019)

Francesco Scorza   University of Basilicata, Italy
Valentin Grecu   Lucia Blaga University on Sibiu, Romania
Jolanta Dvarioniene   Kaunas University, Lithuania
Sabrina Lai   University of Cagliari, Italy

Theoretical and Computational Chemistry and Its Applications (TCCMA 2019)

Noelia Faginas Lago   University of Perugia, Italy
Andrea Lombardi   University of Perugia, Italy

Tools and Techniques in Software Development Processes (TTSDP 2019)

Sanjay Misra   Covenant University, Nigeria

Virtual Reality and Applications (VRA 2019)

Osvaldo Gervasi	University of Perugia, Italy
Sergio Tasso	University of Perugia, Italy

Collective, Massive and Evolutionary Systems (WCES 2019)

Alfredo Milani	University of Perugia, Italy
Valentina Franzoni	University of Rome La Sapienza, Italy
Rajdeep Niyogi	Indian Institute of Technology at Roorkee, India
Stefano Marcugini	University of Perugia, Italy

Parallel and Distributed Data Mining (WPDM 2019)

Massimo Cafaro	University of Salento, Italy
Italo Epicoco	University of Salento, Italy
Marco Pulimeno	University of Salento, Italy
Giovanni Aloisio	University of Salento, Italy

Program Committee

Kenneth Adamson	University of Ulster, UK
Vera Afreixo	University of Aveiro, Portugal
Filipe Alvelos	University of Minho, Portugal
Remadevi Arjun	National Institute of Technology Karnataka, India
Hartmut Asche	University of Potsdam, Germany
Ginevra Balletto	University of Cagliari, Italy
Michela Bertolotto	University College Dublin, Ireland
Sandro Bimonte	CEMAGREF, TSCF, France
Rod Blais	University of Calgary, Canada
Ivan Blečić	University of Sassari, Italy
Giuseppe Borruso	University of Trieste, Italy
Ana Cristina Braga	University of Minho, Portugal
Massimo Cafaro	University of Salento, Italy
Yves Caniou	Lyon University, France
José A. Cardoso e Cunha	Universidade Nova de Lisboa, Portugal
Leocadio G. Casado	University of Almeria, Spain
Carlo Cattani	University of Salerno, Italy
Mete Celik	Erciyes University, Turkey
Hyunseung Choo	Sungkyunkwan University, South Korea
Min Young Chung	Sungkyunkwan University, South Korea
Florbela Maria da Cruz Domingues Correia	Polytechnic Institute of Viana do Castelo, Portugal
Gilberto Corso Pereira	Federal University of Bahia, Brazil
Alessandro Costantini	INFN, Italy
Carla Dal Sasso Freitas	Universidade Federal do Rio Grande do Sul, Brazil
Pradesh Debba	The Council for Scientific and Industrial Research (CSIR), South Africa
Hendrik Decker	Instituto Tecnológico de Informática, Spain

Frank Devai	London South Bank University, UK
Rodolphe Devillers	Memorial University of Newfoundland, Canada
Joana Matos Dias	University of Coimbra, Portugal
Paolino Di Felice	University of L'Aquila, Italy
Prabu Dorairaj	NetApp, India/USA
M. Irene Falcao	University of Minho, Portugal
Cherry Liu Fang	U.S. DOE Ames Laboratory, USA
Florbela P. Fernandes	Polytechnic Institute of Bragança, Portugal
Jose-Jesus Fernandez	National Centre for Biotechnology, CSIS, Spain
Paula Odete Fernandes	Polytechnic Institute of Bragança, Portugal
Adelaide de Fátima Baptista Valente Freitas	University of Aveiro, Portugal
Manuel Carlos Figueiredo	University of Minho, Portugal
Valentina Franzoni	University of Rome La Sapienza, Italy
Maria Celia Furtado Rocha	PRODEB–PósCultura/UFBA, Brazil
Chiara Garau	University of Cagliari, Italy
Paulino Jose Garcia Nieto	University of Oviedo, Spain
Jerome Gensel	LSR-IMAG, France
Maria Giaoutzi	National Technical University, Athens, Greece
Arminda Manuela Andrade Pereira Gonçalves	University of Minho, Portugal
Andrzej M. Goscinski	Deakin University, Australia
Sevin Gümgüm	Izmir University of Economics, Turkey
Alex Hagen-Zanker	University of Cambridge, UK
Shanmugasundaram Hariharan	B.S. Abdur Rahman University, India
Eligius M. T. Hendrix	University of Malaga/Wageningen University, Spain/The Netherlands
Hisamoto Hiyoshi	Gunma University, Japan
Mustafa Inceoglu	EGE University, Turkey
Jongpil Jeong	Sungkyunkwan University, South Korea
Peter Jimack	University of Leeds, UK
Qun Jin	Waseda University, Japan
A. S. M. Kayes	La Trobe University, Australia
Farid Karimipour	Vienna University of Technology, Austria
Baris Kazar	Oracle Corp., USA
Maulana Adhinugraha Kiki	Telkom University, Indonesia
DongSeong Kim	University of Canterbury, New Zealand
Taihoon Kim	Hannam University, South Korea
Ivana Kolingerova	University of West Bohemia, Czech Republic
Nataliia Kulabukhova	St. Petersburg University, Russia
Vladimir Korkhov	St. Petersburg University, Russia
Rosa Lasaponara	National Research Council, Italy
Maurizio Lazzari	National Research Council, Italy
Cheng Siong Lee	Monash University, Australia
Sangyoun Lee	Yonsei University, South Korea

Jongchan Lee	Kunsan National University, South Korea
Chendong Li	University of Connecticut, USA
Gang Li	Deakin University, Australia
Fang Liu	AMES Laboratories, USA
Xin Liu	University of Calgary, Canada
Andrea Lombardi	University of Perugia, Italy
Savino Longo	University of Bari, Italy
Tinghuai Ma	NanJing University of Information Science and Technology, China
Ernesto Marcheggiani	Katholieke Universiteit Leuven, Belgium
Antonino Marvuglia	Research Centre Henri Tudor, Luxembourg
Nicola Masini	National Research Council, Italy
Eric Medvet	University of Trieste, Italy
Nirvana Meratnia	University of Twente, The Netherlands
Noelia Faginas Lago	University of Perugia, Italy
Giuseppe Modica	University of Reggio Calabria, Italy
Josè Luis Montaña	University of Cantabria, Spain
Maria Filipa Mourão	IP from Viana do Castelo, Portugal
Louiza de Macedo Mourelle	State University of Rio de Janeiro, Brazil
Nadia Nedjah	State University of Rio de Janeiro, Brazil
Laszlo Neumann	University of Girona, Spain
Kok-Leong Ong	Deakin University, Australia
Belen Palop	Universidad de Valladolid, Spain
Marcin Paprzycki	Polish Academy of Sciences, Poland
Eric Pardede	La Trobe University, Australia
Kwangjin Park	Wonkwang University, South Korea
Ana Isabel Pereira	Polytechnic Institute of Bragança, Portugal
Massimiliano Petri	University of Pisa, Italy
Maurizio Pollino	Italian National Agency for New Technologies, Energy and Sustainable Economic Development, Italy
Alenka Poplin	University of Hamburg, Germany
Vidyasagar Potdar	Curtin University of Technology, Australia
David C. Prosperi	Florida Atlantic University, USA
Wenny Rahayu	La Trobe University, Australia
Jerzy Respondek	Silesian University of Technology Poland
Humberto Rocha	INESC-Coimbra, Portugal
Jon Rokne	University of Calgary, Canada
Octavio Roncero	CSIC, Spain
Maytham Safar	Kuwait University, Kuwait
Chiara Saracino	A.O. Ospedale Niguarda Ca' Granda - Milano, Italy
Haiduke Sarafian	The Pennsylvania State University, USA
Francesco Scorza	University of Basilicata, Italy
Marco Paulo Seabra dos Reis	University of Coimbra, Portugal
Jie Shen	University of Michigan, USA

Qi Shi	Liverpool John Moores University, UK
Dale Shires	U.S. Army Research Laboratory, USA
Inês Soares	University of Coimbra, Portugal
Elena Stankova	St. Petersburg University, Russia
Takuo Suganuma	Tohoku University, Japan
Eufemia Tarantino	Polytechnic of Bari, Italy
Sergio Tasso	University of Perugia, Italy
Ana Paula Teixeira	University of Trás-os-Montes and Alto Douro, Portugal
Senhorinha Teixeira	University of Minho, Portugal
M. Filomena Teodoro	Portuguese Naval Academy and University of Lisbon, Portugal
Parimala Thulasiraman	University of Manitoba, Canada
Carmelo Torre	Polytechnic of Bari, Italy
Javier Martinez Torres	Centro Universitario de la Defensa Zaragoza, Spain
Giuseppe A. Trunfio	University of Sassari, Italy
Pablo Vanegas	University of Cuenca, Equador
Marco Vizzari	University of Perugia, Italy
Varun Vohra	Merck Inc., USA
Koichi Wada	University of Tsukuba, Japan
Krzysztof Walkowiak	Wroclaw University of Technology, Poland
Zequn Wang	Intelligent Automation Inc., USA
Robert Weibel	University of Zurich, Switzerland
Frank Westad	Norwegian University of Science and Technology, Norway
Roland Wismüller	Universität Siegen, Germany
Mudasser Wyne	SOET National University, USA
Chung-Huang Yang	National Kaohsiung Normal University, Taiwan
Xin-She Yang	National Physical Laboratory, UK
Salim Zabir	France Telecom Japan Co., Japan
Haifeng Zhao	University of California, Davis, USA
Fabiana Zollo	University of Venice Cà Foscari, Italy
Albert Y. Zomaya	University of Sydney, Australia

Additional Reviewers

Adewumi Oluwasegun	Covenant University, Nigeria
Afreixo Vera	University of Aveiro, Portugal
Agrawal Akshat	International Institute of Information Technology Bangalore, India
Aguilar Antonio	University of Barcelona, Spain
Ahmad Rashid	Microwave and Antenna Lab, School of Engineering, South Korea
Ahmed Waseem	Federal University of Technology, Nigeria
Alamri Sultan	Taibah University, Medina, Saudi Arabia
Alfa Abraham	Kogi State College of Education, Nigeria
Alvelos Filipe	University of Minho, Portugal

Amato Federico	University of Basilicata, Italy
Amin Benatia Mohamed	Groupe Cesi, Francia
Andrianov Serge	Institute for Informatics of Tatarstan Academy of Sciences, Russia
Apduhan Bernady	Kyushu Sangyo University, Japan
Aquilanti Vincenzo	University of Perugia, Italy
Arjun Remadevi	National Institute of Technology Karnataka, India
Arogundade Oluwasefunmi	Federal University of Agriculture, Nigeria
Ascenzi Daniela	University of Trento, Italy
Ayeni Foluso	Southern University and A&M College, USA
Azubuike Ezenwoke	Covenant University, Nigeria
Balacco Gabriella	Polytechnic of Bari, Italy
Balena Pasquale	Polytechnic of Bari, Italy
Balletto Ginevra	University of Cagliari, Italy
Barrile Vincenzo	Mediterranean University of Reggio Calabria, Italy
Bartolomei Massimiliano	Spanish National Research Council, Spain
Behera Ranjan Kumar	Indian Institute of Technology Patna, India
Biondi Giulio	University of Florence, Italy
Bist Ankur Singh	KIET Ghaziabad, India
Blecic Ivan	University of Cagliari, Italy
Bogdanov Alexander	St. Petersburg State University, Russia
Borgogno Mondino Enrico Corrado	University of Turin, Italy
Borruso Giuseppe	University of Trieste, Italy
Bostenaru Maria	Ion Mincu University of Architecture and Urbanism, Romania
Braga Ana Cristina	University of Minho, Portugal
Cafaro Massimo	University of Salento, Italy
Capolupo Alessandra	University of Naples Federico II, Italy
Carvalho-Silva Valter	Universidade Estadual de Goiás, Brazil
Cerreta Maria	University Federico II of Naples, Italy
Chan Sheung Wai	Hong Kong Baptist Hospital, SAR China
Cho Chulhee	Seoul Guarantee Insurance Company Ltd., South Korea
Choi Jae-Young	Sungkyunkwan University, South Korea
Correia Anacleto	Base Naval de Lisboa, Portugal
Correia Elisete	University of Trás-Os-Montes e Alto Douro, Portugal
Correia Florbela Maria da Cruz Domingues	Instituto Politécnico de Viana do Castelo, Portugal
Costa e Silva Eliana	Polytechnic of Porto, Portugal
Costa Lino	Universidade do Minho, Portugal
Costantini Alessandro	Istituto Nazionale di Fisica Nucleare, Italy
Crawford Broderick	Pontificia Universidad Católica de Valparaíso, Chile
Cutini Valerio	University of Pisa, Italy
D'Acierno Luca	University of Naples Federico II, Italy
Danese Maria	Italian National Research Council, Italy
Dantas Coutinho Nayara	University of Perugia, Italy
Degtyarev Alexander	St. Petersburg State University, Russia

Dereli Dursun Ahu	UNSW Sydney, Australia
Devai Frank	London South Bank University, UK
Di Bari Gabriele	University of Florence, Italy
Dias Joana	University of Coimbra, Portugal
Diaz Diana	National University of Colombia, Colombia
Elfadaly Abdelaziz	University of Basilicata, Italy
Enriquez Palma Pedro Alberto	Universidad de la Rioja, Spain
Epicoco Italo	University of Salento, Italy
Esposito Giuseppina	Sapienza University of Rome, Italy
Faginas-Lago M. Noelia	University of Perugia, Italy
Fajardo Jorge	Universidad Politécnica Salesiana (UPS), Ecuador
Falcinelli Stefano	University of Perugia, Italy
Farina Alessandro	University of Pisa, Italy
Fattoruso Grazia	ENEA, Italy
Fernandes Florbela	Escola Superior de Tecnologia e Gestão de Bragancca, Portugal
Fernandes Paula	Escola Superior de Tecnologia e Gestão, Portugal
Fernández Ledesma Javier Darío	Universidad Pontificia Bolivariana, Bolivia
Ferreira Ana C.	University of Lisbon, Portugal
Ferrão Maria	Universidade da Beira Interior, Portugal
Figueiredo Manuel Carlos	Universidade do Minho, Portugal
Florez Hector	Universidad Distrital Francisco Jose de Caldas, Colombia
Franzoni Valentina	University of Perugia, Italy
Freitau Adelaide de Fátima Baptista Valente	University of Aveiro, Portugal
Friday Agbo	University of Eastern Finland, Finland
Frunzete Madalin	Polytechnic University of Bucharest, Romania
Fusco Giovanni	Laboratoire ESPACE, CNRS, France
Gabrani Goldie	Bml Munjal University, India
Gankevich Ivan	St. Petersburg State University, Russia
Garau Chiara	University of Cagliari, Italy
Garcia Ernesto	University of the Basque Country, Spain
Gavrilova Marina	University of Calgary, Canada
Gervasi Osvaldo	University of Perugia, Italy
Gilner Ewa	Silesian University of Technology, Poland
Gioia Andrea	University of Bari, Italy
Giorgi Giacomo	University of Perugia, Italy
Gonçalves Arminda Manuela	University of Minho, Portugal
Gorbachev Yuriy	Geolink Technologies, Russia
Gotoh Yusuke	Kyoto University, Japan
Goyal Rinkaj	Guru Gobind Singh Indraprastha University, India
Gümgüm Sevin	Izmir Economy University, Turkey

Gülen Kemal Güven	Istanbul Ticaret University, Turkey
Hegedus Peter	University of Szeged, Hungary
Hendrix Eligius M. T.	University of Malaga, Spain
Iacobellis Vito	Polytechnic of Bari, Italy
Iakushkin Oleg	St. Petersburg State University, Russia
Kadry Seifedine	Beirut Arab University, Lebanon
Kim JeongAh	George Fox University, USA
Kim Moonseong	Korean Intellectual Property Office, South Korea
Kolingerova Ivana	University of West Bohemia, Czech Republic
Koo Jahwan	Sungkyunkwan University, South Korea
Korkhov Vladimir	St. Petersburg State University, Russia
Kulabukhova Nataliia	St. Peterburg State University, Russia
Ladu Mara	University of Cagliari, Italy
Laganà Antonio	Master-up srl, Italy
Leon Marcelo	Universidad Estatal Peninsula de Santa Elena – UPSE, Ecuador
Lima Rui	University of Minho, Portugal
Lombardi Andrea	University of Perugia, Italy
Longo Savino	University of Bari, Italy
Maciel de Castro Jessica	Universidade Federal da Paraíba, Brazil
Magni Riccardo	Pragma Engineering S.r.L., Italy
Mandanici Emanuele	University of Bologna, Italy
Mangiameli Michele	University of Catania, Italy
Marcellini Moreno	Ecole normale supérieure de Lyon, France
Marghany Maged	Universiti Teknologi Malaysia, Malaysia
Marques Jorge	Universidade de Coimbra, Portugal
Martellozzo Federico	University of Florence, Italy
Mengoni Paolo	University of Florence, Italy
Migliore Marco	University of Cassino e del Lazio Meridionale, Italy
Milani Alfredo	University of Perugia, Italy
Milesi Alessandra	Istituto Auxologico Italiano, Italy
Mishra Biswajeeban	University of Szeged, Hungary
Molaei Qelichi Mohamad	University of Tehran, Iran
Monteiro Vitor	University of Minho, Portugal
Moraes João Luís Cardoso	University of Porto, Portugal
Moura Ricardo	Universidade Nova de Lisboa, Portugal
Mourao Maria	Universidade do Minho, Portugal
Murgante Beniamino	University of Basilicata, Italy
Natário Isabel Cristina Maciel	Universidade Nova de Lisboa, Portugal
Nedjah Nadia	Rio de Janeiro State University, Brazil
Nocera Silvio	University of Naples Federico II, Italy
Odun-Ayo Isaac	Covenant University, Nigeria
Okewu Emmanuel	University of Lagos, Nigeria
Oliveira Irene	University of Trás-Os-Montes e Alto Douro, Portugal
Oluranti Jonathan	Covenant University, Nigeria

Osho Oluwafemi	Federal University of Technology Minna, Nigeria
Ozturk Savas	The Scientific and Technological Research Council of Turkey, Turkey
Panetta J. B.	University of Georgia, USA
Pardede Eric	La Trobe University, Australia
Perchinunno Paola	University of Bari, Italy
Pereira Ana	Instituto Politécnico de Bragança, Portugal
Peschechera Giuseppe	University of Bari, Italy
Petri Massimiliano	University of Pisa, Italy
Petrovic Marjana	University of Zagreb, Croatia
Pham Quoc Trung	Ho Chi Minh City University of Technology, Vietnam
Pinto Telmo	University of Minho, Portugal
Plekhanov Evgeny	Russian Academy of Economics, Russia
Poggioni Valentina	University of Perugia, Italy
Polidoro Maria João	University of Lisbon, Portugal
Pollino Maurizio	ENEA, Italy
Popoola Segun	Covenant University, Nigeria
Pratelli Antonio	University of Pisa, Italy
Pulimeno Marco	University of Salento, Italy
Rasool Hamid	National University of Sciences and Technology, Pakistan
Reis Marco	Universidade de Coimbra, Portugal
Respondek Jerzy	Silesian University of Technology, Poland
Riaz Nida	National University of Sciences and Technology, Pakistan
Rimola Albert	Autonomous University of Barcelona, Spain
Rocha Ana Maria	University of Minho, Portugal
Rocha Humberto	University of Coimbra, Portugal
Rosi Marzio	University of Perugia, Italy
Santos Rafael	National Institute for Space Research, Brazil
Santucci Valentino	University Stranieri of Perugia, Italy
Saponaro Mirko	Polytechnic of Bari, Italy
Sarafian Haiduke	Pennsylvania State University, USA
Scorza Francesco	University of Basilicata, Italy
Sedova Olya	St. Petersburg State University, Russia
Semanjski Ivana	Ghent University, Belgium
Sharma Jeetu	Mody University of Science and Technology, India
Sharma Purnima	University of Lucknow, India
Shchegoleva Nadezhda	Petersburg State Electrotechnical University, Russia
Shen Jie	University of Michigan, USA
Shoaib Muhammad	Sungkyunkwan University, South Korea
Shou Huahao	Zhejiang University of Technology, China
Silva-Fortes Carina	ESTeSL-IPL, Portugal
Silva Ângela Maria	Escola Superior de Ciências Empresariais, Portugal
Singh Upasana	The University of Manchester, UK
Singh V. B.	University of Delhi, India

Skouteris Dimitrios	Master-up, Perugia, Italy
Soares Inês	INESCC and IPATIMUP, Portugal
Soares Michel	Universidade Federal de Sergipe, Brazil
Sosnin Petr	Ulyanovsk State Technical University, Russia
Sousa Ines	University of Minho, Portugal
Stankova Elena	St. Petersburg State University, Russia
Stritih Uros	University of Ljubljana, Slovenia
Tanaka Kazuaki	Kyushu Institute of Technology, Japan
Tarantino Eufemia	Polytechnic of Bari, Italy
Tasso Sergio	University of Perugia, Italy
Teixeira Senhorinha	University of Minho, Portugal
Tengku Adil	La Trobe University, Australia
Teodoro M. Filomena	Lisbon University, Portugal
Torre Carmelo Maria	Polytechnic of Bari, Italy
Totaro Vincenzo	Polytechnic of Bari, Italy
Tripathi Aprna	GLA University, India
Vancsics Béla	University of Szeged, Hungary
Vasyunin Dmitry	University of Amsterdam, The Netherlands
Vig Rekha	The Northcap University, India
Walkowiak Krzysztof	Wroclaw University of Technology, Poland
Wanderley Fernando	New University of Lisbon, Portugal
Wang Chao	University of Science and Technology of China, China
Westad Frank	CAMO Software AS, USA
Yamazaki Takeshi	University of Tokyo, Japan
Zahra Noore	University of Guilan, India
Zollo Fabiana	University of Venice Ca' Foscari, Italy
Zullo Francesco	University of L'Aquila, Italy
Žemlička Michal	Charles University in Prague, Czech Republic
Živković Ljiljana	Republic Agency for Spatial Planning, Serbia

Sponsoring Organizations

ICCSA 2019 would not have been possible without tremendous support of many organizations and institutions, for which all organizers and participants of ICCSA 2019 express their sincere gratitude:

Springer Nature Switzerland AG, Germany
(http://www.springer.com)

St. Petersburg University, Russia
(http://english.spbu.ru/)

University of Perugia, Italy
(http://www.unipg.it)

University of Basilicata, Italy
(http://www.unibas.it)

Monash University, Australia
(http://monash.edu)

Kyushu Sangyo University, Japan
(www.kyusan-u.ac.jp)

Universidade do Minho, Portugal
(http://www.uminho.pt)

Contents – Part V

Software Engineering Processes and Applications (SEPA 2019)

A Microservice-Based Health Information System for Student-Run Clinics

Itamir de Morais Barroca Filho[1]([⊠]), Silvio Costa Sampaio[1],
Gibeon Soares Aquino Junior[2], Rafael Fernandes de Queiroz[2],
Dannylo Johnathan Bernardino Egidio[2], Ramon Santos Malaquias[1],
and Larissa Gilliane Melo de Moura[1]

[1] Digtal Metropolis Institute, Federal University of Rio Grande do Norte,
Natal, Brazil
{itamir.filho,silviocs,ramonstmalaquias,larissa.moura}@imd.ufrn.br
[2] Department of Informatics and Applied Mathematics,
Federal University of Rio Grande do Norte, Natal, Brazil
gibeon@dimap.ufrn.br, rfqueiroz.91@gmail.com, dannylojohnathan@gmail.com

Abstract. Student-run clinics are units found in universities and colleges that provide health care to the internal and external public, integrating theoretical knowledge with situations involving treatment provided to real patients, thus reproducing the environment that the student will find in his or her professional life. In this context, this article presents an information system for the management of health services and electronic medical records in student-run clinics called SigSaude. SigSaude is a solution whose architecture is based on microservices, contemplating specialties such as dentistry, psychology, nutrition, and medicine. This system is being used by the student-run clinics of the Federal University of Rio Grande do Norte (UFRN), bringing benefits to the improvement of the quality of patient care and helping teachers and students in the evidence-based teaching-learning process. This system is being used by these clinics and the current results demonstrate the solution's high scalability.

Keywords: Student-run clinic · Microservice · API ·
Electronic medical records

1 Introduction

In the academic context of health, student-run clinics arise from the need to integrate teaching, research and extension activities with health practices. The activities in student-run clinics are usually integrated with the curriculum guidelines of the health professional education in which, in addition to the theoretical disciplines, a set of practical internship components is required. The primary objective of this requirement is to integrate the concepts learned in the classroom and the reality that students will find after they graduate. In this sense,

© Springer Nature Switzerland AG 2019
S. Misra et al. (Eds.): ICCSA 2019, LNCS 11623, pp. 3–16, 2019.
https://doi.org/10.1007/978-3-030-24308-1_1

activities in student-run clinics are assuredly articulated with the reality of the population served, thus reproducing the private practice and training professionals to be ready for this type of performance.

Therefore, student-run clinics consist of an environment associated to an educational institution, in which students perform clinical practices while being taught, under the guidance of a professional who assumes the role of teacher and/or supervisor [1,3].

Another essential feature of student-run clinics is their social role since they serve an economically or geographically disadvantaged population. Usually sheltered in the university environment, student-run clinics provide free treatments to the internal and external community, receiving patients sent from other student-run clinics and health units both in the municipality and macroregion. In fact, in many Brazilian towns, the assistance provided by the student-run clinics guarantee access to health services, which is insufficient and even unavailable in the public network, to a representative number of people.

The activities carried out in the context of a student-run clinic involve different types and natures of information, which need to include all the structures of health care. The maintenance and access to this information, in its turn, takes on even greater importance considering the complicated routine made up of activities that vary according to the academic context. However, there is not much reference in the literature related to health information management systems geared towards this specific student-run clinic environment, that is, of systems capable of establishing a dialogue between the health care practical activities and the curricular activities of the health university courses.

This need is urgent, since, as pointed out by Oliveira [15], we are undergoing social and political changes that affect both the academy and the health services, which has a direct impact on the needs and demands of this area. When it comes to services, there are problems related to the units' physical structure [5]; to the lack of professionalization of the health management; to the physical structure of the communication networks; to the low connectivity in some locations; to the use of diverse information systems; and to the existence of deficient or non-integrated data and records, which, most of the time, are stored in non-standardized paper files, making it difficult to organize and share them with the other individuals involved [8,10].

Seeking to collaborate with the knowledge in this area, this work describes a health information system - SigSaude - based on a microservices architecture, integrated with the administrative and academic management of the university's student-run clinics. The SigSaude aims to incorporate a complex set of services linked to employees with different functions and objectives, without losing its academic vocation.

The university studied was the Federal University of Rio Grande do Norte (UFRN), which offers about 14 health services that are provided through student-run clinics, contributing to the academic training of undergraduate and graduate students. Different types of services/specialties such as dentistry, nutrition, physiotherapy, nursing, psychology, and medicine are provided, which, altogether, totals about 6,000 monthly visits, according to the data supplied by the clinics themselves.

UFRN's student-run clinics, for the most part, do not use a computation system for managing their administrative data, and there is no automated control of the data related to patients and their care. In addition to resulting in a large amount of paper used, this causes a considerable difficulty to maintain and access information. Considering that many of these clinics are distant from each other, the geographic factor is also aggravating their current work model, making it difficult to perform medical referrals and to exchange information between services.

The difficulties described above and the circumstances in which student-run clinics are inserted point out the indispensability of the unification, standardization and easy availability of the patients' data for the services and employees involved in this process. Taking all of this into consideration, the SigSaude proposes the use of the concepts of distributed Electronic Medical Record (EMR) and microservices. The first one aims to aggregate the data that contributes to studies and decision-making [14], while the second one allows to address, in an elegantly and scalable way, the distribution of the EMR data. This article focuses on the concept of microservices architecture.

The ultimate goal of the system described in this work is to make it possible to operate student-run clinics more efficiently, resulting in better training of the students involved in the activities and better treatment for patients.

The remainder of this paper is organized as follows: Sect. 2 presents the microservices architectural model; in Sect. 3, the architecture of the proposed solution is detailed; in Sect. 4, some of the results already obtained in the development of the SigSaude are presented; Sect. 5 brings together some related works; and, finally, Sect. 6 presents the conclusions and directions for future works.

2   Microservices

Microservices are a trend in software architecture that emphasizes the design and development of highly sustainable and scalable software [7]. Dragoni et al. provide a clear distinction between microservices and microservices architecture. Microservices are a cohesive and independent process that interacts through messages, while a microservices architecture is a distributed application in which all of its modules are microservices.

Each microservice is built for a business capacity, runs its processes, and can communicate with other microservices through simple mechanisms such as services APIs [18]. This model aims to achieve an increase in implementation capabilities directly impacting the time and independence of implementation, modifiability, and quality of services [6,16]. Pahl and Jamshidi [16] add that the microservices model favors the decentralization of control and provides greater support to heterogeneity.

Each microservice must exhibit a communication interface so that other microservices in the application ecosystem can exchange data with it. These interfaces often use custom protocols and remote function calls (RFCs) [22]. Gateway APIs are used as intermediaries or points of entry of communication between the microservices [17]. These are usually connected to the internet and use protocols such as HTTP, open standards such as REST or SOAP, and interoperable data exchange technologies, such as XML and JSON [22].

In addition to enabling communication between microservices, the Gateway API also allows the existence of mechanisms for the registration, identification, and discovery of microservices and the control of clients request routes [13]. It is also possible, as an option, to use mechanisms for the management of the identity and data privacy through authentication services such as OAuth [13].

Some trade-offs should also be considered when considering adopting a microservice based architectural model. Among the most important one, Fowler [9] points out that although the microservices' modular structure facilitates the work of large teams, common remote calls in microservices are usually slow and have a considerable risk of failure. Although the independent implementation is a strong point for this architectural model, consistency maintenances in distributed systems are often difficult, which leads to considering that everyone should manage possible consistencies. Finally, the author adds that although microservices provide the freedom to use multiple technologies, frameworks, and data storage resources in their applications, it is essential to have the operational maturity to deal with this universe of various technologies.

The decision to adopt a microservices architecture for the SigSaude was taken given the need to develop an information system with built-in features that could work for many different specialties, and that contemplated the increase in implementation capacity (time and independence), modifiability and quality of services. As a result, the decentralization of control and the greater support for heterogeneity is expected, since different student-run clinics have different demands.

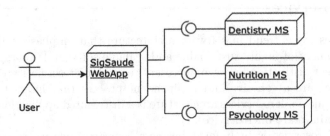

Fig. 1. SigSaude's architecture overview.

3   Solution's Architecture

The architecture of the proposed solution follows the principles of the microservices architecture model. As already mentioned, each student-run clinic has its specific set of services offered. Taking this into consideration, the proposed architecture will allow, for example, a psychology student-run clinic to use only the clinic module and other general management modules, without having to bear the costs of maintaining modules related to other services that are not even used and provided. In another example, the architecture will make it possible to manage instances of each microservice in a flexible way, thus allowing to meet the requirements of a more demanding service.

The structure of the proposed architecture is presented in Fig. 1. In this architecture, the services offered by the student-run clinics are represented by blocks (for example Dentistry MS, Nutrition MS, and Psychology MS, where MS indicates that it is a microservice), where each block represents a self-contained and independent microservice, thus fitting with the assertion [12] that each service must have a single purpose and be responsible for only one of the application's logical context. It is important to clarify that because of space issues, Fig. 1 represents a narrow view of the proposed architecture. Thus, the complete architecture integrates a much higher number of blocks or microservices.

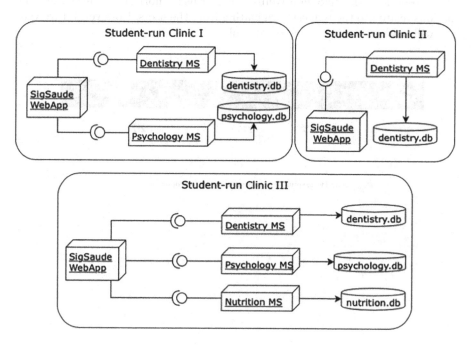

Fig. 2. Implementation architecture in student-run clinics.

The architecture's microservices are organized according to the services offered by each student-run clinic. For example, Dentistry MS represents the microservice of the architecture responsible for the logical processes related to Dentistry services, such as the removal of a patient's teeth. Similarly, the Nutrition MS and the Psychology MS are responsible for the specific rules of each specialty, for example, calculating a patient's body mass index or holding psychological counseling meetings.

In a microservices architecture, it is essential that the components communicate with each other using simple mechanisms [12]. Thus, in Fig. 1, these mechanisms are symbolized by the interfaces linked to the microservices, representing the APIs (Application Programming Interfaces) that provide communication to the microservices to which they are interconnected.

The requests made to the microservices APIs are carried out through the use of another component of the architecture, which is called SigSaude WebApp. For the architecture, this component is a web application responsible for building the interface presented to the user, as well as for intermediating requests to the other microservices. This way, the SigSaude WebApp works as a Gateway API, abstracting all the APIs from the other microservices, receiving requests and designating them to their proper destination. Thus, the SigSaude WebApp assumes the role of orchestrator, controlling the destination and traffic of requests to avoid the congestion of requests sent to the target microservices. Since it is in front of the microservices, the SigSaude WebApp performs authorization/authentication functions related to the requests originating from the users. However, future versions will have to outsource access control.

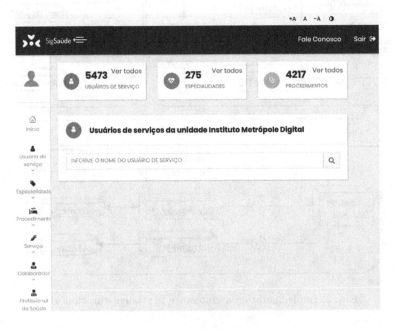

Fig. 3. SigSaude's dashboard.

Student-run clinics usually have several infrastructure problems, which make the deployment of large-scale systems challenging. Some student-run clinics are located in remote locations, where there is no internet with good bandwidth rates, making it difficult to carry out large traffic of data over the network. Another situation found is that some clinics do not have a computer infrastructure like servers with high processing power, thus making it impossible to implement a monolithic system, which requires a lot of storage and processing capacity.

Fig. 4. List of procedures registered in SigSaude.

Again, it should be noted that the use of microservices based on the services offered by student-run clinics will allow the implementation of this health platform with only the microservices needed to attend the specific needs of a student-run clinic. This way, the resources necessary to implement the platform are reduced, since small microservices do not require servers with large storage and processing capacities, nor internet connections with high bandwidth rates, as the information that will travel will be only those that are inherent to the microservice related to the student-run clinic. This reduction in the implementation costs is an important differential of this proposal since most of the student-run clinics offer free care and do not have numerous financial resources.

In the different contexts of student-run clinics, the implementation of the health platform proposed is generally carried out as shown in Fig. 2. In this Figure, each group of microservices represents a context for the student-run clinic, with its own platform implementation, containing its own microservices and database. The SigSaude WebApp component is required in all of the implementation environments, allowing to configure the interface presented to the user according to the environment in which it is implanted.

The group represented by Student-run Clinic II, for example, portrays a simpler scenario for a student-run clinic, which offers only a health service

Fig. 5. List of specialties registered in SigSaude.

(dentistry). This way, only one microservice is made available for it, which performs the logic processing needed for the student-run clinic.

In its turn, the groups presented in Student-run Clinic I and Student-run Clinic III have a larger number of microservices available (dentistry, psychology and nutrition). In this case, these groups represent the contexts of student-run clinics that have greater infrastructure capabilities when compared to the Student-run Clinic II group, considering the number of health services offered by them.

For these student-run clinics scenarios, an architecture based on the monolithic model would be impracticable, since in each context of these student-run clinics, it would be necessary to implement a large system involving all of the services available, including those that are not needed by the clinic because it does not provide the corresponding health service. Each implementation environment will have an instance of the deployment of the architectural structure shown in Fig. 1.

4   Results

The SigSaude was implemented according to the architecture mentioned in the previous section and is already available in many of UFRN's student-run clinics, who are using it every day, feeding the platform with patient registration data, procedures, specialties, services and scheduling control. Up until the moment this article was written, the platform had 5473 patients registered, 275 specialties and 4217 procedures, as shown in the dashboard found in Fig. 3.

Table 1. Metrics assessed in the SigSaude WebApp's code.

Metric	Total	Mean	Std. Dev	Maximum
McCabe Cyclomatic Complexity (avg/max per...)	–	1.365	1.335	19
Number of Parameters (avg/max per method)	–	0.652	0.85	7
Nested Block Depth (avg/max per method)	–	1.106	0.573	4
Afferent Coupling (avg/max per packageFragment)	–	14.1	25.282	111
Efferent Coupling (avg/max per packageFragment)	–	8.55	9.351	30
Instability (avg/max per packageFragment)	–	0.625	0.354	1
Abstractness (avg/max per packageFragment)	–	0.124	0.24	0.9
Normalized Distance (avg/max per packageFragment)	–	0.344	0.318	1
Depth of Inheritance Tree (avg/max per type)	–	1.581	0.943	3
Weighted Methods per Class (avg/max per type)	1729	6.972	9.715	79
Number of Children (avg/max per type)	74	0.298	1.301	9
Number of Overridden Methods (avg/max per...)	22	0.089	0.381	3
Lack of Cohesion of Methods (avg/max per type)	–	0.255	0.382	1.6
Number of Attributes (avg/max per type)	577	2.327	3.452	34
Number of Static Attributes (avg/max per type)	18	0.073	0.478	6
Number of Methods (avg/max per type)	1185	4.778	7.408	74
Number of Static Methods (avg/max per type)	82	0.331	1.623	18
Specialization Index (avg/max per type)	–	0.034	0.177	2
Number of Classes (avg/max per packageFragment)	248	12.4	13.89	57
Number of Interfaces (avg/max per packageFragment)	32	1.6	5.86	27
Number of Packages	20	–	–	–
Total Lines of Code	10415	–	–	–
Method Lines of Code (avg/max per method)	3.809	3.006	4.909	52
Method Lines of Code (avg/max per method)	3.809	3.006	4.909	52

To validate the proposal, the values for the metrics illustrated in Table 1 were collected from the SigSaude WebApp source code and allow to evaluate important characteristics, such as the average of methods in each class, lines of code, number of attributes, method cohesion, number of parameters, etc. Since it is a WebApp, which behaves as an integrating resource for the associated microservices (Gateway API), its numbers are very expressive. Depending on their complexity and purpose, the other microservices may have reduced numbers.

As already reported, each clinic includes the microservices related to them. Figures 4 and 5, respectively, represent some of the procedures and specialties already registered by the users of the UFRN's student-run clinics.

Due to the need for the health systems to have reduced response times, tests were implemented using the J-Meter tool, which makes it possible to easily customize aspects such as workload and duration of testing [4,19].

Thus, requests stress situations were simulated to evaluate SigSaude's scalability. The tests were performed in two moments: the first one with 100 threads, and the second one with 1,000 threads. Each thread, in its turn, executed dozens of requests, totaling 1,700 requests in the first test and 17,000 requests in the second one. Of the requests made, 16 (0.94%) resulted in errors in the first test; for the second test, the number of errors totaled 5,674 (33,38%) because the random characteristic of the generation of requests ended up violating SigSaude's validation rules.

The first test case, which had 1,700 requests, resulted in response times within the acceptable standard - 684 requests were answered in less than 1.5 s, 304 requests were responded between 1.5 and 3 s, and 696 were answered in over 3 s, as shown in Fig. 6.

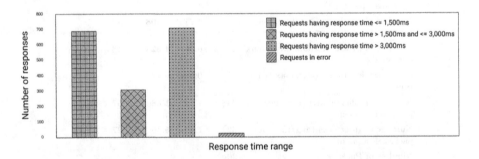

Fig. 6. Overview of the response times for 1,700 requests.

In the second test case, as shown in Fig. 7, 17,000 requests were sent, of which 792 had a response time of less than 1.5 s, 954 took between 1.5 and 3 s, and 9,580 had a response time of more than 3 s.

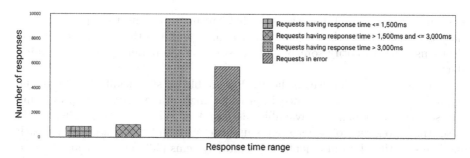

Fig. 7. Overview of the response times for 17,000 requests.

The test results give good indications that the implementation of the microservice based architectural model for the SigSaude performs well, meeting the scalability requirements initially imposed. However, more complex tests should be carried out in the future to confirm these results.

5 Related Works

Although the literature on health management systems is extensive, up until this article was written, it was not possible to find works focused on the specific context of student-run clinics. The papers found in this area focus on proposing hospital management systems, which present dimensions and characteristics that are often incompatible with the environment discussed in this article. Thus, in this section, we present some works that show the need for management systems in student-run clinics, as well as papers that corroborate our choice of using a microservices architecture.

Ali et al. [2] propose a platform based on a microservices model and a WoO (Web of Objects) approach to aid depressive disorders. The WoO approach provides a framework based on IoT services for the Web, virtualizing the objects involved in the application and interconnecting them with their respective physical resources in the infrastructure. The author uses the microservices architecture to reduce the complexity of the project through modular and independent microservices. Thus, each microservice has a specific function in the application, from training models using Machine Learning techniques for the recognition of specific situations of potential users, to services that analyze the user's data searching for characteristics that make it possible to identify symptoms of a depressive disorder.

The tendency of the health community to turn to a complex set of services that incorporate many people with different capabilities and objectives is evidenced in [11]. The work proposes a multi-agent system for health care based on a service-oriented architecture (SOA), which is particularly based on microservices. The microservices of the proposal are based on IoT services. An architecture based on microservices was used to meet the application's scalability requirements, reducing or avoiding overheads in the application messages. The system is equipped with microsensors that capture vital data from patients; this data is transferred to the system that will analyze it and that can make specific decisions, such as notify someone responsible for the patient of some alarming data.

The use of microservices in health has enabled a significant increase in the applications' productivity, since it provides high availability, thus preventing the services from being unavailable, as found in Williams et al. [20]'s work. Also, the segregation of services ends up generating individual security for each module - a critical requirement for hospital systems [20]. Yilong et al. [21] also present a proposal based on microservices to share medical data preserving the patients' privacy. In this work, the author emphasizes that the exchange of medical information is not trivial due to potential privacy intrusions. Thus, the work approaches de-identification techniques, represented as "black boxes," through the use of a microservices architecture, and guarantees the legitimacy of the user through rule-based control access (RBAC).

6   Conclusions and Future Work

This paper discusses the need for an integrated system for the management of health services for student-run clinics and presents, as a solution, the SigSaude. The SigSaude is an initiative from the Federal University of Rio Grande do Norte, which offers many health services such as student-run clinics. Although in it still in its first year, the solution already presents significant results concerning the integration of patient information, schedules, treatments, and patient follow-ups.

The main characteristic of the SigSaude discussed in this article is its design, which is totally microservices-oriented, mainly due to the limitations of the infrastructure for the implementation of large-scale platforms in UFRN's student-run clinics. This way, the clinics only use services that are needed for its context, thus avoiding the waste of resources and increasing the solution's scalability. It is worth noting that despite the integration, each clinic has a different context of use and a certain individuality regarding the services available, so the solution using microservices allows the preservation of the particularities of each clinic and its area of work in the health field.

This work also presents the results of the scalability tests that were performed on the solution. These stress tests were developed and applied to 100 and 1,000 threads simultaneously and the results were considered satisfactory. Taking into consideration the student-run clinics' high demand and the need for availability that the platform needs to meet, the test results suggest that the developed tool can be used by clinics. However, it should be noted that more complex tests should be carried out during the development of the solution.

As future work, there is an intention to apply functionalities for monitoring the patients' clinical evolution, as well as increase the platform's features, including functions like patient care and laboratory and health procedures follow-up. Another important point to be considered in the next phase of the SigSaude is the consolidation of the distributed Electronic Medical Record (EMR). This implies exploring the communication between microservices to draw up the patient's entire history. The EMR will make it possible to reduce bureaucratic processes and customize the patient's care. Other expected functionality is the inclusion of microservices related to research and analysis of health data from the SigSaude's distributed bases.

Acknowledgements. This research was partially supported by the SigSaude Project, funded by the Federal University of Rio Grande do Norte - UFRN. This study was financed in part by the Coordenação de Aperfeiçoamento de Pessoal de Nível Superior – Brasil (CAPES) – Finance Code 001.

References

1. Albuquerque, V., Gomes, A., Rezende, C.H., Sampaio, M., Dias, O., Lugarinho, R.: A integração ensino-serviço no contexto dos processos de mudançãa na formação superior dos profissionais da saúde. REVISTA BRASILEIRA DE EDUCAÇÃO MÉDICA **32**(3), 356–362 (2008)
2. Ali, S., Kibria, M.G., Jarwar, M.A., Kumar, S., Chong, I.: Microservices model in WoO based IoT platform for depressive disorder assistance. In: 2017 International Conference on Information and Communication Technology Convergence (ICTC), pp. 864–866. IEEE (2017)
3. Amaral, A.E., Luca, L., Rodrigues, T., Leite, C., Lopes, F., Silva, M.: Serviços de psicologia em clínicas-escola: revisão de literatura. Bol. psicol. **62**136 (2012)
4. de Camargo, A., Salvadori, I., Mello, R.d.S., Siqueira, F.: An architecture to automate performance tests on microservices. In: Proceedings of the 18th International Conference on Information Integration and Web-Based Applications and Services, pp. 422–429. ACM (2016)
5. Cavalheiro, M.T., Guimarães, A.: Formação para o sus e os desafios da integração ensino serviço. Caderno FNEPAS. Dezembro 2011, vol. 1 (2011)
6. Chen, L.: Microservices: architecting for continuous delivery and DevOps. In: IEEE International Conference on Software Architecture (ICSA) (2018)
7. Dragoni, N., et al.: Microservices: yesterday, today, and tomorrow. Present and Ulterior Software Engineering, pp. 195–216. Springer, Cham (2017). https://doi.org/10.1007/978-3-319-67425-4_12
8. Junior, E., Onofre de Lira, A.C.: Prontuário eletrônico e as perspectivas do e-health. Debates GVsaúde, Debates GVsaúde- Segundo Semestre de 2009 - Número 8 (2009)
9. Fowler, M.: Microservice trade-offs. Dosegljivo (2015). http://martinfowler.com/articles/microservice-trade-offs.html
10. Gonçalves, J., Batista, L., Carvalho, L., Oliveira, M., Moreira, K., Leite, M.: Prontuário eletrônico: uma ferramenta que pode contribuir para a integração das redes de atenção à saúde. Saúde em Debate, Rio de Janeiro, vol. 37, no. 96, pp. 43–50 (2013)
11. Hill, R., Shadija, D., Rezai, M.: Enabling community health care with microservices. In: 2017 IEEE International Symposium on Parallel and Distributed Processing with Applications and 2017 IEEE International Conference on Ubiquitous Computing and Communications (ISPA/IUCC), pp. 1444–1450. IEEE (2017)
12. Lewis, J., Fowler, M.: Microservices: a definition of this new architectural term. Mars (2014)

13. Lu, D., Huang, D., Walenstein, A., Medhi, D.: A secure microservice framework for IoT. In: 2017 IEEE Symposium on Service-Oriented System Engineering (SOSE), pp. 9–18. IEEE (2017)
14. Martins, C., Lima, S.M.: Vantagens e desvantagens do prontuário eletrônico para instituição de saúde. RAS, Abr-Jun 2014, vol. 16, no. 63 (2014)
15. Oliveira, M.: O papel dos profissionais de saude na formacao academica. Olho Magico **10**(2), 37–39 (2003)
16. Pahl, C., Jamshidi, P.: Microservices: a systematic mapping study. In: CLOSER (1), pp. 137–146 (2016)
17. Richardson, C.: Pattern: API gateway/backend for front-end. Google Scholar (2017)
18. Soldani, J., Tamburri, D.A., Van Den Heuvel, W.J.: The pains and gains of microservices: a systematic grey literature review. J. Syst. Softw. **146**, 215–232 (2018)
19. Ueda, T., Nakaike, T., Ohara, M.: Workload characterization for microservices. In: 2016 IEEE International Symposium on Workload Characterization (IISWC), pp. 1–10. IEEE (2016)
20. Williams, C.L., Sica, J.C., Killen, R.T., Balis, U.G.: The growing need for microservices in bioinformatics. J. Pathol. Inf. **7** (2016)
21. Yang, Y., Zu, Q., Liu, P., Ouyang, D., Li, X.: Microshare: privacy-preserved medical resource sharing through microservice architecture. arXiv preprint arXiv:1806.02134 (2018)
22. Yu, Y., Silveira, H., Sundaram, M.: A microservice based reference architecture model in the context of enterprise architecture. In: 2016 IEEE Conference on Advanced Information Management, Communicates, Electronic and Automation Control Conference (IMCEC), pp. 1856–1860. IEEE (2016)

A Systematic Mapping Study on Software Architectures Description Based on ISO/IEC/IEEE 42010:2011

Ademir A. C. Júnior[1]([envelope]) [iD], Sanjay Misra[2] [iD], and Michel S. Soares[1] [iD]

[1] Federal University of Sergipe, Av. Marechal Rondon, s/n - Jardim Rosa Elze,
São Cristóvão, Brazil
{ademiralcj,michel}@dcomp.ufs.br
[2] Convenant University, KM 10 Idiroko Rd, Ota, Nigeria
sanjay.misra@covenantuniversity.edu.ng

Abstract. Software architecture is considered an important area of Software Engineering, as it is useful for managing the development and maintenance of large scale software-intensive systems. Due to Software Architecture importance, the ISO/IEC/IEEE 42010:2011 standard was published in 2011. In this paper, we present a Systematic Mapping Study (SMS) for describing studies that explicitly used the ISO/IEC/IEEE 42010:2011 standard, and identifying which parts of this standard were most considered in the literature. Through the research, we selected 19 papers published between 2007 and September 2018. One interesting result is that ISO/IEC/IEEE 42010:2011 standard has been used, and its presence in papers has increased since 2016. However, parts of the standard are still not considered in practice. Industry and academia can still benefit from learning and improve the use of ISO/IEC/IEEE 42010:2011. Based on our findings, we suggest further research to analyze all the aspects of the standard as well as an industrial study.

Keywords: ISO/IEC/IEEE 42010:2011 · Software architecture ·
Architecture description · Systematic Mapping Study

1 Introduction

Software architecture is considered an important area of Software Engineering, as it is useful for managing the development and maintenance of large scale software-intensive systems [1]. The emphasis of mapping the components and their connectors of a software system is generally recognized, and has led to better control over the design, development, and maintenance of these systems [2].

The software architecture community has developed numerous technologies to support the architecture process (analysis, design, and review) [1]. Besides, in order to facilitate and assist the software architecture documentation, a number of contributions have been made in the last decades in terms of architecture standards, as for, Kruchten 4+1 View Model [3], Siemens' 4 View Model [4]

© Springer Nature Switzerland AG 2019
S. Misra et al. (Eds.): ICCSA 2019, LNCS 11623, pp. 17–30, 2019.
https://doi.org/10.1007/978-3-030-24308-1_2

and Zachman Framework [5]. In addition, a standard was also proposed. Its first version, the ANSI/IEEE 1471-2000, was published as a standard in 2000. Then, it was revised in 2007, and finally published in its current format, the ISO/IEC/IEEE 42010:2011 standard, in 2011.

By reading the ISO/IEC/IEEE 42010:2011 standard, it is clear that it describes many architectural elements in its chapters, including, to mention a few, architecture description, frameworks, viewpoints, relations, rationale, and also the relationship from this specific architectural standard to others, as for instance, the ISO/IEC 12207:2008 [6], which establishes a common framework for software life cycle processes, and ISO/IEC 15288:2008 [7], which establishes a common framework for describing the life cycle of systems created by humans. Therefore, from all these elements, there is no commonly known hierarchy, or at least a notion of minimal architecture, or even which parts most be considered by software architects. In summary, users do not know which elements are the most important ones, and as a result there are elements that are barely mentioned in the literature.

The main objective of this paper is to present a Systematic Mapping Study (SMS) for describing studies that explicitly used the ISO/IEC/IEEE 42010:2011 standard, and identifying which parts of this standard were most considered in the literature.

2   Brief Introduction to ISO/IEC/IEEE 42010:2011 - Systems and Software Engineering - Architecture Description

In this section, we present a brief overview of the standard ISO/IEC/IEEE 42010:2011 [8], which is the focus of our SMS. The ISO/IEC/IEEE 42010:2011 is a new version with improvements of former ANSI/IEEE 1471-2000 and it specifies the best practices for documenting enterprise, system and software architectures.

By considering the terms in Fig. 1, one can notice that systems have architectures that are expressed by architecture descriptions. In addition, Systems have multiple stakeholders who have different concerns. These concerns drive multiple architecture views, and each architecture view consists of architecture models, and adheres to the modeling conventions of its Architecture Viewpoint. A full information of ISO/IEC/IEEE 42010:2011 can be find in the official standard document [8].

3   Research Methodology

This section presents the design and execution of the SMS, which is based on [9]. A SMS provides a structure of the type of research reports and results that have been published by classifying them, and often provides a visual summary, the map of its results [9]. **Besides, in this section it is given the process**

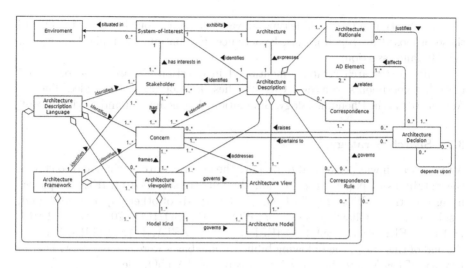

Fig. 1. Conceptual model of an architecture description - Adapted from [8].

for conducting the SMS, which is composed by Research Question (RQ), Research String, Data Source Selection and Selection of Primary Studies. Therefore, all these steps were considered to understand the use of ISO/IEC/IEEE 42010:2011 regarding its most used items.

3.1   Research Questions

The following research question is proposed: "What studies in the literature have used ISO/IEC/IEEE 42010:2011 as a reference for designing their software architectures?". In order to answer this research question, a set of questions is defined, as displayed in Table 1.

Table 1. Research questions

Abbreviation	Question
Q1	When was the ISO/IEC/IEEE 42010:2011 used?
Q2	What was the venue of publication?
Q3	What aspects ISO/IEC/IEEE 42010:2011 are most considered?
Q3.1	Which models were used?
Q4	In which domains was ISO/IEC/IEEE 42010:2011 used?
Q5	What type of validation was considered?
Q6	What type of research strategy was considered?

The domains cited in Question Q4 are the main final activities to which the software architecture will be applied in software and systems development, as for instance, Education, Transportation, Communication, and so on.

Identification of the possible types of validation mentioned in Question Q5 are those proposed in [10]: Analysis, Experience, Evaluation, Example, Persuasion, and Blatant assertion.

Types of research strategy mentioned in question Q6 are those presented in [11]: Experiments, Surveys, Case Studies, Ethnography, Grounded Theory, Action Research, Phenomenology, Simulation, Mathematical and Logical Proof.

3.2   Search Strategy

A test research was performed to prepare the generic search string, and to choose the databases of papers. First of all, the authors searched on IEEE Explorer, using the string "ISO 42010". Then, further words of other papers were found, resulting on the following keywords: ISO 42010, ISO/IEC 42010, IEEE 42010, ISO-IEC-IEEE 42010, ISO/IEC/IEEE 42010, ISO STANDARD 42010. Then, at the end of this stage, the following bibliographic bases were chosen: ACM Digital Library, IEEE Xplore, ScienceDirect, Scopus and WebOfScience.

The defined generic search string is displayed in Table 2.

Table 2. Generic search string.

(**TITLE-ABS-KEY** ("ISO   42010"   OR   "ISO/IEC   42010"   OR "ISO/IEC/IEEE 42010" OR "ISO-IEC-IEEE 42010" OR "IEEE 42010" OR "ISO STANDARD 42010"))

Due to the fact that the first draft of ISO/IEC/IEE 42010:2011 was published in 2007, papers with a date of publication prior to this year were discarded. Also, the inclusion and exclusion criteria were defined to identify relevant works to this research, which are presented as follows:

Inclusion criteria (IC):

– IC1 - Studies that use ISO/IEEC/IEEE 42010:2011 for defining, evaluating, describing, or developing software architectures.

Exclusion criteria (EC):

– EC1 - Duplicated papers;
– EC2 - Secondary study papers;
– EC3 - Papers written in languages other than English;
– EC4 - Posters;
– EC5 - Standards;

The search was conducted on September 12, 2018, returning 128 papers. The results from the databases were exported via *bibtex* file, and imported into tool StArt [12], which assists Systematic Literature Reviews. This tool is used to organize the references of articles, and then all the references were exported to an online spreadsheet, in this case Google Sheets.

4   Results and Analysis

Figure 2 describes the organization of the SMS's steps, and the amount of studies resulting in each one. First, using the adopted support tool and manual analysis, 74 papers were rejected regarding the defined Exclusion criteria.

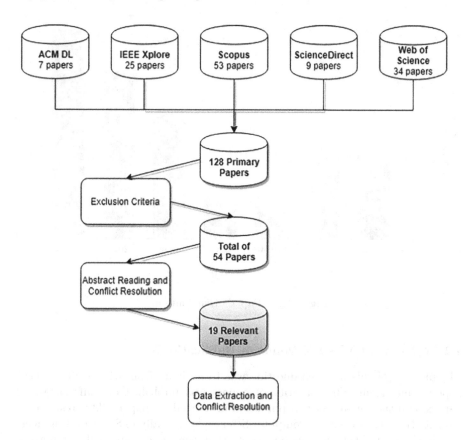

Fig. 2. Representation flow of the SMS.

Second, a selection step was performed. In order to avoid bias, all papers were analyzed independently by two researchers, who applied the defined inclusion and exclusion criteria by reading the title, the keywords and the abstract. At the end of this stage, a meeting was held to resolve doubts or conflicts from the selection, resulting in the final list of 18 papers, 7 from IEEE Xplore, 4 from ScienceDirect, 4 from WebOfScience, 2 from Scopus and 1 from ACM Digital Library.

Finally, data were extracted from the 18 papers in order to answer the questions defined in Table 1. In addition, in the selection phase, data extraction was performed individually by each researcher. Then, at the end of that phase, a meeting was held again to solve doubts or conflicts.

4.1   Q1 - When Was the ISO/IEC/IEEE 42010:2011 Used?

We found that the years of 2016, 2017 and 2018 have the majority of papers, three, four and five respectively, as depicted in Fig. 3. On the other hand, the years that have less papers are 2014 and 2015.

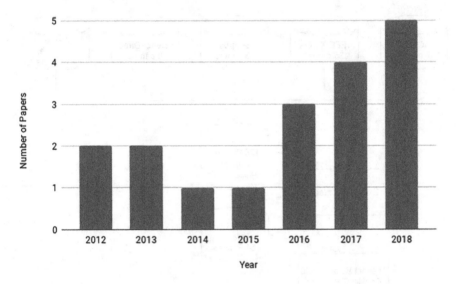

Fig. 3. Q1 - Paper's Distribution.

4.2   Q2 - What Was the Venue of Publication?

The purpose of this research question was to evaluate from what sources these papers came from. The majority of papers was published in conferences, 12 papers, and the remainder was published in journals, 6 papers. This result may indicate that researchers in Computer Science, specifically in Software Engineering, prefer to publish in conferences, or that the papers are still not mature and with enough details to be published in journals. Additionally, there are 17 different locals of publication, just two locals are mentioned twice: Journal of Systems and Software and IEEE International Conference on Software Architecture (ICSA).

This is an important finding of our research, because it allows other researchers to know in which venues articles about ISO/IEC/IEEE 42010:2011 have been published.

4.3   Q3 - What Aspects from ISO/IEC/IEEE 42010:2011 Are Most Considered?

The purpose of this research question is to identify the most used points of the standard ISO/IEC/IEEE 42010:2011 by the researchers. As a research paper most often has a limited number of pages, we infer that the researchers may not write all the possible aspects from the standard. We listed the main ones to be checked on each paper: Stakeholders (Stkh), Concerns (Conc), View, Viewpoint (Vp), Model, Model Kind (M. Kind), Correspondence (Corr), Correspondence Rule (C. Rule) and Rationale.

These aspects may take a considerable area in the selected papers because they require explanation. Thus, it is possible that the authors preferred to omit them, and not necessarily that they were not considered in their research.

Table 3. Aspects of ISO/IEC/IEEE 42010:2011 found in the papers.

Paper	Stkh	Conc.	View	Vp	Model	M. Kind	Corr	C. Rule	Rationale
[13]	•	•					•	•	•
[14]	•	•		•	•	•			•
[15]	•	•	•				•	•	•
[16]	•	•	•	•	•	•	•	•	•
[17]	•	•	•	•					•
[18]	•	•	•		•	•	•		•
[19]	•	•	•		•	•	•	•	•
[20]	•	•	•	•	•	•	•	•	•
[21]	•	•	•	•	•	•	•	•	•
[22]	•	•	•	•	•	•			•
[23]	•	•	•	•	•	•	•	•	•
[24]	•	•	•	•	•	•			•
[25]	•	•	•	•	•	•	•	•	•
[26]	•	•	•	•	•	•			•
[27]	•	•	•	•	•	•			•
[28]	•	•		•	•	•	•	•	•
[29]		•	•	•	•	•	•	•	•
[30]	•	•		•	•	•	•	•	•

The most used aspects are Concerns and Rationales, mentioned by all papers, as depicted in Fig. 4. When defining the stakeholders, concerns came as a consequence. There is one paper, [29], that did not explicitly mentioned stakeholders and all the requirements were extracted from academic literature. Rationales are presented in any software architecture, because they are the reason for decisions.

Stakeholders are the key to any architecture, as they define the main elements of a Software Architecture, 17 papers mentioned this aspect.

The third most mentioned architectural element is Model and Model Kind, 14 out of 18 papers mentioned them. Model and Model Kind refers basically to the type of diagrams, and the most used modeling language is UML, in 10 papers, followed by SysML (3 papers) and SoaML (1 paper). One paper used together UML and SysML, and another used UML and SoaML. This result may be expected because UML is probably the most used modeling language in Software Engineering [31,32].

Another finding of this SMS is that some of the papers that identified the views did not mention what views they used. In contrast, others, explicitly, mention what views they used: [15, 17–19, 22, 24, 27, 29] and [23].

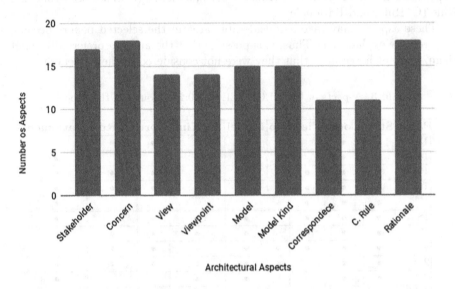

Fig. 4. Q3 - Most considered Architectural Aspects of ISO/IEC/IEEE 42010:2011.

Q3.1- Which Models Were Used? When analyzing the Model Kinds used in the papers, the Use Case, Class and State Machine diagrams are the most mentioned ones, as shown in Fig. 5. This may be an expected result because Use Case diagrams describe scenarios and functional requirements [33], making easier to understand what the system does and give a good means of communication about the system [34]. Furthermore, Class Diagrams can be directly mapped to object-oriented languages, and they are the basis of software construction. Component diagram is the fourth most mentioned model, in four papers, followed by the Sequence diagram, 2 times.

In paper [22], Definition Block and Internal Block diagrams were mentioned. Publication [30] adopted SysML diagrams, and used the following models: Sequence, Package, Use Case, State Machine and Definition Block. As the Sequence, Package, Use Case and State Machine diagrams are part of the UML, they were also included in Fig. 5.

Finally, diagrams mentioned from SoaML were Service Architecture, Participant and Data Exchange.

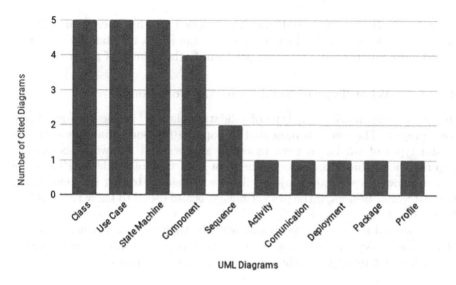

Fig. 5. Q3.1 - UML diagrams that were mentioned on the architectures.

4.4   Q4 - in Which Domains Was ISO/IEC/IEEE 42010:2011 Used?

As depicted in Fig. 6, the Transportation domain is the subject of study in six articles. The second domain in which the standard was applied is Industry.

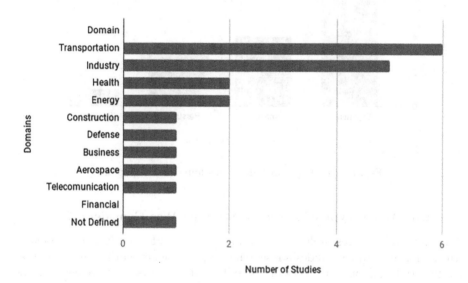

Fig. 6. Q4 - Domains in which the Architecture Description was applied.

ISO/IEC/IEEE 42010:2011 was also applied in the Energy and Health domain. For the rest of the domains mentioned in Fig. 6, the standard was mentioned once. Furthermore, we could not identify the domain of paper [16].

4.5   Q5 - What Type of Validation Was Considered?

In Software Engineering, the type of validation plays a big role for a good software project. The research presented in paper [10] reports that the most successful types of validation were based on analysis and real-world experience. Figure 7 shows that Experience is the most used type of validation. Thus, one way to know if a software project will be successful is testing it, preferably in the real world. Besides, if the project fails, it is also useful to know the problems that cause it.

The second most used type of validation is Analysis with 4 papers. Analysis is also a good type of validation because the authors can show if their solution is worth or not by applying the solution in realistic examples.

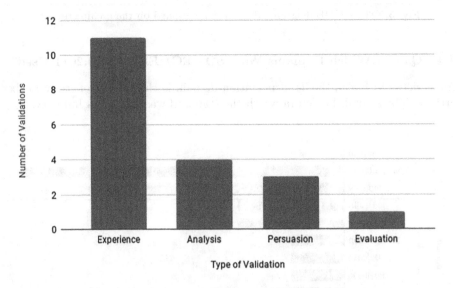

Fig. 7. Q5 - Types of Validations found in the papers.

4.6   Q6 - What Type of Research Strategy Was Considered?

According to [11], a research strategy is an overall plan for conducting a research study, and the strategy guides a researcher in planning, executing, and monitoring the study. Among the types of research strategy proposed in paper [11], we found 3 types in 15 papers of this study. Besides, it was not possible to define the research strategy of 4 papers.

Case Study was found in the majority of papers, in a total of 8 studies. This may be the research strategy near to the real world with less cost. However, the fact that the research is successful in one case does not mean that it will be in any case. Action Research is the second considered one with 5 papers. This research strategy is used to solve problems in a real environment, and most of them was found in industry, health, financial and transportation domains. The last one is simulation, found in the Energy domain.

Based on the definitions offered in [11], the authors could not classify the research in papers [16,19], since they did not provide enough information about the type of research strategy adopted in these papers. Additionally, papers [30] and [29] did not explicitly provided a research strategy, but in their future work, they will consider a case study for their research.

5 Threats to Validity

The results of this research may have been affected by several factors that are categorized as follows.

Selection Bias. Some studies may be included or excluded into the SMS incorrectly. With the purpose of reducing this threat, the research protocol was discussed between the researchers to guarantee a common understanding, and the researchers made decisions together in a meeting for each item that they were in doubt.

Data Extraction. Bias or problem of extraction can influence classifications and the analysis of selected studies. For reducing this bias, the researchers discussed the definitions of each item used to respond the questions. The data extraction form was a spreadsheet composed of 16 columns (data extraction attributes), which was structured as follows: 5 columns related to article identification, 2 columns related to context of the research, and 9 columns related to attributes of ISO/IEC/IEEE 42010:2011.

Generalization. It is possible to generalize the information from this research. Even though the number of papers addressing ISO/IEC/IEEE 42010:2011 standard can be considered small, the search string was wide as possible, to reach the majority of papers in the databases.

External. We can not generalize this information because there is not a significant number of scientific papers addressing the ISO/IEC/IEEE 42010:2011 standard. Furthermore, we may not identify other papers that are suitable to the standard, but do not make reference to it. In order to mitigate this threat, the search string was created to reach as many papers as possible.

6 Conclusions and Future Works

In this paper we presented a Systematic Mapping Study that investigates studies which used ISO/IEC/IEEE 42010:2011 on their software architectures. The most relevant findings from this research are as follows.

First, the number of researches that are using ISO/IEC/IEEE 42010:2011 are increasing since 2016, and most of them are published in conferences. Second, the most used architectural aspects are Stakeholders and Concerns, 18 out of 19 papers mentioned them. Third, UML is the authors' preferred modelling language in software/system architecture, found in 10 papers. Fourth, transportation is the domain in which the standard is most applied, followed by industry, health and energy. Fifth, Experience is the most used type of validation, and Case Study is the most used type of research strategy in projects that used ISO/IEC/IEEE 42010:2011.

The results of this Systematic Mapping Study should provide insights and encourage further research applying ISO/IEC/IEEE 42010:2011 in software architectures.

As a future work, we suggest a further research analyzing all the aspects of the standard. Besides, an industrial study which will analyze companies that use the standard and verify what aspects can be performed.

Acknowledgment. This study was financed in part by the Fundação de Apoio a Pesquisa e Inovação Tecnológica do Estado de Sergipe.

References

1. Falessi, D., Babar, M.A., Cantone, G., Kruchten, P.: Applying empirical software engineering to software architecture: challenges and lessons learned. Empirical Softw. Eng. **15**(3), 250–276 (2010)
2. Bass, L., Clements, P., Kazman, R.: Software Architecture in Practice, 3rd edn. Addison-Wesley Professional (2012)
3. Kruchten, P.B.: The 4+1 view model of architecture. IEEE Softw. **12**(6), 42–50 (1995)
4. Hofmeister, C., Nord, R., Soni, D.: Applied Software Architecture. Addison-Wesley Professional, Boston (2000)
5. Zachman, J.A.: A framework for information systems architecture. IBM Syst. J. **26**, 276–292 (1987)
6. ISO/IEC 12207: 2008(E) IEEE Std 12207–2008 - Redline: systems and software engineering - software life cycle processes - Redline. IEEE (2008)
7. ISO/IEC 15288: 2008(E) IEEE Std 15288–2008 (Revision of IEEE Std 15288–2004) - Redline: ISO/IEC/IEEE International Standard - systems and software engineering System life cycle processes - Redline. IEEE (2008)
8. ISO/IEC/IEEE: Systems and Software Engineering - Architecture Description. ISO/IEC/IEEE 42010:2011(E) (Revision of ISO/IEC 42010:2007 and IEEE Std 1471-2000), pp. 1–46, January 2011
9. Petersen, K., Feldt, R., Mujtaba, S., Mattsson, M.: Systematic mapping studies in software engineering. EASE **8**, 68–77 (2008)
10. Shaw, M.: Writing good software engineering research papers. In: 2003 Proceedings of 25th International Conference on Software Engineering, pp. 726–736 (2003)
11. Johannesson, P., Perjons, E.: An Introduction to Design Science. Springer, Heidelberg (2014)
12. LAPES Laboratory of Research on Software Engineering (LAPES): StArt - State of the Art through Systematic Review (2018). http://lapes.dc.ufscar.br/tools/start_tool. Accessed 8 June 2018

13. Amin, M.S., Blackburn, T., Garstenauer, A.: Deploying a recall mitigation framework for systems engineering. Eng. Manag. J. **30**(1), 42–56 (2018)
14. Chaabane, M., Bouassida, I., Jmaiel, M.: System of systems software architecture description using the ISO/IEC/IEEE 42010 standard. In: Proceedings of the Symposium on Applied Computing, SAC 2017, pp. 1793–1798. ACM, New York (2017)
15. Crichton, R., Moodley, D., Pillay, A., Gakuba, R., Seebregts, C.J.: An architecture and reference implementation of an open health information mediator: enabling interoperability in the rwandan health information exchange. In: Weber, J., Perseil, I. (eds.) FHIES 2012. LNCS, vol. 7789, pp. 87–104. Springer, Heidelberg (2013). https://doi.org/10.1007/978-3-642-39088-3_6
16. Das, A.: Context-aware architecture utilizing computing with words and ISO/IEC/IEEE 42010. SoutheastCon **2016**, 1–6 (2016)
17. Effenberger, F., Hilbert, A.: Towards an energy information system architecture description for industrial manufacturers: decomposition & allocation view. Energy **112**, 599–605 (2016)
18. França, J.M.S., de Lima, J.S., Soares, M.S.: Development of an electronic health record application using a multiple view service oriented architecture. In: Proceedings of the 19th International Conference on Enterprise Information Systems, ICEIS 2017, vol. 2, pp. 308–315 (2017)
19. Gmez, l., Aristizbal, L.M., Zuluaga, C.A., Correa, J.C., Vsquez, R.E.: Development and implementation of a high-level control system for the underwater remotely operated vehicle VISOR3. IFAC-PapersOnLine **50**(1), 1151–1156 (2017). 20th IFAC World Congress
20. Hilliard, R., Malavolta, I., Muccini, H., Pelliccione, P.: On the composition and reuse of viewpoints across architecture frameworks. In: 2012 Joint Working IEEE/IFIP Conference on Software Architecture and European Conference on Software Architecture, pp. 131–140 (2012)
21. Kannengiesser, U., Müller, H.: Towards viewpoint-oriented engineering for industry 4.0: a standards-based approach. In: 2018 IEEE Industrial Cyber-Physical Systems (ICPS), pp. 51–56 (2018)
22. Karkhanis, P., van den Brand, M.G.J., Rajkarnikar, S.: Defining the C-ITS reference architecture. In: 2018 IEEE International Conference on Software Architecture Companion (ICSA-C), pp. 148–151 (2018)
23. Kavakli, E., Buenabad-Chvez, J., Tountopoulos, V., Loucopoulos, P., Sakellariou, R.: WiP: an architecture for disruption management in smart manufacturing. In: 2018 IEEE International Conference on Smart Computing (SMARTCOMP), pp. 279–281 (2018)
24. May, G., Ioannidis, D., Metaxa, I.N., Tzovaras, D., Kiritsis, D.: An approach to development of system architecture in large collaborative projects. In: Lödding, H., Riedel, R., Thoben, K.-D., von Cieminski, G., Kiritsis, D. (eds.) APMS 2017. IAICT, vol. 513, pp. 67–75. Springer, Cham (2017). https://doi.org/10.1007/978-3-319-66923-6_8
25. Musil, J., Musil, A., Weyns, D., Biffl, S.: An architecture framework for collective intelligence systems. In: 2015 12th Working IEEE/IFIP Conference on Software Architecture, pp. 21–30 (2015)
26. Obergfell, P., Oszwald, F., Traub, M., Sax, E.: Viewpoint-based methodology for adaption of automotive E/E-architectures. In: 2018 IEEE International Conference on Software Architecture Companion (ICSA-C), pp. 128–135 (2018)
27. Panunzio, M., Vardanega, T.: An architectural approach with separation of concerns to address extra-functional requirements in the development of embedded real-time software systems. J. Syst. Archit. **60**(9), 770–781 (2014)

28. Van Heesch, U., Avgeriou, P., Hilliard, R.: A documentation framework for architecture decisions. J. Syst. Softw. **85**(4), 795–820 (2012)
29. Vidoni, M., Vecchietti, A.: Towards a reference architecture for advanced planning systems. In: Hammoudi, S., Maciaszek, L., Missikoff, M.M., Camp, O., Cordeiro, J. (eds.) Proceedings of the 18th International Conference on Enterprise Information Systems, (ICEIS), vol. 1, pp. 433–440 (2016)
30. Williams, J.L., Stracener, J.T.: First steps in the development of a Program Organizational Architectural Framework (POAF). Syst. Eng. **16**(1), 45–70 (2013)
31. Hutchinson, J., Whittle, J., Rouncefield, M.: Model-driven engineering practices in industry: social, organizational and managerial factors that lead to success or failure. Sci. Comput. Program. **89**, 144–161 (2014)
32. Chaudron, M.R.V.: Empirical studies into UML in practice: pitfalls and prospects. In: 2017 IEEE/ACM 9th International Workshop on Modelling in Software Engineering (MiSE), pp. 3–4 (2017)
33. Bertolino, A., Fantechi, A., Gnesi, S., Lami, G., Maccari, A.: Use case description of requirements for product lines. In: International Workshop on Requirements Engineering for Product Lines, vol. 2002, p. 12 (2002)
34. John, I., Muthig, D.: Tailoring use cases for product line modeling. In: Proceedings of the International Workshop on Requirements Engineering for Product Lines, vol. 2002, pp. 26–32 (2002)

ArchCaMO - A Maturity Model for Software Architecture Description Based on ISO/IEC/IEEE 42010:2011

Ademir A. C. Júnior[1](✉)(iD), Sanjay Misra[2](iD), and Michel S. Soares[1](iD)

[1] Federal University of Sergipe, Av. Marechal Rondon, s/n - Jardim Rosa Elze,
São Cristóvão, Brazil
{ademiralcj,michel}@dcomp.ufs.br
[2] Convenant University, KM 10 Idiroko Rd, Ota, Nigeria
sanjay.misra@covenantuniversity.edu.ng

Abstract. Academia and Industry have acknowledged that having a fully described software architecture is a crucial asset for software development and maintenance. The description of a software architecture is read by many stakeholders when developing and maintaining complex software systems which are composed by multiple elements, including software, systems, hardware and processes. The software architecture as a development product is useful for technical activities, such as describing the views and concerns of the future software products, as well as for management activities, including allocating tasks to each team and as an input for project management activities. One main issue when describing the software architecture is knowing what elements must be included in the architecture, and at what level of detail. Therefore, it is not unusual that software architects have to deal with difficulties in terms of how to describe the architecture. This paper brings two main purposes: first is the idea of establishing levels of a maturity model for software architectures, which can help in organizing, describing and communicating the software architecture for multiple stakeholders, and, second, a way to evaluate how mature is the software architecture.

Keywords: Software architecture · Maturity models ·
ISO/IEC/IEEE 42010

1 Introduction

Software architecture has been defined in multiple ways since the 1960's. From the first ideas of structuring and decomposing complex systems into more manageable modules [1–3], to modern definitions with focus on cooperating components, decision making [4] and knowledge management (AKM) [5].

Software architecture has been considered by many researchers and practitioners a fundamental asset in software development and maintenance [6–8]. For instance, the authors of a book on documenting software architecture [9] express

© Springer Nature Switzerland AG 2019
S. Misra et al. (Eds.): ICCSA 2019, LNCS 11623, pp. 31–42, 2019.
https://doi.org/10.1007/978-3-030-24308-1_3

that without an appropriate software architecture for the problem to be solved by a software, the project will fail. Other authors also express the difficulties brought by not using correctly a software architecture to handle the complexity of software-intensive systems [10], or the importance of software architectures for developing software systems that are better and more resilient to change when compared to systems developed without a clear architectural definition [11].

However, despite its importance, the process of software architecting, the evaluation of software architectures and even the social impact on the software architecture in an organization are still neglected in software development [8,12, 13]. Creating a reliable, robust software architecture demands effort which will be almost useless in case the architecture is not well-described and understood by technical stakeholders. Software architects need to describe it on the necessary level of detail, trying to solve ambiguity issues, and organize in such a way that it is understandable, and with information that is easy to retrieve.

A case of technical debt occurs when the architectural documentation is insufficient, incomplete, or outdated. One possible reason is due to the contest between agilists and more process-oriented personnel [11,14]. The assumption in this paper is that even though the importance of software architecture is recognized, how to describe, and at what level of detail one has to describe the software architecture, are still open issues in industry. It is frequent that industry practitioners, and even researchers, do not even know how to start to describe the architecture [8], do not know how much architecture to use [15,16], have issues regarding agility in processes and what is named Big Design Up-Front (BDUF) architecture [17], or even which architectural elements are necessary to describe in the software architecture documents [18–20].

One possible solution for describing a software architecture is to rely on models and standards such as Kruchten's 4+1 Model [21] or ISO/IEC/IEEE 42010:2011 [22]. However, the issue here is that in practice it is hard to understand such standards, as they are considered too high-level to be used in practice or too complex to be easily understandable by the software development team.

The proposal in this paper is to describe a model named ArchCaMo to access the level of architectural maturity using ISO/IEC/IEEE 42010:2011 as context. The objective of ArchCaMo is twofold. First, the ArchCaMo model can be used to evaluate current architectures, showing to development personnel at what level of maturity their architecture conforms to. In addition, it is useful for those organizations that are struggling with organizing, describing and communicating the software architecture for multiple stakeholders. For each level of architecture maturity, the organization knows exactly what to expect in terms of activities and deliverables.

Although other maturity models for software architectures were proposed, as described in the next section, to the best of our knowledge, no other models were introduced with focus on ISO/IEC/IEEE 42010:2011.

2   Related Works

Many maturity models were proposed in past decades in order to access capability of organizations and departments of information technology. Among these, SW-CMM and CMMI are well-known, and have been applied to evaluate software development processes in many countries and for a variety of domains.

SW-CMM [23], and later its evolution, Staged CMMI [24], propose evaluation in 5 levels, in which each level includes a number of activities, tasks, goals, processes, practices and so on. Therefore, when an organization is certified at some level, it is possible to know which activities and practices are performed, indicating a level of discipline and organization for software development.

Few works have proposed to evaluate and access maturity levels of software architectures.

For instance, in [25], authors contribute towards establishment of a comprehensive and unified strategy for process maturity evaluation of software product lines, showing the maturity of the architecture development process in two organizations.

Authors of article [26] propose an architectural maturity model framework to improve Ultra-Large-Scale Systems Interoperability. Although the authors present an architectural maturity model, their focus was only on organizing an interoperability maturity model, i.e., the maturity is evaluated from the interoperability point of view, and is not applicable for other architectural purposes.

The US Department of Commerce (DoC) has developed an IT Architecture Capability Maturity Model (ACMM) [27]. The ACMM provides a framework that represents the key components of a productive IT architecture process. Their approach is to identify weak areas and provide an evolutionary path to improving the overall architecture process. The DoC ACMM consists of six levels and nine architecture characteristics.

To the best of our knowledge, no works have described a software architecture maturity model based on ISO/IEC/IEEE 42010:2011, a standard to describe software and system architectures, briefly introduced in the next section. Therefore, novelty here regards not only the proposal of a new architectural capability model for evaluation of software and systems architectures, but also the use of a standard as a guide to the capability model.

ISO/IEC/IEEE 42010:2011 [22] addresses the creation, analysis and sustainment of architectures of systems through the use of architecture descriptions. This standard proposes a conceptual model of architecture description, including concepts such as views, models, concerns, rationale, viewpoints, frameworks and architecture description languages. The standard provides a core ontology for description of software architectures.

Several terms which have some relation to software architecture are defined in the standard. According to the standard *Architecting* is the process of conceiving, expressing, defining, documenting, communicating and certifying proper implementation of, maintaining and improving an architecture throughout a software's life cycle. An *Architecture* is the fundamental concept or properties of a system in its environment embodied in its elements, relationships, and in the principles of its design and evolution.

ISO/IEC/IEEE 42010:2011 does not specify any format for recording architecture descriptions, but it describes the basic context of an architecture description. This context specifies that stakeholders have interests in one or more software systems. These interests, better explained as concerns, include a variety of extra-functional properties, such as maintainability, testability, and modularity, but also project management concerns, including costs, schedule, business goals and strategies. A concern pertains to any influence on a system in its environment. Each system is situated in an environment, which is a context determining the setting and circumstances of all influences upon a software system. The environment of a software system includes developmental, business, technological, operational, organizational, political, economic, regulatory, legal, ecological and social influences.

Each class of stakeholder has more or less interest, depending on how important a concern is regarding their own tasks and roles in the organization. For instance, maintainability is a concern of software developers and architects, and business goals and strategies are concerns for managers. Each system can exhibit many architectures, as for instance, when considered in different environments.

An architecture can be expressed through several distinct architecture descriptions, and the same architecture can characterize one or more software systems, as a software product line sharing a common architecture.

Architecture descriptions have many uses for a variety of stakeholders throughout the system life cycle. For instance, software developers use the architecture description for software design, development and maintenance activities. Clients, acquirers, suppliers and developers use the architecture description as part of contract negotiations, documenting the characteristics, features and design of a software system. Infrastructure personnel use the architecture description as a guide to operational and infrastructure support and configuration management. Managers use the architecture description as a support to software planning activities, such as establishing the schedule, budge, and the team.

A complete description on ISO/IEC/IEEE 42010:2011 can be find in the official standard document [22], and its practical use has been explored by many researchers in past years, for instance in health systems [28,29], industry [30,31], transportation systems [32], business [33], defense [34] and energy [35].

3 ArchCaMo - Architectural Capability Model

Instead of establishing in a rigid way activities, processes and tasks to be followed, in ArchCaMo the idea is to structure the levels in such a way that the organization can decide its own processes for each given practice to be executed at each level.

3.1 How the Levels Are Proposed

The ArchCaMo's levels are based on, essentially, ISO/IEC/IEEE 42010:2011, a Systematic Mapping Study (SMS) executed by the authors, and also the authors' own experience in software architecture.

First, almost all the levels are linked to a topic of the standard. Therefore, we did not change the standard, but we have organized it in such a way that the architecture team can document the software/system's architecture in a sequential manner.

The second reference for ArchCaMo's levels is the SMS. We found initially 128 papers published between 2007 and 2018. After the selection phase, 19 studies expressed that they have used ISO/IEC/IEEE 42010:2011 on their architecture description, thus we identified what aspects/points of the standard were most or least used in these studies. As a result, according to this classification and our knowledge/experience about the standard, we proposed that the most used features of ISO/IEC/IEEE 42010:2011 would be considered in the initial levels and so on.

3.2 ArchCaMo Levels

The ArchCaMo model is defined in 5 levels. The initial level, Level 1, refers to all companies/organizations that do not have a formalized way to define the software architecture, so they may document some aspects that they need or think that is necessary for the project. This level is classified as unstable from the architectural point of view.

Levels 2 and 3. These levels are made up of most relevant aspects that are necessary to describe a software architecture. The following tables describe each level consisting of KAI (Key Architecture Item), the description of the KAI, and the respective reference in ISO/IEC/IEEE 42010:2011.

Table 1. Level 2 - minimum architecture

KAI	Description	Reference in the standard
2.1	Environment is identified	Item 4.2
2.2	Systems of Interest are identified	Item 5.2
2.3	Supplementary information is identified	Item 5.2
2.4	Stakeholders are identified	Item 5.3
2.5	Concerns for each Stakeholder are identified	Item 5.3
2.6	Viewpoints are defined	Item 5.4
2.7	Multiple Views are defined	Item 5.5
2.8	Models are defined	Item 5.6

Table 1 describes the Minimum Architecture, which is the name of Level 2. This table is based on Context of architecture description and Conceptual model of an architecture description of ISO/IEC/IEEE 42010:2011.

Table 2 describes the Defined Architecture, and it is also based on Conceptual model of an architecture description, and Conceptual model of AD elements and correspondences of ISO/IEC/IEEE 42010:2011.

Table 2. Level 3 - defined architecture

KAI	Description	Reference in the standard
3.1	Correspondence rules are identified	Item 5.7.2
3.2	Rationales for decisions are identified	Item 5.8.1
3.3	Concerns related to each decision are defined	Item 5.8.2
3.4	Decisions are managed	Item 5.8.2

Levels 4 and 5. The 2 upper levels represented in Tables 3 (Consistent Architecture) and 4 (Quantified and Improved Architecture) are related to aspects that are needed to improve a software architecture situation in the life cycle that is already structured, but still has possibilities of improvement.

Table 3 describes the Consistent Architecture, based on Conceptual model of an architecture framework, and Conceptual model of an architecture description language of ISO/IEC/IEEE 42010:2011.

Table 3. Level 4 - consistent architecture

KAI	Description	Reference in the standard
4.1	Known inconsistencies are recorded	Item 5.7.1
4.2	Use of Architecture Frameworks	Item 6.1
4.3	Use of Architecture description languages	Item 6.3

Table 4 describes the Consistent Architecture, based on Conceptual model of an architecture framework, and Conceptual model of an architecture description language of ISO/IEC/IEEE 42010:2011.

Table 4. Level 5 - quantified and improved architecture

KAI	Description	Reference in the standard
5.1	Metrics on elements of the other levels are defined	Item 7
5.2	An Architecture Group is established	Page 2[a]

[a] Architecting takes place in the context of an organization ("person or a group of people and facilities with an arrangement of responsibilities, authorities and relationships") [22]

4   ArchCaMo Processes for Each Level

For each level, at least one architectural process is defined. These processes are performed mostly by the architect, or team of software architects that are responsible for the software product.

First of all, we suppose that not all organizations have a defined process for defining, structuring, and evaluating their software architecture. Even though some organizations that have a defined process may not fulfill all the KAI's, it does not mean that their architectural processes and products are irrelevant or insufficient.

4.1   Level 2 - Minimum Architecture

- **P2.1** - Environment is identified. There are many environments, not only the place where the team is coding, but also, for instance, operational environment, development environment, test environment, and so on. Additionally, when defining the environment, this will generate non-functional requirements, and establish rules for the system.
- **P2.2** - System-of-Interest is identified. System in which life cycle is under consideration [36]. One way for identifying the system is the environment in which the system is.
- **P2.3** - Supplementary information is identified. This material shall be specified by the organization or project, which may include: date of issue and status; authors, reviewers, approving authority, or issuing organization; change history; summary; scope; context; glossary; version control information; configuration management information and references [22].
- **P2.4** - Stakeholders are identified. Each stakeholder is defined and ranked for their relative importance for that specific software product. In consonance with [22], these stakeholders shall be considered, and when applicable, identified in the architecture description: users of the system, operators of the system, acquirers of the system, owners of the system, suppliers of the system, developers of the system, builders of the system and maintainers of the system.
- **P2.5** - Concerns for each Stakeholder are identified. For each stakeholder, its relative concerns are identified. In the ISO/IEC/IEEE 42010:2011 documentation, one can find some concerns that should be identified when applicable.
- **P2.6** - Viewpoints are defined. Through interpretation from architectures views it is established the viewpoints which will frame specific established concerns.
- **P2.7** - Multiple Views are defined. Each one of the multiple Views for describing the software architecture is defined to address the concerns held by one or more of its stakeholders.
- **P2.8** - Models are defined. From each viewpoint, models are defined using modelling conventions established by the architecture team, appropriate to the concerns to be addressed. Models are used to answer questions about the system-of-interest.

4.2   Level 3 - Defined Architecture

- **P3.1** - Correspondence rules are identified. These correspondences are used for indicating relations between two or more architecture models, and the rules are used to establish constraints on two or more architecture models.
- **P3.2** - Rationales for decisions are identified. Rationales are written in a list, and the reasons regarding each decision are documented for future reference.
- **P3.3** - Concerns related to each decision are defined.
- **P3.4** - Decisions are managed. Each decision is identified and written using a template defined by the architecture team. All decisions are identified, discussed, and written. At least a spreadsheet is used, but it is better to use a specific software system to keep track of each entry.

4.3   Level 4 - Improved Architecture

- **P4.1** - Known inconsistencies are recorded. An architecture description should record the inconsistencies, and include an analysis of consistency of its architecture models and its views [22].
- **P4.2** - Use of Architecture Frameworks. If the project is using an Architecture Framework, it should include conditions of applicability [22].
- **P4.3** - Use of Architecture Description Languages. The architecture description language should support all the aspects of the system-of-interest [22].

4.4   Level 5 - Quantified and Evaluated Architecture

- **P5.1** - Metrics on elements of the other levels are defined. The software architect evaluates costs and benefits from the metrics, comparing to the other architectures that used ArchCaMo. For each architectural decisions, the architect analyzes the implications, extracting a number of metrics from it.
- **P5.2** - An Architecture Group is established, which is responsible to get information of the state of the art on software architecture. The group seeks to improve the architecture by receiving input from many sources, including research conferences on software architecture, books, articles and reports. The Architecture Group is also responsible for searching for improvements, as for instance, new methods, techniques, languages, processes, and so on, on the theme of software architecture, and try to bring these approaches to be deployed in the organization.

5   Application of ArchCaMo in a Research Paper

This section describes an application of ArchCaMo in a software architecture proposed in an academic research paper. The paper [37] is a work in progress towards the specification of a conceptual architecture of a smart system, for supporting the management of disruptions in the manufacturing domain. Moreover, the work describes system architecture based on a number of interrelated viewpoints according to ISO/IEC/IEEE 42010:2011.

Table 5. ArchCaMO application level 2 in an example

KAI	Description	Reference in the standard	Identification in the paper [37]
2.1	Environment is identified	Item 4.2	Manufacturing Domain
2.2	System-of-Interest is identified	Item 5.2	Smart system for supporting the management of disruptions
2.3	Supplementary information is identified	Item 5.2	Context of the EU-funded H2020 DISRUPT
2.4	Stakeholders are identified	Item 5.3	System users (domain experts, operational managers and decision makers), system administrators, and technology providers (including the suppliers, the developers/integrators, the testers and the maintainers of the system)
2.5	Concerns for each Stakeholder are identified	Item 5.3	The purpose of the system is to support the disruption management lifecycle; The system will be added onto an existing factory ecosystem; The system will be based on a distributed architecture, consisting of loose coupling of (potentially existing) functional components, to enable flexibility in the system components and their functionality. This should reduce the risk for a vendor lock-in
2.6	Viewpoints are defined	Item 5.4	Describes the system main components, their functionality and interfaces; Describes the environment into which the system will be deployed, including dependencies it has on the environment, and the mapping of system components to the environment
2.7	Multiple Views are defined	Item 5.5	Logical view, Informational View and Physical View
2.8	Models are defined	Item 5.6	UML (Class, Component and Deployment)

In this example, displayed in Table 5, we read the research paper looking for any characteristic of the architecture description that follows the maturity model. After all analysis, we found that the description of the system architecture fits in Level 2, the Minimum Architecture. This conclusion may be because this is a short paper, or even it is a work in progress.

The authors did not find evidences for any one of the processes of Level 3, Level 4 or Level 5. Even if one of the KAI of any upper Level is fulfilled, the architecture would still be classified at Level 2.

This paper was chosen among 19 relevant papers found in a Systematic Mapping Study from another research. Even though this is a short paper, this paper was the one with more features following the standard ISO/IEC/IEEE 42010:2011.

6 Conclusion

In this paper, a maturity model for Software Architecture based on the standard ISO/IEC/IEEE 42010:2011, named ArchCaMO, is presented. First, notions about software models and software architecture models are briefly introduced. Then, basic notions of the standard ISO/IEC/IEEE 42010:2011 are presented.

The 5 presented levels of ArchCaMO are based on the described rules of ISO/IEC/IEEE 42010:2011. The initial level, Level 1, considered as unstable, refers to all companies/organizations that do not have a formalized way to define the software architecture. Levels 2 and 3 are made up of most relevant aspects that are necessary to describe a software architecture. Levels 4 and 5 are related to aspects that are needed to improve a software architecture situation in the life cycle that is already structured.

After the levels description, how the levels work through the process is described. To simplify these processes, the authors illustrated with an example, a software architecture published in [37] taken from the literature, showing each aspect of ISO/IEC/IEEE 42010:2011 that they have adopted.

ArchCaMO maturity model evaluates software architectures, providing a direction to the software architecture team of how to manage a description of software architectures from new and legacy systems.

As for future works, our proposal is to evaluate other software architectures in the literature and in companies according to ArchCaMo.

Acknowledgment. This study was financed in part by the Fundação de Apoio a Pesquisa e Inovação Tecnológica do Estado de Sergipe.

References

1. Dijkstra, E.W.: The structure of THE-multiprogramming system. Commun. ACM **26**(1), 49–52 (1968)
2. Parnas, D.L.: On the criteria to be used in decomposing systems into modules. Commun. ACM **15**(12), 1053–1058 (1972)
3. Parnas, D.L.: A technique for software module specification with examples. Commun. ACM **15**(5), 330–336 (1972)
4. Tofan, D., Galster, M., Avgeriou, P., Schuitema, W.: Past and future of software architectural decisions - a systematic mapping study. Inf. Softw. Technol. **56**(8), 850–872 (2014)

5. Capilla, R., Jansen, A., Tang, A., Avgeriou, P., Babar, M.A.: 10 years of software architecture knowledge management: practice and future. J. Syst. Softw. **116**, 191–205 (2016)
6. Garlan, D.: Software architecture: a roadmap. In: Proceedings of the Conference on The Future of Software Engineering, ICSE 2000, pp. 91–101 (2000)
7. Kruchten, P., Obbink, H., Stafford, J.: The past, present, and future for software architecture. IEEE Softw. **23**(2), 22–30 (2006)
8. Garlan, D.: Software architecture: a travelogue. Proc. Future Softw. Eng. FOSE **2014**, 29–39 (2014)
9. Bass, L., Clements, P., Kazman, R.: Software Architecture in Practice, 3rd edn. Addison-Wesley Professional (2012)
10. Oquendo, F.: Software architecture challenges and emerging research in software-intensive systems-of-systems. In: Tekinerdogan, B., Zdun, U., Babar, A. (eds.) ECSA 2016. LNCS, vol. 9839, pp. 3–21. Springer, Cham (2016). https://doi.org/10.1007/978-3-319-48992-6_1
11. Booch, G.: The economics of architecture-first. IEEE Softw. **24**(5), 18–20 (2007)
12. Buchgeher, G., Weinreich, R., Kriechbaum, T.: Making the case for centralized software architecture management. In: Winkler, D., Biffl, S., Bergsmann, J. (eds.) SWQD 2016. LNBIP, vol. 238, pp. 109–121. Springer, Cham (2016). https://doi.org/10.1007/978-3-319-27033-3_8
13. Galster, M., Tamburri, D.A., Kazman, R.: Towards understanding the social and organizational dimensions of software architecting. SIGSOFT Softw. Eng. Notes **42**(3), 24–25 (2017)
14. Yang, C., Liang, P., Avgeriou, P.: A systematic mapping study on the combination of software architecture and agile development. J. Syst. Softw. **111**, 157–184 (2016)
15. Wirfs-Brock, R., Yoder, J., Guerra, E.: Patterns to develop and evolve architecture during an agile software project. In: Proceedings of the 22nd Conference on Pattern Languages of Programs, PLoP 2015, pp. 9:1–9:18 (2015)
16. Waterman, M., Noble, J., Allan, G.: How much up-front? A grounded theory of agile architecture. In: Proceedings of the 37th International Conference on Software Engineering, ICSE 2015, vol. 1, pp. 347–357 (2015)
17. Abrahamsson, P., Babar, M.A., Kruchten, P.: Agility and architecture: can they coexist? IEEE Softw. **27**, 16–22 (2010)
18. Ding, W., Liang, P., Tang, A., Vliet, H.V., Shahin, M.: How do open source communities document software architecture: an exploratory survey. In: 2014 19th International Conference on Engineering of Complex Computer Systems, pp. 136–145 (2014)
19. Graaf, K.A., Liang, P., Tang, A., Van Vliet, H.: How organisation of architecture documentation affects architectural knowledge retrieval. Sci. Comput. Program. **121**, 75–99 (2016)
20. Díaz-Pace, J.A., Villavicencio, C., Schiaffino, S., Nicoletti, M., Vázquez, H.: Producing just enough documentation: an optimization approach applied to the software architecture domain. J. Data Seman. **5**(1), 37–53 (2016)
21. Kruchten, P.B.: The 4+1 view model of architecture. IEEE Softw. **12**(6), 42–50 (1995)
22. ISO/IEC/IEEE: Systems and Software Engineering - Architecture Description. ISO/IEC/IEEE 42010:2011(E) (Revision of ISO/IEC 42010:2007 and IEEE Std 1471-2000), pp. 1–46 (2011)
23. Paulk, M.C., Weber, C.V., Curtis, B., Chrissis, M.B.: Capability maturity model for software (version 1.1). Technical report CMU/SEI-93-TR-024 ESC-TR-93-177, Software Engineering Institute, Pittsburgh, PA (1993)

24. Chrissis, M.B., Konrad, M., Shrum, S.: CMMI for Development: Guidelines for Process Integration and Product Improvement, 3rd edn. Addison-Wesley Professional (2011)
25. Ahmed, F., Capretz, L.F.: An architecture process maturity model of software product line engineering. Innov. Syst. Softw. Eng. **7**(3), 191–207 (2011)
26. Ostadzadeh, S.S., Shams, F.: Towards a software architecture maturity model for improving ultra-large-scale systems interoperability. CoRR, abs/1401.5752 (2014)
27. Meyer, M., Helfert, M., O'Brien, C.: An analysis of enterprise architecture maturity frameworks. In: Grabis, J., Kirikova, M. (eds.) BIR 2011. LNBIP, vol. 90, pp. 167–177. Springer, Heidelberg (2011). https://doi.org/10.1007/978-3-642-24511-4_13
28. França, J.M.S., de Lima, J.S., Soares, M.S.: Development of an electronic health record application using a multiple view service oriented architecture. In: Proceedings of the 19th International Conference on Enterprise Information Systems, ICEIS 2017, Porto, Portugal, 26–29 April 2017, vol. 2, pp. 308–315 (2017)
29. Crichton, R., Moodley, D., Pillay, A., Gakuba, R., Seebregts, C.J.: An architecture and reference implementation of an open health information mediator: enabling interoperability in the rwandan health information exchange. In: Weber, J., Perseil, I. (eds.) FHIES 2012. LNCS, vol. 7789, pp. 87–104. Springer, Heidelberg (2013). https://doi.org/10.1007/978-3-642-39088-3_6
30. Musil, J., Musil, A., Weyns, D., Biffl, S.: An Architecture framework for collective intelligence systems. In: 2015 12th Working IEEE/IFIP Conference on Software Architecture, pp. 21–30 (2015)
31. Van Heesch, U., Avgeriou, P., Hilliard, R.: A documentation framework for architecture decisions. J. Syst. Softw. **85**(4), 795–820 (2012)
32. Karkhanis, P., Brand, M.G., Rajkarnikar, S.: Defining the C-ITS reference architecture. In: 2018 IEEE International Conference on Software Architecture Companion (ICSA-C), vol. 00, pp. 148–151 (2018)
33. Vidoni, M., Vecchietti, A.: Towards a reference architecture for advanced planning systems. In: Hammoudi, S., Maciaszek, L., Missikoff, M.M., Camp, O., Cordeiro, J. (eds.) Proceedings of the 18th International Conference on Enterprise Information Systems (ICEIS), vol. 1, pp. 433–440 (2016)
34. Williams, J.L., Stracener, J.T.: First steps in the development of a Program Organizational Architectural Framework (POAF). Syst. Eng. **16**(1), 45–70 (2013)
35. Effenberger, F., Hilbert, A.: Towards an energy information system architecture description for industrial manufacturers: decomposition & allocation view. Energy **112**, 599–605 (2016)
36. ISO/IEC/IEEE: Systems and software engineering-System life cycle processes (2008)
37. Kavakli, E., Buenabad-Chvez, J., Tountopoulos, V., Loucopoulos, P., Sakellariou, R.: WiP: an architecture for disruption management in smart manufacturing. In: 2018 IEEE International Conference on Smart Computing (SMARTCOMP), pp. 279–281 (2018)

A Survey on the Skills, Activities and Role of the Software Architect in Brazil

Manoela R. Oliveira[1]([⊠]) [iD], Felipe J. R. Vieira[1] [iD], Sanjay Misra[2] [iD],
and Michel S. Soares[1] [iD]

[1] Federal University of Sergipe, Av. Marechal Rondon, s/n - Jardim Rosa Elze,
São Cristóvão, Brazil
manoelareisoliveira@gmail.com, felipejrvieira@gmail.com,
michel@dcomp.ufs.br
[2] Convenant University, KM 10 Idiroko Rd, Ota, Nigeria
sanjay.misra@covenantuniversity.edu.ng

Abstract. Although the skills and knowledge of software architects have already been the subject of some studies in recent years, researchers and practitioners still have not come to a clear consensus about the activities that a software architect is often responsible in practice in order to be considered successful. In recent years, due to occurrence of successive changes and evolution of new technologies, the roles of the architect and even practices related to software architecture have been continuously changed in the software development life cycle. The software architect is expected to possess a diversity of skills. In addition to technical knowledge, domain knowledge and communication skills must be considered. However, there are many job offerings for this position which have in their description skills and roles totally different from the ones already known and considered essential by academic and industry studies. In order to better understand what software architects actually do in their daily activities in practice, and how this resembles or distances themselves from the skills, roles and knowledge cited in the literature as essential, in this article we have conducted a large-scale survey with 536 professionals who currently work or have worked at some period in their careers as software architects. Among the results, it is clear that the roles, responsibilities, activities and tasks performed by software/system architects are still largely unknown and diffuse in organizations, as important tasks to be performed by software architects are still not common sense in industry.

Keywords: Software architect · Industry practice ·
Large-scale survey research

1 Introduction

The discipline of Software Architecture emerged in the past two decades in academia [19] and more recently in software industry [4,8,21,24]. A large number of patterns, frameworks, methods, tools and languages related to activities of

© Springer Nature Switzerland AG 2019
S. Misra et al. (Eds.): ICCSA 2019, LNCS 11623, pp. 43–58, 2019.
https://doi.org/10.1007/978-3-030-24308-1_4

software architecture have been proposed within this period. Even a well-known standard, the ISO/IEC/IEEE 42010 [13], was published. This International Standard specifies the manner in which architecture descriptions of systems are organized and expressed, which confirms the importance of software architecture as a discipline of software engineering.

The role of the software architect has become increasingly common in industry, but the activities, tasks, processes and daily chores related to the software architect became a point of discussion. For instance, do software architects develop source code? How do their work relates to the work of project managers? How long does it take to someone become a (real) software architect? These questions are still subject of debate in academia and industry [1,8] in which patterns and "antipatterns" have been suggested [11,17].

Given the improved importance of software architecture in academic research and industrial practice it is necessary to better understand this role. In this paper we describe a survey about the daily activities performed by professionals who work as software architects in Brazil. The goal is to better understand what software architects actually do in their daily activities in practice, and how this resembles or distances themselves from the skills, roles and knowledge cited in the literature as essential.

The research question in this paper is stated as follows:

RQ - To what extent Software Architect professionals in Brazil perform software architecture activities?

Within this RQ, the idea is to describe, given a number of activities that are known as responsibilities and skills of software architects, searched in the literature, which ones are most performed by software/systems architects working in Brazil.

2 Patterns and Antipatterns of the Software Architect Job

Despite past efforts, we still have little understanding and there is no clear consensus of what software architects do in real-world settings [7]. Several authors have defined software architect patterns and anti-patterns over the past years. Koenig introduced the concept of antipattern in [15], by defining an antipattern just like a pattern, except that instead of a solution it gives something that looks superficially like a solution but is not [15].

Krutchen, in [17], defined as the main antipatterns of software architects: (i) creating a perfect architecture for the wrong system, (ii) creating a perfect architecture, but too hard to implement, (iii) architects in their ivory tower, and (iv) the absent architects. These antipatterns means, respectively, (i) a software architect who is not communicating has a greater probability of not understanding or only gradually understanding the software concerns, (ii) a software architect who does not understand the capability of the implementation team(s) that will create enormous levels of stress and frustration, and will most likely not deliver a quality product in time, (iii) architects that are isolated, not getting enough input from the users and developers, and (iv) the software architect that comes with a complete architecture, out of the blue, which does not relate well to actual problems described in many organizations.

All these antipatterns will experience rejection, because developers must wait for architectural decisions, and no or little architecture design progress is made. Software architects are always away doing other things or fighting fires instead of taking care of architecture. The whole architecture will suffer from immaturity.

Regarding patterns, we have gathered information about definitions of duties, skills, and knowledge of the software architect. We have used definitions from the *Software Engineering Institute* [26] as a reference and performed a literature review with emphasis mainly on articles already recognized about the roles and responsibilities of the software architect, including [11,14,17,20].

After we have evaluated the gathered information, we constructed the following set of activities of the software architect which are considered patterns that the software architect should follow to be considered successful:

1. Define the architecture.
2. Create documents that describe the architecture.
3. Act as a communicator of the software architecture.
4. Make sure everyone is using the proposed architecture.
5. Certify everyone is using the architecture correctly.
6. Make sure that architecture comes out in stages in a timely way so that the overall organization can make progress before it is complete.
7. Certify software and architecture are in synchronization.
8. Certify that management understands the necessary architectural details.
9. Make sure the right modeling is being done, knowing which qualities are going to be met.
10. Assist in tool and environment selection.
11. Identify and interact with stakeholders to make sure their needs are met.
12. Convince stakeholders about the value of the architectural solution.
13. Certify that architecture is not only right for operations, but also for deployment and maintenance.
14. Perform conflict resolution and analyze tradeoffs.
15. Solve technical problems.
16. Maintain and raise the morale of the architecture team.
17. Understand and plan the evolution of architecture.
18. Plan the insertion of new technologies.
19. Manage strategies for identifying and mitigating risks associated with the architecture.
20. Assist in understanding the problem domain.
21. Apply standards already used to solve past problems.
22. Keeping up-to-date with the latest trends.
23. Participate in the planning of projects.
24. Manage individuals and teams.
25. Establish architectural decisions.
26. Think about what impact the decisions have on the current architecture.

27. Act as a technology consultant.
28. Full software life cycle involvement.
29. Assisting product marketing and future product definitions.

3   The Survey

The following sections describe the methods used for conducting the survey.

The web questionnaire for this survey was designed and hosted by the online Google survey service, Google Forms. The questionnaire is composed of thirty-six questions, divided into two different parts. The first part is proposed in order to gather descriptive statistics to summarize the backgrounds of the respondents, and the second part of the survey focused on questions about the functions performed by the software architect in order to answer the research question presented in Sect. 1.

The first six questions are present in part I of the questionnaire, as follows:

1. What is your current job?
2. What is your level of formal education?
3. Number of years of experience in Information Technology related jobs.
4. Number of years in your current position.
5. How many projects are you involved simultaneously in your current job?
6. Do you work currently in which state in Brazil?

The other twenty-nine questions are relative to the twenty-nine patterns presented in Sect. 2. Each activity is measured using multiple response items scored on a 5-point Likert-type scale: 1- Never, 2- Rarely, 3- Sometimes, 4- Often, and 5- Always. The twenty-nine questions about the software architect functions were formulated as affirmative sentences, each sentence representing an item of the patterns found. All Thirty-five questions of parts I and II are mandatory, however we have created a thirty sixth optional and subjective question with the purpose of gathering comments on the routine as a software architect and suggestions for the research.

The first draft of the research instrument was tested and validated by four software architects, all with more than five years of experience in the area, in order to evaluate the understanding of the questions and suggest possible improvements.

After making adjustments from the pilot study and create the revised final version of the questionnaire, the survey was performed between August and September of 2018. Initially, a questionnaire was sent to 3187 professionals who declared their current position on the LinkedIn platform in Brazil as a software architect.

LinkedIn does not allow unlimited inbox messages to be sent to people who are not connected. Therefore, it was necessary to send invitations individually. Each invitation allowed to send a text with a maximum of 300 characters, thus it was necessary to summarize the purpose of the study and the request to participate in the research on the work of the software architect within this small amount of characters.

Then the authors opened each profile individually, clicked on "Connect" and then on "Add Note", inserted the message requesting the answer to the questionnaire and finally clicked on "Send Invitation".

The survey was anonymous, and participation in the survey was voluntary. All invited respondents were informed about the survey with an invitation text describing goals of the study. In addition to the 3187 invitations, the authors have had also the opportunity to submit the questionnaire to the architectural committee of one of the largest software companies in Brazil (a total of forty five members of the committee, about fifteen thousand employees working in Brazil and twenty five thousands all around the world).

Thus, we had a total of 3232 invitations and 536 responses, achieving a response rate of approximately 16.6%. Of the total of 536 responses, 72 respondents also answered the optional question.

4   Results

In this section, the results of our study are presented. We first presented the results of characterization questions. For each question, a graphic was created with the amount of answers referring to each alternative of the question.

Figure 1 depicts the level of education of the study participants. Most study participants have a MBA or other post-graduation course (42,4%). This is an important fact, as it is essential that they stay up to date with new trends and many should have sought better qualification through a professional MBA.

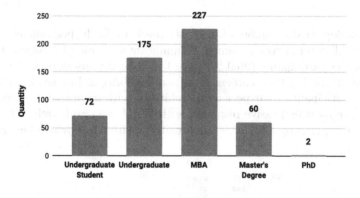

Fig. 1. Level of education

A large part of the study participants (32,6%) have at least completed an Undergraduate course, mostly in Computer Science, Information Systems or Computer Engineering, and 11,9% completed an academic Master's degree in Computer Science. What draws attention to these numbers is the amount of study participants who are still attending an Undergraduate course (13,4%) and the small number of people who have a PhD (0,4%), just 2.

Figure 2 depicts the number of years of IT experience before becoming a software architect. 85.3% of respondents have more than 9 years of experience and 11.8% have between 6 and 8 years, that is, 97% of respondents have more than 5 years of experience in IT. This high percentage shows that usually software architects have been working in industry for a long time and already have personal experience with IT. Of the remaining 3%, 2.6% have between 3 and 5 years and only 0.4% have less than 2 years of experience.

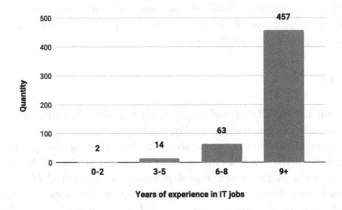

Fig. 2. Years of experience in IT jobs

Figure 3 depicts the number of years of experience in the position as software architects. All alternatives obtained a significant amount of answers. Over a quarter of the participants (26.9 %) have less than 2 years of experience, that is, they are beginning their careers as software architects. In contrast, 15.1% of the study participants are experienced architects, with more than 9 years in the position. The most expressive response, with 37.1%, was from architects with 3 to 5 years of experience, and 20.9% are architects with 6 to 8 years of experience.

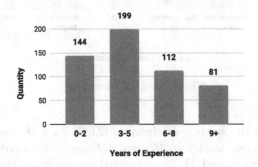

Fig. 3. Years of experience as software architect

Figure 4 depicts the current position of the participants. As suggested in [9], there may be several nomenclatures for the position of architect. It is difficult to distinguish which competencies differentiate one job from the other.

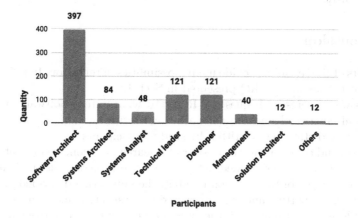

Fig. 4. Current position of participants

According to our filtering through LinkedIn, we know all participants work or have worked at some point of their career as software architects. This question aims to find out how many of them are still performing as software architects. This is a multiple choice question, allowing for more than one option, therefore the sum of percentages exceeds 100. The majority of respondents (74.1%) still works currently as software architects, 15.7% works as systems architects, 18.5% works as software developers, 22.6% works as a technical leader, and a minority works as other jobs titles.

Figure 5 depicts in how many projects the participants are involved simultaneously in their current job. For this question, all alternatives also obtained a significant amount of answers. There were three options, about a third (31,5%)

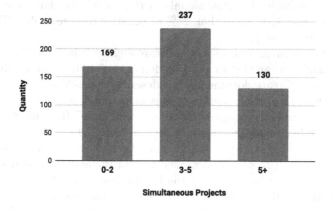

Fig. 5. Amount of projects simultaneous

of the respondents are involved with at most 2 simultaneously, it is inferred that a part of them may be working with only one project. 44.2% are involved simultaneously with 3 to 5 projects and 24.3% are involved with more than 5 projects simultaneously.

5 Discussion

The results of the research provide many possibilities of reflection. In this section, we present the answers to RQ presented in Sect. 1.

To answer the research question RQ, "To what extent Software Architect Professionals in Brazil perform software architecture activities?" we analyzed the answers and statements written by study participants.

To assist and complement the answer of research question, we present Table 1 that gathers the most performed activities by the professionals in their work. Table 1 is composed of the question number, the numbering described in Sect. 2, the percentage of participants who answered the respective question using alternative "Always", "Often" and the sum of percentages of participants who responded to the relative sentence answering "Always" or "Often", in descending order. In this study we considered the sum of alternatives "Always" and "Often" as the total of positive responses to the question.

As can be seen in Table 1, the five activities most executed by software architects in Brazil were: "Think about the impact that decisions have on the current architecture" (26), "Apply standards already used to solve past problems" (21), "Certify that architecture is not only right for operations, but also for deployment and maintenance" (13), "Assist in understanding the problem domain" (20) and "Solve technical problems" (15).

Keeping in mind that the software architect is required to strike a balance between technical knowledge, domain knowledge and communication skills [3, 17], this set of activities corroborates strongly with what is expected from a software architect.

With the similar intention to Table 1, we created Table 2 that gathers the less performed activities by professionals in their work. We have selected only those questions that have more than 25% of negative response rate ("Rarely" + "Never" + "Sometimes").

The five less executed activities by software architects in Brazil were: "Assisting product marketing and future product definitions" (29), "Manage individuals and teams" (24), "Create documents that describe the architecture" (2), "Make sure that architecture comes out in stages in a timely way so that the overall organization can make progress before it is complete" (6) and "Certify that management understands the necessary architectural details" (8).

As depicted in Table 1, question 26 had the highest response rate for the "always" alternative (67.20%) and ranked first in the activity ranking, totaling 95.70% of positive responses. One of the key processes in software architecture is decision making [16, 30]. Therefore, that specific question having a high positive response rate means that software architects in Brazil are probably truly

Table 1. Total positive responses

Question	Always	Often	Always+often
26	67,20%	28,50%	95,70%
21	39,20%	50,40%	89,60%
13	51,10%	35,60%	86,70%
20	38,60%	47,60%	86,20%
15	42,70%	42,00%	84,70%
22	45,70%	38,80%	84,50%
25	32,50%	51,70%	84,20%
10	43,70%	39,70%	83,40%
17	36,90%	43,70%	80,60%
1	34,90%	45,70%	80,60%
3	38,40%	39,20%	77,60%
4	35,60%	40,90%	76,50%
7	30,60%	45,50%	76,10%
18	35,80%	38,50%	74,30%
27	32,10%	41,80%	73,90%
11	33,00%	39,20%	72,20%
5	30,00%	40,70%	70,70%
9	28,70%	41,80%	70,50%
23	29,90%	39,70%	69,60%
16	31,00%	36,60%	67,60%
19	23,50%	43,70%	67,20%
14	20,30%	43,80%	64,10%
12	24,80%	38,80%	63,60%
28	23,10%	38,20%	61,30%
8	24,10%	35,30%	59,40%
6	20,10%	38,60%	58,70%
2	19,40%	35,40%	54,80%
24	21,50%	26,70%	48,20%
29	4,30%	13,40%	17,70%

concerned about the future consequences that may arise in the development and use of the system from their architectural decisions.

Only 67,20% of the respondents have said they always or often worry about risks. According to [27], it has become the architect's role to balance factors such as risk, quality, constraints, and costs when deciding whether to use, buy, or build a component is more advantageous, then this question could have had a more expressive percentage of positive responses.

Table 2. Total negative responses

Question	Sometimes	Rarely	Never	Total negative
29	29,7%	32,5%	20,1%	82,3%
24	29,4%	16,4%	6%	51,8%
2	33,6%	10,3%	1,3%	45,2%
6	29,1%	9,3%	2,8%	41,2%
8	27,8%	9,3%	3,5%	40,6%
28	26,4%	10,6%	1,7%	38,7%
12	25,9%	7,8%	2,6%	36,3%
14	27,6%	6,2%	2,1%	35,9%
19	23,7%	7,3%	1,9%	32,9%
16	23,7%	6,9%	1,9%	32,5%
23	23,7%	6%	0,7%	30,4%
9	20,3%	7,1%	2,1%	29,5%
5	22,6%	6%	0,7%	29,3%
11	21,8%	5%	0,9%	27,7%
27	16,8%	6,7%	2,6%	26,1%
18	19,4%	5,4%	0,6%	25,04%

On sentence 20, "Assist in understanding the problem domain", the index of positive responses was high, 86,20%. It is important that the architect understands very well the domain of the problem so that he/she chooses the architectural details that represent the best solution for each case. Within the architectural decisions theme, 84.20% of respondents affirmed in sentence 25 they always or often "Establish architectural decisions". This is a good result, since the software architecture of a system is the result of a set of architectural decisions [28], and the architect is becoming the manager of architectural knowledge, acting as a facilitator for decision-making and ensuring that decisions are appropriate and coherent to the context of action [30].

Another question with one of the highest rates of positive responses (86,70%) was sentence 13, "Certify that architecture is not only right for operations, but also for deployment and maintenance". This is very important, since the software architecture is constantly evolving and adapting. According to Erder and Pureur [6], architects must have a long-term vision, because the products and software survive even after the end of a project. Even after the software is deployed and being used by the client, there may still be numerous maintenance or addition of new features.

Strengthening the hypothesis about keeping the architect's eye on the future of software, about sentence 17, "Understand and plan the evolution of architecture", 80,60% of the respondents have chosen alternatives always or often.

89,90% of the respondents also responded positively to sentence 21, "Apply standards already used to solve past problems". This is a great result, that almost 90% of architects already have experience and have participated in other projects previously. This is a considerable result, because since most architectural decisions made by architects are made early in the project, they use their experience and abstraction skills to get them [10].

Although most of the respondents seem to be seasoned professionals, they did not stop looking for updates, 86,20% said always or often are keeping up-to-date with the latest trends (question 22), and 74,3% of the respondents always or often plan insertion of new technologies (question 18). Even with a nearly 12% difference between the two questions, this means that even the most experienced architects are still trying to keep up with new trends.

76,50% of the respondents answered positively to sentence 4, making sure everyone is using the proposed architecture, but 18,1% mentioned that they make sure only sometimes. Consequently, almost the same percentage of positive answers from the previous question (76,10%), is sentence 7, "Certify software and architecture are in synchronization". This similarity makes a lot of sense, whereas for both to remain always synchronized, it is necessary for the architect to constantly check whether the architecture that was proposed is actually being used.

When it comes to certifying that the proposed architecture is being used correctly (sentence 5), the result was a bit different. 70,70% of the respondents answered to carry out this activity always or often. Since the number of positive responses was lower than previous sentence "Certify software and architecture are in synchronization", the number of negative responses also increased. 22,60% of the respondents only certify sometimes, and 6,0% answered they rarely certify the architecture is used correctly.

Still following this line of reasoning involving the actual use of the architecture in practice, on question "Make sure the correct modeling is being done, knowing which qualities will be met" (sentence 9), the result is a bit more negative, 29,5% of the respondents choose negatives responses, and 70,50% choose between always or often. However, according to Tofan et al. [28], in their activities, architects need to consider the functional requirements and quality attributes (or non-functional requirements) of software systems. In addition, quality attributes play an important role in the decision-making process, since architects may compromise some quality attributes through tradeoffs (e.g. security versus usability) [28].

A similar example occurs when the subject is architecture definition and documentation. Considering the sentence "I define the software architecture" (sentence 1), 80,60% of respondents chose alternatives always or often, which is a great number of positive answers, but considering the content and importance of the question, since this activity is one of the main activities, and well recognized by several authors [6,17,25]. This percentage may be a little more expressive, and it is only enough to occupy the tenth position in the ranking of questions with the highest percentages of positive answers, as presented in Table 1.

In contrast to the number of professionals who responded positively to sentence 1, the same is not true for sentence 2, "I create documents that describe the architecture". Although documented decisions facilitate the general understanding of a system, architectural knowledge sharing, and evaluation processes [18]. One troubling result is the percentage of negative responses, 45,2% of the respondents answered negatively for sentence 2 and 54,80% choose alternatives always or often. This percentage places sentence 2 within the ranking of questions with a greater amount of negative answers, as depicted in Table 2. There may be a rationale for increasing adoption of agile methodologies with greater focus on coding and less focus on documentation.

One of possible implications is that some architects seem to work isolated. More than a half (51,8%) of respondents answered negatively to manage individuals and teams, (question 24), making this question occupy the second position of the ranking of questions with higher rate of negative answers. As already described in Sect. 1, architects working in isolation is an antipattern, architects in the ivory tower.

Probably this lack of group work influenced the high rate of negative responses to sentences such as "Perform conflict resolution and analyze trade-offs" (question 14), with 35,9%, and "Maintain and raise the morale of the architecture team" (question 16), with 32,5%. Considering this separation between the architect and the team that will develop the software, it is possible that the antipattern "creating a perfect architecture, but too hard to implement" anti-pattern is reached.

One fact that promotes reflections and draws attention is that among the questions with the highest rates of negative responses, as presented in Table 2, most are composed of tasks that require the architect to be involved with the organization or other stakeholders, although sentences such as 3, "Act as a communicator of the software architecture" and 4, "Identify and interact with stakeholders to make sure the needs are met", have received considerable percentages of positive responses, 77,6% and 72,20% respectively.

On sentence 23, "Participate in the planning of projects", 69.60% chose positive answers, which means that many architects (about 30%) in Brazil are not being involved in initial stages of defining the software project. In fact, software architects seem to be less involved even when it comes to business and marketing, apparently an overwhelming majority never even got involved in those steps, as shown in sentence 29, "Assisting product marketing and future product definitions".

Sentence 28, "Full software life cycle involvement" received 38,7% of negative responses. Since software architecture is the central element throughout the software life cycle [29], it is imperative that the software architect has more active participation in all phases of the software life cycle.

It is worth mentioning two other sentences about the architect's involvement with the organization. The first is that 40,6% of the respondents answered negatively to "Certify that management understands the necessary architectural details" (sentence 8), and the second is that 36,3% answered negatively to "Convince stakeholders about the value of the architectural solution" (sentence 12).

This impaired communication with the stakeholders can lead to several problems of understanding and acceptance of the architecture. Perhaps this lack of communication has influenced the amount of negative responses (41,2%) received by the question "Make sure that architecture comes out in stages in a timely way so that the overall organization can make progress before it is complete" (sentence 6). Without transparency and good relationship, it is very difficult for the architecture to be defined in such an efficient way.

Software architects operate in a social and organizational setting with different stakeholders and forces that influence the tasks they perform [7]. As described before, a software architect who is not communicating has a greater probability of not understanding or only gradually understanding the software concerns. Architects should ensure a coherent and sustainable architecture, for which the communication and collaboration skills become very relevant [6].

Regarding the questions about knowledge and technical skills, 73,90% answered they always or often act as a technology consultant (sentence 27), 83,4% mentioned they always or often assist in issues such as selecting environments and tools (sentence 10). The issue on solving technical problems (sentence 15) was very similar (84,70%), being one of the sentences with the highest index of positive answers.

In relation to the subjective question, we separate some significant sentences written by study participants:

"In most companies, it is not always that the architect has an active voice and/or decision-making power. Unfortunately, decisions are made on a time/delivery basis, that is, no matter how much it costs or if it will work, what is important is to deploy on time and show to stakeholders that the software product is there. It is sad when you look back and see a trail of destruction that extends until the project is canceled. And when the project is not canceled, the company coexists with the problems for decades".

"I once heard a phrase that made me think about the job. The most important role of the software architect is to transform business requirements into technical ideas. It is not necessary for the architect to develop, but mainly it is necessary that he/she is the bridge between the product management and the technical team".

"In Brazil, in most software companies, the role of the architect is not well defined, so he/she needs to be involved in all development processes and even often develop everything, he/she has become a senior developer model that we call full stack. This practice compromises the deadlines and quality of software".

6 Threats to Validity

In this study, we address internal, external, construct and conclusion threats to validity.

6.1 Conclusion Validity

By making explicit the thirty-six questions used in the questionnaire and the entire protocol followed to find the architects in LinkedIn and send the questionnaires to be answered, we believe that our results are valid and can be replicated in other countries.

6.2 Construct Validity

In our revision study about the roles, skills and responsibilities of the software architect, we make efforts to gather as much information as possible. Thus, we believe the found patterns represent vastly the patterns dictated by the literature in software architecture.

6.3 External Validity

External Validity refers to the strength of generalization of the study [5]. We cannot disregard the fact that the survey was answered only by professionals through LinkedIn who are working in Brazil, thus the results cannot be easily generalized. Although this is correct, it is important to notice that a large number of these professionals work in multinational companies, besides they have had international experience (MBAs, masters or PhD studied abroad), or even working experience in other countries. Besides, the number of respondents is considerable, when compared to other surveys in Software Engineering research, as for instance, 449 in [12], 258 in [2], 268 in [22] and 99 in [23].

6.4 Internal Validity

Internal Validity refers to how much the data supports the study results. A typical mistake is the misuse of statistical analysis [5]. In this study, we used basic statistics to analyze data, so threats of internal validity are minimal.

7 Conclusion

This study analyzed the understanding of software or systems architects workers about the tasks, activities and skills of the software architect at their daily work. The research consisted of the design, application, and analysis of a survey aiming at finding the understanding of how the profession of software architect is performed by professionals in Brazil.

The vast majority of questions received a high percentage of positive responses. Although some have had a significant amount of negative responses, in the big picture the architects have actually performed much of the activities that are explained in the literature, although the authors also have some differences between what they consider as the role of the software architect, there are some activities that are basically a consensus between them.

However, we could notice, mainly from the sentences of the subjective questions that there is still a lack of understanding about the role of the software architect by the companies, who end up treating the software architect as a senior developer. This study can help the IT recruiters to find professionals who actually have the skills expected from a software architect.

As for future work, the approach used within this research can be used in other countries, or even in a number of countries. Therefore, it will be possible to compare the results between countries, but also to have a higher degree of confidence with results presented in this paper.

References

1. Barroso, A.S., da Silva, J.S.M., Soares, M.S., do Nascimento, R.P.C.: Inuence of human personality in software engineering - a systematic literature review. In: ICEIS 2017 - Proceedings of the 19th International Conference on Enterprise Information Systems, Porto, Portugal, 26–29 April 2017, vol. 3, pp. 53–62 (2017)
2. Besker, T., Martini, A., Bosch, J.: Impact of architectural technical debt on daily software development work – a survey of software practitioners. In: 2017 43rd Euromicro Conference on Software Engineering and Advanced Applications (SEAA), pp. 278–287. IEEE (2017)
3. Correa, B.: How are architects made? IEEE Softw. **30**(5), 11–13 (2013)
4. Cui, X.: Retrospection and perspectives on pragmatic software architecture design: an industrial report. In: Lee, R. (ed.) ICIS 2017. SCI, vol. 719, pp. 13–28. Springer, Cham (2018). https://doi.org/10.1007/978-3-319-60170-0_2
5. Easterbrook, S., Singer, J., Storey, M.A., Damian, D.: Selecting empirical methods for software engineering research. In: Shull, F., Singer, J., Sjøberg, D.I.K. (eds.) Guide to Advanced Empirical Software Engineering, pp. 285–311. Springer, London (2008). https://doi.org/10.1007/978-1-84800-044-5_11
6. Erder, M., Pureur, P.: What's the architect's role in an agile, cloud-centric world? IEEE Softw. **33**(5), 30–33 (2016)
7. Galster, M., Tamburri, D.A., Kazman, R.: Towards understanding the social and organizational dimensions of software architecting. ACM SIGSOFT Softw. Eng. Notes **42**(3), 24–25 (2017)
8. Garlan, D.: Software architecture: a travelogue. In: Proceedings of the on Future of Software Engineering, FOSE 2014, pp. 29–39. ACM, New York (2014)
9. Gorton, I.: Understanding software architecture. In: Gorton, I. (ed.) Essential Software Architecture, pp. 1–15. Springer, Berlin (2011). https://doi.org/10.1007/978-3-642-19176-3_1
10. Hohpe, G., Ozkaya, I., Zdun, U., Zimmermann, O.: The software architect's role in the digital age. IEEE Softw. **33**(6), 30–39 (2016)
11. Hoorn, J.F., Farenhorst, R., Lago, P., Vliet, H.V.: The lonesome architect. J. Syst. Softw. **84**(9), 1424–1435 (2011)
12. Hutchinson, J.E., Whittle, J., Rouncefield, M.: Model-driven engineering practices in industry: social, organizational and managerial factors that lead to success or failure. Sci. Comput. Program. **89**, 144–161 (2014)
13. ISO/IEC/IEEE: ISO/IEC/IEEE 42010 Systems and Software Engineering-Architecture Description, 1st edn. (2011)
14. Klein, J.: What makes an architect successful? IEEE Softw. **33**(1), 20–22 (2016)

15. Koenig, A.: Patterns and antipatterns. Patterns Handb.: Tech. Strat. Appl. **13**, 383–383 (1998)
16. Kruchten, P.: Common misconceptions about software architecture. Rational Edge **1**, 1998–1998 (2001)
17. Kruchten, P.: A what do software architects really do? J. Syst. Softw. **81**, 2413–2416 (2008)
18. Kruchten, P., Capilla, R., Dueñas, J.C.: The decision view's role in software architecture practice. IEEE Softw. **26**(2), 36–42 (2009)
19. Kruchten, P., Obbink, H., Stafford, J.: The past, present, and future for software architecture. IEEE Softw. **23**(2), 22–30 (2006)
20. Microsoft: The Role of an Architect. Architect. J. (15) (2008)
21. Niu, N., Xu, L.D., Bi, Z.: Enterprise information systems architecture-analysis and evaluation. IEEE Trans. Ind. Inf. **9**(4), 2147–2154 (2013)
22. Rahman, A., Partho, A., Meder, D., Williams, L.: Which factors influence practitioners' usage of build automation tools? In: Proceedings of the 3rd International Workshop on Rapid Continuous Software Engineering, pp. 20–26. IEEE Press (2017)
23. Raunak, M.S., Binkley, D.: Agile and other trends in software engineering. In: 2017 IEEE 28th Annual Software Technology Conference (STC), pp. 1–7. IEEE (2017)
24. Ribeiro, F., Rettberg, A., Pereira, C., Steinmetz, C., Soares, M.: An approach to formalization of architectural viewpoints design in real-time and embedded domain. In: 2018 IEEE 21st International Symposium on Real-Time Distributed Computing (ISORC), pp. 59–66, May 2018
25. SEI: Community Software Architecture Definitions (2017). http://www.sei.cmu.edu/architecture/start/community.cfm
26. SEI: Duties, Skills, and Knowledge of a Software Architect (2017). https://www.sei.cmu.edu/architecture/research/previousresearch/duties.cfm
27. Spinellis, D.: The changing role of the software architect. IEEE Softw. **33**(6), 4–6 (2016)
28. Tofan, D., Galster, M., Avgeriou, P., Schuitema, W.: Past and future of software architectural decisions – a systematic mapping study. Inf. Softw. Technol. **56**, 850–872 (2014)
29. Weinreich, R., Buchgeher, G.: Towards supporting the software architecture life cycle. J. Syst. Soft. **85**(3), 546–561 (2012)
30. Weinreich, R., Groher, I.: The architect's role in practice: from decision maker to knowledge manager? IEEE Softw. **33**(6), 63–69 (2016)

Technical and Managerial Difficulties in Postmortem Analysis in Software Projects

Felipe J. R. Vieira(ID), Manoela R. Oliveira(✉)(ID),
Rogério P. C. do Nascimento(ID), and Michel S. Soares(ID)

Federal University of Sergipe, Av. Marechal Rondon, s/n - Jardim Rosa Elze,
São Cristóvão, Brazil
felipejrvieira@gmail.com, manoelareisoliveira@gmail.com,
{rogerio,michel}@dcomp.ufs.br

Abstract. Software is successfully applied in a wide variety of areas. However, software projects have suffered from poor reputation by repeatedly bursting deadlines, costs or failing to fully meet user requirements. Postmortem Analysis is an activity to analyze what happened in projects in search of understanding the failures occurred and the achieved successes. Despite bringing interesting data for improving future projects, Postmortem Analysis is often neglected in organizations. This article seeks to identify and analyze the technical and managerial difficulties that exist in its accomplishment through bibliographical research. As a result, it is possible to conclude that the main difficulties for realizing postmortem activities are the shortage of time, lack of management support, conflicts between stakeholders, difficulty in extracting and collecting data, lack of agreement regarding evaluation criteria, lack of standards for achievement, and lack of useful or efficient historical data.

Keywords: Postmortem · Organizational learning · Software project

1 Introduction

Software is successfully applied in a wide variety of areas. It supports and facilitates the activities of individuals and organizations in their daily routines. Modern world is highly dependent on software. However, software projects have been suffering from poor reputation [13,17,22,23] by repeatedly bursting deadlines, costs or failing to fully meet user requirements. There are reports of software flaws reaching billions of dollars, as well as failures that have caused accidents and damage to human life [7,8,27].

An approach to understanding the causes of software project failures is to conduct postmortem analysis [3,6,14,21]. This analysis is a collective learning activity which can be organised for projects either when they end a phase or are terminated [10,14]. The main motivation is to reflect on what happened

© Springer Nature Switzerland AG 2019
S. Misra et al. (Eds.): ICCSA 2019, LNCS 11623, pp. 59–69, 2019.
https://doi.org/10.1007/978-3-030-24308-1_5

in the project to improve future practices for the individuals and teams that participated in the project, as well as the organization as a whole. Other terms may also represent this type of processes, such as project retrospective, lessons learned, and postproject review.

Since the 1990s, this method of analysis has already been recognized as a practice that guarantees competitive advantage to companies [18]. Birk *et al.* [2] mentioned that the postmortem analysis is an excellent method for knowledge management by capturing experiences and improvement suggestions from completed projects and works even in small and medium-sized companies that do not have large budgets. Several researches have been developed in order to improve this form of analysis in software projects [1, 5, 9, 10]. Even so, the answers to understanding why software projects fail are often neglected in organizations [1, 11, 12, 14], and so are not readily available.

Failure to perform postmortem analysis makes it difficult to identify indicators for improving organizations. For example, the knowledge acquired in this analysis allows modifying and improving the software development process [16], as well as identifying critical points before and during project execution [1, 14]. Sommerville [24] reports that it is possible to improve the software process because many organizations may include outdated techniques or do not take advantage of the best software engineering practices in industry. Therefore, applying techniques that aid in detection of failure points is important for prioritizing improvement actions and increasing the effectiveness of software construction activities.

Knowledge Management is a large interdisciplinary field that provides methods that simplify the process of sharing, distributing, creating, capturing and understanding of a company's knowledge [4], allowing the organization to modify its behavior in order to reflect new knowledge and ideas.

Thus, with the premise that postmortem analysis is an important tool for improvement of realization of software projects and is often neglected, according to reports found in the literature, this work aims to identify and list the main technical and managerial difficulties for its accomplishment. For this, a bibliographic research was carried out in several scientific databases in the area of Computer Science and Management.

The reminder of this paper is structured as follows. Section 2 presents the background and general theories on postmortem analysis and knowledge management. Section 3 describes the research method. Sections 4 and 5 are respectively related to the technical and managerial difficulties in the postmortem analysis, and Sect. 6 summarizes findings and suggests future work on the topic.

2   Background

This section briefly describes the concepts of postmortem analysis and presents the phases that define its process, then it is explained how knowledge is transmitted in an organization through the theory of Knowledge Management.

2.1   Postmortem Analysis

Postmortem analysis is a collective learning activity which main motivation is to reflect on what happened in the project [10]. The objective is to identify the success and failure points of previous projects to acquire knowledge that will allow improvement in execution of future projects. This analysis can be performed when a phase ends or when a project is terminated. Lessons learned make it possible to improve the individuals and teams that participated in the project, as well as the organization as a whole [10,14].

Postmortem Analysis is a relevant tool for project teams to collectively identify communication gaps and practices to improve future projects [3]. Postmortem analysis in software projects provides an excellent method for knowledge management, due to the high feasibility for continuous improvement and corrective actions development [2,14].

There are variations in relation to the objective and degree of formality in the execution of a postmortem analysis. It can be focused on collecting experiences related to a simple activity, the phase of a process, or acquiring the available experiences of a project as a whole [25]. Data collection can be performed through semi-structured interviews, informally, or through a multi-step process using formal methods [25].

For a postmortem analysis a well-defined process is required [9] which can generally be simplified into four phases [1]:

1. Data collection - Data are collected from team members through interviews and questionnaires, or a combination of the two. Project documentation can also be used as a source for data collection;
2. Workshop meeting - With some members who participated in the current project, a meeting is held using formal analysis methods, such as structured discussions, root cause analysis and fishbone diagrams, to elicit tacit knowledge from participants [1];
3. Data analysis - In this phase the lists with positive and negative points of project are analyzed, creating an order of impact in the project, statistical methods can be used to aid in the process. This phase can be performed during a workshop meeting or separately;
4. Present results - Results are presented to members of the organization in order to allow others to use lessons learned in the development of future projects.

The common phases of the processes heavily depend on participation of the project team members and the subjective opinions expressed by them [1]. The role of documentation is not so important when compared to the role of workshops and interviews. Thus, most studies on postmortem analysis of projects have used methods that require active participation of project staff or their combination using project documentation.

Even though it is an important activity for improving project development, postmortem analysis in software projects is often neglected [1,11,12,14], which highlights the need to disseminate such practice. However, for postmortem analysis to be more commonly performed in organizations, factors that make it impossible or difficult to execute must be found and effective measures must be taken.

2.2 Knowledge Management

Knowledge Management can be defined as a method that simplifies the process of sharing, distributing, capturing and understanding a company's knowledge [4]. The purpose of these efforts is to provide the employees of the organization with the knowledge that they need to maximize their effectiveness, thereby expanding the capacity of the organization [19].

In the Knowledge Management, the word "knowledge" is usually classified into tacit and explicit knowledge [10]. These two forms of knowledge make up the epistemological dimension in the creation of organizational knowledge [20]. Tacit knowledge comes from interactions of the individuals that constitute the organization, through exchange of experiences, ideas, emotions and conversations. Explicit knowledge is what can be represented in a textual or symbolic way, by means of manuals, norms, formal documents, and thus easily found and stored [4, 19].

Knowledge is in constant conversion, going from tacit to explicit, from explicit to tacit, and also being transformed from tacit to tacit, and from explicit to explicit [20]. Each of these conversions has a particular definition.

- Socialization - is the transference of tacit knowledge to another person, in which there is exchange of experiences between individuals, which can occur through observation, imitation and practice [4];
- Externalisation - is the process of converting tacit into explicit knowledge, usually triggered by dialogue or collective reflection, but can also be the result of individual reflection [10];
- Combination - occurs through reconfiguration of existing knowledge leading to new knowledge. It is the gathering and systematization of formal knowledge from different sources that are reorganized by separating, adding, combining and classifying explicit knowledge [10];
- Internalisation - means to take externalised knowledge and make it into individual tacit knowledge in the form of the mental models or technical know-how [4].

Organizations can not create knowledge alone. Tacit knowledge of individuals constitutes the basis of knowledge creation of organizations, and it is fundamental that the organization mobilizes tacit knowledge created and accumulated at the individual level [20]. This tacit knowledge is propagated by the organization through knowledge conversion and condensed at higher ontological levels.

For Nonaka and Takeuchi [20], the ontological dimension of knowledge is composed of individual, group, organization and inter-organization. Creation of organizational knowledge begins in the individual and is disseminated, expanding interaction groups that cross boundaries between sections, departments, divisions and organizations, establishing a spiral process.

Understanding these dimensions ensures better visualization of how knowledge moves in projects and organizations, making it possible to learn from projects that have already been completed. For example, in the postmortem analysis at the epistemological level, two conversions are widely used: socialization and externalization [10]. At the ontological level, postmortem analysis facilitates dissemination of knowledge from the individual level to the organizational level.

3 Research Method

For the development of this paper an exploratory research was carried out by means of a bibliographical survey on the topics Postmortem Analysis and Knowledge Management. The motivation was to gather information on the subject and delimit the field to be studied.

In examining the subject, it has been identified that postmortem analysis in projects is often neglected [1,11,12,14]. However, the difficulties that led to its non-achievement are often neglected in these articles.

Given the perception of this gap, the main objective of the research is to understand and map what are the difficulties that inhibit the accomplishment of this type of analysis. Knowledge of these difficulties makes it possible to mitigate risks when executing postmortem analysis, a practice that allows improvement of organization and competitive advantage through lessons learned.

Three knowledge bases were used: ACM Digital Library, IEEE Xplore and ScienceDirect, as well as Google Scholar as a tool to increase search comprehensiveness.

With the objective of mapping only recent articles that would bring current experiences, only articles published starting from year 2012 are considered. However, the established criterion was disregarded because few articles - only nine - meet this restriction.

The difficulties found in the articles were categorized into two types: technical difficulties and managerial difficulties. Separation into two types of difficulties expanded the discussion on the subject, because solving the technical part is only part of the overall solution, both difficulties influence each other over time. Managerial support through elements of organizational, operational structures, and engaging communication is critical to organizational learning.

This division made possible a better understanding of the difficulties. These are presented and discussed in the following sections.

4 Technical Difficulties

The main technical difficulties to perform postmortem analysis are presented in this section. At the end, Table 1 presents a summary of technical difficulties mapped from literature.

4.1   Lack of Standards for Performing the Analysis

In summary, the postmortem analysis process consists of four phases: data collection, workshop meeting, data analysis and present results [1]. Several papers that aim to improve this form of analysis in the projects were published [1,5,9,10].

However, in the literature, the lack of methodological support [14] and the lack of an effective method that will yield good results without the need of external consultants or experts [5], are cited as difficulties to carry out this activity.

As presented, there are papers that propose improvements for the postmortem analysis, however some articles [5,14] indicate that the lack of standards is still a problem. It is suspected that the proposed processes fail to meet the specificities inherent in some types of projects or particularities of the team. Thus, a standardization of tools, techniques, and processes would help both the team and the organization, since the necessary steps would be known to each team member.

4.2   Collection and Data Extraction

Few aspects of the knowledge that is generated during a project is made explicit through documentation. It requires the knowledge that those involved have of the project. However each individual has only the vision of a part of the whole, this can produce incorrect conclusions about the project [3,14]. For example, in a software development team, there are several roles, such as software architect, test analyst and infrastructure analyst, among others.

It is common that each professional specialization is concerned only with their specific activities. This is a common situation, but it can become a problem if professionals do not share their knowledge, when necessary, with other team members.

Ahonen and Savolainen [1] emphasize that the common phases of postmortem analysis processes heavily depend on participation of project team members and the subjective opinions expressed by them. It is important to collect and extract as much as possible of tacit knowledge present in project members.

Growth in the number of distributed development teams creates major challenges for conducting retrospective projects [15]. It is increasingly common for teams to be distributed in different cities within the same country, or even in different countries. Language barriers can not be disregarded, even among professionals with fluency in the same language, as it is known that there are idioms or terms that can cause different understandings.

Performing data collection and extraction is critical to quality analysis, as finding out which practices should be strengthened and which should be abandoned in future projects is not a trivial task in complex systems, particularly on large, lengthy projects [9], resulting from feedback and dynamic, systemic effects [26].

4.3   Useful and Efficient Histories of Postmortem Analysis

When project retrospective results are not used and knowledge is not disseminated among members and teams, those involved become dissatisfied with the process [10]. This makes it difficult to conduct future postmortem analysis because leaders and the analysis itself lose credibility with the team, turning a tool for organizational learning into something meaningless for the organization.

Having historical information that is useful and easily accessed is fundamental to the incentive of its realization [26]. The link between analysis and future projects must be well-understood [9] so that the benefits of performing postmortem analysis can be realized.

Collaborative tools such as wikis, blogs, institutional portals, or decision support systems are relevant to mitigate such difficulty. Development of techniques and tools that seek to solve this problem help both the team, since this will visualize the results of the work spent, as well as the management, since it makes it possible to observe the return of investment occurred in the project.

Table 1. Technical difficulties encountered in performing postmortem analysis

Difficulties	Authors
Lack of standards for performing the analysis	[5, 14]
Collection and data extraction	[3, 14, 15]
Useful and efficient histories of Postmortem analysis	[9, 26]

5   Managerial Difficulties

Main managerial difficulties to perform postmortem analysis are presented in this section. At the end, Table 2 presents a summary of managerial difficulties mapped from literature.

5.1   Lack of Specific Schedule for Conducting the Analysis

The greatest difficulty presented in papers is insufficient time [1, 3, 5, 10, 12, 14, 26]. Because it is an activity performed when a phase ends or when a project is terminated, postmortem analysis in many cases does not have a dedicated timetable for its accomplishment, and if it does, it ends up being deferred in detriment of other activities to be completed due to eventual delays in schedule.

Project team members frequently do not have time for meetings, or for sessions to review lessons learned [5, 10], and they happen to be reallocated to other projects before they are done. Glass [12] claims that professionals in the field of Software Engineering are constantly busy and they rarely have time to think about how development could be going better, not just faster.

Taking time to perform postmortem analysis is important because most processes use methods that require active participation of project staff or their combination with the use of project documentation [1].

However, Bjarnason *et al.* [3] warned that even if project members take the time for a retrospective, it can be hard to correctly remember and jointly discuss past events in a constructive way. It is important to use a schedule with activities carried out in the project to guide the meetings and participation of members.

Since the results provided by postmortem analysis are beneficial to the organization as a whole, using simplified or lightweight version can be a possible solution when time is a constraining factor [5]. However, the results may fall short.

5.2 Lack of Agreement Regarding the Criteria to Be Evaluated

In carrying out the analysis it is necessary that the project criteria that will be evaluated are presented in a clear way. The workshop facilitator should state the objectives of the meeting, if possible, describing the process to be followed [10]. Clarity of the process mitigates risks of meetings being unproductive and having an ineffective environment for sharing lessons learned.

This risk occurs because in organizations that do not have the culture of retrospective project, those involved may feel threatened to share poor project experiences, generating an evaluation and critical environment, rather than learning and sharing. Responsible management should make it clear that the goal is to analyze the process as a whole, not people in an individualized way.

Another risk is that members of the meeting emphasize only the negative aspects of the project, forgetting to strengthen the good practices that have occurred to be repeated in future projects.

A well-defined process of carrying out the postmortem analysis, its phases and criteria, allows those stakeholders to feel secure and protected to share the learning that occurred during the project [9], enabling the conversion of tacit knowledge into explicit and disseminating it through the organization.

5.3 Conflict Between Stakeholders and Information Bias

When the organization does not have a culture of knowledge sharing, conflicts between stakeholders may occur and information provided may hide project events.

One of the concerns in conducting postmortem analyzes is the honest sharing of what happened in the project and the experiences gained. But in projects that have failed, there is a natural disincentive within the organization to conduct a postmortem analysis, it also creates apprehension for individuals preparing to participate in the meeting [1,9], causing them to become defensive or seeking guilty. Retrospective of the project can turn into an emotional outburst, rather than a constructive discussion on how to improve practice.

It is important to emphasize that postmortem analysis is based on personal experience in events that occurred in the project. The risk of incorrect conclusions is present, because considerations made by those involved observe only a part of the whole that is the project [3,14]. This vision of the project may be biased even because some team members may not want to participate in the process because they do not wish to do a self-assessment.

To create a good environment for conducting an analysis where there are no distortions and biases in members' responses, Dingsøyr [10] suggests that managers should not participate in the project retrospective team, because beyond activities needed for the retrospective will be assessing individual performance of those involved, which may prevent lessons learned from developing the project. In this way, the retrospective meeting should be clearly separated from any personal performance assessment [10].

5.4   Lack of Management Support

In order to carry out postmortem analysis, it is essential that there be management support for its implementation. Pressures for delivery of results [9], too busy teams [12,14], lack of motivation to invest financial, human and time resources in closed projects [26], immediate reallocation from one project to another without time to discuss what was learned during implementation [3] may make it impossible to create retrospective. Due to the lack of support, over time the details and sequence of events are forgotten, losing an important input for organizational improvement [3].

Even if in organizations there is a process for postmortem analysis, if it is not supported by management, it is seldom used in practice [10], and when its results are not used and knowledge disseminated, those stakeholders begin to show dissatisfaction with the process [10], being only a bureaucratic step.

Table 2. Managerial difficulties encountered in performing postmortem analysis

Difficulties	Authors
Lack of specific schedule for conducting the analysis	[1,3,5,10,12,14,26]
Lack of agreement regarding the criteria to be evaluated	[9,10]
Conflict between stakeholders and information bias	[1,3,9,10,14]
Lack of management support	[3,9,10,12,14,26]

6   Conclusion

This article had as objective to identify and to indicate which are the difficulties for accomplishment of postmortem analysis. Through a bibliographical research a set of difficulties were identified and classified into two categories: technical difficulties and managerial difficulties. This classification allowed better understanding of the issue and the proposals that overcome such difficulties.

This paper identified that, even though there are some processes to perform postmortem analysis, the lack of better methodological support prevents this practice. It also clarified that in a retrospective, tacit knowledge is what brings additional learning to organizations. Therefore, ways to capture this knowledge must be well executed and encouraged. It also showed that use of faster and more efficient means of accessing the information generated in postmortem analyzes motivates achievement of the same information both at the operational level and at the managerial level.

In relation to managerial difficulties, the lack of a specific schedule was the difficulty that most appeared in articles. The lack of clear criteria and a well defined process were also mentioned as difficult because they allowed dispersion of those involved and did not direct the meeting to points that bring benefits to construction of knowledge. Conflict among those involved may also be a risk to achievement as it may inhibit participation of members or encourage search for guilty parties. Finally, if there is no support from management for dissemination of this practice, not allocating resources necessary for its realization, it becomes impracticable.

This research provided better understanding of existing difficulties and synthesized this information in two tables. However, a threat to validity is the limited amount of articles that addresses the issue. In order to reduce this threat, the restriction of publication starting from year 2012 was disregarded, considering only the relevance of the published article. This fact even shows shortage of research on difficulties in performing postmortem analysis.

As for future works, a set of templates will be proposed to help individuals to extract information from postmortem analysis of projects. The objective is the standardization in activities of collection and extraction of data, which enables creation of a history that is easily accessible. This work will help to mitigate some of the technical difficulties. Another work to be developed, will be a framework that allows accomplishment of postmortem analysis that can be adapted to reality of a specific organization seeking to reduce the managerial difficulties reported in these works.

References

1. Ahonen, J.-J., Savolainen, P.: Software engineering projects may fail before they are started: post-mortem analysis of five cancelled projects. J. Syst. Softw. **83**(11), 2175–2187 (2010)
2. Birk, A., Dingsoyr, T., Stalhane, T.: Postmortem: never leave a project without it. IEEE Softw. **19**(3), 43–45 (2002)
3. Bjarnason, E., Hess, A., Svensson, R.-B., Regnell, B., Doerr, J.: Reflecting on evidence-based timelines. IEEE Softw. **31**(4), 37–43 (2014)
4. Bjørnson, F.-O., Dingsøyr, T.: Knowledge management in software engineering: a systematic review of studied concepts, findings and research methods used. Inf. Softw. Technol. **50**(11), 1055–1068 (2008)
5. Bjørnson, F.-O., Wang, A.-I., Arisholm, E.: Improving the effectiveness of root cause analysis in post mortem analysis: a controlled experiment. Inf. Softw. Technol. **51**(1), 150–161 (2009)
6. Cerpa, N., Verner, J.-M.: Why did your project fail? Commun. ACM **52**(12), 130–134 (2009)

7. Charette, R.-N.: Why software fails [software failure]. IEEE Spectr. **42**(9), 42–49 (2005)
8. Charette, R.-N.: IT's fatal amnesia. Computer **50**(2), 86–91 (2017)
9. Collier, B., DeMarco, T., Fearey, P.: A defined process for project post mortem review. IEEE Softw. **13**(4), 65–72 (1996)
10. Dingsøyr, T.: Postmortem reviews: purpose and approaches in software engineering. Inf. Softw. Technol. **47**(5), 293–303 (2005)
11. Duffield, S., Whitty, S.-J.: How to apply the systemic lessons learned knowledge model to wire an organisation for the capability of storytelling. Int. J. Proj. Manag. **34**(3), 429–443 (2016)
12. Glass, R.-L.: Project retrospectives, and why they never happen. IEEE Softw. **19**(5), 111–112 (2002)
13. Jørgensen, M.: A survey on the characteristics of projects with success in delivering client benefits. Inf. Softw. Technol. **78**(Supplement C), 83–94 (2016)
14. Lehtinen, T.-O., Mäntylä, M.-V., Itkonen, J., Vanhanen, J.: Diagrams or structural lists in software project retrospectives an experimental comparison. J. Syst. Softw. **103**(Supplement C), 17–35 (2015)
15. Lehtinen, T.-O., Virtanen, R., Viljanen, J.-O., Mäntylä, M.-V., Lassenius, C.: A tool supporting root cause analysis for synchronous retrospectives in distributed software teams. Inf. Softw. Technol. **56**(4), 408–437 (2014)
16. Lehtinen, T.-O., Itkonen, J., Lassenius, C.: Recurring opinions or productive improvements—what agile teams actually discuss in retrospectives. Empirical Softw. Eng. **22**(5), 2409–2452 (2017)
17. Linberg, K.-R.: Software developer perceptions about software project failure: a case study. J. Syst. Softw. **49**(2–3), 177–192 (1999)
18. Menke, M.-M.: Managing R&D for competitive advantage. Res.-Technol. Manag. **40**(6), 40–42 (1997)
19. Mitchell, S.-M., Seaman, C.-B.: Could removal of project-level knowledge flow obstacles contribute to software process improvement? A study of software engineer perceptions. Inf. Softw. Technol. **72**(Suppl. C), 151–170 (2016)
20. Nonaka, I., Takeuchi, H.: The Knowledge Creating Company: How Japanese Companies Create the Dynamics of Innovation. Oxford University Press, New York (1995)
21. Politowski, C., Fontoura, L.-M., Petrillo, F., Guéhéneuc, Y.-G.: Learning from the past: a process recommendation system for video game projects using postmortems experiences. Inf. Softw. Technol. **100**, 103–118 (2018)
22. Savolainen, P., Ahonen, J.-J., Richardson, I.: Software development project success and failure from the supplier's perspective: a systematic literature review. Int. J. Proj. Manag. **30**(4), 458–469 (2012)
23. Sharon, I., Soares, M.S., Barjis, J., van den Berg, J., Vrancken, J.L.M.: A decision framework for selecting a suitable software development process. In: International Conference on Enterprise Information Systems, pp. 34–43 (2010)
24. Sommerville, I.: Software Engineering. Pearson, Boston (2011)
25. Stålhane, T., Dingsøyr, T., Hanssen, G.K., Moe, N.B.: Post mortem – an assessment of two approaches. In: Conradi, R., Wang, A.I. (eds.) Empirical Methods and Studies in Software Engineering. LNCS, vol. 2765, pp. 129–141. Springer, Heidelberg (2003). https://doi.org/10.1007/978-3-540-45143-3_8
26. Williams, T.: Identifying the hard lessons from projects - easily. Int. J. Proj. Manag. **22**(4), 273–279 (2004)
27. Zhivich, M., Cunningham, R.-K.: The real cost of software errors. IEEE Secur. Privacy **7**(2), 87–90 (2009)

Customer Feedback Prioritization Technique: A Case Study on Lean Startup

Syeda Sumbul Hossain[1]([✉]), S. A. M. Jubayer[2], Shadikur Rahman[1],
Touhid Bhuiyan[1], Lamisha Rawshan[1], and Saiful Islam[1]

[1] Daffodil International University, Dhaka, Bangladesh
{syeda.swe,shadikur35-988,lamisha.swe,saiful35-865}@diu.edu.bd,
t.bhuiyan@daffodilvarsity.edu.bd
[2] Wardan Tech Ltd., Dhaka, Bangladesh
xubayernil@gmail.com

Abstract. Nowadays, a startup is being very popular and entrepreneurs are increasing day by day. Though we are watching many successful startups e.g. Dropbox, Amazon, Viber and so on, the list of unsuccessful startups is very long. Who is being successful they must have their own strategy, which they apply in their startup and get success. In lean startup strategy, the customers give feedbacks about the startup and the owner understands the demand of customers by collecting feedback from customers and provides service according to the feedback. On the other hand, all the feedbacks from the customers are not important for a startup project. So it is needed to separate or prioritize feedbacks which are needed to execute the startup project. But there are not sufficient techniques for prioritizing the feedbacks collected from customers. By conducting a systematic mapping study and a case study (interview and observation is used), we propose a technique which will be used to prioritize customer feedback in lean startup. This technique will be helpful for the startup projects to become successful.

Keywords: Lean startup · Customer · Feedback · Prioritization technique

1 Introduction

Software engineering is a specific domain in engineering where software is developed by following appropriate principles, procedures, and methodologies. From the very beginning of software development to maintaining of the developed product, all steps are covered according to software engineering, that ensures a solution that is reliable, usable, maintainable and meets the customer requirements properly. From the very first stage to the last stage of system development, it shows a systematic and disciplined way to develop the system properly. Moreover, customer support must be given after system publishing. Most of the time customer support is like as maintaining the system, fixing the bugs, updating

S. Misra et al. (Eds.): ICCSA 2019, LNCS 11623, pp. 70–81, 2019.
https://doi.org/10.1007/978-3-030-24308-1_6

system features according to customer demands [1]. Nowadays, people want to launch startup where those people are known as entrepreneurs. This enterprise could be a technology-based startup or anything else. But most of the time a large number of entrepreneurs and their startup cannot be successful. Eric the writer of the Lean Startup book, think that the number of unsuccessful startups is very high [3]. Again, it is mentioned 75% of startups is unsuccessful [2]. A startup starts with a unique idea and launches the new product based on the idea in a very uncertain condition. A startup is always started for the unknown customer and customer demands always changed [3]. The entrepreneur does not know that the customer will like the product or not. Nowadays, many entrepreneurs use a way to reduce the nonsuccessive ration of startup by using a methodology which is called 'lean startup'. The lean startup 100 methodology helps the entrepreneurs to test their idea to the customer by interviewing them in several ways. They able to justify their ideas before launching their product for the customer when the following lean startup. Customer feedback has played an important role in a lean startup [2]. To use customer feedback on startup is not a very old concept, but very effective for every startup project. If the startup able to fulfill the user or customer expectation, then the startup can be successful, though being successful is a continues process. If the customer is not satisfied with the service on startup, then it could be the end of the startup. A startup has not finished after publishing the product in the market because it may not meet the customer demands properly. When the customers use the product they may have some others demands which they expect on a startup product again, they may dislike some features and do not use those features which is a waste in the lean startup [2]. It is important to know the feedback of customers to be successful in the startup world.

At present, the customer feedback is not a new concept for ensuring the system usability and availability. But all the feedback from customers is not required to execute. It is needed to select the proper feedback for execution on startup service. Otherwise, the wrong feedback may be selected for execution. There are not sufficient resources to select the proper feedback or to prioritize the feedback which is given by the customers of startup. This could be a big problem when the number of the startup is large. So that the intention of this research is to propose a model for prioritizing the feedback of customers for making the system more usable. Therefore, we prepare the research question as:

RQ: *How practitioners prioritize customer feedback on lean startup?*

The rest of the paper is organized as follows. In Sect. 2 we present related work. In Sect. 3, research method that was used to data collection which is followed by results in Sect. 4. Discussion and conclusion presented in Sects. 5 and 6 respectively.

2   Related Work

The concept of using customer feedback on startup is not very new idea, where one of a principle of a lean startup is 'Learn', which may compare to customer feedback [3]. Every startup can improve its level when they use customer feedback properly on a startup project. To find out the areas of improvement can be identified from the feedback which is given by different customers [2,4]. Using feedback in a startup is not a very old idea, for this reason, there are insufficient resources to work with the customer feedback, mainly how to use the feedback properly. According to the search result of different database about the topic of this work, the researcher cannot find any method or framework which is suggested to prioritize customer feedback for a lean startup. But everywhere it is said that the feedback from customers is important for the improvement of startup. In [16] represents a model for lean startup. Opti4Apps [17] a development model, which is mainly user-centric feedback revealing approach, for lean development to achieve high software quality for any startups. By conducting semi-structured interviews from three Finnish software companies, this [18] paper shows benefits, challenges and some recommendations for practising lean startups. Focusing on the customer satisfaction, an Axiomatic Design [19] is proposed for verifying the customer needs for lean startups.

3   Research Methodology

In this research, two research methods have applied. First one is a systematic mapping study and the second one is a case study. The case study is conducted based on the data which is found in first research method. The overview of research methodology is given in Fig. 1.

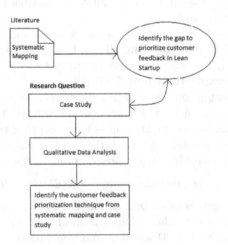

Fig. 1. Research overview

3.1 Systematic Mapping Study

The systematic mapping study is used in this research to find out the related research work and reduces the possibility of research bias. According to Kitchenham [5], a systematic map is a method that can be conducted to achieve an overview of a particular research area. The Systematic mapping study is used to identify the current study of the research area. It is used to find out research gaps to contribute in the research area. The following steps are proposed in the systematic mapping study [5,6].

3.1.1 Sys-Map Step 1: Definition of Research Questions (Research Scope)

In the systematic mapping study, the research question is the main key factor rather than in a systematic review [8]. The research question has to manipulate in such way that reflects the main and secondary goal of the systematic mapping of the study [5,6]. This is essential to identify the quantity and related works and result according to the research questions [8]. Following these guidelines, the researcher has specified a research question (RQ) in the field of the lean startup project.

3.1.2 Sys-Map Step 2: Formulation and Execution of Search Queries (All Studies)

The search string has to make according to research scope. The search strings are used to find the primary studies from digital sources or databases. The purpose of this search strategy is to identify and formulate search terms, define search process and resources to be searched [5,6].

Search Strategy- Lean Startup, Customer, Feedback and Prioritization have multiple dimensional contexts. It is observed that, multiple studies stated a keyword in different terms and values. Therefore, snowballing approach [9] is performed to manipulate all possible related keywords. Search strings are specified systematically drawn through the following steps:

- All the possible keywords are recognized by looking over titles, abstracts and index terms of studies.
- Relevant papers are identified by scope area and intervention in terms of research question [9].
- Thesaurus is used to find synonyms for keywords.
- Search strings are specified systematically by using Boolean operators such as AND, OR etc.

Search Strings- ("Customer" OR "Customers" OR "User" OR "Users") AND ("Feedback" OR "Feedbacks") AND ("Prioritization" OR "Priority" OR "Prioritize") AND ("Lean Startup" OR "Lean Start Up").

Both manual and automated search is conducted for this research. Different websites have searched for finding out relevant resources.

3.1.3   Sys-Map Step 3: Screening of Studies (Relevant Studies)

To find out the relevant studies inclusion and exclusion criteria is used in this research. Those papers are included which are relevant to the research question, those papers are not taken which are not relevant to the research question. The following steps are followed to find out relevant studies:

- The primary studies written in English and not to be duplicated.
- In the second step the title and abstract are used to find relevant studies. If those are not clear, then introduction and conclusion section could be acknowledged.
- The relevant studies that are in full text and clear those should be included. If they are not available (either digital or printed copy), then they should be excluded.
- The relevant studies should be included which are matched with the research area.

3.1.4   Sys-Map Step 4: Developing Classification Scheme (Key Wording Using Title, Abstract and Index Terms)

Classification schemes are used to shape the objectives of our research. According to Kitchenham [7], key-wording is done in two steps. First, the researcher read the title and abstract to find the keywords and concept that reflect the contribution of research also reduce the time and effort. This is the foundation level of classification scheme. Second, if abstract and title is not clear, then the researcher read the introduction and conclusion to take a depth knowledge of papers in detail.

3.1.5   Sys-Map Step 5: Data Extraction Process and Mapping of Studies (Systematic Map)

After completing classification scheme, the related study was mapped according to plans of classification scheme. The studies are listed and from all of those listed studies, the duplicated studies have been removed.

3.2   Case Study

Qualitative research is an approach which is used to understand the phenomenon and to solve the 'how' or 'why' problem. Qualitative research helps to know the background reason, opinions and motivations. The purpose of this research is to provide such a way for startup projects so that they able to identify a statistical data of customer feedback prioritization methodology.

In this research, the exploratory single case study is used. As exploratory case study is more appropriate where in-depth and detail knowledge is not available [10]. Participation and structured are two types of observation. In participation, researcher needs to involve with the selected case and in structured researcher need to look from outside of the selected case [10, 11]. The researcher involved with the team to perform the participatory case study. In this process, the researcher has got a depth understanding about the process because the researcher has become a part of the daily routines, events, rituals and interactions with the company [11].

3.2.1 Sampling

The startup company, which is investigated named it as Alpha. Because that startup company does not want to publish their name in this research. The Alpha company only provides the team structure of the feedback collection team and customer feedback decision making team. That is shown in following Table 1 The customer feedback collector collect feedbacks from customers once in a month using email, phone calls, Skype. After collection of feedback the team makes known the lead engineer. They discuss about the feedback in meeting where three to five members include based on the feedback types. The CEO and the lead engineer must attend at the meeting. They discuss about the feasibility of the collected feedback. Then they make decisions which feedback needs to implement first and which is not needed to implement at all.

Table 1. Different teams of alpha

Team name	Team member
Customer feedback collection	1
Customer feedback decision	Not fixed (Usually 3 to 5 including lead engineer and CEO)

3.2.2 Interview Design

This is the most common format of data collection in qualitative research. According to Oakley, qualitative interview is a type of framework in which the practices and standards be not only recorded, but also achievable, challenged and as well as reinforced [12]. Most of the qualitative research interviews are either semi-structured, lightly structured or in-depth [13]. In this research the researcher conducted a semi-structured so that the interview section could be more flexible and follow up questions can arise. The researcher has some predefined questions for the interview.

3.2.3 Data Collection

The researcher performed four working day participatory observation case study to find the answer to our research question. After getting in-depth knowledge about the research area, the researcher also performed semi-structured interviews with the feedback collection team and with the leader of the feedback decision making team. Overview of this single case study is given Table 2.

Table 2. Research activity

Activity	Participants	Focus area
Observation	Customer feedback collection team Customer feedback decision making team	Focus on customer feedback, feedback collection process, feedback priority process
Interview	Customer feedback decision making team leader	Challenges to collect feedback, decision making to implement the feedback

Six types of data collection technique proposed by Yin [15]: documents, archived records, structured interviews, direct observation, participatory observation and artifacts. Firstly, the researcher performed participatory observation to get data. After gathering knowledge and data, reviews some demo email document where the feedback collection team asks for feedback to the customer. The researcher maintains a notebook to write down daily observational data so that those can help future linkup between our findings. Data also collected from some demo email document. During this observation on of the researcher maintain communication with team leader over the phone call and face to face discussion to know more about customer feedback prioritization techniques they have used in their lean startup. Secondly, a face to face semi-structured interview with the team leader was performed which lasts for 30 min. The interview topic covers the feedback prioritization technique, where customer feedback is given priority first, how to set the value of customer for startup and some follow up questions.

3.2.4 Data Analysis

The data are collected from different data sources. But that data can not be understandable by the reader. Well organized data help the reader to understand the context or the purpose of research clearly [14]. Both researcher documented the result of the interview together. We used qualitative data analysis technique which is called thematic data analysis technique. Both researcher revisited the recorded interview multiple times and triangulate this with the data which is collected in observations. Using mind mapping tools (e.g Xmind) our findings are

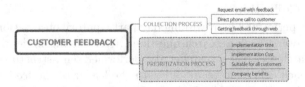

Fig. 2. A map of customer feedback

mapped for better visualization (See Fig. 2). The research question is mapped by several research methodologies and steps. Every step is mentioned in Table 3.

Table 3. Mapping of research questions to research methodology

Research questions	Research step	Research methodology
How practitioners prioritize customer feedback on lean startup?	To identify the techniques of feedback prioritization, which is collected from customers on a lean startup project?	Systematic mapping Case study Qualitative data analysis

4   Results

In this section, the results are reported along with categorization based on the research theme. The findings from observation is outlined. An overview of different findings is listed in Table 4.

Table 4. Findings from case study

Dimensions	Findings
Feedback collection	Email; Website; Phone calls; Online calls
Feedback priority	Team meeting; Customer value; Implementation time;
Techniques	Implementation cost; Suitable for all customers

The team usually uses emails, websites and talks to customer for collecting their feedback about the service customers are used. The team notes down all the collected feedback and documented those feedbacks to discuss in the meeting. When the sufficient feedbacks are collected, then they decide to call a meeting to discuss and make decisions about collected feedbacks. In the meeting, minimum three to five members are present. In every meeting the CEO and the lead engineer must be participating. In our observation, we have found that the feedback collector team presents the collected feedbacks in the meeting and make acknowledged the team about the customers and customer's feedbacks. At the meeting the members discuss various issues about the collected feedbacks and make a decision to implement customer feedback based on the value of customer in this project, the implementation time of feedbacks and the implementation cost.

4.1   Feedback Collection Process

The feedback collection team where the minimum member can be only one, the team collects feedbacks from customers in every month. Most of the time they use email for collecting feedbacks from their customers. They ask their customer about the service they are using through email and they note down the feedback given by the customer even if the customer does not reply they also note it down. The website is also used to get feedbacks from customers. They ask their customers about the services through the website. Sometimes they use phone calls and Skype calls depends on customers choose. If customer wants to give feedbacks over voice call only then they use this process.

4.2   Feedback Selection

Feedback selection is an important part for every startup. This startup team is always concern about customer's comments and feedbacks. When the feedbacks are collected from customers, they call a meeting to discuss about collected feedback. In this meeting they select the feedbacks from all of the collected feedback. The CEO, engineer head and other members discuss about the feasibility of collected feedbacks. They give priority the customer value, the development time and cost of feedbacks, the necessity of feedbacks for all customers than a single customer, the business benefit of collected feedbacks for this project is important. Measuring all of those issues they select feedbacks to be implemented from all feedbacks which are collected from customers. The startup project controller thinks that, those customers who are using their service more than others; they are most valuable customer for this project. They always give priority to those customers and give priority to their feedbacks for future release. If the customer has social value or brand value, not a prime user of this project, they also rated as a valued customer for this project. Those feedbacks are not selected which are more costly and take more times to be implemented. This is an important issue for giving priority or prioritizes the customer feedback. If the customer feedbacks take more time that must be a cause for increase cost. So they discuss the possible implementation time and cost of feedbacks before select feedbacks. If the collected feedbacks are not adding any value for all of the users or a maximum number of users then those feedbacks are not selected. They think that, their startup should be comfortable and useable for all of their targeted customers. If feedbacks are demanded by a customer which is not important for others at all, they skip this feedback of that customer for that time. They store this feedback for future; it may be used in the future, but not at this time.

Their main purpose to make profit from the market using their project. If any feedback does not meet the purpose of the project or does not profitable this feedback is not accepted at this meeting. It is observed that the selection of feedbacks must depend on the above issues. At that meeting they ensure that the selected feedbacks will add value for their project for a long run. After this feedback selections meeting the selected feedbacks are delivered to the development team for implementation.

5   Discussion

In every startup feedback is very crucial for the improvement of the startup project. The customers of startup project give feedbacks after using the service provided by the startup. In this research it is agreed with the startup project team that feedback plays a very important rule for the improvement of startup, but the most important thing is, the necessary feedback should be identified by the project operator. This also agreed with them, that every startup has its own way to identify those feedbacks which are important for the improvement of startup, in other words, every startup prioritizes their collected feedbacks which are collected from customers in their own way. Most of the time few techniques for prioritizing feedback matched with each others. After the observation by the researcher in this research, the researcher categorized the feedback prioritize technique in two major parts. The first one is related to the project and the last one is related to the customers. Which is related to the company that may be called as Look At Them process or LAT process and the second one may be called as Look At Me process or LAM process. After the categorization of the feedback prioritization process, the researcher proposes a new process which is depended on LAT and LAM process and named this new process as Look At Star process or LAS process.

5.1   Look at Them Process or LAT Process

The researcher are observed that, the startup project team always concerned about their customer. They try to listen them and try to provide service as their customer demand. They collect feedback from their startup user or customer for implementing those feedbacks. This agreed that, when the feedback is collected from customers the value of the customer for this project should be noted. The customer value depends on the type of startup project. The project team decides which customers are valuable to them. Again, the feedbacks may not be taken even if those are given by the valuable customers when those feedbacks are not usable for most of the customers of startup project. If those kinds of feedbacks are selected which may be used by a few of the startup's customers that may be costly for the startup, because most of the time that kind of service may not be profitable for startup project. When the feedback does not come from valuable customer, but that may be used by most of the customers in this project, then that kind of feedbacks may be taken for implementation.

5.2   Look at Me Process or LAM Process

Feedbacks are collected from customers and implemented for using by customer on a startup project for making profit and ensure the stability of the startup project. This is identified from the startup project team that, if the feedback takes much time to be implemented, most of the time that kind of feedback should not be taken for implementation. If that kind of feedback is taken, then it may be a reason for the expenses of extra money, which may increase the cost of startup project. It would be a good idea when those kind of feedbacks is taken for implementation which may be implemented within a short time. The implementation time is directly related to the cost of the startup project. Those kinds of feedbacks should not be selected which have no relationship with the startup goals, though it is from valuable customers.

5.3 Look at Star Process or LAS Process

LAT and LAM process are divided the feedbacks into two major parts. Now to make feedback prioritize, it is needed to make a scale for LAT and LAM process. The scale has a maximum value of five stars. When the feedbacks are divided into LAT and LAM, that time those feedbacks must be given a start mark where the maximum start is five. After dividing and giving stars to all feedbacks then all the feedbacks need to be sorted according to their star, where the most given star feedback will be placed at number one. Then the implementation team will look at the stars of the feedback for future execution.

6 Conclusion

The summary of all activities and the outcome of this research is discussed in this section. The main purpose of this research is to find out the prioritization techniques of customer feedback on lean startup. These techniques will be helpful for the startup projects to become successful. When the technique will be used in the lean startup project, the time and cost will be reduce of startup. The systematic mapping study and case study methodology is used in this research. The following sections are the summary of the findings of research question:

The gap of research is found out through systematic mapping study. The research question is established after the systematic mapping study. The relation between customer and lean startup is described in different studies. It is also described that the feedback of customer is most important for the lean startup project. It is found that there is not any proper technique used to prioritize the feedback of customers for future execution, which is motivated to find out a prioritization technique of customer feedback.

The case study methodology is used in situations when the depth knowledge of any research area is not available. According to the research question the depth knowledge of this research area is not sufficient. So case study needed to conduct for this research. Interview and observation are used to collect data for this research. By conducting interviews it is identified that, the investigated company has used their own process to prioritize the customer feedback for their startup project. When they prioritize feedback they consider that is that customer value, time and cost of implementation feedback, the suitability of feedback for all customers. The researcher proposes a new technique for prioritize customer feedback after conduction interviews and observation. Where in the first phase it is needed to use LAT and LAM process and in the last phase it is needed to used LAS process.

References

1. Sommerville, I.: Software Engineering. Addison-Wesley, Boston (2007)
2. Blank, S.: Why the lean start-up changes everything. Harvard Bus. Rev. **91**(5), 63–72 (2013)
3. Hart, M.A.: The lean startup: how today's entrepreneurs use continuous innovation to create radically successful businesses Eric Ries, 320 p. Crown Business, New York (2011)
4. Myyryläinen, M., Hämäläinen, H.: Lean startup approach for innovative corporate culture (2014)
5. Petersen, K., et al.: Systematic mapping studies in software engineering. In: EASE, vol. 8 (2008)
6. Mujtaba, S., et al.: Software product line variability: a systematic mapping study. School of Engineering, Blekinge Institute of Technology (2008)
7. Kitchenham, B.: Procedures for performing systematic reviews, vol. 33, no. 2004, pp. 1–26. Keele University, Keele, UK (2004)
8. Budgen, D., et al.: Using mapping studies in software engineering. In: Proceedings of PPIG, vol. 8. Lancaster University (2008)
9. Jan, N., Ibrar, M.: Systematic mapping of value-based software engineering: a systematic review of value-based requirements engineering (2010)
10. Razzak, M.A., Ahmed, R., Mite, D.: Spatial knowledge creation and sharing activities in a distributed agile project. In: 2013 IEEE 8th International Conference on Global Software Engineering Workshops (ICGSEW). IEEE (2013)
11. Musante, K., DeWalt, B.R.: Participant Observation: A Guide for Fieldworkers. Rowman Altamira, Lanham (2010)
12. Oakley, A.: Gender, methodology and people's ways of knowing: Some problems with feminism and the paradigm debate in social science. Sociology **32**(4), 707–731 (1998)
13. Mason, J.: Linking qualitative and quantitative data analysis. In: Analyzing Qualitative Data, pp. 89–110 (1994)
14. Basit, T.: Manual or electronic? The role of coding in qualitative data analysis. Educ. Res. **45**(2), 143–154 (2003)
15. Yin, R.K.: Case Study Research: Design and Methods. Sage Publications, Thousand oaks (2009)
16. Sauvola, T., et al.: Continuous improvement and validation with customer touchpoint model in software development. In: ICSEA 2018, p. 62 (2018)
17. Elberzhager, F., Holl, K., Karn, B., Immich, T.: Rapid lean UX development through user feedback revelation. In: Felderer, M., Méndez Fernández, D., Turhan, B., Kalinowski, M., Sarro, F., Winkler, D. (eds.) PROFES 2017. LNCS, vol. 10611, pp. 535–542. Springer, Cham (2017). https://doi.org/10.1007/978-3-319-69926-4_43
18. Salas Martinez, M.: Good Practices of the Lean Startup Methodology: Benefits, Challenges and Recommendations (2016)
19. Girgenti, A., et al.: An axiomatic design approach for customer satisfaction through a lean start-up framework. Procedia CIRP **53**, 151–157 (2016)

Meta-Analysis of Researches of STEAM with Coding Education – in Korea

Jeong Ah Kim and HeeJin Kim[✉]

Department of Computer Education, Catholic Kwandong University,
579BeonGil 24, Gangneung, KangWon, Korea
{clara, akddl4}@cku.ac.kr

Abstract. We thought that programs applied with programming (coding) and creative/convergence education (STEAM) which are representative educational trends in the 4th industrial revolution era, are very useful strategy for improving the problem solving capabilities and creativeness. We need well-defined process for developing the IT-based STEAM program and well-defined evaluation criteria to verify the program. In this paper, we tried to analyze the previous related researches to identify the process and evaluation tools for IT-based STEAM program design.

1 Introduction

In the case of STEM that began in the US, it was aimed at enhancing students' academic achievement related to STEM subjects, inducing interest in related subjects, and encouraging female and ethnic minority students to enter science and engineering. In Korea, despite high academic achievement compared to other countries, STEM education was started to improve efficacy, confidence, and interest in relatively low science learning and to solve the phenomenon of students avoiding science and engineering [1]. The IT-centered STEAM education program has been proven to help students understand the principles of science and mathematics concepts through solving math and engineering problems through their own real-life experiences and knowledge utilization [2]. From 2015, coding education was enforced into the curriculum of elementary school. Then, form the 2018, coding education was involved as individual subject into middle school. Therefore, we thought that it was necessary what topics have been studied and what kinds of research areas were interested in IT-based STEAM education.

We select 16 thesis of master and ph.D degree from the riss.net which is the knowledge repository in Korea. We searched the paper with the keywords such as STEAM, coding, programming, and computational thinking. 19 papers were retrieved but 3 papers are not related with programming education so that we excludes them. In this paper, we surveyed 16 papers and analyzed them with 6 perspectives: (1) degree of school, (2) Subject of STEAM and tools of coding education, (3) Goals of the research, (4) strategies of research and course design, (5) Type of contents designed in each researches, (6) Evaluation methods. In Sect. 2, we described the background knowledge of STEAM and coding education. In Sect. 3, we summaries the research results of

© Springer Nature Switzerland AG 2019
S. Misra et al. (Eds.): ICCSA 2019, LNCS 11623, pp. 82–89, 2019.
https://doi.org/10.1007/978-3-030-24308-1_7

17 papers. We explains our results of meta-analysis in Sect. 4 and discuss the future research directions in Sect. 5.

2 Background Domain

2.1 STEAM Education

STEAM education has its roots in STEM education, which is at the heart of US education reform. STEM was used as an acronym for Science, Technology, Engineering, and Mathematics at the National Science Foundation (NSF). As it continuously appeared in education policies or education related issues, it has gained attention in science education all over the world. STEM education emphasizes the convergence and practice of STEM-related subjects in order to secure competitiveness in the age of globalization suitable for the changes and challenges of the 21st century [3]. In 2011, Korea's Ministry of Education, Science and Technology announced its plans to implement STEAM education which increases understanding, interest, and the potential of science and technology in elementary and secondary schools with the objective of realizing talent power by cultivating creative talents in science and technology in its work report (Ministry of Education, Science and Technology, 2011; Ministry of Education, Science and Technology, 2010). STEAM, which added arts (including the humanities in a broad sense) activities to the STEM education in the United States and the United Kingdom has become a term for convergence talent education in Korea. The Ministry of Education, Science and Technology (2011) defined STEAM an educational program that enhances students' interest and understanding of science and technology and fosters STEAM literacy and problem-solving skills based on science and technology. The Korea Foundation for the Advancement of Science and Creativity (a) defines STEAM as "education to develop students' interest and understanding of science and technology and to develop STEAM Literacy based on science and technology and real-life problem-solving skills."

2.2 Software Education

Computational thinking is the process of thinking about how to solve the various complex problems that humans face in real life, and it is a comprehensive thinking process to solve the problem-solving process effectively and efficiently through the powerful capabilities provided by computing devices. Computational thinking is emphasized as a core competency that a learner should have in the 21st century, where computing technology is the backbone of society and people need the ability to use it to solve complex problems. It is recognized as a fundamental skill such as reading, writing, and counting that everybody must know [4]. Computational thinking is the ability to correctly analyze a given problem into a logical, critical, or creative thinking problem and solve it. Based on the definition of computational thinking, it is composed of 5 computational components including algorithm, decomposition, generalization, abstraction, and evaluation [5].

3 Survey of Related Research

Kim [1] developed a STEAM education program that integrates science subjects and programming for elementary school students to develop a programming-oriented STEAM education program for enhancing computational thinking. We proposed and suggested digital storytelling, physical computing, and scientific writing as ideas to appropriately converge programming and STEAM's curriculum learning in a programming-oriented STEAM education program. Four STEAM educational programs were proposed and developed for elementary school students according to the objectives of various curriculum management, and their effects were verified by using test tools such as creativity, logical thinking ability, and interest in science.

In order to understand mathematics curriculum, Kim [6] developed a SW Convergence Mathematics Instruction Program based on computing thinking. SW Convergence Mathematics Instruction was defined as a program that allows students to think creatively and learn on their own to solve problems efficiently through computational principles and learned computing technologies when mathematical problems are given. We analyzed how SW Convergence Mathematics Instruction affects attitude, mathematical creativity, mathematical problem-solving ability of elementary and middle school students.

Kim [7] developed STEAM teaching and learning materials for mathematically gifted students using random numbers and physical computing, analyzed the effects of the developed data on students' STEAM core competency improvement, and confirmed the suitability of the developed teaching and learning materials. Based on the development criteria of STEAM teaching and learning materials, development direction and learning goals were set up and 20-period teaching and learning materials for middle school mathematic gifted students were developed. In order to verify the validity of the developed gifted teaching and learning materials for mathematics, we observed participation in the class situation and measured the change using the STEAM core competency evaluation framework. In addition, we examined the changes of learners through pre and post tests by using convergence problem solving ability tests and future talent competency tests.

Yu [8] implemented programming based experiential activities in consideration of developmental stage and characteristics of elementary students. Lego WEDO robots were selected as an educational tool that not only motivates and attract students' interests but that is also easily manipulated. A STEAM program using Lego WEDO was developed and applied to two 6th grade classes. The effect of participant learners on computing thinking ability was analyzed. After applying 13 periods of STEAM programs, the pre and post computational thinking scores were compared and levels of satisfaction were surveyed. The computational thinking ability evaluation was carried out with self-developed items that were reviewed by experts in terms of performance and analysis, algorithms and codes, generalization, structuring, and data analysis.

Although the most effective education is algorithm and programming education for the improvement of creative problem solving, Lee [9] suggests that the development of teaching and learning methods for programming education is very scarce and relies on traditional methods. STEAM-based education approaches from the integrated viewpoint of how it relates to various subjects in one problem centering on real life problems. STEAM-based education can be a teaching and learning strategy to improve creative problem-solving ability. A STEAM based robot programming educational process was developed and applied to secondary students gifted in informatics. STEAM learning was compared with disciplinary robot programming lessons focused on acquiring concepts and the effects on creative problem-solving abilities were inspected.

Yoo [10] developed the STEAM-based learning materials for robot use for creativity enhancement for elementary gifted students. Through studies that verify the effects of applying this, we selected the robot-based learning subject suitable for elementary school gifted students and designed the lesson to achieve the learning goal. The effects of creativity were inspected.

Han [11] argued that SW Convergence Education for increasing creativity, communication ability, consideration, conversion ability in students must be implemented, and suggested a SW coding-based convergence program for elementary students gifted in science. After applying this to elementary students gifted in mathematics/sciences, the validity was verified through the effectiveness test.

Lee [12] developed and applied middle school mathematics statistics unit and Python Programming Convergence Instructions (STEAM) according to the contents system and achievement standard of the information department and mathematics department The problem-solving ability, the programming interest, and the pre-test and post-test of mathematical interest were examined to verify the effects of the statistical-python fusion class on problem solving ability, programming interest, and interest in mathematics.

Lee [13] developed a STEAM-based education program that can be applied in the field by combining the content of science subjects with scratch that can be easily accessed by learners. The effects of STEAM-based education programs using scratch on the creativity and the positive characteristics related to science of elementary school students were verified.

Hong [14] developed SW convergence education program using scratch that can be applied for a long time and verified how ICT literacy and SW awareness of elementary school students are affected.

Sung [15] practiced intelligent robot-driven programming directly and claimed that creative robots can be trained to adapt to the student's competence, understand and apply algorithms, and naturally acquire logical thinking and creativity. It is proved that the students become more interested in learning with their sense of accomplishment and self-confidence that they can feel when they operate correctly according to the control program they designed with the robot they made. For this purpose, a program was designed to improve storytelling ability by designing and creating various structures using frames and rivets with Tami, an intelligent educational robot consisting of convergence contents of science, technology, engineering, art and mathematics.

In order to increase the interest of mathematics, Kim [16] developed a STEAM-based mathematics learning program using scratch, focusing on mathematics. After analyzing contents of mathematics learning contents and STEAM, we developed a mathematical learning program using scratch by applying a model of convergence learning. The developed program was applied to students in the first year of high school to verify the effect on high school students' interest in mathematics.

Shin [17] developed a creative STEAM education program using scratches for use in elementary schools and examined and verified the changes in creativity and learner response as applied to actual school sites. The state of elementary school students was classified into cognitive, affective, and behavioral domains. The most difficult units were identified through questionnaires and the selected magnetic field unit was classified into STEAM elements.

Na [18] developed the STEAM program using unplugged computing techniques on the subject of social studies subjects and applied it to elementary schools to verify the improvement of creative problem-solving ability.

Jung [19] developed and applied the STEAM education program in the arts field to enhance creativity. Since the arts subjects such as Korean language, music, and art are the subjects preferred by female students, the STEAM program proved that female students brought a change in their attitudes toward computers. It is significant that the existing STEAM education program was developed based on science and mathematics, while the STEAM education program centered on the arts area was developed and applied.

4   Meta-Analysis of Related Researches

In Korea, teachers for elementary school are graduated from National university of Education. To improve the problem solving capabilities and computational thinking, coding education was involved in elementary curriculum from 2015 in Korea. 65% papers (11 papers) were the results for elementary schools. Just 1 papers was written with the experimental results with high school students. The subject of STEAM with coding were science, mathematics, art, social studies, and Korean Language (Table 1).

Table 1. Subjects of STEAM and coding education

	Science	Math	Painting	Social studies	Music	Ethics	Korean language
# of researches	6	5	4	2	1	1	1
Ratio (%)	37.5	31.3	25.0	12.5	6.3	6.3	6.3

The tools of STEAM with coding were scratch, unplugged, Lego-wedo, Physical computing, Robot programming, and Python. The ratio of Scratch was highest but various tools were adopted for researches.

The goals of many researches were to improve the interests and creativity of each subject (Table 2). Some researches tried to improve the general creativity and problem solving capabilities. Not many researches considered of the computational thinking.

Table 2. Analysis of research goals

	Outcomes & creativity of subject	Creativity	Problem-solving	Computational thinking	Self-effectiveness
# of researches	6	7	4	2	1
Ratio (%)	37.5	43.8	25.0	12.5	6.3

Almost researches designed the course of 14 h and more. It means that many researches was designed for after-school activities and the some part of regular class. 2 researches suggested the course design for very long courses of 36 h. These 2 researches were designed for regular class in elementary school. Just 5 researches applied the instructional systems design (ISD) framework and the other researches applied just their own design strategy. Just 3 researches were evaluated their studies by own questionnaire or evaluation tools. The other researches were evaluated with well-defined evaluation tools. The most popular evaluation tools were Torrance's creativity evaluation tools (A type) and simplified version for creative problem-solving capability checklist introduced by Korean Educational Development Institute. The Aiken Attitude to Mathematics Scales was used to evaluate the improvement of interest and cre-ativeness in Math and science subject. All researches provided syllabus for suggested program. Some researches provided detail syllabus and course materials.

5 Discussions

Convergent programs with programming (coding) and STEAM are very powerful and useful paradigm for creative/convergence education. In Korea, elementary and sec-ondary schools have tries to implement STEAM education for increasing the under-standing, interest, and the potential of science and technology. Also coding education was embedded for improving the problem-solving capability. Actually, coding edu-cation might be powerful tool for engineering in STEAM and also practical tool for STEAM education. In this paper, we tried to analyze the trends of IT-based (coding) STEAM education researches in Korea since we tried to develop the program for high school students. After coding education was involved as regular course in elementary schools, many researches related IT-based STEAM education was suggested. So far, not many researches are launched for high schools. Also, math and science were the major subjects for convergence with coding since these subjects are considered as critical subject for creativeness. There are not many researches about art including language education and problem-based learning. From the analysis of related research, we suggested further researches appropriate instructional systems design process and strategies and more verified evaluation framework for various objectives of program.

References

1. Kim, T.H.: STEAM education program based on programming to improve computational thinking ability. Ph.D thesis, Jeju National University of Education (2015)
2. Choi, H.: Design and development of software-based fusion STEAM board. Mater Degree, KyuingIn National University of Education (2015)
3. Yakman, G., Kim, J.: Using BAKUK to teach purposefully integrated STEM/STEAM education. In: 37th Annual Conference International Society for Exploring Teaching and Learning, Atlanta, Georgia (2007)
4. Wing, J.M.: Computational thinking. Commun. ACM **49**(3), 33–35 (2006)
5. Selby, C., Woollard, J.: Computational Thinking: The Developing Definition (2013). http://eprints.soton.ac.uk/356481. Accessed 23 June 2014
6. Kim, M.: The effects of the mathematics class that converged SW on mathematical attitude, mathematical creative ability and mathematical problem solving ability of elementary and middle school students. Master Degree, Ajou University (2018)
7. Kim, H.S.: Development and application of teaching-learning materials on STEAM using random number and physical computing for mathematically gifted students. Master Degree, Korea National University of Education (2018)
8. Yoo, S.: The effect of STEAM program using LEGO WEDO on computational thinking of elementary school students. Master Degree, Seoul National University of Education (2018)
9. Lee, H.: The effect of STEAM-based robot programming education on the creative problem-solving skills of secondary information gifted students. Master Degree, Korea National University of Education (2015)
10. Yoo, S.: The effects of STEAM-based learning using a robot for improving gifted primary school student's creativity. Master Degree, Korea National University of Education (2013)
11. Han, D.-H.: Development of STEAM program based on SW coding for the Mathmatical & Scientific Gifted of Elementary School. Mater Degree, KyuingIn National University of Education (2018)
12. Lee, D.Y.: Effects of middle school mathematical statistics area and Python programming STEAM instruction on problem solving ability and curriculum interest. Master Degree, GongJu National University of Education (2018)
13. Lee, J.H.: Development and application of STEAM based education program using scratch. Master Degree, Jeju National University of Education (2012)
14. Hong, J.M.: The effect of convergent software education program using scratch on elementary students' ICT literacy and their awareness of software education. Mater Degree, KyuingIn National University of Education (2015)
15. Sung, Y.S.: Study of implementation scheme of STEAM learning model through intelligent robot design based on scratch. Master Degree, JunBuck National University of Education (2017)
16. Kim, E.J.: The development and application of mathematics program based on STEAM using scratch for the first grade high school students. Master Degree, Korea National University of Education (2013)
17. Shin, S.K.: The development and application of creative STEAM program using scratch for elementary school. Master Degree, Daegu National University of Education (2012)

18. Na, W.Y.: The effect of STEAM education program using unplugged computing on creative problem-solving abilities in elementary students. Mater Degree, KyuingIn National University of Education (2016)
19. Jung, S.B.: Application and effect analysis of arts area STEAM education program: focused on the scratch programming. Master Degree, Jeju National University of Education (2016)

Component Architecture of mHealth Service Platform

Jeong Ah Kim and DongGi Kim(✉)

Catholic Kwandong University, 579BeonGil 24, Gangneung,
GangWonDo 25601, Korea
clara@cku.ac.kr, remaindk0@gmail.com

Abstract. The area of mobile healthcare (mHealth) is expected to expand from disease treatment to various areas, such as disease prevention, telemedicine, and universal health promotion. Under such vertical and horizontal medical industry expansion, the mHealth concept for the improvement of the quality of medical services, such as telemedicine and medical record automation, will become the keyword of the industry while mobile devices and networks will be advanced. In this paper, architecture of mHealth is suggested for multi-product, small-quantity production and a majority constitution by small manufacturers.

Keywords: Mobile health service · Architecture · Software platform

1 Introduction

The mHealth, a medical healthcare service that utilizes mobile technologies, is attracting much attention because it can create new service values by combining the existing healthcare areas with IT and mobile technologies [1]. Major advanced countries are implementing various policies to activate the mHealth industry as well as U-Healthcare, and they are developing services, such as telemedicine, management of patients with chronic diseases, and medical video conferencing, by combining the medical field with ICT to reduce medical expenses. In the mHealth area, devices, software, and services are combined in various forms. Therefore, various stakeholders participate in the area, and thus, convergence based on standard technologies is required [2]. In addition, even non-experts should be able to develop easily services customized to various consumers. The considerations for activating the development of mHealth mobile apps are as follows: ① the applications must be connected to various types of bio-signal measuring instruments, ② the bio-signal measuring instruments must perform accurate and efficient measurements at home or on the move, ③ the measured data must be linked seamlessly to the integrated mHealth service center, ④ the measured data must be analyzed using various techniques to provide results that are easy to see, and ⑤ non-experts in programming must be able to develop mobile apps if they have service planning capabilities.

As for the necessity for a development platform in consideration of the characteristics of the medical device manufacturing area for mHealth, the medical device manufacturing industry, an essential mHealth element, is characterized by multi-product,

S. Misra et al. (Eds.): ICCSA 2019, LNCS 11623, pp. 90–96, 2019.
https://doi.org/10.1007/978-3-030-24308-1_8

small-quantity production and a majority constitution by small manufacturers. In addition, there are various items to be dealt with. Owing to these characteristics, it is difficult to derive specialized assistance for each device manufacturer, which is required for the development of mHealth mobile apps and capable of developing various business models. ISO/IEEE standards were established for pulse oxymeters, blood pressure monitors, thermometers, scales, blood glucose meters, and activity meters. The optimal data exchange protocol area between devices and managers was adopted as a standard in the transmission area. Basic channel electrocardiograms, respiration rate, blood coagulation test, insulin pumps, and cardiovascular fitness meter are under progress for standard establishment. Based on these standards, the interoperability between devices must be performed by providing the mHealth service platform and linkage methods between the standards and each device. There is a necessity for platforms that can support monitoring and consulting services among the mHealth areas since they are expected to create the highest demand in the next five years. In these service areas, it is necessary to develop a platform that can support the development of apps that meet Time-To-Market and stable service quality. Environments that support the development of mobile apps for non-experts in programming are emerging. The examples include open and commercial tools, such as App Inventor, Rud Dev, and MobiCart. Since they are environments that support the development of general-purpose mobile apps, effort is required to develop devices for mHealth services, elements that can provide linkage with mHealth servers, and process analysis results; therefore, they are not suitable for mHealth service planners and developers to use. Based on the environmental concept that supports the development of the existing general-purpose mobile apps, mobile app-developing environments specialized for mHealth are required. This study aims to analyze the characteristics of mobile apps specialized for mHealth in terms of architecture and to propose the architecture that can support such characteristics. In Sect. 2, the characteristics of mobile medical services are examined. In Sect. 3, architecture drivers required to provide mobile medical services are defined. In Sect. 4, the required architecture design results are explained. In Sect. 5, conclusions on future utilization methods and verification are presented.

2 Related Research

"Telehealth Project" of the U.S., "Telecare Project" of the UK, "iN2015" of Singapore, "AAL Project" of EU, and "u-Japan Project" of Japan are the representative examples of such policies. While the area requires a high level of expertise, the market is growing due to the combination of healthcare and mobile IT technologies, the demand for mobile applications, and the rapid increase in related products. In particular, the importance and growth of mHealth based on mobile applications can be expected. That the FDA announced guidelines on medical mobile applications is proof. Over 13,600 consumer healthcare applications are registered in application stores, and their average price is USD 2.05. There are approximately 40,000 applications that support multi-platforms, 70% of which are related to personal health and fitness, and 30% are applications for medical experts (source: APEC Health Forum, 2012). While mHealth has the benefits of reducing health monitoring costs and improving efficiency as well as medical accessibility, there is still no specific business model. Although the mobile health apps market has a high growth potential due to its benefit of not restraining consumers, the difficulty in forming consumers is a limitation. At the moment, selling apps through app stores is the only business model, and it does not have a significant value in terms of revenue. The most realistic alternative to overcome this situation is to develop mHealth apps in connection with device manufacturers. Developing various app functions based on the accurate understanding of devices and measurement contents is presented here as a business model. The necessity, barriers, and success factors of the development of mHealth apps are as follows. Previously, the largest barriers were the vulnerability of data security, a lack of standards, and the inaccuracy of discovery, but it is now expected that these problems can be addressed by the distribution of smart devices, an increase in user demand, and the development of patient-customized care medical methodology (source: resrech2guidance mHealth App Developer Economics survey 2014, n = 2032). Remote patient management systems are provided to large hospitals, such as Pusan National University Hospital and Gyeongsang National University Hospital, and over 200 small hospitals. The mobile diabetes management service (high care) for managing health through mobile phones or internet is provided to patients. Isoo UBcare Co., Ltd. developed MDoctor (Mobile Healthcare solution) and began the mobile diabetes commercial services for general patients. Healthpia began the diabetes measurement service in 2004, and its "diabetes phone" co-developed with LG Electronics and Infopia in July 2006 received an approval from the FDA in the U.S. Humana launched "GoldWalker," a 99-cent mobile game. This game was classified into a fitness application because the game continued only when the gamer actually walked. In Japan, Fujitsu developed a technology for checking the pulse in real time using the face photograph taken by a camera built in smartphones and tablet PCs. eHealth Aces Pvt in India developed an app service that connects users to doctors and released it in Google Play. It is provided in a price range from 9 to 2,49 rupees, and it can be linked easily to other medical services provided by eHealth Aces Pvt. [3] introduced most popular app for mHealth. Recent studies show that mobile devices and apps can support a variety of routine medical tasks including clinical reference, drug dose calculation, patient education, accessing medical records, and clinical decision support [4, 5].

3 Architecture Driver

In this study, an architecture was developed for the mHealth mobile platform, which can identify components for mHealth services (sensor component, measurement data analysis component, patient care guideline component, inference component, and visualization component) and create mHealth mobile apps based on scenarios that may activate their development. For this, architecture drivers were identified as shown in Table 1 by analyzing the current mHealth services and technical trends.

Table 1. Architecture driver

Trends and Goals	Description
1. Service creation possibility	• Generation of visual programming environment so that non-experts in programming can easily develop mobile apps if they have creative mHealth service plans • Creation of visual development tools that provide methods for intuitively developing desired mHealth services • Services can be developed by assembling common and product-specialized components from the mHealth service platform
2. Scalability of the care guidelines	• The increasing importance of evidence-based medical services, which provide better health performance, expand the uniformity of the quality of treatment, and suppress the growth of healthcare expenses by providing patients with more effective and safer interventions • The essential application of evidence-based medical services as technical innovation for reducing the costs of acquisition, storage, processing, and searching of various data to be utilized in mHealth services • The defining of the potential range of evidence-based medical services in mHealth services is necessary, considering medical law and clinical environments • The nursing protocol for providing evidence-based mHealth services must have a form (CIP: Computer Interpretable Protocol) that can be understood by computers • Forms suitable for the CIP definition are defined based on various forms following the existing nursing protocol • For the evidence-based care service customized to patients, the nursing protocol must be created in accordance with the forms for CIP
3. Visualization of analysis information	• The commonly required visualization methods in mHealth services are Chart, Graph, and Gauge • Components for visualizing the analysis information are expanded based on the existing open source components
4. Analysis of accumulated information	• Various forms of analysis must be supported by defining basic analytical features as the functions for sensor-based data analysis • Avg, SD, Rec, Sm, Int, PSD, MF, MPF, FFT, RMS, Wavelet
6. Data collection from medical sensors	• Development of sensor modules for measuring bio-signals, such as ECG, EMG, EEG, ENG, EOG, and ERG, as well as sensor modules for measuring temperature, blood pressure, respiration, and pulse
	• Design that enables the implementation of high-precision filter circuits and channel expansion
	• Design of a circuit capable of implementing signal amplification and attenuation functions

4 Component Identification for mHealth Architecture

4.1 Builder Component and Visualization Framework

This environment can add contents required for mHealth based on JS/HTML 5 and Open Source Code. It implemented the visible component based on the common component modeling method and design the screen generator component through web authoring tools based on the HTML 5 technology. The detailed component design is shown in the Fig. 1.

4.2 Care Guideline Framework

This component can easily create the nursing protocol for mHealth. It defines the service range and method, taking into consideration the legal regulations of mHealth and risk elements from the medical perspective. They are defined by the range of services provided by the Clinical Decision Support Service (CDSS), which constitutes an axis of the existing medical information system, and the technical and legal restrictions of mHealth. As the nursing protocol must be defined in the CIP form for evidence-based services in mHealth, the framework contains the procedure and methods required for CIP creation. The framework is defined in the following figure as the nursing protocol for processing hypertension and metabolic syndrome, which are the most representative chronic diseases, so that it can be created and used as a reference model in the future for the scalability of the knowledge. Figure 2 show the several example of care guidelines.

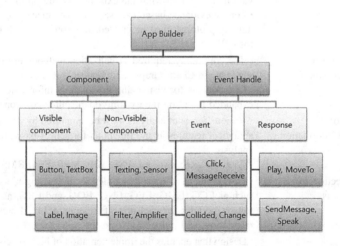

Fig. 1. Component of visual builder

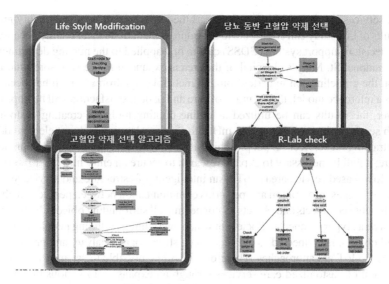

Fig. 2. Guideline components

4.3 Medical Sensor Framework

The bio-potential signal measurement sensor module and dms sensor module are built into the components to measure the ECG, EMG, and EEG signals from the human body so that the output of built-in sensors can be used easily. They are also designed so that the setting value of each sensor can be easily modified. Moreover, they are defined so that the Universal Sensor Interface function can be implemented. The Notch Filter and Band Pass Filter components are elements for implementing the digital filter function. They are designed to enable high-precision filter circuit implementation and channel expansion. A band pass filter is used to remove the power noise. The ECG, EMG, and EEG amplification modules are components constituting an amplification circuit capable of measuring signals, and they implement the amplification and atten-uation functions. The Low Pass Filter and High Pass Filter modules enable high-precision filter circuit implementation and channel expansion. They remove the power noise using the Band Pass Filter, and the Low Pass Filter is used to remove the signal noise. It was verified that multiple biometric data, such as the heartbeat and pulse, can be easily monitored through bio-sensor nodes.

5 Conclusion and Future Research

This study proposed a mHealth service platform architecture capable of integrating the information obtained from medical devices with evidence-based medical services and supporting the co-development and co-brand-based construction of small-scale multi-product medical sensor manufacturers. It is expected that the mHealth service platform can be utilized as the basis of the co-marketing required of small-scale manufacturers to efficiently pioneer the market under global competition. The importance of evidence-based medical services is continuously increasing as the importance of medical quality grows. The results of this study can contribute to the improvement of medical quality because the clinical decision support system (CDSS) can be first applied to the nursing department of the International St. Mary's Hospital. If the area is expanded to pressure sores and falls, based on the guidelines on hypertension and metabolic syndrome, which has been proposed as a reference model, the accuracy of care and patient satisfaction will be improved. Moreover, the results can be utilized as online training tools for creating customized mHealth services; they can be used in mHealth service planning and unit element development training for services for people majoring in biomedical engineering and nursing. In the future, it will be necessary to expand research to secure an entry into other Internet of Things (IoT)-based service areas. IoT is an intelligent infrastructure and service technology that exchanges information and performs communication between people and objects as well as between objects and objects by connecting all surrounding objects. In the future, there will be a Hyper Connected Society in which everything, including people, processes, data, and objects, is connected to create, collect, store, share, analyze, and predict information as the IoT era approaches. Therefore, it will be possible to secure a basis for the development of customized care services through an expansion to various targets other than medical sensors.

References

1. Kay, M., Santos, J., Takane, M.: mHealth new horizons for health through mobile technologies. World Health Organ. **64**, 66–71 (2011)
2. Estrin, D., Sim, I.: Open mHealth architecture: an engine for health care innovation. Science **330**(6005), 759–760 (2010)
3. Labrique, A.B., Vasudevan, L., Kochi, E., Fabricant, R., Meh, G.: mHealth innovations as health system strengthening tools: 12 common applications and a visual framework. Glob. Health Sci. Pract. **1**(2), 160–171 (2013)
4. Becker, S., et al.: mHealth 2.0: experiences, possibilities, and perspectives. JMIR mhealth uhealth **2**(2), e24 (2014)
5. Lewis, T.L., Wyatt, J.C.: mHealth and mobile medical apps: a framework to assess risk and promote safer use. J. Med. Internet Res. **16**(9), e210 (2014)

An Architectural Approach
to the Precedent-Oriented Solution of Tasks
in Designing a Software Intensive System

Petr Sosnin[✉], Sergey Shumilov, and Aleksandr Ivasev

Ulyanovsk State Technical University,
Severny Venets, Str. 32, 432027 Ulyanovsk, Russia
sosnin@ulstu.ru, mars@mv.ru, nevskei@yandex.ru

Abstract. The paper presents an approach to architectural modeling focused on its use for the development of functional components of a software intensive system (SIS), each of which is associated with the solution of a specific design task. To ensure the independence of proposed architectural modeling from the specificity of a certain SIS, the approach is focused on creating a complex of specialized means called TASK, which is intended for solving the design tasks in the workplace of a member of the design team. The specificity of the complex consists in forming by the designer for any solved task its reusable model (model of a precedent), which is included in the experience base applied in the design process of a certain SIS or their family. The prototype version of the TASK was developed in the personified version of the toolkit WIQA, which provides the solution of design tasks at the conceptual stage of the development of the SIS. This version of objectifying the approach is specifically implemented in a prototype form so that it can be used as a sample that can be fitted for architectural modeling of any design tasks when developing any SIS.

Keywords: Architectural modeling · Designing · Precedent model · Project task · Prototyping · Software intensive systems

1 Introduction

Professionally mature development of a modern SIS is unthinkable without the mandatory construction and operational use of its architectural representation (Architecture Description, AD), which is considered to be a very important version of the existence of the SIS, demanded at all stages of its life cycle. Most importantly, this version is the first (earliest) representation of the SIS, which can be tested as a whole. Moreover, this wholeness must express the essential features of the SIS, and, usually, in forms that contribute to a constructive understanding of them by those persons (stakeholders), concerns of which should be taken into account in the SIS project.

In all subsequent versions of the SIS-existence, the requirements integrated into AD must be coordinated without fail, preserving the wholeness embedded in AD, which may change on the course of developing the SIS, but only if there are very serious reasons for this. Thus, the AD artifact in its current state captures those interconnected

S. Misra et al. (Eds.): ICCSA 2019, LNCS 11623, pp. 97–107, 2019.
https://doi.org/10.1007/978-3-030-24308-1_9

high-level requirements, which are prohibited from being changed at lower levels of detail, since possible changes in AD are too expensive decisions for the process of developing the SIS.

The high importance of artifacts of the AD-type has found expression in standards that integrate the experience of architectural modeling of systems with software. Among such standards, a special place is occupied by the IEEE-1497: 2000 standards and its extension ISO/IEC/IEEE 42010: 2011. The standards are based on the formation of the system S ({Vj}) of "architectural views" (Views, {Vj}), based on the "points of view" (Viewpoints, {VPk}) specified in the architectural description of the project. This description must include all specifications that should be materialized for each modeled view Vj in the developed SIS. It should be noted that behind each architectural view is its graphic (typically block-and-line) image or diagram with the necessary description.

In the development of a specific SIS, the responsibility for constructing an artifact lies with the architect, who possesses the necessary competencies and uses specialized tools that ensure executing the role of the "architect." The article proposes a version of architectural modeling, focused on its use by the designer in solving design tasks, and such use contributes to the achievement of the positive effects of such modeling not only from the activity of the architect but also on other members of the designers' team.

The proposed version of the architectural approach is aimed at using useful "architectural views" on the design process from the "point of view of working with design task." The implementation of the architectural approach has led to the development of specialized tools, the prototyping of which was implemented in the instrumental environment OwnWIQA, intended for supporting the conceptual activity of the designer in individual working with project tasks [1]. The toolkit OwnWIQA provides uniting its instances into complexes in the corporate network of the SIS development for providing the work in designers' group.

2 Question-Answer Approach to Solving the Project Tasks

For many years, we investigated the processes of conceptual designing the SISs in conditions of the operational interactions of designers with experience and its models. This stage of designing was chosen because it directly involves working with semantic (conceptual) objects, the system of which must be materialized in the form of a conceptual project of SIS before its programming. Also, in practice, this stage is usually the source of costly semantic errors due to personal and collective problems with understanding, or, in other words, this stage is subject to the negative influence of human factors, especially when the designers face new tasks in their operative actions [2].

In the course of the research, some versions of the toolkit WIQA were developed, the continuous improvement of which was facilitated by its architecture, which was based on a system of architectural views on the (conceptual) project of the SIS. In investigated views onto the system, the central place occupies the task-oriented structuring of the project and the question-answer interactions of designers with experience in the process of solving the project tasks.

A special place in the systematization of views on a project is the construction of their instances for specific projects, for which designers can use the specialized instrumental mechanisms of mapping the main entities of the operational space of designing onto the semantic memory of the question-answer type.

As a result of mappings OF a project, a corresponding conceptual space is formed in which the construction and integration of species instances and their use is carried out. The features of the conceptual space of the project in the network version of the NetWIQA toolkit and its personalized version of OwnWIQA are described in detail in the publications [1] and [3].

To date, the potential of WIQA toolkit versions provides some representations of the tasks used in the activities shown in Fig. 1. In actions with these representations, the components are objectified in similar forms of question-answer nets (QA-nets) localized in the conceptual space of the SIS-project.

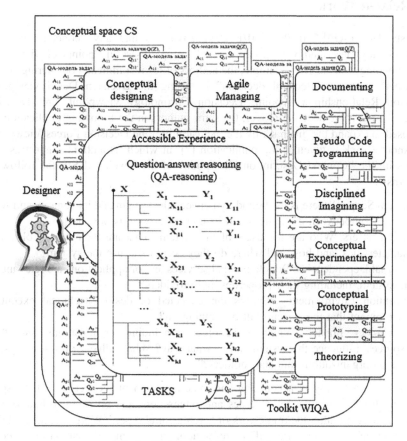

Fig. 1. Basic applications of QA-nets

To increase the efficiency of work with such components, they are integrated into the system of architectural views on that what is understood as the task/In its turn; it led to implementing the next step in the development of the toolkit OwnWIQA – to its extension by the subsystem called TASK.

The diagram, which reflects the (potential) work of a designer with a task, specifically uses the term "point of view", for which the following definition is introduced in ISO/IEC/IEEE 42010: 2011 - "a set of samples, templates, and agreements for building one type of architectural views. It identifies stakeholders whose problems are reflected in the point of view, as well as guidelines, principles, and template models for building the relevant views" [4].

Namely, in the first place, it is proposed to link the system of "points of view" with an integrated set of typical diagram types (templates) of the "task", and secondly, to integrate the subsystem TASK into the environment of the OwnWIQA for effective work with project tasks in the conceptual space of the project of any developed system.

3 Related Works

The standard ISO/IEC/IEEE 42010: 2011 envisages that any "concern" may be architecturally described with a coordinated group of useful "points of view" and corresponding "views." For example, the authors of [5] recommend considering such a construct as an "architectural decision" by using the Decision Detail viewpoint, Decision Relationship viewpoint, Decision Chronology viewpoint, and Decision Stakeholder Involvement. Moreover, the same authors in the following publication [6] proposed to expand the given set by the inclusion in it the Decision Forces Viewpoint.

Another trick is given in the publication [7], in which its authors suggest associating with the "Context Description Viewpoint" of the developed SIS the following concerns:

1. System Scope: Where is the boundary between the system and its context, and what interactions between the system and its context cross this boundary?
2. System Users: Who are the users of the system; what are their types, roles, and characteristics; and how and where do they access and use the system?
3. External Dependencies: Which external services and/or applications are relevant for the system, including their properties and providers?
4. Execution Environment: What is the expected or desired technical execution environment that the system will be running on?
5. Stakeholder Impact: Which stakeholders, including organizations and their resources, influence the system and in what way? What influence does the system have on organizations and stakeholders?"

Another possibility of accounting and materialization of "concerns" is their specification, distribution of a set of types and integration of a set of (distributed) constituent concerns within the framework of "architectural types." With such a possibility they associate an "aspect-oriented" representation and the materialization of concerns [8].

The real practice of architectural decisions is discussed in the industrial case study published in [9]. The current retrospection view on the theory and practice of architectural descriptions is presented in the paper [10].

In our version of the architectural approach to the precedent-oriented solution of the design task, their groups, and systems, it was decided to use all the cited possibilities for recording, specifying and realizing the "concerns" and "architectural views" chosen for the development of the subsystem TASK. Note that if the project tasks of any SIS are solved in the OwnWIQA-environment, then the "concerns" and "architectural views" processed in the subsystem TASK will be taken into account and materialized in each instance of the task. So, they will be inherited by the created SIS, firstly, at the conceptual stage of its development, and secondly, in reusable applications of solutions. Thus, the version of the architectural approach presented in the article is created to solve design tasks of the SIS, but its instrumental materialization is used by the authors to build the subsystem TASK of the toolkit OwnWIQA.

4 Distribution of Tasks in the Conceptual Space of the Project

For the set of architectural views that make up the architecture of the developed SIS, it is required to be coordinated so that they form integrity corresponding to the theory of the SIS-project [3]. Since the theory of the project and the architecture of the SIS are built in parallel on the course of designing, they complement each other. Moreover, each architectural view must be the correct application of the project theory, and prompts its development, providing an interpretation of theoretical constructs and contributing architectural understanding.

Which means that it is useful to include the view from the viewpoint of theorizing in a coherent set of architectural views materialized in the OwnWIQA, the structure of which is shown in Fig. 2.

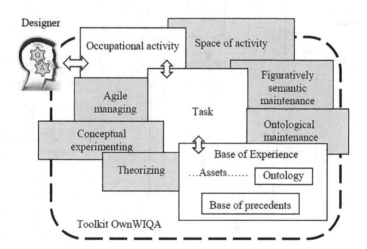

Fig. 2. Structure of the toolkit OwnWIQA from the viewpoint of working with tasks

In Fig. 2, there are no links between the blocks, but for the blocks, we use two colors ("white" and "gray") to separate the main line of designer' activity (white color) from the accompanying actions (gray color).

The main line of activity focuses on solving the project task, on the course of which the designer interacts with the necessary experience and its models that are accumulated in the Base of Experience. In the frame of such activity, the designer builds the reusable descriptions of the solved tasks (models of precedents) that are placed in the Base of Precedents. Indicated blocks of the main activity lead to the corresponding architectural views objectified in the OwnWIQA.

In actions of the main line, the designer uses automated support (blocks marked in gray) that help to increase the quality of working with tasks, their groups, and systems. Such blocks objectify an additional subset of the architectural views on work with project tasks in the toolkit OwnWIQA.

Below, we clarify the proposed version of the architectural approach to precedent-oriented work with project task only for the block TASK integrated all mastered reflections of the task onto QA-memory of the toolkit OwnWIQA. Namely, with this block, we bind the subsystem TASK, the architectural structure of which is schematically shown in Fig. 3.

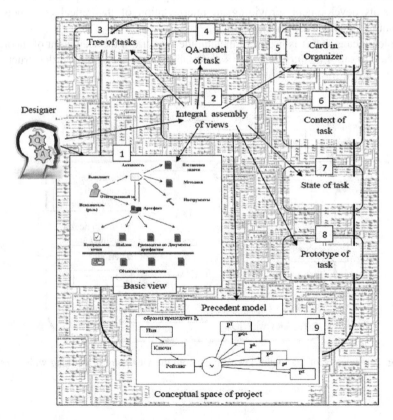

Fig. 3. The system of architectural views of the "task"

In the proposed version of the complete set of views on the task and their integration into a single whole, the following requirements were used:

1. For mastered activities noted in Fig. 1, all typical models of the task must find their expressions in the integral set of architectural views.
2. Each additional view of the task must be configured for its use in the semantic memory of the OwnWIQA environment.
3. Samples of typical views for a task and their integral set should be placed in the conceptual space [11] of the corresponding project.

Based on these requirements, a set of architectural views was selected. They are shown in Fig. 3 where names of views suggest what they are responsible for in the process of conceptual solution of the design task. Several indicated views found their informational descriptions in papers [1] and [3]. For this reason, below we concern only decisions for architectural views with numbers one, two and nine.

5   Prototyping of Architectural Solutions

A very important part of the OwnWIQA is a set of tools for programming in pseudo-code intended for two purposes:

- tools allow users (and therefore creators) of OwnWIQA to expand the functional potential of this toolkit;
- using these tools, one can build simple applications or application prototypes by programming a suitable shell above the OwnWIQA.

These possibilities helped us to develop a prototype version of the TASK linking prototypes for architectural views shown in Fig. 3. In this section, we will demonstrate

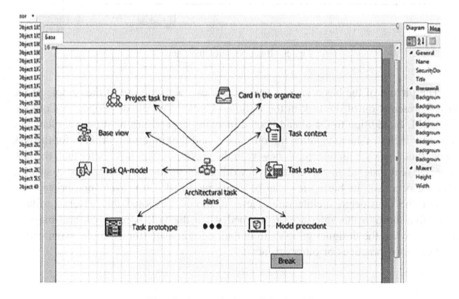

Fig. 4. Integral view of the "task"

what is behind pseudo-code prototyping for architectural views 1, 2, and 9. Let's start with the integral view, the visual (interface) form of which is shown in Fig. 4.

It should be noted, that Figs. 3 and 4 reflects only the projection of the TASK on visually accessible models of a design task, with which the designer interacts in the process of solution, applying activities and other artifacts of the scheme presented in Fig. 2. Among these models, very important places occupy those of them that belong to the main line of the designer's activity. One of these models corresponds to the basic view, the interface form of which is presented in Fig. 5.

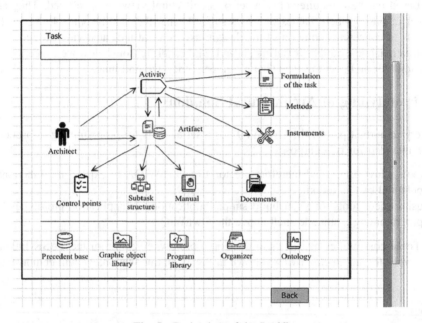

Fig. 5. Basic view of the "task"

The picture of the basic view is specially drawn with the use of the sample of the visual presentation of the task in the Rational Unified Process developed in Corporation IBM. In addition to the already noted indexing capabilities of structural elements, this view includes the navigation button "Back" and the (input/output) field for the task name, that binds the architectural view with the corresponding task. After that, the task instance is registered in the catalog of work tasks in the Organizer. For a specific instance of a task, its basic view can be easily modified if it proves appropriate.

For the considered architectural view, it should be noted that several artifacts accessible through this interface are formed when the task is resolved, and they are available when the designer go to them in their current state (for example, statement of the task, used practices or other artifacts).

All elements of the interface form of the basic view are also indexed. Some of them lead to software agents, each of which ensures the identity of the declarative components of the task that are used in other views. For example, one of these agents provides the identity of the current version of the task statement in the basic view and in the corresponding model of the precedent, which is built in the course of solving the task.

Another major artifact of the main line of designer's actions is the precedent model, the architectural view of which is shown in Fig. 6, where icons are clarified by names of components integrated into the precedent model.

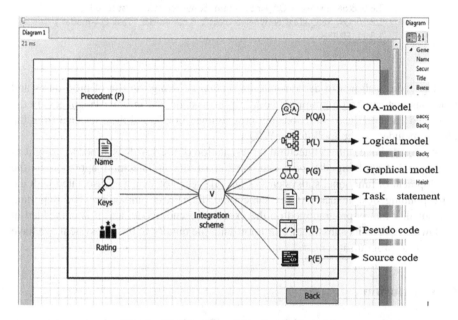

Fig. 6. Visualization of the precedent model

The structure of the model and the details of its components, taking into account their operational formation, are discussed in detail in [12]. For this architectural view, it is also important to ensure the identity of the content and structure of the available and processed conceptual objects represented by QA-nets.

To ensure the identity, we developed a utility for copying of QA-objects into a specialized buffer memory for subsequent loading from this memory onto the necessary place occupied by the corresponding view. The implementation of such utility includes operations of export and import of QA-nets with their intermediate representation in the form of XML-files. The necessary work is performed by the following pseudocode program:

```
◢ Z 1.8. BUF
    ▷ Q 1.8.1. &mynewproject& := QA_GetAreaId("Buffer object");
    ◢ Q 1.8.2. IF &mynewproject&< 0 THEN BEGIN
          Q 1.8.2.1. &mynewproject& := QA_CreateArea("Buffer object");
        ▷ Q 1.8.2.2. END
    ▷ Q 1.8.3. QA_DeleteNode(&mynewproject&, 0)
    ▷ Q 1.8.4. &myproject& := QA_GetAreaId("Diagram");
    ▷ Q 1.8.5. &qaid& := QA_FindQAItem (&myproject&, "First task")
    ▷ Q 1.8.8. QA_CopyQATree(&myproject&, &qaid&, &mynewproject&, 0)
    ▷ Q 1.8.9. &qanewid& := QA_FindQAItem (&myproject&, "First task")
    ▷ Q 1.8.10. QA_SetQAText(&mynewproject&, &qanewid&, "Task QA-model")
    ▷ Q 1.8.11. FINISH
```

The code is shown to demonstrate its syntax, allowing the use of procedures and functions that can be programmed both in pseudo-code and in other languages. In the presented code, the used functions are programmed in C#, and they selected from the library included in the toolkit OwnWIQA.

As noted above, the architectural representation of the TASK is aimed at using it as a sample for applying the proposed version of the architectural approach to the development of functional subsystems of any SIS, each of which is associated with the corresponding design task. At the same time, the TASK embodies very important functionality that is programmed on the executed pseudo code, and it is embedded in the OwnWIQA as its subsystem. For improving the quality of this subsystem, we have an intent to program it on C#.

6 Conclusion

The successful development of the modern SIS is almost impossible without the creation of its architectural description that is the source of numerous positive effects in all stages of designing. Usually, any artifact of this type is interpreted as a version of the SIS existence that discloses its structure and content in understandable forms helping to discover possible semantic errors. Building the architectural description for the SIS is a very qualified work that must be fulfilled by the architect or their group.

In any case, the architect solves a set of specialized tasks. Considering the usefulness of the architect's actions and their results, we develop the simplified version of tools that provide the use of the architectural approach in a precedent-oriented solution of project task at the individual workplace. The feature of the approach is the use of the system of architectural views on the task in the project.

The proposed version of architectural views is realized as the prototype version of means (called TASK) with the use of the toolkit OwnWIQA intended for the conceptual solution of project tasks. To simplify the possibility of adjusting the TASK by its users, we developed it with the use of drawn interfaces and pseudocode programming embedded into the toolkit OwnWIQA.

The kernel of the TASK consists of the basic architectural view integrating essential components of the task to be solved, and the precedent-oriented view accumulating the necessary models of the task for its reusable application.

Acknowledgments. This work is supported by the Russian Fund for Basic Research (RFBR) with Grants # 18-07-00989a, 18-47-730016 p_a, 18-47-732012p_мк, and Ministry of Science and High Education with the State Contract №2.1534.2017/4.6.

References

1. Sosnin, P.: Experience-Based Human-Computer Interactions: Emerging Research and Opportunities, p. 294. Hershey, IGI-Global (2017)
2. Clarke, P., O'Connor, R.V.: The situational factors that affect the software development process: towards a comprehensive reference framework. J. Inf. Softw. Technol. **54**(5), 433–447 (2012)
3. Sosnin, P.: Substantially evolutionary theorizing in designing software-intensive systems information, Switzerland, vol. 9, no. 4, paper № 91 (2018)
4. ISO/IEC/IEEE 42010:2011 Systems and software engineering - Architecture description, pp. 1–46 (2011)
5. Bedjeti, A., Lago, P., Lewis, G.A., Boer, R.D.D., Hilliard, R.: Modeling context with an architecture viewpoint. In: IEEE International Conference on Software Architecture (ICSA), pp. 117–120 (2017)
6. Van Heesch, U., Avgeriou, P., Hilliard, R.: Forces on architecture decisions - a viewpoint. In: Proceedings of the 2012 Joint Working IEEE/IFIP Conference on Software Architecture and European Conference on Software Architecture, pp. 101–110. IEEE Computer Society, Washington, DC, USA (2012)
7. Van Heesch, U., Avgeriou, P., Hilliard, R.: A documentation framework for architecture decisions. J. Syst. Softw. **85**(4), 795–820 (2012)
8. Hilliard, R.: Using aspects in architectural description. In: Moreira, A., Grundy, J. (eds.) EAW 2007. LNCS, vol. 4765, pp. 139–154. Springer, Heidelberg (2007). https://doi.org/10.1007/978-3-540-76811-1_8
9. Dasanayake, S., Markkula, J., Aaramaa, S., Oivo, M.: Software architecture decision-making practices and challenges: an industrial case study. In: Proceedings of 24th Australasian Software Engineering Conference, pp. 88–97 (2015)
10. Cuesta, C.E., Garlan, D., Pérez, J. (eds.): ECSA 2018. LNCS, vol. 11048. Springer, Cham (2018). https://doi.org/10.1007/978-3-030-00761-4
11. Sosnin, P.: Question-answer nets as a valuable source of information in designing the software intensive system. In: 25th Telecommunications Forum, TELFOR 2017 - Proceedings, pp. 1–4 (2017)
12. Sosnin, P.: Precedent-oriented approach to conceptually experimental activity in designing the software intensive systems. Int. J. Ambient Comput. Intell. **7**(1), 69–93 (2016)

Galactic Swarm Optimization Applied to Reinforcement of Bridges by Conversion in Cable-Stayed Arch

Camilo Vásquez[1], Broderick Crawford[1], Ricardo Soto[1],
José Lemus-Romani[1(✉)], Gino Astorga[2], Sanjay Misra[3],
Agustín Salas-Fernández[1], and José-Miguel Rubio[4]

[1] Pontificia Universidad Católica de Valparaíso, Valparaíso, Chile
{camilo.Vasquez.e,jose.lemus.r,juan.salas.f}@mail.pucv.cl,
{broderick.crawford,ricardo.soto}@pucv.cl
[2] Universidad de Valparaíso, Valparaíso, Chile
gino.astorga@uv.cl
[3] Covenant University, Ota, Nigeria
sanjay.misra@covenantuniversity.edu.ng
[4] Universidad Tecnológica de Chile INACAP, Santiago, Chile
jrubiol@inacap.cl

Abstract. The scouring of piers bridges, caused by hydraulic action, is one of the main risks that the structure suffer over the years. One of the methods in development is to change the structure of the bridge incorporating a upper cable-stayed arch, which allows to implement vertical and network hangers in charge of lifting the original bridge board. For this it is necessary to optimize the order and the adjustment magnitudes tension of the hangers. To solve this problem we implemented a software for optimization which uses Galactic Swarms Optimization, which is inspired by the movement of the stars, which is inspired by the movement of the stars, galaxies and superclusters under the influence of gravity. When comparing the results obtained with other approximate techniques, we can observe from the diagrams of distribution of instances that level two of the algorithm does not have the necessary and expected capacity to solve or leave from a local optimum.

Keywords: Reinforcement of bridges · Metaheuristics ·
Galactic Swarm Optimization · Combinatorial optimization

1 Introduction

The collapse of the beam bridge is a great threat. 70% of the bridges collapse by hydraulic action, of which 35% collapse by scouring their piers [7]. One of the possibilities to avoid the collapse of the bridges is to use reinforcement techniques, such as the one proposed by Matías Valenzuela in his doctoral thesis [10], the bridging method by means of cable-stayed arch conversion. This method allows

© Springer Nature Switzerland AG 2019
S. Misra et al. (Eds.): ICCSA 2019, LNCS 11623, pp. 108–119, 2019.
https://doi.org/10.1007/978-3-030-24308-1_10

the change of the structure making a new configuration of the bridge, implementing hangers active and passive, in charge of lifted the original bridge board. The tension of the hangers must be done sequentially.

For this, it is necessary to optimize the order and the magnitudes of adjustment of the tension of the hangers. To solve the problem raised, the Galactic Swarm Optimization (GSO) algorithm will be used. The GSO algorithm simulates the movement of stars, galaxies and superclusters in the cosmos. The stars are not evenly distributed in the cosmos, but are grouped into galaxies that in turn are not evenly distributed. On a sufficiently large scale, the individual galaxies appear as point masses. The attraction of stars within a galaxy to large masses and galaxies to other large masses is emulated in the GSO algorithm. The results obtained by GSO will be compared with other optimization techniques.

The metaheuristics implemented in very complex problems is not something new [2,3,9], while the use of these techniques for problems related to bridges is not [4,6,11].

This paper is ordered as follows, in Sect. 2 the problem to be solved is presented, in Sect. 3 the metaheuristic to be implemented, in Sect. 4 the results obtained together with the corresponding statistical analysis to compare performance, ending with the Sect. 5 with the conclusions of the work.

2 Problem

One of the most important problems presented by bridges crossing river channels is the undermining of their piers. The most important consequence is the total collapse of the structure, generating high human and economic costs. As a result of this, several systems of inspection, monitoring and maintenance of the submerged bridge infrastructure have been implemented.

There are several statistics worldwide that confirm this fact. The work developed by [7] states that 70% of bridge collapses have a cause in hydraulic action, where scouring reaches 35%.

The reinforcement of bridges is proposed as a methodology, which directly attacks the problem of undermining. The reinforcement consists of a arch that goes over the bridge, from end to end, which by means of hangers supports the board. The proposed method has advantages of cost and time, also presents problems from the engineering point of view. For constructive reasons, the tension of the hangers can not be performed simultaneously, so they must be done in sequential order. In addition, excessive stress can cause damage to the structure, instability or collapse of it. This is why we are facing a direct problem of optimization. What is the proper tension order? And with what magnitude should the hangers hold?

A bridge before reinforcing it is functional and is constructed in such a way that it supports both the board and the effort it makes in the passage of vehicles along it, that is, the bending of it. Because of this we will use the original bridge as a reference, so when installing the arc and tensioning the hangers, the objective is to minimize the tension difference. It is expected that the tension in each longitudinal fraction of the bridge will vary depending on the order and magnitude of tension of the upper hangers, so a full search does not seem to be a good option. It is worth mentioning that a structural system of cable-stayed arch is hyperstatic and interdependent, that is, the modification of a tension redistributes the efforts in the whole structure.

To solve problems of high computational complexity like this one, several algorithms have been developed inspired by the behavior of nature, such as genetics (GA), swarms, flowers, among others. In this research it will be use Galactic Swarm Optimization (GSO) [8] to find order and magnitude of the stress, which is a metaheuristic algorithm based in population and inspired by the movement of stars, galaxies and superclusters of galaxies in the cosmos.

For the modeling of the bridge and the problem itself, we will use SAP2000, a software for the analysis and design of structures, which allows the API to pass information from a metaheuristic technique to the bridge, as well as request from them properties and relevant information of the structure [1]. The API contains pre-defined functions that can be invoked from a library in different programming languages, allowing a realistic modeling of the bridge. The bridges, meanwhile, are pre-designed in the software for optimization to separate their design and structuring of the optimization algorithm.

2.1 Objetive Function

The objective function is defined as the summation of the difference tense of both top and low, for each one of K cuts and each one of the 2 beams, as described by the equation:

$$min \sum_{i=1}^{2} \sum_{k=1}^{k} |\sigma o_{i,k} - \sigma m_{i,k}| \tag{1}$$

Where $\sigma o_{i,k}$ is the tension of the original bridge on beam i and on the cut k. Meanwhile, $\sigma m_{i,k}$ it is the modified bridge tension in beam i and in cut k. This function is evaluated for both the lower and higher tensions of the board, and the objective is to minimize the differences. In the ideal and utopian case, the optimum is 0, since it would represent absolute equality between the efforts of the original bridge and the modified one, maintaining all of its properties and completely eliminating the problem of scour.

2.2   Constraints

The problem have constraints that must be met to satisfy the objective function

- The hangers cannot be jacking simultaneously.

$$ord_1, ord_2, .., ord_n \in \{1, 2, ..., n\} \tag{2}$$

$$ord_w \neq ord_j \; ; \; \forall j, \omega \; con \; j \neq \omega; \; j, \omega \in \{1, 2, ..., n\} \tag{3}$$

- The effort of the modified bridge deck should not pass the limits of the Band Admissible Modified (BAM):

$$\sigma m \geqslant \sigma o \tag{4}$$

$$\sigma m \geqslant fct \tag{5}$$

$$\sigma m \leqslant fcmax2 \; \text{(in intermediate stages)} \tag{6}$$

$$\sigma m \leqslant fcmax \; \text{(in final stages)} \tag{7}$$

Where:
- σm is the tension (top or bottom) of the modified bridge.
- σo is the tension (top or bottom) of the original bridge.
- fct is the maximum tension to traction admissible for the concrete.
- fcmax is the maximum tension to admissible compression for the concrete.
- fcmax2 is the maximum tension to compression for the concrete, extended.

Any tension on the modified bridge deck that is not inside the BAM described from the original model is discarded because can generate damage to the bridge.

3   Galactic Swarm Optimization

GSO is based on PSO, the original algorithm is inspired by swarms like the behavior of flocks of birds and fish, which is a defense mechanism to confuse predators. The GSO algorithm simulates the movement of stars, galaxies and superclusters of galaxies in the cosmos, the distribution of stars in the universe is not done uniformly, however they are grouped into galaxies that in turn are not distributed homogeneously, the attraction of stars within a galaxy to large masses and galaxies to other large masses are emulated in the GSO algorithm as follows:

- Individuals in each subpopulation who are attracted to better solutions in the subpopulation according to the PSO algorithm
- Each subpopulation is represented by a better solution found by the subpopulation and treated as a superswarm
- Superswarm comprises the best solutions found in each subpopulation moving to the PSO algorithm.

The swarm and superswarm movement can be achieved since it is population-based, providing multiple exploration and exploitation cycles by dividing the search in terms of offers, providing the algorithm with more opportunities to accurately locate a local minimum, in the first level it is considered the exploratory phase where potential local minimums are identified, the second level of the GSO algorithm is the exploratory phase which uses the best solutions already calculated by the sub swarms considering the information already calculated in the first level.

The swarm is a set X of D-Tuples that contains $(\chi_j^{(x)} \in R^D)$ that consists of M partitions, called subswarms X_i, each of size N, X is randomly initialized within the search space $[x_{min}, x_{max}]^D$.

Each subswarm independently explores the search space, the declaration for updating the velocity and the position are:

$$V_j^{(x)} \leftarrow \omega_1 + C_1 R_1(P_j^{(x)} - \chi_j^{(x)}) + C_2 R_2(g^{(i)} - \chi_j^{(x)}) \tag{8}$$

$$\chi_j^{(x)} \leftarrow \chi_j^{(x)} + V_j^{(x)} \tag{9}$$

Algorithm 1. GSO

---

1   Level 1 Initialization: $\chi_j^{(i)}$, $v_j^{(i)}$, $p_j^{(i)}$, $g^{(i)}$ within $[x_{min}, x_{max}]^D$ randomly.
2   Level 2 Initialization: $v^{(i)}$, $p^{(i)}$, g within $[x_{min}, x_{max}]^D$ randomly.
3   **for** $EP \leftarrow$ *1 to EP_{max}* **do**
4   　　Begin PSO: Level 1
5   　　**for** $i \leftarrow$ *1 to M* **do**
6   　　　　**for** $k \leftarrow$ *0 to L_1* **do**
7   　　　　　　**for** $j \leftarrow$ *1 to N* **do**
8   　　　　　　　　$v_j^{(i)} \leftarrow \omega_i v_j^{(i)} + c_1 r_1(p_j^{(i)} - \chi_j^{(i)}) + c_2 r_2(g^{(i)} - \chi_j^{(i)})$;
9   　　　　　　　　$\chi_j^{(i)} \leftarrow \chi_j^{(i)} + v_j^{(i)}$;
10 　　　　　　　　**if** $f(\chi_j^{(i)}) < f(p_j^{(i)})$ **then**
11 　　　　　　　　　　$p_j^{(i)} \leftarrow \chi_j^{(i)}$
12 　　　　　　　　**if** $f(p_j^{(i)}) < f(g^{(i)})$ **then**
13 　　　　　　　　　　$g^{(i)} \leftarrow p_j^{(i)}$;
14 　　　　　　　　**if** $f(g^{(i)}) < f(g)$ **then**
15 　　　　　　　　　　$g \leftarrow g^{(i)}$;
16 　　　　　　　　**end**
17 　　　　　　**end**
18 　　　　**end**
19 　　　　**end**
20 　　**end**
21 　　**end**
22 　　Begin PSO: Level 2
23 　　Initialize Swarm $y^{(i)} = g^{(i)}$: 1,2,...,M;
24 　　**for** $k \leftarrow$ *0 to L_2* **do**
25 　　　　**for** $l \leftarrow$ *1 to M* **do**
26 　　　　　　$v^{(i)} \leftarrow \omega_2 v^{(i)} + c_3 r_3(p^{(i)} - y^{(i)}) + c_4 r_4(g - y^{(i)})$;
27 　　　　　　$y^{(i)} \leftarrow y^{(i)} + v^{(i)}$;
28 　　　　　　**if** $f(y^{(i)}) < f(p^{(i)})$ **then**
29 　　　　　　　　$p^{(i)} \leftarrow y^{(i)}$;
30 　　　　　　**if** $f(p^{(i)}) < f(g)$ **then**
31 　　　　　　　　$g \leftarrow p^{(i)}$;
32 　　　　　　**end**
33 　　　　**end**
34 　　**end**
35 　**end**
36 **end**

The best solutions participate in the next stage of clustering creating a new superswarm

$$y^{(i)} \in Y : i = 1, 2, ..., M \qquad (10)$$

$$y^{(i)} = g^{(i)} \qquad (11)$$

In this second stage of clustering the velocity and the position are updated according to the following expression.

$$v^{(i)} \leftarrow \omega_2 v^{(i)} + C_3 R_3 (p^{(i)} + y^{(i)}) + C_4 R_4 (g - y^{(y)}) \qquad (12)$$

$$y^{(i)} \leftarrow y^{(i)} + v^{(i)} \qquad (13)$$

where $p^{(i)}$ is the best staff in relation to the vector $y^{(i)}$, is defined ω_2, r_3 and r_4 in a similar way in the equations. In the first level, g indicates us as the best global and is not updated unless the search finds us one better and this is indicated as a global best of the subswarm.

4   Computational Results

As a first step we must carry out an implementation of the GSO algorithm, the solution vector has the positions of hangers and the magnitude of tights that must be applied, Table 1 show us an example how to represent a solution vector, this representation was proposed by Valenzuela for the reinforcement of bridges by cable-stayed arch.

Table 1. Example of solution vector

Position 1	Position 2	Position 3	Magnitude 1	Magnitude 2	Magnitude 3
3	1	2	0,99	0,87	0,28

In the previous example, the solution indicates that hanger 3 will first test with a magnitude of 99% of its total capacity. Then, hanger 1 with a magnitude of 28% of its total capacity will be tested and so on, remember that if we have N hangers we will have N magnitudes, for this example we choose a N = 3.

4.1 Parameter Settings Used in Experiments

It is necessary to clarify that all instances where executed with the same settings that show us Table 2 for GSO, which was obtained through the parametric scanning technique.

Table 2. GSO parameters

Population	Particles	M	N	L1	L2	EPmax	c1	c2	c3,c4
16	16	3	3	10	5	20	1	2	2,05

4.2 Computational Results

GSO for Bridges reinforcement was implemented in Python 3.6 and executed in a Personal Computer running Windows 10 on Intel core i5-2450M CPU (2.5 Ghz), 4 GB of RAM. Each instance was executes 15 times. After 28 days we got the results proposed by GSO, Table 3 show us the order of the hangers and the magnitude of each instance that must be tensed.

4.3 Comparing Ressults

We proceed to compare the Fitness obtained by GSO against Black Hole (BH). In Table 3, the first comparison of the Fitness obtained in GSO compared with BH is made, in this first comparison we can see that BH obtains better results than GSO, instances AB-TCV, CC-TCV and CR-AA10.

Table 3. Fitness comparison of AB-TCV, CC-TCV and CR-AA10

#	AB-TCV		CC-TCV		CR-AA10	
	BH	GSO	BH	GSO	BH	GSO
1	517068,78	529200,60	520682,20	527060,41	517761,81	519494,37
2	524023,77	530211,73	520212,17	527303,87	514470,31	519266,95
3	524821,68	530061,40	520538,00	527834,13	517102,87	520307,33
4	520848,21	528982,32	524706,86	526450,57	517088,90	521410,82
5	520622,78	529420,80	522918,41	527208,89	514502,45	518775,94
6	520152,44	528410,12	518616,05	527399,37	511024,81	520978,36
7	517564,07	530047,57	519413,56	527084,65	516154,93	521187,18
8	523623,83	530784,11	524143,33	528874,63	512943,62	522132,29
9	519373,56	529621,11	522562,15	528226,65	515740,37	525596,65
10	524246,51	531688,83	515930,44	528306,50	512584,97	523154,52
11	523785,40	528014,20	520447,93	528675,52	517126,96	520018,54
12	520203,82	530353,34	523472,34	531062,87	516430,95	520474,21
13	520872,27	530180,50	517694,83	528173,91	514210,37	523051,55
14	518973,97	531445,54	519115,91	528109,73	513743,60	522499,51
15	522447,22	530585,53	515608,06	527803,39	512808,82	519816,41

In Table 4, the BH aptitude is compared with the GSO. In the instances HW-TCV, PT-TCV and PV-TCV, we can see that BH obtains better results compared with GSO.

Table 4. Fitness comparation of HW-TCV, PT-TCV and PV-TCV

#	HW-TCV		PT-TCV		PV-TCV	
	BH	GSO	BH	GSO	BH	GSO
1	518227,34	527961,52	526676,11	530629,71	521950,83	531314,18
2	518554,72	528067,86	519411,92	532261,71	523427,99	532787,87
3	521443,88	527742,47	525110,87	530873,89	523381,04	532459,42
4	518566,59	528248,59	520610,73	530893,66	524362,17	530547,87
5	516990,68	527836,18	524252,03	531887,35	520927,57	531665,44
6	522992,53	527892,94	520560,47	530988,44	525788,70	531611,54
7	522006,56	528272,14	523880,06	532110,56	518788,67	532980,62
8	519225,68	528719,51	525204,20	532565,11	521114,47	533992,99
9	520271,78	528395,84	523880,06	531777,87	523983,25	533430,95
10	523204,08	529802,91	520863,04	534283,32	522809,15	532294,35
11	520515,56	529823,21	522029,40	532478,93	522648,28	532266,30
12	519526,11	529434,44	522617,22	533405,46	521351,71	531424,12
13	517752,37	528505,20	518340,35	533742,99	523941,25	531446,67
14	521967,48	529975,94	517173,90	531376,60	517407,41	533571,92
15	521974,26	527659,89	518891,31	532841,54	520202,02	531187,13

In Table 5, the BH aptitude is compared with the GSO. In the instances RC-AA10, RD-AA10 and TC-TCV, we can see that again BH obtains better results in comparison with the GSO.

Table 5. Fitness comparation of RC-AA10, RD-AA10 and TC-TCV

#	RC-AA10		RD-AA10		TC-TCV	
	BH	GSO	BH	GSO	BH	GSO
1	514019,85	518737,96	517038,97	523745,78	519824,40	536659,43
2	514605,63	518378,62	519226,40	522347,77	519571,13	537237,85
3	517856,01	520511,92	513572,50	524090,89	524103,15	537710,92
4	517790,49	521976,81	512678,64	522025,96	521301,71	536943,11
5	514457,07	520494,80	511665,24	522714,47	522386,88	537360,60
6	514508,11	522145,48	517200,65	523148,52	522834,91	536770,49
7	510072,74	520155,20	515799,79	521575,51	522191,19	536218,72
8	514272,05	519629,90	516494,40	523663,98	519926,61	539349,44
9	515619,91	520425,45	511107,49	525045,23	522591,31	538048,60
10	513847,14	520283,77	514930,92	523703,71	521634,82	537776,72
11	514603,89	522717,67	509176,30	522197,22	523052,42	538490,51
12	513776,52	521214,74	512632,11	523920,74	524989,00	536447,97
13	514564,78	520679,18	508556,02	523448,38	525268,02	536403,85
14	511927,54	522722,21	521000,00	524393,51	520641,95	536528,36
15	513593,24	521267,85	513408,64	521249,26	519598,17	537071,14

Finally, in Table 6, BH is compared with GSO in the instances VC-TCV and WR-TCV, observing similar results to the instances previously compared.

Table 6. Fitness comparation of VC-TCV and WR-TCV

#	VC-TCV		WR-TCV	
	BH	GSO	BH	GSO
1	517454,84	527373,52	521210,45	528830,37
2	516764,75	527174,76	519448,38	528816,50
3	526420,20	528192,99	519880,23	529534,30
4	523586,26	527802,89	519204,81	529416,28
5	517878,92	528666,35	526646,98	529143,40
6	521676,41	528720,57	523896,15	530172,24
7	515963,27	529040,68	519162,74	529313,30
8	524091,12	528679,67	522611,37	529544,89
9	520710,80	530326,24	522236,03	529608,69
10	520958,23	528896,13	518685,87	527664,26
11	522523,26	528854,60	521471,35	529841,96
12	521104,33	529145,63	523417,26	528941,97
13	521939,46	528667,78	525384,95	530628,27
14	521888,84	527765,76	520876,22	530696,92
15	520548,39	526734,62	522051,32	530893,56

The Table 7 describe us each instance with the minimum value of fitness of GSO and BH.

Table 7. Fitness differences

Instance	Min GSO	Min BH	Difference
AB-TCV	528014,2050	517068,779	10945,4260
CC-TCV	526450,57	515608,056	10842,514
CR-AA10	518775,9410	511024,809	7751,1320
HW-TCV	527659,8893	516990,684	10669,2053
PT-TCV	530629,7060	517173,901	13455,8050
PV-TCV	530547,8720	517407,41	13140,4620
RC-AA10	518378,6210	510072,744	8305,8770
RD-AA10	521249,2605	508556,024	12693,2365
TC-TCV	536218,7240	519571,134	16647,5900
VC-TCV	526734,6176	515963,267	10771,3506
WR-TCV	527664,2601	518685,865	8978,3951

4.4   Instance Distribution

We will compare the distribution of the samples of each instance through a violin plot that shows the full distribution of the data.

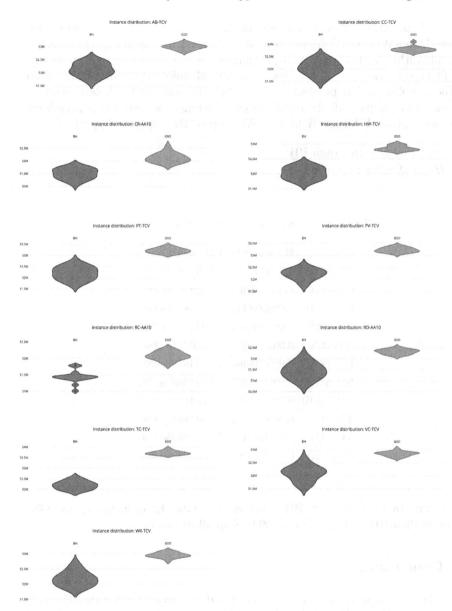

Although GSO privileges exploration as exploitation, we can deduce that according to all the cases studied, the second level of PSO is not enough to be able to leave a local optimum, and it is less effective when converging compared to BH.

4.5   Statistical Tests

We perform the statistical tests between the mentioned algorithms BH and GSO. Where Kolmogorov-Smirnov-Lilliefors test allows us to analyze the normality of our 15 executions of each instance, obtaining a non-parametric distribution. While Mann-Whitney-Wilcoxon test [5] It is used to buy the performance of each algorithm for this particular problem.

The test carried a p-value of less than 0.05, therefore H0 cannot be assumed, so the samples are independent of each other. To evaluate the heterogeneity of samples and compare all the results of each instance we used a non-parametric test called Mann-Whitney-Wilcoxon. We propose the following hypotheses:

- H_0: GSO is better than BH
- H_1: States the opposite.

Table 8. p-value Mann-Whitney-Wilcoxon test

Instance	GSO vs BH	BH vs GSO
AB-TCV	0.999998467	1.53348888e-006
CC-TCV	0.999998467	1.53348888e-006
CR-AA10	0.999998467	1.53348888e-006
HW-TCV	0.999998467	1.53348888e-006
PT-TCV	0.99999847	1.5296211e-006
PV-TCV	0.999998467	1.53348888e-006
RC-AA10	0.999998467	1.53348888e-006
RD-AA10	0.999998467	1.53348888e-006
TC-TCV	0.999998467	1.53348888e-006
VC-TCV	0.999998467	1.53348888e-006
WR-TCV	0.999998467	1.53348888e-006

As we can see in Table 8, BH is better than GSO in all instances and GSO is better than BH with an error of 99.99% in all instances.

5   Conclusion

According to the statistical analysis performed we can concluded that the GSO is not better than BH to solve the problem of bridge reinforcement through conversion of cable-stayed arch. We can observe in the distribution diagrams of instances that level two of the GSO algorithm does not have the necessary and expected capacity to solve or leave from a local optimum. In order to improve the search capacity of the algorithm, it is necessary that the exploration capabilities of the second level must be enhanced, as well as a better adjustment of the parameters in the applied algorithm. This it can be discussed in a future work.

References

1. Sap2000. http://www.csiespana.com/software/2/sap2000
2. Crawford, B., Soto, R., Berrios, N., Olguín, E., Misra, S.: Cat swarm optimization with different transfer functions for solving set covering problems. In: Gervasi, O., et al. (eds.) ICCSA 2016. LNCS, vol. 9790, pp. 228–240. Springer, Cham (2016). https://doi.org/10.1007/978-3-319-42092-9_18
3. Crawford, B., Soto, R., Johnson, F., Misra, S., Paredes, F.: The use of metaheuristics to software project scheduling problem. In: Murgant, B., et al. (eds.) ICCSA 2014. LNCS, vol. 8583, pp. 215–226. Springer, Cham (2014). https://doi.org/10.1007/978-3-319-09156-3_16
4. García-Segura, T., Yepes, V.: Multiobjective optimization of post-tensioned concrete box-girder road bridges considering cost, CO_2 emissions, and safety. Eng. Struct. **125**, 325–336 (2016)
5. Mann, H.B., Whitney, D.R.: On a test of whether one of two random variables is stochastically larger than the other. Ann. Math. Stat. **18**, 50–60 (1947)
6. Martí, J.V., García-Segura, T., Yepes, V.: Structural of precast-prestressed concrete U-beam road bridges based on embodied energy. J. Clean. Prod. **120**, 231–240 (2016)
7. Muñoz, E., Valbuena, E.: Los problemas de la socavación en los puentes de colombia. Revista de Infraestructura Vial, numeral, p. 15 (2006)
8. Muthiah-Nakarajan, V., Noel, M.M.: Galactic swarm optimization: a new global optimization metaheuristic inspired by galactic motion. Appl. Soft Comput. **38**, 771–787 (2016)
9. Soto, R., et al.: Autonomous tuning for constraint programming via artificial bee colony optimization. In: Gervasi, O., et al. (eds.) ICCSA 2015. LNCS, vol. 9155, pp. 159–171. Springer, Cham (2015). https://doi.org/10.1007/978-3-319-21404-7_12
10. Valenzuela, M.: Refuerzo de puentes de luces medias por conversión en arco atirantado tipo network. PhD thesis, Universitat Politècnica de Catalunya, Barcelona, España, February 2012
11. Yepes, V., Martí, J., García-Segura, T., González-Vidosa, F.: Heuristics in optimal detailed design of precast road bridges. Arch. Civil Mech. Eng. **17**(4), 738–749 (2017)

A Systematic Literature Review for Service-Oriented Architecture and Agile Development

James Taylor Faria Chaves[(✉)] and Sergio Antônio Andrade de Freitas[(✉)]

University of Brasilia, Darcy Ribeiro Campus, Brasília, DF, Brazil
jameschaves@gmail.com, sergiofreitas@unb.br

Abstract. This research presents a Systematic Literature Review (SLR) involving Agile Methods and Service-Oriented Architecture (SOA). Is this combination of solutions capable of handling rapid changes in the environment, business objectives, and requirements? To answer this question and give confidence to this review, a rigorous protocol was followed and relevant studies were selected, data were extracted and analyzed. Some studies propose a mature solution, although they do not present data that are more consistent and capable of being evaluated. Other studies are superficial. In addition, few studies have gone through the protocol. So the main conclusion is that combining SOA and Agile methods can be a good way to solve the problem, but more studies are needed.

Keywords: Agile methods · Service-Oriented Architecture (SOA) ·
Systematic Literature Review (SLR) · Software engineering

1 Introduction

Service-Oriented Architecture (SOA) and Agile development methods. This is the combined solution that some researchers and practitioners are using to address the need for rapid change in environment, business goals, requirements, and even customer interests. This Systematic Literature Review (SLR) evaluated and interpreted relevant searches that address this solution to see if that combination is able to handle the problem.

Through a rigorous protocol, some studies were selected and analyzed from three points of view. It was evaluated the solutions proposed by the researchers and how they addressed the problems involving SOA based applications with agile development. It was also evaluated how the concepts of the agile methodology were used and what SOA principles were addressed. Information about the distribution of publications over the years and the type of paper sources have also been extracted to assess the importance of the subject in the area of software engineering.

Despite the interest of the subject, only 18 studies passed the review protocol. Also, none of them presented a consistent evaluation of the results. However, they

© Springer Nature Switzerland AG 2019
S. Misra et al. (Eds.): ICCSA 2019, LNCS 11623, pp. 120–135, 2019.
https://doi.org/10.1007/978-3-030-24308-1_11

demonstrated the importance of the theme. All studies presented a problem to be solved, and they all concluded that the SOA and Agile solution would meet, at least in part, the issues raised. Therefore, due to the small number of studies and the needs presented, one of the conclusions of this review is that more studies need to be done to better understand the phenomena and their implications.

Section 2 provides an overview of SLR, SOA, and Agile Methods concepts. Section 3 explains the research methods used to carry out this review. Section 4 presents the results of the extraction data from the accepted studies. Section 5 addresses the research questions of this review and Sect. 6 presents the final conclusions.

2 Background

2.1 Systematic Literature Review

Systematic Literature Review (SLR) is an instrument used for synthesizing evidence in some research area [29]. It is a rigorous methodology of review of research results. Its purpose is to aggregate all existing evidence on a research question. The origin of SLR was in medicine researchers [22]. Kitchenham [21] presented a guideline for performing SLR in Software Engineering that was derived from existing guidelines used by medical researches. According to Kitchenham [21]:

"A systematic literature review is a means of identifying, evaluating and interpreting all available research relevant to a particular research question, or topic area, or phenomenon of interest. Individual studies contributing to a systematic review are called primary studies; a systematic review is a form a secondary study."

The SLR has more scientific value than a simple literature review due to its methodological rigor. The reasons for performing a SLR are to summarize the existing evidence concerning a treatment or technology, to identify any gaps in current research in order to suggest areas for further investigation and to provide a framework/background in order to appropriately position new research activities [21].

2.2 Agile Development

A light method for software development can be understood as a method that the needs and goals of the stakeholders drive the development and enable the rapid and flexible development of software. The processes and tools itself are less important than deliverables, people, developers and stakeholders, communication, and the ability to adapt to change. This type of method has to be iterative, incremental, cooperative and adaptable to changes in environments and requirements. The search for this type of software development method led to the "agile methods" that were stated in the Agile Manifesto, published in 2001 [2] where seventeen developers and consultants representatives of light methods for software development met to discuss better ways of developing software.

There are many methods of software development that claim to be agile such as SCRUM, Dynamic Systems Development Method (DSDM), Adaptive Software Development (ASD), Internet Speed Development (ISD), Lean Software Development (LSD), Crystal Clear, Extreme Programming (XP), Feature-Driven Development (FDD), Pragmatic Programming (PP), and so on [13,16,18,36,37]. Even Rational Unified Process (RUP was used by some authors as an agile method [19,30]. Each has its own phases and life cycles, and some methods do not even well define the phases of development.

2.3 Service-Oriented Architecture

Organizations have their own business goals and they need software systems to satisfy those goals, sometimes with crosscutting stakeholders concerns. One of the key challenges to building systems that meet the goals of large numbers of stakeholders is integrating and reusing existing systems, while adding new functionality to support the business processes and to respond to changes in the business. Software Architecture is a bridge between those goals and the final resulting system, and comprehends the set of structures needed to reason about the system, which comprise software elements, relations among them, and properties of both [12,24]. In the ending of the 20th century, new approaches to system architecture have emerged which aim to structure a complex system around units of capability, called services [5].

This is the context in which Service-Oriented Architecture (SOA) is placed, that has emerged as a widely accepted solution to this challenge allowing a homogeneous enterprise-wide solution satisfying objectives that include an easy and flexible integration with legacy systems and simplifying business processes. Software architecture can be composed by several design patterns simultaneously to reach its goal and SOA is a paradigm, a design pattern, not a complete architecture. This design pattern was already being used since the beginning of 1990s, mainly in Simple Object Access Protocol (SOAP) [14,41] form. In the mid 2000s, the Representational State Transfer (REST) [33,41] form began to spread and today its hard do say witch proportion news applications are made in one or other form, existing intermediary forms, between both [41]. SOA is a sort of architecture that uses standards-based infrastructure to forge large-scale systems out of loosely coupled, inter-operable services, distributed, invocable, publishable and business oriented that can act like providers, consumers or Information Technology (IT) elements that join providers and consumers. SOA can create systems-of-systems by mapping existing systems into services, then orchestrating communication between the services. New functionality can be created by either adding new services or modifying communication among existing services with low costs, innovators services to clients, agile adaption, and reaction to opportunity and weakness competitiveness [5,6,17,26,35].

SOA can also be understood as an architectural style and uses services as building blocks to embrace changes in the business environment by composing of services and creating composite services already existing with applications in a technology heterogeneous environment. The business and technical processes are implemented as services and each service represents a particular functionality that maps explicitly to a step in a business process [3]. In this way, service can be understood as any task or function provided by an organization, aligned to business, well defined and isolated from other tasks (autonomy principle) [14] and Service orientation help organizations consistently deliver sustainable business value, with increased agility and cost effectiveness, in line with changing business needs [4]. In general, the basic Service Consumer software is simply a browser or browser-like "thin client", with little or no application software stored locally.

Erl [14] presents the eight principles that a service-oriented solution should follow:

1. Standardized Service Contract: a service should express its purpose and capacities through a contract;
2. Service Loose Coupling: the dependencies among the service's contract, implementation and consumers should be minimal;
3. Service Abstraction: a service should hide its implementation details to keep its consumers loosely coupled;
4. Service Reusability: services should be corporate resources, agnostic to functional contexts;
5. Service Autonomy: a service should have control over its environment and resources, while remaining isolated from other services;
6. Service Statelessness: services should only hold state information when necessary in order to not compromise its availability or scalability;
7. Service Discoverability: services should be easily discovered and understood to foster reuse;
8. Service Composability: it should be possible to create services from the composition of other services in order to produce sophisticated solutions according to business needs requirements and fostering reuse of existing assets

Service-Oriented Architecture (SOA) is not just a set of services connected together. The services consumers and the services providers are connected through an infrastructure responsible to implementing many of the principles of SOA, such as discoverability and composability, as well as responsible for transforming data according to standardized service contracts and dealing with security issues [14].

3 Research Method

In this Systematic Literature Review (SLR) it was used the guidelines proposed by Kitchenham [21] and Kitchenham and Charters [23] and thus, the next steps where followed:

1. Planning the review:
   (a) Identification of the need for a review
   (b) Developing a review protocol
2. Conducting the review:

(a) Identification of research
(b) Selection of primary studies
(c) Study quality assessment
(d) Data extraction & monitoring
(e) Data synthesis
3. Reporting the review

A review protocol is a written plan that is completed before the review begins and it describes every aspect of the review from the background, the rationale for the survey, to the final report. A predefined protocol reduce the possibility researcher bias and provides a means by which the review itself can be repeated or updated at a later date to include subsequent publications [21,25]. According to Kitchenham [21] the background is the rationale for the survey, explain the need for the review. In this paper the background is showed in the Sect. 2. In the following subsections, it is presented the elements of the review according to the developed review protocol and some additional planning information.

3.1   Research Questions

The primary and secondary research questions elaborated for this study are:

1. Primary Research Question (RQ01): What Agile solutions are proposed for developing Service-Oriented Architecture (SOA) based Applications?
   – Population: all roles in software development process;
   – Intervention: agile Processes for development SOA based applications.
   – Control: processes for traditional software development;
   – Outcomes: set of processes, frameworks, models, and techniques for developing SOA based applications with Agile methods.
2. Research Question (RQ02): What phases of the agile life cycle are the studies covering?
3. Research Question (RQ03): What common principles of Service-Oriented Architecture (SOA) are the studies covering?

The RQ02 and RQ03 research questions complement the RQ01 research question. The research question RQ01 tries to answer what kind of contribution the studies bring, process, method, tool, etc. In addition, the RQ02 research question seeks to identify at which phases of the life cycle is the focus of the studies and the RQ03 research question is concerned with identifying how common principles of SOA are addressed in the studies.

3.2   Search String and Data Sources

To compose the search string the main words and synonyms were identified. Table 1 describes these synonyms. At first, other synonyms were tried, such as Extreme Programming (XP), SCRUM, Lean Software Development (LSD), and Crystal, but these synonyms did not add much, and sometimes brought undesirable works. In addition to the selected synonyms, the words "architecture",

Table 1. Search synonyms

Agile Development	Service-oriented Architecture
Agile Method	SOA
Agile Programming	Service-Based Architecture (SBA)
Agile Process	Service-Oriented Computing (SOC)
Agile Practice	Webservice
Agile Requirement	Representational State Transfer (REST)
Agile Technique	Simple Object Access Protocol (SOAP) Service-based

"computing", "system", and "application" were added to limit the result only to the type of study desired.

All of the used electronic data sources work with a well know structure to ask about electronic papers, using the operator 'OR' to include synonyms for each search term, and the operator 'AND' to link together each set of synonyms. Thus, the search string used was:

((*SOA* OR *SBA* OR *SOC* OR *webservice** OR *"web service"* OR *"web services"* OR *REST* OR *SOAP* OR ((*"software-oriented"* OR *"Software oriented"*) AND (*architecture* OR *computing*)) OR ((*"service-based"* OR *"service based"*) AND (*application** OR *system*))) AND (*"AGILE DEVELOPMENT"* OR *"AGILE MANUFACTURING"* OR *"AGILE METHOD"* OR *"AGILE PROGRAMMING"* OR *"AGILE PROCESS"* OR *"AGILE PRACTICE"* OR *"AGILE REQUIREMENT"* OR *"AGILE TECHNIQUE"*))

Only the electronic data sources depicted in Table 2 were used. Each data source has its own peculiarity to do the search, so the search string above needed to be adapted for each case, but without losing its essence.

Table 2. Data sources

Source	URL
IEEE	https://ieeexplore.ieee.org
ACM	https://dl.acm.org/
Web of Science	https://www.isiknowledge.com
Springer	https://link.springer.com/
Science Direct	https://www.sciencedirect.com
Scopus	https://www.scopus.com

3.3   Study Selection and Data Extraction

Table 3 depicts the selection criteria used in this review. Some criteria are "Automatically identified" and all electronic data sources used in this review provide advanced search tools that allow filtering of automatic criteria. Even though the

Table 3. Study selection criteria

Studies' inclusion criteria
- Automatically identified
- Published and available in electronic data sources
- Contain search keywords in the title, abstract or author keywords
- In English
- All publication years
- Personally identified
- About SOA development using Agile Development Method
- Have to be more than four pages
Studies' exclusion criteria
- Studies that cite SOA and Agile although it isn't the main purposes to explain about development SBA using agile
- Papers which are obviously not related to the research questions in this protocol
- Papers that are application domain specific

original data source search tool does not provide all the necessary features, some parameters are easy to identify in standalone tools, such as an electronic data sheet.

Other criteria for inclusion and exclusion of studies, not "Automatically identified", were identified through a careful reading of the authors title, abstract and keywords. Some studies were excluded late, in the data extraction phase, during the full reading. This was because a conservative criterion was used in this selection phase: *'in case of doubt the study remains'*.

The State of the Art through Systematic Review (StArt)[1] tool was used to aid in data extraction. This tool helps to organize all the work and its two main features are that it follows the protocol proposed by Kitchenham [21] and its local database is a SQLite database[2], which allowed to directly access the tables and work with the data in a Structured Query Language (SQL)[3] way.

3.4   Data Synthesis Strategy

Viewing all collected data is not the best way to understand the data. For the synthesis, the data was stratified the by year, paper sources, and type of solution presented. Table 4 shows the fields used to assist in extracting data.

To classify the solutions found in the studies, they were grouped in phases, or processes, of the software development life-cycle, that is, in which stage of the development life cycle the proposed solution fits best. Proposed by Kitchenham and Charters [23], the reciprocal translation method [28] was used. The processes found in the studies were classified into groups of related processes. But first, it

---

[1] http://lapes.dc.ufscar.br/tools/start_tool.

[2] https://www.sqlite.org.

[3] https://en.wikipedia.org/wiki/SQL.

Table 4. Data extraction fields

Data field	Purpose
Reviewer	Name of reviewer
Title	Name of study
Authors	Study authors
Publication source	Where the paper was published, name of journal, conference, etc.
Publication type	Is the paper a conference paper, journal paper, etc.?
Year of publication	When study was published
Research question	Research question(s) of the study
Study focus	Primary objective of the study
Processes	Process described in the study
Findings/conclusions	Main conclusions from the study
IS valid	Was it a valid study?

was necessary to choose a specific development life-cycle to be used by a pattern. The options to chose were the life-cycles related to SOA or those related to Agile development.

Defining a life-cycle for agile software development is more difficult as agile in essence does not follow a rigorous process, as it can be seen in the Manifesto for agile software development [2]. By the manifesto it is possible to see that processes, tools, comprehensive documentation, negotiation of contracts, and following a plan is not the most important. Thus the development meta-model SOA proposed by Lane and Richardson [25] has been chosen. In this meta-model, the phases are 'Analysis and Design (AD)', 'Construction and Testing (CT)', 'Deployment and Provisioning (DP)' and 'Implementation and Monitoring (IM)'.

4   Data Extraction Results

After the planning phase and with the protocol at hand, it was time to execute the review, select the studies and extract and analyze the data. Data extraction occurred during August 2018. Each data source has its own search tools with its own characteristics. The search query had to be adapted to take full advantage of the potential of each tool.

In the first phase, 146 studies were selected, already discounting the duplicate papers, that is, papers that were available in more than one data source. All abstracts were read and a total of 124 studies were rejected. The main reason for the rejection was that while the studies cited SOA and Agile, the main goal was not to address the development of SOA based application using Agile methods. Then, 22 studies have gone into the data extraction phase.

In data extraction phase, the full text of the 22 studies was read and the extraction form based in Table 4 was filled. At this phase, 4 papers were rejected. Although these papers addressed SOA and Agile methods, they did not address any of the three research questions. Then, 18 studies remained. They are the objects of this review, listed in Table 5.

Table 6 shows the solutions of each study bound to its respective phase in the meta-model after the process of reciprocal translation. Most of the solutions were linked in the 'Analysis and Design' phase of the meta-model. In this type of solution, the authors pay special attention to the definition of the system architecture and its components, linked to the business processes. The 'Construction and Test' phase of the meta-model also received a lot of attention from the researchers, especially regarding the development process itself. Two studies addressed a solution to governance and one to security. The 'Deployment and Provisioning' phase received only 2 studies. The 'Execution and Monitoring' phase did not receive any solution. This demonstrated that most authors were more interested in delivering products and less on how to maintain them. All solutions have presented concepts based on agile methods in general or on specific development methods, such as Rational Unified Process (RUP) or Extreme Programming (XP).

Although the research has not limited the origin of the paper, no book or book chapter has been selected. Most of the paper came from the Conference

Table 5. Categorical data extracted from selected studies

Study	Source	Year	Solution	Meta-model	Q1	Q2	Q3
[1]	CP	2014	Framework/Model	AD/CT/DP	Y	Y	
[7]	SP	2013	Approach/Other	CT	Y	Y	Y
[8]	CP	2012	Approach/Framework	AD/CT	Y		
[9]	WP	2013	Framework	CT	Y		
[10]	JP	2017	Model	AD/CT/DP	Y		
[11]	JP	2010	Process	CT	Y	Y	
[12]	CP	2007	Model/Process	AD	Y		Y
[15]	CP	2011	Framework	CT	Y		
[19]	JP	2003	Approach	AD/CT	Y		
[20]	JP	2008	Approach	AD	Y		
[24]	CP	2005	Other	AD	Y		
[30]	CP	2013	Process	AD/CT	Y	Y	
[31]	CP	2008	Framework	AD/CT	Y		
[32]	CP	2010	Model	CT	Y		Y
[34]	JP	2012	Approach	AD	Y		
[38]	CP	2017	Approach	AD/CT	Y		
[39]	CP	2010	Model	AD	Y		
[40]	SP	2016	Other	AD	Y		Y

CP - Conference Paper/JP - Journal Paper
SP - Symposium Paper/WP - Workshop Paper

Table 6. Reciprocal translation detail

Analysis and Design (AD)	
Framework to design, implementation and deployment of SOA*	[1]
Solution to defining architecture	
Analysis, Architecture Elaboration, Granularity Identification	[10]
SOA Based Model Driven Rapid Development Architecture	[39]
BPMN model	[8]
Composition and orchestration of services	[20]
Establish a Core SOA Architecture	[34]
Architecture Description Language for SOA	[40]
Continuous refactoring' of an SOA	[24]
Service integration	[12]
Solution to defining business process	
SCA model	[8]
Analysis of enterprise business	[8]
Assembling business processes	[8, 10]
Targeting the stakeholder goals (TROPOS and MAP)	[19]
Solution to defining components	
Automatic code generation making domain models instantly executable*	[38]
Identification of the granularity of business components	[8]
Assembling business components	[8, 10]
Design (RUP)	[30]
Creation Services (XP)	[30]
Composition Services (XP)	[30]
Interface Prototype Driven Development (IPDD)*	[31]
Construction and Testing (CT)	
Solution do development	
Framework to design, implementation and deployment of SOA*	[1]
Automatic code generation making domain models instantly executable*	[38]
Development of component operations	[8, 10]
Development (RUP)	[30]
Maintenance (RUP)	[30]
Interface Prototype Driven Development (IPDD)*	[31]
Guidelines and best practices for SOA agile development	[7]
Managing change in software development (XP)	[19]
Specifying the software development process (RUP)	[19]
Agile model-driven development	[11]
Solution to governance	
E-governance system	[32]
Agile Methods governance	[9]
Solution to security	
Security framework for SOA with Agile development	[15]
Deployment and Provisioning (DP)	
Deployment	[10]
Framework to design, implementation and deployment of SOA*	[1]
Execution and Monitoring (EM)	

*The solution appear in more than one phase

Paper (CP) and Journal Paper (JP). This type of paper represents the latest in terms of publications in Computer Science. According to Montesi and Owen [27] "conference publication can measure the ability to innovate and propose new ideas, whereas journal publication can more strongly contribute to building a knowledge basis".

The studies are distributed between the years 2003 and 2017, and the peak is between the years 2010 and 2013, 9 studies. Between the years 2014 and 2016, only 3 studies and in the year 2017, 2 studies. This distribution of publication trend is following the Gartner Hype-Cycle[4]. It seems that today the subject is moving from the 'Slope of Enlightenment' to the 'Plateau of Productivity'. It is a sign of maturity of the subject. No study from the year 2018 appears in this review. This may state that the interest of the subject is decreasing or the data sources did not index the studies for the year 2018 when the data were extracted. In the future, in a possible repetition of this review, this doubt can be clarified.

5   Discussion of Research Questions

The previous section presented a general analysis of the data distribution. It was assessed what the data could explain without touching on the subject of the review itself. This section continues to analyze the data, now addressing the specific research questions.

5.1   RQ01: What Agile Solutions Are Proposed for Developing Service-Oriented Architecture (SOA) Based Applications?

Table 5 shows the type of results and the phase of the meta-model in which they were classified by the reciprocal translation process. Although all studies have addressed the RQ01, some authors have explored SOA and Agile to address issues related to business objectives and rapid changes in requirements, in the environment, and even the customer, as an alternative to traditional monolithic systems [8,9,11,12,31]. But, other authors only addressed the need to deal with the SOA and Agile itself. They assumed that the problem itself would be the combination of these two concepts. They did not explain the need to use them. [7,15,19,20,24,30,34,39].

Although some studies have presented artifacts or experiments, none of them presented results or data capable of allowing any type of validation for the readers. The general conclusion of the authors is that the proposed solutions are able to solve the initial problems presented by them. In Rong *et al.* [31], for example, the authors presented a Service-Oriented Framework of Interface Prototype Driven Development. They did a comparison between two similar projects developed by the same team. Project 'A' used the proposed framework, meanwhile the project 'B' did not. They concluded the project that used the proposed framework supports an instant response to requirements changes and improves

---

[4] https://en.wikipedia.org/wiki/Hype_cycle.

the quality and efficiency of analysis and design for data-centered application system, but, no data was presented that allow the readers to evaluate the results stated by the author.

Wang et al. [39] presented the 'SOA based Model-driven Rapid Development Architecture - SMRDA'. The authors presented a combination of SOA, Modeldriven Architecture (MDA), proposed by Object Management Group (OMG) and agile methods. They applied the SMRDA in a software education management platform. They concluded that the combination of SOA and MDA approaches is the main trend of modem software development in enterprise applications. The key of which, is modeling services correctly, and applying agile development technique.

Karam et al. [20] presented a tool called 'VisualWebC' (short for Visual Web Composition) to support the visual composition of Web services. The authors concluded that their approach presents several significant advantages, such as the creation of web applications with complex functionality with relatively little effort and time.

Chehili et al. [9] presented a platform called FraSCAti to be used with their proposed framework, the FASOAD, a Framework for Agile Service-Oriented Architectures Development. This FraSCAti platform was presented by the authors int an previous study. The authors also did a case study in a High Educational domains.

In Christou et al. [11] the authors presented an example using the Agile Unified process (AUP) in a process of a bank.

Abdelouhab et al. [1] concluded that a major benefit of the Agile-UCD-SOA (Agile & user centric SOA) framework is that it leads to highly flexible and agile software that should be able to meet rapidly changing business needs.

Chehili et al. [8] concluded that their approach, with successive division of the project, the customer involvement, and the acceptance test parts of the architecture can meet the terms of the manifesto of agile methods.

Shahrbanoo [34] concluded that their approach is not only practical but also viable and valuable to develop agile architecture in an agile way since it is an easy approach to apply and also emphasizes on customer involvement. All the authors concluded by the success of their proposed solutions, but there is no way to evaluate the results.

Although Chehili et al. [10] did not present a way to validate their results, they presented a mature work, perhaps because it is a more recent work. ASOS-DeM (Agile and Service Oriented Software Development Method) aims to overcome the complexity of web-based development projects by dividing it into subprojects to allow the application of agile methods' practices. Defines how an SOA agile development project should be executed by a self-organizing team. Describes the concepts that may be used in an SOA project such as 'Artifacts', 'Tasks' and 'Roles'. Address development, analysis, architecture elaboration, granularity identification, components assembling, deployment and integration tests, and business processes assembling.

5.2 RQ02: What Phases of the Agile Life Cycle Are the Studies Covering?

Many of the solutions are linked to the general concepts of agile methods. Some have borrowed specific methods used in methodologies that claim to be agile, such as Extreme Programming (XP), Lean Software Development (LSD), and Rational Unified Process (RUP).

Although some studies have adopted well-known development process tactics, few studies have addressed specific phases of agile development. Abdelouhab *et al.* [1] addressed design, implementation and deployment phases. Rao *et al.* [30] addressed exploration, planning, iterations to release, productionizing, maintenance, and death. Carvalho and Azevedo [7] construction phase. Christou *et al.* [11] inception, elaboration, construction, and transition phases. These results seems to corroborate the idea that defining the life-cycle in agile development methods is more difficult than in traditional development processes. Being agile is respecting other things besides processes and tools itself.

5.3 RQ03: What Common Principles of Service-Oriented Architecture (SOA) Are the Studies Covering?

Like agile phases, few studies addressed specifics SOA principles. Zúñiga-Prieto *et al.* [40] addressed service loose coupling and service composability. Roy and Debnath [32] addressed standardized service contract, service loose coupling, and service abstraction. Demchak *et al.* [12] addressed service loose coupling and service composability. The only one study that addressed all 8 SOA principles was Carvalho and Azevedo [7], standardized service contract, service loose coupling, service abstraction, service reusability, service autonomy, service statelessnes, service discoverability, and service Composability.

Service-Oriented Architecture (SOA) presents a high level of complexity and what had been observed is that few authors have entered into SOA's core. Maybe they should have put more emphasis on the details, more attention to SOA principles.

6 Conclusion

All studies in this review have presented at least one type of solution to address the development of Service-Oriented Architecture (SOA) based application with Agile methods. These studies have shown that this subject is important, worthy of study and is entering a period of maturity. However, there is a gap between research and practice. None of the studies presented a substantial result with data that can be analyzed. Few studies have attempted to present a well-defined process, although this seems to be a feature of agile methods, SOA needs some rigor in its development because of its complexity. However, this does not disqualify the combined SOA and agile methods solution. More studies need to be done, but it seems to be a promising way. This review is yet another piece to help along this way.

References

1. Abdelouhab, K.A., Idoughi, D., Kolski, C.: Agile & user centric SOA based service design framework applied in disaster management. In: 2014 1st International Conference on Information and Communication Technologies for Disaster Management (ICT-DM), pp. 1–8 (2014). https://doi.org/10.1109/ICT-DM.2014.6917792
2. Alliance, A.: Agile manifesto, vol. 6, no. 1 (2001). http://www.agilemanifesto.org
3. Arsanjani, A., Holley, K.: The service integration maturity model: achieving flexibility in the transformation to SOA. In: 2006 IEEE International Conference on Services Computing (SCC 2006), p. 515 (2006). https://doi.org/10.1109/SCC.2006.104. https://ieeexplore-ieee-org.ez54.periodicos.capes.gov.br/document/4026979/
4. Arsanjani, A., et al.: The SOA manifesto. SOA Manifesto, p. 35, October 2009. http://serviceorientation.com/soamanifesto/original
5. Bass, L.: Software Architecture in Practice. Pearson Education India (2007)
6. Bianco, P., Kotermanski, R., Merson, P.F.: Evaluating a Service-Oriented Architecture. Research Showcase @ CMU 1 September 2007. http://repository.cmu.edu/sei
7. Carvalho, F., Azevedo, L.G.: Service agile development using XP. In: Proceedings of 2013 IEEE 7th International Symposium on Service-Oriented System Engineering, SOSE 2013, pp. 254–259 (2013). https://doi.org/10.1109/SOSE.2013.25
8. Chehili, H., Boufaida, M., Seinturier, L.: An agile approach for service-oriented architectures. In: ICSOFT, pp. 468–471 (2012)
9. Chehili, H., Seinturier, L., Boufaida, M.: FASOAD: a framework for agile service-oriented architectures development. In: Proceedings of International Workshop on Database and Expert Systems Applications, DEXA, pp. 222–226 (2013). https://doi.org/10.1109/DEXA.2013.28
10. Chehili, H., Seinturier, L., Boufaida, M.: An evolutive component-based method for agile development of service oriented architectures. Int. J. Inf. Syst. Serv. Sect. (IJISSS) **9**(3), 37–57 (2017)
11. Christou, I., Ponis, S., Palaiologou, E.: Using the agile unified process in banking. IEEE Softw. **27**(3), 72–79 (2010). https://doi.org/10.1109/MS.2009.156
12. Demchak, B., Farcas, C., Farcas, E., Krüger, I.H.: The treasure map for Rich Services. In: 2007 IEEE International Conference on Information Reuse and Integration, IEEE IRI-2007, pp. 400–405 (2007). https://doi.org/10.1109/IRI.2007.4296653
13. Dybå, T., Dingsøyr, T.: Empirical studies of agile software development: a systematic review. Inf. Softw. Technol. **50**(9), 833–859 (2008). https://doi.org/10.1016/j.infsof.2008.01.006. http://www.sciencedirect.com/science/article/pii/S0950584908000256
14. Erl, T.: SOA: Principles of Service Design, vol. 1. Prentice Hall, Upper Saddle River (2008)
15. Farroha, D., Farroha, B.: Developing corporate services in an agile environment. In: Proceedings of IEEE Military Communications Conference MILCOM, pp. 1535–1540 (2011). https://doi.org/10.1109/MILCOM.2011.6127525
16. Highsmith, J., Cockburn, A.: Agile software development: the business of innovation. Computer **34**(9), 120–127 (2001). https://doi.org/10.1109/2.947100
17. Idoughi, D., Kerkar, M., Kolski, C.: Towards new web services based supervisory systems in complex industrial organizations: basic principles and case study. Comput. Ind. **61**(3), 235–249 (2010)

18. Inayat, I., Salim, S.S., Marczak, S., Daneva, M., Shamshirband, S.: A systematic literature review on agile requirements engineering practices and challenges. Comput. Hum. Behav. **51**, 915–929 (2015). https://doi.org/10.1016/j.chb.2014.10.046. http://www.sciencedirect.com/science/article/pii/S074756321400569X

19. Ivanyukovich, A., Gangadharan, G.R., D'Andrea, V., Marchese, M.: Towards a service-oriented development methodology. Trans. SDPS **1**, 10 (2003)

20. Karam, M., Dascalu, S., Safa, H., Santina, R., Koteich, Z.: A product-line architecture for web service-based visual composition of web applications. J. Syst. Softw. **81**(6), 855–867 (2008). https://doi.org/10.1016/j.jss.2007.10.031

21. Kitchenham, B.: Procedures for performing systematic reviews. Keele University 33(TR/SE-0401), Keele, UK, 28 (2004). http://www.scm.keele.ac.uk/ease/sreview.doc

22. Kitchenham, B., Brereton, O.P., Budgen, D., Turner, M., Bailey, J., Linkman, S.: Systematic literature reviews in software engineering - a systematic literature review. Inf. Softw. Technol. **51**(1), 7–15 (2009). https://doi.org/10.1016/j.infsof.2008.09.009

23. Kitchenham, B., Charters, S.: Guidelines for performing systematic literature reviews in software engineering. Engineering **2**, 1051 (2007). https://doi.org/10.1145/1134285.1134500

24. Krogdahl, P., Luef, G., Steindl, C.: Service-oriented agility: an initial analysis for the use of agile methods for SOA development. In: 2005 IEEE International Conference on Services Computing (SCC 2005) Vol-1, vol. 2, pp. 93–100 (2005). https://doi.org/10.1109/SCC.2005.86

25. Lane, S., Richardson, I.: Process models for service-based applications: a systematic literature review. Inf. Softw. Technol. **53**(5), 424–439 (2011). https://doi.org/10.1016/j.infsof.2010.12.005

26. Meijer, E., Bierman, G.: A co-relational model of data for large shared data banks. Commun. ACM **54**(4), 49 (2011). https://doi.org/10.1145/1924421.1924436

27. Montesi, M., Owen, J.M.: From conference to journal publication: how conference papers in software engineering are extended for publication in journals. J. Am. Soc. Inf. Sci. Technol. **59**(5), 816–829 (2008)

28. Noblit, G.W., Hare, R.D., Hare, R.D.: Meta-Ethnography: Synthesizing Qualitative Studies, vol. 11. Sage, Thousand Oaks (1988)

29. Petersen, K., Vakkalanka, S., Kuzniarz, L.: Guidelines for conducting systematic mapping studies in software engineering: an update. Inf. Softw. Technol. **64**, 1–18 (2015). https://doi.org/10.1016/j.infsof.2015.03.007

30. Rao, G.S., Krishna, C.V.P., Rao, K.R.: Rational unified process for service oriented application in extreme programming. In: 2013 Fourth International Conference on Computing, Communications and Networking Technologies (ICCCNT), pp. 1–6 (2013). https://doi.org/10.1109/ICCCNT.2013.6726586. http://ieeexplore.ieee.org/document/6726586/

31. Rong, H., Zhou, N., Jin, M., Wu, J.: Research on service-oriented framework of interface prototype driven development. In: 2008 International Conference on Computer Science and Software Engineering, vol. 2, pp. 552–557 (2008). https://doi.org/10.1109/CSSE.2008.362

32. Roy, S., Debnath, M.K.: Designing SOA based e-governance system using eXtreme Programming methodology for developing countries. In: 2010 2nd International Conference on Software Technology and Engineering, vol. 2, pp. 2–277 (2010). https://doi.org/10.1109/ICSTE.2010.5608805. https://ieeexplore.ieee.org/abstract/document/5608805/

33. Severance, C.: Roy T. fielding: understanding the REST style. Computer **48**(6), 7–9 (2015)
34. Shahrbanoo, M.: An approach for agile SOA development using agile principals. Int. J. Comput. Sci. Inf. Technol. **4**(1), 237–244 (2012). https://doi.org/10.5121/ijcsit.2012.4118
35. Shi, S.S.B., Stokes, E., Byrne, D., Corn, C.F., Bachmann, D., Jones, T.: An enterprise directory solution with DB2. IBM Syst. J. **39**(2), 360–383 (2000). https://doi.org/10.1147/sj.392.0360. http://ieeexplore.ieee.org/ielx5/5288519/5386991/05387000.pdf?tp=&arnumber=5387000&isnumber=5386991
36. Timperi, O.: An Overview of Quality Assurance Practices in Agile Methodologies. Soberit. Hut.Fi 650 (2004)
37. Vallon, R., da Silva Estácio, B.J., Prikladnicki, R., Grechenig, T.: Systematic literature review on agile practices in global software development. Inf. Softw. Technol. **96**, 161–180 (2018). https://doi.org/10.1016/j.infsof.2017.12.004. http://www.sciencedirect.com/science/article/pii/S0950584917302975
38. Wang, B., Rosenberg, D., Boehm, B.W.: Rapid realization of executable domain models via automatic code generation. In: 2017 IEEE 28th Annual Software Technology Conference (STC), pp. 1–6 (2017). https://doi.org/10.1109/STC.2017.8234464
39. Wang, B., Wen, C., Sheng, J.: A SOA based model driven rapid development architecture - SMRDA. In: 2010 2nd International Conference on Education Technology and Computer, ICETC 2010, vol. 1, pp. 421–425 (2010). https://doi.org/10.1109/ICETC.2010.5529218
40. Zúñiga-Prieto, M., Insfran, E., Abrahão, S.: Architecture description language for incremental integration of cloud services architectures. In: Proceedings of 2016 IEEE 10th International Symposium on the Maintenance and Evolution of Service-Oriented and Cloud-Based Environments, MESOCA 2016, pp. 16–23 (2016). https://doi.org/10.1109/MESOCA.2016.10
41. Zur Muehlen, M., Nickerson, J.V., Swenson, K.D.: Developing web services choreography standards - the case of REST vs. SOAP. Decis. Support Syst. **40**(1 SPEC. ISS.), 9–29 (2005). https://doi.org/10.1016/j.dss.2004.04.008

Integrating the Scrum Framework and Lean Six Sigma

Anacleto Correia[1]([⊠]) [iD], António Gonçalves[1] [iD],
and Sanjay Misra[2] [iD]

[1] CINAV, Alfeite, 2810-001 Almada, Portugal
cortez.correia@marinha.pt
[2] Covenant University, Ota, Ogun State, Nigeria

Abstract. Lean Six Sigma approach has been a successful manufacturing quality improvement tool. In the last decades, it has helped many services and product industries to achieve better performance and higher results. No wonder that the approach has aroused the interest of the software development industry. As result, some software companies have been trying to adopt Lean Six Sigma in their development processes, specifically in conjunction with agile methods. Based on some of these experiences this paper intends to propose the integration in the Scrum method the quality procedures defined on the Lean Six Sigma (LSS). By complementing the current generic quality procedures of Scrum method with more formalized and well-proven quality measures from LSS we intend to improve the efficacy and efficiency of Scrum.

Keywords: Agile methodology · Scrum · Lean Six Sigma · Software quality

1 Introduction

Among software development methodologies, agile methodologies, anchored by the values and the principles of the Agile Manifesto, claim their suitability to better manage software development lifecycle. The manifesto highlights a set of values an agile methodology should embody, inter alia, the relevance of individuals and their interactions, the need of a continuous delivery of working software, collaboration with customer and the fast response to change. Among these several lightweight development methods, there is Scrum.

In IT related domains, Scrum has been used to develop software, hardware, embedded software, networks of interacting function, autonomous vehicles. Scrum has also been widely used for products, services, and the management of organizations, such as, schools, government, marketing, or the operation of a process, and almost everything we use in our daily lives, as individuals and societies. As happened with other agile methods, Scrum provides practices that help companies building the right product, at a certain moment, and empowering the teams to continuously redesign the released products, optimizing its value throughout development, and allowing it to address, in each moment, the customers' expectation. Therefore, the main aim of the methodology is to deliver what is needed at appropriate time in each iteration of the development cycle.

© Springer Nature Switzerland AG 2019
S. Misra et al. (Eds.): ICCSA 2019, LNCS 11623, pp. 136–149, 2019.
https://doi.org/10.1007/978-3-030-24308-1_12

Scrum methodology for software development can be successfully applied in context of unclear customer's requirements, tight deadlines and budgets. However, besides the benefits associated to the use of Scrum, and agile technologies in general, concerns can be raised regarding the procedures embedded in the methodology that could ensure an effective measurement of gains in quality, productivity and business satisfaction.

This paper is an attempt to include in the empirical approach for software development methodology Scrum, prescriptive techniques for defining and improving products, processes and services with a focus on reduction of defects and failures, on variation and waste elimination, prioritizing, in a planned and objective way, the achievement of quality and financial results, found in Lean Six Sigma (LSS) methodology.

This paper is organized as follows: in the next section we describe the fundamentals of the Scrum framework, either in its static perspective, with a light ontology depicting its main concepts and their relationships, as well using a dynamic representation of a process model representing the main activities developed iteratively. In Sect. 3 the fundamentals of the Lean approach are described, as well as the Six Sigma method for quality. Both approaches are merged in the Lean Six Sigma method, which are presented also according the same two perspectives previously used (static and dynamic). The section four synthetizes how the integration between Scrum and Lean Six Sigma can be achieved. The work ends by drawing some conclusions and foreseeing future work.

2 Scrum Framework

2.1 Overview

Scrum is a process framework that can embody within it, various processes and techniques on complex products. Scrum intends to give efficacy to product management and development techniques in order to continuously improve the product, the team, and the working environment [1]. Scrum was initially developed for managing and developing products. The method was proved especially effective in iterative and incremental knowledge transfer.

The essence of Scrum is a small team of people. The individual team is highly flexible and adaptive. These strengths continue operating in single, several, many, and networks of teams that develop, release, operate and sustain the work and work products of thousands of people. They collaborate and interoperate through sophisticated development architectures and target release environments.

2.2 Scrum Model

In this section we formalize the main concepts of Scrum [2], as well the relationship among them, through the light ontology presented in Fig. 1.

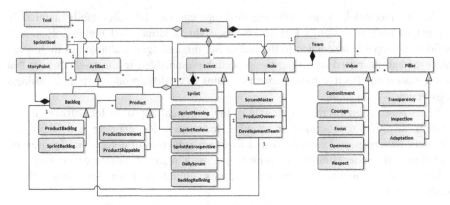

Fig. 1. The model of Scrum.

Each component within the Scrum framework serves a specific purpose. The *Rules* of Scrum bind together the *Events* and *Artifacts*, and govern the relationships and interaction between them, anchored by the *Values* and *Pillars* of the framework.

The Scrum's *Values* of *Commitment, Courage, Focus, Openness* and *Respect* should be embodied and lived by the *Team*. Successful use of Scrum depends on people becoming more proficient in living these five values.

The *Team* has self-organized and cross-functional members each of one with specific *Role*. They tend to choose the best way to accomplish their work, rather than being directed by others outside the team, and rely on having internally all competencies needed to accomplish the work without depending on external team's members. The team deliver a *Product* iteratively and incrementally, maximizing opportunities for feedback. Incremental deliveries (*ProductIncrement* or *ProductShippable*) ensure that a working product version is always available after each *Sprint*.

Relate with the *Values*, the Scrum's *Pillars* of *Transparency, Inspection,* and *Adaptation* are instantiated to bring trust for stakeholders. Through *Transparency* it is required the definition of aspects, based on agreed standards, in order that stakeholders can share a common understanding of the process. Scrum users must frequently inspect *Artifacts* to detect undesirable variances. The *Inspection* should be performed by skilled inspectors at defined point of work. If there are aspects of the process that deviate outside acceptable limits, conducting to unacceptable *Product*, the process or the *Product* being built must be subject of *Adaptation*, i.e. to an adjustment so deviation can be minimized.

The *Roles* played by members of the *Team* are the *ProductOwner*, the *DevelopmentTeam*, and a *ScrumMaster*. The *ProductOwner* is responsible for maximizing the value of the product resulting from work of the *DevelopmentTeam*.

The *ProductOwner* is the person responsible for managing the *ProductBacklog* and represent the desires of those wanting a *Product*. The *DevelopmentTeam* consists of people who do the work for delivering a *ProductIncrement* at the end of each *Sprint*. Only members of the *DevelopmentTeam* create the *ProductIncrement*. The *DevelopmentTeam* is structured and empowered to organize and manage its own work in order to optimize the overall efficiency and effectiveness. The *ScrumMaster* is responsible for promoting and supporting Scrum, which is attained by helping the *Team* understanding Scrum theory, practices, rules, and values.

The *Sprint*, the core of Scrum, is a maximum duration activity during which a useable and potentially releasable *Product* is created. *Sprints* have same durations throughout a development effort, with a new *Sprint* starting immediately after the conclusion of the previous. Prescribed *Events* are used in Scrum to create regularity and to minimize the need for meetings not defined in Scrum. All events in Scrum are time-boxed. A *Sprint* contains as prescribed events for inspection and adaptation the *SprintPlanning*, *DailyScrum*, the *SprintReview*, and the *SprintRetrospective*. The *Sprint* is the container of all these events as well as the regular *DevelopmentWork*. Each event in Scrum, other than the *Sprint* itself, is an opportunity to inspect and adapt a functionality, therefore, specifically designed to enable *Transparency*, *Inspection* and *Adaption*.

The *Sprint* is a kind of a mini-project that aims to accomplish a *SprintGoal*, which is embodied by an *Artifact*, that can be planned, designed, built, and be the result *ProductIncrement*.

In Scum, the *Backlog* is a kind of *Artifact*, that consists of an ordered list of what is needed in the *Product*. It is the repository of requirements for any changes to be made to the *Product*. The *ProductOwner* is responsible for the *ProductBacklog*, including its content, availability, and ordering. The *ProductBacklog* evolves as the product and the environment in which it will be used evolves since the initially requirements. The *ProductBacklog* constantly changes to identify what the product requirements to be appropriate, competitive, and useful.

The *ProductBacklog* lists all features, functions, requirements, enhancements, and fixes that constitute the changes to be made to the product in future releases. *ProductBacklog* items have the attributes of a description, order, estimate, and value. *ProductBacklog* items often include test descriptions that will prove its completeness when *ProductShippable*. As a product is used and gains value, and the marketplace provides feedback, the *ProductBacklog* becomes a larger and more exhaustive list. Requirements never stop changing, so a *ProductBacklog* is a living *Artifact*. Changes in *StoryPoints* (business requirements), market conditions, or technology may cause changes in the *ProductBacklog*.

The *ProductIncrement* is the sum of all the *ProductBacklog* items completed during a *Sprint* and the value of the *ProductIncrements* of all previous *Sprints*. At the end of a *Sprint*, the new *ProductIncrement* must be accepted, which means it must be in a useable condition and meet the *Team*'s terms of acceptance. So, the *ProductIncrement* is a body of inspectable, done work at the end of the *Sprint* towards the *SprintGoal*.

Multiple *Teams* often work together on the same *Product*. One *ProductBacklog* is used to describe the upcoming work on the *ProductShippable*. A *ProductBacklog* attribute that groups items may then be employed.

2.3   Scrum's Process Framework

After the static representation of Scrum made in previous section, Fig. 2 presents a dynamic view of the same process through a BPMN process model. There, one can see that after collecting the business requirements and prioritize them, the *ProductOwner* (bottom lane) discusses the objective that each *Sprint* should achieve and the *ProductBacklog* items that, when the *Sprint* is completed, allow to achieve the *SprintGoal*. The work to be performed in the *Sprint* is planned at the *SprintPlanning*. This plan is usually created by the collaborative work of the entire *Team*.

The *ScrumMaster* (middle lane) ensures that the *SprintPlanning* takes place and whether attendants understand its purpose. The *DevelopmentTeam* (top lane) works to forecast the functionality that will be developed during the *Sprint*. The entire *Team* collaborates on the work of the *Sprint*. The input to the *SprintPlanning* meeting is the *ProductBacklog*, the latest *ProductIncrement*, projected capacity of the *DevelopmentTeam* during the *Sprint*, and past performance of the *DevelopmentTeam*. The number of items selected from the *ProductBacklog* for the *Sprint* is solely up to the *DevelopmentTeam*. Only the *DevelopmentTeam* can assess what it can accomplish over the upcoming *Sprint*. During *SprintPlanning* the *Team* also crafts a *SprintGoal*. The *SprintGoal* is an objective that will be met within the *Sprint* through the implementation of the *ProductBacklog*, and it provides guidance to the *DevelopmentTeam* on why it is building the *ProductIncrement*.

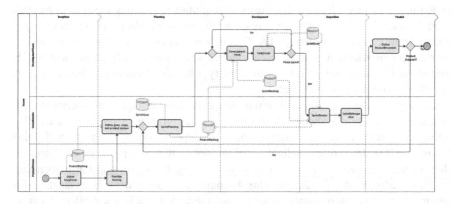

Fig. 2. The Scrum's process framework.

Having set the *SprintGoal* and selected the *ProductBacklog* items for the *Sprint*, the *DevelopmentTeam* will transform the requirements into a working *ProductIncrement* during the *Sprint*. The *ProductBacklog* items selected for the *Sprint* plus the plan for delivering them is called the *SprintBacklog*.

The Work starts by designing the system and may be of varying size, or estimated effort. However, enough work is planned during *SprintPlanning* for the *DevelopmentTeam* to forecast what it believes it can do in the upcoming *Sprint*. Work planned for the first days of the *Sprint* by the *DevelopmentTeam* is decomposed by the end of the *SprintPlanning* meeting. The *DevelopmentTeam* self-organizes to undertake the work in the *SprintBacklog*, both during *SprintPlanning* and as needed throughout the *Sprint*.

The *ProductOwner* can help to clarify the selected *ProductBacklog* items and make trade-offs. If the *DevelopmentTeam* determines it has too much or too little work, it may renegotiate the selected *ProductBacklog* items with the *ProductOwner*.

The *SprintGoal* is an objective set for the *Sprint* that can be met through the implementation of *ProductBacklog*. It provides guidance to the *DevelopmentTeam* on why it is building the *ProductIncrement*. It is created during the *SprintPlanning* meeting. The *SprintGoal* gives the *DevelopmentTeam* some flexibility regarding the functionality implemented within the *Sprint*. The selected *ProductBacklog* items deliver a coherent function, which can be the *SprintGoal*. The *SprintGoal* can be any other coherence that causes the *DevelopmentTeam* to work together rather than on separate initiatives.

As the *DevelopmentTeam* works, it keeps the *SprintGoal* in mind. In order to satisfy the *SprintGoal*, it implements functionality and technology. If the work turns out to be different than the *DevelopmentTeam* expected, they collaborate with the *ProductOwner* to negotiate the scope of *SprintBacklog* within the *Sprint*.

The *DailyScrum* is a time-boxed event, within the *Sprint*, for the *DevelopmentTeam* held every day. During the *DailyScrum* the *DevelopmentTeam* plans work for the next work day. This optimizes team collaboration and performance by inspecting the work since the last *DailyScrum* and forecasting upcoming *Sprint* work.

The *DevelopmentTeam* uses the *DailyScrum* to inspect progress toward the *SprintGoal* and to inspect how progress is trending toward completing the work in the *SprintBacklog*. Every day, the *DevelopmentTeam* should understand how it intends to work together as a self-organizing team to accomplish the *SprintGoal* and create the *ProductIncrement* by the end of the *Sprint*.

The *DevelopmentTeam* often meet immediately after the *DailyScrum* for detailed discussions, or to adapt and re-plan, the rest of the *Sprint*'s work. *DailyScrum*s improve communications and improve the *DevelopmentTeam*'s level of knowledge. This is a key inspect and adapt meeting.

A *SprintReview* is held at the end of the *Sprint* to inspect the *ProductIncrement* and adapt the *ProductBacklog* if needed. During the *SprintReview*, the *Team* and stake-holders collaborate about what was done in the *Sprint*. Based on that and any changes to the *ProductBacklog* during the *Sprint*, the *DevelopmentTeam* collaborate on the next things that could be done to optimize value. The result of the *SprintReview* is a revised *ProductBacklog* that defines the probable *ProductBacklog* items for the next *Sprint*. The *ProductBacklog* may also be adjusted overall to meet new opportunities.

The *SprintRetrospective* is an opportunity for the *Team* to inspect itself and create a plan for improvements to be enacted during the next *Sprint*. The *ScrumMaster* ensures that the event takes place and that attendants understand its purpose. The purposes of the *SprintRetrospective* are: (1) to inspect how the last *Sprint* went with regards to people, relationships, process, and tools; (2) identify and order the major items that went well and potential improvements; and, (3) to create a plan for implementing improvements to the way the *Team* does its work.

The *ScrumMaster* encourages the *Team* to improve the development process and practices to make it more effective for the next *Sprint*. During each *SprintRetrospective*, the *Team* plans ways to increase product quality by improving work processes or adapting the definition of acceptance, if appropriate and not in conflict with product or organizational standards.

By the end of the *SprintRetrospective*, the *Team* should have identified improvements that it will implement in the next *Sprint*. Implementing these improvements in the next *Sprint* is the adaptation to the inspection of the *Team* itself. Although improvements may be implemented at any time, the *SprintRetrospective* provides a formal opportunity to focus on inspection and adaptation. Also, it is conducted a *ProductBacklog* refinement by adding detail, estimates, and order to items in the *ProductBacklog*. Higher ordered *ProductBacklog* items are usually clearer and more detailed than lower ordered ones, and therefore deemed for selection in the next *SprintPlanning*. *ProductBacklog* items usually acquire this degree of transparency through the above described refining activities. This is an ongoing process in which the *ProductOwner* and the *DevelopmentTeam* collaborate on the details of *ProductBacklog* items. So, during *ProductBacklog* refinement, items are reviewed and revised.

The *DevelopmentTeam* is responsible for all estimates. The *ProductOwner* may influence the *DevelopmentTeam* by helping it understand and select trade-offs, but the people who will perform the work make the final estimate.

At any point in time in a *Sprint*, the total work remaining in the *SprintBacklog* can be summed. The *DevelopmentTeam* tracks this total work remaining at least for every *DailyScrum* to project the likelihood of achieving the *SprintGoal*. By tracking the remaining work throughout the *Sprint*, the *DevelopmentTeam* can manage its progress.

Since Scrum is based on transparency decisions to optimize value and control risk are made based on the perceived state of the *Artifact*s. To the extent that transparency is complete, these decisions have a sound basis. To the extent that the *Artifact*s are incompletely transparent, these decisions can be flawed, value may diminish and risk may increase.

The *ScrumMaster* must work with the *ProductOwner*, *DevelopmentTeam*, and other involved parties to understand if the *Artifact*s are completely transparent. A *ScrumMaster* can detect incomplete transparency by inspecting the *Artifact*s, identifying patterns, and detecting differences between expected and real results. The *ScrumMaster*'s job is to work with the *Team* and the organization to increase the transparency of the *Artifact*s.

When a *ProductBacklog* item or a *ProductIncrement* is described as acceptable, the *Team* must understand and agree in what it means to ensure transparency. This is the definition of acceptance for the *Team* and is used to assess when work is complete on the *ProductIncrement*.

The same definition guide the *DevelopmentTeam* in knowing how many *ProductBacklog* items it can select during a *SprintPlanning*. The purpose of each *Sprint* is to deliver *ProductIncrement*s of potentially releasable functionality that adhere to the *Team*'s current definition of acceptable.

*DevelopmentTeam*s deliver a *ProductIncrement* with useable functionality every *Sprint*, so a *ProductOwner* may choose to immediately release it. If the definition of acceptable for a *ProductIncrement* is part of the conventions, standards or guidelines of the development organization, the *Team* must support it.

3 The Lean Six Sigma Approach

Lean [3] and Six Sigma philosophy had separate origins. While Six Sigma was started as an approach to reduce operational variation and defects, Lean thinking enabled elimination of waste and reduction of cycle time. The primary focus of Six Sigma is on effectiveness whereas Lean focuses on efficiency. As an integrated strategy, Lean Six Sigma has become a method for the excellence of systems by enabling the break-through improvement in every part of the system through process enablement, cost reduction, and increased benefits [4].

Typical Lean Six Sigma is aimed at reducing variation, defects, and waste, as well as improving process speed for existing processes and systems. These principles can be applied in a proactive manner to prevent defects and waste, while minimizing the impact of variation and enabling process speed. This is done in the context of designing and developing processes, products, and systems.

In the following sections we dive into the details of Six Sigma and Lean, in order to extract the concepts and procedures that are depicted in the static model of Lean Six Sigma (Fig. 3) and the dynamic process model of Lean Six Sigma Methodology (Fig. 4). These models will be used in Sect. 4 for integration of quality procedures of Lean Six Sigma Methodology and Scrum.

3.1 Six Sigma

Six Sigma is a management approach which creates an environment where the methodology is applied as a business strategy. Therefore, Six Sigma is a disciplined process that focuses on delivering products with a consistent quality. The strength of Six Sigma is the continuous improvement process underpinned by three Pillars: *change empowerment, training of resources* and *top management support.*

The target of Six Sigma are operational business processes. A *Process* consists of four parts, *Input, Activities, Output,* and *Feedback.* The *Output* (y) is the final product delivered to an internal or external customer, while the *Input* (x) is any resource put into a process to be transformed as result. Any change in the inputs causes changes in the output, i.e., $y = f(x)$. Each Input can be classified as of the *Type*: Controllable (C), Non-Controllable (NC), Noise (N), and Critical (X). An important aspect of the process is the *Feedback.* Feedback helps in process control, because it suggests changes to the inputs. Each process should be designed to attain an output according to the requirements of the customer.

Six Sigma is implemented by a cycle of activities known as *DMAIC* (Define, Measure, Analyze, Improve, and Control). In the activities of *Define*, the problem statement and the plan for the improvement initiative are defined. In Six Sigma, in addition to defining the problem, the Six Sigma project team is also gathered in this phase. The activities of *Measure* collect the data from the process and determines the current quality and operational performance levels. Also, the measurement criteria (e.g. how to measure, when to measure, and who will measure) is established. In the activities of *Analyze*, the business process and the data generated from the measurement activity are studied to understand the root causes of the problem. In the activities of *Improvement*, possible improvement actions are identified and prioritized. These are then tested and the enhanced action plan is finalized. In the last activities, related to *Control*, the Six Sigma team goes for a full-scale implementation of the improvement action plan and sets up controls to monitor the system in order to sustain the gains. In the *DMAIC* cycle of problem-solving focused teams are assigned to a well-defined project that directly influences the organization's bottom line with customer satisfaction and increased quality being by-products.

There are several levels in the Six Sigma team structure. The level of *Champions*, with mandate from top management for the improvement initiatives. They identify the scope of projects, design the deployment strategy, support cultural change, and coach *MasterBlackBelts*. At next level *MasterBlackBelts* train and coach *BlackBelts*, *Gree-Belts*, as well as *FunctionalLeaders* of the organization. Another level, in the Six Sigma structure, is addressed by *BlackBelts*. They apply strategies to specific projects, and lead teams to execute projects. Finally, *GreenBelts* support the *BlackBelts* by participating in project teams performing day-to-day jobs related to their work area, as well as training junior *YellowBelts*.

Six Sigma defines some core *Concepts* and *Measures*, such as Opportunity, Defect, Specification limits, Rolled Throughput Yield (RTY), and Defects per Million Opportunity (DPMO). An Opportunity is defined as every chance for a process to deliver an output that is either *right* or *wrong*, as perceived by the customers. A Defect is defined as every result of an opportunity that does not meet customer specifications and does not fall within the Specification limits, delimited by an Upper Specification Limit (USL) and Lower Specification Limit (LSL). RTY is a measure of process efficiency expressed as percentage. DPMO is also known as Non-Defect per Million Opportunities (NPMO) and is a measure of process performance.

Specific *Tools* are employed in the *Activities* of the *DMAIC* process. The *Define* uses tools such as Supply, Input, Process, Output, Customer (SIPOC) Diagram, Voice of Customer (VOC), Critical to Quality (CTQ) Trees, Quality Function Deployment (QFD), Failure Mode and Effects Analysis (FMEA), Cause and Effect (CE) Matrix, and Project Charter. The *Measure* uses tools such as GAGE R and R Variables, Run Charts or Control Charts, Cp, Cpk, Sigma level (Z Level) and Defects per Million Opportunity (DPMO), and Anderson Darling Test. The tools used in the *Analyze* are Simple Linear Regression (SLR), Pareto Charts, Fishbone Diagram, FMEA, and Multi-Vari Charts or Hypothesis Tests. In the *Improve*, the tools that can be used are Brainstorming, Piloting and FMEA, and Design of Experiments (DOE). The *Control* activity uses tools such as Control Charts, Control Plan, and Measurement System Analysis (MSA) Re-analysis. Some of these tools can be used interchangeably between the activities.

The benefits of Six Sigma are the fact that the *DMAIC* process eliminates the root cause of problems and defects in processes. The solution can go through the creation of robust products that mitigate the impact of a variable input or output on a customer's experience. Using Six Sigma reduces variation in a process and thereby reduces wastes in the same process. It ensures customer satisfaction and provides process standardization. Rework is substantially reduced because one gets it right the very first time. Furthermore, users' requirements are key for Six Sigma.

3.2   Lean

The Lean approach, instantiated by the Toyota production system, is based on five *Pillars*: (1) *Value*, which means the specification of value from the point of view of the customer; (2) *Stream*, by the identification of all the steps in the stream of value and eliminating waste; (3) *Flow*, by allowing the value to flow without discontinuity; (4) *Pull*, by letting the customer be the one to pull value from the process; (5) *Continuous improving* of the process in search of perfection.

Lean thinking uses a slightly different approach to problem solving than Six Sigma approach. Progress is made through the execution of events, wherein a small group of employees assemble together through an incremental and continuous improvement, a process, through a series of quick and focused sessions (*Kaizen events*). This approach intends that the team leave the mentality of long-cycle-time project and gain a mindset for action. The Kaizen approach for execution can be synthetized in the following cycle: (1) *Map* out the *As-Is* of the process and create a baseline; (2) *Establish* a vision for the *to-be* state; (3) *Identify* the gaps and establish opportunities for improvement; (4) *Implement* changes and remove waste from the system; (5) *Evaluate* results and institutionalize continuous improvement.

The key thinking behind the Lean approach is to produce what is needed for the customer, when it is needed, with the minimum amount of resources. Lean achieves this by addressing eight types of wastes: (1) *Waiting* (90 percent of artifact's life is spent in this state); (2) *Overproduction* (producing more than what is necessary); (3) *Rework* (e.g. editing, approving, revising); (4) *Motion* (any movement that does not change the characteristics of the product); 5. *Processing* (when a transformation exceeds the required); (6) *Inventory* (the need of extra space and additional handling); (7) *Intellect* (means not taking advantage of the thinking power and knowledge base of human resources); (8) *Transportation* (the unnecessary movement of parts, material or work-in-process from one operation to another).

3.3   Lean Six Sigma

Lean advocates argue that Six Sigma does not directly address speed, flow, and waste within processes. Six Sigma supporters, on the other hand, pointed out that Lean approach is not capable of solving variation problems or process optimization issues. The logical answer to the dilemma is Lean Six Sigma – the combination of the approaches to organizational performance.

Lean Six Sigma is the improvement methodology that combines the best of the Lean concepts and Six Sigma tools, merged in the model of Fig. 3. The emphasis is on obtaining the best of both improvement methodologies, while minimizing any potential weaknesses. The emphasis is on taking advantage of the value generation focus offered by the Lean method, while maintaining the statistical rigors of the Six Sigma methodology.

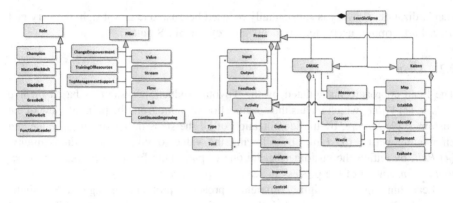

Fig. 3. The model of Lean Six Sigma.

The idea behind adoption of the Lean Six Sigma approach is to enable the organization with a common language, framework, methodology, and process to operating processes, developing and producing products easily and efficiently. The integrated approach of Lean Six Sigma, as depicted in Fig. 4, optimizes the value-creation process and maximizes shareholder value by achieving the fastest rate of improvement in cost, quality, process speed, safety, and customer satisfaction.

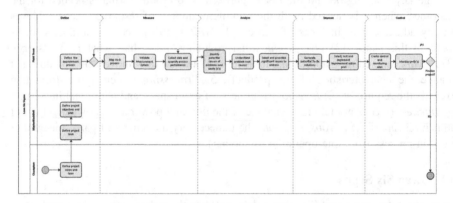

Fig. 4. Process of Lean Six Sigma Methodology.

4 Integration of LSS in Scrum

At the problem-solving level, Lean Six Sigma is a project-driven methodology. The projects executed under the methodology follow the DMAIC process. The aim of Lean Six Sigma is to identify the areas of variation, isolate root causes, optimize processes and thereby reduce or minimize the impact of variation in the products, processes, and services. Variation causes uncertainty, risk, and potential defects.

With the use of the Scrum in software development the aim is to achieve productivity and quality of the process. For assessing productivity in software development, one must consider the time spent on activities such as coding, testing, bug fixes and deployment of software solution. When assessing the productivity indicator, it is important to consider its relationship with quality. For example, non-compliance, of delivered product, with defined quality standards, result in new tasks for corrections and, consequently, the extension of the development time in order to obtain the intended quality levels.

At the end of a Sprint, the review and retrospective meetings serve as input for the identification of tasks, as well as positive and negative aspects of the Sprint. The results of those meetings are inputs for the use of techniques from LSS, to attain the performance indicators specified by the client. Based on these results, the causes and effects of faults are identified, prioritized and measures with techniques from LSS. The measurements performed are inputs to statistical analyses leading to the definition of more effective action plans. Through the implementation of these plans, the processes are set by enabling continuous improvement and the progressive alignment of performance and quality to the needs and expectations of the customer for the Sprints. The Product Backlog integrates the requirements related with improvements, identified as result of the Sprints, as well as the set of items resulting from the application of the techniques from LSS methodology, during the Sprints.

The integration of the LSS and Scrum intends, through the DMAIC cycle, to contribute for the improvement of productivity and quality indicators of the process undertaken by the Scrum [5]. The set of techniques of LSS methodology suggested to be used in the Sprint, are the following:

Define: (1) inclusion, on the terms of the contract, of the scope and objectives of the use of the LSS, assessment of the associated financial impacts, and definition of the LSS functions of team members alignment with the project; (2) initial assessment of the performance indicator, using descriptive statistics as the baseline of the problem.

Measure: (1) the SIPOC diagram is used to identify the relevant elements of the project for improvement before starting work; (2) each process object of Sprint should be mapped and documented, by including inputs and outputs, the tasks involved, the people accountable, the time spent in the activities, and the granular procedures that are part of these activities; (3) build an cause and effect diagram and analysis for the issues of the process pointed out during the Sprint, Daily Scrum, review and retrospective meetings. In addition to this analysis, map also the relationships between causes and activities, as well as inputs and outputs of the development process; (4) the cause and effect matrix is used to list and prioritize the inputs of the process with the customer's requirements, based on process maps. The purpose of the matrix is to show the process entries that are associated with the characteristics of quality, to assist in the identification of critical inputs; (5) the effort and impact matrix is used for a cost-benefit analysis and prioritization of tasks based on customer's requirements. The matrix is built through the evaluation of the impact on the result of the performance indicator compared to the effort required to perform the improvements; (6) assessment of the initial capacity by determining the value of the corresponding process capability sigma and DPMO; (7) evaluation of the measuring and inspection systems which allows the quantification of reliability of data to obtain.

Analyze: (1) the Fault Tree Analysis diagram is used for the analysis of root causes of specific failures; (2) the analysis of the critical inputs of processes can be made using, for example, regression analysis to model the relationship between two or more variables. The correlation coefficient can explain the degree by which an independent variable explains the variation of dependent variable, and whether the association between the variables is positive or negative.

Improve: (1) build an action plan, for identification of actions, during the Daily Scrum, review and retrospective meetings of the team; (2) update the initial SIPOC considering the implementation of the action plan; (3) update the process map after the implementation of the action plan; (4) the effectiveness of performed actions of improvement is assessed by the final capability of processes.

Control: Build the control plan from the analyses of critical inputs, that really impact on the result of the performance indicator, then transfer the monitoring of the improvements made to the people responsible for the processes.

In order to achieve the proposed integration, the procedures from LSS to be undertaken by Scrum are of the following:

- *Perform the DMAIC cycle of LSS in Sprints*: for each improvement project a Product Backlog is created based on the phases of the DMAIC cycle. The Backlog prioritization can be accomplished based on either users' requirements or analysis of causes of defects/failures of current processes. This analysis enables the prioritization of improvements based on cost-benefit assessment subject to client's needs, undertaken in the current Sprint or future Sprints, in order to achieve productivity and quality gains;
- *Use of process maps in the creation of Sprint Backlogs*: these maps are used in Sprint Backlogs' planning serving as a Work breakdown structure, providing a perspective of the activities that need to be added to the Sprint. The use of these maps allows for the review of processes, the team's training in procedures, assists in the identification of problems, improving internal communication and decreasing the time of Sprints' planning;
- *Identification of causes of defects or faults through the review meetings and retrospectives*: part of the defects or flaws pointed out by team or customer are related to problems in the process. These problems can be analyzed by the team in technical meetings, generating inputs to create cause and effect diagrams. During the analysis of these problems, the use of process maps facilitates the mapping of the causes to the steps and inputs the processes, as well as the identification of critical sources of poor performance of the indicator (e.g. the number of bugs found in the first test cycles);
- *Prioritization of Product Backlogs*: from the analyses carried out with the techniques of the LSS, corrective actions and improvements are prioritized in the Product Backlog by the Product Owner. The prioritization amongst the backlog items for improvements and new developments depend on the decisions of the Product Owner, which need to be aware of the customer needs, the development processes and the techniques of LSS;

- *Use of LSS techniques to improve utilization of the Scrum*: an assessment of the current state of the use of the Scrum is done through a survey to the team and the client. The result of the survey will assist in the identification of strengths and weaknesses. Based on the weak points, improvement projects are defined and initiated.

5 Conclusion

This work intended to integrate the Scrum and Lean Six Sigma methods. By complementing the generic quality procedures of Scrum method with formalized quality measures from LSS in order to improve the efficacy and efficiency of Scrum regarding software development.

The work is developed by describing the fundamentals of the Scrum framework, either in its static perspective, by depicting in a model its main concepts and their relationships, as well as through a dynamic representation of the main activities developed iteratively in Scrum. The same approach was followed to synthetize the fundamentals of the Lean Six Sigma method. The main concepts of this method were also presented through a class model (static perspective) and a process model (dynamic perspective). Those representations of the Scrum framework and Lean Six Sigma method allow the comparison of the approaches in order to supplement the Scrum framework with Lean Six Sigma quality procedures.

The future work intended to perform is the validation, in a real context of a Scrum project, the instantiation of the integrated LSS procedures.

Acknowledgments. This work was supported by Portuguese funds through the Center of Naval Research (CINAV), Portuguese Naval Academy, Portugal.

References

1. Sutherland, J., Schwaber, K.: The scrum guide. The definitive guide to scrum: the rules of the game (2013)
2. Mundra, A., et al.: Practical scrum-scrum team: way to produce successful and quality software. In: Proceedings of 13th International Conference on Computational Science and Its Applications, pp. 119–123. IEEE (2013)
3. Womack, J.P., et al.: Machine That Changed the World. Simon and Schuster, New York (1990)
4. Jugulum, R., Samuel, P.: Design for Lean Six Sigma: A Holistic Approach to Design and Innovation. Wiley, Hoboken (2010)
5. Cunha, T.F.V., et al.: SLeSS: a Scrum and Lean Six Sigma integration approach for the development of software customization for mobile phones. Proceedings of 25th Brazilian Symposium on Software Engineering, pp. 283–292. IEEE (2011)

Hardware and Software System for Hydric Estimation and Crop Irrigation Scheduling

Karen Daza, Jorge Hernandez, and Hector Florez[✉][iD]

Universidad Distrital Francisco Jose de Caldas, Bogotá, Colombia
kgiselledaza@gmail.com, jehernandezrodriguez@gmail.com,
haflorezf@udistrital.edu.co

Abstract. In hydroponic crops located in underdeveloped countries, the hydric estimation is usually done manually and empirically; however, based on tropical climate, the ideal factors regarding temperature and humidity for each plant can be different. Thus, hydric estimation must be different depending on the plants because it depends on the plants species, type of soil, variety in the diameter of the roots, among others. Therefore, the hydric estimation must be done plant by plant in order to achieve a right development of every plant in a desired crop. In this paper, we present an approach based on software and hardware components integration, which is able to calculate the crops evapotranspiration and to make hydric estimation based on the ideal factors of each plant and the experimental data collected from each species in order to minimize the use of water in irrigation processes and to ensure the right development of plans.

Keywords: Hydric estimation · Crop irrigation ·
Hardware and software

1 Introduction

Agriculture has a fundamental role in the economic development of underdeveloped countries, where the main function is focused on providing food and the necessary resources for the development of other activities. The study and contributions made in this field are very important for countries in order to have the possibility of excelling in the production and export of agricultural products. Then, the control of the water allows the diversification of crops, stabilizes and increases their performance allowing more seasons of good harvests. Moreover, improved water control enables crop diversification, stabilizes and increases crop yields, and enables more cropping seasons [8].

Most crops do not have intelligent irrigation systems, which decreases the probability of finding a system to measure the hydric need of each plant taking into account their ideal factors such as soil temperature and humidity. This

© Springer Nature Switzerland AG 2019
S. Misra et al. (Eds.): ICCSA 2019, LNCS 11623, pp. 150–165, 2019.
https://doi.org/10.1007/978-3-030-24308-1_13

causes that the irrigation is done sporadically wasting large amounts of water. Depending on the type of crop or species, the amount of water needed tends to vary; then, sometimes the soil absorbs the greatest amount of liquid, since plants have a certain time to absorb what is necessary for their development.

When irrigation is done manually, water dissipation is high because usually this process is done until the soil has a large quantity of liquid. However, not all chemical processes in plants are the same due to some of them absorb water faster than others. For the case of hydroponic crops, which in most cases are urban crops, normally people do not have the necessary time or knowledge to perform the proper calculation that integrates the necessary factors to validate the water needs for each plant, which would affect the crop by lack or excess of water.

We think it is important to contribute to agricultural development through automation. Then, we intend to reduce water consumption in crops based on automated processes. With this in mind, based on this work, we provide farmers of hydroponic crops a tool for calculating the amount of water and the scheduling irrigation plant by plant. As a result, throughout the development of the harvest, the irrigation becomes an automatic process, which is monitored by farmers. In addition, for each plant, farmers can adjust attributes in the configuration of the system in order to optimize the estimation.

The paper is structured as follows. Section 2 presents the main concepts of crop irrigation. Section 3 presents the related work. In Sect. 4, we illustrate the proposed approach. Section 5 presents the results. Finally, Sect. 6 concludes the paper.

2   Crop Irrigation

Irrigation is the watering of land by artificial methods. Without irrigation, agriculture is limited by the availability and reliability of naturally occurring water from floods or rain. There are different types of irrigation to perform this function. For instance, by drip, by sprinkler, and by microject. Each one has a characteristic that makes it the most effective method according to the crop features. Nevertheless, in most cases, surface drip method required less water [4].

2.1   Hydroponic Crops

A hydroponic crop is the combination of different methods to replace the soil. The technology reduces land requirements for crops by 75% or more, and water use by 90%. Crop nutrients are contained and recycled; then, no residual salts are lost to environment. In addition, herbicides use is non-existent as well as pesticides are natural vegetable sprays and barriers [3].

2.2   Evapotranspiration

Evapotranspiration (ET) is the combination of two separated processes: evaporation and transpiration. The ET is calculated to determine the exact amount of water that is being lost in the atmosphere. On the one hand, evaporation is the process whereby liquid water is converted to steam and removed from the evaporating surface. The water evaporates from surfaces such as rivers, lakes, vegetation, or even the pavement. On the other hand, the transpiration consists of the vaporization of liquid water contained in plant tissues [2]

ET is expressed in millimeters (mm) per unit of time and indicates the water lost in a cultivated area. Table 1 shows the factors that influence the ET, which are the climatic variables, the types of crops, and the environmental conditions of the land.

Table 1. Factors that influence ET

Factor	Description
Climate variables	Radiation, air temperature, atmospheric humidity, and wind speed
Crop	The type of crop and the stage of development must be considered when it is about estimating evapotranspiration
Environmental conditions	Low soil fertility, limited use of fertilizers, diseases and soil parasites can limit the development of the crop and reduce ET

Reference crop ET (ETo) is the rate of evapotranspiration from a hypothetical reference crop with an assumed crop height of 0.12 m (4.72 in), a fixed surface resistance of $70 \, \text{s} \, \text{m}^{-1}$ ($70 \, \text{s} \, 3.2 \, \text{ft}^{-1}$) and an albedo of 0.23, closely resembling the evapotranspiration from an extensive surface of green grass of uniform height, actively growing, well-watered, and completely shading the ground [7].

In addition, The relation between ETo and ET with a certain surface allows making the relation with other surfaces by removing the process of defining the ET level for each crop and period. Then, it is important to study the rate of ET in the atmosphere regardless of the type of crop and stage considering that the crop does not have water stress or diseases

The following concepts are required for the calculation of ETo.

- **Average temperature of the environment** (T_{hr}). It is the average between the maximum and the minimum air temperature observed during a period of 24 h.
- **Saturation pressure of steam at air temperature** $(e^0(T_{hr}))$. It is the pressure of the gaseous phase for a temperature, in which the liquid water and the steam are in dynamic equilibrium.
- **Saturation pressure of steam** (e_s). It is the average of the vapor saturation pressure at maximum temperature and the vapor saturation pressure at minimum average air temperature

- **Relative Humidity** (HR). It is the division between the amount of water that the air has at certain temperature and the amount of water that it could contain if it is saturated at the same temperature.
- **Actual steam pressure derived from the temperature of the dew point** (T_d). It is the steam saturation pressure at the dew point temperature due the dew point temperature is the temperature that air needs to be cooled in order to be saturated.
- **Slope of steam pressure curve** (Δ). It is the the ratio between the saturation pressure of steam and the temperature.
- **Atmospheric pressure** (p): It is the pressure exerted by the weight of the earth's atmosphere, which is is expressed in kilo pascals (kPa).
- **Latent heat of vaporization** (L_v): It is the energy required to change a mass of liquid water unit to water steam under constant pressure and temperature.
- **Psychometric constant** (γ): It represents the air as the mixture of two gases that do not react with each other and behave almost like two ideal gases: dry air and water steam.
- **Wind speed in relation to height** (U_2): For computing the evapotranspiration and determining how it varies in time, it is necessary to express it as the average over a certain interval of time based on the wind speed.
- **Extraterrestrial radiation** (R_a): It is the daily solar radiation that is received on a horizontal surface located at the upper limit of the atmosphere.
- **Solar radiation** (R_s): It is the energy coming from the sun, which is provided by the reactions of the hydrogen in the nucleus of the sun by nuclear fusion and emitted by the solar surface.
- **Net solar radiation or long wave** (Rl_N): The amount of long wave energy emission is proportional to the absolute temperature of the surface raised to the fourth power. The net energy flow that leaves the earth's surface is less than the calculated and given by the Stefan-Boltzmann law due to the absorption and radiation returned from the sky.
- **Net radiation** (R_n): It represents the sum of all contributions of short and long-wave radiation flows that enter and leave the surface.
- **Density of soil heat flow** (G): It measures the amount of energy transferred through the soil. Since the heat flux of the soil is small compared to the net radiation and for time periods G, it is estimated because when the soil heats, it depends on the net radiation.

ET of the crop under standard conditions (ETc) is the calculation of the ET of any crop when it has optimal soil conditions, abundant fertilizer, and without diseases. It is calculated from climatological data

2.3   Hydric Estimation

It is the process of subtracting the outputs and adding the water inputs. The inputs are: precipitation, amount of water in the previous irrigation, capillary ascent, and superficial inlet drainage. The outputs consist of ET, percolation losses, and output drainage. The soil water balance is calculated in the Decision Support System for Agrotechnology Transfer (DSSAT) [6] based on crop models in order to evaluate the possible yield reduction caused by soil and plant water deficits [10].

3   Related Work

For the design of crop irrigation systems it is necessary to analyze the context. The peak irrigation requirement for a project or farm will depend on both the pattern of the reference ET rate and the distribution of the crop coefficient curves for the crops of interest during the growing season [10].

Zhang et al., [14] built a hardware and software scheme for the calculation in real time of ET and automatic irrigation based on the period of the crop and climatic data. To obtain them, a hardware component that sends the data to a watering server was installed. The controller in the crop determines the moment of the irrigation and performs the calculations for the water balance according to the time of harvest and the ET obtained. Our approach does not measure the factors by crop, but it does by plant, which is better for the crop.

Shah et al., [11] created a network of wireless sensors (WSN) for the harvesting grapes. The main reason for this study is to relate the requirements of optimal irrigation in terms of water savings. Sensors were deployed at a grid of 30 m by 30 m. Each node was able to transmit/receive packets to other nodes inside a well-defined transmission range of 30 m. The network collects data on humidity and PH of the soil, environment temperature, and humidity. Based on the information of said variables, decision making is made at a central node. However, in hydroponic crops there is no natural soil to optimally install a sensor mesh; then, our approach uses sensors that can go to each plant in the crop.

In Umair et al., [13], authors describe an approach for irrigation based on an artificial neural network as a control unit. Inputs of sensors located in the crop feed the network. The main function of this is to maintain the ideal moisture in front of to the real humidity of the soil. They conclude that the project fails due to limitations in the controller.

Zheng et al., [15] performed a hardware and software architecture, where installed subnodes operate through a web platform. The cloud server makes connections with the controlling subnode every minute and inquires the latest unexecuted controlling instructions, which are sent by the cloud server to the subnode. Daily, the system recompile the data stored for the calculation of ET and water balance. The hydric estimation is done by harvest and not by plant as we are considering in this project.

Shamshirband et al., [12] calculated evapotranspiration using the cuckoo search algorithm (CSA) using climate data against four ANN computer models: ANN, ANN CSA, ANFIS, and ANFIS CSA. They successfully established that the optimized version of ANFIS using CSA has better results than the ANFIS model in the training and testing phases for calculating the ETo.

4   Proposed Approach

In this project, we proposed an approach based on the integration of hardware and software components through a communications flow. A prototype was created in order to access to each plant of the crop through a coordinate system allowing accessing to every plant in real time. It performs the process for water estimation taking into account the temperature, plant humidity, crop ET, ideal factors of the plant, and the floor space for each plant.

4.1   System Architecture

Our solution consists in an environment made up of several hardware and software artifacts. Each artifact has a main function and a direct communication with another artifact. The architecture is presented in Fig. 1. It includes four artifacts: central system, client application, master component, and slave component.

- **Central system.** It has the process for sending requests to the master component. It consists in searching the plants with programmed irrigation during the day. Based on this, it sends a request to the slave component to measure temperatures and humidity to calculate the ET.

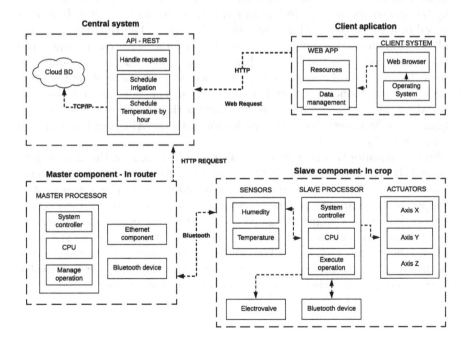

Fig. 1. System architecture

This environment consists of two components, the API-REST developed with the loopback framework for Node.js[1], which has communication through TCP/IP protocol to the second components that is a non-relational database created in MongoDB[2] that stores the information from sensors, irrigation, data of the plants, and data of farmers.

In addition, the API-REST manages three modules: (a) *handle request*, which is a listener that responds the requests of the clients, (b) *schedule irrigation*, which is a process that obtains the necessary data to sort the humidity measures and generates the corresponding irrigation to the plants of the crop, and (c) *schedule temperature by hour*, where the request is sent to the master component to take the room temperature every hour throughout the day.

- **Client application.** It is the interface for the farmer to consult the quantity of water irrigated to each plant, to create plants, and to sort irrigation. This interface has been developed with the framework Vue.js[3], which provides a web application deployed in a web browser and manages the data. Finally, it provides the necessary resources for the services of the system such as (a) management of ideal factors of each plant, (b) validation of positions for irrigation and humidity, (c) search of plants to order irrigation at any moment, (d) configuration of crop data, and (e) irrigation control for each plant per month and per day.

- **Master component.** It constantly queries the API-REST for the not performed operations and sends this data to the slave component. It is supported by the master processor, which is an arduino located in the router. It is composed of a Bluetooth module and arduino Ethernet. The Bluetooth module allows communication between the master and the slave components. For this communications the Bluetooth module was selected for two main reasons. The former is because the slave component must move along the crop; thus, a wired connection would limit its movement. The latter is because based on the arduino architecture, the Bluetooth connection is easy to configure. The Ethernet allows communication with the API-REST in order to find new tasks.

- **Slave component.** It is in the crop waiting for tasks sent by the master component. Based on the received data, its functions are: go to the plant, perform moisture-temperature measurement, and irrigate plants. This component is supported by an arduino for the execution of operations. The software core is designed to execute an incoming operation and send a response to the master component. The actuator component consists of three axes (x, y, z) for the movement towards each plant. The control system converts the analog signals of the humidity and temperature sensors into digital signals. The electrovalve is operated by time, when the operation is to irrigate a plant.

---

[1] https://nodejs.org/en/.
[2] https://www.mongodb.com/.
[3] https://vuejs.org/.

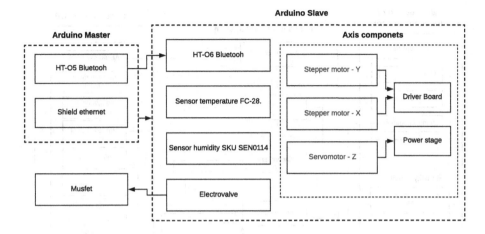

Fig. 2. Hardware subsystem architecture

Electronic Prototype. The electronic prototype is a hardware system that integrates several electronic devices. Mainly, it includes the arduino in the slave component, which operates at 5 V, in which two sensors are implemented: humidity *FC-28* and temperature *DHT11*. In addition, a Bluetooth device *HC-06*, which will sends information and receives requests. The prototype also includes two steeper motors that work at 12 V for x-axis and y-axis. They move the device to the desired position. Moreover, it includes a servomotor for the z-axis. Finally, there is an electrovalve that works at 12 V. On the other side, we have the arduino in the master component, which works at 5 V, in which an Ethernet is implemented for connecting to internet and receiving API-REST requests that will be sent through the Bluetooth device *HC-05*. Figure 2 presents the described hardware architecture.

4.2 Hydric Balance Process

In order to irrigate every plant of the crop, the system must obtain the necessary parameters for the hydraulic need, presented in Fig. 3, which has three elements: data required of measurements DB sensors, data required DB, and process in central system.

Data Required DB. This element is a database that stores all parameters of the crop, plant, and irrigation in order to provide all required information for calculating the amount of water needed by each plant in the irrigation process.

Data Required Measurements Sensors DB. These element is used to store the information obtained by the readings based on the sensors installed in the hardware. Sensors are able to read temperature and humidity for each plant in the crop.

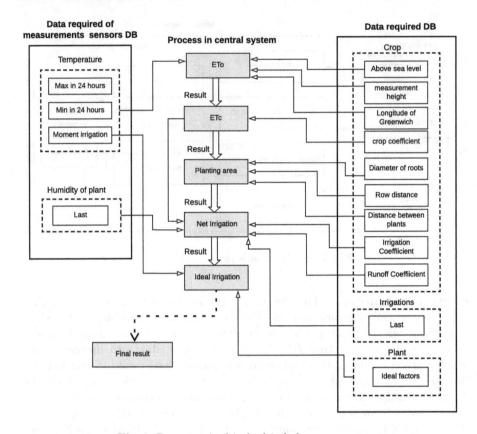

Fig. 3. Data required in hydric balance process

Process in Central System. This element consists of a flow of sub-processes for making calculations based on some input variables in order to obtain an output. These sub-processes are:

– **Evapotranspiration reference ETo**: It is the first sub-process to be carried out. It consists of four inputs and one output, which is the ETo. Equation 1, which is FAO Penman-Monteith [16], was implemented for time periods.

$$ET_0 = \frac{0,48\Delta(R_n - G) + \gamma\frac{37}{Thr+273}u_2(e^0(T_{hr}) - e_a)}{\Delta + \gamma(1 + 0,34u_2)} \tag{1}$$

where:

ET_o	Reference evapotranspiration (mm hour^{-1})
T_{hr}	Air temperature in one hour (°C)
G	Density of heat flow in the soil (MJ m^{-2} hour^{-1})
R_n	Net radiation of the crop surface (MJ m^{-2} hour^{-1})
γ	Psychometric constant (kPa °C^{-1})
Δ	Slope of the steam precision curve (kPa °C^{-1})

U_2 Wind speed at a height (ms^{-1})
$e^0(T_{hr})$ Pressure of vapor saturation at air temperature (kPa)
e_a Real steam pressure (kPa)

The temperatures Max - Min are used to calculate Thr. Based on that, we can calculate $e^0(T_{hr})$, the *saturation pressure* (e_s), and also the *steam pressure* $(e_s - e_a)$. From this, the average temperature is used to calculate the slope of the steam precision curve (Δ). In order to calculate whether data that depend on the location of the crop, the information in the database regarding sea level and longitude-latitude coordinates are used. Based on this information, we can also calculate the *extraterrestrial radiation* (R_a). Finally the ETo is calculated.

- **Evapotranspiration of the crop under standard conditions ETc:** It refers to the crop with the following conditions: no environmental factors, good fertilization, and good conditions for crop development. Then, the input *crop coefficient* (K_c) is used to relate the ETo with the ETc, which generates an output that corresponds to ETc.
- **Planting area:** It is the third process of water balance, which consists of three inputs and one output. The first input is *Diameter of roots* (r) used to determine the floor area used by each plant. The second input is *Row distance* (dh), which is the distance covered by each row. The third input is *Distance between plants* (dpl), which defines the distance between plants in the row. Based on these, the result of the planting area is generated.
- **Net irrigation:** The fourth process consists of five inputs. The first input comes from ETc, which in the water balance is the main loss of water. The second input is last of humidity, which is obtained from the prototype before calculating the irrigation. Based on this, the calculation of the Eto is validated. The third input is *irrigation coefficient* (K_r), which determines the performance, transportation, and failures in the irrigation. The fourth input is *Runoff coefficient* (K_e), which is related to the *precipitation* (P) of rain that the crop has had as an additional water gain. The last input is last irrigation, which is the last amount of water applied.
- **Ideal irrigation:** It is the fifth process to perform. It consists of two inputs: the first input is the temperature at the time of irrigation and the second input is ideal factors stored by plant (humidity, temperature and amount of water). Based on them, we know wheather or not the plant is in condition to receive irrigation.
- **Final result:** If it is necessary to water the plant, the final result is the calculation of time in which the device will irrigate. It is determined with the volume of the hose and according to the flow or quantity of water calculated in the previous steps.

4.3 System Coordinates

The device makes two displacements for calculating the water balance. The first displacement is made to read the humidity of the plant, while the second displacement is made at the time of irrigation. In the crop, each plant has a dropper,

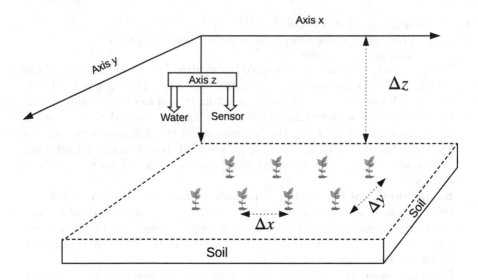

Fig. 4. Coordinate system in the crop.

where the water is deposited to perform the drip irrigation. There are three axes (x, y, z), where Axes x, y are used for the displacement Δx and Δy respectively. The axis z is used to irrigate. Figure 4 presents the Cartesian plane implemented in the crop. It illustrates two elements for the axis z: the first one is the electrovalve for the irrigation and the second one is the humidity sensor.

4.4   Communication

The client application has a direct communication to the central system. Master and slave components communicate through Bluetooth using a data format created for this project in order to avoid data loss. Then, when the master sends information to the slave, the slave produces a response and viceversa; nevertheless, if the master or the slave go offline, the response is not received; then, the action is sent again and when the offline device goes online they recover the communication.

The central system responses using JSON format. Then, each component has a process to generate this format depending on the type of the response requested. The fundamental part of the project is in the communication between the master and the slave components. The master component is constantly consulting the API-REST as well as the operations that are carried out in the future. Table 2 presents the data that the master must send to the slave to perform the operation depending on the type, i.e., humidity reading, temperature reading, go to plant or make irrigation. Once data is sent to the slave, it returns the responses of the response slave column.

Table 2. Data between Master slave

Operation (op)	Data	Response slave
Temperature	type op	Measurement temperature
Humidity	type op, Pos x, Pos y	Measurement humidity
Go to plant	type op, Pos x, Pos y	Ok
Irrigation	type op, Pos x, Pos y, Time irrigation	Volume water

5 Results

We performed a case study, which correspond to the implementation of the system in one crop established in Bogota, Colombia, located at the coordinates: North Latitude: $4^o35'56''$ and West Longitude: $74^o04'51''$. The temperatures from December to March are high, but from April to October are lower. The height at sea level is 2.625 m. Tomato was taken as a study crop. The relative humidity ranges was between 70% and 80%. Root length density ranged was between 0.5 cm and 1.5 cm [9]. The ideal tomato temperature can be divided into three stages:

- Germination. According to [1], the temperature for germination is between 16 and 30 °C.
- Growth development. According to [1], the temperature for growth development is between 12 and 30 °C.
- Fructification. The ideal temperature is between 15 and 22 °C.

Then, in general, the values between 18.3 and 32.2 °C were considered ideal air temperatures for tomato during the growing season [5].

We tested the system in a crop composed of thirty plants. The distance between rows was 0.7 m and the distance between plants was 0.4 m. The crop was observed from the day 55 for the fructification stage. We studied ten plants of the thirty plants of the crop. Five plants were irrigated using the system, while other five plants were irrigated manually. During 30 days the system made the water balance for the five selected plants and manual irrigation was carried out for other plants. The irrigation was done every day at 6:00 am by drip establishing different water levels.

Humidity is measured from 0% to 100%, where 0% means that the soil is completely dry and 100% is completely wet. Throughout the process of plant development, humidity must be maintained between 40% and 70% as ideal factor.

On the one hand, Fig. 5 shows the humidity of the five plants irrigated manually, where the highest humidity was 98% achieved by the plants 2 and 3, while the lowest humidity was 0.3% achieved by the plant 3. On the other hand, Fig. 6 shows the humidity of the five plants irrigated by the system, where the highest humidity was 71.76% achieved by the plant 5, while the lowest humidity was 39.63% also achieved by the plant 5.

With this in mind, we can observe that the humidity levels for the plants irrigated by the system are in almost all cases between the ideal factors i.e.,

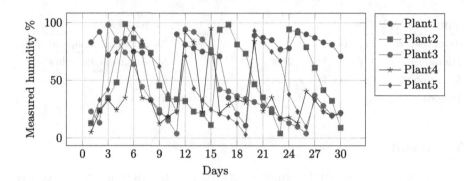

Fig. 5. Humidity measured in plants irrigated manually

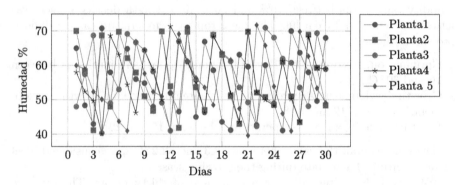

Fig. 6. Humidity measured in plants irrigated with the system

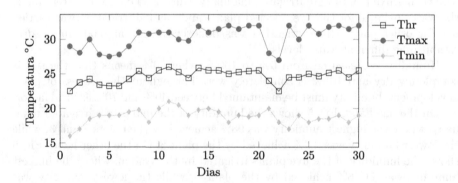

Fig. 7. Experimental temperature readings.

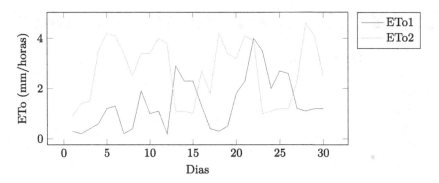

Fig. 8. Experimental data ETo.

between 40% and 70%, while the humidity levels for the plants irrigated manually are out of the ideal factors. Thus, based on the experimentation and the corresponding results, the system ensures a better irrigation process and also saving water in the crop.

In addition, Fig. 7 presents the average (*Thr*), minimum (*Tmin*) and maximum (*Tmax*) temperature per day for this period of time. These readings were obtained by the sensor installed in the prototype. Thus, the temperature oscillates between 32.00 and 16.00 °C.

Figure 8 presents the *ETo* readings in two time ranges: 06.00–07.00 (ETo1) and 14.00–15.00 (ETo2) during the thirty days. These results were dependent on *Thr* according to the min and max temperature readings 24 hours back. Then, in the crop the *Eto2* was higher in the days 1 to 13, 16 to 21 and 28 to 30. For *Eto1* it oscillated between 0.2 to 4.0 (mm/hour) and for *Eto2* it had a variation between 0.9 to 4.6 (mm/hour).

5.1 Information System

We developed a information system called *RIWA*. It reports the amount of water to each selected plant. In addition, it shows the name of the plant to which the ET calculation is made, the humidity, and the temperature at the moment of irrigation. It also informs the date in which the process was done, as shown in Fig. 9

In addition, *RIWA* allows creating the plants that are in the crop and those that the farmer wants to add. Each plant includes the attributes: name, species, alias, ideal factors such as temperature, humidity, and the amount of water. Moreover, we can simulate a crop in the system, where we can locate the plants in the area.

For the information system, we used Node.js for two reasons: it executes asynchronous processes for each operation in irrigation scheduling after saving data in order to allow the master component order operations with these values and it pulls out data in JSON format from requests HTTP in components communication.

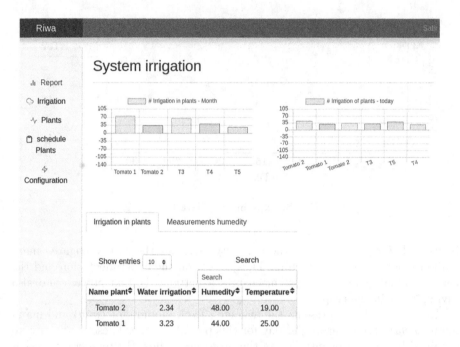

Fig. 9. Irrigation report

6   Conclusions

Based on the hardware and software system proposed, farmers can have an important tool to control the irrigation of a crop. In addition, this project facilitates the work of the farmers, since they do not have to develop the irrigation activity empirically because the prototype allows scheduling irrigation.

Using the input data, farmers can calibrate the irrigation estimate plant by plant. For the given temperatures and data of the crop, the *ETo* oscillated between 0.2 and 4.6 (mm/hour), the humidity of the plants under study was between 40% and 70%, which is considered optimal for their development. The water applied to all plants had a common margin of 2%. We think it was because they are all of the same species and ground. For future studies, it is necessary to carry out tests with different kinds of plants and soil, increase the distance between plants and rows in order to have a wider margin to irrigate plant by plant.

The experiments results allow concluding that irrigation is better in the morning when the temperatures is lower because it uses less water due to water loss by evapotranspiration ETo is lower.

References

1. Adams, S., Cockshull, K., Cave, C.: Effect of temperature on the growth and development of tomato fruits. Ann. Bot. **88**(5), 869–877 (2001)
2. Allen, R., Pereira, L., Raes, D., Smith, M.: Guidelines for computing crop water requirements. Geophysics **156**, 178 (1998)
3. Bradley, P., Marulanda, C.: Simplified hydroponics to reduce global hunger. In: World Congress on Soilless Culture: Agriculture in the Coming Millennium, vol. 554, pp. 289–296 (2000)
4. Camp, C.: Subsurface drip irrigation: a review. Trans. ASAE **41**(5), 1353 (1998)
5. Everhart, C.: The complete guide to growing tomatoes: a complete step-by-step guide including heirloom tomatoes (back-to-basics gardening) (2010)
6. Hoogenboom, G., et al.: Decision support system for agrotechnology transfer version 4.0. University of Hawaii, Honolulu, HI (2004). (CD-ROM)
7. Irmak, S., Haman, D.Z.: Evapotranspiration: potential or reference. IFAS Extension, ABE **343**, 1–3 (2003)
8. Joe Stevens, B.K.: Trends and outlook: agricultural water management in Southern Africa country report South Africa, pp. 10–18. International Water Management Institute (2015)
9. Machado, R.M., Maria do Rosàrio, G.O.: Tomato root distribution, yield and fruit quality under different subsurface drip irrigation regimes and depths. Irrig. Sci. **24**(1), 15–24 (2005)
10. Ritchie, J.: Soil water balance and plant water stress. In: Tsuji, G.Y., Hoogenboom, G., Thornton, P.K. (eds.) Understanding Options for Agricultural Production, vol. 7, pp. 41–54. Springer, Dordrecht (1998). https://doi.org/10.1007/978-94-017-3624-4_3
11. Shah, N., Das, I.: Precision irrigation sensor network based irrigation. In: Problems, Perspectives and Challenges of Agricultural Water Management, pp. 217–232. InTech, Rijeka (2012)
12. Shamshirband, S., et al.: Estimation of reference evapotranspiration using neural networks and cuckoo search algorithm. Am. Soc. Civ. Eng. **142**(2), 1–12 (2015)
13. Umair, S.M., Usman, R.: Automation of irrigation system using ANN based controller. Int. J. Electr. Comput. Sci. IJECS-IJENS **10**(02), 41–47 (2010)
14. Zhang, S., Wang, M., Shi, W., Zheng, W.: Construction of intelligent water saving irrigation control system based on water balance. IFAC-PapersOnLine **51**(17), 466–471 (2018)
15. Zheng, Q., Zhu, F., Mao, C., Lv, X.: A smart irrigation decision support system based on cloud, pp. 1–10. Undergraduate, Hohai University, Nanjing, China (2014)
16. Zotarelli, L., Dukes, M.D., Romero, C.C., Migliaccio, K.W., Morgan, K.T.: Step by step calculation of the penman-monteith evapotranspiration (fao-56 method). Institute of Food and Agricultural Sciences, University of Florida (2010)

Electronic Medical Information Encryption Using Modified Blowfish Algorithm

Noah Oluwatobi Akande[1]([✉]), Christiana Oluwakemi Abikoye[2],
Marion Olubunmi Adebiyi[3], Anthonia Aderonke Kayode[1],
Adekanmi Adeyinka Adegun[4], and Roseline Oluwaseun Ogundokun[1]

[1] Data and Information Security Research Group,
Computer Science Department, Landmark University,
Omu-Aran, Kwara, Nigeria
akande.noah@lmu.edu.ng
[2] Computer Science Department, University of Ilorin, Ilorin, Kwara, Nigeria
[3] Department of Computer and Information Sciences,
Covenant University, Ota, Nigeria
[4] Discipline of Computer Science,
University of Kwazulu-Natal, Durban, South Africa

Abstract. Security and privacy of patients' information remains a major issue of concern among health practitioners. Therefore, measures must be put in place to ensure that unauthorized individual do not have access to this information. However, the adoption of digital alternative of retrieving and documenting medical information has further opened it up to more attacks. This article presents a modified blowfish algorithm for securing textual and graphical medical information. The F-function used in generating round sub-keys was strengthened so as to produce a strong key that could resist differential attacks. Number of Pixel Change Rate (NPCR) and Unified Average Changing Intensity (UACI) of 98.85% and 33.65% revealed that the modified algorithm is sensitive to changes in its key and also resistive to differential attacks. Furthermore, the modified algorithm demonstrated a better encryption and decryption time than the existing blowfish algorithm.

Keywords: Data and information security · Decryption · Encryption ·
Medical information security · Modified blowfish algorithm

1 Introduction

The advancement in Information and Communication Technologies (ICT) have caused a major shift from traditional means of medical information archiving to the electronic or digital alternative. Electronic Medical Information (EMI) entails the use of state-of-the-art ICT tools in retrieving the needed information about a patients' health condition with a view to facilitate a faster, easier, efficient and cost effective healthcare practices. While a vast majority of patients want to use digital devices to monitor their health conditions, medical practitioners also believe that EMI will facilitate effective sharing of medical information among medical practitioners and health care information technology systems without location being a barrier [14]. However, the use of these

© Springer Nature Switzerland AG 2019
S. Misra et al. (Eds.): ICCSA 2019, LNCS 11623, pp. 166–179, 2019.
https://doi.org/10.1007/978-3-030-24308-1_14

ICT tools has raised security concerns about the confidentiality, integrity and availability of EMI. The content and nature of data available in health care industries have made them vulnerable to theft and data fraud [16]. A KPMG survey reported that 81% of 223 US healthcare organizations and 110 million patients in the US had their data breached in 2015 [18]. Despite the massive threats recorded by healthcare industries across the world in 2016, 95% of healthcare organizations still do not use any software for information security governance or risk management [24]. Therefore, healthcare sector faces a larger attacks and threats than other sectors perhaps for financial gains, political interest or to expose security flaws [22]. In addition, the effect of this security breach is not limited to patients' and medical personnel's psychological distress but could also result in financial loss and reputation harm [12, 28]. Though authors [20] and [32] identified Denial of Service (DoS), ransomware, malware, cryptographic attacks, privilege escalation, injection and web security exploits as some of the techniques used by attackers to infiltrate EMI, new techniques are being employed daily. Therefore, authors in [1] opined that the most effective way to secure data from attackers is to either protect the medium through which information is being sent or to put measures in place to secure the actual information being sent. To this effect, the use of biometrics, encryption, firewalls and smartcards as some security techniques that could be used to secure EMI was proposed in [3]. However, according to [30], the best approach to securing EMI is via cryptographic techniques. Leveraging on this, a modified blowfish cryptographic algorithm for encrypting and decrypting EMI is proposed in this research. Blowfish is one of the symmetric cryptographic techniques which has been widely employed to secure data. As an unpatented and license-free encryption algorithm, blowfish is known to be the fastest and simplest symmetric cryptographic algorithm [9, 19]. However, in addition to blowfish being best appropriate for instances where the key remains constant [27], it does not provide authentication and non-repudiation [10]. Blowfish key generation process depends on its Feistel function (F-Function). The default F–function uses two OR operation and one XOR operation in generating the needed key for each rounds. This article reports a modified blowfish algorithm which is aimed at further strengthening the weak keys limitation of blowfish algorithm. This was achieved by replacing the existing blowfish F-Function which uses use two XOR and one OR operation with a F-function that uses two XOR and one OR operation.

2 Existing Blowfish Algorithm

Traditional blowfish algorithm is a 64-bit symmetric block cipher that encodes an input plaintext one block at a time. As a symmetric cryptographic algorithm, the same key length that ranges from 32 bits to 448 bits is used for both encryption and decryption. The cryptographic process of blowfish algorithm majorly involves data encryption and key expansion [15, 29]. The data encryption is achieved with a 16-round Feistel network which splits the input data block into two equal halves before carrying out encryption in multiple rounds. Furthermore, the key expansion involves the use of four 32 bits S-boxes and a P-array that comprises of eighteen 32-bit sub-keys which are generated before the data encryption and decryption [2]. For the sub-key generation, blowfish algorithm uses a F-function; this splits a 32-bit plaintext into four equal parts. Each 8-bit sub-division is then converted into a 32-bit data stream using the S-box. The resultant 32-bit data from each 8-bit sub-division is finally XORed together to produce the final 32-bits output. This shows that the F-function is an integral part of the blowfish encryption and decryption process. The F-function used for sub-key generation is shown in Fig. 1:

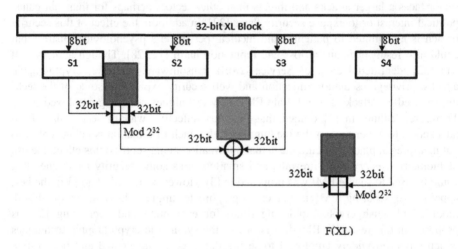

Fig. 1. Existing blowfish function F

Similarly, the algorithm below is used for the sub-keys generation:

(a) start
(b) Set the P-array to be empty then assign a fixed string to the four S-boxes. The strings are made up of hexadecimal digits: P1 = 0x243f6a88, P2 = 0x85a308d3, P3 = 0x13198a2e, P4 = 0x03707344, etc.
(c) Carry out a XOR operation between P1 and the first 32 bits of the key, P2 and the second 32-bits of the key until all the bits of the whole P-array has been XORed.
(d) Using subkeys generated in (c), encrypt all-zero strings with blowfish algorithm.
(e) Replace P1 and P2 with the result generated in (d).
(f) Use Blowfish algorithm to encrypt the output of (d) with the modified subkeys generated in (c)
(g) Replace P3 and P4 with the result generated in (f).
(h) repeat this process until all entries in P array has been changed.
(i) Stop

2.1 Encryption and Decryption

The main goal of blowfish algorithm is to make a message undecipherable by a third party, this is called encryption while decryption attempts to restore an encrypted message back to its original state. The encryption and decryption process are similar except that the P-arrays (P0, P1 ... P17) are used in reverse during the decryption process. However, the key used for encryption remains unchanged and are still used for the decryption process. The pseudocode for blowfish encryption is given as:

Step 1: Split the input 64bit data into xL and xR where each half contains 32-bit half data

Step 2: Repeat steps (a) to (c) while i = 1 to16

(a) Carry out XOR operation between xL and P[i].

(b) Compute the F-function of xL such that:

$$F(xL) = ((S_1 + S_2, \bmod 2^{32}) \text{ xor } S_3) + S_4, \bmod 2^{32}$$

(c) XOR F(xL) with xR.

Step 3: Swap xR and xL.
Step 4: Carry out XOR operation between xR and P[16].
Step 5: Carry out XOR operation between xL and P[17].
Step 6: Merge xR and xL.

The pseudocode for the decryption process is given as:

Step 1: Split the input 64bit data into xL and xR where each half contains 32-bit half data

Step 2: Repeat steps (a) to (c) while i = 16 to1

(a) Carry out XOR operation between xL and P[i].

(b) Compute the F-function of xL such that:

$$F(xL) = ((S_1 + S_2, \bmod 2^{32}) \text{ xor } S_3) + S_4, \bmod 2^{32}$$

(c) XOR F(xL) with xR.

Step 3: Swap xR and xL.
Step 4: Carry out XOR operation between xR and P[1]
Step 5: Carry out XOR operation between xL and P[0].
Step 6: Merge xR and xL.

3   Related Works

Several encryption techniques have been used to secure EMI which could be textual, audio as well as images. Medical image encryption using cosine number transform was proposed by Lima, Madeiro, and Sales [21]. The technique was aimed at correcting rounding-off errors that may cause discrepancies between original and encrypted images. the key sensitivity of the technique was evaluated by attempting to decrypt the cipher with a wrong key that is slightly different from the right one. The number of pixels change rate measured revealed that the image obtained with a wrong key is completely different from the original image. The technique was also shown to be secure against entropy attack as well as known-plaintext and chosen- plaintext attacks. Also, an adaptive medical image encryption technique using an improved chaotic mapping was proposed by Chen and Hu [6]. In addition to securing medical images, the technique was aimed at overcoming the flaws of the existing chaotic image encryption algorithm. Initially, logistic sine chaos mapping was used to scramble the plain image. Afterwards, the scrambled image was divided into 2-by-2 sub blocks before encrypting each sub-block. Information entropy, correlation coefficient, key space analysis and the plaintext sensitivity of the technique revealed that the technique actually overcame the lack of diffusion limitation of existing chaotic image encryption algorithm. A novel way of hiding EMI inside medical images to be encrypted before being transmitted over a network was proposed by Masilamani [23]. Encryption/ decryption and data hiding keys were embedded into a separate block of the secret message before a block-wise image encryption process was used to encrypt the cover image. A trained SVM model was used to extract the secret message along with the keys. The execution time and time complexity measured were on the higher side perhaps due to the complexity of the technique proposed. Ismail, Said, Radwan, Madian, and Abu-elyazeed [13] also proposed a generalized Double Humped (DH) logistic map using Pseudorandom Number Key (PNK) generation. The PNK was used in the encryption of biomedical images before sending them on a network. A very low correlation coefficients obtained from the original and encrypted images confirmed the encryption strength of the proposed technique. Also, the key sensitivity analysis of the encryption technique revealed that it is highly sensitive to every small change in the key parameters.

Furthermore, a two-dimensional (2D) logistic-sine-coupling map image encryption technique was proposed by Hua, Jin, Xu and Huang [11]. The technique designed a permutation algorithm to permutate the image pixels to different rows and columns after which a diffusion algorithm was used to spread the plain-image on the encrypted image. A higher encryption efficiency was recorded when the proposed technique was compared to other encryption techniques. Bai et al. [4] also proposed an encryption technique for securing EMI obtained from patients' Body Area Network (BAN). QRS complex of the electrocardiogram signal was used to extract vital signs from the patients' BAN, these vital signs were used to create the initial key before the key stream was generated using linear feedback shift register. Dynamic key updating and low energy consumption are the major advantages of the proposed technique. Blowfish algorithm has also been widely employed to secure medical images. such could be seen in the works of Kondawar and Gawali [17] who employed blowfish algorithm to secure EMI retrieved from a patient's wearable device. An ARM7 LPC2138 Microcontroller was programmed to synchronize the activities of several sensors connected to it.

However, blowfish algorithm was used to encrypt the retrieved data before forwarding it to the receiver section through the RF module. The secret key used for the encryption and decryption process would have been shared among the authorized medical personnel. Blowfish algorithm was also employed for textual information encryption by Raigoza [31]. The research aimed at determining if the size of original files do change after encryption. Also, they seek to know the point at which the execution time will change when ASCII values of input files change between 32 to 126. Results obtained revealed that the file size remains unchanged after encryption for input strings with lengths in multiples of 16 i.e. 16, 32, 48, 64 etc. Also, encryption and decryption times remains stable when there is a change in ASCII value. Furthermore, Panda [27] also employed blowfish to encrypt binary, text and image input files. Performance evaluation results obtained revealed that encryption time, decryption time and throughput increased with an increase in size when binary, text and image input files were used.

To improve the limitations of existing blowfish algorithm, several attempts at modifying blowfish algorithm have been reported in the literature. Nur, St, Darlis and Si [26] implemented a modified blowfish algorithm on Field-Programmable Gate Array (FPGA) for textual information encryption. The number of rounds required in the existing blowfish algorithm was reduced to 4 and 8 rounds while the key size was changed from 448 bit to 384 bit. Performance evaluation carried out revealed that lesser encryption time was recorded when 4 rounds were used compared to when 8 and 16 rounds were used. Also, lesser encryption rounds yielded greater throughput which means that a high encryption time will yield more throughputs. It was also observed that larger key lengths require more resources on FPGA.

Moreover, Hazra [10] employed blowfish and Diffie-Hellman techniques for image and file encryption. Blowfish algorithm was used to generate the secret key while using Diffie-Hellman protocol was used to generate a share private key to be used by the users over an unsecured network. With this technique, encrypted data can only be read by intended parties as a two level security system was developed. Similarly, a hybrid blowfish-MD5 and RSA-MD5 was presented by (Chauhan and Gupta [5]). Both hybridized algorithm was used for textual information encryption. Performance evaluation result obtained revealed that the size for the encrypted file increases for both hybridized algorithms but the execution time of Blowfish-MD5 was lesser when compared to RSA-MD5 algorithm. Blowfish algorithm was also modified for image encryption by Ali and Abead (2016). The multi sub-keys needed for encryption was generated from five instead of four S-boxes. The correlation coefficient of the algorithm and the number of pixels change rate revealed that the modified algorithm performed better than existing blowfish algorithm. Similarly, the F-Function of blowfish algorithm was optimized for encryption by Christina and Joe [8]. The F-function of the optimized blowfish algorithm has two S-boxes instead of four in the existing blowfish algorithm. Also, one XOR operation was used in the F-function in contrary to two additions and one XOR operations needed in the existing blowfish algorithm. However, a high execution time was recorded with the optimized blowfish technique though a high throughput was achieved. Conclusively, a comparative analysis of DES and blowfish algorithms was carried out by Nie and Zhang [25]. Results obtained revealed that the existing blowfish algorithm encrypts faster than DES but it requires a larger memory than DES. This is certainly because of the memory required by the F-Function to generate the sub keys and authors were of the opinion that memory requirements could limit the use of blowfish for smart card applications and other memory constrained applications.

4   Methodology

To improve the existing blowfish algorithm, its F-function which is used to generate the round sub-keys was modified. Existing F-function in Eq. 1 uses two OR operations, one XOR operation and four s-boxes.

$$F(xL) = \left((S_1 + S_2, \ mod \ 2^{32}) \ xor \ S_3 \right) + S_4, \ mod \ 2^{32} \tag{1}$$

However, the modified F-function in Eq. 2 uses two XOR operations, one OR operation and four S-boxes.

$$F(xL) = \left(((S_1 \ xor \ S_2) + S_3, \ mod 2^{32}) \ xor \ S_4 \right) \tag{2}$$

The modified F-Function is further illustrate with Fig. 2.

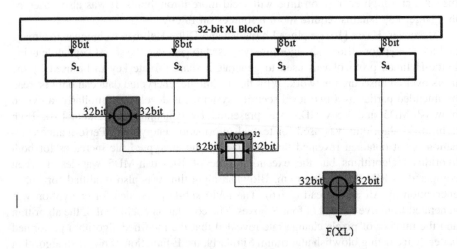

Fig. 2. F-Function of the modified blowfish algorithm

The pseudocode for the modified Blowfish Encryption is given as:

Step 1: Split the input 64bit data into xL and xR where each half contains 32-bit half data

Step 2: Repeat steps (a) to (c) while i = 1 to16

(a) Carry out XOR operation between xL and P[i].
(b) Compute the F-function of xL such that:

$$F(xL) = \left(\left(\left(S_1 xor S_2\right) + S_3, mod2^{32}\right) xor\, S_4\right)$$

XOR F(xL) with xR.

Step 3: Swap xR and xL.
Step 4: Carry out XOR operation between xR and P[16]
Step 5: Carry out XOR operation between xL and P[17].
Step 6: Merge xR and xL.

The pseudocode for the modified blowfish decryption is given as:

Step 1: Split the input 64bit data into xL and xR where each half contains 32-bit half data
Step 2: Repeat steps (a) to (c) while i = 16 to1

(a) Carry out XOR operation between xL and P[i].
(b) Compute the F-function of xL such that:

$$F(xL) = \left(\left(\left(S_1 xor S_2\right) + S_3, mod2^{32}\right) xor S_4\right)$$

F(xL) is XORed with xR.

Step 3: Swap xR and xL.
Step 4: Carry out XOR operation between xR and P[1]
Step 5: Carry out XOR operation between xL and P[0].
Step 6: Merge xR and xL.

The modified Blowfish Algorithm was employed to secure EMI of patients; textual and graphical information were considered. The implementation was carried out in MATLAB R2015a programming environment on a Dell Inspiron 15 N3000series; 500 GB, 4 GB RAM, core i3, 1.7 GHz Dual processor.

5 Results and Discussion

The graphical user interface used for EMI documentation is shown in Fig. 3. Patients medical records are captured using the interface. A patient id is automatically generated for each patient using the first letter of each name, the sex and their age. Also, an image can be uploaded to illustrate the patients' ailment. A secret key used for the encryption and decryption would have been distributed among authorized personnel. Once this key is supplied, the EMI can be encrypted as well as decrypted.

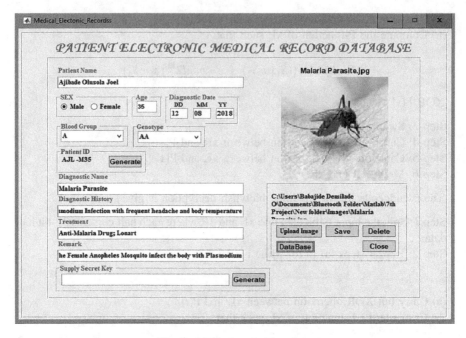

Fig. 3. Medical record interface

As expected, the saved EMI can also be retrieved by authorized medical personnel once the secret key has been supplied. Figure 4 illustrates an encrypted EMI that was decrypted.

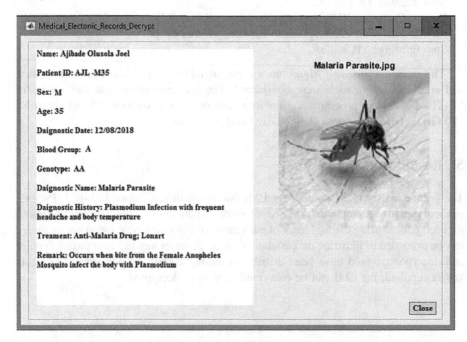

Fig. 4. Decrypted medical record

An attempt to access a decrypted EMI with a use a wrong secret key yields an unreadable message as shown in Fig. 5.

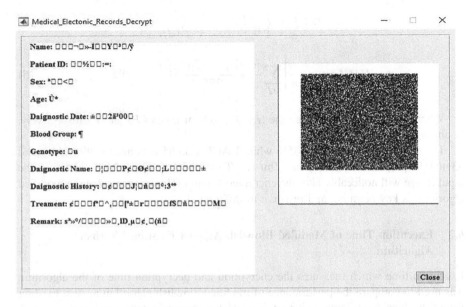

Fig. 5. Decrypted medical record with wrong secret key

6 Performance Evaluation

Depending on the amount of information available to the intruders, four classical types of attacks were reported by Ismail et al. [13]. Cipher text only attack occurs when an intruder attempts to deduce the secret key using the cipher text. Known plaintext attack occurs when the intruder attempts to deduce the secret key form the plain text and its corresponding cipher text available to him. Chosen plain text attack occurs when the intruder could access the encryption system, therefore an attempt is made to generate a cipher text with a plain text available to him. In the chosen cipher text attack, the intruder could access the decryption system, therefore an attempt is made to deduce a plain text from the cipher text available to him. Therefore, an encryption system must be evaluated against these attacks.

6.1 Differential Attack Analysis

This was used to confirm the strength of an encryption algorithm and also to ensure that the encryption system is resistive to any attacks that may arise from a compromise to the plain text or cipher text. Therefore, the diffusion performance of the algorithm could be determined using the Number of Pixel Change Rate (NPCR) and the Unified Average Changing Intensity (UACI). NPCR measures the change in pixel numbers between two images while UACI measures the average difference in intensity between two images. NPCR and UACI can be measured using Eqs. 3, 4 and 5 respectively:

$$NPCR = \frac{\sum_{i,j} D(i,j)}{m \times n} \times 100\% \tag{3}$$

$$D(i,j) = \begin{cases} 1, & c_1(i,j) \neq c_2(i,j) \\ 0 & c_1(i,j) = c_2(i,j) \end{cases} \tag{4}$$

$$UACI = \frac{1}{m \times n} \left[\sum_{i,j} \frac{|C_1(i,j) - C_2(i,j)|}{255} \right] \times 100\% \tag{5}$$

Where $P1(i,j)$ and $P2(i,j)$ are the $(i,j)th$ pixels of images $P1$ and $P2$ respectively, m and n are the pixels width.

The computed NPCR is 98.85% while UACI is 33.65% as against 99.6094% and 33.4635% proposed by Deng and Zhu [7]. This revealed that a slight change in the input image will noticeably alter the encrypted version. This confirms that the modified algorithm is key sensitive and resistive to differential attacks.

6.2   Execution Time of Modified Blowfish Against Existing Blowfish Algorithm

Execution time which measures the encryption and decryption time of the algorithm was used to compare the performance of modified blowfish algorithm against existing Blowfish algorithm. Comparative analysis of the execution time as shown in Fig. 6 revealed that the modified blowfish algorithm encrypts faster than existing blowfish algorithm. Also, the analysis of the decryption time shown in Fig. 7 revealed that the modified blowfish algorithm decrypts faster than existing blowfish algorithm.

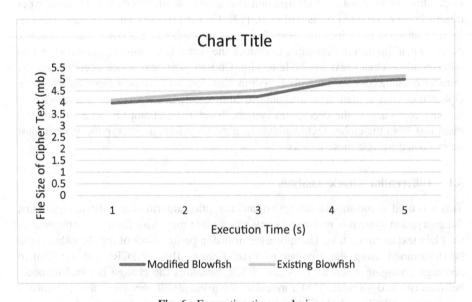

Fig. 6. Encryption time analysis

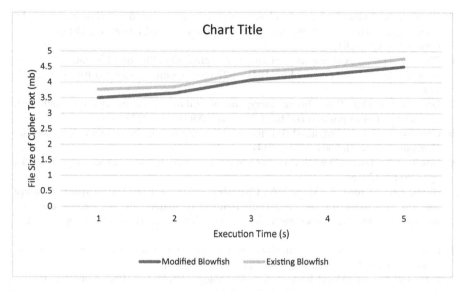

Fig. 7. Decryption time analysis

7   Conclusion

Electronic medical information is a sensitive information about the state of health of a patient and they need to be kept away from unauthorized individuals. Despite the limitations of blowfish algorithm, it can still keep these EMI secured from intruders. An attempt to improve the deficiencies of existing blowfish algorithm by modifying its F-function has been presented in this article. Differential Attack Analysis carried out has shown that the modified algorithm is secured against plaintext and cipher text attacks. Also, a comparative analysis between the modified and the existing blowfish algorithm has also shown that the modified version has a better execution time than the existing one. Other ways of improving the blowfish algorithm can be further explored towards increasing its encryption strength.

References

1. Christiana, A.O., Adeshola, G.Q., Oluwatobi, A.N.: Implementation of textual information encryption using 128, 192 and 256 bits advanced encryption standard algorithm. Ann. Comput. Sci. Ser. **15**(2), 153–159 (2017)
2. Alabaichi, A.M.: Security Analysis of Blowfish Algorithm, September 2013. https://doi.org/10.1109/ICoIA.2013.6650222
3. Andriole, K.P.: Security of electronic medical information and patient privacy: what you need to know. J. Am. Coll. Radiol. **11**(12), 1212–1216 (2014). https://doi.org/10.1016/j.jacr.2014.09.011
4. Bai, T., et al.: A lightweight method of data encryption in BANs using electrocardiogram signal. Future Gener. Comput. Syst. (2018). https://doi.org/10.1016/j.future.2018.01.031

5. Chauhan, A., Gupta, J.: A novel technique of cloud security based on hybrid encryption by Blowfish and MD5. In: 4th International Conference on Signal Processing, Computing and Control (ISPCC) (2017)
6. Chen, X., Hu, C.: Adaptive medical image encryption algorithm based on multiple chaotic mapping. Saudi J. Biol. Sci. **24**(8), 1821–1827 (2017). https://doi.org/10.1016/j.sjbs.2017.11.023
7. Deng, X.H., Zhu, C.X.: Image encryption algorithms based on chaos through dual scrambling of pixel position and bit. J. Commun. **35**(3), 216–223 (2014)
8. Christina, L., Joe, I.: Optimized Blowfish encryption technique. Int. J. Innov. Res. Comput. Commun. Eng. **2**(7), 5009–5015 (2014)
9. Gowda, S.N.: Using Blowfish encryption to enhance security feature of an image, vol. 200, pp. 126–129 (2016)
10. Hazra, T.K., Mahato, A., Mandal, A., Chakraborty, A.K.: A hybrid cryptosystem of image and text files using Blowfish and Diffie-Hellman techniques. In: 8th Annual Industrial Automation and Electromechanical Engineering Conference (IEMECON), pp. 137–141 (2017)
11. Hua, Z., Jin, F., Xu, B., Huang, H.: 2D logistic-sine-coupling map for image encryption. Sig. Process. (2018). https://doi.org/10.1016/j.sigpro.2018.03.010
12. ICIT: Institute for Critical Infrastructure Technology. Hacking healthcare in 2016: lessons the healthcare industry can learn from the OPM breach (2016). http://icitech.org/wp-content/uploads/2016/01/ICIT-Brief-Hacking-Healthcare-IT-in-2016.pdf
13. Ismail, S.M., Said, L.A., Radwan, A.G., Madian, A.H., Abu-elyazeed, M.F.: Generalized double-humped logistic map-based medical image encryption. J. Adv. Res. **10**, 85–98 (2018). https://doi.org/10.1016/j.jare.2018.01.009
14. Jack, M.: Survey : 64 percent of patients use a digital device to manage health. Mobi Health News (2018)
15. Kaur, A., Singh, G.: A random selective block encryption technique for secure image cryptography using Blowfish algorithm. In: 2018 Second International Conference on Inventive Communication and Computational Technologies (ICICCT), pp. 1290–1293 (2018)
16. Keckley, P.H.: Privacy and security in health care : a fresh look. Deloitte Center for Health Solutions, pp. 1–20 (2013)
17. Kondawar, S.S., Gawali, D.H.: Blowfish algorithm for patient health monitoring. In: International Conference on Inventive Computation Technologies (ICICT), pp. 1–6 (2016)
18. KPMG: Health care and cyber security: increasing threats require increased capabilities (2015). https://assets.kpmg.com/content/dam/kpmg/pdf/2015/09/cyber-health-care-survey kpmg-2015.pdf
19. Landge, I.A.: VHDL based Blowfish implementation for secured embedded system design, pp. 3–7 (2017)
20. Langer, S.G.: Cyber-security issues in healthcare information technology. J. Dig. Imaging **2016**(October 2016), 117–125 (2017). https://doi.org/10.1007/s10278-016-9913-x
21. Lima, J.B., Madeiro, F., Sales, F.J.R.: Signal processing: image communication encryption of medical images based on the cosine number transform. Sig. Process. Image Commun. **35**, 1–8 (2015). https://doi.org/10.1016/j.image.2015.03.005
22. Martin, G., Martin, P., Hankin, C.: Cybersecurity and healthcare : how safe are we ? **3179**, 4–7 (2017). https://doi.org/10.1136/bmj.j3179
23. Masilamani, V.: ScienceDirect reversible reversible data data hiding hiding scheme scheme during during encryption encryption using using machine machine learning learning. Proc. Comput. Sci. **133**, 348–356 (2018). https://doi.org/10.1016/j.procs.2018.07.043
24. Netwrix Research Lab: 2017 IT Risks Report (2017)

25. Nie, T., Zhang, T.: A study of DES and Blowfish encryption algorithm. In: IEEE Region 10 Conference (TENCON 2009), pp. 1–4 (2009)
26. Nur, K., St, P., Darlis, D., Si, S.: An implementation of data encryption for Internet of Things using Blowfish algorithm on FPGA 2. In: 2nd International Conference on Information and Communication Technology (ICoICT), pp. 75–79 (2014)
27. Panda, M.: Performance Analysis of Encryption Algorithms for Security, pp. 278–284 (2016)
28. Park, E.H., Kim, J., Wile, L.L., Park, Y.S.: Factors affecting intention to disclose patientsÕ health information. Comput. Secur. (2018). https://doi.org/10.1016/j.cose.2018.05.003
29. Patel, P., Patel, R., Patel, N.: Integrated ECC and Blowfish for smartphone security. Proc. Comput. Sci. **78**(December 2015), 210–216 (2016). https://doi.org/10.1016/j.procs.2016.02.035
30. Quist-Aphetsi, K., Laurent, N., Anca, C.P., Sophie, G., Jojo, M.E., Nii, N.Q.: A cryptographic technique for security of medical images in health information systems. Proc. Comput. Sci. **58**, 538–543 (2015). https://doi.org/10.1016/j.procs.2015.08.070
31. Raigoza, J.: Evaluating performance of symmetric encryption algorithms, pp. 1378–1381 (2016). https://doi.org/10.1109/CSCI.2016.257
32. William, J.G., Adam, F., Adam, L.: Threats to information security—public health implications. New Engl. J. Med. **377**, 1–3 (2017)

A Deep Convolutional Encoder-Decoder Architecture for Retinal Blood Vessels Segmentation

Adegun Adekanmi Adeyinka[1], Marion Olubunmi Adebiyi[2],
Noah Oluwatobi Akande[3(✉)], Roseline Oluwaseun Ogundokun[3],
Anthonia Aderonke Kayode[3], and Tinuke Omolewa Oladele[4]

[1] School of Computer Science, University of Kwazulu-Natal,
Durban, South Africa
[2] Department of Computer and Information Sciences,
Covenant University, Ota, Nigeria
[3] Bioninformatics Research Group, Computer Science Department,
Landmark University, Omu-Aran, Kwara, Nigeria
akande.noah@lmu.edu.ng
[4] Computer Science Department, University of Ilorin, Ilorin, Kwara, Nigeria

Abstract. Over the last decades, various methods have been employed in medical images analysis. Some state-of-the-arts techniques such as deep learning have been recently applied to medical images analysis. This research proposes the application of deep learning technique in performing segmentation of retinal blood vessels. Analyzing and segmentation of retina vessels has assisted in diagnosis and monitoring of some diseases. Diseases such as age-related fovea degeneration, diabetic retinopathy, glaucoma, hypertension, arteriosclerosis and choroidal neovascularization can be effectively managed by the analysis of retinal vessels images. In this work, a Deep Convolutional Encoder-Decoder Architecture for the segmentation of retinal vessels images is proposed. The proposed method is a deep learning system composed of an encoder and decoder mechanism allows a low resolution image set of retinal vessels to be analyzed by set of convolutional layers in the encoder unit before been sent into a decoder unit for final segmented output. The proposed system was evaluated using some evaluation metrics such as dice coefficient, jaccard index and mean of intersection. The review of the existing works was also carried out. It could be shown that the proposed system outperforms many existing methods in the segmentation of retinal vessels images.

Keywords: Retinal vessels · Deep learning · Convolutional layers · Encoder · Decoder · Images · Segmentation

1 Introduction

Over the years, retinal blood vessels have been revealed to contain rich features that could be used to diagnose many deadly diseases such as Diabetes Retinopathy (DR), Hypertensive Retinopathy (HR), glaucoma, cataract etc. Growth of false blood vessels

© Springer Nature Switzerland AG 2019
S. Misra et al. (Eds.): ICCSA 2019, LNCS 11623, pp. 180–189, 2019.
https://doi.org/10.1007/978-3-030-24308-1_15

are pointer to the presence of DR while a measure of the Arteriovenous Ratio (AVR) could be used to detect and grade the presence of HR and glaucoma [1, 2]. AVR is a function of the Central Retinal Venular Equivalent (CRVE) and Central Retinal Artery Equivalent (CRAE) of the retinal blood vessels. Therefore, how to segment retinal blood vessels with a view to extract features that could facilitate the diagnosis of pathological signs has been a growing field of research. However, segmenting the components of retinal has been a difficult task especially when the retinal contains pathological signs [3]. Therefore, automated approach to retinal blood vessels segmentation is being explored by researchers towards segmenting these components. Various automated segmentation techniques such as Deep machine learning [4, 5]; supervised neural network [6, 7]; U-net based Convolutional neural network [8, 9]; Deep neural network [10–12] have been employed in the literature with an acceptable level of accuracy. However, a more accurate segmentation technique is still being craved for by researchers as well as medical practitioners. Image analysis and segmentation carried out based on deep learning methods has produced improved results with a very high accuracy [4]. This article presents a deep learning technique that uses encoder–decoder mechanism for retinal blood vessels segmentation.

2 Related Works

In the last decade, there have been a lot of research about the application of deep learning for medical image analysis. Some works have been particularly carried out in the segmentation process of medical image analysis most especially retina images using state-of-the arts techniques.

Authors in [13] carried out a review of existing methods in retinal blood vessels segmentation. They categorized the methods into: kernel-based techniques, vessel-tracking, mathematical morphology-based, multi-scale, model-based, adaptive local thresholding and machine learning. A Convolutional Neural Network (CNN) architecture for the segmentation of blood vessels fundus images was proposed by authors in [9]. The architecture was derived from U-Net architecture that implements an encoder-decoder architecture. A segmentation accuracy of 97.90% was achieved when the technique was evaluated with DRIVE dataset. Also, a trainable pre-weighted neural network termed Frangi-Net was employed for retinal blood vessel segmentation in [7]. The technique was tested with healthy, DR and glaucomatous retinal images. An accuracy of 84%, 82% and 84% were recorded with the healthy, DR and glaucomatous retinal images respectively. Authors in [14] also proposed a multi-scale convolutional neural network structure and label processing approach for the segmentation of retinal blood vessel. Their method used two different scale image segments to generate input for two deep convolutional networks. A sensitivity, specificity and accuracy of 78.90%, 98.83% and 97.10% were achieved with healthy retinal images available in STARE database while 78.43%, 98.37% and 96.90% was achieved with pathological retinal images available in the same STARE database.

Another model consisting of a combination of CNN and Long Short Term Memory (LSTM) was proposed to perform segmentation on retinal OCT images [5]. CNN was applied to extract layers of interest image and also extract the edges and LSTM was applied to trace the layer boundary. Their model was trainable and applicable to minimal data. A pixel wise mean absolute error of 1.30 ± 0.48 was achieved when the technique was evaluated on three publicly available databases. Similarly, a multiscale and multi-level deeply supervised convolutional network with short connections was developed for retinal vessel segmentation in [6]. Short connections were used to transfer semantic information between the layers. Both forward and backward short connections were used for passing low level information and the proposed method was applied on DRIVE dataset.

CNN and Conditional Random Fields (CRFs) were combined into an integrated deep network to develop a model called Deep Vessel system to achieve state-of-the-art retinal vessel segmentation performance [16]. The model was experimented on DRIVE, STARE, and CHASE DB1 datasets. A segmentation accuracy and sensitivity of 95.23%, 76.03%; 95.85%, 74.12% and 94.89%, 71.30% were recorded with DRIVE, STARE, and CHASE DB1 datasets respectively.

A deep neural network (DNN) that uses max-pooling layers (MPCNNs) instead of subsampling or down sampling was also used for retina images segmentation [10]. The MPCNN mapped input samples into output class probabilities using hierarchical layers to extract features and fully connected layers to classify extracted features. An accuracy of 94.66% and an area under receiver operating characteristics curve of 97.43% were recorded.

Encoder-decoder based convolutional network architecture for semantic pixel-wise segmentation of retinal images was developed [11]. The network adapted the well-known SegNet model that learns high dimensional feature maps. This provided pixel wise segmentation of retinal abnormalities by assigning particular object class label. The technique was evaluated using MESSIDOR dataset. A mean accuracy of 99.24% was achieved for exudates segmentation, 88.65% for cotton wool spots segmentation and 97.86% for haemorrhages.

A fully convolutional network (FCN) for retinal layers' segmentation on retinal optical coherence tomography (OCT) images was developed [8]. Fan et al. [17] introduced a hierarchical image matting model for retinal blood vessel segmentation. The continuous and extendible characteristics of retinal blood vessels was incorporated into the image matting model. The performance of the technique was carried out on DRIVE datasets and an accuracy of 0.881 was obtained.

An intelligent blood vessel segmentation technique that could track vessels in the presence of occlusion was presented in [17]. The technique used hidden markov model for the vessel segmentation. When evaluated on DRIVE dataset, an AUC of 0.9 was achieved. In the same vein, convolutional neural network was employed for retinal blood vessel segmentation in [18]. When the performance was carried out on DRIVE dataset using ROC curve, an accuracy of 0.9802 was achieved. Condition random field was employed in [19] to reduce the number of encoders and decoders used by U-Net for a more improved retinal blood vessel segmentation. The improved segmentation technique was validated on DRIVE dataset while ROC curve was used for the performance evaluation. A segmentation accuracy of 0.9748 was achieved.

3 Methodology

3.1 Dataset

The proposed method was evaluated on publicly available retinal image dataset known as Digital Retinal Images for Vessel Extraction (DRIVE) [15], It contains 80 color fundus images. The images were further divided into a training set containing 57 samples and a test set, both containing 27 image samples. The training set and the testing set also come with their respective ground truth labels.

3.2 Model Implementation

The software used for the model implementation includes:

- Python Version 3.5
- Keras 2
- Tensor flow backend
- Scikit-image Version 0.14.1

The experimental platform is a personal computer equipped with an Intel Core i7 processor with ten (10) 3.4 GHZ cores, 16 GB memory and NVIDIA Tesla K40c GPU with Ubuntu 16.04 operating system.

3.3 General Architecture of the Proposed System

The proposed deep convolutional encoder-decoder model architecture adapts the popular U-Net model that implements a contemporary classification network into fully convolutional networks. It operates by learning from pixels to pixels in an end-to-end manner. Training image dataset and corresponding ground truth image dataset serves as the input into the system. These will be taken through the other sections of the system such as data preparation section and the learning and training section. The form of training employed is a supervised form of training whereby the target goal in the form of the ground truth images is supplied together with the input images. After a period of training, the validation image data set will now be fed into the system for the expected predictions. The output data from the prediction will finally be compared with our target goals for accuracy and the performance metrics evaluated.

The architecture is composed of the following major sections:

Data Preparation Section

The training image data set and the corresponding ground truth image data set were used to train the model simultaneously. The images were resized into 96 × 96 dimension, after which they were resampled to remove every form of noise. The ground truth serves as the expected output and the training set serves as the input to train the system. The input datasets (training and validations sets) and the ground truth are located in an online repository called DRIVE dataset. The sample training image data set and ground truth images are illustrated in Figs. 1 and 2 below.

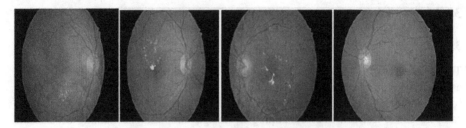

Fig. 1. A sample retina training image data set

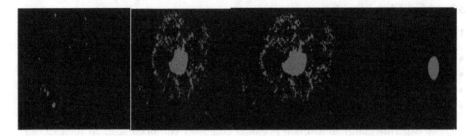

Fig. 2. The corresponding ground truth images

Learning and Training Section:
In this section, we have the encoder units and the decoder units.

Encoder:
The encoder is made up of set of convolution layers and pooling layers. Features extraction from the input image takes place at the convolution layer and the pooling layers reduce the resolution of the image feature maps. In this model, the encoder applies Rectified Linear Unit (RELU) activation function.

Each encoder uses the Max-pooling to translate invariance over small spatial shifts in the image and combine this with Subsampling to produce a large input image context in terms of spatial window. This method reduces the feature map size and this leads to image representation that is noisy with blurred boundaries. The restoration is done by decoder as the output image resolution must be the same as input image.

Decoder:
The decoder ensures that the image resolution of image set from the encoder units is increased to the initial resolution status. It is also made up of set of convolution layers. Each of the layers in the decoder stage corresponds to the layer in the encoder i.e. for each of the encoders there is a corresponding decoder which up samples the feature map using the already stored max-pooling indices. Sparse feature maps of higher resolutions are then produced. These are fed through the training section to produce dense feature maps.

Prediction:
The prediction section of this model is performed by predicting pixel-wise labels for an output which has the same resolution as the input image. The last part of the decoder is

connected to a softmax classifier which classifies each pixel. The sparse feature maps restored from the original resolution are then fed to the softmax classifier to produce the final segmentation.

Output:
The final segmented images are generated at this section. These are stored with preds as the output name. The performance of the model is also evaluated at this section. The model is described by the diagram in Fig. 3.

The layout of encoder-decoder architecture is illustrated with Fig. 3.

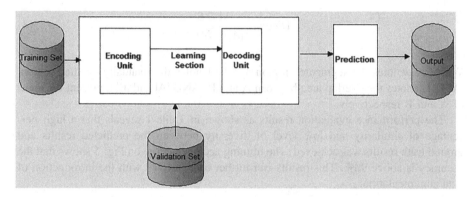

Fig. 3. Layout diagram of a proposed segmentation method for retina images analysis

3.4 Experimental Results and Analysis

The performance of the proposed model was evaluated and the results displayed below. The segmentation accuracy has been assessed by comparing the predicted results with the manual version. The final results of the validation image set used for testing segmentation are compared with the ground truth.

The metrics can be described as stated below:

- Positive Predictive Value (PPV): amount of prediction that turns positive. This was measured using Eq. 1:

$$PPV(A, B) = \frac{|A \cap B|}{|A|} \tag{1}$$

- Intersection of Union (IoU): this is also known as Jaccard similarity coefficient; it describes the similarity measured over two image sets. This can be calculated using Eq. 2:

$$IOU(A, B) = \frac{|A \cap B|}{|A| \cap |B|} \tag{2}$$

- Sensitivity: also known as true positive rate (TPR) Sensitivity: This is the proportion of actual positives which were predicted positive. It can be defined as the proportion of images which were predicted to belong to a class with respect to all the images that truly belong in the class.

$$\text{Sensitivity} = \frac{|A \cap B|}{|B|} \tag{3}$$

- Dice Coefficient: also shows similarity measure and it is related to Jaccard index. This was measured using Eq. 4:

$$\text{Dice} = \frac{|A \cap B|}{(|A| \cap |B|) \div 2} \tag{4}$$

Where A denotes the segmented region and B denotes the manually labelled region, |A∩B| denotes the overlap area between A and B, AND |A| and |B| represent the areas of A and B respectively.

The performance evaluation results as shown in Table 1 reveals that a high percentage of similarity and low level of diversity between the predicted results and ground truth results was achieved. The training accuracy curve on Fig. 5 shows that the accuracy is above 90%. This results can further be improved with the introduction of data augumentation.

Table 1. Performance evaluation of the proposed model

Performance metrics	Dice coefficient (%)	Intersection of union (%)	Positive predictive value (%)	Sensitivity (%)
Proposed model	82.23	72.23	96.5	96.5

The final segmented output is presented in the Fig. 4:

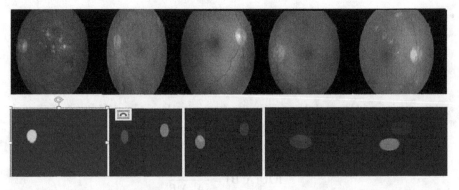

Fig. 4. The figure contains the validation image set and the predicted segmented image results from the proposed model.

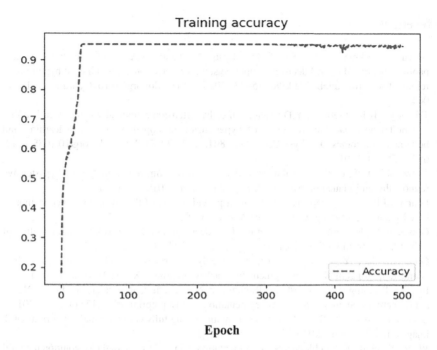

Fig. 5. The figure shows the accuracy curve of the proposed model when trained on retina images dataset.

4   Conclusion

In this work, a novel deep learning method and its application on segmentation of retina images for detection and diagnosis of some diseases has been investigated. The review of the existing works was also carried out. The proposed model was evaluated and analyzed. This paper shows that the proposed model gave a better performance over the existing techniques. The encoder–decoder mechanism in this model can be improved on in the future works where ensemble methods with some other state-of-the arts techniques can also be explored. Application of data augmentation techniques will also improve the performance of the proposed system because limited data was used for the experiments. The detailed methodology which has been broken into learning, encoder, decoder, prediction was fully explored.

References

1. Akbar, S., Akram, M.U., Sharif, M., Tariq, A., Khan, S.A.: Arteriovenous ratio and papilledema based hybrid decision support system for detection and grading of hypertensive retinopathy. Artif. Intell. Med. **90**, 15–24 (2018). https://doi.org/10.1016/j.artmed.2018.06.004
2. Triwijoyo, B.K., Pradipto, Y.D.: Detection of hypertension retinopathy using deep learning and boltzmann machines detection of hypertension retinopathy using deep learning and boltzmann machines. J. Phys: Conf. Ser. **801**, 1–7 (2017). https://doi.org/10.1088/1742-6596/755/1/011001
3. Oluwatobi, A.N., et al.: Vascular networks segmented from retinal images of hypertensive retinopathy and glaucoma patients. J. Eng. Appl. Sci. (2019, in press)
4. Pound, M.P., et al.: Deep machine learning provides state-of-the-art performance in image-based plant phenotyping. GigaScience **6**, gix083 (2017)
5. Gopinath, K., Rangrej, S.B., Sivaswamy, J.: A deep learning framework for segmentation of retinal layers from OCT images. arXiv preprint arXiv:1806.08859 (2018)
6. Guo, S., Gao, Y., Wang, K., Li, T.: Deeply supervised neural network with short connections for retinal vessel segmentation. arXiv preprint arXiv:1803.03963 (2018)
7. Fu, W., Breininger, K., Würfl, T., Ravikumar, N., Schaffert, R., Maier, A.: Frangi-Net: a neural network approach to vessel segmentation. arXiv preprint arXiv:1711.03345 (2017)
8. Ben-Cohen, A., et al.: Retinal layers segmentation using fully convolutional network in OCT images. RSIP Vision (2017)
9. Wang, X., et al.: Retina blood vessel segmentation using a U-net based Convolutional neural network. In: Procedia Computer Science: International Conference on Data Science (ICDS 2018), Beijing, China, 8–9 June 2018 (2018)
10. Melinščak, M., Prentašić, P., Lončarić, S.: Retinal vessel segmentation using deep neural networks. In: VISAPP 2015 (10th International Conference on Computer Vision Theory and Applications) (2015)
11. Badar, M., Shahzad, M., Fraz, M.M.: Simultaneous segmentation of multiple retinal pathologies using fully convolutional deep neural network. In: Nixon, M., Mahmoodi, S., Zwiggelaar, R. (eds.) MIUA 2018. CCIS, vol. 894, pp. 313–324. Springer, Cham (2018). https://doi.org/10.1007/978-3-319-95921-4_29
12. Kang, S.H., Park, H.S., Jang, J., Jeon, K.: Deep neural networks for the detection and segmentation of the retinal fluid in OCT images. National Institute for Mathematical Sciences, Daejeon, Korea, 34047
13. Almotiri, J., Elleithy, K., Elleithy, A.: Retinal vessels segmentation techniques and algorithms: a survey. Appl. Sci. **8**(2), 155 (2018)
14. Li, M., Ma, Z., Liu, C., Zhang, G., Han, Z.: Robust Retinal blood vessel segmentation based on reinforcement local descriptions. Biomed. Res. Int. **2017**, 9 (2017)
15. Staal, J., Abràmoff, M.D., Niemeijer, M., Viergever, M.A., Van Ginneken, B.: Ridge-based vessel segmentation in color images of the retina. IEEE Trans. Med. Imaging **23**(4), 501–509 (2004)
16. Fu, H., Xu, Y., Lin, S., Kee Wong, D.W., Liu, J.: DeepVessel: retinal vessel segmentation via deep learning and conditional random field. In: Ourselin, S., Joskowicz, L., Sabuncu, M. R., Unal, G., Wells, W. (eds.) MICCAI 2016. LNCS, vol. 9901, pp. 132–139. Springer, Cham (2016). https://doi.org/10.1007/978-3-319-46723-8_16
17. Fan, Z., et al.: A hierarchical image matting model for blood vessel segmentation in fundus images. In: Computer Vision and Pattern Recognition, pp. 1–10 (2017). http://arxiv.org/abs/1701.00892

18. Hassan, M., Amin, M., Murtza, I., Khan, A., Chaudhry, A.: Robust hidden Markov model based intelligent blood vessel detection of fundus images. Comput. Methods Programs Biomed., 193–201 (2017). http://doi.org/10.1016/j.cmpb.2017.08.023
19. Güleryüz, M.Ş., Ulusoy, İ.: Retinal vessel segmentation using convolutional neural networks. In: IEEE 26th Signal Processing and Communication Applications Conference, pp. 1–4 (2018)

Context Data Preprocessing for Context-Aware Smartphone Authentication

Sangjin Nam[1] ⓘ, Suntae Kim[1](✉) ⓘ, Jung-Hoon Shin[1],
Jeong Ah Kim[2], and Sooyong Park[3]

[1] Department of Software Engineering, CAIIT, Chonbuk National University,
567 Baekje-daero, Deokjin-gu, Jeonju-si, Jeollabuk-do, Republic of Korea
{potter930, stkim, shinjh}@jbnu.ac.kr
[2] Department of Computer Education, Catholic Kwandong University,
Beomil-ro 579 beon-gil, Kangneung-Si, Kangwon-Do, Republic of Korea
clara@cku.ac.kr
[3] Department of Computer Science and Engineering, Sogang University,
35 Baekbeom-ro, Mapo-gu, Seoul, Republic of Korea
sypark@sogang.ac.kr

Abstract. This paper proposes an approach to carrying out context data pre-processing gathered from smartphone users to support context-aware authentication. Context-aware authentication is a technique to implicitly authenticate a smartphone user using contextual data (e.g., call log, location) without explicitly requesting the user's any actions. In order to enable context-aware authentication, a user's contextual data should be carefully processed for learning user's past contextual patterns in consideration of user's hourly, daily, weekly or monthly behaviors. In this paper, we gathered contextual data from 200 voluntary smartphone users for about 2 years and showed what the appropriate contextual data is preprocessing for performing context-aware authentication.

1 Introduction

Recently, most of the people use diverse mobile devices in their daily life. Among them, a smartphone is considered as the most popular devices because it basically can be used as a communication tool, and also people can use diverse complementary services in the single device [4, 5]. The growth of the use of the smartphone has caused an increase of the demand of user authentication techniques in the smartphone applications, as it has its own authentication methods and steps [3].

Most of the applications in a smartphone apply the id/password scheme for user authentication. However, the *id/password* scheme has a big and broad issue that it relies on the human's memory so that it is easy to forget. Some of the applications that handle secure data (e.g., bank or stock trading accounts) use a *digital certificate* issued by the public certificate authority or the *OTP* (One-Time-Password) scheme for user authentication. However, the digital certificate scheme forces a user to issue the certificate from the central authority with a complicated certificate issue process, and the OTP scheme needs extra devices and network bandwidth to get the one-time-password [1, 2, 10]. In addition to these, the diverse *biometric methods* [6] based on sensors of

© Springer Nature Switzerland AG 2019
S. Misra et al. (Eds.): ICCSA 2019, LNCS 11623, pp. 190–202, 2019.
https://doi.org/10.1007/978-3-030-24308-1_16

the smartphone have been proposed, but it contains another issue regarding the low accuracy of the sensors and negative effects of the environmental factors such as illumination, humidity, etc.).

In order to address the issues, the context-aware authentication, so-called implicit authentication, techniques based on user's contextual data have recently been studied [6–9]. This technique uses call history record or location data that can be easily collected from a smartphone, carrying out the user authentication by comparing the past historical context data to the recent delta t time context data. However, the performance of the authentication technique highly relies on the preprocessing of the context data to appropriately characterize the user's behaviors.

This paper proposes the context data preprocessing technique for context-aware smartphone authentication. It consists of three steps. First, we introduce several types of context data that can be gathered from the smartphone and discuss its characteristics. Then, the gathered data is preprocessed in the three steps: (1) unification of the time unit for serializing the context data, (2) location data preprocessing, and (3) n-dimensional aggregation of the context data. The last step is to measure the quality of the preprocessed context data by applying statistical techniques. After the three-step preprocessing, diverse context-aware authentication schemes [6–9] may achieve higher performance. As the evaluation, we collected 200 voluntary smartphone users for about 2 years and showed the result of the sensitivity analysis with several data preprocessing parameters.

The rest of the paper is organized as follows: Sect. 2 introduces a representative authentication technique and discuss its pros and cons. Section 3 presents context data preprocessing technique composing of three major steps. Section 4 describes how we obtained the high-quality context-aware data obtained from the voluntary users with tuning the parameters. Section 5 concludes this paper.

2   Related Work

This section introduces several traditional authentication techniques and discusses its pros and cons. Also, it presents background on the context-aware authentication and its data preprocessing approaches.

2.1   Authentication Techniques

In this section, we introduce several traditional authentication approaches such as ID/Password, OTP, digital certificate and biometric technique and discuss its pros and cons. The ID/Password is the most popular and broadly used user authentication scheme not only in the smartphone but also in the general computers. This scheme is fast and relatively easy because a user just enters the password matched with his/her id as shown in Fig. 1(a). However, the scheme can work only if the user should memorize the pair of information. Because of this, most users tend to memorize several pair of id/password, otherwise, they consistently use a single id/password throughout applications. Furthermore, the application like Google Chrome provides a feature that keeps a user's id/password of a specific web site, which causes another security breach of the system. Additionally, in case of that a user forgets the pair of information, the user should carry out many tedious steps in order to recover the information [10, 13].

The OTP (One-time password) scheme is an authentication technique where a password is valid during only one login session, which is generally used as the complementary authentication. Figure 1(b) presents the steps of OTP. Once a user in OTP requests a one-time password to the application, the application generates a one-time password, and sends it back to the user. If the password that the user enters and that generated by the application is the same, the user is valid. Although its security level seems to be high thanks to the temporal password, a user should have an extra device or extra system (e.g., email) to obtain the password. Thus, it should rely on the other authentication scheme for the extra device or system accordingly. And also, it should spend extra cost to obtain the temporal password [11].

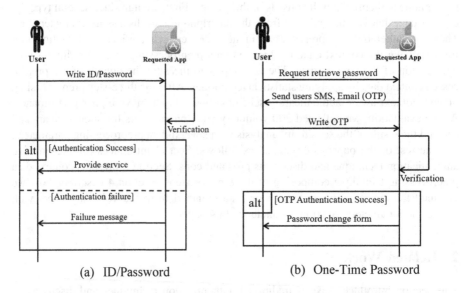

(a) ID/Password   (b) One-Time Password

Fig. 1. The ID/password and OTP authentication scheme semantics

In addition to the two authentication scheme, the digital certificate is considered as a powerful authentication technique that is broadly used in the financial industry [21]. This technique depends on the certificate authority that generates the user's pair of keys. As shown in Fig. 2, the user should submit user's document that can guarantee his/her identity to an organization connected to the certificate authority and carry out the several steps to get the user's pair of keys issued by the certificate authority. A user should regularly update the digital certificate, as it is only valid during a certain period of time. Once the user keeps the digital certificate issued by the certificate authority, he/she provides the certificate to the application with its corresponding password, and then the application requests the authority to validate the certificate and the password. This digital certificate authentication scheme contains several issues: (1) the digital certificate is usually stored in the local storage and is likely to be stolen; (2) it must use a specific application (e.g., a web browser); and, (3) a user has to perform several steps in offline to issue the digital certificate.

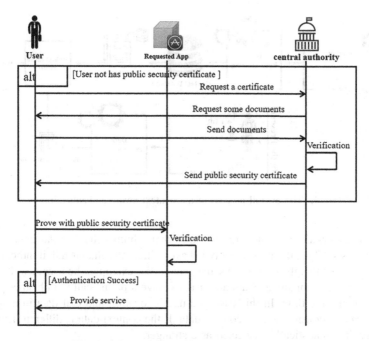

Fig. 2. The digital certificate scheme semantics

Recently, the biometric approach starts to be broadly used due to its convenience. The approach first stores the biometric information (e.g., fingerprint, iris, or face) [12–14] and authenticate a user with the pattern matching technology between the stored and the entered. The iris recognition approach [15] is a biometric identification that uses pattern recognition of each human's iris. Also, the face recognition approach has similar steps for the user's authentication, but the recognition success rate is not very high because the glasses and lighting have an heavy influence on the recognition. The fingerprint approach needs an extra device to capture the user's fingerprint, and its recognition rate depends on the humidity and hands foreign matters.

2.2 Context-Aware Authentication

The context-aware authentication, so-called implicit authentication, techniques based on user's contextual data have recently been studied [6–9]. This technique uses call history record or location data that can be easily collected from a smartphone, carrying out the user authentication by comparing the past historical context data to the recent delta t time context data. Figure 3 presents the overall process of context-aware authentication. First, a user just uses his/her own device (e.g., smartphone) that has several sensors. The device collects diverse user's contextual data (e.g., *CDR (Call Data Record), Location, App Usages*). Second, the contextual data is processed in several ways and stored in the *context database*. Third, the user who wants to access specific application requests it to authenticate him/herself. The application compares the user's recent context to that of the context database using *Authentication Model*. If two data sets have a huge gap, the application denies the user's access, otherwise, it allows it.

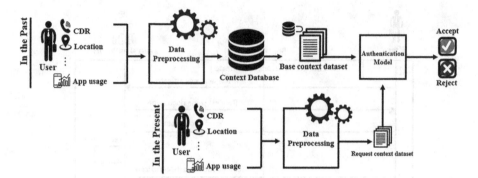

Fig. 3. The overall process of the context-aware authentication

The context-aware authentication assumes that a human has similar behaviors on the regular basis. Thus, if a user recently behaves differently than usual, it indicates that it needs to suspect that the user is the same person. For example, the user A wakes up at 7 am, goes to the company at 8 am and usually have a phone call with his/her parents during the commute time. In this case, the user's location and call data in a specific time span can be considered as a context data. If the context data is different from that of the user, it is statistically suspected as a stranger.

Shi *et al.* [7] carried out the data preprocessing with context data aggregation based on the time-of-day, day-of-week, and separated the data into two groups: *good events* and *bad events*. The good event indicates the system event (e.g., call or location) that is already known. For example, the *incoming* or *outgoing* call number is one of the contact numbers stored in the smartphone. For the location, if the current location is the location that the user frequently stayed before, it is considered as a good event. Based on the good/bad event aggregation, the paper computes the authentication score as the following equations:

- $Score_{Positive} = \prod_i^n p(\Delta Time\ of\ Good\ Event\mid Time\ of\ day)_i$
- $Score_{negative} = \prod_i^n p(\Delta Time\ of\ Bad\ Event\mid Time\ of\ day)_i$
- $Score = Score_{GoodEvent} - Score_{BadEvent}$

In this approach, the data preprocessing indicates data aggregation or density based on the time span (e.g., time-of-day, day-of-week). It only considers the gap between two sets of events in a specific time span without considering the importance of type of event (e.g., call data vs. location).

Kayacik *et al.* [9] suggested similar context-aware authentication techniques. They established the authentication model with the special model and temporal model. In order to support the model, they created the context database with sensor data in associated with time as well as location. All sensor data are first grouped in terms of the specific time span and location, and then the data is statistically scored by the probability density functions (pdf) and conditional probability as below:

- $Score = \dfrac{\sum_i^n pdf(degree\ of\ sensor\mid Time\ of\ Day)_i}{n}$

3   Context Data Preprocessing Technique

This section proposes the data preprocessing technique for the context-aware authentication, composing of three steps: (1) data collection, (2) context data preprocessing, and (3) statistical quality evaluation of the data. From the following subsections, we present a detailed explanation.

3.1   Data Collection

Data collection is the first step of the context-aware authentication in the smartphone. The smartphone has several sensors and useful information that can be used as a user' context. It may be impossible to guarantee individual identity with just a single context data, but a combination of several context data may increase the precision of the authentication. The possible context data that can be used for the context-aware authentication is summarized as below:

- *CDR (Call Data Record)* is a set of incoming and outgoing calls in the smartphone. In the time of a day or a week, the user tends to make phone calls to similar people on the regular basis. Because of this, CDR is one of the possible context data. CDR data is composing of *types of calls* such as incoming and outgoing, *timestamp*, *receiver number*, *receiver name*, and *call duration*.
- *Location Data* indicates a user's location composing of a *latitude* and *longitude* information collected by GPS (Global Positioning System). It is considered as the most appropriate data for the context-aware authentication [7]. The location data consists of the latitude, longitude, altitude by the timestamp. Thus, it can be used to extract user's location moving patterns, the major spot where the user stays and how long.
- *SMS (Simple Text Message)* is another candidate. The data is composed of not only text message itself, but also the received time. Sometimes, this data contains very important contents for the authentication (e.g., authentication key issued by the authentication authority). However, SMS tends to contain diverse spam messages. Thus, the outgoing text message is generally used for authentication.
- *App Usage* indicates a history of a user's application usage. Like CDR and location data, a user tends to use similar applications depending on the location and time so that it is very useful information for context-aware authentication.
- *Typing Pattern* denotes a user's key input pattern of the smartphone virtual keyboard. Depending on the user, the key input speed, the typo frequency is different. Some of the research used to use this data for user authentication [13].

3.2   Context Data Preprocessing

This subsection describes how the context data is processed for context-aware authentication. Among the candidate data set mentioned in the previous subsection, we selected the CDR and location data as the key data set for the context-aware authentication. This is because those are the most representative and fundamental data that most of the smartphone support. In addition, the literature [7] showed the two datasets characterizes the user's context very well. The context data preprocessing consists of three steps as presented in Fig. 4. First, it starts with the unification of the timestamp for the diverse context data. Then, the location data is specially processed, because the longitude and latitude are quite fine-grained, it is inappropriate to use context-aware authentication. Based on the data, the hierarchical aggregation is performed depending on the appropriate time span.

3.2.1   Unification of the Time Unit

The first step is the unification of the time unit, aiming at the serialization of all contextual data at the end of this step. Depending on the context data from different smartphones, the time data format is very different. For example, some of the data has the time format 'yyyy-MM-dd HH:mm:ss.SSS' and other has a Unix timestamp composed of 10 digit numbers. Thus, it is inevitable to make the time format the same for serializing all system events depending on its occurring time.

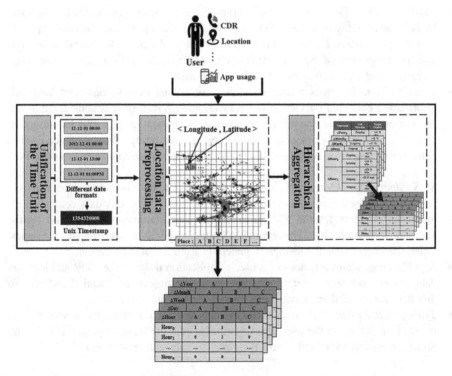

Fig. 4. The steps of the data preprocessing for context-aware authentication

3.2.2   Location Data Preprocessing

Location Data indicates a user's location composing of a *longitude* and *latitude* information collected by GPS. By using the location data, we can extract the user's location moving patterns and major spot where the user stays and how long he/she does in the stop. However, as the longitude and latitude is very small number composed of 10^{-10} (e.g., 46.5212053706, 6.6190893676), it is not efficient to use them to compare two locations directly. There might be several possible approaches to preprocessing location data. One of them is applying the clustering approaches of machine learning such as K-Means [16] or agglomerative hierarchical clustering [17]. However, it is a hard problem to decide the appropriate cluster number, and also the clustering approach loses too much information for the location.

Another possible approach is to make a grid map based on the latitude and longitude as shown in Fig. 5. Depending on the α that indicates the number of cells of the entire world, the place is simply computed like the equation in the figure. Thus, we need to decide the appropriate α. In case of the $\alpha = 10^7$, 0.001×0.001 of the latitude and longitude gap indicates the 100 m $\times$ 80 m size cell in the real world. In the evaluation section, the α is obtained by the sensitivity analysis.

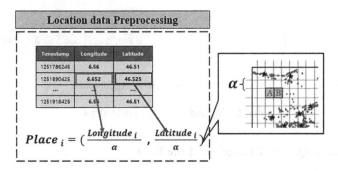

Fig. 5. Location data preprocessing

3.2.3 Hierarchical Aggregation

This step is a hierarchical aggregation of the serialized context data with grid-mapped location data. It starts with making a feature vector composed of context data that occurs during $\Delta Time$. Figure 6(a) denotes the aggregation steps of the CDR and location context data occurred during the fundamental time span (e.g., 1 h or 2 h). In the figure, the left tables are the raw CDR and location data, and then those are grouped into the $\Delta Time$ base (see the two tables in the center column). Then, the two data are merged into one table, and each data are aggregated and placed at each column. Thus, the one row of $\Delta Time$ denotes the number of context data that occurred during the time span. It should be noted that $\Delta Time$ is considered as the minimal time of gathering the context data for requesting authentication.

The next step is a hierarchical aggregation from the fundamental time span aggregation. If the fundamental time span is 1 h, the hierarchical aggregation time span might be 1 day or 2 days, 1 week or 1 month as shown in Fig. 6(b). The levels of the hierarchy is decided to the experiment, however, we can imagine that the $\Delta Time$ and the levels of hierarchical aggregation should characterize a human's life pattern.

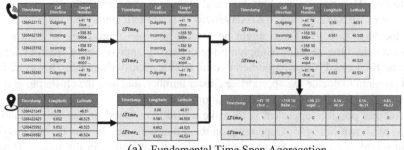

(a) Fundamental Time Span Aggregation

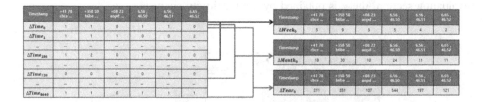

(b) Hierarchical Aggregation

Fig. 6. Hierarchical aggregation steps

3.3   Statistical Quality Evaluation of the Data

After aggregating context data, the data quality should be evaluated. As the context-aware authentication is an approach to comparing the recent context data to the past context data, the recent context data indicates the context data gathered during $\Delta Time$ and the past context data can be the past data gathered during $\Delta Time$ and the result of hierarchical aggregation. The high-quality data denotes that the recent and past context data should have the same mean and variance for the same user. Otherwise, the mean and variance are different for the different user. Thus, the α and $\Delta Time$ should be decided to make high-quality data.

Statistically, *Two-Sample T-Test* is the approach to statistically check if the means of two sets of data is the same or not. Thus, the *p-value* greater than 0.05 of the T-Test denotes that the means of the two data sets statistically are the same [18]. For checking if the distribution (i.e., variance) of the two sets of data, we can apply F-Test where we can consider that distribution of two sets of data is statistically the same if the p-value is greater than 0.05 [19]. We can guess that the recent smartphone user is the same user with the past if the p-value resulting from T-Test and F-Test of the recent context data and the past context data is greater than 0.05. Otherwise, the recent and past users are different. To make the two tests passed for the same user's context data, we should decide the parameters α and $\Delta Time$.

4   Experiment: Real-World Context Data

In this section, we present an experiment on the data preprocessing for the real-world context data. Thus, we first introduce the context data set and then present how we obtain the best parameters to have high-quality context data using the statistical approach. Finally, we discuss the result in the last subsection.

4.1   Experimental Setting

We have applied our approach to the MDC (Mobile Data Challenge) dataset [20], which is a collection of smartphone data such as accelerometer, network connections, calendar, CDR as well as GPS gathered from about 200 users for two years from 2012. We extracted the five user's context data, because only small number of the user's data has complete and location data during the period. Table 1 presents the data set.

Table 1. The number of the five smartphone user's dataset

User ID	Number of CDR	Number of GPS	Number of Data
5938	7	1931	1938
5973	3	1717	1720
5928	6	922	928
5976	32	814	846
6177	10	797	807
...	...	...	...

4.2   Experiment Result

We carried out the MDC data preprocessing according to the aforementioned steps: (1) unification of the timestamp, (2) location data preprocessing, and (3) hierarchical aggregation. Then, we tried to find the best parameters such as α and the $\Delta Time$ by

Table 2. Experiment result

α	Request data	base data	F-test p-value	Average of F-test p-value	T-test p-value	Average of T-test p-value
10^8	1hour	1 hour before	3.6735E-05		0.572925	
	2hour	2 hour before	0.1	0.033345578	0.6197	0.456889815
	1day	1 day before	1.4798E-267		0.178044444	
	1hour	the same hour before 1 week	0.3719		0.879433333	
	2hour	the same hour before 1 week	3.96E-01	0.460938095	9.70E-01	0.942544444
	1day	The same weekday of last	0.615414286		0.9787	
	1week	last week	0.113677778	-	0.934966667	-
	1month	last month	2.37E-02	-	9.16E-01	-
10^7	1hour	1 hour before	0.036021898		0.87131	
	2hour	2 hour before	0.015502372	0.017174757	0.8531125	0.702263056
	1day	1 day before	6.5065E-171		0.382366667	
	1hour	the same hour before 1 week	1.63158E-09		0.704514286	
	2hour	the same hour before 1 week	0.321257143	0.107085715	0.962828571	0.648505952
	1day	The same weekday of last	1.10893E-44		0.278175	
	1week	last week	0.635525	-	0.9754625	-
	1month	last month	0.0935	-	0.912333333	-

applying the F-Test and T-Test statistical techniques. We performed the experiment with two α 10^7 and 10^8, the five $\Delta Time$ 1 h, 2 h, 1 day, 2 days, 1 week and 1 month. Also, we compared the request data (recent data) to the diverse past data (base data) of the same user. Table 2 summarized the result.

The first row of Table 2 can be understood as the follows: (1) the location separated by the 100 m × 80 m grid ($\alpha = 10^8$), (2) we compared the two data sets, each of which is the recent 1 h data and the 1 h before the 1 h, (3) the variance of the two sets is different and the mean is the same, because the p-value of F-test is less than 0.05, and the p-value is greater than 0.05. In order to make the data valid for the context-aware authentication, most of the p-value of F-Test and T-Test should be greater than 0.05. Thus, we can conclude that comparison between 1 h – 1 h before is not appropriate though the two means are the same.

We highlighted the data set which has the p-value less than 0.05 with the bright red color in the table. According to the result, most of the means in the comparison is the same (see the result of T-Test) and the variance (i.e., distribution) is different. Also, the result of F-Test in case of $\alpha = 10^7$ indicates the comparison has a different distribution, though the two data set is from the same user. Also, we can recognize a comparison between 1, 2 h, 1 day and the same hour before 1 week and the same weekday of the last provides better data quality.

According to the experiment result, we can conclude that the 100 m × 80 m grid map of the location provides better performance, and aggregating the data depending on the week, and comparison data such as 1 h, 2 h to that before 1 week showed better performance. Thus, we can conclude that the hierarchical aggregation should be 1 h, 1day, 1week, 1 month, and 1 year as shown in Fig. 7.

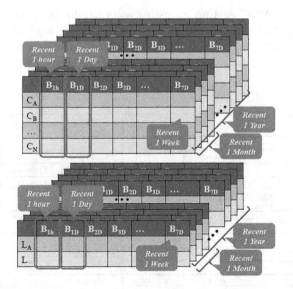

Fig. 7. Appropriate hierarchical aggregations

5   Conclusion

In this paper, we proposed the data preprocessing approach for context-aware authentication in a smartphone. For the authentication, we first summarized the candidate context data that can be gathered from the smartphone. Then, we proposed the three-step data preprocessing approach consisting of (1) unification of the time unit for serializing the context data, (2) location data preprocessing, and (3) n-dimensional aggregation of the context data. For the evaluation, we applied our approach to the MDC dataset and showed how we obtained the best parameters by using F-Test and two sample T-Test. As future work, we have a plan to enhance our approach more so that we will establish the model of context-aware authentication and implement it.

References

1. Herley, C.: So long, and no thanks for the externalities: the rational rejection of security advice by users. In: Proceedings of SACMAT (2009)
2. Hulsebosch, J.R., Salden, H.A., Bargh, S.M., Ebben, P.W.G., Reitsma, J.: Context sensitive access control. In: Proceedings of SACMAT (2005)
3. Nachenberg, C.: A window into mobile device security: examining the security approaches employ. SSR (2011)
4. Whitney, L.: Smartphones to dominate PCs in Gartner forecast. CNET Business Tech News (2010)
5. Rainie, L., Anderson, J.: The Future of the Internet III. Pew Internet Project (2008)
6. Zhang, F., Kondoro, A., Muftic, S.: Location-based authentication and authorization using smartphone. TrustCom (2012)
7. Shi, E., Niu, Y., Jakobsson, M., Chow, R.: Implicit authentication through learning user behavior. In: Burmester, M., Tsudik, G., Magliveras, S., Ilić, I. (eds.) ISC 2010. LNCS, vol. 6531, pp. 99–113. Springer, Heidelberg (2011). https://doi.org/10.1007/978-3-642-18178-8_9
8. Markus, J., Shi, E., Golle, P., Chow, R.: Implicit authentication for mobile devices. USENIX (2009)
9. Hilmi, G.K., Just, M., Baillie, L., Aspinall, D., Micallef, N.: Data driven authentication: on the effectiveness of user behaviour modelling with mobile device sensors. MoST (2014)
10. Lamport, L.: Password authentication with insecure communication. Commun. ACM **24**(11), 770–772 (1981)
11. Huang, C.-Y., Ma, S.-P., Chen, K.-T.: Using one-time passwords to prevent password phishing attacks. J. Netw. Comput. Appl. **34**(4), 1292–1301 (2011)
12. Xi, K., et al.: A fingerprint based bio-cryptographic security protocol designed for client/server authentication in mobile computing environment. Secur. Commun. Netw. **4**(5), 487–499 (2011)
13. Nilesh, A., Salendra, P., et al.: A review of authentication methods. Int. J. Sci. Technol. Res. **5**(11), 246–249 (2016)
14. Bhatia, R.: Biometrics and face recognition techniques. Int. J. Adv. Res. Comput. Sci. Softw. Eng. **3**, 93–96 (2013)
15. Kak, N., Gupta, R.: Iris recognition system. Int. J. Adv. Comput. Sci. Appl. **1**, 34–40 (2010)
16. Hartigan, J.A., Wong, M.A.: A k-means clustering algorithm. J. Roy. Stat. Soc. Ser. C (Appl. Stat.) **28**(1), 100–108 (1979)

17. William, H.E.D., Edelsbrunner, H.: Efficient algorithms for agglomerative hierarchical clustering methods. J. Classif. **1**, 7–24 (1984)
18. Snedecor, G.W., Cochran, W.G.: Statistical Methods. 8th edn. Iowa state University Press (1989)
19. Shen, Q., Faraway, J.: An f test for linear models with functional responses. Statistica Sinica **14**, 1239–1257 (2004)
20. Mobile Data Challenge (MDC) Dataset: Dataset Distribution Portal. https://www.idiap.ch/dataset/mdc. Accessed 6 Feb 2019
21. Perlman, R.: An overview of PKI trust models. IEEE Netw. **13**(6), 38–43 (1999)

Extending and Instantiating a Software Reference Architecture for IoT-Based Healthcare Applications

Itamir de Morais Barroca Filho[1]([✉]), Gibeon Soares Aquino Junior[2],
and Thais Batista Vasconcelos[2]

[1] Digital Metropolis Institute, Federal University of Rio Grande do Norte,
Natal, Brazil
itamir.filho@imd.ufrn.br
[2] Department of Informatics and Applied Mathematics,
Federal University of Rio Grande do Norte, Natal, Brazil
{gibeon,thais}@dimap.ufrn.br
http://www.imd.ufrn.br, http://www.dimap.ufrn.br

Abstract. The Internet of Things (IoT) is making possible the development of applications in many markets, such as buildings, home, industrial and healthcare. Concerning the healthcare market, there are a lot of challenges in the design, development, and deployment of these applications, such as interoperability, availability, usability, and security. To contribute to solve the aforementioned challenges, we proposed a software reference architecture, named *Reference Architecture for IoT-based Healthcare Applications (RAH)*, to systematically organize the main elements of this domain, its responsibilities and interactions, promoting a common understanding of these applications' architecture. RAH presents software architectural solutions (i.e., architectural patterns and tactics) documented using architectural views. This work aims to present RAH and instantiate it to design the software architecture of an IoT-based healthcare platform for intelligent remote monitoring of the patient's health data.

Keywords: Internet of Things (IoT) · Healthcare ·
Reference architecture · Software architecture

1 Introduction

New technologies can change lives! That is what is happening with the use of the Internet of Things (IoT). The IoT denotes a trend where a large number of embedded devices employ communication services offered by Internet protocols. Many of these devices, often called "smart objects" or "things", are not directly operated by humans but exist as components in buildings or vehicles, or are spread out in the environment [1]. Thus, the basic idea of this paradigm is

© Springer Nature Switzerland AG 2019
S. Misra et al. (Eds.): ICCSA 2019, LNCS 11623, pp. 203–218, 2019.
https://doi.org/10.1007/978-3-030-24308-1_17

the pervasive presence, around all users, of a variety of things - such as Radio-Frequency IDentification (RFID) tags, sensors, actuators, mobile phones, etc. Through unique addressing schemes, things are able to interact with each other and cooperate with their neighbors to reach common goals [2]. It is estimated that by 2025, 80 billion IoT devices will be online, creating 180 ZB of data [3]. This myriad of connected things, the data captured by them, and the connectivity between them is making possible the development of IoT applications in various markets, such as transportation, buildings, energy, home, industrial, and healthcare.

Concerning the healthcare market, this paradigm is reshaping modern healthcare, connecting everything to the Internet, shifting "from anytime, anyplace connectivity for anyone" to "connectivity for anything". The IoT can be the main enabler for distributed healthcare applications, thus having a significant potential to contribute to the overall decrease of healthcare costs, while increasing the health outcomes. Moreover, IoT-based healthcare applications are projected to provide the biggest economic impact. These applications, such as mHealth and telecare, which help to afford medical wellness, prevention, diagnosis, treatment and monitoring services to be delivered efficiently through electronic media, are expected to create about $ 1.1–$ 2.5 trillion annually in global economy growth by 2025 [4].

There are a lot of challenges in the development and deployment of this kind of application, such as (i) **interoperability** [5,6]: there are heterogeneous sources of data, the devices' protocol is not open, so a given device cannot be integrated to another (or multiple) applications, and there are also different studies and proposals for patient monitoring at hospitals or personal monitoring at home; (ii) **availability** [5]: several applications do not provide a way to ensure that they are available when needed; (iii) **usability** [7]: most existing home healthcare systems have drawbacks, such as simple and few functionalities, weak user interaction, and poor mobility; (iv) **security** [5]: many existing systems lacks of permission control, privacy, and data anonymity, etc; (v) **flexibility** [8]: existing products cannot autonomously adapt to usage scenarios, such as assisted living, intelligent buildings, smart transportation, energy, healthcare, or entire supply chains; (vi) **productivity** [8]: IoT-based healthcare services need to extend toward predictive maintenance and proactive enhancements, improving uptime and, thus, productivity.

In short, the complex and heterogeneous nature of the IoT-based healthcare applications makes their design and development difficult. It also causes an increase in the development cost, as well as hampers interoperability among existing systems. Thus, a strategy to design a software reference architecture to systematically organize the main elements of IoT-based healthcare applications, its responsibilities, and interactions, promotes a common understanding of these applications' architecture. A reference architecture (RA) is used as a basis to design concrete architectures in multiple contexts, serving as an inspiration or standardization tool [9]. Nowadays, the increasing complexity of software, the need for efficient and effective software design processes, and the need for high levels of system interoperability, demands for reference architectures to systematically organize the software design process, applying an architecture-centric development approach.

Considering the challenges associated to the development of IoT-based healthcare applications, the main objective of this paper is to present and instantiate a reference architecture, named *Reference Architecture for IoT-based Healthcare Applications* (RAH) [10], designed to improve the common understanding and systematization of the IoT-based healthcare applications' architectural design, and to offer guidelines for the development of these applications. The Reference Architecture presented in this paper is an extension of an initial version presented by Barroca and Aquino [10].

The rest of this paper is organized as follows: in Sect. 2, related works are reviewed. RAH reference architecture is described in Sect. 3. Section 4 describes the case study used to apply RAH to design and develop an IoT-based healthcare application, named PAR, for intelligent remote monitoring of patients in critical situation. Finally, the final remarks and future works are presented in Sect. 5.

2   Related Work

This section discusses about the existing reference architectures for the Internet of Things (IoT). These architectures were identified through the conduction of an exploratory review. Currently, to the best of our knowledge, there is no specific reference architecture for IoT-based healthcare applications. Identifying and structuring an architecture or model is a long and tedious process with much effort to abstract from specific needs and technologies. Such a reference can serve as an overall and generic guideline [8].

In the IoT context, the applications have been based on fragmented software implementations for specific systems and use cases, and usually they do not follow reference architectures. The need for reference architectures in industry has become tangible with the fast-growing number of initiatives working toward standardized architectures. These initiatives aim to facilitate interoperability, simplify development, and ease implementation [8]. There are three major reference architectures found in the literature for IoT: IoT-A [11], IIRA [12], and WSO2 [13]. These reference architectures work with concepts, such as IoT domain and IoT service, trying to address as many IoT applications scenarios as possible.

IoT-A Reference Architecture is, among others, designed as a reference for the generation of compliant-IoT concrete architectures that are tailored to one's specific needs [14]. It is an abstract framework that comprises of a minimal set of unifying concepts, axioms and relationships for understanding significant connections among entities of the IoT domain. IIRA is a standard-based open architecture for Industrial IoT (IIoT) systems. IIRA maximizes its value by having broad industry applicability to drive interoperability, to map applicable technologies, and to guide technology and standard development. The architecture description and representation are generic and at a high level of abstraction to support broad applicability in industry. IIRA distills and abstracts common characteristics, features and patterns from use cases defined in the Industrial Internet Consortium (IIC), as well as elsewhere. The WSO2's reference architecture consists of a set of components organized in layers and cross-cutting layers [13].

IoT-A RA argues the need to address the following quality attributes: interoperability, availability, security, performance, and scalability. However, it does not present the components defined to meet these attributes and, it does not present an evaluation in a real system. IIRA is at a level of abstraction that excludes architectural elements and requirements whose evaluation requires specificities only available in concrete systems, not presenting what are the addressed quality attributes. The WSO reference architecture highlights the scalability and security quality attributes mapping them into proprietary components of the WSO2 platform. Moreover, it was not found examples of how to instantiate these reference architectures into concrete architectures, and their evaluation.

Finally, the idea to address as many IoT applications requirements and scenarios as possible, without specifying the quality attributes required for the IoT-based healthcare applications or the components that address these requirements, make it difficult to use these reference architectures as guidelines for the development of these applications. Moreover, these reference architectures for IoT-based applications are too generic and abstract, and they do not focus on IoT-based healthcare applications. Therefore, currently, to the best of our knowledge, there is no reference architecture for the IoT-based healthcare domain.

3   A Reference Architecture for IoT-Based Healthcare Applications

As presented in Sect. 1, there are a lot of challenges related to the development and deployment of IoT-based healthcare applications, such as interoperability [5,6], availability [5], usability [7], security [5], flexibility [8], and productivity. Regarding interoperability, the overview of the papers presented by Barroca and Aquino [15] showed that 93% of the described new solutions would demand a change in the existing healthcare hardware and software. Although, there are many proposed protocols and different studies about IoT-based healthcare applications [15], a shared goal to produce an interoperable system adopting open standards for healthcare, for example HL7 [16], and a seamless framework to be easily deployed in any given scenario for healthcare is still missing [6]. In this scenario, the current state-of-the-art comprises independent IoT-based healthcare applications that do not interoperate and communicate with other applications. With the perspective of expanding these applications market and consequently the development of new solutions, this problem will grow significantly.

In this context, one of the possible cause for the lack of interoperability and communication between IoT-based healthcare applications is the absence of a software reference architecture (SRA) to serve as a guideline for the design of their architectures. SRA facilitates the development process, acting as a means of standardization and making modular configuration and interoperability with IoT-based healthcare solutions from different suppliers possible. Finally, its existence would provide a standardized view for these applications architecture which facilitates communication between the potential stakeholders (business professionals, software developers).

Therefore, we designed a software reference architecture for IoT-based healthcare applications, named *Reference Architecture for IoT-based Healthcare Applications (RAH)*, to serve as a guideline for the design of these applications' architectures [10]. It systematically organizes the main elements of these applications, its responsibilities and interactions, promoting a common understanding of these applications' architecture. RAH is defined based on a set of functional and nonfunctional requirements (quality attributes) related to IoT-based healthcare applications. These requirements were extracted from existing publications collected through the study presented by Barroca and Aquino [15]. This SRA was previously presented by Barroca and Aquino [10], but it is updated and instantiated in this work.

This section presents the proposed software reference architecture for IoT-based healthcare applications. It is structured as follows: in Sect. 3.1, it is described the requirements of a reference architecture for IoT-based healthcare applications, specifying the functional and nonfunctional requirements (quality attributes). Section 3.2 describes RAH, the software reference architecture for IoT-based healthcare applications.

3.1 Requirements of a Reference Architecture for IoT-Based Healthcare Applications

In this section, it is discussed the functional and nonfunctional requirements that must be addressed in RAH. The functional requirements express the functionalities that must be supported by an IoT-based healthcare application. The study presented by Barroca and Aquino [15] was used to define these requirements. The nonfunctional requirements must be addressed in the development of an IoT-based healthcare application. To define the nonfunctional requirements of a reference architecture for IoT-based healthcare applications, it was used the list of quality attributes of information systems presented by Bass et al. [17], as well as the existing publications presented by Barroca and Aquino [15]. Based on these list of requirements, the first version of RAH was defined. In this section, a set of extended functional and non-functional requirements of IoT-based healthcare applications is presented.

Functional Requirements. According to Bass et al., the functional requirements state what the system must do, and how it must behave or react to runtime stimuli [17]. Thus, the functional requirements of IoT-based healthcare applications consist of monitoring the patient's body and environment [15]. Regarding the body monitoring, the applications use sensors attached to the patient's body and capture data from: *Electrocardiogram (ECG)*, *Blood pressure*, *Blood glucose*,

Heart rate, Oxygen saturation, Temperature, and *Breathing rate.* To monitoring the environment, the applications use sensors deployed in the patient's environment to capture data from *temperature, light, humidity, location, body position, motion data, SpO_2, atmospheric pressure and CO_2* [15]. They are important because the environment conditions can directly affect the patient's treatment.

Quality Attributes (Nonfunctional Requirements). The quality attributes or nonfunctional requirements are qualifications of the functional requirements or of the overall product. A qualification of a functional requirement is an item such as how fast a function must be performed, or how resilient it must be to erroneous input. A qualification of the overall product is an item such as the time to deploy the product or a limitation on operational costs [17]. Thus, the main nonfunctional requirements/quality attributes of IoT-based healthcare applications are [15]: *Availability, Interoperability, Performance,* and *Security.*

3.2   RAH - Reference Architecture for IoT-Based Healthcare Applications

From the requirements of a reference architecture for IoT-based healthcare applications, which were previously defined, RAH was designed. The stakeholders for this reference architecture are systems analysts, software architects and developers of IoT-based healthcare applications. RAH is presented in the layered view in Fig. 1. The layered view is based on the layered style, which reflects a division of the software into layers that represent a group of modules offering a cohesive set of services [18]. More information about its views and services can be found in https://par.imd.ufrn.br/services.

This reference architecture is composed of five layers: **Sensing, Middleware, Services, Applications** and **Quality Attributes.** Interacting with the Sensing Layer, there are patients with devices to capture their biometrics and environment data. Interacting with the Applications Layer there are the users, such as physicians, hospital administrators, nurses, family, patients, pharmaceutical and clinical staff, that can be using an IoT-based healthcare application.

The *Sensing Layer* is responsible for monitoring the patient's body and environment, and is composed of the following components:

1. *Devices*: it is a hardware component that represents the devices used for monitoring the patient's body and environment. For instance, for the patient's body monitoring sensors to capture heart rate, temperature, etc, and for the environment monitoring, the devices are sensors that capture data related to temperature, light, humidity, SpO_2, pressure, and CO_2.
2. *Gateway Component*: it is a software component that receives data from the *Devices* and makes them available to the *Middleware Layer*. This component is composed of the *Raw Data Receive Service, Raw Data Send Service, Filter Service, and Network Service.*

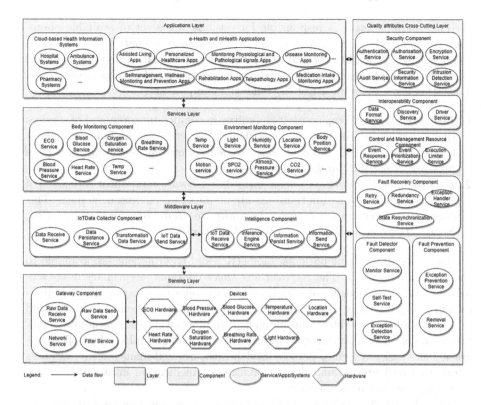

Fig. 1. Layered view of the RAH reference architecture.

Regarding the *Middleware Layer*, it is responsible for receiving the patient's sensors and environment data from the *Sensing Layer*, processing it, persisting it and making it available for the *Services Layer*. This layer is composed of the following components:

1. *IoTDataCollector Component*: it is a software component that receives the raw data sent by the *Gateway* component. It is composed of *Data Receive, Data Persistence, Transformation, IoT Data Send* services. Thus, this component is responsible for persisting, processing and transforming the raw data in a data format that are understandable by the *Intelligence* component.
2. *Intelligence Component*: it is a software component that receives data from the *IoTDataCollector* component and uses inference engines to classify and persist the intelligent information in a repository. This intelligent information can be specific alerts configured by the clinical staff for the patients, or automatic alerts detected by the use of Artificial Intelligence techniques. This component also sends information to the *Services Layer*, and it is composed of *IoT Data Receive, Inference Engine, Information Persist and Information Send* services.

The *Services Layer* is responsible for establishing a set of available operations related to the consumption of the patients monitored data (body and environment) by the applications. It centralizes access to data providing a bridge between the applications in the *Application Layer* and the *Middleware Layer*. Thus, this layer is composed of the following components:

1. *Body Monitoring Component*: it is a software component composed of services that provides information about patients' biometrics data. This component is composed of *ECG, blood glucose, oxygen saturation, breathing rate, blood pressure, heart rate, and temperature* services.
2. *Environment Monitoring Component*: it is a software component composed of services that provides informations about patients' environment data. This component is composed of *light, humidity, location, body position, motion, SpO_2, atmospheric pressure, CO_2, and temperature* services.

Thus, the data about patients' biometrics and environment are available to the *Applications Layer*. The *Applications Layer* contains the primary usage scenarios of IoT-based healthcare applications. Therefore, these examples of applications are grouped in cloud-based health information systems, e-Health, and mHealth applications. The cloud-based health information systems are for hospitals, ambulance, and pharmacy systems. The e-Health and mHealth applications are for the assisted living, personalized healthcare, self-management, wellness monitoring and prevention, disease monitoring, medication intake monitoring, telepathology, and rehabilitation.

The *Quality Attributes Cross-Cutting Layer* is responsible for features that make IoT-based healthcare applications secure, interoperable, available, and efficient. Its components address availability, interoperability, performance, and security. It is important to emphasize that because of the responsibility of this layer, it interacts with the *Applications, Services, Middleware*, and *Sensing* layers. Therefore, it is composed of the following components:

1. *Security Component*: it is a software component responsible for protecting patients data and information from unauthorized access while still providing access to people (patients, clinical staff, family, and physicians), systems and services that are authorized. It is composed of *authentication, authorization, encryption, audit, security information, and intrusion detection* services.
2. *Interoperability Component*: it is a software component responsible for allowing the IoT-based healthcare applications to have the ability to exchange data (syntactic interoperability), and also to interpret the data being exchanged (semantic interoperability). It is composed of *data format, discovery, and driver* services.
3. *Control and Management Resource Component*: it is a software component responsible for the performance of IoT-based healthcare applications. This performance regards to the response time and IoT-based healthcare applications ability to meet timing requirements. It is composed of *event response, event prioritization, execution limiter* services.

4. *Fault Recovery Component*: it is a software component related to availability and faults recoveries of IoT-based healthcare applications. It is composed of *retry, redundancy, exception handler, and state resynchronization* services.
5. *Fault Detector Component*: it is a software component related to availability and faults detections of IoT-based healthcare applications. It is composed of *monitor, self-test and exception detection* services.
6. *Fault Prevent Component*: it is a software component related to availability and faults preventions of IoT-based healthcare applications. It is composed of *exception prevention and removal* services.

4   A Case Study of Development of an IoT-Based Healthcare Application

This section presents the evaluation of RAH. For this evaluation a case study was conducted aiming to search evidence to test the hypothesis that RAH can be used to design an IoT-based healthcare application. For this, the case study research process presented by Runeson and Host [19] was followed.

4.1   Case Study Design

To assess RAH, the software architecture of PAR was designed as an instance of such reference architecture. PAR is an IoT-Based healthcare platform to integrate patients, physicians and ambulance services [20] in order to promote better care and fast preventive and reactive urgent actions for patients in a critical situation. It is composed of five modules: *Remote Patient and Environment Monitoring, Patient Healthcare Data Management, Patient Health Condition Management and Emergency and Crisis Management*. This platform was developed considering the need to transfer the healthcare from the hospital (hospital-centric) to the patient's home (home-centric) and is based on RAH (Reference Architecture for IoT-based Healthcare Applications).

Objective. The main objective of this case study is to validate the suitability of RAH to support the software architecture design of IoT-based healthcare applications capable of addressing their requirements.

Research Question (RQ). Can a software architecture of an IoT-based healthcare application be designed by using RAH?

4.2   Collecting Evidence

Nine people participated of this case study during its conduction: (i) The software architect of RAH, in charge of verifying the correct conduction of the instantiation process of RAH, and responsible for collecting and analyzing the evidence to answer the RQs; (ii) the software architect of PAR, responsible

Table 1. Functional requirements of PAR and RAH's components and services.

Id	Functional requirements	RAH's component and services
FR01	Remote body monitoring of patients: ECG, heart rate, oxygen saturation, temperature, breathing rate	RAH's body monitoring component: ECG, heart rate, oxygen saturation, temperature, and breathing rate services
FR02	Remote environment monitoring of patients: temperature and humidity	RAH's environment monitoring component: temperature and humidity services
FR03	Patient healthcare data management: records data of patients, physicians, nurses, health insurance, health condition, history of monitoring and emergency alerts	RAH's cloud based health information systems: Hospital systems
FR04	Patient's health condition management: definition of critical levels for the values read by the sensors	RAH's cloud based health information systems: Hospital systems
FR05	Emergency and crisis managements: patient's health condition and the services that should be alerted in case of emergency	RAH's cloud based health information systems: Ambulance systems; RAH's e-health and mhealth applications

for conducting and documenting the instantiation process; (iii) five developers responsible for supporting the requirements elicitation and implementation of PAR; and (iv) two registered nurses assisting the domain analysis activity. The remainder of this section presents the information collected at conducting each procedure described in Sect. 4.1.

Procedure 1 - Documenting the Platform Software Architecture Design. In this procedure, the scope and architectural design of PAR were established. PAR is an IoT-based healthcare platform for intelligent remote monitoring of patients in a critical situation and was developed considering the necessity to transfer the healthcare from the hospital (hospital-centric) to the patient's home (home-centric). This platform integrates patients, physicians, and ambulance services to promote better care and provide fast preventive and reactive urgent actions. It addresses challenges like interoperability, performance, security, and availability.

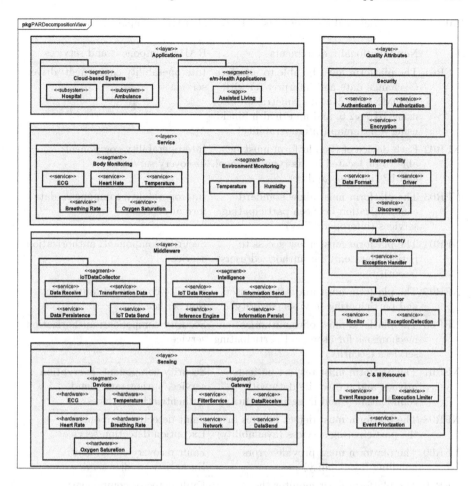

Fig. 2. PAR decomposition view as an instance of RAH.

The two registered nurses involved in the case study were responsible to define with the developers and architects the requirements of PAR. In total, 05 functional requirements and 12 nonfunctional requirements were defined for PAR. These functional requirements are summarized in Table 1. The software architecture of PAR identified what are RAH's services and components that address these functional requirements. Stakeholders identified in the context of PAR are the patient, family, physician, nurse, hospital and ambulance operators.

Regarding non functional requirements (quality attributes), the software architecture of PAR identified what are RAH's services and components that address these requirements. Thus, the non functional requirements and RAH's components and services are summarized and presented in Table 2. The number of monitored patients (19) proposed in NFR12 is based on the current capacity of the Intensive Care Unit (ICU) of the Onofre Lopes Hospital of the Federal

Table 2. Non functional requirements of PAR and RAH's components and services.

Id	Non functional requirements	RAH's component and services
NFR01	The platform must be able to interface (exchange data and interpret it) with an OMNI 612 Multiparametric Monitor using HL7 v2.6, and an eHealth Shield using a hashmap (interoperability)	Interoperability component: driver service
NFR02	Each device of the platform must be able to be located by its type, protocol, and IP (interoperability)	Interoperability component: discovery service
NFR03	The platform must allow standard communication between participating services (interoperability)	Interoperability component: data format service
NFR04	The platform must allow access to patient data only for authorized users (security)	Security component: authorization service
NFR05	The platform must authenticate users and participating services (security)	Security component: authentication service
NFR06	The platform must offer authorization mechanisms for users and participating services (security)	Security component: authorization service
NFR07	The platform must respect patients privacy and protect its data with confidentiality and integrity (security)	Security component: encryption service, authorization and authentication services
NFR08	The platform must detect failures in the participating services (availability)	Fault detector component: Exception detection service
NFR09	The platform must provide errors handling (availability)	Fault recovery component: Exception handler service
NFR10	The platform must monitor the participating services and devices (availability)	Fault detector component: monitor service
NFR11	The platform must be aware of its situation, and prevent and correct internal faults and failures (availability)	Fault detector component: monitor service
NFR12	The platform must be able to monitor 19 patients and to handle 133 transactions per second (performance)	Control and management resource component: event response, prioritization and execution limiter services

University of Rio Grande do Norte. The nurses participating in this case study work at this hospital, and suggested that this platform should be able to handle the current capacity of this ICU. The number of transactions (133) proposed in NFR12 is based on the 19 patients and the necessity of PAR to monitor ECG, heart rate, oxygen saturation, temperature, breathing rate, temperature, and humidity (NFR01 and NFR02). This results in 19 patients with 7 monitored data per second (one for each sensor).

Based on the requirements documents and RAH reference architecture, PAR's software architect designed PAR architecture instantiating the identified elements of RAH. Figure 2 presents PAR decomposition view. This view presents PAR in a fragmented way, beyond the layers and components of PAR Layered View, it details the PAR's services. This view was created by the PAR software architect following the requirements, and selecting which services of RAH would be instantiated for PAR. The importance of PAR decomposition view is the simplicity of the presentation of PAR fragmented in services, without showing its relationships, that are the focus of the following architecture views, designed from this decomposition. The services of RAH selected for the components are necessary to achieve the functional and nonfunctional requirements of PAR.

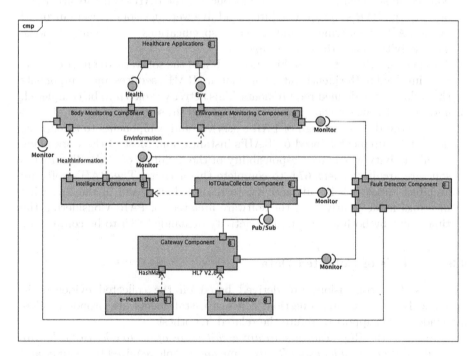

Fig. 3. PAR component and connector view.

PAR component and connector view is presented in Fig. 3. In this view, it is possible to note the following PAR quality attributes: interoperability and availability. Interoperability can be achieved in the communication between the devices and the Gateway component, which allows connection with different device types and different data flows. Availability can be achieved through the presence of the Fault Detector component, which monitors the PAR components, to identify any anomalies in their behavior. Regarding the data flow presented in this view, it starts with the devices sending the raw data (HL7 V2.6 and

HashMap) to the Gateway. The Gateway packages the data, it defines the packet headers and sends them to the IoTDataCollector (IDC). The IDC will receive the data packets, persist and treat them so that the output to the Intelligent Component is like IoTData.

Therefore, the Intelligent Component will apply its rules of inference about the IoTData, so that this data is semantically understood and presents information about the health status of a patient. The service layer components (Body and Environment Monitoring) act as interfaces that abstract the requests for information about patients' health and the environment in which they are accommodated. Finally, this information reaches the applications and is presented to the end users of PAR.

Resources - This procedure took 118 h:

1. Nine persons, of which two were nurses, one was the RAH's software architect, one was the PAR's software architect and five were developers, were involved in the PAR's requirements and use cases specifications and documentations. This activity took 26 h to be completed.
2. Two persons, the software architect of PAR and the software architect of RAH were involved in the identification of what are RAH's services and components that address the defined requirements. This activity took 9 h to be completed.
3. Two persons, the software architect of PAR and the software architect of RAH were involved in the design of PAR's services and components to attend the defined requirements, based on RAH's instantiation. Most of the work made in this activity was under responsibility of the architect of PAR. The PAR's software architect spent 67 h to complete this activity. The RAH's software architect spent 16 h in this activity, to resolve doubts and in the reviewing meetings made jointly with the software architect of PAR. Considering the time spent by both architects, this activity demanded 83 h to be completed.

4.3 Analysis of Collected Data

In this section conclusions are derived based on the collected evidences in Sect. 4.2. For the research question, conclusive statements are proposed offering evidence to support or refute the related hypothesis.

To answer the RQ - *Can a software architecture of an IoT-based healthcare application be designed by using RAH?*, time and people required to conduct and document the instantiation of RAH was registered. Therefore, at the end of the Procedure 1, presented in Sect. 4.2, information about time spent and people involved to design software architecture of PAR was detailed.

To support the hypothesis that *RAH allows to design software architectures of IoT-based healthcare applications*, the concrete software architecture of PAR was designed, as an instantiation of RAH. In this procedure, presented in Sect. 4.2, the requirements and architectural elements of PAR were mapped into requirements and architectural elements of RAH. This mapping, presented in Tables 1 and 2, shows that each requirement of PAR is under the responsibility of at least one component and service of RAH. Figure 2 presents the services and components instanced of RAH for PAR.

Moreover, the architectural views of PAR were created following the guidelines and views of RAH, as presented in Figs. 2 and 3. With these evidences, it is possible to affirm that RAH allowed the design of the software architecture of PAR, an IoT-based healthcare application. However, additional instantiations of RAH for the design of concrete architectures of IoT-based healthcare applications must be performed to offer more evidence to support this hypothesis.

Finally, as presented in the Procedure 1, the RAH's software architect spent 16 h to resolve doubts and in the reviewing meeting made jointly with the software architect of PAR. The PAR's software architect spent 67 h to complete this instantiation of RAH and documentation of PAR. It is possible that this time could be less if there were a specific instantiation process to use with RAH. A video presenting PAR is available in https://par.imd.ufrn.br/video, and its architectural views are presented in https://par.imd.ufrn.br/views. The source code of PAR is available in https://projetos.imd.ufrn.br/iothealthcareplatform/.

5   Conclusions and Future Works

This paper presented an extended version of an initial proposal of RAH. This new consolidated version is instantiated in this paper through a case study involving 9 specialists in grounding the application using RAH as a basis for the development process. RAH was designed mainly using as input a systematic mapping study presented by Barroca and Aquino [15]. This study allowed us to extract the main characteristics (functional and nonfunctional requirements), protocols and challenges related to healthcare applications.

The applicability of RAH was assessed using evidence by conducting an instantiation process to design and implement PAR, an IoT-based healthcare application for intelligent remote monitoring of patients in a critical situation. Although the obtained results were positive, replications of the case study can be conducted in different types of applications. The components and services developed for PAR can be reused in new IoT-based healthcare applications. Thus, the update of RAH to support code generation of the instanced software architectures, providing common components and services can help in the instantiation of new applications.

Finally, many opportunities for research emerged during the development of this work. They represent perspectives of future research that can contribute to the areas of e-Health, IoT-based healthcare applications, and software architecture. Some of them are described as follows: development framework for IoT-based healthcare applications; RAH as middleware for IoT-based healthcare applications; and RAH as a product line architecture.

References

1. Arkko, J., McPherson, D., Tschofenig, H., Thaler, D.: Architectural considerations in smart object networking (2015)
2. Atzori, L., Iera, A., Morabito, G.: The internet of things: a survey. Comput. Netw. **54**(15), 2787–2805 (2010)

3. IDC. IDC FutureScape: worldwide it industry 2017 predictions (2017). https://www.idc.com/getdoc.jsp?containerid=us41883016

4. Al-Fuqaha, A., Guizani, M., Mohammadi, M., Aledhari, M., Ayyash, M.: Internet of things: a survey on enabling technologies, protocols, and applications. IEEE Commun. Surv. Tutor. **17**(4), 2347–2376 (2015)

5. Doukas, C., Maglogiannis, I.: Bringing IoT and cloud computing towards pervasive healthcare. In: 2012 Sixth International Conference on Innovative Mobile and Internet Services in Ubiquitous Computing (IMIS), pp. 922–926. IEEE (2012)

6. Khattak, H.A., Ruta, M., Di Sciascio, E.: CoAP-based healthcare sensor networks: a survey. In: Proceedings of 2014 11th International Bhurban Conference on Applied Sciences & Technology (IBCAST), Islamabad, Pakistan, 14th–18th January, 2014, pp. 499–503. IEEE (2014)

7. Kevin, I., Wang, K., Rajamohan, A., Dubey, S., Catapang, S.A., Salcic, Z.: A wearable internet of things mote with bare metal 6LoWPAN protocol for pervasive healthcare. In 2014 IEEE 11th International Conference on Ubiquitous Intelligence and Computing, pp. 750–756. IEEE (2014)

8. Ebert, C., et al.: Reference architectures for the internet of things. IEEE Softw. 112–116 (2016)

9. Muller, G.: A reference architecture primer. Eindhoven University of Technology, Eindhoven, White paper (2008)

10. Barroca Filho, I.M., de Aquino Junior, G.S.: A software reference architecture for IoT-based healthcare applications. In: Gervasi, O., et al. (eds.) ICCSA 2018. LNCS, vol. 10963, pp. 173–188. Springer, Cham (2018). https://doi.org/10.1007/978-3-319-95171-3_15

11. Bassi, A., et al.: Enabling Things to Talk. Springer, Heidelberg (2016). https://doi.org/10.1007/978-3-642-40403-0

12. Lin, S.W., Crawford, M., Mellor, S.: The industrial internet of things volume G1: reference architecture. Industrial Internet Consortium (2017)

13. Fremantle, P.: A reference architecture for the internet of things. WSO2 White paper (2014)

14. Bauer, M., et al.: IoT reference model. In: Bassi, A., et al. (eds.) Enabling Things to Talk, pp. 113–162. Springer, Heidelberg (2013). https://doi.org/10.1007/978-3-642-40403-0_7

15. de Morais Barroca Filho, I., de Aquino Junior, G.S.: IoT-based healthcare applications: a review. In: Gervasi, O., et al. (eds.) ICCSA 2017. LNCS, vol. 10409, pp. 47–62. Springer, Cham (2017). https://doi.org/10.1007/978-3-319-62407-5_4

16. HL7.org. Health level seven (2017)

17. Bass, L., Clements, P., Kazma, R.: Software Architecture in Practice, 3rd edn. Addison-Wesley, Boston (2013)

18. Bachmann, F., et al.: Documenting Software Architectures: Views and Beyond. Addison-Wesley Professional, Boston (2011)

19. Runeson, P., Host, M.: Guidelines for conducting and reporting case study research in software engineering. Empir. Softw. Eng. **14**(2), 131–164 (2009)

20. Barroca Filho, I.M., de Aquino Junior, G.S.: Proposing an IoT-based healthcare platform to integrate patients, physicians and ambulance services. In: Gervasi, O., et al. (eds.) ICCSA 2017. LNCS, vol. 10409, pp. 188–202. Springer, Cham (2017). https://doi.org/10.1007/978-3-319-62407-5_13

Artificial Intelligence Techniques for Electrical Load Forecasting in Smart and Connected Communities

Victor Alagbe[1], Segun I. Popoola[1,2(✉)] ⓘ, Aderemi A. Atayero[1] ⓘ,
Bamidele Adebisi[2] ⓘ, Robert O. Abolade[3], and Sanjay Misra[1] ⓘ

[1] IoT-Enabled Smart and Connected Communities (SmartCU) Research Cluster,
Covenant University, Ota, Nigeria
victor.alagbe@stu.cu.edu.ng, atayero@covenantuniversity.edu.ng
[2] Department of Engineering, Manchester Metropolitan University,
Manchester M1 5GD, UK
segun.i.popoola@stu.mmu.ac.uk, b.adebisi@mmu.ac.uk
[3] Department of Electronic and Electrical Engineering,
Ladoke Akintola University of Technology, Ogbomoso, Nigeria
roabolade@lautech.edu.ng

Abstract. Electricity consumption has been on a rapid increase world-wide and it is a very vital component of human life in this age. Hence, reliable supply of electricity from the utility operators is a necessity. However, the constraints that electricity supplied must be the same as electricity consumed puts the burden on the utility operators to make sure that demand is equal to supply at any point in time in smart and connected communities. Load forecasting techniques, therefore, aim to resolve these challenges for the operators by providing accurate forecasts of electrical load demand. This paper reviews current and mostly used short term forecasting techniques, drawing parallels be-tween them; and highlighting their advantages and disadvantages. This paper concludes by stating that there is no one-size-fits-all technique for load forecasting problems, as appropriate techniques depend on several factors such as data size and variability and environmental variables. Different optimization techniques can be used whether to reduce errors and its variations or to speed up computational time, hence resulting in an improved model. However, it is imperative to consider the tradeoffs between each model and its different variants in the context of smart and connected communities.

Keywords: Artificial Intelligence · Load forecasting · Smart city ·
Neural network · Support Vector Machine

1 Introduction

Electricity consumption has been on a rapid increase worldwide and it is a very vital component of human life in this age. Several studies have shown the presence of direct correlation between growth in Gross Domestic Product (GDP) and

© Springer Nature Switzerland AG 2019
S. Misra et al. (Eds.): ICCSA 2019, LNCS 11623, pp. 219–230, 2019.
https://doi.org/10.1007/978-3-030-24308-1_18

increase in energy consumption. A study of seventeen countries in Africa over a thirty-year period found a correlation between GDP and electricity consumption with varying amount of causality [1]. A seventeen-year study period of seventeen industries in Taiwan revealed a bi-directional causality effect and showed that increase in electricity consumption by 1% resulted in a corresponding 1.72% increase in GDP [2]. Electricity generation at any time need to be equal to the electricity consumption to prevent huge losses. However, energy demand can be highly infrequent and varies greatly; hence, there is a need to accurately forecast load demand of users to allow for adequate planning. Load forecast can be divided into three forecast periods, the short term which varies from less than one hour to one-week, medium term from one month to one year, and long term forecast from one year to ten years. Short Term Load Forecast (STLF) is very important in energy planning and management for ensuring optimum supply and consumption of data without wasting resources. However the load series is characterized by non-linearity, non-stationary and seasonal variations, hence making accurate forecast hard to achieve [3]. Also, STLF models are found to be affected by weather conditions due to the strong correlation between weather variables and electricity consumption [4]. In this review, we discussed relevant sections of literature which attempted to solve the short-term load forecast challenge with diverse models, drawing up parallels and similarities between them.

Load forecast techniques generally can be classified into two: parametric and non-parametric techniques. The parametric techniques are based on the assumptions that sampled data follow a probability distribution based on a fixed set of parameters and include linear regression, exponential smoothing, auto regressive moving average (ARMA) etc. While non-parametric techniques – which consist mainly of Artificial Intelligence – have flexible parameter sets which may increase or decrease depending on new information. Such examples include Support Vector Machine (SVM), Artificial Neural Networks (ANN), Extreme Learning Machine (ELM) etc. These techniques however have different strengths and weaknesses as pertaining to the research problem at hand.

This paper reviews current and mostly used short term forecasting techniques, drawing parallels between them; and highlighting their advantages and disadvantages. This paper concludes by stating that there is no one-size-fits-all technique for load forecasting problems, as appropriate techniques depend on several factors such as data size and variability and environmental variables. Different optimization techniques can be used whether to reduce errors and its variations or to speed up computational time, hence resulting in an improved model. However, it is imperative to consider the tradeoffs between each model and its different variants in the context of smart and connected communities.

2   State-of-the-Art Computational Intelligence Techniques

2.1   Artificial Neural Networks

ANN draws its inspirations from the human nervous system. It consists of large array of artificial neurons interconnected with each other. Each neuron has an input, output, weight and threshold in a bio-mimicry of the brain neurons. ANN is defined as a large array of parallel combinations of simple processing units which are highly capable in modifying their parameters through a learning process in response to their environment to capture information [5]. ANN has advantage in not being explicitly programmed but in being trained hence, allowing it to capture and recognize invariance between variables which it was not trained for [6].

The neuron in an artificial neural network serves as the basic computing element. The neuron has a set of inputs which are passed into it with their respective weights which are then summed together and passed through an activation function and bias which determines its output. This output can be the final output or input to another neuron in the next layer.

A neural network primarily comprises of three layers which are: input, hidden and output layer. A network with no hidden layer is referred to as Single Layer Neural Network (SLNN) while a network with one or more hidden layer is Multilayer Perceptron (MLP). Neural networks, however, has different forms which vary largely from Feedforward NN, Recurrent NN, Convolutional N etc. and are usually trained using Backpropagation algorithm, Levenberg Marquardt algorithm etc.

2.2 Support Vector Machine

SVM was first introduced in by Boser et al. [7] as a training algorithm which maximizes the margin between the decision boundaries and the training patterns. The SVM were mainly inspired by statistical learning algorithm, based on risk minimization principles [8]. SVM is used to create separating hyperplane optimally with the feature space in higher dimension and in which subsequent findings can be grouped into different subsets [9]. SVM can also be used with non-linear boundaries as stated in [10], by transforming them to linear boundaries on a higher dimensional plane.

The SVM has found increased use in research and industry as it very effective in solving non-linear problems [11], and have demonstrated good performance in regards to preventing over-fitting leading to improved performances in solving time-series problems [12]. Over-fitting occurs when the learning algorithm learns too much from the data and become unable to generalize with new data sets. However, the SVM suffers from computational inefficiency as large computational resources are needed for higher dimensional feature space which is resolved using "kernel trick" [13]. Kernels are functions which modify how similarities are calculated between functions by representing inner products of observation rather than the actual observation.

The Support Vector Regression (SVR) however, is a form of SVM centered on regression, built and developed to minimize structural risks [14]. This is achieved by reducing the probability of the model from the training examples will achieve minimal error when introduced to new examples. The best solution to this risk minimization is achieved when the convex criterion function is reduced.

2.3 Fuzzy Logic

Fuzzy Logic can be said to be a form of Boolean logic that can be used to handle partial truth values i.e. values that are not completely true or false. This is derived from humans' reasoning methods which are not exact in nature but approximate. The theory of fuzzy sets, which is a generalization of classic theory of sets serves as the fundamental mathematical basis of fuzzy logic [15]. The switch of an object from classic theory to fuzzy logic theory is realized through the membership function, which can be triangular, Gaussian, trapezoidal etc. A fuzzy application is made up of four distinct layers: input; rule evaluation or inference; composition or aggregation of outputs; and defuzzification or output layers [16].

2.4 Extreme Learning Machine

ELM is a modern learning algorithm which was proposed in [17] by Huang et al. for feed forward neural networks with single hidden layer (SLFN) as an improvement in learning speed over traditional algorithms with the model exhibiting better generalization performance. In ELM, the input weights and hidden biases of the network are not tuned but randomly generated; hence, enabling the transformation of nonlinear system to linear system [18]. ELM has been implemented in several applications such as regression, classification, clustering, feature selection etc. The network layout of an ELM consist of the input layer as the first layer; a hidden layer which is activated by weighted projections of the input to non-linear sigmoid units as the second layer; and the output layer which comprises of units wi [19].

3 Current Trends and Research Directions

3.1 Neural Network for Electrical Load Forecasting

In using ANN for sub-hourly electricity usage forecast in commercial buildings, Chae et al. [20] used time indicator, environmental and operational data gotten from the metering infrastructure for three buildings with one utility billing system. The variable selection analysis was done with Random Forest yielding five variables: day type, outdoor dry-bulb temperature, outdoor relative humidity, operational condition and time indicator, together with previous electricity usage which were used as the predictor variables after which the model was built with Bayesian regularized neural network with Levenburg-Marquart (LM) back propagation algorithm. The result revealed that additional hidden layers and increased time delay resulted into better performance of the model with reduced average MSE and the min-max error range. In predicting day-ahead peak load demand for the Iranian National Grid, authors in [21] proposed an hybrid method comprising of wavelet decomposition and ANN. The high and low frequency components of the data were first captured using wavelet decomposition while the ANN which was optimized with genetic optimization was then used for each component. The peak demand was then determined by reconstructing the low and high components. Results demonstrated better MAPE forecast errors and applicability of the model in real-time applications due to acceptable processing time.

In [22], Generalized Regression Neural Network (GRNN) was implemented to solve the non-linearity problem in which STLF is one of such. To select the spread parameter which determines the performance of GRNN, the fruit fly optimization decreasing step (SFOA) was employed; and this was integrated with weather variables and the periodicity of the short-term load to build a credible model. The model when com-pared to a Back Propagation NN yielded better performance in accuracy (SFOA-GRNN RMSE = 0.0018 vs. BPNN RMSE = 0.024), stability and convergence speed.

In [23], Khwaja et al. used Bagged Neural Network, which creates multiple sets of a dataset by sampling randomly with dataset, trains on each dataset and averages the results with an aim to improve on the performances of single neural network by reducing errors variation and estimation errors. The data used was collected from the New England Pool region using historical temperature data, load pattern history, hour of the day, day type etc. The model demonstrated consistent results when the multiple sets of ANN are more than or equal to 50, with appreciable performance regarding reduced MAPE compared to other techniques like single ANN, bagged regression trees, ARMA etc. However, a similar STLF in [24] using Boosted Neural Networks, BooNN – a process which uses several iterations of multiple ANN models and then minimizes the error in each iteration – which was trained with the Levenberg–Marquardt backpropagation (LMB) and the same datasets from New England Pool showed a better forecasting error and minimum variation when benchmarked with ANN, Bagged NN and other techniques; with reduction in computational time compared to BNN.

The backpropagation training algorithm is commonly used for feed-forward neural network, however, it has high energy, low rates of convergence, and poor generalization of the neural network [25]. Ozerdem et al. in [26] forecast hourly load supply using feedforward neural network. The authors developed two models, the first a feedforward neural network with particle swarm optimization and the other trained with back propagation learning algorithm using data from an energy company based in North Cyprus. The results demonstrated the suitability of the two networks for modelling energy demand with the back-propagation network achieving higher performance on MAE and MSE while the particle swarm optimized model achieved faster convergence with twice as fast training speed. The authors concluded on the choice of particle swarm optimized models for faster development of models limited impacts on error metrics performance.

Authors in [27] proposed a novel deep feedforward neural network for STLF. Evaluation of the model with three case studies of daily electricity consumption of cities in China showed the better forecasting accuracy of the proposed model com-pared to gradient boosting and random forest. The result also demonstrated the influence of weekly, monthly, and weather-related variables on electricity consumption of households. Also, He in [28] developed a deep neural network model for STLF by processing the multiple types of input features individually and extracting the information using convolution neural networks (CNN), and modelling the implicit dynamics using recurrent components. Results on hourly loads of a city in North China showed flexibility and superiority of the method.

In predicting energy demand for smart grid, the authors in [29] proposed the use of neural network optimization approach. Using real time data from Pecan Street Inc, CNN was first used in predicting the energy demand and then Particle Swarm Optimization and Genetic Algorithm were used to optimize the results of the CNN model. The authors discovered from observing the results that the NNGA was better suited for short term energy predictions (achieving MSE of 0.391 compared to 0.495 of NNPSO) while the NNPSO was suited for long term (MSE of 0.408 compared to 0.429 of NNGA).

Authors in [30] proposed a new prediction method using Self-Recurrent Wavelet Neural Networks (SRWNN) as the forecast engine and Levenberg-Marquardt as the learning algorithm. The model was used to forecast hourly load demand of a building in a micro-grid. Results of the forecast showed that the SRWNN outperformed other forecasting models and demonstrated the ability of SRWNN to effectively adapt to variations and non-smooth behavior of the time series. The authors in [31] made use of the Advanced Wavelet Neural Network (AWNN) for very short term load forecast. The AWNN decomposes the complex load series into different frequencies and predict them separately. Evaluation of the model with Australian and Spanish electricity load data revealed that AWNN was the most accurate model for both datasets when compared with other models such as NN, LR, MTR etc.

In predicting the medium to long term load demand of commercial and residential buildings at 1 h resolution, Rahman et al. in [32] proposed two deep Recurrent Neural Network (RNN) models, which are also used for inputting missing data. Results predicting the load demand of the Public Service Building in Utah showed that the RNN models performed better in predicting the electric load profiles of buildings than a three-layer multi-layered perception model with the data imputation scheme performing better too with higher accuracy. In comparing the performances of SVM and ANN, the authors in [33] explored the data driven performance of ε-SVM Regression (ε-SVM-R) based on Radial Basis Function (RBF) and polynomial kernel; and two Nonlinear Autoregressive Exogenous Recurrent Neural Networks (NARX RNN) of different depths. Result using historical data of heating and cooling load demand of a non-residential district in Germany demonstrated the advantage of NARX RNNs over ε-SVM-R using computational time and accuracy as metrics.

Ruiz et al. in [34] proposed an Elman Neural Network model, a form of RNN together with genetic algorithm which optimized the weights of the model to forecast electricity consumption of public buildings with the aim of increasing energy efficiency and hence result in energy savings. The proposed model was based on electricity consumption data collected from buildings in University of Granada. The test results of the model showed a 61% improvement benchmarked against the NAR and NARX models, with MSE of 0.005085 for model without temperature and 0.004413 for model including temperature.

Furthermore, Ko et al. in [35] proposed a hybrid method comprised of RBF Neural Network (RBFNN), SVR and Dual Extended Kalman Filter (DEKF). The SVR is firstly used to deduce the initial parameters and the neural network's structure while the DEKF is the learning algorithm used to optimize the parameters determined by the SVR; the optimized RBFNN is then finally used to perform the forecast. Using da-tasets form the Taipower Company with three case scenarios to evaluate the multi-day ahead forecast of the hybrid model, the proposed model SVR-DEKF-RBFNN demonstrated better forecasting performances in robustness, stability and accuracy when compared to other hybrid methods such as DEKF-RBFNN and gradient descent RBFNN (GRD-RBFNN).

3.2 Support Vector Machine for Electrical Load Forecasting

Kernel-based methods such as the SVR has shown tremendous success in STLF applications. However, the performance of such methods depends on choosing suitable kernel functions for the learning target. Che and Wang in [36] proposed a combinational method in addressing this issue using datasets from New South Wales and California with differing characteristics to compare the proposed model with other individual SVR models that are kernel-based. The result showed that the combined model, P-KSVR-CM, a combination of four kernel functions – linear, Gaussian, tanh and polynomial kernels resulted in an increased in forecasting accuracy when compared to the best performing individual SVR models.

Chen et al. in forecasting hourly load demand of a non-stationary operated hotel developed hybrid support vector regression model combined with multi-resolution wavelet decomposition (MWD) in [37]. The WMD which was used to remove random noises from the load series and to better illustrate the special periodic features. Results of the model with and without MWD were compared, and the MWD was found to reduce the deviations slightly only when ε the non-sensitive loss function is higher than 0.1. In comparison, operating under the belief that good feature selection is very import in influencing prediction accuracy, Yang et al. in [38] used the Auto Correlation Function (ACF) for its feature selection while the Least Squares Support Vector Machines (LSSVM) was used for the forecast and was optimized using the Grey Wolf Optimization (GWO) and Cross Validation (CV). The proposed model, AS-GCLSSVM was used for the week ahead half hourly load forecast and results demonstrated the effectiveness of the approach in improving forecasting accuracy compared with other benchmark models though, the algorithm is time consuming and complicated.

Meanwhile, Niu et al. in [39] proposed the ant colony optimization so as to reduce the processing of large datasets and the resultant slow processing speed. The optimization technique is employed to discover optimal feature subsets in the data resulting in more accurate selection compared to other techniques like PCA, entropy-based feature selector etc. Using the selected features in forecasting short term load with Support Vector Regression, the novel method achieved better forecasting accuracy compared to single SVM and BPNN highlighting the importance of using data mining techniques for SVM-learning system.

Tong et al. in [40] proposed a deep learning theory in order to handle massive data accumulated from different sensors. The model firstly processes the features from the historical load and temperature datasets using stacked denoising auto-encoders (SDA). The model then trains a support vector regression for day-ahead load fore-cast. Observations from the model showed the capabilities of the model to describe and forecast the load tendency with better accuracy and minimal error. Comparison of the model with SVR and ANN also revealed better performance with low MAPE values. In demonstrating the applicability of online support vector for STLF, Vrablecová et al. in [41] compared the accuracy performances of ten state of the art model using Irish CER dataset. The results showed that tree-based ensemble methods such as random forests, bagging etc. achieved similar or superior forecasting accuracy than the online SVR. Furthermore, online SVR had comparable accuracy result with other online load forecast methods. To improve efficiency and computational accuracy, Li et al. in [42] proposed a the use of sub-sampled support vector regression ensemble (SSVRE). The SSVRE was also combined with swarm optimization learning thereby ensuring that each individual SVR ensemble has enough diversity for STLF. The results showed the superior performance and reduced uncertainties of the SSVRE model. Furthermore, a Guassian SVM short term load forecasting was developed by Zheng et al. in [43] operating on the basis that of the admissible translation-invariant function of SVM of pth-derivative Gaussian wavelet when p is an even number. The method was constructed with the wavelet kernel function and the parameters were optimized using stochastic focusing search (SFS) algorithm. The results showed a better forecasting accuracy compared to Morlet wavelet SVM and Gaussian SVM with the lowest MAPE and MRE.

To address the non-linearity of electric load caused by seasonal variations. The authors in [44] proposed a novel decomposition-ensemble model containing SVM, Single Spectrum Analysis (SSA), Autoregressive Moving Average (ARIMA) and cuckoo search algorithm. Using half-hourly datasets from New South Wales and Singaporean hourly load datasets, the proposed model resulted into higher forecasting accuracy compared to eight other models such as SVM, CS-SVM, BNN, SSA-SVM etc.; with all performance metrics of half-hourly loads better than the hourly loads, indicating the strength of SSA-SVM-CA in its robustness.

3.3   Fuzzy Logic for Electrical Load Forecasting

The authors in [45] used the triangular fuzzy-number models for forecasting. The first being the triangular fuzzy-number grey model (TFGM) which is used for TF series having poor fluctuation, and others being an amended TFGM with BP neural networks (NNTFGM) and the SVMTFGN. The result of load forecast in a district in China showed a better performance of the amended models with smaller MREs (NNTFGM = 7.54%, SVMTFGN = 7.99%) compared to the 23.74% of the TFGM.

Coelho et al. in [46] proposed a self-adaptive evolutionary model for STLF in a micro-grid environment, by applying a bio-inspired optimizer called GES to determine the weights' optimal values and fuzzy rules. The result of the meta-heuristics model showed better forecast accuracy with lesser computation time compared with other hybrid model in [47] with low variations in the forecast errors, with the model being suitable for micro and large grids.

In forecasting the short term thermal power demand of HVAC, the authors in [48] proposed an estimation method for the usage activity pattern of the HVAC. The authors used Recurrent NN for the dynamic activity prediction together with ANFIS for the demand prediction model. The use of specialized modeling structure in instances where power demand is not readily available was validated by the results in respect of accuracy and performance of the model.

3.4 Extreme Learning Machine for Electrical Load Forecasting

Chen et al. in improving the accuracy of forecasts of the ELM model in [49] used a novel method optimized with the empirical mode decomposition which removed noises and decomposed the load series together with mixed method of RBF and UKF kernel for optimum selection of kernels which greatly influence the performance of ELM. The novel method resulted in better accuracy than RBF-ELM, UKF-ELM, mixed ELM etc.; and verification of the model using three datasets showed similar results.

In order to solve the challenge caused by small capacity and higher randomness in micro-grids, the authors in [47] proposed a hybrid model with parameter optimization. The model which included EMD for time series decomposition, EKF and KELM for prediction algorithms and PSO for optimization polled results with high accuracy and efficiency using four different datasets. However to improve accuracy and achieve low reduction rates, the authors in [50] developed a Data Framework Strategy to construct features pool and the genetic algorithm binary improved cuckoo search for lowest reduction rates. The authors then used the ELM as the forecasting model and the hybrid model achieved a high and robust accuracy with minimum number of effective features used.

4 Conclusion

Computational Intelligence techniques have proved important and extremely useful in forecasting energy demand in the short term for effective operation of the grid by the utility operators. Review of past works have shown that there is no one coat fits all in the short term forecast problem as each model has its own merits and demerits; and different datasets have different peculiarities. However, basic fundamentals for solving the short term forecast problems for future works can be inferred.

The reviewed works in this paper has expounded on the importance of data pre-processing which includes imputation of missing variables and treating of outlier values, as these errors in the data which are regarded to as noise may affect severely the performance of the model. Furthermore, there is also the need feature engineering. This is a process whereby variables which are very significant and with high correlation to the variable to be forecast are chosen to improve the learning abilities of the model and hence its performance. Also, there are evidences of weather variables in improving the accuracy of load forecast models, as there are correlations between electricity consumption and weather conditions.

Furthermore, different optimization techniques can be used whether to reduce errors and its variations or to speed up computational time, hence resulting in an improved model. However, it is imperative to consider the trade-offs between each model and its different variants in the specific context it will be used in before committing to a short-term load forecast model.

References

1. Wolde-Rufael, Y.: Electricity consumption and economic growth: a time series experience for 17 African countries. Energy Policy **34**(10), 1106–1114 (2006)
2. Lu, W.-C.: Electricity consumption and economic growth: evidence from 17 Taiwanese industries. Sustainability **9**(1), 1–15 (2016)
3. Mohan, N., Soman, K.P., Sachin Kumar, S.: A data-driven strategy for short-term electric load forecasting using dynamic mode decomposition model. Appl. Energy **232**, 229–244 (2018)
4. Amara, F., et al.: Household electricity demand forecasting using adaptive conditional density estimation. Energy Build. **156**, 271–280 (2017)
5. Haykin, S.: Neural Networks: A Comprehensive Foundation. Prentice Hall, Upper Saddle River (1999)
6. Luger, G.F.: Artificial Intelligence: Structures and Strategies for Complex Problem Solving, 6th edn. Pearson (2009)
7. Boser, B.E., Guyon, I.M., Vapnik, V.N.: A training algorithm for optimal margin classifiers. In: Proceedings of the 5th Annual ACM Workshop on Computational Learning Theory (1992)
8. Vapnik, V.N.: An overview of statistical learning theory. IEEE Trans. Neural Netw. **10**(5), 988–999 (1999)
9. Kuster, C., Rezgui, Y., Mourshed, M.: Electrical load forecasting models: a critical systematic review. Sustain. Cities Soc. **35**, 257–270 (2017)
10. Auria, L., Moro, R.A.: Support Vector Machines (SVM) as a Technique for Solvency Analysis. DIW Berlin, German Institute for Economic Research (2008)
11. Zhao, H.X., Magoulés, F.: A review on the prediction of building energy consumption. Renew. Sustain. Energy Rev. **16**(6), 3586–3592 (2012)
12. Hong, T., Fan, S.: Probabilistic electric load forecasting: a tutorial review. Int. J. Forecast. **32**(3), 914–938 (2016)
13. Adhikari, R., Agrawal, R.K.: An introductory study on time series modeling and forecasting (2013)
14. Smola, A.J., Schölkopf, B.: A tutorial on support vector regression. Stat. Comput. **14**(3), 199–222 (2004)
15. Elias, C.N., Hatziargyriou, N.D.: An annual midterm energy forecasting model using fuzzy logic. IEEE Trans. Power Syst. **24**(1), 469–478 (2009)

16. Chen, S.X., Gooi, H.B., Wang, M.Q.: Solar radiation forecast based on fuzzy logic and neural networks. Renew. Energy **60**, 195–201 (2013)
17. Huang, G.-B., Zhu, Q.-Y., Siew, C.-K.: Extreme learning machine: a new learning scheme of feedforward neural networks. In: IEEE International Joint Conference (2004)
18. Zhu, Q.-Y., et al.: Evolutionary extreme learning machine. Pattern Recogn. **38**(10), 1759–1763 (2005)
19. Tissera, M.D., McDonnell, M.D.: Deep extreme learning machines: supervised autoencoding architecture for classification. Neurocomputing **174**, 42–49 (2016)
20. Chae, Y.T., et al.: Artificial neural network model for forecasting sub-hourly electricity usage in commercial buildings. Energy Build. **111**, 184–194 (2016)
21. Moazzami, M., Khodabakhshian, A., Hooshmand, R.: A new hybrid day-ahead peak load forecasting method for Iran's National Grid. Appl. Energy **101**, 489–501 (2013)
22. Hu, R., et al.: A short-term power load forecasting model based on the generalized regression neural network with decreasing step fruit fly optimization algorithm. Neurocomputing **221**, 24–31 (2017)
23. Khwaja, A.S., et al.: Improved short-term load forecasting using bagged neural networks. Electr. Power Syst. Res. **125**, 109–115 (2015)
24. Khwaja, A.S., et al.: Boosted neural networks for improved short-term electric load forecasting. Electr. Power Syst. Res. **143**, 431–437 (2017)
25. Zhang, J., et al.: Enhancing performance of the backpropagation algorithm via sparse response regularization. Neurocomputing **153**, 20–40 (2015)
26. Ozerdem, O.C., Olaniyi, E.O., Oyedotun, O.K.: Short term load forecasting using particle swarm optimization neural network. Procedia Comput. Sci. **120**, 382–393 (2017)
27. Guo, Z., et al.: A deep learning model for short-term power load and probability density forecasting. Energy **160**, 1186–1200 (2018)
28. He, W.: Load forecasting via deep neural networks. Procedia Comput. Sci. **122**, 308–314 (2017)
29. Muralitharan, K., Sakthivel, R., Vishnuvarthan, R.: Neural network based optimization approach for energy demand prediction in smart grid. Neurocomputing **273**, 199–208 (2018)
30. Chitsaz, H., et al.: Short-term electricity load forecasting of buildings in microgrids. Energy Build. **99**, 50–60 (2015)
31. Rana, M., Koprinska, I.: Forecasting electricity load with advanced wavelet neural networks. Neurocomputing **182**, 118–132 (2016)
32. Rahman, A., Srikumar, V., Smith, A.D.: Predicting electricity consumption for commercial and residential buildings using deep recurrent neural networks. Appl. Energy **212**, 372–385 (2018)
33. Koschwitz, D., Frisch, J., van Treeck, C.: Data-driven heating and cooling load predictions for non-residential buildings based on support vector machine regression and NARX Recurrent Neural Network: a comparative study on district scale. Energy **165**, 134–142 (2018)
34. Ruiz, L.G.B., et al.: Energy consumption forecasting based on Elman neural networks with evolutive optimization. Expert Syst. Appl. **92**, 380–389 (2018)
35. Ko, C.-N., Lee, C.-M.: Short-term load forecasting using SVR (support vector regression)-based radial basis function neural network with dual extended Kalman filter. Energy **49**, 413–422 (2013)
36. Che, J., Wang, J.: Short-term load forecasting using a kernel-based support vector regression combination model. Appl. Energy **132**, 602–609 (2014)

37. Chen, Y., Tan, H., Song, X.: Day-ahead forecasting of non-stationary electric power demand in commercial buildings: hybrid support vector regression based. Energy Procedia **105**, 2101–2106 (2017)
38. Yang, W., Kang, C., Xia, Q., et al.: Short-term probabilistic load forecasting based on statistics of probability distribution of forecasting errors. Autom. Electr. Power Syst. **30**(19), 47–52 (2006)
39. Niu, D., Wang, Y., Wu, D.D.: Power load forecasting using support vector machine and ant colony optimization. Expert Syst. Appl. **37**(3), 2531–2539 (2010)
40. Tong, C., et al.: An efficient deep model for day-ahead electricity load forecasting with stacked denoising auto-encoders. J. Parallel Distrib. Comput. **117**, 267–273 (2018)
41. Vrablecová, P., et al.: Smart grid load forecasting using online support vector regression. Comput. Electr. Eng. **65**, 102–117 (2018)
42. Li, Y., Che, J., Yang, Y.: Subsampled support vector regression ensemble for short term electric load forecasting. Energy **164**, 160–170 (2018)
43. Zheng, Y., Zhu, L., Zou, X.: Short-term load forecasting based on Gaussian wavelet SVM. Energy Procedia **12**, 387–393 (2011)
44. Zhang, X., Wang, J.: A novel decomposition-ensemble model for forecasting short-term load-time series with multiple seasonal patterns. Appl. Soft Comput. **65**, 478–494 (2018)
45. Zeng, X.-Y., et al.: Triangular fuzzy series forecasting based on grey model and neural network. Appl. Math. Model. **40**(3), 1717–1727 (2016)
46. Coelho, V.N., et al.: A self-adaptive evolutionary fuzzy model for load forecasting problems on smart grid environment. Appl. Energy **169**, 567–584 (2016)
47. Liu, N., et al.: A hybrid forecasting model with parameter optimization for short-term load forecasting of micro-grids. Appl. Energy **129**, 336–345 (2014)
48. Sala-Cardoso, E., et al.: Activity-aware HVAC power demand forecasting. Energy Build. **170**, 15–24 (2018)
49. Chen, Y., et al.: Mixed kernel based extreme learning machine for electric load forecasting. Neurocomputing **312**, 90–106 (2018)
50. Jiang, P., Liu, F., Song, Y.: A hybrid forecasting model based on date-framework strategy and improved feature selection technology for short-term load forecasting. Energy **119**, 694–709 (2017)

Computational Investigation of Consistency and Performance of the Biochemical Network of the Malaria Parasite, *Plasmodium falciparum*

Marion Adebiyi[1,2], Bolaji Famuyiwa[3], Abayomi Mosaku[4],
Roseline Ogundokun[1(✉)] (iD), Olaolu Arowolo[1], Noah Akande[1],
Adekanmi Adegun[1], Aderonke Kayode[1], Ayodele Adebiyi[1,2],
and Ezekiel Adebiyi[2]

[1] Department of Computer Science, Landmark University,
Omu Aran, Kwara, Nigeria
ogundokun.roseline@lmu.edu.ng
[2] Department of Computer and Information Sciences,
Covenant University, Ota, Nigeria
[3] College of Information and Communications Technology,
Bells University of Technology, Ota, Nigeria
[4] European Bioinformatics Institute, Cambridge, UK

Abstract. Malaria has been a problem in the public health sector and Sub-saharan African. The most prevalent symptoms of this disease is caused by *Plasmodium falciparum,* a blood borne pathogen, there has also been a disclosure of resistance to anti malaria drugs in *Pf*. An intimate process of acquiring insight to an organism's metabolism is to analyze her network topology deploying computational techniques.

In this research, the Flux Balance Analysis (FBA) of the metabolism of malaria parasite, *Plasmodium falciparum* that has been converted to a System Biology Markup Language (SBML) format in another work (Segun et al. 2014) was used to predict the metabolic activities and to investigate the consistency of the multi-compartment biochemical metabolic network of the parasite using FASIMU software.

With a projected output in view, a flux-balance computation was first deployed on an energy model and redox metabolism of the human red blood cells to learn the internal structure of FASIMU, this was a simpler model compared to *Plasmodium falciparum* model. The results of the analysis generated a file that consists of the flux values, reaction identifiers, equilibrium constants adopted and the concentration values. It was also discovered that transporters conveyed metabolites among the various cellular compartments of the organism. Further results of the flux balance analysis of the compartmented *Plasmodium falciparum* metabolic network generated a comprehensive list of target metabolites indispensable to the growth of the organism, which have been confirmed by recent literature. It is evident that the results generated from this research represent a significant step towards discovering drug targets.

Keywords: *Plasmodium falciparum* · *FASIMU* ·
Computational investigation · Biochemical network · Malaria parasite

© Springer Nature Switzerland AG 2019
S. Misra et al. (Eds.): ICCSA 2019, LNCS 11623, pp. 231–241, 2019.
https://doi.org/10.1007/978-3-030-24308-1_19

1   Introduction

The name given to Malaria was invented in Italy and it is interpreted to mean "bad air was the root cause of the disease" (WHO 2004). Malaria is not a new disease caused by infection with protozoan parasites which belongs to the genus *Plasmodium* transmitted by the female *Anopheles* specie mosquitoes (Francis 2010). Its a severe mosquito-borne disease and a potentially life threatening illness conveyed to humans by the bite of the female *Anopheles* mosquito (NaTHNaC 2010), "*Anopheles* has over 420 different species of which about 50 are medically significant vectors of malaria" (Stürchler 2008). *Anopheles* biting patterns and the parasite/disease transmitted differ depending on world region and species, but malaria parasite, *Plasmodium falciparum Pf.* transmission occurs mostly between dusk and dawn. *Anopheles gambiae*, the main malaria transmitting mosquito in West Africa, is identified to be very active indoors once its midnight (NaTHNaC 2010). A single-celled parasite from this genus *Plasmodium* is what causes malaria, this specie of *plasmodium* has not less than 100 diverse species in existences and is capable of transmitting malaria to other mammalian host, humans inclusive (NIH 2010).

Often symptoms of malaria include headache, malaise, weakness, cough, muscle pain, and diarrhea. Malaria caused by *Plasmodium falciparum* can aggravate to become a serious and dangerous illness if not diagnosed and treated on time, leading to cerebral malaria, kidney failure and severe anemia, which can eventually end in coma and death. (NaTHNaC 2010). It is described as the major human parasitic disease, and still a core source of morbidity, and death, especially in the third world countries. WHO in 2015 reported that malaria makes up for about 438 000 deaths, and 90% of this deaths are from Africa despite the 60% global decline, this is against the reports that death rates may keep increasing yearly" (Krogstad 1996). People who are mostly at risk are those with no or little protective immunity against the disease (WHO 2008). In areas such as Africa, south of the Sahara where there is high transmission, the most susceptible groups are young children, who have not yet built immunity to malaria, pregnant women, whose immunity is affected by pregnancy, particularly during the first two trimesters and pregnancies, and finally travellers coming from areas with little malaria spread. (WHO E Science 2010).

A metabolic network can simply be represented as a list of reactions. Metabolic networks depict every known possible path that connects cellular compounds to one another by the use of biochemical transformations (Chalancon et al. 2013). Understanding the functions of a metabolic network and a good grasp of its topological properties is very essential. By constructing a metabolic network of *P. falciparum* based mainly on data extracted from different biological database, and integrating it sufficiently with supporting experimental data, it might produce a model that will replicate the inner workings of the organism (Ginsburg 2006). Poolman grouped the techniques for analysing metabolic networks into two: structural and kinetic analysis (Poolman et al. 2004).

Jeffrey (2010) defined Flux Balance Analysis as a structural modelling mathematical method for analysing the flow of metabolites within a metabolic network. Flux-balance analysis of the whole organism metabolic networks of *P. falciparum* has been used to predict essential reactions and thus drug targets (Huthmacher et al. 2010).

2   Methodology

FASIMU is a command line adapted software for flux distribution calculation was deployed to implement this system, it is an extremely flexible computation environment for various flux-balance analysis, it calculates flux distributions using varieties of the most popular FBA algorithms (Baird 2013; Biomed Central 2013), and uses the optimization capabilities of free Linear Programming (LP) solve and GNU Linear Programming Kit (GLPK) and commercial solvers CPLEX, Linear, INteractive, and Discrete Optimizer (LINDO) (Andreas et al. 2011). "The results can be visualized in Cytoscape or BiNA using newly developed plugins" (www.sbml.org). Motivation to use FASIMU includes an opportunity to be incorporated on some level of the operating system, it distinctly out-stands other similar tools with the idea of a summarizing description file for flux-balance simulations (Biomed Central 2013). The extracted metabolic network from various databases was compiled in a semi-automated manner using System Biology Markup Language (SBML) format (Adebiyi et al. 2014). Moreso, it has a well defined protocol for network analysis and allows Incorporation of effective commercial and free solvers (www.Biomedcentral.com). It permits simple application of new algorithmic solutions (Andreas 2011) and faster.

Structural modelling was deployed in analysing the extracted metabolic network, which has been compiled and converted to SBML format (Adebiyi et al. 2014); this network was extracted and tested for consistency. A compartmentalized metabolic network was needed for this work to be able to create specific location or cellular addresses for which processes should occur, to impound metabolites from participating in undesirable reactions, to establish physical boundaries for biological processes that enable the cell to carry out different metabolic activities at the same time and finally, to generate a specific micro-environment to temporally regulate a biological process (Andreas 2007).

FBA was used to calculate the flow of metabolites through the metabolic network and it also investigated the metabolic capability of the cellular system. Justifiably, structural modelling was preferred because despite that kinetic modelling can offer a more accurate description of an organism's metabolism than structural but at the same time it is substantially more difficult because is a larger scope for errors when constructing kinetic models and finding errors can take a long time (Hayton and Su 2004). Literature shows that it is currently not suitable for malaria research. Kinetic modelling of large-scale metabolic networks is extremely difficult which is traceable to the scarcity of particular enzyme rate data (Afonso 2006).

Furthermore, large problems can become computationally expensive and the resulting systems are frequently unstable and give results that are difficult to trust. There is an easy and effective substitute for analysis of metabolic capabilities of cellular systems which is flux balance analysis (Constraint-based reconstruction and analysis) (Klann et al. 2011). There is insufficiency of Kinetic data obtainable for the simulation of networks, constraining the number and size of systems in various species that can be analyzed via this approach (Raman and Chandra 2009).

To deploy FBA, the following processes were carried out step wisely,

I. The Metabolic reactions were illustrated as a stoichiometric matrix (S), with size m * n. Each row of the stoichiometric matrix denotes one distinct compound (aimed at a system with m compounds) and each column denotes one reaction (n reactions).

II. The values in each of the columns are the stoichiometric coefficients of the metabolites partaking in a reaction. With every metabolite produced, there is a positive (+) coefficient.

III. A phenotype was described in a biological objective function structure that is applicable to the network being considered. Mathematically, an 'objective function' is to quantitatively state the amount each reaction put in to the phenotype. The mathematical illustrations of the metabolic reactions together with the objective describe a system of linear equations. In flux balance analysis, linear programming is applied to mathematically solve these linear equations (Orth 2010).

FBA seeks to maximize or minimize an objective function $Z = c^T v$, which could be several linear combination of fluxes. c = vector of weights representing the amount each reaction v (for example, biomass reaction when simulating maximum growth) put in to the objective function (www.ncbi.nlm.nih.gov). Through the optimization of objective functions, FBA found a single optimal flux distribution that lies on the edge of the allowable solution space (Dal'Molin et al. 2010).

3   Implementation and Results

3.1   To Run the Consistency Check of the Metabolic Network

The network was checked accordingly for consistency and capability to generate important metabolites by modifying the subsequent set of biochemical reactions and transport processes to realize a consistent network; this was justified by flux balance simulations to achieve metabolic processes. The first step was completed by substituting highly defined metabolites by more typical metabolites, using a physically compiled list of substitutions. However, if the same metabolite appears with uncommon IDs in reactions, one of the IDs is selected to substitute alternative IDs. Reactions having generic terms were either eliminated or substituted by more definite reactions. Lastly, reaction duplets that previously existed in the initial data or were produced by the consistency procedure were deleted (Sabrina et al. 2007).

The consistency check process made sure that reactions with neither generic stoichiometry (the quantitative relationship between reactants and products) nor reaction duplets existed. To connect related reactions, equivalent metabolites were verified to have the same level of specificity.

3.2   Fasimu Functions Demonstrated on a Small Human Erythrocyte Model

In this test, flux-balance computation was demonstrated on a model of the energy and redox metabolism of human red blood cells (Schuster and Holzhutter 1995), thereby learning the internal structure of a FASIMU session and applying several of the implemented algorithms available. This was a simpler model compared to the *E.coli* and *Plasmodium falciparum* simulation (Fig. 1).

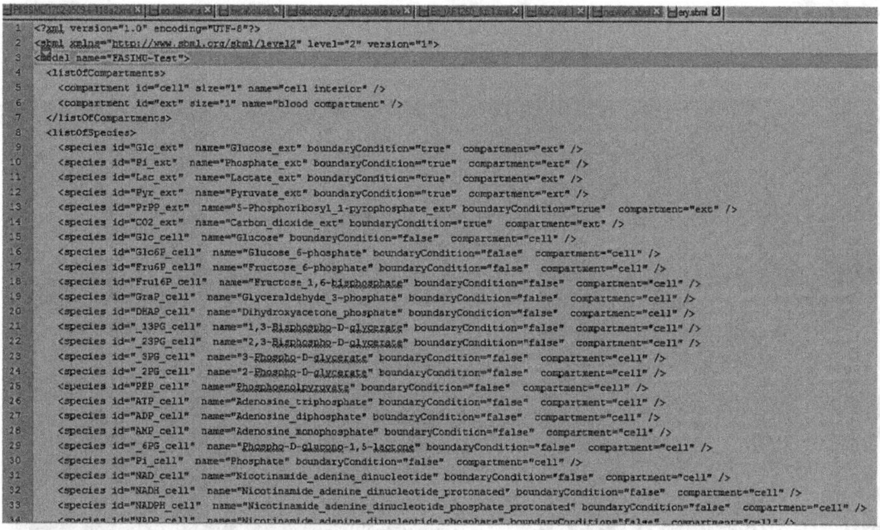

Fig. 1. SBML file for the Human Erythrocyte

Several files have been generated from the SBML file which was used for the simulations. The SBML file is not regarded any more.

This file shows all flux distributions of a computation series. The flux distributions are separated by lines with many # characters followed by the name of the simulation. In the next line there is a description of the system boundaries of this particular simulation. The next line gives a short comment whether a solution is computed with optional comments from the solver. Additionally warnings are shown here. Then the solution is given in a tab-separated format. The first column provides the name of the reaction (www.alecjacobson.com). The second column provides the flux value (www.alecjacobson.com). Note that zero fluxes are not recorded in the solution. Next column gives the equilibrium constant just for information, then the reaction written with metabolite identifiers follows. FASIMU can also be ordered to write them with metabolite names given in the file metabolites: most conveniently this can be done in the initial start-up of

For computations where the thermodynamic feasibility is checked a section follows given hypothetical concentrations which are compatible with the flux distribution.

The fourth column holds possible reaction names given in the file reaction-names. For computations where the thermodynamic feasibility is checked a section follows given hypothetical concentrations which are compatible with the flux distribution (Scuster et al. 1999; Schuster et al. 2000).

3.3 The Output of the Evaluation.txt

See Fig. 2.

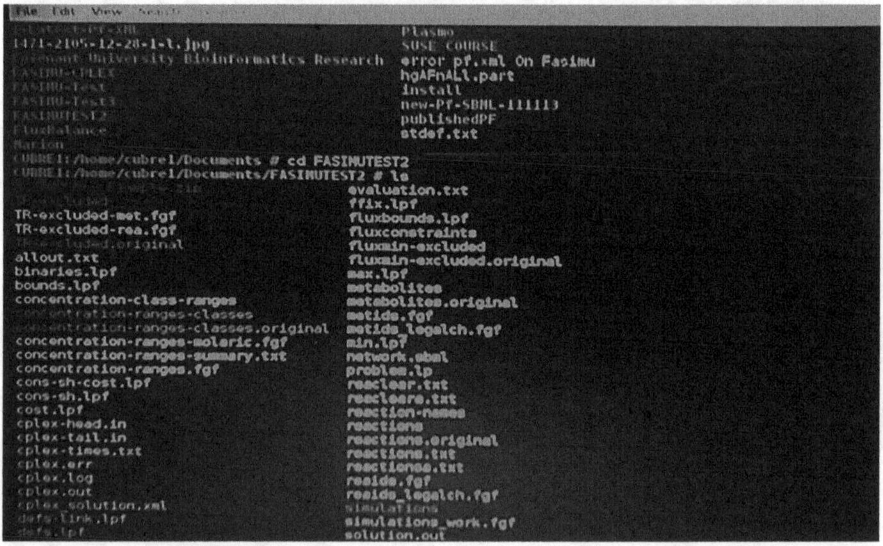

Fig. 2. Screenshot of the Output of the demonstration FASIMU Functions on Human Erythrocyte Model

3.4 Validating and Analyzing the Network

Constraints were defined to make sure essential biomass precursors such as phospholipids are generated, which are required for the parasite reproduction (Huthmacher et al. 2010). In this case;

- i. Mass balance constraints: metabolite production and consumption rates are equal
- i. Boundary constraints: that limited nutrient uptake/excretion
- ii. Internal constraints: that limited the flux through reactions within the organism, transport reactions were introduced only where it is needed.
- iii. Thermodynamically reaction constraints: irreversibility of reactions

More constraints were added to compel the network to generate a set of target metabolites essential for the growth of the organism. Constraints were also included to reduce the amount of active reactions whose survival is not sustained by genome annotations. This was important as data obtain from the BioCyc database include reactions exclusive of any associated gene and are present in *P.falciparium*.

Some of the constraints involved were Constraints −Glc_ext ... −8 <= Glc_ext <= 8 interpreted as the glucose exchange flux between (−8,8), not (−8,0). Constraints stddef ... %O2_ext is interpreted as Oxygen uptake allowed in the file stddef.txt. FASIMU equilibrium constants were used as weights for the backward fluxes in the flux minimization and to implement the thermodynamic feasibility constraint. The Gibb's free energies was not given directly, so we computed the equilibrium constants with this formula

$$K_{eq} = e^{-\frac{\Delta G_r^0}{RT}} \tag{1}$$

Where
R - the universal gas constant
T - is the absolute temperature (FASIMU model has a fixed temperature)
eq - Equilibrium Constant
Gr - Gibb's free energies

Solution space is more restricted as a result of Constraints gotten from thermodynamics and cellular environment conditions. More constraints were added to compel the network to generate a set of target metabolites essential for the growth of the organism.

3.5   Defining Objective Functions for the Analysis

Mathematically, an 'objective function' is used to quantitatively define how much each reaction contributes to the phenotype. In flux balance analysis, these linear equations are solved using linear programming. FBA maximize or minimize the objective function.

The Objective function defined in FBA analysis of the *plasmodium falciparum*

i. *Minimize ATP production*: This objective is stated to determine conditions of optimal metabolic energy efficiency.

ii. *Minimize nutrient uptake*: is used to determine the conditions under which the cell will perform its metabolic functions while consuming the minimum amount of available nutrients.

iii. *Maximize metabolite production*: to determine the biochemical production capabilities of *plasmodium falciparum*.

- FASIMU allowed flexibility in the description of objectives and constraints; so sequence of execution was calculated, varying the objectives and constraints of the automatically generated results. More results are available at the appendices section. The ensuing set of biochemical reactions and transport processes was modified to achieve a consistent network verified by flux balance simulations to implement metabolic processes. The metabolic capabilities of the cellular system of the parasite was investigate, this allowed us to evaluate unknown fluxes in metabolic networks according to the cellular constraints. The simulation was successful; the essential metabolites that must be exchange over the system boundary was successfully extracted and these set of target metabolites was established from literature to be indispensable to the growth of the organism, *Plasmodium falciparum*. Hence the network is valid.
- **less allout.txt** shows the list of the essential metabolites that must be exchanged over the system boundary of the parasite.

The allout.txt output is available at the Appendix IX section of the project (Fig. 3).

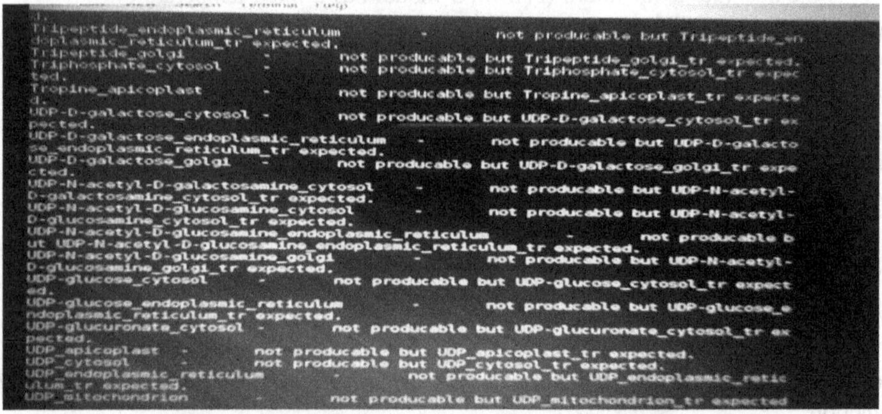

Fig. 3. Screenshot of the Output of the demonstration FASIMU *Pf*

The results provided us with the list of some of the essential metabolites that should be exchanged over the system boundary of a valid *Plasmodium falciparum* network. Table 1 below.

Table 1. Results obtained from the analysis of the *Pf* network, listing the essential metabolites/compound names, structure, compartments where they belong and their known function.

Compound	Compound-Name	Compound Structure	Compartment	Functions
ATP_regeneration	Adenosine Triphosphate		Cytosol	ATP plays a central role in energy exchanges in *plasmodiumfalciparu*, serves as the main donor of free energy. They are present in the glycolytic pathway. (Hutmatcher et al., 2010)
GSH	Glutathione		Cytosol	*Plasmodium falciparum* exhibits an intense gluta-thione metabolism. Glutathione plays a role not only in antioxidative defence and in maintaining the reducing environment of the cytosol. (Becker et al., 2003)
Hsp90 protein	Heat shock protein 90		Cytosol, Mitochondrion	The Hsp90 protein parasite Plasmodium falciparum is critical for the survival; it is proven that the anti-Hsp90 drug geldanamycin is toxic to P. falciparum growth. (Lelièvre et al., 2010)

4   Conclusion

This work presents an FBA analysis of the compartmented metabolic network of *Plasmodium falciparum* System Biology Mark-up Language (SBML) format and FASIMU tools; this provided us with information on transporters that transferred metabolites between the different cellular compartments of the organism. This serves as input or a promising starting point for further drug targets and development and target discovery. It is a functional description of the network in terms of essential metabolites that must be exchanged over the system boundary of *Plasmodium falciparum* network. The result of the compartmented metabolic network in SBML format validated by flux balance approach generated a set of target metabolites established from literature to be essential to the growth of this organism and this presents a promising point (input) for further drug target and development.

References

Segun, A.F., et al.: Computational biology and bioinformatics in Nigeria. PLOS Comput. Biol. **10**(4) (2014). https://doi.org/10.1371/journal.pcbi.1003516

Francis, E.G.C.: History of the discovery of the Malaria parasites and their vectors. Parasites Vectors BioMed Central Part Springer Nature **3**(5) (2010). https://doi.org/10.1186/1756-3305-3-5

Afonso, A., et al.: Malaria parasites can develop stable resistance to artemisinin but lack mutations in candidate genes *atp* (encoding the sarcoplasmic and endoplasmic reticulum Ca^{2+} ATPase), *tctp*, *mdr1*, and *cg10*. Antimicrob. Agents Chemother. **50**(2), 480–489 (2006)

Andreas, H., Sabrina, H., Hermann-Georg, H.: Including metabolite concentrations into flux balance analysis: thermodynamic realizability as a constraint on flux distributions in metabolic networks. Biomedcentral Bioinform. Syst. Biol. **1**, 23 (2007)

Andreas, H., Sabrina, H., Andreas, G., Christoph, G., Hermann-Georg, H.: FASIMU: flexible software for flux-balance computation series in large metabolic networks. Biomedcentral Bioinform. **12**, 28 (2011)

Baird, J.K.: Effectiveness of antimalarial drugs. N. Engl. J. Med. **352**, 1565–1577 (2005)

Baird, J.K.: Evidence and implications of mortality associated with acute *Plasmodium vivax* malaria. Clin. Microbiol. Rev. **26**(1), 36–57 (2013)

WHO: Update on malaria terminology. http://www.who.int/malaria/mpac/mpac-sept2015-terminology-annex2.pdf?ua=1

Chalancon, G., Kruse, K., Babu, M.M.: Metabolic networks, structure and dynamics. In: Dubitzky, W., Wolkenhauer, O., Cho, K.H., Yokota, H. (eds.) Encyclopedia of Systems Biology. Springer, New York (2013). https://doi.org/10.1007/978-1-4419-9863-7

Sturchler, D., Sturchler, M.P.: Global epidemiology of malaria. In: Schlagenhauf, P. (ed.) Travelers' Malaria, 2nd edn, pp. 9–35. BC Decker, Hamilton (2008)

Orth, J.D., Bernhard, P.: Systematizing the generation of missing metabolic knowledge. Biotechnol. Bioeng. **107**(3) (2010). https://doi.org/10.1002/bit.22844

Dal'Molin, C.G., Quek, L., Palfreyman, R.W., Brumley, S.M.: AraGEM, a genome-scale reconstruction of the primary metabolic network in Arabidopsis. Plant Physiol. **152**(2) (2010). https://doi.org/10.1104/pp.109148817

Hutmacher, D.W., Loessner, D., Rizzi, S., Kaplan, D.L., Mooney, D.J., Clement, J.A.: Can tissue engineering concepts advance tumor biology research? NCBI Pub Med Trends Biotechnol. **28** (3), 125–133 (2010). https://doi.org/10.1016/j.tibtech.2009.12.001

Lelievre, B., Catherine, D., Mikael, D.: Qualitative and Quantitative Analysis of Chemotherapy Preparations. Euro. J. Hosp. Pharm. **16**(4), 33–38 (2010)

NIH: National Expert Panel on Diagnosis and Management (2010)

Becker, K., Friedrich, A.W., Lubritz, G., Weilert, M., Peters, G., Von Eiff, C.: Prevalence of genes encoding pyrogenic toxin superantigens and exfoliative toxins among strains of Staphylococcus aureus isolated from blood and nasal specimens. J. Clin. Microbiol. **41**, 1434–1439 (2003)

Ginsburg, H.: Progress in in silico functional genomics: the malaria Metabolic Pathways database. Trends Parasitol. **22**(6), 238–240 (2006)

Hayton, K., Su, X.Z.: Genetic and biochemical aspects of drug resistance in malaria parasites. Curr. Drug Targets Infect. Disord. **4**(1), 1–10 (2004)

Raman, K., Chandra, N.: Flux balance analysis of biological systems: applications and challenges. Brief Bioinform. PubMed **10**(4), 435–449 (2009). https://doi.org/10.1093/bib/bbp011

Huthmacher, C., Hoppe, A., Bulik, S., Holzhutter, H.-G.: Antimalarial drug targets in Plasmodium falciparum predicted by stage-specific metabolic network analysis. Biomedcentral Bioinform. **4**, 120 (2010)

Hyde, J.E.: Drug-resistant malaria-an insight. Fed. Eur. Biochem. Soc. J. **274**(18), 4688–4698 (2007)

Jeffrey, D.O., Ines, T., Bernhard, P.: What is flux balance analysis? Nat. Biotechnol. **28**(3), 245–248 (2010)

Klann, M., Lapin, A., Reuss, M.: Agent-based simulation of reactions in the crowded and structured intracellular environment: Influence of mobility and location of the reactants. Biomedcentral Syst. Biol. **5**(1), 71 (2011)

Krogstad, D.J.: Malaria as a reemerging disease. Epidemiol. Rev. **18**, 77–79 (1996)

Kuntzer, J., et al.: BN++ - a biological information system. J. Intergr. Bioinform. **3**(2), 34 (2006)

Poolman, M.G., Assmus, H.E., Fell, D.A.: Applications of metabolic modelling to plant metabolism. J. Exp. Bot. **55**, 1177–1186 (2004)

Sabrina, H., Andreas, H., Hermann-Georg, H.: Pruning genome-scale metabolic models to consistent and functional networks. Genome Inform. **18**, 308–319 (2007)

Schuster, S., Dandekar, T., Fell, D.: Detection of elementary flux modes in biochemical networks: a promising tool for pathway analysis and metabolic engineering. Trends Biotechnol. **17**(2), 53–60 (1999)

Schuster, S., Fell, D.A., Dandekar, T.: A general definition of metabolic pathways useful for systematic organization and analysis of complex metabolic networks. Nat. Biotechnol. **18**(3), 326–332 (2000)

Schuster, S., Holzutter, H.G.: Use of mathematical models for predicting the metabolic effect of large-scale enzyme activity alterations. Application to enzyme deficiencies of red blood cells. Eur. J. Biochem. **229**(2), 403–418 (1995)

Vinay, S.K., Madhukar, S.D., Costas, D.M.: Optimization based automated curation of metabolic reconstructions. Biomedcentral Bioinform. **8**, 212 (2007)

World Health Organization: Global Burden of Disease. WHO Library Cataloguing-in-Publication Data (2004). ISBN 978 92 4 156371 0

World Health Organization: Malaria cases and deaths in Africa World Malaria Report. WHO Library Cataloguing-in-Publication Data, Geneva (2008). ISBN 978 92 4 156371 0

BioCyc. Summary of Plasmodium falciparum, Strain 3D7, version 16.5. BioCyc: Database Collection (2012). http://biocyc.org/PLASMO/organism-summary?object=PLASMO. Accessed 7 Feb 2013

BioMed Central: Flux Balance Analysis: FASIMU Software (2013). www.biomedcentral.com. Accessed July 2013

Look And Feel Java Platform SE 7. Oracle Documentation (2012). http://docs.oracle.com/javase/7/docs/api/javax/swing/LookAndFeel.html. Accessed 26 May 2012

NaTHNaC. Health information sheet on malaria (2010). http://www.nathnac.org/pro/factsheets/malaria.htm

Software Platforms for Systems Biology SBML.org, December 2010. http://sbml.org/Events/Workshops/The_1st_Workshop_on_Software_Platforms_ for_Systems_Biology

U.S. Department of Health and Human Services. National Institutes of Health National Institute of Allergy and Infectious Diseases NIH Publication No. 07-7139 (2007). www.niaid.nih.gov

Xampp. Version 1.8.2/PHP 5.4.27 (2013). https://www.apachefriends.org/download.html. Accessed 16 Mar 2013

Investigating Evolution in Open Source Software

Jordan McDonald and Des Greer[✉] ⓘ

Queen's University Belfast, Belfast BT7 1NN, UK
{jmcdonald23, des.greer}@qub.ac.uk

Abstract. Lehman's well-known laws of software evolution have existed since the early 1980's and although they have been nuanced, augmented and discussed many times since then, software and software development practices have changed dramatically since then, not least due to the rise and popularity of open source software (OSS). OSS is written collaboratively with the process and products publically observable, whereas the original laws were derived based on a very different context. The question then arises if Lehman's laws apply to modern day OSS software. The GitHub repository is the most comprehensive source of OSS projects and is used here to obtain data on how OSS projects have evolved. This work uses one hundred open source projects hosted on GitHub. Metrics are obtained via the provided API, using a purpose-built workbench and several of Lehman's laws are evaluated using the data available. Coupled with a critique of how judgements can be made from the data available, the study has discovered that the evidence does not support many of the laws. An important proviso with such an approach is the limitation on what data can be extracted and/or inferred from the GitHub API. Nonetheless, there is enough of a challenge made to the laws to warrant further study and a need to revisit some of the laws in the context of open source development.

Keywords: Open source software · Software evolution · Repository mining · Empirical software engineering

1 Introduction

Evolution of Open Source Software products is very different from closed source projects yet almost all investigations leading to Lehman's laws of Software Evolution has been based on closed-source projects [1, 2]. Thus there is scope for re-investigating the applicability of these laws in modern open source software projects.

Lehman's first three laws of software evolution were formulated in the mid-1970s arising from a study on IBM data from 1968. Further laws were added in 1980, 1991 and 1996 [3, 4]. Collectively the laws attempt to describe and explain the factors that drive growth and development of software as well as the forces that lead to reduced progress. The goal of this paper is to examine these laws in the context of modern open source projects hosted on GitHub, with a dataset extracted via the GitHub API. GitHub is a hosting service designed for collaboration on a centralized repository of source code. Any user of the website can 'Clone' any public repository and read or alter the code, this serves as the backbone of modern open source development and helps facilitate the 'fork

© Springer Nature Switzerland AG 2019
S. Misra et al. (Eds.): ICCSA 2019, LNCS 11623, pp. 242–256, 2019.
https://doi.org/10.1007/978-3-030-24308-1_20

and pull' model of development. In addition to code hosting, collaborative code review, and integrated issue tracking, GitHub has integrated social features. Users are able to subscribe to information by "watching" projects and "following" users, resulting in a feed of information on those projects and users of interest [5].

At the time of writing, GitHub claims to host over 100 million projects with 31 million developers [6] which would make it the largest host of source code in the world. This coupled with the easily accessible GitHub API, which can be used to obtain data on commits, code churn, issues, watchers and pulls, among other metrics, means that GitHub provides an obvious foundation to examine Lehman's laws as they apply to Open Source Software (OSS).

This paper will perform a large scale analysis of open source projects hosted on GitHub, extracting data at the repository level in order to determine how well the selected Lehman's laws hold. The next section will provide some background to the study, Sect. 2 will describe the background to the work, Sect. 3 will describe the methodological aspects of the study. Section 4 will discuss the results of the work while Sect. 5 will discuss the validity of the study. Finally, in Sect. 6 we provide attempt to draw conclusions from the work and identify possible further work.

2   Background and Related Work

2.1   Laws of Evolution

Lehman's laws have undergone multiple changes. Lehman originally qualified the application of such laws by distinguishing between three categories of software – S-programs, P-programs and E-Programs [3]. In this paper we will limit the scope to E-programs, the reasonable assumption being that the collaborative projects selected will be of this type i.e. broadly "computer applications in the *real world*" [4]. There is, of course, a small probability that sampled GitHub projects will be S or P-type but both of these types are less obvious candidates for collaboration via GitHub due to the static nature of the problems they solve [7]. Table 1 provides a summary of the relevant laws as they apply to E-type systems. Laws 4, 5, and 8 do not lend themselves to this type of study and so are not included.

Table 1. Lehman's laws of software evolution (Greyed not studied).

	Law description
1	(1974) **"Continuing Change"** - a system must be continually adapted or it becomes progressively less satisfactory
2	(1974) **"Increasing Complexity"** - as a system evolves, its complexity increases unless work is done to maintain or reduce it
3	(1974) **"Self-Regulation"** - system evolution processes are self-regulating with the distribution of product and process measures close to normal
6	(1991) **"Continuing Growth"** - the functional content of a system must be continually increased to maintain user satisfaction over its lifetime
7	(1996) **"Declining Quality"** - the quality of a system will appear to be declining unless it is rigorously maintained and adapted to operational environment changes

2.2   Related Work

Attempts at general data mining from GitHub have been prominent in recent years, Kalliamvakou et al. [5] focused on avoiding common pitfalls in GitHub mining and concluded that there is valuable data to be found if these are avoided. More generally, there is a systematic literature review on the evolution of open source projects, where the authors examine the data sets utilised, sources of the data and research trends in recent years [8]. The authors found that Lehman's laws do not hold in certain cases, with individual laws in the research yielding contradicting results for OSS projects.

Yu and Mishra [9] investigated the quality of evolving software by mining bug reports and provide evidence to confirm law seven. Sheoran et al. [10] investigated "watchers" on GitHub. The paper looks at the contributors to a project, tracking the process of a user becoming a watcher to finally contributing to a project, finding that this process accounts for a huge bulk of the tested projects eventual contributors. Another study on this topic was conducted by Ben et al. [11] which performed visualisation on metrics related to commits, low level code statistics and lines of code on a single project, but this restriction limits the generality of the research. Gousios et al. [12] look in depth at the GitHub 'fork and pull' model of development on a sample of 291 projects. The metrics utilised are among the widest ranging, considering feature sets for the pull request itself, the project and the developers involved. An analysis was made on what projects utilise this model, the turnover rate of pull request and why requests are rejected. Borges et al. [13] provide insight into what constitutes project popularity on GitHub making use of the starring mechanism. Bissyandé [14] analyses issues as part of open source software, correlating the data with watchers, forks and other metrics.

A similar study to that presented in this paper was conducted on a long running FLOSS project, glibc inside a SCM repository with over 20 years of history [7]. The paper also centres on Lehman's laws and makes use of commits, lines of code and files changed to represent evolution. A downside to this study is single project focus. A nine project study is used in [15] with a focus on long running projects. The findings, based on code level metrics only confirmed the laws of continuing change and continuing growth for all programs but gave evidence that the other six laws were sometimes violated. Skoulis et al. [16] also delves into software evolution and Lehman's laws, however from the context of databases. Rather than confirm or challenge the laws they offer general observations on the evolution process and its influences. Work also exists looking at the evolution of the Linux kernel [17]. This study found that several of Lehman's laws were supported.

There has also been an extensive study of the Eclipse development environment by Mens et al. [18]. They analysed the source code of Eclipse, for example capturing differences between releases and relating these with various quality measurements. They found strong support for laws one and six but only partial support for law two. This support for laws one and six from Eclipse data is repeated in [19], as well as qualified support for law eight but not for the other laws, where they state that the evidence is contradictory.

It also important to consider relevant research that focuses on the laws outside of the given OSS context. There is some evidence to support Lehman's laws in a refactoring based development approach [20]. This study uses a single project case study and concludes that the laws apply in this context.

Prior studies that are similar to the approach in this paper have limitations such being based on a single (or just a few) project or being very specific in scope. By contrast this study will use a large data set with variation in the language.

3 Methodology

3.1 Research Questions and Hypotheses

In order to provide scope and direction to the research we have defined research questions with multiple hypotheses that will attempt to draw out appropriate relationships for each law with the metrics extracted via the GitHub API. Each (alternative and null) hypothesis is also accompanied by justification and reasoning which explain the choice of metric used for each law. Inevitably, we will have to resort to proxy measures since many of the concepts in the laws are not directly measureable. Hence for each hypothesis we will give a justification for the metric(s) used. Indeed several of the laws are difficult to assess from solely GitHub data. In that case we have omitted to study laws 4, 5 and 8.

> **RQ** – Is it possible using data extracted from the GitHub API to determine if OS software evolution over time reflects Lehman's laws?
>
> H_1a – If the number of commits decreases the number of star gazers will also reduce (laws 1 & 6).
>
> H_10 – There is no relationship between the number of stargazers and the number of commits.
>
> **Justification** – In this particular case a caveat should be noted. Stargazer count is a reflection of developers rather than users (GitHub is not designed for end users). However, OSS developers typically exists as a result of user demand. Indeed it is also often the case that an OSS user is also a developer. The assumption can be made that if a developer stops stargazing the software has become less satisfactory. Commits can be used to represent changes made to the code.
>
> H_2a – Total lines of code increases as a software system evolves (law 2).
>
> H_20 – Total lines of code will not increase as a software system evolves.
>
> **Justification** – To represent complexity LOC provides a convenient measure. There is good support in the literature [21] to show that LOC and McCabe's Cyclomatic Complexity have a stable linear relationship. Extending to use other complexity measures remains in plans for future work.
>
> H_3a – Issues, additions and deletions over time for are normally distributed (law 3).
>
> H_30 – Issues, additions and deletions over time are not normally distributed.
>
> **Justification** – To capture the essence of 'self-regulation', issue counts were chosen as a suitable metric. This represents how 'processes' are managed by the developers and forms the focal point for communication and decision making on code changes. The product of software evolution can be assessed via code output, at the lower level of addition and deletion counts.
>
> H_4a – Project issues increase as code churn decreases (law 7).

H₄0 – There is no relationship between project issues and code churn.

Justification – To capture the declining quality of a software system, issues is an appropriate measure. As quality declines it seems intuitive that more issues will be created by developers. Code churn will be represented by LOC, which satisfies the need for rigorous maintenance to prevent a decline in quality.

3.2   Project Selection

Figure 1 demonstrates the project selection process. The ten languages have been chosen based on a ranking system [22]. These derived (based on total active repositories, both public and private but excluding forks) as of August 2015: JavaScript, Java, Ruby, PHP, Python, CSS, C++, C#, C, and HTML. GitHub's advanced search facility allows descending ordering of the 'most stars' for a programming language. Each sequential project is then evaluated against two criteria.

a. Duration of project life on GitHub, with a five year threshold, arbitrarily chosen to ensure evolution can be mapped over a sustained period of time.

b. It is very common for projects to use multiple programming languages. However GitHub allows users to examine a project for the breakdown of languages utilised. Using this, each project had to meet a 50% target language affinity requirement. This process was applied to two hundred projects in total, the final dataset of one hundred was then randomly selected with the intent of taking ten projects from each programming languages group of twenty.

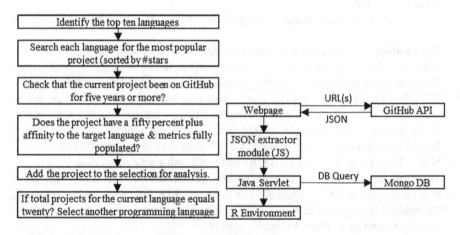

Fig. 1.   GitHub project selection process and GitHub extraction workbench architecture

3.3   Data Collection

GitHub provides a robust API which is ideal for mining the data associated with a project. The current version of the API is version 3, and all requests are performed over HTTPS, the data is returned in a JSON format which allows simple parsing of the required metric. A workbench (Fig. 2) has been devised which will handle the automated collection of the data for each of the one hundred projects and to execute statistical functions. The method utilised to collect GitHub data used AJAX as implemented in the JQuery JavaScript library, and then once processed data was stored in a MongoDB database. In order to test hypotheses, various statistical methods are provided via the R environment [23] which was integrated into the workbench.

3.4   Data Analysis

Each metric is associated with an accompanying time series that signifies the start of a weekly interval. The dataset itself is organised into a vector with each point containing weekly counts of the frequency of the metric in that particular time period. Some data points may have gaps between frequencies that exceed the weekly structure, therefore padding has been introduced to fill the gaps in a project as required, in this case each padded weekly interval will be assigned a zero to signify no activity in that period. To ensure the integrity of the research the first six months for each projects have been 'trimmed'. This is reasonable since many projects that have origins that predate the GitHub platform. This also removes the possibility of initial 'dump' of data from a pre-existing source thus polluting the results with the potential for significant statistical outliers. The metrics that will be extracted from the API in order to quantify the analysis are listed below.

- Stargazers - Repository Starring is a feature that lets users bookmark repositories. Stars are shown next to repositories to show an approximate level of interest.
- Commits - A commit, or "revision", is an individual change to a file or set of files.
- Additions & Deletions
- Issues - Issues are suggested improvements, tasks or questions related to the repository.
- Issues Comments – Messages that a user has attached to a specific issue.
- LOC – total lines of code at a certain time point.
- Growth Rate – how much a metric changed per time interval.

3.5   Statistical Analysis

Growth Rate. This concept has significant relevance. We use it in tandem with an LOC metric to test H_2. We can express growth rate and average growth rates as percentages.

Growth Rate - $G = ((X - Y) \div Y) \times 100$

Average Growth Rate - $G = ((X \div Y)^{1 \div n} - 1) \times 100$ where X = current value, Y = past value, n = total samples

Shapiro Wilk Test. This particular test will be applied to the three metrics stated for H_3, in order test for normality. As per tradition, we set alpha at a 95% confidence level i.e. alpha = 0.05.

Cross Correlation. To adequately test H_1 and H_4 a cross correlation will be performed which will quantify the relationship between two time series by identifying lags of series x that will be useful predictors of series y. In the case of this research, multiple lag values will be considered to determine if a change in one metric weeks prior will have an impact on a series weeks in the future, in other words to determine if x leads y. We have used the R package cross correlation function *ccf*(...) [23].

4   Results and Discussion

4.1   H$_1$a: If the Number of Commits Decreases the Number of Star Gazers Will also Reduce

A lagged cross correlation was performed with multiple different values in order to determine if and when the impact of making a change i.e. a commit will have a direct effect on the number of stargazers, and in particular what duration after a commit the change is felt most significantly. The results of this experiment are shown in Table 2 for a lag from −9 to 0 weeks.

The results show a clear relationship between the amount of the lag applied to the commits and the percentage of positive correlations that have been attained between the lagged commit count and the present stargazer count. As the lag is increased (in this context each increment represents the count of commits a week further into the past) the amount of correlation begins to decrease which indicates that the further apart the commit frequency in a particular week from the present stargazer count, the less impact it will have on the amount of stargazers. It is possible that in the case of extreme lag applied that the effect of that change has already been felt at some point in the interim, therefore it may have already changed the count of the stargazers in a positive or negative way. If we now consider the inverse of this trend it appears that if changes in the amount of commits contributed to the project are recent (0 lag to −4 lag) the amount of stargazers is more likely to correlate which would suggest that the amount of commits made recently has a greater bearing on the number of stargazers than those which typically happened over a month prior. If we consider this from a potential stargazer's point of view it stands to reason that they will be more likely to 'star' or 'unstar' the project based upon the recent changes that have been made to the system rather than those that happened in points in time beyond a few weeks due to having a greater investment in commits that have more immediate effects on the project.

Table 2. % Positive cross correlation at different lag intervals for #Commits and #Stargazers

Lag amount	% Positive correlations between #commits and #stargazers
0	60%
−1	61%
−2	57%
−3	60%
−4	60%
−5	54%
−6	55%
−7	55%
−8	50%
−9	51%

Regarding accepting or discarding the null hypothesis, the value in the case of all lags is not conclusive enough to be able to determine this. An argument could be made that the lesser lag values support the hypothesis. In particular, the −1 commit lag which is the best performing correlation percentage with stargazers indicates that the optimum time is week before the stargazers react to the commit count and decide whether to remain stargazers or to stop following the project. Figure 2 visualises the distribution of correlation values at different lag intervals, highlighting the almost random nature obtained, thus supporting the null hypothesis. Table 2 shows the mean correlation values for each lag interval and while all remain positive the significance of lag interval is evidently minor. Therefore, we cannot reject the null hypothesis.

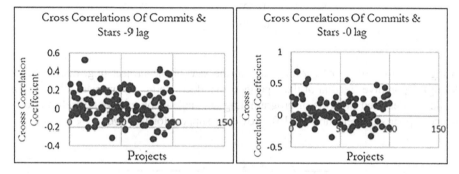

Fig. 2. Distribution of correlation for the two extreme lag intervals

Law one and six both state that in order to maintain user satisfaction the project will need to continually change and grow to maintain user satisfaction. A reason why this does not apply to the context of the GitHub platform could be attributed to the starring process which serves as a repository 'bookmark' for the user to show an level of interest that does not extend to receiving notifications etc. about the project. This would suggest that independent of the amount of commits (change) made the user will continue to remain starred until they have a reason to change that stance (become less satisfied)/stop supporting the project which highlights a clear disconnect between these particular laws and the GitHub platform (Table 3).

4.2   H$_2$a – Total Lines of Code Increases as a Software System Evolves

LOC metrics were organised into a vector and a growth rate algorithm applied to determine the average percentage growth for each week from the first and last week's LOC total. Thus from 100 projects, 100 growth rate values were generated, allowing the assessment of the percentage of projects that increased in size over time. Figure 3 visualises the results of this process. The majority of the projects increase in size as the software system evolves. This is generally to be expected since as time progresses the demand for new functionality is intuitively expected and will be constant in order to support the user base. However, there remain several projects that produced contrary results and reduced in size. Law two states that this could be the side effect of work

Table 3. Mean cross correlation for stargazers and commits organised by interval

Lag interval	Mean cross correlation for #commits and #stargazers
0	0.0321
−1	0.0258
−2	0.0266
−3	0.0307
−4	0.0336
−5	0.0381
−6	0.0461
−7	0.0367
−8	0.0607
−9	0.0701

being done to actively reduce or maintain the size of the project (e.g. due to refactoring). Upon investigation of the 7 projects that decrease in size, no particular pattern could be identified in terms of programming language or otherwise. Overall, the evidence supports the rejection of H_20, providing support for law two.

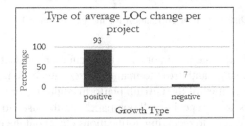

Fig. 3. Number of projects where LOC increased or decreased over time

4.3 H_3a – Issues, Additions and Deletions Over Time for Are Normally Distributed

To capture the essence of the third law three metrics would have to be considered to represent the 'products and process measures' and the 'self-regulating' keywords, in this case additions/deletions in tandem with issues was chosen. In order to determine if these measures were close to normal the Shapiro-Wilk test of normality was leveraged for each metric extracted from the 100 sampled projects. Again the 100 calculated p-values were compared with an alpha of 0.05.

Table 4 shows the overall results showing clearly that we cannot reject the H_30 hypothesis. Rather, evidence points to the non-normality of the data and counters law three despite threshold relaxations from the traditional 0.05. We also conducted an Anderson-Darling statistical test for normality and found a similar result. The

Table 4. Percentage of sampled distributions with varying alpha values for normality using Shapiro-Wilk

Alpha	Percentage of issues	Percentage of deletions	Percentage of additions
0.01	88%	100%	100%
0.02	90%	100%	100%
0.03	90%	100%	100%
0.04	91%	100%	100%
0.05	94%	100%	100%

non-normality may reflect the nature of open source development in which changes to the master branch can be made dynamically at any time, as a consequence of this it is possible that there will be periods where no change to the code is made. As a result of this the amount of additions and deletions may fluctuate from week to week with no consistency in the amount of code change, depending on the nature of the change which could vary from a minor bug fix to integrating a new feature. The OSS paradigm thrives upon contribution from distributed collaborators at any point in time, pull requests are monitored by the core projects team but a change is reviewed and accepted at any arbitrary point in time which disrupts the normality of additions and deletions.

4.4   H₄a – Project Issues Increase as Code Churn Decreases

We have limited the scope of our study to what can be extracted via the GitHub API. Further studies are ongoing looking at separate metrics for source code quality and its relationship to software change as determined from GitHub. Nonetheless, for completeness we have made the link from quality to the number of issues that occur in each weekly interval. LOC change will be used to assess code churn. To determine if a decrease or stagnation in the lines of code will lead to an increased number of issues (or vice versa) in the set of projects a cross correlation was again applied with various lag parameters tested to supplement the analysis. The main target was to evaluate each generated correlation value and count the amount of times for each of the one hundred projects that a negative correlation occurs, this has been expressed as a series of percentages in Table 5.

A pattern can be observed which shows the overall percentage increasing as the LOC lag is moved further into the past. This indicates that an increase/decrease in the LOC of a project will have a greater impact on the amount of issues over an extended period of time rather than immediately. Logically this makes sense as introducing new features in the past may typically spawn issues that were not immediately evident to the core team and may quickly to come to the surface following extensive usage and feedback from the user base. This would explain why the amount of positive correlations decrease as the lag is increased as a new feature may be introduced that has a side effect that produces bugs whereas if the −9 lag is considered the amount of issues will have decreased as the potential problems will have already been fixed by the present point in time from that initial change to lines of code.

Table 5. Percentage of correlations for different lags that are negative

Lag amount	Percentage of negative correlations **
0	32%
−1	33%
−2	32%
−3	32%
−4	35%
−5	35%
−6	37%
−7	37%
−8	36%
−9	38%

If the percentages themselves are considered it indicates that the amount of negative correlations in this context is the minority result, rather than changes in lines of code decreasing the amount of issues in most cases the amount of issues increase (or rather than stagnation/decrease in LOC introducing more issues, it reduces the amount of issues). This brings up a possible facet of open source development that may contribute to this phenomenon, typically a subset of the core team reviews pull requests and decides on whether to merge them or not. This potentially isolates a sizeable proportion of the contributors who have no input on what is accepted. Therefore, it is likely that in hindsight after the pull request was accepted and it has been extensively utilised that issues arise after an arbitrary amount of time. Table 5 suggests that considering the LOC further into the past has a lesser impact towards issues than immediate changes. Overall this suggests that an increase to lines of code is more likely to spawn an issue than stagnation or a decrease. This could be a result of introducing new features which could have only been tested in isolation by the core team and when exposed to the public give rise to more issues. On the other hand, a reduction in LOC could be a result of refactoring or removing dead code, thereby improving the software and preventing future problems.

To conclude reference should be made back to the hypothesis to determine an outcome, the results in Table 5 provide evidence which disputes law seven in most cases. Figure 4 shows a distribution of values that appear random indicating little support for H_4. Further, this claim which albeit contrast with the significant negative presence as seen in Table 5 shows only a minor affinity towards a positive correlation in the case of a mean.

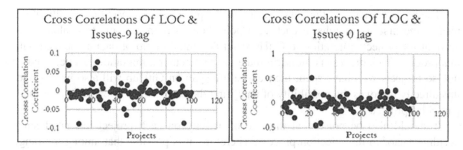

Fig. 4. Distribution of correlations at different lag points

5   Validity Discussion

5.1   Construct Validity

Due to a focus on the metrics that can be attained from the GitHub API, Lehman's laws had to be interpreted into hypotheses that represent the intent of each law as accurately as possible. In some cases logical metrics were available such as using stargazers to measure 'satisfaction', however in other cases there is room for dispute. An example of this is evidenced in law two 'increasing complexity' this study represents complexity as lines of code, however it is also possible to choose more appropriate measures such as McCabe's cyclomatic complexity which would involve delving into lower level metrics at the code base, which is beyond the scope of this initial study. Hypothesis six focuses on quality, the metric that has been attached to this law is issues and its relationship with code churn (additions and deletions) but in reality this is a much coarser grain aspect. A more complete study could account for testing code coverage, architecture, count of bugs among others.

In most cases the percentage values yielded at each lag interval indicate that a negative correlation is the majority result supporting the idea that the number of issues is to an extent driven by the volume of comments. Therefore the more a project team utilises a feedback system the more likely that the code will improve. It is difficult to explain why that in most cases a significant subset of the projects do not adhere to this principle, the size and make up of each team a transient factor that cannot be quantified in this context. In addition to this it is possible that as interaction via comments increases that this will lead to the discovery of additional issues that are associated with the current point of discussion.

The evaluation process for each hypothesis should also be taken into account, for H_1 and H_4 a binary threshold was used to generate the percentages at each lag interval. This does not account for the strength of each individual correlation value and how significant it may be, for example based on upon the scatter graphs provided in each of those hypotheses a broad subset of the data in most cases is focused around the zero point and may often times is extremely close to either being positive or negative. This lack of precision, while useful for stimulating a discussion may represent values that do no lean either way to supporting or refuting the hypotheses as significance is not easy to evaluate.

The pre-processing of the dataset also has the potential to impact the validity of the results, the first six months of each data point being trimmed from the evaluation to account for projects migrating to GitHub and the initial dump of data associated with that process. This process is indiscriminate of the whether a migration has occurred or not, so projects who have spent their entire life span on GitHub will also be targeted, this directly removes the possibility of analysing the early stages of evolution for these particular projects.

It should also be noted that the rate of activity on each project has not been a deciding factor in the selection process. Therefore, it is possible that among the range of projects there will be some that are maintained much more effectively than others, this is dependent on factors such as the size of the team actively working on the project and the amount of general user collaboration on GitHub. This might lead to cases where the activity of the team itself becomes a driver of software evolution, which this study does not account for and could be an avenue for future work.

5.2   External Validity

While the random selection of a fairly large set of projects was made the study would benefit from repetition before any attempt is made to generalise the findings. The study targeted the most popular projects on GitHub as representative of typical open source development. This is open to dispute and the findings may not necessarily apply to all projects e.g. less popular projects. We also targeted popularity as defined by developer attention rather than attention from users.

5.3   Conclusion Validity

Using the results, in most cases it is difficult to unequivocally support or refute a law. The main contributions of the paper are therefore in the discussion of the results and support or otherwise for Lehman's laws. In some cases, (e.g. H_2 and H_3) the results provide clear support or refutation However the other hypotheses remain much more debateable.

6   Conclusions

The goal of this paper was to evaluate Lehman's Laws of software evolution via usage of the GitHub API. Our research question on whether it is possible using data extracted from the GitHub API to determine if OS software evolution over time reflects Lehman's laws is answered. There is much that can be extracted to help study software evolution and to evaluate Lehman's laws and tools can be built that make the process of data extraction, transformation and analysis relatively straightforward. The experience shows that the data that can be extracted from GitHub is insufficient to conclusively test Lehman's laws. A much richer dataset, perhaps including data on downloads, on defects or on quality would produce much more useful results.

On support or otherwise for Lehman's laws we found contradictory evidence in all cases studied except for laws 2 and 3. For H_2 i.e. that the total lines of code increases as a software system evolves we can reject the null hypothesis and therefore find support for law two. On the other hand, we found evidence to support H_30. Here the evidence seems to clearly reject law three since we found in our study that issues, additions and deletions over time were not normally distributed.

Our findings are often similar to those in related work as discussed in Sect. 2. The work by Gonzalez-Barahona [7] also found support for law two and also questioned the validity of law three. Similar to our work they have found the evidence for the other laws to be inconclusive and, interestingly, question the falsifiability of the laws, especially given the need to use proxy measures such as LOC for complexity. The work by Mens et al. [18] and Fernandez-Ramil [19] on Eclipse found support for laws one and six, but otherwise found their data inconclusive. They did find partial support for law two depending on the complexity metric used. The message here may be that support or otherwise for Lehman's law depend on the indicators used. As an example there is no agreement on how to measure such things as complexity or satisfaction. Even more so the best measures are not always practicable and proxy measures must be used.

Overall, in our findings, based on results from a dataset of 100 open source projects, only one of the hypotheses provide enough evidence to support the laws investigated. The discussion for why this occurs often reflects the context of open source development and the GitHub platform itself which are aspects of software evolution that Lehman's laws did not foresee. However, utilising only data that can be extracted from the API at the repository level imposed certain restrictions on the nature of each hypotheses interpretation therefore further work into this topic could be explored that integrates a detailed analysis of the code base itself in order to supplement these findings. We are also looking to extend work on causes of change [24, 25] as it applies to OSS. In addition to this future contribution may entail presenting an alternative to Lehman's laws which fully consider the open source paradigm and establish a set of rules that account for the variations in this approach from traditional software development.

References

1. Paulson, J.W., Succi, G., Eberlein, A.: An empirical study of open-source and closed-source software products. IEEE Softw. **30**, 246–256 (2004)
2. Greer, D., Conradi, R.: Software project initiation and planning - an empirical study. IET Softw. 3(5), 356–368 (2009)
3. Lehman, M.M.: On understanding laws, evolution, and conservation in the large-program life cycle. J. Syst. Softw. **1**, 213–221 (1980)
4. Lehman, M.M.: Laws of software evolution revisited. In: Montangero, C. (ed.) EWSPT 1996. LNCS, vol. 1149, pp. 108–124. Springer, Heidelberg (1996). https://doi.org/10.1007/BFb0017737
5. Kalliamvakou, E., Gousios, G., Blincoe, K., Singer, L., German, D.M., Damian, D.: The promises and perils of mining github. In: Proceedings of 11th Working Conference on Mining Software Repositories, pp. 92–101 (2014)
6. GitHub Features (2019). https://github.com/features. Accessed 31 Mar 2019

7. Gonzalez-Barahona, J.M., Robles, G., Herraiz, I., Ortega, F.: Studying the laws of software evolution in a long-lived FLOSS project. Softw. Evol. Process **26**(7), 589–612 (2014)
8. Syeed, M., Hammouda, I., Syatä, T.: Evolution of open source software projects: a systematic literature review. J. Softw. **8**(11), 2815–2829 (2013)
9. Yu, L., Mishra, A.: An empirical study of Lehman's law on software quality evolution. Int. J. Softw. Inform. **7**(3), 469–481 (2013)
10. Sheoran, J., Blincoe, K., Kalliamvakou, E., Damian, D., Ell, J.: Understanding 'watchers' on GitHub. In: Proceedings of 11th Working Conference on Mining Software Repositories, pp. 336–339 (2014)
11. Ben, X., Beijun, S., Weicheng, Y.: Mining developer contribution in open source software using visualization techniques. In: Proceedings of 3rd International Conference Intelligent System Design and Engineering Applications (ISDEA), pp. 934–937 (2013)
12. Gousios, G., Pinzger, M., van Deursen, A.: An exploratory study of the pull-based software development model. In: Proceedings of the 36th International Conference on Software Engineering, pp. 345–355 (2014)
13. Borges, H., Valente, M.T., Hora, A., Coelho, J.: On the Popularity of GitHub Applications: A Preliminary Note. arXiv:1507.00604 (2015). Accessed 31 Mar 2019
14. Bissyandé, T.F.: Got issues? Who cares about it? An investigation of issue trackers of 105 projects. In: Proceedings of IEEE 24th International Symposium on Software Reliability Engineering, pp. 188–197 (2013)
15. Neamtiu, I., Xie, G., Chen, J.: Towards a better understanding of software evolution: an empirical study on open-source software. J. Softw. Evol. Process **25**, 193–218 (2013)
16. Skoulis, I., Vassiliadis, P., Zarras, A.: Open-source databases: within, outside, or beyond Lehman's laws of software evolution? In: Jarke, M., et al. (eds.) CAiSE 2014. LNCS, vol. 8484, pp. 379–393. Springer, Cham (2014). https://doi.org/10.1007/978-3-319-07881-6_26
17. Israeli, A., Feitelson, D.G.: The Linux kernel as a case study in software evolution. J. Syst. Softw. **83**(3), 485–501 (2010)
18. Mens, T., Fernández-Ramil, J.: The evolution of Eclipse. In: Proceedings of International Conference Software Maintenance, pp. 386–395 (2008)
19. Fernandez-Ramil, J., Lozano, A., Wermelinger, M., Capiluppi, A.: Empirical studies of open source evolution. In: Mens, T., Demeyer, S. (eds.) Software Evolution, pp. 263–288. Springer, Berlin (2008). https://doi.org/10.1007/978-3-540-76440-3_11
20. Stroulia, E., Kapoor, R.: Metrics of refactoring-based development: an experience report. In: Wang, X., Johnston, R., Patel, S. (eds.) OOIS, pp. 113–122. Springer, Heidelberg (2001). https://doi.org/10.1007/978-1-4471-0719-4_13
21. Graylin, J., Hale, J., Smith, R.K., Hale, D., Kraft, N.A., Ward, C.: Cyclomatic complexity and lines of code: empirical evidence of a stable linear relationship. J. Softw. Eng. Appl. **2**(3), 137–143 (2009)
22. La, A.: Language Trends on GitHub. https://github.com/blog/2047-language-trends-on-github. Accessed 31 Mar 2019
23. RFoundation: The R Project for Statistical Computing. https://www.r-project.org/. Accessed 31 Mar 2019
24. McGee, S., Greer, D.: A software requirements change source taxonomy. In: 4th International Conference on Software Engineering Advances, ICSEA 2009, Includes SEDES 2009: Simposio para Estudantes de Doutoramento em Engenharia de Software (2009)
25. McGee, S., Greer, D.: Towards an understanding of the causes and effects of software requirements change: two case studies. Requir. Eng. **17**(2), 133–155 (2012)

Development of an Alumni Feedback System for Curriculum Improvement in Building Technology Courses

Adedeji Afolabi[1(✉)], Emmanuel Eshofonie[2], and Faith Akinbo[1]

[1] Department of Building Technology, Covenant University, Ota, Nigeria
adedeji.afolabi@covenantuniversity.edu.ng
[2] Centre for Systems and Information Services,
Covenant University, Ota, Nigeria

Abstract. In this fast-paced world, the needs of the world of work and the global market is changing at an unprecedented speed. Therefore, institutions of higher learning need to constantly adjust their programs to fit into these needs. The study aimed to develop an alumni feedback system for curriculum improvement in Building Technology courses. The study highlighted the benefits of an alumni feedback system compared to a manual questionnaire method or other methods of curriculum improvement. The web-based system was designed through use case and system block diagrams. Thereafter, the web-based system was programmed using HTML, CSS, MySQL and PHP. Screenshots of the web-based system was presented. The alumni feedback system comprises of background information of the alumni, perception test on the impact of the course content and a review of the course content for curriculum improvement. Since this is a preliminary study, future studies would be based on analyzing data obtained in the database in terms of the numerical and text data. This study can be adapted for other programmes for the purpose of curriculum improvement.

Keywords: Construction industry · Curriculum · Web-based systems

1 Introduction

It is common to evaluate students on different parameters after a course has been taught. However, another insight is produced when they have graduated and encountered the real world and the world of work. The reality that sets in is if they can actually apply what has been learnt in the four walls of their university. [1] suggested that due to the fast-paced changing strata in the needs of the world of work and the global market generally, institutions of higher learning need to constantly adjust their programs. [2] added that this is the first rule of sustainability, where universities are current in terms of the product and services they are dishing out to their customers. The customers in this case is the world of work while the products are the seasoned graduates that have been groomed with tested and up-to-date curriculum.

Taking this study to the Nigerian context, [3] argued with over 200 tertiary institutions, the products are most times unemployable. They attributed this to the outdated

© Springer Nature Switzerland AG 2019
S. Misra et al. (Eds.): ICCSA 2019, LNCS 11623, pp. 257–265, 2019.
https://doi.org/10.1007/978-3-030-24308-1_21

school curricula and lack of employable skills. [4] argued that the educational system must move away from the era of chalk and talk, rather focus on the industry needs to build employable graduates. Researchers such as [5] and [6] noted that unemployment has been the most socio–economic challenge gripping developing nations such as Nigeria. This most times is linked to curricula of higher institutions. The curriculum should be such that help graduates to fit into the world of work or be creators of jobs. Rather than waiting on the government in developing countries, the onus is on schools of higher learning to re-strategize on how to ensure that their graduates are employable and also create employment for others. In developed countries, the higher institutions have deeply taken initiatives to create graduates that are ready for the workplace as a result of listening to the needs of industries [7]. [8] opined university researchers in developed countries are able to observe the need trends of industries and examine their importance in improving the state of the nation's economy and technological advancements. What better way to understand the needs of the real world than viewing it from the eyes of the Alumni in comparison with the present curriculum.

The case for the building technology curriculum is centred on its relevance in oiling the necessary housing and urban infrastructure needed in developing nations, menace of building collapse and other un-professional conduct that negatively affect the image of the construction industry. Nigeria for instance struggles in these things. This study posits that if one of the root causes of these negative attributes of the Nigerian con-struction industry is associated with the outdated curriculum, then there is need for a review. The construction sector is looking for raw talents that are able to assume the required positions within organizations with little or no need of retraining [9]. These employable recruits will be able to fill the skill gap that exists in the construction sector. For employers of labour, [7] noted that a skill deficient graduate will lead to a loss and poor output for the firm. The construction industry is so critical in using graduates that have the required skills because of the nature of the products in terms of housing and other civil infrastructure [10]. The role of universities should not end in producing academically sound graduates but additionally ensuring that they are desirable to employers. This is one of the numerous roles of a robust and sustainable educational curriculum. Therefore, the study intends to develop of an alumni feedback system for curriculum improvement in Building Technology courses.

2 Review of Related Literature

In the study by [11], they argued that graduates from Nigeria's tertiary institutions have not been able to meet employers' needs. [12] stated that this is against the idea of quality education of creating job creators rather than job seekers. Sadly, [11] opined that many of Nigeria's graduates find it difficult to eloquently communicate and con-fidently defend their certificates on the job without adequate retraining. Statistically, [13] reported that only 10% of students that graduate annually become employed immediately. This points to the gap that exist in the Nigerian education curriculum system.

Several studies have pointed to the need for university-industry partnership in curriculum development. Interestingly, the alumni of university bodies have become part of the industry and being former students that have passed through the university courses have become rich source of curriculum improvement. [1] studied the impact of alumni feedback on a masters' programme in engineering based courses. Their study was able to assess the relevance of the program, the suitability of the objectives outlined in the program and the expected outcomes from graduates. However, the study used a paper-based method in form of a well-structured questionnaire. Similarly, [14] measured the impact of using alumni as an assessment tool for curriculum improvement in mechanical engineering programs. This study posits that the process can be automated. This is sustainable, can give instant and faster feedback. The result can be analyzed on the spot, whereby improvements can be effected immediately.

The study by [15] developed an alumni feedback systems for adult education among alumni. Their study advised that in the face of stiff competition and dwindling funds for universities there is need for innovative approach in improving their school's performance and service delivery. Using an alumni feedback system is not limited to curriculum improvement. [15] noted that it can be useful in managing alumni-university relationships, obtain latest industry information as regards the courses, supply of information as regards vacant employment positions in the industry and developing new programs that can engender lifelong learning among alumni. [16] evaluated the veterinary curriculum using an alumni-based approach on expected attributes of graduates from the program. [17] reported that some accrediting bodies usually suggest that programs intermittently engage outside evaluation for program improvement. In the study by [17], they used an unnamed online survey directed at graduates from over a decade for curriculum improvement in obstetrics and gynecology. From all the reviews, automating the process of the alumni feedback system is better than the paper-based method. This is so, in that, response can be stored, retrieved easily and processed faster.

3 System Design and Implementation

The alumni feedback system for curriculum improvement was designed as a web-based system which has a home interface and a database system. In order to design the web-based form, the use case diagram and a system block diagram was developed. Figure 1 showed the use case diagram of the alumni feedback system for curriculum improvement. In Fig. 1, there are majorly two users; the lecturer and the alumni completing the online form and curriculum improvement section.

Secondly, a system block diagram was designed as shown in Fig. 2. This helped to describe the pattern of the interface that was developed. In Fig. 2, a URL is provided to the alumni who are able to complete their background information, take the perception test on the course and help review curriculum content for improvement purposes. The lecturer on the other hand can access the back end of the web-form to obtain the content of the curriculum improvement through the database and analyse the content.

Using the use case diagram and the system block diagram, the study developed the web-based interface for alumni feedback system for curriculum improvement in building technology courses. Adopting the interactive database framework by [18–20] as shown in Fig. 3, the web-interface was designed using HTML and CSS, while the

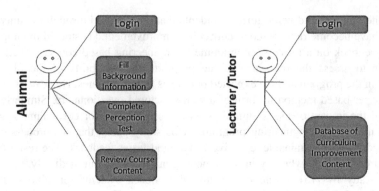

Fig. 1. Use case diagram of the alumni feedback system for curriculum improvement. Source: Author's Design

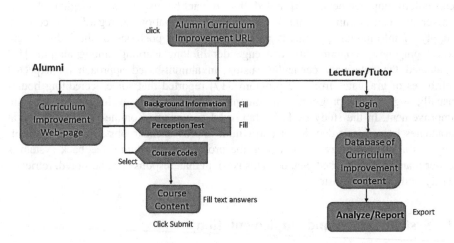

Fig. 2. System Block diagram for alumni feedback system for curriculum improvement. Source: Author's Design

database for the curriculum improvement was designed using MySQL. The connection platform for the web-interface and database system was achieved using PHP programming language.

A snippet of the PHP programming code is shown in Fig. 4. The preliminary work is accessible via the link http://bigtorch.com.ng/AlumniFeedback/index.php. The details in the link is presented in Screenshot as presented in Figs. 5, 6, 7 and 8. Figure 5 showed the background information of the alumni.

Background such as gender, program, email, year of graduation, grade at graduation and status of practice in the Building profession were requested. The second part of the alumni feedback system sought answers on their perception about the impact and usefulness of the course content on their present practice. The study used a 5-point Likert scale on the perception of the students to the course content. The parameters used in this section were adapted from [1, 14–17]. The third section of the

Platform 1
COLLECT
HTML
web-interface
Platform 2
PROCESS
PHP
connection
Platform 3
STORE
MySQL
database

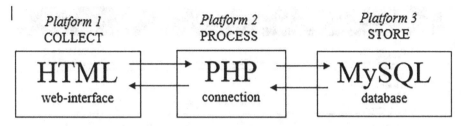

Fig. 3. Interactive framework for the web-based system. Source: [18]

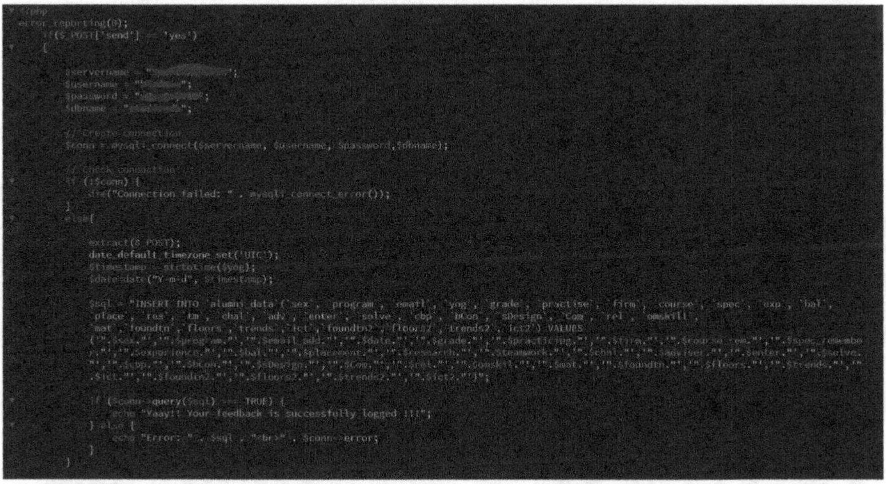

Fig. 4. Screen shot of the programming language used. Source: Author's Design

web-interface highlighted all the courses in Building technology from 100 level–500 level. The alumni are advised to select a course they would like to review the content and suggest ways to improve the teaching and delivery of the course content. Upon completion of the details, the alumni submits the responses which can be accessed via the database by the lecturer/tutor.

This ongoing research designed the web-based alumni feedback system to improve instructor's pedagogy and help in curriculum improvement towards producing employable graduates. Comparing this study with previous studies in [1, 14, 15], this study prescribed a web-based system rather than a paper-based questionnaire method. As the university graduates from this tertiary institutions are dispersed in different locations around the world, the web-based system gives them the opportunity to contribute to curriculum improvement for the younger generation. The alumni curriculum improvement link can be shared via emails, WhatsApp and on the Departmental website. Further studies in this light would analyse the feedback from the database of the alumni feedback system and analysing the empirical data would present to the instructor the needed changes that needs to be in place for better pedagogy.

Covenant University

Alumni Feedback Form (College Of Building)

Academic Year: 2018-19

Dear Eagles,

We are glad to have had you spend some time with us in Covenant University. We would love to have your opinion about our curriculum in Building Technology from your perspective now that you are part of the industry. Your input will help shape Kings and Queens in Hebron. Feel free as your identity would be kept private.

* Required

1. Male: ○ Female: ○ *

2. Program: *

[Enter Program]

3. Email: *

[Enter Email]

4. Year Of Graduation*

[dd-----yyyy]

5. Grade upon Graduation: *

○ First Class; ○ Second Class Upper; ○ Second Class Lower; ○ Third Class;

6. Are you presently practicing Building Technology? * Yes ○ No ○

7. If Yes, What is your role in your firm?*

[Enter your role]

8. Do you recall any course (s) in Building Technology (BLD) that has been useful in construction? *

Yes ○ No ○

9. If Yes, Please specify?*

[Specify]

Fig. 5. Background information of Alumni in the Feedback system. Source: Author's Design

Please kindly indicate the one that applies to courses in Building Technology using
5 = Strongly Agree, 4 = Agree, 3 = Neutral, 2 = Disagree, 1 = Strongly Disagree

S/N	Parameters	5	4	3	2	1
1	Overall Educational Experience was satisfactory	●	●	●	●	●
2	There was balance between theory and practical	●	●	●	●	●
3	The program helped to quickly secure a placement in the industry	●	●	●	●	●
4	Independent research work was adequate	●	●	●	●	●
5	Teamwork was encouraged	●	●	●	●	●
6	The courses were intellectually challenging	●	●	●	●	●
7	My level adviser was helpful in the study	●	●	●	●	●
8	Entrepreneurship was encouraged	●	●	●	●	●
9	The study helped me solve problems faster and better	●	●	●	●	●
10	Teaching of Computer-based programs are adequate in the courses	●	●	●	●	●
11	The business aspect of construction was well taught	●	●	●	●	●
12	The structural aspect of building design was taught	●	●	●	●	●
13	Communication skills were enhanced	●	●	●	●	●
14	The courses are applicable/relevant to real life situations	●	●	●	●	●
15	There were enough materials for the courses	●	●	●	●	●
16	Organizational and managerial skills were developed	●	●	●	●	●

Fig. 6. Perception test on the impact of Building Technology courses. Source: Author's Design

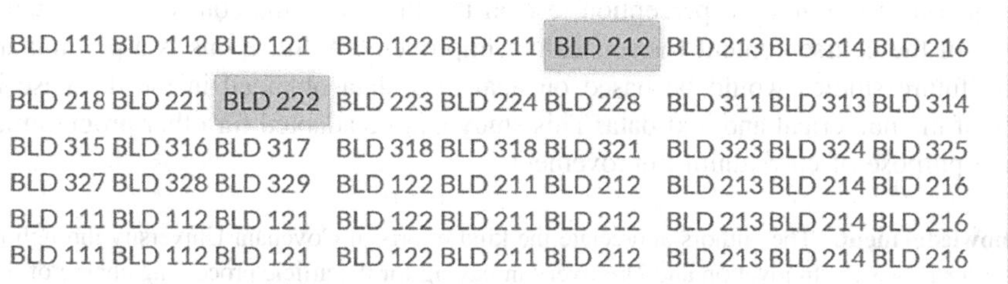

BLD 111 BLD 112 BLD 121   BLD 122 BLD 211 BLD 212 BLD 213 BLD 214 BLD 216

BLD 218 BLD 221 BLD 222 BLD 223 BLD 224 BLD 228   BLD 311 BLD 313 BLD 314

BLD 315 BLD 316 BLD 317   BLD 318 BLD 318 BLD 321   BLD 323 BLD 324 BLD 325

BLD 327 BLD 328 BLD 329   BLD 122 BLD 211 BLD 212   BLD 213 BLD 214 BLD 216

BLD 111 BLD 112 BLD 121   BLD 122 BLD 211 BLD 212   BLD 213 BLD 214 BLD 216

BLD 111 BLD 112 BLD 121   BLD 122 BLD 211 BLD 212   BLD 213 BLD 214 BLD 216

Fig. 7. List of course codes in Building Technology in the Feedback system. Source: Author's Design

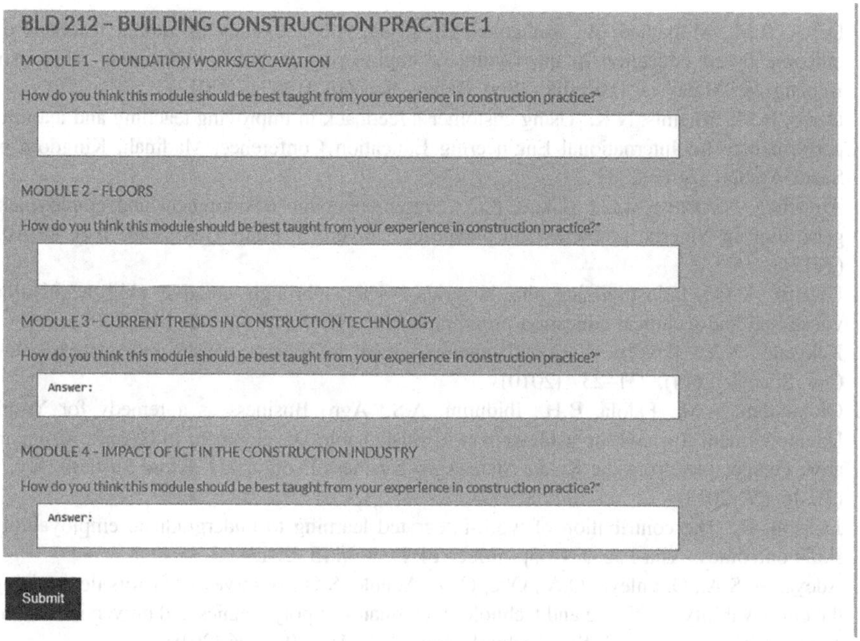

BLD 212 – BUILDING CONSTRUCTION PRACTICE 1

MODULE 1 - FOUNDATION WORKS/EXCAVATION

How do you think this module should be best taught from your experience in construction practice?*

MODULE 2 - FLOORS

How do you think this module should be best taught from your experience in construction practice?*

MODULE 3 - CURRENT TRENDS IN CONSTRUCTION TECHNOLOGY

How do you think this module should be best taught from your experience in construction practice?*

Answer:

MODULE 4 - IMPACT OF ICT IN THE CONSTRUCTION INDUSTRY

How do you think this module should be best taught from your experience in construction practice?*

Answer:

Submit

Fig. 8. Sample of a selected course code showing course content to be reviewed. Source: Author's Design

4   Conclusion

The study present the aspect of curriculum improvement through the online participation of alumni feedback in Building Technology courses. The study highlighted the benefits of an alumni feedback system compared to a manual questionnaire method or other methods of curriculum improvement. The web-based system was designed through use case and system block diagrams. Thereafter, the web-based system was programmed using HTML, CSS, MySQL and PHP. Screenshots of the web-based system was presented. The alumni feedback system comprises of background information of the alumni, perception test on the impact of the course content and a review of the course content for curriculum improvement. Since this is a preliminary study, future studies would be based on analysing data obtained in the database in terms of the numerical and text data. This study can be adapted for other programmes for the purpose of curriculum improvement.

Acknowledgement. The authors appreciate the kind efforts of Covenant University through its Centre for Research, Innovation and Discovery in paying for the article processing charge of this article.

References

1. Deros, B.M., Mohamed, A., Mohamed, N., Ihsan, A.K.: A study of alumni feedback on outcome based education in the faculty of engineering & built environment, Universiti Kebangsaan Malaysia. Procedia – Soc. Behav. Sci. **60**, 313–317 (2012)
2. Deros, B.M., Khamis, N.K.: Using customer's feedback in improving teaching and learning performance. In: International Engineering Education Conference, Madinah, Kingdom of Saudi Arabia, 16–19 2009
3. Anyadike, N., Emeh, I.E.J., Ukah, F.O.: Entrepreneurship development and employment generation in Nigeria: problems and prospects. Univers. J. Educ. Gen. Stud. **1**(4), 88–102 (2012)
4. Uwaifo, V.O.: Industrializing the Nigerian society through creative skill acquisition vocational and technical education programme. Int. NGO J. **4**(4), 142–145 (2009)
5. Kakwagh, V.V., Ikwuba, A.: Youth unemployment in Nigeria: causes and related issues. Can. Soc. Sci. **6**(4), 231–237 (2010)
6. Olokundun, A.M., Falola, B.H., Ibidunni, A.S.: Agro Business as a remedy for Youth Unemployment towards the achievement of Sustainable Development in Nigeria: Comparative Perspectives from the Kwara State Agro Business Economy. J. Econ. Sustain. Dev. **5** (3), 46–57 (2014)
7. Jackson, D.: The contribution of work-integrated learning to undergraduate employability skills outcomes. Asia-Pac. J. Coop. Educ. **14**(2), 99–115 (2013)
8. Adeyemo, S.A., Ogunleye, O.A., Oke, C.O., Adenle, S.O.: A survey of factors determining the employability of science and technology graduates of polytechnics and universities in the Nigerian labour market. J. Sci. Technol. Educ. Res. **1**(5), 99–106 (2010)
9. Afolabi, A.O., Oyeyipo, O.: The perception of future decision-makers on the building profession. Malays. Constr. Res. J. **21**(1), 55–73 (2017)
10. Afolabi, A.O., Ojelabi, R.A., Oyeyipo, O., Tunji-Olayeni, P.F., Omuh, I.O.: Integrating software development courses in the construction curriculum. Turkish Online J. Educ. Technol. **2017**(Special Issue), 215–225 (2017)
11. Eneh, A.N., Eneh, O.C.: Rethinking the curriculum of Nigerian university education: functionality challenges. Sustain. Hum. Dev. Rev. **7**(1–4), 39–55 (2015)
12. Makinde, J.K.A.: We are on to all-round excellence in Ojewale Olu. Tell Mag. (2007)
13. Gyamfi, C.C.: Minister bemoans youth unemployment. Guardian Newspaper (2006)
14. Younis, N.: Impact of alumni feedback on the curriculum. In: Proceedings of the 2002 American Society for Engineering Education Annual Conference & Exposition, pp. 1–9 (2002)
15. Chen, C., Chung-Ming, L.: Applying an alumni feedback system to adult education and the school management value chain. J. Hum. Resour. Adult Learn. **9**(2), 143–151 (2013)

16. Cobb, K.A., Brown, G.A., Hammond, R.H., Mossop, L.H.: Alumni-based evaluation of a novel veterinary curriculum: are Nottingham graduates prepared for clinical practice. Vet. Rec. Open **2**, 1–9 (2015)
17. Curran, D., Xu, X., Dewald, S., Johnson, T.R.R., Reynolds, R.K.: An alumni survey as a needs assessment for curriculum improvement in obstetrics and gynecology. J. Graduate Med. Educ. **11**, 317–321 (2012)
18. De Wolf, C.: Material quantities in building structures and their environmental impact. Unpublished MSc. thesis, Department of Architecture, Massachusetts Institute of Technology (MIT), USA (2014)
19. Afolabi, A., Fagbenle, O., Mosaku, T.: IT management of building materials' planning and control processes using web-based technologies. In: Rocha, Á., Correia, A.M., Adeli, H., Reis, L.P., Costanzo, S. (eds.) WorldCIST 2017. AISC, vol. 570, pp. 12–19. Springer, Cham (2017). https://doi.org/10.1007/978-3-319-56538-5_2
20. Afolabi, A.O., Fagbenle, O., Ojelabi, R., Amusan, L., Tunji-Olayeni, P., Daniyan, V.: Development of a web-based human resource sourcing system for labour only contracts. In: Construction Research Congress 2018: Construction Information Technology - Selected Papers from the Construction Research Congress 2018, April 2018, pp. 736–746 (2018)

e-Maintenance Framework for Strategic Asset Management in Tertiary Institutions

Adedeji Afolabi[1]([⊠]), Ibukun Afolabi[2], Emmanuel Eshofonie[3],
and Faith Akinbo[1]

[1] Department of Building Technology, Covenant University, Ota, Nigeria
adedeji.afolabi@covenantuniversity.edu.ng
[2] Department of Computer and Information Sciences,
Covenant University, Ota, Nigeria
[3] Centre for Systems and Information Services,
Covenant University, Ota, Nigeria

Abstract. Tertiary institutions require buildings such as its senate building, classrooms, laboratories, administrative rooms, hostels and other offices in order to function. Providing and maintaining these buildings require a lot of planning and capital investment. The study examined the prospects of using e-Maintenance platform for strategic asset management in tertiary institutions. This study noted that adequate maintenance of the building infrastructural base of tertiary institutions is crucial for sustainability in the face of dwindling funds in the education sector. In order to automate the e-Maintenance process for strategic maintenance of the institution's building maintenance, a use case diagram, system block diagram, sequence diagram and activity diagram were designed and presented in this study. Three (3) main users are essential in the sequence of operation of the e-Maintenance platform. These users represent the building occupants, the facility manager and the management personnel; for effective oversite and performance monitoring. The methodology of this research includes using the combination of HTML, CSS and the C-Sharp programming language for the interface design and server side scripting while MySQL was the database platform used for storing and retrieving the data used for the application. In conclusion, the study developed an e-Maintenance framework for strategic asset management in tertiary institutions.

Keywords: Asset management · Automation · Construction industry ·
e-Maintenance · Web-based systems

1 Introduction

Tertiary institutions require buildings such as its senate building, classrooms, laboratories, administrative rooms, hostels and other offices in order to function. Providing and maintaining these buildings require a lot of planning and capital investment. The dwindling funds available to tertiary institutions means that adequate attention is given to the available infrastructure within the university, as providing new ones may become difficult. The asset gathered by the tertiary institutions need to be strategically managed over the years through proper maintenance to ensure they are continually attractive and

© Springer Nature Switzerland AG 2019
S. Misra et al. (Eds.): ICCSA 2019, LNCS 11623, pp. 266–277, 2019.
https://doi.org/10.1007/978-3-030-24308-1_22

meet the competitive environment universities try to compete in. In the study by [1] strategic infrastructure asset management is defined as the process by which organization achieves its goals by ensuring that its asset meets the needs of its changing customers.

Crucial to asset management is operational improvement, satisfaction of the customer using the facilities, improved productivity, quality asset and positive environmental impact. To achieve this, maintenance is at the centre of strategic asset management. Maintenance cost on the other hand continues to increase. The study by [2] stated that maintenance cost can account for up to 40% of the total operating cost of an organization. To think that the maintenance cost of a conglomerate increased from 200 billion dollars to 600 billion dollars in the space of 10 years [3]. This means that without adequate planning for maintenance, it can break or ruin a business [4]. As tertiary institutions continue to increase its capacity and asset base to cater for the needs of its students, there is need for adequate maintenance of its asset. Tertiary institutions have embraced the use of information and communication technologies. This can be applicable for maintenance monitoring and feedback mechanism. Other e-technologies adopted by tertiary institutions can be seen in works by [5–8].

An easy definition of the term e-Maintenance is put forward by [9] as the process of integrating existing traditional maintenance strategies with the innovation of information and communication technologies (ICTs). From this definition, [10] asserted that e-Maintenance is able to provide the necessary maintenance support in terms of information on resources needed for the maintenance works, services needed to be carried out and the personnel allocation in order to take proactive and informed decision. The process of e-Maintenance helps users to log in from anywhere in the world to take remote actions. In this, maintenance operations can be setup, controlled and the performance of the maintenance personnel monitored and evaluated [11]. The study by [12] added that e-Maintenance technologies ensures transparency and efficiency by integrating the business process of an organization with a collaborative maintenance environment. The maintenance process becomes lean and downtime is minimized as much as possible. The use of the internet-based network ensures data and information flow for easy decision making in maintenance of university's asset. With the prospects of e-Maintenance, the study developed an e-Maintenance framework for strategic asset management in tertiary institutions.

2 Review of Related Literature

Different definitions exist for e-Maintenance in diverse studies [9, 10, 13]. A major similarity in the description of e-Maintenance is the use of ICTs within a firm's maintenance strategy or plan. The study by [13] stated that different types of e-Maintenance platforms exist and in different capacities as used in diverse industries. In the study by [4], their e-Maintenance system was a condition monitoring module that receives data from sensors attached on the device needing maintenance services. With the emergence of artificial intelligence (AI), predictive maintenance can be detected through condition monitoring/prognosis of equipment and buildings [13]. The prospects of this remote sensing in e-Maintenance has been heavily utilized in the automobile industry, aerospace industry, power and other manufacturing industries. Examples of the e-Maintenance systems in operation include, Condition Monitoring Multi Agent System (COMMAS) was designed for a smart electrical plant [14] and a chemical processing plant [15], an expert system using vibration analysis to identify faults in the manufacturing industry [16], the use of Radio Frequency Identification (RFID) technology with microchips and antenna in many other industries [17] and instant email notification as used by computer or gadget manufacturing companies [18]. In the aerospace industry, [19] reported that a communication platform was developed to remotely fix their aircraft's computers.

The study by [10] examined the advantages and barriers to an efficient use of e-Maintenance. Their study showed that e-Maintenance offers the opportunity to develop new maintenance systems within an organization, improve support systems and help define new maintenance activities. Additionally, [13] argued that firms are able to increase their competitive advantage over their counterparts through a well-managed e-Maintenance platform. The article by [20] opined that smart companies are able to optimize the performance of their asset base through process reliability. In that, [13] pointed out the advantage of a 24-hour feedback system and centralization of data. A major challenge to the maintenance feedback mechanism is the need to provide an easy to manage database due to the high volume of information it has to store and process [10]. The study by [4] asserted that people management is key while planning for maintenance works. e-Maintenance helps to create a collaborative environment among the building occupants, facility managers, technicians and the management. By this economic goals are realized by companies that implement e-Maintenance systems through reduced maintenance process cost by increasing maintenance identification time and duration of maintenance intervention and preventing downtime [4]. They referred to it as an enhancer of zero downtime performance in business operations.

3 System Design

According to [10], for e-Maintenance to succeed, the existing maintenance system within an organization needs to be studied for efficient models and process to be drafted in e-Maintenance technologies. In tertiary institutions in Nigeria, due to the enormous investment in building infrastructure, there is a dedicated department that handles maintenance services within the institution. In some places, they are referred to as the Works Department while in the area under study, it is referred to as the Physical Planning Department (PPD). Every maintenance unit in each tertiary institution has its own mode of carrying out its maintenance works in terms of sourcing for maintenance resources, delegation of personnel and carrying out of the maintenance activity. The similarity amongst the tertiary institution is the goal of maintaining its asset at a minimum cost. The e-Maintenance framework designed in this study is for a private institution in South-West Nigeria.

The existing maintenance complaint technique used in the tertiary institution chosen is a paper-based method using a job card for asset management. The study posit that the process can be automated thereby ensuring speed, easy data storage and retrieval, process monitoring and evaluation. A sample of the job card is presented in

Fig. 1. In Fig. 1, essential components are highlighted such as date, location, type of work required and a brief description of the maintenance challenge. This was designed by the Physical Planning Department within the private tertiary institution.

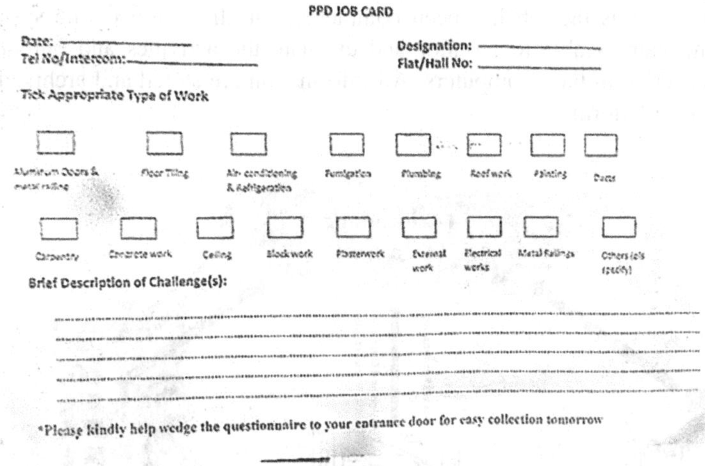

PPD JOB CARD

Date: ——————————   Designation: ——————————
Tel No/Intercom:——————————   Flat/Hall No: ——————————

Tick Appropriate Type of Work

☐ Aluminum Doors & metal railing ☐ Floor Tiling ☐ Air-conditioning & Refrigeration ☐ Fumigation ☐ Plumbing ☐ Roof work ☐ Painting ☐ Docts

☐ Carpentry ☐ Concrete work ☐ Ceiling ☐ Blockwork ☐ Plasterwork ☐ External work ☐ Electrical works ☐ Metal Railings ☐ Others (as specify)

Brief Description of Challenge(s):

....
....
....
....

*Please kindly help wedge the questionnaire to your entrance door for easy collection tomorrow

Fig. 1. Sample of Job Card used for Maintenance purposes (sourced from the private institution)

In order to automate the e-Maintenance process for strategic maintenance of the institution's building maintenance, a use case diagram, system block diagram, sequence diagram and activity diagram were designed and presented in this study. From Fig. 2, there are three (3) main users of the system. The first user is the building occupant, either in a Fig. 2 showed the use case diagram for the e-Maintenance portal in strategic asset management. Office space, residential apartment, hostel or other administrative building including the health centre. The other users are the Facility Manager and the Management personnel in charge of the Physical Planning Department (PPD) or a Personnel in the Senate either the Registrar or any other authorized person.

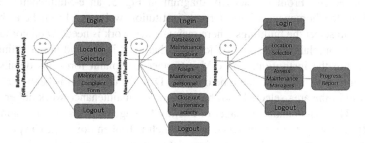

Fig. 2. Use case diagram for e-Maintenance portal in strategic asset management

Figure 3 showed the system block diagram for the e-Maintenance portal. Essentially, the e-Maintenance system is a web-based system that receives information from the building occupants who lodges maintenance issues required within their space. The Facility Manager is able to access the system from anywhere. The Facility Manager attached to each building asset accesses teach complaint from the building occupants and assigns them to the appropriate job personnel. The maintenance activity would be close out as soon as the job has been completed. The final user of the system; the Management team is able to monitor and evaluate the activities and output of the facility manager from their computers. All information are stored and archived on the e-Maintenance platform.

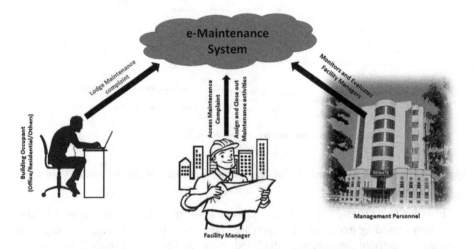

Fig. 3. System block diagram for the e-Maintenance portal

Figure 4 showed the sequence diagram of the flow of information. In the sequence diagram, there are 3 phases through the 8-point step from initiation of the e-Maintenance compliant to the evaluation process.

Figure 5 showed the activity diagram of the e-Maintenance system for strategic asset management. From the activity diagram in Fig. 5, an e-Maintenance URL is provided on the homepage of the tertiary institution webpage. From here, building occupants can select the buildings where maintenance work is needed and complete the maintenance complaint forms i.e. the job card that exist in the traditional maintenance process within the institution. The e-Maintenance complaint form has details of the Description of the complaint, the type of work, Date the complaint is been made, exact location within the area selected and the status of the maintenance work either open or closed out. The Maintenance manager or Facility Manager (FM) is able to login via the same URL and view the maintenance work which is broken down into Type of work, the description of the complaint, location, date, status and assign. The assign section helps the Maintenance manager or FM to allocate jobs to the appropriate quarters of skilled labour required. Once the job is completed, the Maintenance Manager or FM is

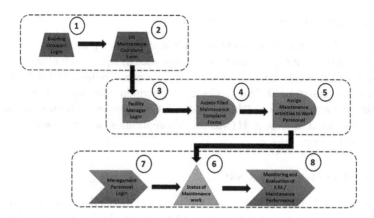

Fig. 4. Sequence diagram of the flow of information

able to close out the maintenance activity on the e-Maintenance portal. The Management or Personnel appointed to serve as an oversite function to monitor and evaluate the activities of the Maintenance manager or FM. The Management function is able to view activities that are still pending and closed out. The contact details in terms of email and contact number of the Maintenance manager or FM is made available on the platform for easy communication to sort out pending maintenance issues.

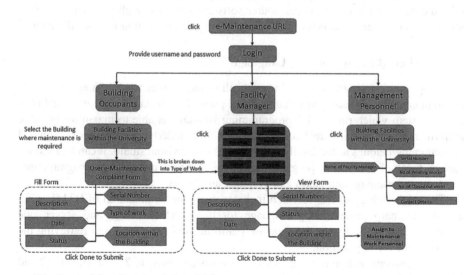

Fig. 5. Activity diagram of the e-Maintenance system for strategic asset management

4   System Implementation

This section gives a brief overview of the tools used in the coding of the application software. The various tools used in the development of the system are as follows:

4.1 Hyper Text Mark-up Language (HTML)

HTML is a markup language used in the development of web pages. Markup languages are usually written with angled brackets and tags such as <p> which means paragraph, <br> which means break, <body> which means the main contents that will be viewed on the browser and so on. HTML codes can be written with any text editor and are saved using the file extensions ".htm or .html". Once they have been saved any web browser can be used to view it. HTML for this application was written using sublime text as the text editor.

4.2 Cascading Style Sheet (CSS)

CSS is used to add some styling to HTML tags. The particular framework used was Bootstrap. The extension for css file is.css and external style sheets can be added using the html <link> tags. It helped to enforce the behavior of several of the entities of the application.

4.3 MySQL

In order to design the database management system (DBMS) for the e-maintenance system, MySQL (Structured Query Language) was used. Using MySQL helped to store the data in separate tables rather than putting each of them in a large warehouse. This is organized for speed, scalability, reliability and easy-to use. A database is a collection of related data. This is a free and open source software and runs on all platforms. MySQL also performs several functions. This was used in this application to store the data.

4.4 C-Sharp(#) Programming Language

The programming language used for controlling the system was C-Sharp (#). A C# program can contain managed or unmanaged parts. The managed code is fussed over by the system which runs it. C# programming language is able to maximize possible performance, and enable direct access to parts of the underlying computer system. C# programming belongs to the family of languages in the visual studio. It can be used for various types of application programming some of which include web programming, windows programing, animation and graphics and so on.

The methodology of this research includes using the combination of HTML, CSS and the C-Sharp programming language for the interface design and server side scripting while MySQL was the database platform used for storing and retrieving the data used for the application.

In the implementation of the e-Maintenance system, Figs. 6, 7, 8, 9, 10, 11, 12 and 13 showed the screenshots of the developed e-Maintenance platform. The users of the platforms follows the activity diagram described in Fig. 5.

Fig. 6. Portal Homepage for e-Maintenance system

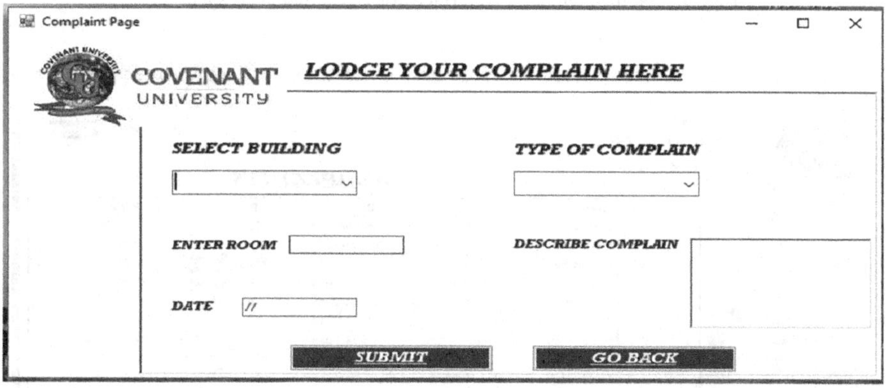

Fig. 7. User complaint page for e-Maintenance system

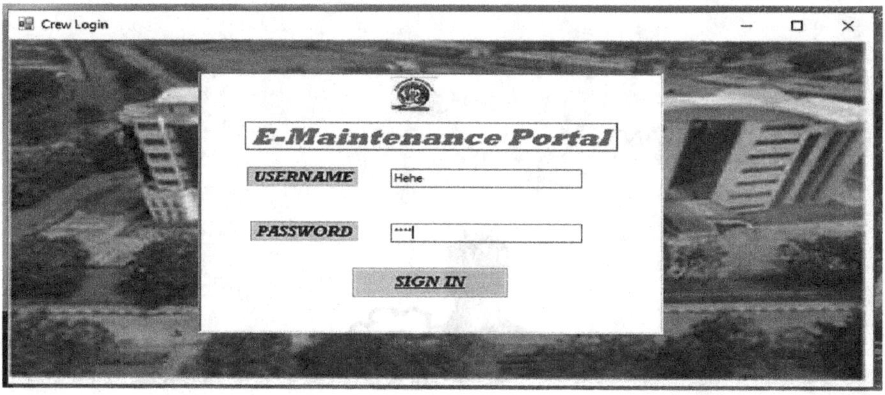

Fig. 8. Facility Manager Login page for e-Maintenance system

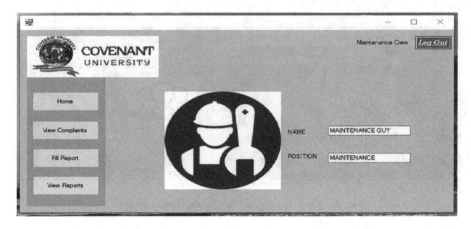

Fig. 9. Facility Manager Interface for e-Maintenance system

Fig. 10. Summary Complaint Interface for e-Maintenance system

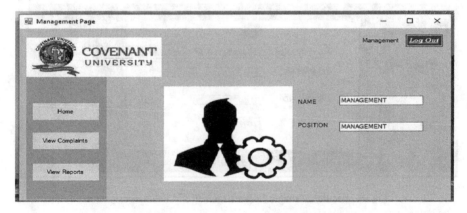

Fig. 11. Management Interface for e-Maintenance system

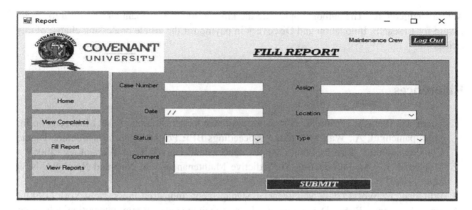

Fig. 12. Fill Report Interface for e-Maintenance system

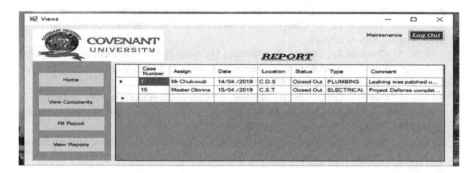

Fig. 13. View Report Interface for e-Maintenance system

5 Conclusion

The study examined the prospects of using e-Maintenance platform for strategic asset management in tertiary institutions. This study noted that adequate maintenance of the building infrastructural base of tertiary institutions is crucial for sustainability in the face of dwindling funds in the education sector. In order to automate the e-Maintenance process for strategic maintenance of the institution's building maintenance, a use case diagram, system block diagram, sequence diagram and activity diagram were designed and presented in this study. Three (3) main users are essential in the sequence of operation of the e-Maintenance platform. These users represent the building occupants, the facility manager and the management personnel; for effective oversite and performance monitoring. For future study, the e-Maintenance platform should be developed, having an interactive interface and a database. The effectiveness should also be measured against the existing tradition method of obtaining maintenance feedback within the institution.

Acknowledgement. The authors appreciate the kind efforts of Covenant University through its Centre for Research, Innovation and Discovery in paying for the article processing charge of this article.

References

1. Too, E.G., Betts, M., Arun, K.: A strategic approach to Infrastructure Asset Management. In: Sirikijpanichkul, A., Wai, S.H. (eds.) Proceedings BEE Postgraduate Infrastructure Theme Conference 2006, Gardens Point Campus, Queensland University of Technology (2006)
2. Mobley, R.K.: An Introduction to Predictive Maintenance. Van Nostrand Reinhold, New York (1990)
3. Wireman, T.: World Class Maintenance Management. Industrial Press, New York (1990)
4. Han, T., Yang, B.-S.: Development of an e-maintenance system integrating advanced techniques. Comput. Ind. **57**, 569–580 (2006)
5. Afolabi, A., Ojelabi, R., Amusan, L., Adefarati, F.: Development of a web-based building profession career panel as a guidance information system for secondary school students. In: International Conference on Computing Networking and Informatics (ICCNI), pp. 1–10. IEEE, Lagos, Nigeria (2017)
6. Afolabi, A., Owolabi, D., Ojelabi, R., Oyeyipo, O., Aina, D.: Development of a web-based tendering protocol for procurement of construction works in a tertiary institution. J. Theoret. Appl. Inf. Technol. **95**(8), 1595–1606 (2017)
7. Afolabi, A., Oyeyipo, O., Ojelabi, R., Amusan, L.: Construction professionals' perception of a web-based recruiting system for skilled labour. J. Theoret. Appl. Inf. Technol. **96**(10), 2885–2899 (2018)
8. Afolabi, A., Ibem, E., Aduwo, E., Tunji-Olayeni, P., Oluwunmi, O.: Critical success factors (CSFs) for e-Procurement adoption in the Nigerian construction industry. Buildings **9**(47), 1–18 (2019)
9. Li, Y., Chun, L., Nee, A., Ching, Y.: An agent-based platform for web enabled equipment predictive maintenance. In: Proceedings of IAT 2005 IEEE/WIC/ACM International Conference on Intelligent Agent Technology, Compiègne, France (2005)
10. Adolfo, C-M., Benoit, I., Eric, L.: On the concept of E-maintenance. Information and communication technologies applied to maintenance. Review and current research. Reliab. Eng. Syst. Saf. **93**(8), 1165–1187 (2008)
11. Hung, M., Chen, K., Ho, R., Cheng, F.: Development of an e-Diagnostics/maintenance framework for semiconductor factories with security considerations. Adv. Eng. Inform. **17** (3–4), 165–178 (2003)
12. Hausladen, I., Bechheim, C.: E-maintenance platform as a basis for business process integration. In: Proceedings of INDIN04, 2nd IEEE International Conference on Industrial Informatics, Berlin, Germany, pp. 46–51 (2004)
13. Chowdhury, S., Akram, A.: E-maintenance: opportunities and challenges. In: Proceedings of IRIS 2011, pp. 68–81 (2011)
14. Mangina, E.E., McArthur, S.D.J., McDonald, J.R.: The use of a multi-agent paradigm in electrical plant condition monitoring. In: 2001 Large Engineering Systems Conference on Power Engineering. Conference Proceedings (LESCOPE 2001). Theme: Powering Beyond 2001 (Cat. No. 01EX490), pp. 31–36 (2001)
15. Sun, J.G., Yang, X.B., Huang, D.: Multi-agent based distributed chemical process monitoring and diagnosis. In: Proceedings of 2002 International Conference on Machine Learning and Cybernetics (Cat. No. 02EX583), vol. 2, pp. 851–856 (2002)

16. Ebersbach, S., Peng, Z.: Expert system development for vibration analysis in machine condition monitoring. Expert Syst. Appl. **4**(1), 291–299 (2008)
17. Angeles, R.: RFID technologies: supply-chain applications and implementation issues. Inf. Syst. Manag. **22**(1), 51–65 (2005)
18. Intelligent Remote Device management. http://www.canon.com.au/en-au/Business/Software-Solutions/Service/eMaintenance. Accessed 05 Feb 2019
19. Dassault to Provide Cutting Edge Support Through Falcon 'E-Maintenance' Program. http://www.dassaultfalcon.com/whatsnew/shared/w_prelease_details.jsp?DOCNU M=131145. Accessed 05 Feb 2019
20. Lee, J.: A framework for next generation e-maintenance system. In: Proceedings of the Second International Symposium on Environmentally Conscious Design and Inverse Manufacturing, Tokyo, Japan (2001)

Scenes Segmentation in Self-driving Car Navigation System Using Neural Network Models with Attention

Kirill Sviatov[1]([⊠])[iD], Alexander Miheev[1], Daniil Kanin[1],
Sergey Sukhov[2], and Vadim Tronin[1]

[1] Ulyanovsk State Technical University, Severny Venetc, 32, Ulyanovsk, Russia
{k.svyatov,v.tronin}@ulstu.ru, a.miheev@simcase.ru,
dan-kan@mail.ru
[2] Ulyanovsk Branch of the Institute of Radio Engineering and Electronics,
V. A. Kotelnikov of Russian Academy of Science, Moscow, Russia
s_sukhov@hotmail.com

Abstract. The article describes the design process of a software module for the road signs recognition used for the self-driving car, developed at the Ulyanovsk State Technical University (UlSTU) at the Faculty of Information Systems and Technologies in cooperation with the Faculty of Mechanical Engineering. One of the main tasks to be solved when creating technical vision systems based on neural networks, including for self-driving cars, is to create a training dataset sufficient to train network models. At the same time, in the task of semantic segmentation of the scene, the preparation of a large train set may require considerable effort for manual labeling. The article describes a convolutional network model with a soft attention mechanism, which is trained for the classification task with the possibility of extracting an attention mask from the internal network state, which can be used for semantic image segmentation. This approach can significantly reduce the cost of data labeling.

Keywords: Artificial intelligence · Neural networks · Machine learning ·
Computer vision · Attention networks · Self-driving car

1 Introduction

The design process of automatic control systems of mobile robots includes many tasks such as objects detection in a visual flow of sensors data for orientation in space, scene analysis and path planning [1]. Moreover, in most cases, it is not enough to detect the presence of an object in the image. It is necessary to detect its position to get spatial features for the calculation of the distance between sensor and object or the distance between several objects.

In case of a small number of identified objects classes, the localization problem in neural network models can be reduced to predicting a series of binary masks for each

---

This work was supported by RFBR Grant 18-47-732004 p_мк and 18-47-732005 p_мк.

S. Misra et al. (Eds.): ICCSA 2019, LNCS 11623, pp. 278–289, 2019.
https://doi.org/10.1007/978-3-030-24308-1_23

class: the mask takes nonzero values at the position in the image where the object of the corresponding class is found by the model's decision [2]. Such a task has a name "semantic segmentation" and typical solution to this problem is using models based on convolutional neural networks of the "image to image" type [3, 4]. These models contain the block "encoder", which performs convolution, and the block "decoder", which performs the deconvolution of abstract features from the hidden state space into an image mask [5].

Such kind of models needs a large labeled dataset of masks. In this article, synthetically generated dataset is described. The location and area of each character were known for each generated image in this dataset. In many practical problems with a complex data structure, such labeling process need considerable labor costs [6]. In this paper, the method of training models with a small amount of labeled data will be described.

2 Literature Review

Training process of models with a small amount of labeled data is very hard and this is an actual problem in the field of machine learning. There are many approaches for solving this problem: semi-supervised learning [17, 18], transfer learning [19], active learning [16], etc. Generation of extra synthetic data similar to data from a specific domain is a common and good approach in case of automation of such processes. For example, heuristic generation of training data using external knowledge bases, patterns, rules, or other classifiers [20, 22]. Such approaches are called weak supervision. Recently, a new method was proposed under such an approach: data was generated according to the rules of a certain probability distribution based on the Generative Adversarial Networks (GAN) [21]. This approach is different from fixed approaches, where data is generated on the basis of a given function, but so-called "labeling functions" are needed for it. In [20], weak supervision was used to generate data on medical articles and books, but the primary filtering was performed by heuristics. This paper proposes to automate the stage of "labeling functions" on the example of the image segmentation task using neural networks.

Today, there are many neural network architectures and their modifications which are intended to improve the accuracy and speed of neural networks, improve their ability of convergence to the optimal solution, or increase the level of generalizability. A perspective and powerful approach to solving more complex tasks (for example, generation of textual descriptions from an image, recognition of the context and relations between objects), as well as the achievement of higher quality results is the attention model [7, 8]. The model with attention converges to the right solution for a long time, but this only affects the duration and computational complexity of the training process, but not the speed of the trained neural network.

The idea of the attention methods has biological premises. A human brain solves many complex tasks faster than a computer algorithm due to the fact that all objects do not process simultaneously, but selectively, i.e. complex input pattern is divided into segments and processed separately [13–15]. The attention method in neural networks works in a similar way [12, 24]. Of course, the real processes in the human brain are much more complicated [23], but it is not necessary to copy the biological prototype completely. For example, the convolutional neural network model takes only a few aspects from biology, but it made a breakthrough in machine learning.

In the training process, the model of soft attention network generates a mask of importance for abstract features. Unlike the features themselves, this mask is generated not by local convolutions, but by estimating the contribution of all features to the result of a function. Since certain abstract features correlate with certain classes of objects, it can be assumed that the mask of importance will assume a high value in those positions where the signs have a greater influence on the result of the function. In the case when the function solves the classification problem, each output label (class) will correlate with a certain mask, which is planned to be used as a segmentation mask of an object.

Modifying the "encoder-decoder" architecture by the model of pyramidal attention was proposed by Li [9]. This allows improving the quality of segmentation. But the model described in this article uses a network with attention in the formulation of the classification problem for automatic segmentation of the required objects. It is not necessary to create a labeled selection of masks with the location of the object with this model since the network itself generates maps of importance (attention).

To evaluate the advantages of the proposed approach, the developed model is compared with the following:

1. **The classical convolution network** is a standard model for obtaining a basic level of accuracy in the classification of objects without taking into account the segmentation of the scene.
2. **U-Net Segmentation** [10] based on the typical U-Net architecture [5] for solving the problem of character recognition. A typical U-Net structure includes a coding block (first part of the network) that compresses the sign space, and a decoding block (second part of the network) that expands the sign space into a new image.
3. **The Soft Attention Convolution Network** [7].
   There are several modifications of attention networks. One of the first was the "hard attention" model [8], after than the "soft attention model" (AttRNN) [7] was proposed. Its authors developed a method for better interpretability of attention masks, which is important for solving the segmentation problem. Also, the soft attention model converges to a solution quickly, while the accuracy is lower than the accuracy of the hard attention model.
   The main idea of attention neural networks is the extra filtering or weighting of internal representations (hidden attribute space) for significant reducing the weight of factors that have little impact in a particular context. Thus, the subsequent layers of the network get a more compact number of combinations (have a denser distribution), and this increases the model accuracy.
   The AttRNN developers used the network model with attention to generate a textual image description. In this article, the attention mechanism is used for classification and subsequent image segmentation for recognizing traffic signs. Thus, the AttRNN model was transformed.

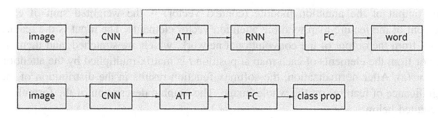

Fig. 1. The structure of the initial network with soft attention (above) and the structure of the proposed network (below)

Figure 1 shows the structural diagrams of the original AttRNN and the segmentation network (AttSeg):

- "Image" is the original image provided as the input of the network.
- "CNN" - module with the convolutional part.
- "FC" - fully connected layer.
- "Class prop" - the probability vector of the target class.
- "Word" - generated text description.
- "ATT" is a block of attention that receives the last set of feature maps from the convolutional network. It weighs the importance of these feature maps, which allows selecting only those pixels of the original image and only those features that are considered important at the moment.

Attributes, that were transformed according to their importance, are sent to the RNN. RNN is a recurrent network that generates a hidden vector which describes the next area of attention (the next most important weighing criterion) and the output vector of features. Output signs, received from the recurrent network, are collected and transformed into word codes after a series of such actions (vector representation of words) to get a text description of the image.

3   Methodology

The offered architecture of a neural network allows to exclude a recurrent unit, and get the probability vector of the target class ("class prop") after the first forward propagation process.

The attentional mechanism in this architecture is represented by a sequential block in the calculations graph of neural network (Fig. 2). It is another layer along which both feed forward calculations and gradient back propagation can be carried out. The mathematical expectation of the desired context vector $\hat{z}_t$ can be calculated as follows:

$$\mathbb{E}_{p\left(s_{t|a}\right)}\left[\hat{Z}_t\right] = \sum_{i=1}^{L} \alpha_{t,i} a_i \tag{1}$$

where $\alpha_{t,i}$ is the section of elements by the index t in the feature map with index i from the feature map set obtained from the convolutional block; a_i - the attention vector; L is the number of feature maps; t is the index of the element in the section of feature maps.

The output of the attention module (context vector) is the weighted sum of each element of the feature map with the attention vector elements. The input is the feature maps from the output of the convolutional network, which are stretched, and then the vector from the elements of each map at position t is matrix-multiplied by the attention vector (a). After normalization, the softmax function results in the distribution of the significance of features on the whole image. The graphic description of the formula is presented below.

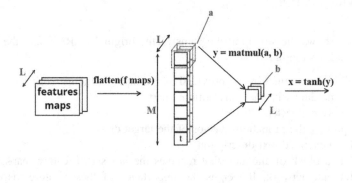

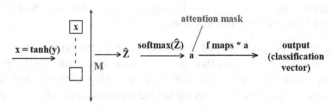

Fig. 2. The attention mechanism.

The code of the attention mechanism in Python language using the tensorflow framework as a library for building a neural network graph is presented below:

```
m_list = [tf.tanh(tf.matmul(conv_unstack[i], Wa)) for i in
range(len(conv_unstack))]
m_concat = tf.concat([m_list[i] for i in
range(len(conv_unstack))], axis = 1)
self.alpha = tf.nn.softmax(m_concat)
z_list = [tf.multiply(conv_unstack[i], tf.slice(self.alpha, (0,
i), (-1, 1))) for i in range(len(conv_unstack))]
z_stack = tf.stack(z_list, axis = 2)
z = tf.reduce_sum(z_stack, axis = 2)
```

This code continues the computational graph of the convolutional network.

The attention vector a_i can be interpreted as a mask of the desired object if could be translated into a square form. The elements of this mask are the influence (weight) coefficients (from 0 to 1) of each position t of the attribute cards on the target variable. The attention vector takes into account all feature maps in position t. During the training process, the attention vector "learns" the patterns in feature maps combinations. The features of a certain sign have a stronger effect on a certain class label on the output. So, the mask highlights relevant pixels on the original image by higher weight values.

The task of road signs recognizing, was selected for experiments as a part of the general task of objects recognizing in the road environment. Six road signs, which were selected for the experiments, are shown in Fig. 3.

Fig. 3. Road signs reference images

The task implies the detection of a sign in a complex scene where different objects are mixed in the original image. Besides, the sign occupies a small area of the image. There is also a sample with real images of the scenes, which was used as a test set. The sample was obtained after the competition of small self-driving cars "Autonet 18+" in the Russian robotic festival "Profest 2018" (Fig. 4).

An augmented train set was generated for network training by placing of road signs images on top of random images: roads, buildings, and other objects similar to real images from car cameras (for example, Fig. 5).

A train set size of 21380 images was generated from 6 road signs and 727 backgrounds. The generation parameters were as follows:

- Turn of signs: from −60 to 60°.
- Scaling of signs: from 12% to 70% of the image.
- Standard Gaussian noise was applied to 50% of the images.
- Proportions of signs: random compression across from 100% to 70%.
- Change in chromaticity of backgrounds in HSV format: 15% of changes in hue and 60% in total of changes in saturation and brightness.

Fig. 4. Real data example

Fig. 5. Generated data example

Several versions of models with different hyperparameters were created (Table 1) for the experiments to compare the results of their work.

The following model instances were used (the convolution size was 5×5 on all networks):

- Simple Convolution Net A (Conv A).
- Simple Convolution Net B (Conv B).
- Segmentation U-Net A (Seg A): the deconvolutional layers mirror the convolutional ones.
- Segmentation U-Net B (Seg B): the deconvolutional layers mirror the convolutional ones.
- Segmentation U-Net C (Seg C): the deconvolutional layers mirror the convolutional ones.

Table 1. Tested models parameters

Parameters	Conv A	Conv B	Seg A	Seg B	Seg C	AttSeg A	AttSeg B
Convolutional layers	32, 64, 128	32, 64, 128, 256, 512	20, 40, 60, 80	32, 64, 128	32, 48, 64, 96, 128, 160	32, 64, 128	32, 48, 64, 128, 256
Fully- connected layers in the middle of network (number of neural units)	256	256	100	256	–	128	256

Following characteristics were used to evaluate the quality of the model:

- The classification accuracy, estimated as the relative number of right answers among the entire data set. The classification accuracy was calculated on a test set, when the model doesn't have examples from this domain when training.
- The processing time of one image in milliseconds.
- The segmentation quality, evaluated by standard accuracy metrics (seg precision), completeness (seg recall) and proportion of correct answers (seg accuracy). The segmentation quality was calculated on a validation set, i.e., the model did not have specific examples when training, but have data from this domain. Nevertheless, one can evaluate the behavior on the test set from the quality of classification and visual examples:

$$precision = \frac{tp}{tp + fp} \tag{2}$$

$$recall = \frac{tp}{tp + fn} \tag{3}$$

$$accuracy = \frac{tp + tn}{tp + tn + fp + fn} \tag{4}$$

where:

- *fp (false positive)* - the number of pixels on which the model detects a road sign, but there was no sign on the image.
- *fn (false negative)* - the number of pixels on which the model doesn't detect a road sign, but there was a road sign on the image.
- *tp (true positive)* - the number of pixels on which the model detects a road sign, and there was a road sign on the image.
- *tn (true negative)* - the number of pixels on which the model doesn't detect a road sign, and there was no sign on the image.

Table 2. Models testing results

Metric	Conv A	Conv B	Seg A	Seg B	Seg C	AttSeg A	AttSeg B
Accuracy, %	22	91	75	92	**97**	95	94
Time, ms	0,04	0,1	0,04	0,04	0,04	0,13	0,05
Seg precision	–	–	97,90	98,92	**99,43**	33,38	22,06
Seg recall	–	–	91,82	91,29	**96,86**	95,79	81,25
Seg accuracy	–	–	99,15	99,18	**99,76**	85,99	79,15

The results of models testing (Table 2) shows the following: despite the fact that the precision metric for the AttSeg A model is 3 times lower than the same metric for the Seg C model, the first model has almost the same recall value and a high response rate of correct answers 85,99%. The low level of the precision metric is due to the fact that the model captures the extra zone around the real road sign and the area of this zone relative to the square of the road sign is significant (Fig. 8). But regarding the area of the entire image, the percentage of errors is small (seg accuracy) and false negative responses (False negative) are small, that indicates the model stability and high forecast confidence. It is clear from Figs. 6, 7 and 8 that the AttSeg A model has a sufficient level of quality. It can be argued that it works well for the segmentation task without manual labeling of masks. The network copes with this task on its own, and it has fewer layers and parameters than in a fully connected or convolutional network architecture.

Increasing the number of layers in AttSeg B does not give a quality improvement since the feature maps become very small, so improving the model results becomes the goal of further work.

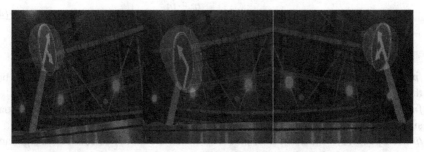

Fig. 6. An example of road signs segmentation by the Attention network (all signs are marked with a mask of the same color)

Fig. 7. An example of road signs segmentation by the U-net (all signs are marked with a mask of the same color)

Fig. 8. An example of road signs segmentation by the Attention network from street view for real self-driving car (all signs are marked with a mask of the same color)

The training process stopped because of a lack of resources when accuracy did not change after two epochs in a row by more than 0.25%. AttSeg trained for the longest, not only from the point of view of computing resources but also from the point of view of convergence (58 epochs against 20 epochs for the segmentation network). At the same time, starting from the 40th epoch, AttSeg was overfitted, and the attention mask began to cover the entire picture, so the results were collected before the overfitting.

It should also be noted that an attention mask is a fractional number, but in order to simplify the unambiguous interpretation, the threshold cropping is performed at 0.5, that is, those mask values that are below the threshold are equal to zero.

4 Conclusion

The paper explains that the network with attention can be used as an alternative to networks such as "encoder-decoder" (image-to-image) to solve the segmentation problem as a special case of the classification problem. Thus, it is possible to save significant resources on the labeling of segments in the train set and make labeling for only class key features.

Despite the fact that the training set doesn't have segment markings, training in the style of classification tasks, the network itself trained how to select important objects that are closely associated with the target class. Thus, it can be argued that the modified network with a soft attention mechanism is capable of quite well to solve the problem of objects segmentation in automatic mode without special labeling, being trained in the classification mode (accuracy = 85.99%, recall = 95.79%, precision = 33.38%). All this allows eliminating labor costs for creating a labeled segmented sample.

At the same time, the performance of such a network is comparable to the performance of a segmentation network, which is especially important for mobile platforms used in self-driving cars.

In this article number of assumptions was made that defines the tasks for the following work:

1. Avoid network overfitting;
2. Improve segmentation accuracy;
3. Check the network with several objects of the same class at the same time;
4. Check the network with several classes of objects simultaneously.

References

1. Siam, M., Gamal, M., Abdel-Razek, M., Yogamani, S., Jagersand, M., Zhang, H.A.: Comparative Study of Real-time Semantic Segmentation for Autonomous Driving. http://openaccess.thecvf.com/content_cvpr_2018_workshops/papers/w12/Siam_A_Comparative_Study_CVPR_2018_paper.pdf
2. Николенко, С., Кадурин, А., Архангельская, Е.: Глубокое обучение. – СПб. : Питер (2018). – 480 с
3. Isola, P., Zhu, J., Zhou, T., Efros, A.: Image-to-Image Translation with Conditional Adversarial Networks. https://arxiv.org/abs/1611.07004
4. Goodfellow, I., Bengio, Y., Courville, A.: Deep Learning. MIT Press, Cambridge (2016)
5. Ronneberger, O., Fischer, P., Brox, T.: U-Net: Convolutional Networks for Biomedical Image Segmentation. https://arxiv.org/pdf/1505.04597.pdf
6. Kaschub, C.: Digging into the complexity of the data labeling challenge. https://www.oreilly.com/ideas/digging-into-the-complexity-of-the-data-labeling-challenge
7. Xu, K., et al.: Show, Attend and Tell: Neural Image Caption Generation with Visual Attention. https://arxiv.org/pdf/1502.03044.pdf
8. Mnih, V., Heess, N., Graves, A., Kavukcuoglu, K.: Recurrent Models of Visual Attention. https://arxiv.org/pdf/1406.6247.pdf
9. Li, H., Xiong, P., An, J., Wang, L.: Pyramid Attention Network for Semantic Segmentation. http://bmvc2018.org/contents/papers/1120.pdf
10. Oliveira, G.L., Bollen, C., Burgard, W., Brox, T.: Efficient and Robust Deep Networks for Semantic Segmentation. https://lmb.informatik.uni-freiburg.de/Publications/2017/OB17a/oliveira17ijrr.pdf
11. Iglovikov, V., Shvets, A.: TernausNet: U-Net with VGG11 Encoder Pre-Trained on ImageNet for Image Segmentation. https://arxiv.org/pdf/1801.05746.pdf (2018)
12. van de Laar, P., Heskes, T., Gielen, S.: A Neural Model of Visual Attention. Neural Networks: Artificial Intelligence and Industrial Applications. Springer, London (1995). https://link.springer.com/chapter/10.1007/978-1-4471-3087-1_23

13. Bundesen, C.: A theory of visual attention. Psychol. Rev. **97**(4), 523–547 (1990)
14. Johnston, W.A., Dark, V.J.: Selective attention. Ann. Rev. Psychol. **37**, 43–75 (1986)
15. Fukushima, K.: A neural network model for selective attention in visual pattern recognition (1986). https://link.springer.com/article/10.1007/BF00363973
16. Druck, G., Settles, B., McCallum, A.: Active Learning by Labeling Features (2009). https://aclweb.org/anthology/D09-1009
17. Salimans, T., Goodfellow, I., Zaremba, W., Cheung, V., Radford, A., Chen, X.: Improved Techniques for Training GANs. arXiv:1606.03498 (2016). http://papers.nips.cc/paper/6125-improved-techniques-for-training-gans.pdf
18. Laine, S., Aila, T.: Temporal ensembling for semi-supervised learning. arXiv:1610.02242 (2016)
19. Augenstein, I., Vlachos, A., Maynard, D.: Extracting Relations between Non-Standard Entities using Distant Supervision and Imitation Learning (2015). https://www.aclweb.org/anthology/D15-1086
20. Ratner, A., Varma, P., Hancock, B., Ré, C.: Weak Supervision: A New Programming Paradigm for Machine Learning (2019). http://ai.stanford.edu/blog/weak-supervision
21. Zhou, Z.-H.: National Key Laboratory for Novel Software Technology Nanjing University, Nanjing 210023, China. A Brief Introduction to Weakly Supervised Learning. https://pdfs.semanticscholar.org/3adc/fd254b271bcc2fb7e2a62d750db17e6c2c08.pdf
22. Sun, Y.-Y., Zhang, Y., Zhou, Z.-H.: Multi-Label Learning with Weak Label. https://pdfs.semanticscholar.org/4642/916ee5c2697356d02afdb3cd13b30b8051ba.pdf
23. Zangemeister, W.H.: Clinical neuroscience aspects of visual attention and cognition. https://www.elsevier.com/books/visual-attention-and-cognition/zangemeister/978-0-444-82291-8
24. Vaswani, A., et al.: Attention Is All You Need. arXiv:1706.03762 (2017)

Evolutionary and Adaptive Elderly Care Ecosystem

Thais A. Baldissera[1,2(✉)] and Luis M. Camarinha-Matos[1]

[1] Faculty of Science and Technology and UNINOVA-CTS,
NOVA University of Lisbon, Campus de Caparica, 2829-516 Caparica, Portugal
{tab,cam}@uninova.pt
[2] Instituto Federal Farroupilha, Santa Maria, RS 97050-685, Brazil

Abstract. Personalized care services for each individual are typically required in the aging process. Considering this domain, a collaborative elderly care ecosystem (ECE) is proposed to support the provision of composite services that may combine contributions from multiple service providers. A personalized solution is built through of services composition, tailored to the individual customer (senior), respecting her/his requirements, preferences, lifestyle, and constraints. An additional issue the ecosystem must deal with is the problem of evolution, as individual's care needs are not static over time. Consequently, the care services need to evolve accordingly to keep the elderly's requirements satisfied. This process of services' adaptation is challenging since many services can be dependent on each other, and there are various constraints that need to be observed before adaptating and enacting new services. In this paper, we exploit socio-technical aspects of service adaptation in the context of elderly care ecosystems. Starting with a service personalization method previously proposed (SCoPE method), we presented an adaptive and evolutionary system (SEvol) based on the MAPE-K methodology. The SEvol method considers customer's inputs and suggests evolution plans. In the end, a workflow diagram is presented considering the main processes of ECE demonstrating the roles of the ECE environments and the main stakeholders, according to three stages: preparation, execution and monitoring phase.

Keywords: Elderly Care Ecosystem · Service Evolution ·
Service Composition and Personalization · Collaborative Networks

1 Introduction

Recent studies in the field of aging indicate that the seniors population worldwide is constantly growing [1–3]. In Europe, elderly population already represents 24% of the population (175 millions of persons), in contrast to 16% of youngsters (117 millions) [3]. While it is expected that the general Europe's populace decreases over the years, current trends indicates that the quantity of seniors will reach rates of 27.2% of the populace by 2050 [4].

In the well-being and aging context, a collaborative Elderly Care Ecosystem (ECE), in line with the notion of a Collaborative Business Ecosystem, "has the potential to provide an environment where personalized services might increase customer

© Springer Nature Switzerland AG 2019
S. Misra et al. (Eds.): ICCSA 2019, LNCS 11623, pp. 290–305, 2019.
https://doi.org/10.1007/978-3-030-24308-1_24

satisfaction, and give service providers access to new opportunities, share costs and risks, and strengthen their business" [5]. In this context, Collaborative Networks are the cornerstone of collaboration initiatives among service providers. To accomplish these objectives, composition and rating of care and assistance services should meet particular needs, since customer care needs can be attended in distinct forms, considering various providers. This paper proposes a method to address this need.

The remainder of this article is organized as follows: the Elderly Care Ecosystem is introduced in Sect. 2. The Service Composition and Personalization Environment (SCoPE) method is also briefly mentioned. Section 3 introduces the ECE evolution system represented by the Service Evolution (SEvol) method. The ECE processes are described in Sect. 4. Finally, the conclusions are presented in Sect. 5.

2 Elderly Care Ecosystem - ECE

In general, a number of technologies has been employed to support organizations to work together better. The ubiquitous use of open distributed systems, such as internet-based systems, enables efficient distributed businesses process, faster time to market, and practical development through global economy [3]. In dynamic environments, such as found in health services, organizations are constantly comfronted to efficiently collaborate with other enterprises and compose personalized offers without losing quality and competitiveness.

In this context, we can resort to the concept of collaborative network (CN) which is defined as "an alliance constituted of a variety of entities (e.g. organizations and people) that are largely autonomous, geographically distributed, and heterogeneous in terms of their operating environment, culture, social capital and goals, but that collaborate to better achieve common or compatible goals, and whose interactions are supported by a computer network" [6].

A particularly relevant kind of CN is a Business Ecosystem (BE). A BE can be identified as a "long-term strategic alliance which tries to preserve local specificities, tradition, culture, and frequently benefit from local government incentives, involving a complex interplay of collaboration and competition around producers, consumers, regulators, and support entities" [7, 8].

One specific example of BE is given by the term Digital Business Ecosystem [3], which is also inspired on biological ecosystems, but with a stronger emphasis on the perspective of technological support. Furthermore, the term Collaborative Business Ecosystem (CBE) was introduced to emphasize the "collaborative environment" perspective [9–11]. The CBE is based on Collaborative Networks discipline and supports enterprises with collaborative tools to assist on the mitigation of organizations' weaknesses while strengthen their know-how. As a result, organizations offering composite (integrated) care services in the ECE is expected to leverage their competitive advantage to customer agreement.

Our concept of Elderly Care Ecosystem (ECE) represents a particular case of a CBE. It includes various elements of a collaborative environment (administration, broker, virtual organization, planner, and coordinator), and specific elements that characterize it as an "Elderly Care Collaborative Network", specifically the customers (seniors), customer's request and requirements, customer's care needs, ECE services, and ECE service providers, including others [11–13]. Figure 1 presents the ECE environment domain diagram highlighting four ECE subsystems: ECE Manager System, ECE Information System, ECE Personalization System, and ECE Evolution System, and the three phases involved in the operationalization of ECE: Preparation phase, Execution phase, and Monitoring phase.

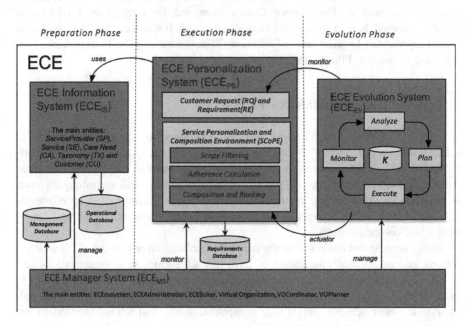

Fig. 1. ECE environment domain diagram

The *Preparation phase* corresponds to the creation of ECE and definition of its rules and functionalities within a collaborative environment. It involves (i) representing the main body of information and knowledge, (ii) the target audience identification, the considered stakeholders, specifically partners in the several areas (entity of support, entity of regulation, private institutions, governmental companies, freelancing professionals, caregivers, etc.) which are members of ECE, (iii) human and ICT resources, (iv) business and management rules; and (v) characterizing the available services. Based on a number of templates this phase involves creating the taxonomy of care need goals, identifying the service provider profile, service profile, and customer profile. The main subsystems responsible for the *Preparation phase* are the *ECE Manager System* (ECE_MS) and the *ECE Information System* (ECE_IS). ECE_MS is consolidated through the pillar of collaborative networks and the ECE_IS is more detailed in the next sections in the current chapter.

The *Execution phase* relates to the process of composition and personalization of services, including the ranking of the offered pairs (services and demand (customer care needs)). The main actuator subsystem at this stage is the *ECE Personalization System* (ECE_PS) which involves the Service Composition and Personalization Environment

(SCoPE method). This method comprises three steps: scope filtering, service adherence calculation, and service composition and ranking.

The Service Composition and Personalization Environment (SCoPE) was proposed in our previous work [5]. The method is composed of three main stages: (1) Scope Filtering – responsible for matching and filtering service and providers considering the care needs taxonomy, (2) Adherence Calculation – responsible for the outcomes of the first rating of services and providers considering their fitness for a specific customer, and (3) Service Composition and Ranking – responsible for recommending a solution list of providers. Figure 2 presents the SCoPE overview.

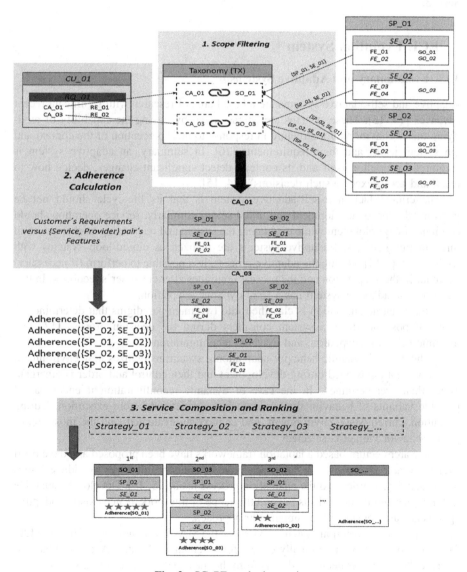

Fig. 2. SCoPE method overview

The *Monitoring phase* implements the *ECE Evolution System* (ECE$_{EV}$) that supports the service evolution and monitoring in the *ECE Service Personalization* (ECE$_{PS}$) environment. ECE$_{EV}$ supports the Service Evolution (SEvol) method. Considering the dynamic environment and stages of life of the elderly, the *ECE broker* analyses the situation and adapts the services to fit each new context. In this way, SEvol evolves an existing care solution to cope with the new customer's life stage (e.g. handling new customer inputs, new or obsolete care needs, technological issues, new business strategies of service providers, etc.). The detailed process of the self-adaptive system approach for service evolution into ECE (ECE$_{EV}$ and the SEvol method) is presented in Sect. 3.

3   ECE Evolution System

3.1   Evolutionary and Adaptive Systems

Adaptive and self-adaptive systems are a broad area of research with significant recent advances [14, 15]. These systems are characterized by having the capability of modifying their behavior and/or structure in response to their perception of the context and the system itself, and their requirements [16]. In summary, an adaptive system is "required to monitor itself and its context, detect significant changes, decide how to react, and act to execute such decisions" [14, 15].

The critical fact in a self-adaptive system is that its life-cycle should not be interrupted after its development and initial set up. Similarly, service operation should continue after deployment while evaluating the system and responding to changes at all time. In this sense, self-adaptive systems are realized as closed-loop systems with feedback loop [14]. During the adaptive process, it is possible to perform (if necessary) a human-in-the-loop action and the process continues after customer's feedback. In this situation, the adaptive system has a semi-dynamic adaptation.

Semi-dynamic adaptation is classified into two main paradigms that determine the range of possible states a system considers during the decision process [17, 18]: dynamic behavior adaptation, and dynamic reconfiguration.

In the case of dynamic behavior adaptation a system recognizes new environment conditions not envisioned during development and then control and order is emergent rather than predetermined. In the case of dynamic reconfiguration it encompasses possible variants of behavior that are somehow predefined before execution. During execution, current state, environment, and context are evaluated, and the most appropriate behavior variant is selected.

Some architecture-based adaptation frameworks have been proposed and developed over the years. They represent either academic or industry initiatives to address issues on the self-* properties and the adaptation process itself [15, 19]. Developing adaptive technologies and frameworks is beyond the scope of this work, hence existing adaptive approaches are considered to support our approach.

The proposed evolution system is based on the MAPE-K control loop structure [20, 21]. This control loop traditionally covers four elements: Monitor, Analyze, Plan and Execute. "Monitor" collects the details from the managed resources (e.g., sensors data, customer's information, configuration property settings, etc.). The monitor function gathers information, filter it and aggregate it (besides normalizing) until detect a condition that requires analysis. "Analyze" function is responsible for complex data analysis and reasoning based on the conditions detected by monitoring phase. If some modification is necessary, a change request is invoked to the plan function. The "Plan" organizes the actions needed to achieve the target goals and creates (or selects) a process that will enact the modifications. Finally, "Execute" functions operationalize the modifications by executing the planned actions on managed resource. This is accomplished with the use of specific effectors.

3.2   SEvol Method

In the elderly care ecosystem domain, and for each new context change, the proposed ECE Evolution System analyses the situation (in collaboration with the relevant stakeholders) and adapts the service to fit that new context. In other words, the Service Evolution (SEvol) method supports the solution evolution to cope with the new life stage. Under this perspective, the notion of evolutionary service [22–26] means that the provided service is adapted to the senior's needs, and to any changes that affect the senior's life context.

Following MAPE-K, the SEvol method is based on a control loop composed of four main stages: (i) monitoring events that occur in the surrounding physical and social context (i.e., both context changes and messages exchanged between stakeholders); (ii) analyzing monitored data against solution requirements to identify need of adaptation; (iii) devising an evolution strategy that reconciles current solution with a new customer's context; and (iv) enacting such strategy while minimizing disturbances caused by suggested solutions. These stages are identified in the i* rationale strategic model (see Fig. 3) that provides an intentional description of processes in terms of process elements and the rationales behind them [27].

The main actor is *Evolution System* (A-04 in Fig. 3) that is supported by additional elements of the model: *Context sensor* (A-01), *Agent* (A-02), and *Contextual actuator* (A-03). In more detail:

- *Context sensor* (A-01) is seen as a computational entity (hardware and software) providing raw data about the elderly environment. For instance, a bracelet that determines the current location of the customer or other stakeholders (e.g., who deliver/execute the care service), the sensor that determines the temperature and humidity levels in specific places, the smart communicator's automatic incoming/outgoing calls, etc.
- *Agent* (A-02) represents each of the actors who need to be monitored to ensure that they deliver according to their role in the ecosystem and send feedback about their acts. These agents may represent a senior, her/his guardian or caregiver, the coordinator of the virtual organization, VO (who manages the care service delivery for this senior), a service provider (which is part of a VO), etc. *Agents* are linked to the *Evolution System* (A-04) through inputs provision to identify a new request or through choices made in the human interaction. For instance, a substitution of a resource may be solicited by a service provider.

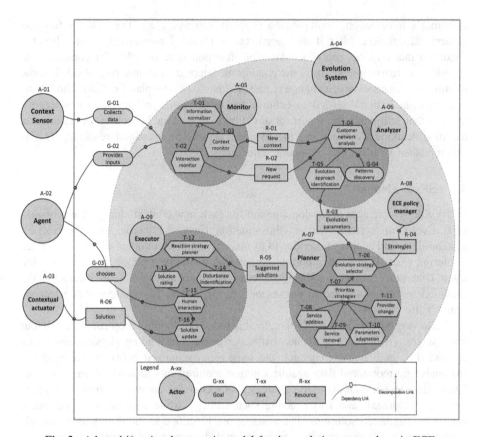

Fig. 3. Adapted i* rationale strategic model for the evolution system loop in ECE

– *Evolution System* (A-04) provides the self-adaptation capabilities of our model. This actor is split into four sub-actors:

Sub-actor *Monitor* (A-05) receives the information from agents (*Agent* (A-02)) and sensors (*Context Sensor* (A-01)). The inputs from the agents can be of several origins, for instance, from the customer and his/her family and guardian, or from the ECE, mainly originated in the Virtual Organization (VO) coordination, ECE management, or service provider. The inputs from sensors represent data about the elderly environment, for instance, information about senior's sleep analysis. Examples of outcomes are (i) the identified new care need, (ii) indication that a care need is no longer present, and (iii) indication that service changes the delivery parameters.

Sub-actor *Analyzer* (A-06) receives, from *Monitor* (A-05), information about the current elderly context living (*New context* (R-01) or *New request* (R-02)) and observes the pattern identifying the solution parameters that need to evolve.

Sub-actor *Planner* (A-07) selects evolution strategies to be adopted by the ECE policy manager (A-08), and ranks suggested solutions. The proposed solution evolution approach in ECE is based on (1) composition (or decomposition) of the current solution

(*Service addition* (T-08) or *Service removal* (T-09)); (2) solution parameters change (*Parameters adaptation* (T-10)), for instance, delivery conditions; or (3) the change of the entity responsible for the care service delivery (*Provider change* (T-11)).

Sub-actor *Executor* (A-09) changes the behavior of the managed resource using effectors based on the actions recommended by the *Planner* (A-07). Notice that evolution should not be considered a new personalization since it does not seek the better possible results from scratch, but instead seeks a satisfactory solution with the least possible disturbance to the customer (that is already used to the specific characteristics of current solution).

More details about these four sub-actors are presented in the following subsections.

Sub-actor Monitor. The *Monitor*'s (A-05) purpose is to identify relevant changes in the physical and social context, notifying the *Analyzer* actor (A-06). To collect inputs, the *Monitor* relies on context sensors and agents. Distinct tasks are needed to carry out the *Monitor*'s goal:

The task *Information normalizer* (T-01) initiates the monitoring function, taking its input from sensors or agents. The collected data and provided inputs are normalized to a "common language" that expresses the information on a context model (see Fig. 4).

The *Collects data* (G-01) and *Provides inputs* (G-02) are required by the Monitor's tasks: *Interaction monitor* (T-02) and *Context monitor* (T-03).

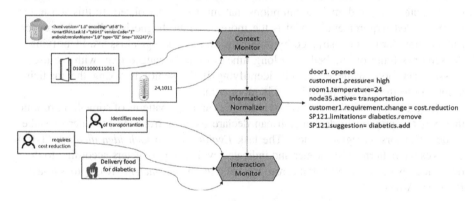

Fig. 4. Overview of *Information normalizer* task

The *Interaction monitor* (T-02) processes the status of existing non-standard data and exposes it through *New request* (R-02). For instance, a service provider will no longer deliver a specific service, or the customer wants to lower the price of a solution.

The *Context monitor* (T-03) computes information related to context and establishes *New context* (R-01). For example, if the customer has a medical appointment and her/his location is not moving, this information is sent (He/she did visit the doctor), or he/she is five days without leaving home, not participating in routine meetings (indicating signs of isolation, a possible new care need.)

Figure 4 sketches how the *Information normalizer* (T-01) works. Some inputs are sent in different formats: an XML file from the smart t-shirt, binary raw data from the door, CSV (comma-separated values) data from the thermometer, change of request from the customer activating (or disabling) care needs, customer is changing the constraints, and a service provider removing a limitation or adding an application suggestion.

Normalization demands the definition of a translation plan for each raw data format. If the task sources provide data in standard formats (e.g., XML file from the smart t-shirt), transformation schemes can be defined using a transformation language (e.g., XSLT – eXtensible Stylesheet Language Transformation).

If the house entrance door is closed (e.g. door.status = closed) and an event such as open(door, time i) happens, the *Context Monitor* (T-03) converts these data in terms of a shared context environment changing the status of the entrance door to open (door. status = open) – representing a *New context* (R-01): "door1.opened". A the other hand, if the customer identifies a new need (e.g. need of transportation), the *Iteration monitor* (T-02) processes events related to context and exposes this requirement - representing a *New request* (R-02): "node35.active = transportation".

Sub-actor Analyzer. Sub-actor *Analyzer* (A-06) is responsible for checking current information about the *Evolution System* (A-04) collected by the Monitor.

The role of requirements to the *Customer network analysis* (T-04) is to specify the goals that should (or should not) be achieved by certain agents, the plans these agents can execute, and the domain assumptions that must not be violated. In this sense, the more detailed requirements model is the more accurate diagnosis will be. Moreover, agents' granularity is constrained by pragmatic and technological issues. Identifying if the senior is lying on the bed for a long time is trivially gauged (e.g. with the use of pressure sensors), while effectively identifying if the senior is taking the medicine according to the current prescription is more complex.

The goal *Patterns discovery* (G-04) identifies and sets patterns of something routine that was not previously declared. It can declare patterns from the provider or stake-holders (sensors, caregivers, etc.). The task *Evolution approach identification* (T-05) observes the patterns of customer and indicates evolution parameters according to their relevance level, and provides the resource *Evolution parameters* (R-03) to sub-actor *Planner* (A-07).

Sub-actor Planner. *Planner* (A-07) analyses *Evolution* parameters (R-03) selecting the evolution strategies to this context serving as a system interface with ECE policy manager (A-07) that handles policies defined by ECE managers. *Evolution strategy selector* (T-06) receives the *Strategies* (R-04) from *ECE policy manager* (A-07) and prioritizes these solutions considering the ECE policies and goals (subtask *Prioritize strategies* (T-07)). The suggested strategies for solution evolution are based on the following tasks: *Service addition* (T-08), *Service removal* (T-09), Parameters adaptation (T-10), and *Provider Change* (T-11). In the end, a resource *Suggested solutions* (R-05) is sent to the sub-actor Executor (A-09).

In our work, the evolution (or adaptation) is mainly based on direct inputs of customer. We consider as primary inputs to the evolution process: (a) the identified new care need, (b) identification that a care need is no longer present, or (c) identification that service changes the delivery conditions.

The proposed service evolution strategy in ECE is based on composition (or decomposition in case of service removal) of the current solution or the parameter change of delivery conditions. For each primary input, the detailed strategy is presented below (more details in [25]).

- **Situation (a): adding a care need x.** The newly added care need is covered by current solution of the customer; therefore, adding a new care need implies the adaptation of the integrated {service, provider} pairs. It is possible to classify this adaptation into two categories: (a1) Identifying (in the current solution) a {service, provider} pair that covers the new care need (the solution is not changed). (a2) Adding a new {service, provider} pair that covers the new care need. So the process should identify if the current solution satisfies the new care need. If so, the process ends. Otherwise, the service and provider fragments which cover the new care need x are identified in order to extend the current solution (based on the adherence level resulting from SCoPE method).

- **Situation (b): removal of a care need x.** This removal should not affect the current solution for the other care needs. So, two cases are considered: (b1) Removal of {service, provider} pair that covers the x care need (if this pair does not cover any other need). (b2) Change of {service, provider} pair that jointly covers x and other care needs (for instance a care need y). The immediate removal of a {service, provider} pair fragment (without prejudice to current solution) can only be done if it is exclusively attending the x care need. In this situation (b1), the {service, provider} pair fragment is eliminated along with the obsolete care need, and the calculation of the solution adherence is updated. Otherwise (b2), the {service, provider} pair fragment that is attending care needs x and y goes through a new process of calculating the adherence (SCoPE method) considering now only the care need that stays (y). The fragment can be updated if there is a better service adherence to y. The adherence is calculated by the SCoPE process. This process can be repeated when other care needs are also covered by the same fragment.

- **Situation (c): modifying parameters of a care need.** In this situation, the customer's care needs remain the same. However, specific requests are modified in ECE. For example, the customer usually requires a transportation service once a week, but for the next month, it will be twice a week (frequency parameter); the customer had a collective transportation service, but now she/he wants private transportation (service features parameter), etc. The evolution plan to change a care need parameter involves two stages: (c1) Identify the parameter which should be changed checking if the new value is available for the current solution, (c2) Find a {service, provider} pair available that attends the new parameter.

Sub-actor Executor. The sub-actor Executor (A-09) executes the action and the solution is adapted according of new requirements. The task Reaction strategy planner (T-12) calculates the rating of the evolutionary solution (task Solution rating (T-13)) and identifies the disturbance in relation to the old solution (task Disturbance identification(T-14)). In the next step, the human-in-the-loop phase is started and the ECE broker and the customer confirm (or decline) the new proposed solution (task Human interaction (T-15)), and the solution is updated (task Solution update (T-16)).

4 ECE Processes

As previously mentioned in Sect. 2, the ECE environment supports three main processes associated to care services: Preparation, Execution and Monitoring, and uses four environments: ECE Information System and ECE Manager System (briefly presented Sect. 2), ECE Personalization System and ECE Evolution System (presented in the Sect. 3).

To demonstrate the integration of environments and their roles step by step a workflow diagram is presented in Fig. 5. This diagram illustrates the main process flow split in five lanes (ECE Manager System, Customer, Service Provider, ECE Personalization System and ECE Evolution System). A brief description of each process of Fig. 5 is presented in the Table 1.

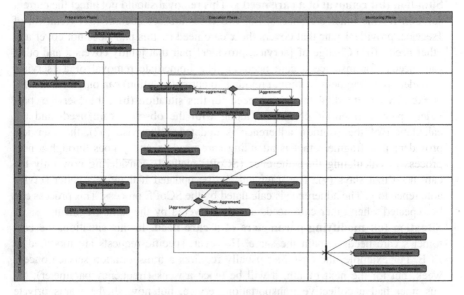

Fig. 5. ECE workflow diagram divided into five lanes

To illustrate the applicability of the proposed ECE framework, Table 2 presents a summary of a practical application scenario relating the main ECE process.

Table 1. Brief description of each sub-process of Fig. 5

Phase	ID	Activity	Lane	Description
Preparation	1.	ECE Creation	ECE Manager System	ECE definition of its rules and functionalities. Characterization of ECE elements profile templates identifying the proposed care needs taxonomy.
Preparation	2a.	Input Customer Profile	Customer	Customer profile implementation. Registering a customer.
Preparation	2b.	Input Provider Profile	Provider	Service provider profile implementation. Registering a service provider.
Preparation	2b1.	Input Service Identification	Provider	Service profile implementation. Registering a service linking with the provider.
Preparation	3.	ECE Validation	ECE Manager System	Validation of all the elements to start the execution process. There is at least one item in each profile (or a minimum established in the ECE Creation).
Preparation	4.	ECE Initialization	ECE Manager System	Release to wait a customer's input.
Execution	5	Customer Request	Customer	Filling out customer choices and preferences. Collecting of data for the service request.
Execution	6a.	Scope Filtering	ECE Personalization System	Filtering of potential services to attend customer request based on care need taxonomy.
Execution	6b.	Adherence Calculation	ECE Personalization System	Calculating the adherence between customer request and potential services found in scope filtering activity.
Execution	6c.	Service Composition and Ranking	ECE Personalization System	Building the matrix of proposed solutions to customer ranking by service adherence.
Execution	7.	Service Ranking Analysis	Customer	Analyzing of the proposals presented if it is in accordance with what the customer intends (in the-human-in-the-loop action). If not, return to the initial form of execution form (activity 5. Customer Request). If so, proceed to Service Selection.
Execution	8.	Solution Selection	Customer	Human-in-the-loop for confirmation of selected solution.
Execution	9.	Service Request	Customer	After customer favourable evaluation, approval is given to submit the solution to the involved service providers.
Execution	10.	Request Analysis	Provider	The business partners (which are member of the CN) respond to the customer request.
Execution	10a.	Receive Request	Provider	Provider analyses data and adjusts business strategy if necessary.
Execution	11a.	Service Enactment	Provider	Delivery of Service Solution.
Execution	11b.	Service Rejected	Provider	There was no agreement between the partners in the provision of the service. Return to form 7. Service Ranking Analysis.
Monitoring	12a.	Monitor Customer Environment	ECE Evolution System	Identifying new care needs or obsolete care needs of the customer.
Monitoring	12b.	Monitor ECE Environment	ECE Evolution System	Promoting addition or removal of services, addition or removal of service providers, and ECE Manager is changing rules or strategies.
Monitoring	12c.	Monitor Provider Environment	ECE Evolution System	Service provider is doing update on its services.

Table 2. ECE process in a practical application scenario

ECE's Activities (main)	Scenario					
2a. Input Customer Profile	[(idCustomer:c1; name:Robert; gender:male; geographicalArea: Lisbon; guardian:[Marco:son]; limitations:[{diabetic, memory less, cardiac]; maximumInvestiment:100; tecnhologicalKnowledge:low)]					
2b. Input Provider Profile	[(idProvider:p1; name:ALLCorporation; geographicalArea:world; services:{s1, s2, s3}; rating:5;) ; (idProvider:p2; name:EldCareCorporation; geographicalArea:Europe; services:{s1, s4, s5}; rating:4;)]					
2b1. Input Service Identification	[(provider:{idProvider:p1, idProvider:p2}), (service:{idService:s1, name: Security_Guard_service; careNeed: {diseaseMaintenance; high; safety: high}; p1.cost:40; p2.cost:30; area:independentLiving ; …})]; [(provider:{idProvider:p1}), (service:{idService:s2, name:MyMonitor careNeed: {safety; veryHigh}; cost:40; area:health; ...}); ({idService:s3, name:Agenda; careNeed:{diseaseMaintenance; low; safety: medium }; cost:40; area: indepentedentLiving; …}) [(provider:{idProvider:p2}), (service:({idService:s4, name:TotalControl; careNeed:{diseaseMaintenance; high;}; cost:100; area: health; …..}) ({idService:s5, name:HelpYou; careNeed:{diseaseMaintenance; medium; safety: high}; cost:75; area: health/independentLiving; ....})					
5. Customer Request	[(idCustomer:c1; careNeed:({diseaseMaintenance,high},{safety, veryHigh}); requirement:({cost,soft,≤,100};{tecnhologicalUsability,soft,=,high})]					
6b. Adherence Calculation (more details in [5])	Service, provider	diseaseMaintenance	safety	*adherence*	Cost	Cost-Benefit Ratio (%)
	sp$_{11}$	0.885	0.622	0.75	40 €	1,71
	sp$_{12}$	0.184	0.782	0.48	30 €	1.60
	sp$_{21}$	0.000	0.927	0.46	40 €	1.15
	sp$_{31}$	0.345	0.451	0.39	85 €	0.46
	sp$_{42}$	0.767	0.000	0.38	100 €	0.38
	sp$_{52}$	0.639	0.791	0.71	75 €	0.95
6c. Service Composition and Ranking (more details in [5])	Solutions	diseaseMaintenance	*Safety*	*adherence*	Cost	Cost-Benefit Ratio (%)
	Solution 1	sp$_{11}$	sp$_{21}$	0.906	80 €	1.113
	Solution 2	sp$_{52}$		0.715	75 €	0.953
	Solution 3	sp$_{11}$	sp$_{52}$	0.838	115 €	0.729
	Solution 4	sp$_{42}$	sp$_{21}$	0.847	140 €	0.605
8. Solution Selection	[(idCustomer:c1;) (Strategy:humanInTheLoop); (solution:Solution1:{sp11,sp22}, ad:0.906;cost:80)]					
12a. Monitor Customer Environment	newRequest:[(idCustomer:c1; careNeed:({diseaseMaintenance,high}); requirement:({cost,soft,≤,50};{tecnhologicalUsability,soft,=,high})]					
8. Solution Selection	[(idCustomer:c1;) (Strategy:serviceRemoval); (Solution:newSolution:{sp11}, ad: 0.885;cost:40)]					

5   Conclusions

In this paper, we present a view about the influence of evolutionary and adaptive systems identifying the MAPE-k control loop structure. We propose a service evolution method (SEvol) to support the adaptation process (evolution) of current customer's solution to new requests.

Following MAPE-K, the SEvol method is based on a control loop composed of four main stages: (Monitor) monitoring events that occur in the surrounding physical and social context; (Analyzer) analyzing monitored data against solution requirements to identify need of adaptation; (Planner) devising an evolution strategy that reconciles current solution with a new customer's context; and (Executor) enacting such strategy while minimizing disturbances caused by suggested solutions. The K corresponds to the current customer's solution. Providing an intentional description of processes in terms of process elements and the rationales behind them, the Evolution System was explained through an i* rationale strategic model. In the end, a workflow diagram is presented considering the main processes of ECE, demonstrating the roles of the ECE environments and the main stakeholders, separated in the three stages of: preparation, execution and monitoring. In addition, a practical application scenario is presented in the main ECE process to evaluate our approach. This proposal is intended to provide an adaptive system that can work well with an ECE framework to service personalization and evolution.

Ongoing developments include the assessment of the proposed method within a real elderly care ecosystem.

Acknowledgements. The authors acknowledge the contributions of the Portuguese FCT-Strategic program UID/EEA/00066/2019 for providing partial financial support for this work.

References

1. Kearney, A.T.: Understanding the Needs and Consequences of the Ageing Consumer (2013). The Consumer Goods Forum. https://www.atkearney.com/documents/10192/682603/Under standing+the+Needs+and+Consequences+of+the+Aging+Consumer.pdf/6c25ffa3-0999-4b 5c-8ff1-afdca0744fdc. Accessed 10 Feb 2019
2. Fengler, W.: The End of the Population Pyramid (2014). http://www.economist.com/blogs/ graphicdetail/2014/11/daily-chart-10. Accessed 10 Feb 2019
3. Gartner, I.: Gartner's 2018 Hype Cycle for Emerging Technologies Identifies Three Key Trends That Organizations Must Track to Gain Competitive Advantage (2018). http://www. gartner.com/doc/2847417?refval=&pcp=mpe#a-1321928256. Accessed 12 Jan 2019
4. Bureau, P.R.: 2018 World Population Data (2018). http://www.worldpopdata.org/index.php/ map. Accessed 12 Jan 2019
5. Baldissera, T.A., Camarinha-Matos, L.M.: SCoPE: service composition and personalization environment. Appl. Sci. **8**(11), 2297 (2018)
6. Camarinha-Matos, L.M., Afsarmanesh, H.: Classes of collaborative networks. In: Encyclopedia of Networked and Virtual Organizations, I.S. Reference, Editor, USA, pp. 193–198 (2008)

7. Camarinha-Matos, L.M., Afsarmanesh, H., Boucher, X.: The role of collaborative networks in sustainability. In: Camarinha-Matos, L.M., Boucher, X., Afsarmanesh, H. (eds.) PRO-VE 2010. IAICT, vol. 336, pp. 1–16. Springer, Heidelberg (2010). https://doi.org/10.1007/978-3-642-15961-9_1

8. Camarinha-Matos, L.M., Rosas, J., Oliveira, A.I., Ferrada, F.: A collaborative services ecosystem for ambient assisted living. In: Camarinha-Matos, L.M., Xu, L., Afsarmanesh, H. (eds.) PRO-VE 2012. IAICT, vol. 380, pp. 117–127. Springer, Heidelberg (2012). https://doi.org/10.1007/978-3-642-32775-9_12

9. Camarinha-Matos, L.M.: Collaborative Business Ecosystems and Virtual Enterprises: IFIP TC5/WG5.5 Third Working Conference on Infrastructures for Virtual Enterprises … in Information and Communication Technology). Springer, Heidelberg (2013)

10. Graça, P., Camarinha-Matos, L.M.: The need of performance indicators for collaborative business ecosystems. In: Camarinha-Matos, L.M., Baldissera, T.A., Di Orio, G., Marques, F. (eds.) DoCEIS 2015. IAICT, vol. 450, pp. 22–30. Springer, Cham (2015). https://doi.org/10.1007/978-3-319-16766-4_3

11. Baldissera, T.A., Camarinha-Matos, L.M.: Towards a collaborative business ecosystem for elderly care. In: Camarinha-Matos, L.M., Falcão, A.J., Vafaei, N., Najdi, S. (eds.) DoCEIS 2016. IAICT, vol. 470, pp. 24–34. Springer, Cham (2016). https://doi.org/10.1007/978-3-319-31165-4_3

12. Baldissera, T.A., Camarinha-Matos, L.M.: Services personalization approach for a collaborative care ecosystem. In: Afsarmanesh, H., Camarinha-Matos, L.M., Lucas Soares, A. (eds.) PRO-VE 2016. IAICT, vol. 480, pp. 443–456. Springer, Cham (2016). https://doi.org/10.1007/978-3-319-45390-3_38

13. Baldissera, T.A., Camarinha Matos, L.M., DeFaveri, C.: Designing elderly care ecosystem in collaborative networks environment. In: International Conference on Computing, Networking and Informatics. IEEE, Ota (2017). Editor

14. Salehie, M., Tahvildari, L.: Self-adaptive software: landscape and research challenges. ACM Trans. Auton. Adapt. Syst. 4(2), 1–42 (2009)

15. de Lemos, R., et al.: Software engineering for self-adaptive systems: a second research roadmap. In: de Lemos, R., Giese, H., Müller, H.A., Shaw, M. (eds.) Software Engineering for Self-Adaptive Systems II. LNCS, vol. 7475, pp. 1–32. Springer, Heidelberg (2013). https://doi.org/10.1007/978-3-642-35813-5_1

16. Laddaga, R., Robertson, P.: Self adaptive software: a position paper. In: SELF-STAR: International Workshop on Self-* Properties in Complex Information Systems (2004)

17. Shelton, C.P., Koopman, P., Nace, W.: A framework for scalable analysis and design of system-wide graceful degradation in distributed embedded systems. In: Proceedings of the Eighth International Workshop on Object-Oriented Real-Time Dependable Systems, (WORDS 2003) (2003)

18. Macedo, P.A.P.: Models and Tools for Value Systems Analysis in Collaborative Environments. Universidade Nova de Lisboa, Monte da Caparica (2011)

19. Brun, Y., et al.: Engineering self-adaptive systems through feedback loops. In: Cheng, B.H. C., de Lemos, R., Giese, H., Inverardi, P., Magee, J. (eds.) Software Engineering for Self-Adaptive Systems. LNCS, vol. 5525, pp. 48–70. Springer, Heidelberg (2009). https://doi.org/10.1007/978-3-642-02161-9_3

20. IBM: An architectural blueprint for autonomic computing. In: IBM White Paper (2006)

21. Arcaini, P., Riccobene, E., Scandurra, P.: Modeling and analyzing MAPE-K feedback loops for self-adaptation. In: Proceedings of the 10th International Symposium on Software Engineering for Adaptive and Self-Managing Systems. IEEE Press (2015)

22. O'Grady, M.J., Muldoon, C., Dragone, M., Tynan, R., O'Hare, G.M.: Towards evolutionary ambient assisted living systems. J. Ambient Intell. Hum. Comput. 1(1), 15–29 (2010)

23. Hong, J., Suh, E.-H., Kim, J., Kim, S.: Context-aware system for proactive personalized service based on context history. Expert Syst. Appl. **36**(4), 7448–7457 (2009)
24. Brown, A., Johnston, S., Kelly, K.: Using Service-Oriented Architecture and Component-Based Development to Build Web Service Applications. Rational Software Corporation, San Jose (2002)
25. Baldissera, T.A., Camarinha-Matos, L.M.: Services evolution in elderly care ecosystems. In: Camarinha-Matos, L.M., Afsarmanesh, H., Rezgui, Y. (eds.) PRO-VE 2018. IAICT, vol. 534, pp. 417–429. Springer, Cham (2018). https://doi.org/10.1007/978-3-319-99127-6_36
26. Marcos-Pablos, S., García-Peñalvo, F.J.J.S.: Technological ecosystems in care and assistance: a systematic literature review. Sensors **19**(3), 708 (2019)
27. Yu, E.S., Mylopoulos, J.: From ER To "aR"—modelling strategic actor relationships for business process reengineering, pp. 125–144. Ph.D. thesis. University of Toronto, Toronto – Canadá (1995)

Software Engineering Methodologies for the Evaluation and Monitoring of Projects of Higher Education Students

Susana Flores[1]([✉]), Claudia Torrero[1], Everardo Torrero[2],
Lamia Handam[1], and Silvana Flores[1]

[1] TNM/Instituto Tecnológico de La Laguna, 27000 Torreón, COAH, Mexico
msfloresa@correo.itlalaguna.edu.mx
[2] MAQTEC, Gómez Palacio, DGO, Mexico

Abstract. The change of strategies in teaching in Higher Education motivated the present work. With the application of cooperative and collaborative learning in the classroom, better results were obtained in the subject Research Workshop II, which is taught in Higher Education in Engineering. The work applying cooperative and collaborative learning impacted on the way to evaluate the participants, generating the need to find a way that allowed to have the elements to know who was contributing, which team progressed slower according to the program, as well as their peers in the development of the research project. In recent years in a significant number of companies dedicated to Information Technology and Communications have incorporated agile methodologies to manage different projects in very diverse branches, but especially in Software Engineering. In particular, the methodology used is Scrum. Therefore, Scrum was incorporated to develop students' projects, but also to evaluate the progress that students are making in the development of projects. With the incorporation of Scrum, better results have been obtained in the projects that the students develop, they and the evaluator are aware of the progress and delays they have in achieving them, in order to take actions that allow the products requested to be completed in a timely manner the curricular program of the subject.

Keywords: Cooperative and collaborative learning · Agile methodologies · Scrum

1 Introduction

The complexity of the last subject of research of the three that are taught in engineering careers at the University, has caused that traditional teaching-learning strategies are redirected by alternatives that allow the teacher to cover all the subjects of the study program. The subject, which includes the elaboration of prototypes, theses, articles presented in congresses and research forums, posters, slide presentations among others. These practices are applied in a 16-week course, where sixth, seventh, eighth and ninth semester students participate and sometimes apprentices from different areas come together, but mainly from the Computer Systems Engineering degree.

© Springer Nature Switzerland AG 2019
S. Misra et al. (Eds.): ICCSA 2019, LNCS 11623, pp. 306–315, 2019.
https://doi.org/10.1007/978-3-030-24308-1_25

The work begins in 2014, at which time the master teaching strategy is changed by cooperative and collaborative learning strategies, to organize the young people in the work they will develop during the semester. In addition, communication was incorporated beyond the classroom through social networks to follow up on the deliverables of the groups formed and to establish and maintain communication with them outside the classroom. This decision was made with the idea that the instructor could cover all the points indicated by the curriculum of the subject and the students had a better understanding of them. Thanks to the fact that better results were obtained in the scope of the subjects of the program of the subject, in advances of prototypes, elaboration of documentation, participation in specialized forums, it was decided to continue along this path.

The incorporation of different strategies in the classroom presents a problem for the management of the projects, the monitoring of the team work, the deliverables and the evaluation. Therefore, it was decided to incorporate Software Engineering methodologies so that students and professors had clarity in the scope of the work developed, to know in which part of the project the students were participating, to review advances in research documentation and prototype development, and thus having more elements for the evaluation of the participating students.

Agile methodologies have a high degree of flexibility and tolerance to frequent changes, increasing the probability of success in development processes. Mundra, Misra and Dhawale, consider that one of the factors that influences that agile methodologies lead to a good development, is the work in small groups, from four to ten collaborators, which allows a support collaboration between those that make up the team, plus it has been proven that small teams work better than large development teams [1].

In the following sections, we present the review of the literature that was made in relation to collaborative and cooperative work, learning strategies, surveys, projects and research that have been conducted on agile methodologies, ending with the results that have been achieved to date, by including SCRUM in the projects of the students and in the evaluation of the developments made.

2   Methodology

2.1   Cooperative and Collaborative Learning

Cooperative and Collaborative Learning (CL) has been defined as an instructional model that can teach diverse content at different grade levels. Students work in small, structured and heterogeneous groups to master the content of a subject [1]. From time immemorial, the Jews expressed in their holy book about teaching that a person will learn better if they have a partner that facilitates learning and in turn facilitate learning [2, 3]. On the other hand, the human history survival has been possible thanks to the cooperation of its members. It was not the individual advantage that made it possible, but the group. Regarding education Kagan and Kagan (2009) consider that cooperative learning contributed to solving the educational crisis that for several years had education in the United States [4].

As characteristics of the CL, the small trained groups work and cooperate to achieve shared objectives maximizing personal achievement, unlike competitive and individualistic learning, in which one works to achieve a goal and a qualification without taking other colleagues into account [5].

The report made by Cohen, Brody and Sapon-Shevin, is related to the growing need to innovate teaching in classrooms, taking the proposal to include cooperative learning as a pedagogical option for learning. Therefore, many educational programs have increased the number of opportunities for teachers and students to experience cooperative and collaborative teaching and learning. That's why according to Cohen, Brody and Sapon-Shevin in education who works as a team has greater chances of success [6].

The vision of Ferreiro on cooperative learning is given from three perspectives, one in which the CL penetrates education and teaching. The other is to consider it as an educational model, to be used in all the components of the educational institution. Finally, it can be seen as a strategy that can be used in the classroom [7].

In cooperative learning the teacher performs functions as a mediator, enabling the student to learn to move from a state of not knowing, can do, to being another qualitatively superior one of knowing, of knowing how to do and being. In this other point of view, the teacher as mediator moves the apprentice in his area of potential development, stimulating the development of his learning potentialities while correcting the non-assimilated cognitive functions. This is how in the environment parents, friends and teachers are mediators, facilitating the transition from a real initial state to a potentially awaited state. In sum, in CL the mediator (a) favors learning, (b) stimulates the development of potentialities, (c) modifies deficient cognitive functions, (d) fosters the movement of an initial state of not knowing, doing, and being in a way that transcends the here and now [2].

Starting from the vision of cooperative learning as a learning strategy, the teacher should assume a role of mediator and be supplied with new skills that allow students to achieve joint achievements. A similar case represents the CL for the students, since for them it represents a change and they must learn to work cooperatively.

2.2 Learning Strategies

Páez, proposes several definitions of learning strategies, beginning with that of Poggioli (cited in Páez), which considers them as cognitive plans to achieve a successful performance. On the other hand, Schunk (cited in Páez), with a global vision, includes them as part of learning activities, considering them as techniques to maintain a better learning environment. Said author also considers that the strategies are the forms that are followed to reach the learning objectives. On the other hand, Dallimore, Herstentein and Platt (cited in Páez) see them as a means by which the quality of participation and effectiveness of the discussion in the classroom is increased by an active facilitation that allows the Students to present their experiences and add ideas. The authors also consider the value that teachers bring to the learning environment by asking effective questions. All this will produce constructivist contributions in the teaching process [8].

2.3 Agile Methodologies

In the development of software projects, the cost overruns for software projects, the late delivery of products, excessive documentation, the non-inclusion of changes arising in the development process in the requirements of the systems are mentioned. Due to this, in order to try to amend this problem in the year 2001, 17 people from different companies such as Extreme Programming, SCRUM, DSDM, Adaptive Software Development, Crystal, among others, meet in Utha, looking for a solution to the programming directed by the documentation and driven by "heavyweight" software development processes. The Manifesto for Agile Software Development, agreed by all participants, arises from that meeting [9]. In the Agile Software Development Manifesto, individuals and their interactions are valued more, the work of software development that works, the collaboration with the client, as well as the response to the changes present in the life of software development.

Thanks to the success in the development of software products, the simplicity of its methods and its flexibility, agile methodologies in particular SCRUM have been adopted by large companies including Fuji-Xerox, Honda, Canon and Toyota. The case of Toyota shows an increase of four times its productivity and twelve times in the quality of the competitors, this was shown by Sutherland, Anton, Jack and Niklai on the 2007 [10].

In 2016, Uskov, Kondamudi, Krishnaiah and Singh rely on the 7th Annual State of Agile Development Survey, to justify collaborative work, and propose changes to the academic curricular program in engineering education, which includes topics, tools, curricular content, laboratory practices with a focus on the design and development of software and information systems for computers [11]. Among the questions included in the survey conducted by VersionOne in the 7th Annual State of Agile Development Survey, more than 4000 users about any agile methodology are; the agile methodology used, the agile technique used, causes of failure to follow an agile methodology, in what type of projects Kanban uses, who practices the agile management portfolio, among many concepts that were present in the survey [12]. The source used by Uskov et al. of the report, is related to the benefits experienced by users when using agile methodologies, reporting that 90% of respondents felt much better in the ability to manage the change in priorities, 85% reported that their productivity increased, 84% obtained better visibility in the improvement of the project, 84% reported an increase in morale in the work team, 81% reported that the quality of the software increased, 80% considered that the risks were reduced, the 79% thought that the product came faster to the market, 79% had a better experience in the alignment of IT and business objectives, 76% felt a simpler development process, in 74% it improved and increased the engineering discipline, and software maintenance and extensibility were also increased, finally 67% managed the agile methodology in distributed teams [11, 12].

There is another study, that of Caeiro et al., Related to the adoption of lean and agile methodologies in the universities of four countries: Greece, Portugal, Spain and Estonia. They conducted this study because they consider it important that students prepare in these methodologies, given their current application in the business world. They found that in addition to traditional teaching, it is now common to use active learning methods such as problem-based learning (PBL) and the use of simulations and serious games such as "Dice of Debt" or "Scrum Game". These games and simulations were designed to be played in teams, face to face, finding them appropriate for ICT subjects or e-learning situations [13].

2.4   SCRUM

The survey financed by VersionOne, in the question of what agile methodology is used in the company; Scrum and its variants appear with 72%, far above any other methodology present [12]. In an article presented by Srivastava, Bhardwaj and Saraswat in 2017, it is mentioned that agile methodologies have been better for a faster and more effective software development and they find that the adoption of these methodologies has helped companies achieve better levels of CMM in the organization. They describe the SCRUM methodology as a personalized way of working to conduct different projects in which the requirements are selected in a flexible way, without a predetermined path to follow [14].

Schwaber quoted in [16], presents the basic principles of the methodology:

- "The incremental development of the project requirements in short and fixed time blocks.
- Prioritization of the requirements by value for the client and development cost of each iteration.
- Empirical control of the project. At the end of each iteration, the client is shown the real result obtained, so that he can make the necessary decisions based on what he observes and the context of the project at that moment. The team synchronizes daily and makes the necessary adaptations.
- The empowerment of the team that is committed to deliver some requirements and for which the necessary authority is granted to organize their work.
- The systematization of collaboration and communication.
- The timeboxing of project activities to help in decision-making and obtain results" [15].

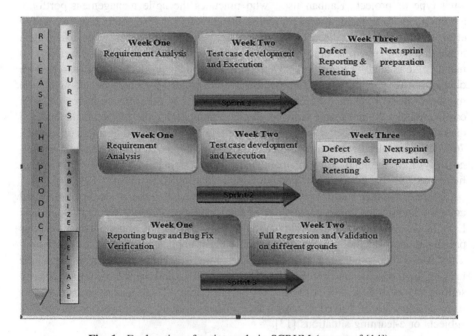

Fig. 1. Explanation of sprint cycle in SCRUM (source of [14])

In SCRUM there are several roles, to carry out a very close collaboration in the development of the project, they are: (1) Product Owner, (2). Master Scrum and (3). Team Scrum. Each role has a specific task; thus, the task of the Master Scrum (MS), is to eliminate the obstacles that arise in the development of the project. The Team Scrum (TM), is formed by developers, testers and other experts from other fields, which lead to develop a product that satisfies the client. Tasks are divided into small blocks, called sprints. A sprint is assigned a small group of people, who will carry out the task. The task to be performed is documented in a sprint backlog and is determined by the Product Owner, calling them user stories. They are associated with the sprint planning which includes methods to finish the sprint [16] cited by [14, 18]. At the end of the day, a meeting is held to review whether the assigned task was achieved or advanced. The goal of each sprint is to release a potential product. The meeting with the Product Owner is done at the end of the sprint, presenting the finished product, for review [14]. The objectives of the sprint cannot be changed, however, in the following sprints new features can be added to the project [17] cited in [14]. A normal SCRUM cycle is presented in Fig. 1.

3 Results

The beginning of the investigation dates to 2014, initially SCRUM was not incorporated, in the projects developed by the students, nor as a way to evaluate the projects carried out by the trained work teams. However, since the first semester in which cooperative and collaborative learning was used quantitatively and qualitatively, they began to have better results in the projects carried out by the students. By incorporating SCRUM, young people have greater clarity in what is being done, progress is made faster in the objectives defined in the projects, better documentation of these is achieved, participating in local and national forums and congresses (Table 1).

Table 1. Project management results.

Semester	Total projects	Finished projects
Jan–Jun 2014	8	1
Aug–Dec 2015	5	5
Jan–Jun 2016	6	5
Aug–Dec 2016	5	3
Jan–Jun 2017	4	3
Aug–Dec 2017	4	3
Jan–Jun 2018	3	3
Aug–Dec 2018	4	4

The projects developed by the students have been diverse, so they have built projects of home automation, e-Commerce, Machine Learning, Machine Vision, Virtual Reality, help to motor recovery of people, layout of buildings, among others, in Fig. 2, some of them are shown.

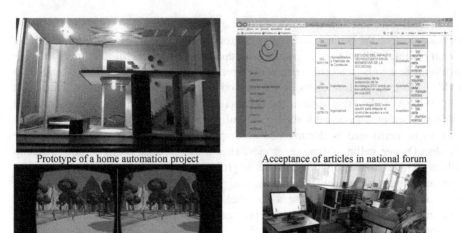

Prototype of a home automation project	Acceptance of articles in national forum
Virtual Reality Project	Student interacting with his project

Fig. 2. Examples of products generated by students

In Table 2, an extract of the methodology that was used in a layout project that was prepared in the semester Aug-Dec 2018 by a team of students of the subject is presented.

Table 2. Overview of the general sprint of a layout project.

Sprint:	General
Team scrum	Anuar Sánchez
	Liliana Gallegos
	David Villanueva
	Ricardo Rea
Master scrum	Ricardo Rea
Backlog	Acquire necessary knowledge of Unity
	Download software Unity
	Download software Sketchup
	Obtain plane of the Institute (general distributions)
	Establish standard measures of buildings
	Capture of the elements of each building
	Digitization of buildings
	Digitization of other structures (green areas, vegetation, fences).
	Export elements from Sketchup to Unity
	Unification of the components
	Configure point of view
	Road configuration

From the general sprint, this in turn was divided into several sprints, in which the Scrum Masters were rotated, until reaching several specific objectives. It is worth mentioning that the last sprints could not be made due to lack of adequate equipment. In Fig. 3, some buildings of the layout made are shown.

Fig. 3. Layout of some buildings

In Table 3, the pending's of the first sprint of another Project in which SCRUM was used for its elaboration are shown.

Table 3. Estimating the pending of the first sprint.

Pendings	Estimate in size (small, medium, large)
Design screen for CISCO phones	Large
List of places to be called test	Medium
Installing the Internet Explorer browser with version 7 on the machines in which the system is to be used	Medium
Configuring a server with Apache system, using PHP and MySQL	Medium
Phone 7945, 7965 or 7975 available for development integration	Small
Creation and configuration of the users in the call manager to be able to interact and to inject to the phones	Large
Running label injection on the remote phone	Large
Running label injection on the local phone	Large

The use of SCRUM, to evaluate the work of the students, has been very useful, since the evaluator in this way knows the work carried out by each participant and the quality that each sprint contributes to the final work. The progress meetings face to face with the different work groups are held each week, achieving personalized attention, in which progress and jams of the work are detected and with the social networks a less formal monitoring of the work that the students are doing is maintained. For those groups with progress problems, more meetings face to face are held during the week, from two to three meetings, so that they can keep pace with classmates.

4   Conclusions

The change of paradigm in the teaching in the matter Research Workshop II, to the cooperative and collaborative learning, generated better results in the learning of the students. Even as indicated in Table 1, in the semester Jan–Jun 2014, only one project was completed, the rest achieved better results than the work done individually. In the following semesters, cooperative and collaborative learning continued, with an area of opportunity in the way teams were evaluated. Better products were obtained by the student teams, however, the elements to evaluate the students were not very clear. This led to a revision of the Agile Methodologies, used in a good number of companies dedicated to Information and Communication Technologies in different types of projects. The results that have been obtained since the beginning of using Scrum have allowed for a better control of the progress and results of the projects prepared by the students. Several projects have begun to be presented in research forums, articles have been prepared for congresses, prototypes are available, documentation of a thesis is reached in the majority at 80% and in very few cases at 100%; even when 90% of students start their project in the subject. Another thing that was detected is that the students stay very motivated during the course and some have continued with their work beyond the final semester. We also consider that it is very important that they are given the necessary tools, devices and equipment for the development of their work, which sometimes go beyond the budget for this.

References

1. Mundra, A., Misra, S., Dhawale, C.A.: Practical scrum scrum team: way to produce successful and quality software. In: 13th International Conference on Computational Science and Its Applications, Barcelona, ESpaña (2013)
2. Dyson, B., Casey, A.: Cooperative Learning in Physical Education: A Research Based Approach. Routledge, London (2012)
3. Ferreiro, R., Espino, N.: El ABC del aprendizaje cooperativo. Trabajo en equipo para aprender y enseñar, México: Trillas (2013)
4. Cassany, D.: Aprendizaje cooperativo para ELE (2004). upf.edu. Accessed 2014
5. Kagan, S., Kagan, M.: Kagan Cooperative Learning. Kagan Publishing, San Clemente (2009)
6. Johnson, D., Johnson, R.: Introduction to cooperative learning. An overview of cooperative learning EUA: Cooperative Learning (2009). Accessed 02 Dec 2016
7. Cohen, E., Brody, C., Sapon-Shevin, M.: Teaching Cooperative Learning. State University New York, New York (2004)
8. Ferreiro Gravie, R.: Nuevas alternativas de aprender y enseñar, México: trillas (2009)

9. Paéz, I.: Estrategias de aprendizaje-investigación documental. Laurus **12**, 254–266 (2006)
10. Beck, K., et al.: History: The Agile Manifesto. Agile Alliance, 11 February 2001. agilemanifesto.org/history.html. Accessed 02 Dec 2018
11. Uskov, V., Kondamudi, R., Krishnaiah, D., Singh, U.: Innovative agile project management curriculum for engineering education. In: 2016 IEEE Global Engineering Education Conference (EDUCON), Abu Dhabi UAE (2016)
12. VersionOne. Agile Made Easier, 7th Annual State of Agile Development Survey (2013). https://www.versione.one/pdf/7th-Annual-State-of-Agile-Development-Survey.pdf. Accessed 20 Aug 2017
13. Rodríguez, M.C., Vázquez, M.M., Tslapatas, H., de Carvalho, C.V., Jesmin, T., Heidmann, O.: Introducing lean and agile methodologies into engineering higher education. In: 2018 IEEE Global Engineering Education Conference (EDUCON), Santa Cruz de Tenerife, Canary Islands, Spain (2018)
14. Srivastava, A., Bhardwaj, S., Saraswat, S.: SCRUM model for agile methodology. In: International Conference on Computing, Communication and Automation, Greater Noida, India (2017)
15. Souza Mariz, L.M.R., Franca, C., da Silva, F.: An empirical study on the relationship between the use of agile practices and the success of software projects that use scrum. In: Brazilian Symposium on Software Engineering, Salvador, Bahia, Brasil (2010)
16. Albaladejo, X.: Qué es SCRUM (2005). https://proyectosagiles.org/que-es-scrum. Accessed 2016
17. Rubin, K.S.: Essential Scrum: A Practical Guide to the Most Popular Agile Process. Addison-Wesley, Boston (2012)
18. Schwaber, K.: Agile Project Management with Scrum. Microsoft Press, USA (2004)
19. Maifiesto por el Desarrollo Ágil de Software, Agile Alliance, 11 Feb 2001. agilemanifesto.org/iso/es/principles.html. Accessed 02 Dec 2018
20. Arrova Dewi1, D., Muniandy, M.: The agility of agile methodology for teaching and learning activities. In: 8th Malaysian Software Engineering Conference, Langkawi, Malaysia (2014)

A Web Framework for Online Peer Tutoring Application in a Smart Campus

David Akobe[1], Segun I. Popoola[1,2]([⊠]) [iD], Aderemi A. Atayero[1] [iD],
Olasunkanmi F. Oseni[3], and Sanjay Misra[1] [iD]

[1] IoT-Enabled Smart and Connected Communities (SmartCU) Research Cluster,
Covenant University, Ota, Nigeria
david.akobe@stu.cu.edu.ng, atayero@covenantuniversity.edu.ng
[2] Department of Engineering, Manchester Metropolitan University,
Manchester M1 5GD, UK
segun.i.popoola@stu.mmu.ac.uk
[3] Department of Electronic and Electrical Engineering,
Ladoke Akintola University of Technology, Ogbomoso, Nigeria
ooseni@lautech.edu.ng

Abstract. Peer tutoring is a unique and efficient method of teaching that has been widely investigated. Related works in the literature ranges from cross-age peer tutoring, peer tutoring for the disabled, reciprocal peer tutoring, to peer tutoring for children. One unique method that has been scarcely documented, however, is peer tutoring with the aid of the Internet. In this paper, therefore, a web framework is proposed for online peer tutoring application in a smart campus. The peer tutoring web application identifies two key target users: the tutor and the tutee. The tutors will help in teaching other students; they are responsible for accepting requests from tutees and in turn holding tutoring sessions for the tutees. They also have the responsibility of uploading important documents to the platform which are accessible to tutees. On the other hand, the tutees search for the tutors with prowess in their course of need and make a request for a tutoring session. They also have access to the materials uploaded by the tutors. The peer tutoring web application is designed in such a way that the web browser communicates with the web server by making Hyper Text Transfer Protocol (HTTP) request to the server. The proposed framework consists of the client-side and the server-side which are connected by the web browser. In essence, web-based peer tutoring application will go a long way in improving students' academic performance in a more efficient manner.

Keywords: Peer tutoring · Web application · E-learning ·
Smart campus

1 Introduction

Peer tutoring is a unique teaching technique; it consists of two or more students working together and teaching each other rather than learning from a teacher's

S. Misra et al. (Eds.): ICCSA 2019, LNCS 11623, pp. 316–326, 2019.
https://doi.org/10.1007/978-3-030-24308-1_26

direct instruction [1]. In a world where the role of Information and Communication Technology (ICT) in the delivery of instruction in a university has been truly explosive, peer tutoring provides a unique academic solution for poor performing students as it involves the acquisition of knowledge or skill through active helping and supporting among student equals or matched companions [2,3]. Peer tutoring ensures that every student is carried along at their own pace [4]. It is an adept method that not only benefits students who want to achieve better grades in school, but it is also helpful for higher level achieving or skilled students [5]. It provides an effective and efficient way to improve social and conduct aptitudes such as communication and sharing amongst classmates and pairs, which are all critical proficiency.

Peer tutoring has also been said to improve student's self-esteem [6]. Proper implementation of the peer tutoring framework in classrooms will ensure that teachers are able to individualize instruction for each student, giving each student in the class-room the opportunity to be actively engaged in learning at the same time [1]. Peer tutoring can be classified into various forms: class-wide peer tutoring, cross-age peer tutoring [7], peer tutoring implemented with the aid of the Internet [8], and reciprocal peer tutoring which involves reciprocity and mutuality [9]. Peer tutoring has a lengthy history of success in classrooms [10], and it is an effective strategy which is successful in improving student academic performance [7].

Peer tutoring is a unique and efficient method of teaching that has been widely investigated. In this paper, the concept of peer tutoring is well explained with the hope of applying it in a smart campus environment. Then, various approaches employed in implementing peer tutoring in the literature are discussed under the following categories: class-wide; cross-age; reciprocal; and Internet-based peer tutoring approaches. Finally, a web framework is proposed for online peer tutoring application in a smart campus.

2   The Concept of Peer Tutoring

Peer tutoring involves two pupils: a tutor and a tutee. The students educate one another usually in minute groups. These gatherings are cautiously sorted out and monitored by an educator or coordinator in a classroom setting. Peer tutoring is not just a viable and effective method for enhancing both the guide's and tutees' academic performance; it likewise empowers them to be free and independent. It, furthermore, emancipates the teachers, permitting them the opportunity to assess the peer tutoring process in the class [11]. A broad definition given in [12] stated that peer tutoring "involves people from similar social groupings who are not professional teachers helping each other to learn and learning themselves by teaching". Peer tutoring is a dynamic, enjoyable strategy that empowers interests and it offers an elective, yet powerful, method for learning [13].

According to Topping [14], peer mentoring is an old practice that dates back to Greece. A crude definition for it at that time is one in which the peer tutor was considered as a surrogate educator in the learning transmission process. It was later under-stood that the communication between companions was fairly unique relative to the on between an instructor and student. Consequently, a superior definition was coined out stating that it is the process in which highly gifted students helped other students who were inadequate in specific proficiency. This interaction can, however, be coordinated by an instructor. Topping [14] identified that the evolution of peer tutoring over the years made it more difficult to find a suitable definition for the process. The previous definitions were vague explanations of what the whole process entailed. He, therefore, concocted a fairly wide definition of the peer mentoring process featured in [12]. His definition, however, failed to take cognizance of the benefits that the process provides to the tutor and tutee. Topping categorically structured peer tutoring into ten proportions, of which three important dimensions pertinent to this study are listed namely: (a) Year of study – The author [12] distinguished that guides and tutees could either be the same or different year students; (b) Role continuity - He stated that the tutor's and tutee's roles should be interchangeable, and not immutable. He suggested that there be a form of reciprocity and mutuality in the tutoring process; (c) Tutor qualities - It was realized that the generalization that the tutors were expected to be the best students in class.

3   Taxonomy of Peer Tutoring Methodologies

3.1   Class-Wide Peer Tutoring

Class-wide peer tutoring is a form of peer tutoring that has been implemented in various educational systems. It is structured in a way that allows students to form pairs or groups in a classroom setting. In each pair, one student assumes the role of a tutor while the other student assumes the role of a tutee. Incentives are usually included as a way to further motivate students to perform excellently as they assume their roles [16].

Hall et al. [15] implemented a class mentoring framework at the Juniper Gardens Youngster's venture to enhance the guidance for minority, distraught, and leaning-impaired kids. The authors proposed three principles in the implementation of the class-wide peer tutoring framework: (a) the "opportunity to respond concept"; (b) successive connection between educator and classroom precursors; and (c) attitude scrutiny. The first principle used was the "opportunity to respond concept". The requirement for this idea emerged because of the absence of active participation by kids who were tasked with the instructor's exercise from the educational modules, amid an oral cognizance class [17]. Due to this limitation in the conventional teaching system, the authors identified a vital condition for scholarly accomplishment which they defined as a course of action in which there was a successive connection among educator and classroom precursors and scholar acknowledgement. This turned out to be the core of the "opportunity to respond" model. The authors demonstrated the efficacy of this model by moving the tykes to another classroom for learning- impaired students. In this case, six minutes of oral perusing practice was conducted every day. This resulted in an increase of comprehension reading speed by 31.5 words per minute in addition to the original 15.2 words per minute. On the other hand, error rate diminished by 7.4 blunder words from an original 9.8 blunder words per minute. The authors also took note of the issue in growing the framework as identified by Elliott and Delquadri [16]. This was reported as a way of accomplishing similar impact in customary classrooms that had a greater multi-faced nature because of the heterogeneity of pupil's aptitude levels and expansive numbers. They further provided a suitable solution to this loophole by enabling friends administer to their colleagues reacting. Every youngster in a class therefore could get 10 min of direct practice time on each key instructional ability, regardless of whether it was math, vocabulary, oral perusing, or perception. Another principle that was used in the class-wide mentoring framework involved selection of scholarly target practices and aptitudes that instructors would use to decide a youngster's advancement.

Delquadri et al. [17] discovered that in choosing educator assigned practices for guidance, there was a high probability that those practices would be kept by the instructional environment and turn out to be progressively utilitarian for the tyke [17]. The final principle employed by the authors was that of attitude scrutiny. The authors structured the tutoring scheme in such a way that the instructor could deliberately audit the tyke's execution gains. This afforded the instructor the chance to give understudy acknowledgement and acclaim, separately, without method, and hence enhanced the kid's self-esteem without the instructor knowing. In conclusion, the authors noted that the class wide peer mentoring strategies are still undergoing changes and development by various researchers. However, the strategy has proven to be a successful instructional technique for enhancing student's scholastic fulfillment.

Kamps et al. [18] also implemented a class-wide peer tutoring scheme at the Juniper Gardens children's venture. This involved students with autism. Three students with autism paired with three other non-disabled students participated in the class-wide peer tutoring scheme set up by the authors. The main aim of the tutoring scheme was to improve the social skills of the students with autism whilst improving the oral fluency, perusing skills, and overall academic performance of the students. The authors discovered that the class-wide peer tutoring scheme was indeed an adequate and profitable procedure for improving the aforementioned skills in students. The students with autism as well as the non-disable tutors also showed a welcome gesture towards this approach and expressed their intent to participate in the scheme yet again.

3.2   Cross-Age Peer Tutoring

It is no small fact that peer coaching or tutoring is an adept instructional technique that has the advantage of individualizing content based on pupils needs, while taking into account broad input and ensuring immense assignment commitment [19]. An impeccable definition of peer tutoring would be an understudy intervened instructional methodology, organized so that one understudy is in charge of giving guidance to another understudy in a particular area of expertise [20]. It should be noted that the two understudies would have a mutual connection such as being within similar age brackets. The practice of clarifying ideas and realities to other students is shown to help mentors create and fortify their own aptitudes [21]. Cross-age peer coaching, however, nullifies the mutual connection by making use of a more seasoned mentor who shows a more youthful tutee [22].

Greene et al. [23] applied this form on peer tutoring with fluency-based instruction approaches to facilitate increment in science aptitudes of students going to class-rooms in distraught areas. Forty-four members formed the sample size. The members chosen were between the ages of eight and twelve. A lead experimenter backed by a second teacher educated the members. Both experimenter and the extra teacher were ace level students finishing college postgraduates' studies in Applied behavior analysis. The experimenter gave instructional courses in recurrence-building and mentoring mediation to the second teacher before and after the intercession period. Cheat sheets which comprised of focused math problems were provided to the second teacher with the answers to the math problems written in reverse on the sheet. The sheets were flashed and the tutee was required to see the math truth on the sheet and afterwards state the appropriate response that was imprinted on the switch of the card. The exploratory gatherings by the authors indicated the capacity of students to advance through the meditation with many accomplishing a decent number of familiarity points amid an 8-week intercession period. Huge contrast on mean post-test scores between the trial and control aggregate were found for the Mathematics familiarity subset and on familiarity with target math problems. This distinction turned out to be concurrent with a past research demonstrating the viability of cross-age peer coaching [24] and familiarity base intercession [25] to build familiarity with science skills. The authors were able to expand on past research on cross age peer tutoring, demonstrating that it is in reality and affecting strategy for enhancing arithmetic aptitudes of students. The conclusion was that although there might be constrained advantages for coaches or tutors, the utilization of cross-age peer coaching and familiarity-based guidance has huge advantages for more youthful tutees.

3.3   Reciprocal Peer Tutoring

Peer mentoring can either involve reciprocity and mutuality or not [9]. Mutuality is a critical component of peer mentoring that prevents tutee dependency and absolute tutor superiority. It also encourages exchange of information between tutee and tutor [25]. Reciprocity helps engender social interactions, and promotes characteristics such as participation, cooperation and solidarity [26]. Reciprocal peer tutoring is, therefore, a form of peer tutoring that employs the two aforementioned unique components.

Miravet et al. [9] investigated the effects of this form of companion mentoring in a school setting. The sample size was a total of 85 students enlisted in a predefined course to guide and mentor others. A non-exploratory descriptive design which en-tailed no purposeful control of the variable and ensured that observations were carried out in a natural habitat. A discussion group was formed with only 39 participants out of the total 85. The discussion group was formed to enable participants discuss the effects, advantages, and argue for or against reciprocal peer tutoring [27]. Five other separate groups engaged in discussions centered around self-concept and attitudes of solidarity. Data were gathered from the various discussion groups and MaxQda 10 was the software program used to structure the descriptive analysis of the gathered data. The discourse that took place amongst group members revealed that students saw themselves as being equipped for clarifying subject content, searching for data, and setting up important talk forums; activities that were formally only pertinent to teachers. The authors also realized that they possessed the capacity to explain a topic to a fellow student [28]. Students felt independent; this correlated with the examination made in [29]. It was concluded that reciprocal peer tutoring was indeed very effective in a school setting.

3.4 Internet-Based Peer Tutoring

Computer-aided mentoring is one important but scarcely documented companion mentoring methodology. Researchers have featured the beneficial outcomes of pupil-to-pupil interaction on pupil motivation, learning and diligence in courses and educational modules [30]. On the other hand, computer-aided peer mentoring is still rarely documented. However, this method has the potential to acquaint expansion in distance, web and mixed courses [10].

In a research conducted by Evans and Moore [8], computer-aided mentoring was explored and applied by developing an electronic peer coaching framework known as Online Peer-Assisted Learning (OPAL). Figure 1 shows the process flow of the online peer tutoring platform. The first process in OPAL begins with answering a question. Once a student answers a question or problem correctly, he or she is granted access into "pool" of tutors. Once in, the student can post a "tutoring ticket" anonymously to the platforms database, indicating his or her accessibility and readiness to teach the question or problem for which he or she is eligible. This provides tutees with a pool of eligible and expert tutors to select from. A tutoring ticket contains records of the tutors instructing history, and length of previous tutoring sessions. A unique inclusion in the platform is that of virtual interaction. The mentoring session itself may occur over the web by means of skype, email or other social engines. The tutor and the tutee are also admonished to make video reflections of the tutoring sessions as a form of verification that the session took place. The process formally ends when the tutee answers the proposed question and is granted access to the tutor pool. Student gains were measured using a survey in which students were asked to utilize a 5-point Likert scale to rate their leaning increases due to the tutoring sessions received [31]. The authors further reckoned that it was inconclusive to rely on students' general perceptions only. The authors were able to mitigate student dissatisfaction by ensuring proper hierarchy and organization of topics and using a "gate structure" which helped to rule the possibility of having incompetent tutors. The survey also suggested a few key factors that contributed to the learning gains of students. The coaching process gave them the confidence to

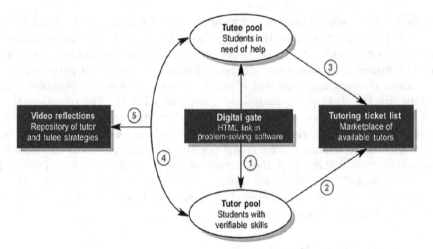

① Students who answer problems correctly gain the ability to tutor on those problems.

② Eligible tutors post "tickets" indicating their availability and willingness to tutor.

③ Students seeking help for a particular problem respond to a tutoring ticket from the list.

④ The tutor helps the tutee understand the problem and answer it correctly.

⑤ Tutor and tutee record video reflections on their teaching and learning experiences.

Fig. 1. Process flow of the online peer tutoring platform [8]

attempt problems that they previously feared. The platform also helped students expand their knowledge base. The videos made by the students during the session enabled students to express their thoughts and make corrections to the teaching methods.

4   Proposed Web Framework for Online Peer Tutoring

The peer tutoring web application identifies two key target users: the tutor and the tutee. The tutors help teach other students; they are responsible for accepting requests from tutees and in turn holding tutoring sessions for the tutees. They also have the responsibility of uploading important documents to the platform which are accessible to tutees. On the other hand, the tutees search for the tutors with prowess in their course of need and make a request for a tutoring session. They also have access to the materials uploaded by the tutors.

The proposed web architecture shown in Fig. 2 is hinged on sever-side programming. The peer tutoring web application is designed in such a way that the web browser communicates with the web server by making Hyper Text Transfer Protocol (HTTP) request to the server. The proposed framework consists of the client-side and the server-side which are connected by the web browser. The client side consists of the web pages seen on the browser after the requested has been sent to the server. The requests usually consist of a Uniform Resource

Locator (URL) which contains a method that defines the required action. Semantic User Interface (UI) provided the framework for the front-end design of the web application to ensure lighter web pages. The front end (client-side) and the back end (Server-side) of the web application are linked via a server-side programming language such as C#. Figure 2 depicts the communication between the client and the server in server-side programming. The Cascade Style Sheet (CSS) is usually on the web, as in the case of the peer tutorial web application which uses semantic UI for all its styling. Programming languages that can be used for the client side include HTML, JavaScript, and CSS while the languages used for the server-side include PHP, Python, C# and NodeJS.

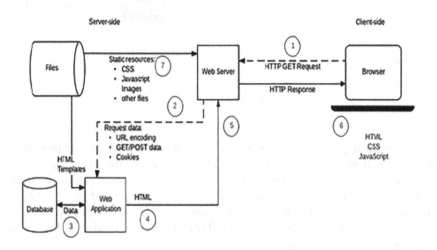

Fig. 2. Proposed web framework

Figure 3 shows the process flow of the peer tutorial web application. The login and register platform for each of the pages can be designed using semantic UI. Structured Query Language (SQL) authentication can be used for login authentication. The SQL authentication works by comparing the username and password typed by the user on the front-end with the data stored in the database. If they both matches, the user is granted access to the platform. If they do not match, however, an error message is displayed on the page. The Admin section is the first and most important section of the peer tutorial application. The administrator performs four major functions: (a) adding programs to the database; (b) adding courses to the Database; (c) editing a tutor or tutees details; and (d) granting permission for the tutee to view an uploaded material.

Semantic UI provided the forms and styles for the webpage, the front end was connected to the database using connection strings. The first step was to acquire the connection string after the creation of the necessary tables for the databases, this was followed by initializing the connection string, and running the query, function or method (this was initialized in the code on the server-side). Lastly, the connection was closed and catch was placed to detect errors

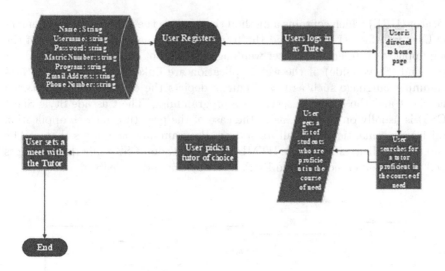

Fig. 3. Proposed web framework

if any. The tutor page consists of five tabs; Requests tab which displays all the requests that have been made by tutees, Materials tab which allows the tutor to upload documents for the tutee to view, the Profile tab which allows the tutor edit his personal details, the prowess page which allows the tutor update his course proficiency and the logout tab, which redirects the Tutor to the login page. Each entry on the front-end is stored directly in the database, through the use of the connection strings.

The tutee page consists of four tabs: Profile tab which allows the tutee update details; History tab which displayed the list of requests approved by a tutor; the Search tab which enables the tutee search for a tutor proficient in a course of need or a material uploaded by a tutor which might be helpful for that course; and the Logout tab which redirects the tutee to the login page.

5   Conclusion

In this paper, various peer tutoring forms and techniques have been explained with emphasis on the importance and success of each method of peer tutoring implemented in the literature. It became obvious that computer-aided peer tutoring is one method of peer tutoring that is scarcely documented. However, computer-aided peer tutoring framework holds unique techniques that would go a long way in improving students' academic performance.

In the light of the above, a web framework was proposed for online peer tutoring application in a smart campus. The peer tutoring web application identifies two key target users: the tutor and the tutee. The tutors help teach other students; they are responsible for accepting requests from tutees and in turn holding tutoring sessions for the tutees. They also have the responsibility of uploading important documents to the platform which are accessible to tutees. On the other hand, the tutees search for the tutors with prowess in their course of need and make a request for a tutoring session. They also have access to the materials uploaded by the tutors.

The peer tutoring web application is designed for smart campus in such a way that the web browser communicates with the web server by making HTTP request to the server. The proposed framework consists of the client-side and the server-side which are connected by the web browser. The client side consists of the web pages seen on the browser after the requested has been sent to the server. The requests usually consist of a URL which contains a method that defines the required action.

Acknowledgement. This work was carried out under the IoT-Enabled Smart and Connected Communities (*SmartCU*) research cluster of the Department of Electrical and Information Engineering, Covenant University, Ota, Nigeria. The research was fully sponsored by Covenant University Centre for Research, Innovation and Development (CUCRID), Covenant University, Ota, Nigeria.

References

1. Plotnick, E.: Trends in Educational Technology. ERIC Digest (1996)
2. Sideridis, G.D., et al.: Classwide peer tutoring: effects on the spelling performance and social interactions of students with mild disabilities and their typical peers in an integrated instructional setting. J. Behav. Educ. **7**(4), 435–462 (1997)
3. Topping, K.J.: Trends in peer learning. Educ. Psychol. **25**(6), 631–645 (2005)
4. Dineen, J.P., Clark, H.B., Risley, T.R.: Peer tutoring among elementary students: educational benefits to the tutor 1. J. Appl. Behav. Anal. **10**(2), 231–238 (1977)
5. Harris, V.W., Sherman, J.A.: Effects of peer tutoring and consequences on the math performance of elementary classroom students 1. J. Appl. Behav. Anal. **6**(4), 587–597 (1973)
6. Miller, D., Topping, K., Thurston, A.: Peer tutoring in reading: the effects of role and organization on two dimensions of self-esteem. Br. J. Educ. Psychol. **80**(3), 417–433 (2010)
7. Pigott, H.E., Fantuzzo, J.W., Clement, P.W.: The effects of reciprocal peer tutoring and group contingencies on the academic performance of elementary school children. J. Appl. Behav. Anal. **19**(1), 93–98 (1986)
8. Evans, M.J., Moore, J.S.: Peer tutoring with the aid of the Internet. Br. J. Educ. Technol. **44**(1), 144–155 (2013)
9. Miravet, L.M., Ciges, A.S., García, O.M.: An experience of reciprocal peer tutoring at the university. Procedia-Soc. Behav. Sci. **116**, 2809–2812 (2014)
10. Olmscheid, C.: The effectiveness of peer tutoring in the elementary grades (1999)
11. Gyanani, T., Pahuja, P.: Effects of peer tutoring on abilities and achievement. Contemp. Educ. Psychol. **20**(4), 469–475 (1995)
12. Topping, K.: Tutoring. International Academy of Education Genf, Switzerland (2000)
13. Alegre Ansuategui, F.J., Moliner Miravet, L.: Emotional and cognitive effects of peer tutoring among secondary school mathematics students. Int. J. Math. Educ. Sci. Technol. **48**(8) 1185–1205 (2017)

14. Topping, K.J.: The effectiveness of peer tutoring in further and higher education: a typology and review of the literature. High. Educ. **32**(3), 321–345 (1996)
15. Hall, R.V., et al.: The importance of opportunity to respond in children's academic success. In: Mentally Handicapped Children: Education and Training, pp. 107–140 (1982)
16. Elliott, M., Delquadri, J.C.: Rearranging the Instructional Format to Increase Opportunity to Respond in the Basal Reading Series with Minority Children (1981)
17. Delquadri, J., et al.: Classwide peer tutoring. Except. Child. **52**(6), 535–542 (1986)
18. Kamps, D.M., et al.: Classwide peer tutoring: an integration strategy to improve reading skills and promote peer interactions among students with autism and general education peers. J. Appl. Behav. Anal. **27**(1), 49–61 (1994)
19. Dufrene, B.A., et al.: Monitoring implementation of reciprocal peer tutoring: identifying and intervening with students who do not maintain accurate implementation. Sch. Psychol. Rev. **34**(1), 74–87 (2005)
20. Robinson, D.R., Schofield, J.W., Steers-Wentzell, K.L.: Peer and cross-age tutoring in math: outcomes and their design implications. Educ. Psychol. Rev. **17**(4), 327–362 (2005)
21. Mitchell, R.J., et al.: Effects of fourth and second graders' cross-age tutoring on students' spelling. Reading Psychol. **37**(1), 147–166 (2016)
22. Stenhoff, D.M., Lignugaris/Kraft, B.: A review of the effects of peer tutoring on students with mild disabilities in secondary settings. Except. Child. **74**(1), 8–30 (2007)
23. Greene, I., Mc Tiernan, A., Holloway, J.: Cross-age peer tutoring and fluency-based instruction to achieve fluency with mathematics computation skills: a randomized controlled trial. J. Behav. Educ. **27**(2), 145–171 (2018)
24. Hawkins, R.O., et al.: Applying a randomized interdependent group contingency component to classwide peer tutoring for multiplication fact fluency. J. Behav. Educ. **18**(4), 300 (2009)
25. Gallagher, E.: Improving a mathematical key skill using precision teaching. Irish Educ. Stud. **25**(3), 303–319 (2006)
26. Lázaro, A.M.: La conducta prosocial. Cuadernos de trabajo social (9) 125 (1996)
27. Gómez, A., Jose, M.: La investigación educativa: claves teóricas (2007)
28. Dávila, L., Adamelia, S.: La tutoría como programa que favorece la formación integral. Presencia Universitaria **5**(10), 48–55 (2015)
29. Schleyer, G., Langdon, G., James, S.: Peer tutoring in conceptual design. Eur. J. Eng. Educ. **30**(2), 245–254 (2005)
30. Johnson, D.W.: Student-student interaction: the neglected variable in education. Educ. Res. **10**(1), 5–10 (1981)
31. Seymour, E., et al.: Creating a better mousetrap: on-line student assessment of their learning gains. In: National Meeting of the American Chemical Society (2000)

Use of Blockchain Smart Contracts in Software Engineering: A Systematic Mapping

Faizan Tariq and Ricardo Colomo-Palacios$^{(\boxtimes)}$

Faculty of Computer Sciences, Østfold University College,
Postboks 700, 1757 Halden, Norway
{faizant,ricardo.colomo-palacios}@hiof.no

Abstract. A smart contract is one of the safest mechanisms in the form of computerized and authorized legitimate commitment between two parties. This form of securing commitments has been gaining popularity on the last years in a variety of fields. However, and maybe because of its relative novelty, there is not a clear understanding of its possibilities. This study is aimed to cover the usage, benefits and challenges on the use of Blockchain Smart Contracts in Software Engineering in the form of a Systematic mapping. The most common use of the smart contracts is to work as a digital code that plays the role of a mediator, which removes human intervention. The availability of professionals in this area is a reported challenge along with the client's trust on usability with respect to security. Besides, this paper identifies various difficulties that have not been yet addressed by existing methodologies. As a consequence of our findings, more practical use of this system can open doors for further research.

Keywords: Smart contracts · Software engineering · Block chain

1 Introduction

Blockchain technology is becoming the key solution to provide reliability and security without any need for central supervisory authority to validate a panoply of transactions. Blockchain is a decentralized transaction and data management technology based solution developed initially for Bitcoin cryptocurrency [1]. Literature reported a wide set of blockchain applications ranging from cryptocurrency, financial services, risk management, Internet of Things to public and social services [2], naming just a few of the most important and reported fields of application. Nevertheless, and in spite of its popularity there are reported challenges of this technology such as scalability and security problems still not tackled [3].

Blockchain is a technology that provides an environment to create distributed decentralized applications, which are meant to complete transactions between two parties without any involvement of any third party. It's a peer-to-peer network where the transaction or a mutual goal can be achieved without relying on a third party [4]. This term "blockchain" is the system on which Bitcoin transactions are being completed. Rooted in the technological needs of Bitcoin, nowadays it is the most commonly used application of Blockchain technology [1].

© Springer Nature Switzerland AG 2019
S. Misra et al. (Eds.): ICCSA 2019, LNCS 11623, pp. 327–337, 2019.
https://doi.org/10.1007/978-3-030-24308-1_27

This technology works on distributed ledger technologies (DLT), where, multiple entities hold a copy of ledger and all participants are naturally permitted to contribute. These transactions are stored in a distributed ledger in a series of blocks [5] and participants are called nodes. All the nodes in the network have a copy of all the transactions occurred in the network. In DLT all the nodes agree on a common truth, as the correctness of ledger, any change in the ledger made by any node have to be accepted by all other participants in the network [6].

Smart contracts are small pieces of codes, which are executed when a certain specified condition comes true. These smart contracts are written in Turing-complete languages that run on the blockchain platform [6]. We can say that, it's a self-executable digital contract that releases digital payments once the conditions fulfill the requirements. There are many blockchain platforms available to write the smart contracts but the most used are Ethereum based [7]. There are many fields in which smart contracts are being used but in our systematic mapping we will only focus on the use of smart contracts in software engineering.

In recent years we have seen a huge increase in the number of software development companies, numbering more than 100k software and I.T companies including small and medium-sized [8]. One can say that software companies arena is dominated by small and medium size organizations [9]. Now every company wants to have more clients but the domains are getting more complex and in a wider range, and small companies cannot have enough employees to cover all the fields or business aspects. To meet these requirements, outsourcing to third-party contractors is a regular practice is software arena [10]. However, in global software development several concerns appear including real competence to perform the work to be done and trust appear apart from traditional issues like requirements stability. This later problem is even more tangible in global settings [11]. In this scenario, smart contracts can play a crucial role in outsourcing governance so none of the parts can breach or make changes to the contract [8].

This interaction between smart contracts and software engineering seem to be a promising field to researchers and practitioners alike. However, in spite of the attractiveness of the field and its potential, to the best of authors' knowledge, there is not a systematic literature review devoted to identify opportunities and potential problems in this interaction. Literature devoted efforts in literature reviews on Blockchain [1] or smart contracts [7] both from a general or business specific perspective [12–17], however, as stated before there are not previous literature reviews on Blockchain based smart contracts and their application in Software Engineering. This paper is aimed to bridge this research gap.

The objective of this systematic mapping is to research the use of smart contracts in software engineering. We aim to study the prospective problems or opportunities facing in software engineering, while using smart contract. The mapping study will help us to find the problems in blockchain based smart contracts in software engineering and its possible solutions.

2   Research Methodology

The systematic mapping method was used to explore the studies related to the use of blockchain based smart contracts in software engineering. Our study follows the guidelines by Petersen et al. [18]. By means of this work, we will be able to find the exact studies to map, the important papers and articles that will help us to answer our research questions. The purpose of this study is to structure and characterize the state of the practice on smart contracts applied to software engineering, analyzing previous works published in the literature to provide an overview of the topic and to help discover potential gaps for future research. Due to the breadth of the topic, a systematic mapping study was selected by authors to identify and categorize all relevant research papers (referred to as primary studies) related to this topic. Authors followed these steps to conduct the systematic mapping.

Process steps

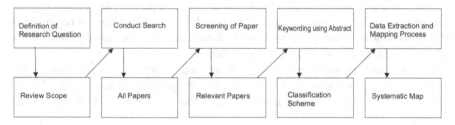

Outcomes

Fig. 1. Systematic mapping process

We followed the steps specified in the Fig. 1 to perform the systematic mapping. The process starts with defining the research questions and searching for relevant papers, followed by screening of papers, reading the abstract and extraction of data for mapping. All the steps produce results accordingly and the final result is in fact, a systematic map of the topic.

2.1   Goals and Research Questions

The goal of our research is to gain an insight into the problems and opportunities of using Blockchain smart contracts in software engineering. So in order to get an overview of this subject in a structured and sound way, authors define three research questions.

RQ-1:   What are the challenges or benefits of using Blockchain based smart contracts in software engineering?

RQ-2:   What are the most reported uses of blockchain based smart contract in software engineering?

RQ-3:   What aspects of software engineering are most affected by initiatives in blockchain based smart contracts?

2.2   Study Protocol

Regarding the keywords for the search, after some exploratory searches using different combination of keywords, the researchers jointly established the final string to be used in the search for papers in the databases. Although small modifications in the syntax were performed, the general string was:

("smart contract") AND ("blockchain") AND ("software engineering")

With regards to databases, the following databases were used to find relevant literature on the topic:

- ACM Digital Library (http://dl.acm.org)
- IEEE Explore (https://explore.ieee.com)
- SpringerLink (https://link.springer.com)
- ScienceDirect (https://www.sciencedirect.com/)
- Wiley Online Library (https://onlinelibrary.wiley.com).

This set of sources was chosen by authors, given that they are among the most relevant sources of articles within the broad field of computing and because they are accessible using institutional accounts. The search was performed at the beginning of 2019 in the aforementioned databases using Zotero as a reference management tool in order to store studies and also to avoid duplications.

Inclusion and exclusion criteria were stablished in order to exclude articles and studies which are not relevant to answer research questions stated before. Table 1 depicts the inclusion and exclusion criteria that authors implemented in this systematic mapping:

Table 1. Inclusion and exclusion criteria fort the mapping

Inclusion criteria	Exclusion criteria
The papers are in software engineering area in which the research scope being the use of blockchain smart contracts in this filed	Studies not written in English
The full text of the paper is available	The full text of the paper is not available
The paper is related to smart contracts problems or challenges in software engineering	The papers are from other fields of Computer Science
The paper is showing the possible solutions of smart contract problems in software engineering	Non-technical papers

We applied the following three filters to identify the specific papers answering our research questions:

- **Filter 1:** The resulting papers of the search string, have been scanned by reading the title, keywords, abstract, results, conclusion, number of citations, and year of publication and by applying inclusion/exclusion criteria from Table 2.
- **Filter 2:** We then read full text of the papers that passed the filter 1.

- **Filter 3:** We studied the papers that we filtered out from filter 2. Then we included those papers, which actually describe the benefits and challenges of use of Smart Contracts in Software Engineering.

For our study, authors followed a systematic mapping, depicted in Fig. 2. In this regard, we used keywords to reduce the time needed to map the classification scheme to make sure that we include all the studies, which are related to our research. This search contains two steps. In the first step we read the abstracts and keywords of the selected papers to check the contribution of that paper, identifying what are the main goals of each paper and what aspects it is exploring. This helps to classify the papers in categories. When abstracts not enough to get the understanding of the selected paper then the reviewer can also go through the introduction and conclusion of the papers. Finally, when the keywords have been chosen, then they can be clustered to form categories for the map.

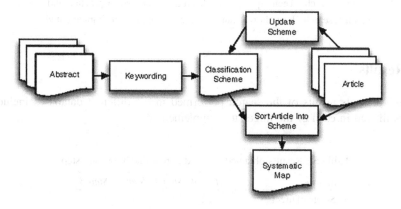

Fig. 2. Classification scheme

In our study, authors classify papers into three different categories, Research Scope, contribution type and research type. Each consisting of a set of categories to which we can map the papers. These categories are presented and defined in the following tables:

Table 2. Research scope

Category	Description
Possible uses	In this category, only the uses of the smart contracts are discussed
Opportunities	This category contains articles with different opportunities
Compatibilities	This category includes compatibility of the smart contracts in current software engineering practices
Aspects	This category includes aspects, which are influenced by mart contracts in software engineering

Table 3. Contribution type

Category	Description
Process	A process describes the activities, action and their work flow
Tool	A software tool is developed to support different aspect of software variability
Model	How things should be done is describe in this model
Technique	It is used to achieve the specific task. It could come accompanied with a support tool

Table 4. Research type

Category	Description
Solution proposal	In which the solution of the problem is proposed
Opinion paper	Someone express the personal opinion
Experience paper	What and how something has been done in practice
Validation research	Technique not yet been implemented in practice and novel
Evaluation research	It is shown that how the techniques are implemented

3   Results

Table 5 presents results of the search performed in the different databases including papers filtered in each of the three steps implemented:

Table 5. Results obtained in the different databases and steps

Source	Initial	Step 1	Step 2	Step 3
ScienceDirect	22	13	1	1
IEEE	25	0	0	
ACM Digital Library	142	11	11	7
Wiley (Online Library)	4	0	0	0
Springer	178	4	4	0
TOTAL	*371*	*28*	*16*	*8*

Apart from results themselves, it is also worth to present frequencies in each aspect. That is, the Analysis of the outcomes presenting the frequencies of publications for each category. It results in concluding which categories have been highlighted in past research and then, to find gaps and possibilities for future research work. This is further demonstrated by x-y coordinates scatterplots with bubbles in category intersections. The size of the bubble depends on the number of articles that are pair in each category, corresponding to the bubble coordinates. Figure 3 presents the information in a graphical way:

During the classification process, we sorted the articles to the scheme adopted. In this process, we used Excel where we classified different articles in classes defined previously in Tables 2, 3 and 4. The analysis shows the frequency of the papers in the past and the research gaps in these. To show this research frequency graphically, we used bubble plot. Bubble plot is a two-dimensional plot where observation data is shown in circles. The size of the bubble shows the number of articles or papers in each category in Fig. 3.

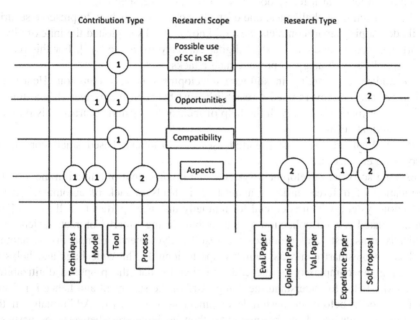

Fig. 3. Bubble plot of the distribution of contributions among the three criteria

The plot clearly shows that the number of Experience papers, Solution proposal and Processes are more in numbers. All of these papers are with different opportunities and aspects. In research type we found more papers in Experience and opinion papers. Whereas in contribution type, we found more papers which are describing the process. There are fewer papers in other aspects and opportunities, therefore a need to do further research in those areas.

4   Analysis and Discussion

In this section, research questions are answered in an isolated way by authors as follows:

RQ-1: What are the challenges or benefits of using Blockchain based smart contracts in Software Engineering?

A set of challenges when applying Blockchain based smart contracts in software engineering was reported by literature. The first challenge is the need to find recognized professionals with specialized skill in Blockchain and software engineering at the same time [19]. This talent shortage has an impact in industry and affects software process in a negative way [5].

On the other hand, the main purpose of using Smart Contract is to enhance software security. To prove this, some testing is required to check whether the Smart Contract is able comply with legal systems involved. Then Blockchain transactions also have to test that it really does not allow to double spending.

In perspective of challenges, one of the key challenges is how to preserve security while developing smart contracts. Several known attacks exploited the inflexibility of smart contracts in attempts to steal digital currency from users [7]. For this reason, there should be a strategy to prevent such attacks.

Nowadays outsourcing in software development is very common. Hence, the developer and employers need to establish trust between themselves. It's a difficult task to do it manually but, with the help of inclusion of smart contracts this problem can be mitigated [6].

RQ-2: What are the most reported uses of blockchain based smart contract in software engineering?

In existing software development systems, the involvement of human in the loop for verification of different tasks is a must. This leads to lack of automated reward collection system, which is crucial for mutually untrusted parties to collaborate [20]. An automated reward collection system is built using Smart Contract, which automatically runs tests and produces the results. Cyclometric complexity is another application of smart contracts, which helps to identify the code bugs and helps in predicting the complexity of the code. Similar to that, the proposed digitizability complexity helps to understand the complexity of the statement and hence it refrains complex codes before the design/development state starts [5]. Additionally, if the developer is outsourced by the employer, then, to build trust between the parties a smart contract based system is introduced. Through this, both the developer and employer are able to benefit from a secured relationship [8].

RQ-3: What aspects of software engineering are most affected by initiatives in blockchain based smart contracts?

Singi in [21] stated that software development is becoming a distributed process rapidly, with small teams working virtually from their locations. When they work on projects, sometimes they add third party codes in software products without reporting to their team lead. This could lead to a low quality of the final product, which is not good for the company's reputation. To comply with this, a blockchain and smart contract based infrastructure is proposed. This will keep track of the developers who will add third party code or components to the final product. So, if that open source code is non-compatible, it will advise them with regards to best practices and mitigating actions. Before the development process begins, the consultants can check the coding complexity involved in the development process using smart contracts [5]. If a new piece of software is required to be developed or just modified, then the employer just can upload his work with the reward and the developer who will be interested will accept it. Then he will develop the software and deliver to get his reward. So, there will be no need of any mediator company between employer and employee [8].

5 Conclusions, Limitations and Future Work

In this paper we illustrated the use of blockchain based smart contracts in software engineering. The main motivation of this study was to examine how the smart contracts can be beneficial for software engineering and underline possible rooms of improvement of fields of research. Maybe the most important aspect underlined by our study is the need of competence in the field. Although talent wars are not new in software arena e.g. [22], our study underlines the need to develop professionals in the area. This leads to identify avenues of research in the talent management but also in the educational field.

The aim of this study was to structure and characterize the state of the practice on software engineering and smart contracts, analyzing previous works published in the literature to provide an overview of the topic and to help discover potential gaps for future research. For that purpose, the authors decided to use a general search string to not bias the study towards any specific field inside software engineering. However, including in the scope of this research knowledge areas inside software engineering (e.g. Requirements Engineering) would have provided a richer set of primary studies and should be considered for a future work.

Finally, another aspect that could threat this study is researcher bias. This could have affected the selection of primary studies, their classification and the accuracy in data extraction. To reduce this threat of validity, both researchers devoted their time in the selection and classification of primary studies designing and implementing a protocol for the inclusion and exclusion criteria along as resolving disagreements by discussion.

References

1. Yli-Huumo, J., Ko, D., Choi, S., Park, S., Smolander, K.: Where is current research on blockchain technology?—A systematic review. PLoS ONE **11**, e0163477 (2016). https://doi.org/10.1371/journal.pone.0163477
2. Zheng, Z., Xie, S., Dai, H.-N., Chen, X., Wang, H.: Blockchain challenges and opportunities: a survey. Int. J. Web Grid Serv. **14**, 352–375 (2018). https://doi.org/10.1504/IJWGS.2018.095647
3. Zheng, Z., Xie, S., Dai, H., Chen, X., Wang, H.: An overview of blockchain technology: architecture, consensus, and future trends. In: 2017 IEEE International Congress on Big Data (BigData Congress), pp. 557–564 (2017). https://doi.org/10.1109/BigDataCongress.2017.85
4. Hegedus, P.: Towards analyzing the complexity landscape of solidity based Ethereum smart contracts. In: 2018 IEEE/ACM 1st International Workshop on Emerging Trends in Software Engineering for Blockchain (WETSEB), pp. 35–39 (2018)
5. Pradeepkumar, D.S., Singi, K., Kaulgud, V., Podder, S.: Evaluating complexity and digitizability of regulations and contracts for a blockchain application design. In: Proceedings of the 1st International Workshop on Emerging Trends in Software Engineering for Blockchain, pp. 25–29. ACM, New York (2018). https://doi.org/10.1145/3194113.3194117

6. Wang, P., Liu, X., Chen, J., Zhan, Y., Jin, Z.: QoS-aware service composition using blockchain-based smart contracts. In: Proceedings of the 40th International Conference on Software Engineering: Companion Proceedings, pp. 296–297. ACM, New York (2018). https://doi.org/10.1145/3183440.3194978

7. Macrinici, D., Cartofeanu, C., Gao, S.: Smart contract applications within blockchain technology: a systematic mapping study. Telemat. Inform. 35, 2337–2354 (2018). https://doi.org/10.1016/j.tele.2018.10.004

8. Król, M., Reñé, S., Ascigil, O., Psaras, I.: ChainSoft: collaborative software development using smart contracts. In: Proceedings of the 1st Workshop on Cryptocurrencies and Blockchains for Distributed Systems, pp. 1–6. ACM, New York (2018). https://doi.org/10.1145/3211933.3211934

9. Sanchez-Gordon, M.-L., O'Connor, R.V., Colomo-Palacios, R.: Evaluating VSEs viewpoint and sentiment towards the ISO/IEC 29110 standard: a two country grounded theory study. In: Rout, T., O'Connor, R.V., Dorling, A. (eds.) SPICE 2015. CCIS, vol. 526, pp. 114–127. Springer, Cham (2015). https://doi.org/10.1007/978-3-319-19860-6_10

10. Casado-Lumbreras, C., Colomo-Palacios, R., Ogwueleka, F.N., Misra, S.: Software development outsourcing: challenges and opportunities in Nigeria. J. Glob. Inf. Technol. Manag. 17, 267–282 (2014). https://doi.org/10.1080/1097198X.2014.978626

11. Colomo-Palacios, R., Casado-Lumbreras, C., Soto-Acosta, P., Misra, S., García-Peñalvo, F.J.: Analyzing human resource management practices within the GSD context. J. Glob. Inf. Technol. Manag. 15, 30–54 (2012)

12. Wang, Y., Han, J.H., Beynon-Davies, P.: Understanding blockchain technology for future supply chains: a systematic literature review and research agenda. Supply Chain Manag. Int. J. 24, 62–84 (2018). https://doi.org/10.1108/SCM-03-2018-0148

13. Queiroz, M.M., Telles, R., Bonilla, S.H.: Blockchain and supply chain management integration: a systematic review of the literature. Supply Chain Manag. Int. J. (2019). https://doi.org/10.1108/SCM-03-2018-0143

14. Taylor, P.J., Dargahi, T., Dehghantanha, A., Parizi, R.M., Choo, K.-K.R.: A systematic literature review of blockchain cyber security. Digit. Commun. Netw. (2019). https://doi.org/10.1016/j.dcan.2019.01.005

15. Li, J., Greenwood, D., Kassem, M.: Blockchain in the built environment and construction industry: a systematic review, conceptual models and practical use cases. Autom. Constr. 102, 288–307 (2019). https://doi.org/10.1016/j.autcon.2019.02.005

16. Drosatos, G., Kaldoudi, E.: Blockchain applications in the biomedical domain: a scoping review. Comput. Struct. Biotechnol. J. 17, 229–240 (2019). https://doi.org/10.1016/j.csbj.2019.01.010

17. da Silveira, F., Neto, I.R., Machado, F.M., da Silva, M.P., Amaral, F.G.: Analysis of Industry 4.0 technologies applied to the health sector: systematic literature review. In: Arezes, P.M., et al. (eds.) Occupational and Environmental Safety and Health. SSDC, vol. 202, pp. 701–709. Springer, Cham (2019). https://doi.org/10.1007/978-3-030-14730-3_73

18. Petersen, K., Vakkalanka, S., Kuzniarz, L.: Guidelines for conducting systematic mapping studies in software engineering: an update. Inf. Softw. Technol. 64, 1–18 (2015). https://doi.org/10.1016/j.infsof.2015.03.007

19. Porru, S., Pinna, A., Marchesi, M., Tonelli, R.: Blockchain-oriented software engineering: challenges and new directions. In: 2017 IEEE/ACM 39th International Conference on Software Engineering Companion (ICSE-C), pp. 169–171 (2017). https://doi.org/10.1109/ICSE-C.2017.142

20. Rocha, H., Ducasse, S.: Preliminary steps towards modeling blockchain oriented software. In: Proceedings of the 1st International Workshop on Emerging Trends in Software Engineering for Blockchain, pp. 52–57. ACM, New York (2018). https://doi.org/10.1145/3194113.3194123

21. Singi, K., Pradeepkumar, D.S., Kaulgud, V., Podder, S.: Compliance adherence in distributed software delivery: a blockchain approach. In: 2018 IEEE/ACM 13th International Conference on Global Software Engineering (ICGSE), pp. 126–127 (2018)

22. Radant, O., Colomo-Palacios, R., Stantchev, V.: Analysis of reasons, implications and consequences of demographic change for IT departments in times of scarcity of talent: a systematic review. Int. J. Knowl. Manag. **10**, 1–15 (2014). https://doi.org/10.4018/ijkm.2014100101

SPLide: An Integrated Development Environment Supporting Software Product Lines

Ockhyun Paek[1(✉)], Taeho Lee[1], and Jin-Seok Yang[2]

[1] Weapon System Software Reliability Technology Division,
Agency for Defense Development, Yuseong, P.O. Box 35,
Daejeon 34186, Republic of Korea
{ohpaek, thlee}@add.re.kr
[2] SPID, 18F, 145, Gasan digital 1-ro, Geumcheon-gu,
Seoul 08506, Republic of Korea
edward@espid.co.kr

Abstract. SPLide is an integrated development environment for applying software product line to Korean weapon system software development. SPLide supports feature-oriented software development lifecycle. Development of the weapon system software has been made based on a single software development process. Engineers reuse some of the code, common modules and algorithms from previously developed software to increase productivity. However, legacy software is not designed for reuse and cannot be effectively reused. This necessitated strategic reuse, and we developed a tool to support systematic software reuse by applying software product line engineering. In this paper, we propose an integrated development environment that can apply feature-oriented software product line engineering to efficiently develop various weapon system software.

1 Introduction

Weapon systems are generally developed in the form of assembling and integrating dozens of components into one system. Each component can be installed and operated in a variety of similar weapon systems for various purposes through addition, modification, and improvement of functions. Therefore, there exists software that can be commonly used according to the functions of target systems.

Conventional weapon system software has been developed through a process of requirements analysis, design, implementation and testing of a single system without considering systematic reuse. Engineers have partially reused existing design, implementation, and testing artifacts. However, in this way, it is difficult to build up reusable assets in similar areas in the future. This is because a single software development process does not consider the diversity that can occur in terms of customer, environment, infrastructure, and so on.

The SPL platform is the foundation for developing one or more applications with diversity. Tool support is necessary for SPL platform development for various weapon

© Springer Nature Switzerland AG 2019
S. Misra et al. (Eds.): ICCSA 2019, LNCS 11623, pp. 338–348, 2019.
https://doi.org/10.1007/978-3-030-24308-1_28

system domains. There are several studies related to the SPLE methodology and the tools that support it [1–4, 9, 10 and 11]. We developed weapon system SPL processes and tools to comply with the weapon system software development process [5] and to expand with various SW development tools. SPLide is a tool to support all phases of weapon system SPLE processes.

Section 2 describes the components and functions of SPLide, and Sect. 3 introduces the application of SPLide through a simple GCS project.

2   SPLide

We first introduce the overview of the tool and explain how it supports SPLE process. Then, each of modules comprising the tool is explained in detail.

2.1   Overview of SPLide

SPLide supports all phases for weapon system SPLE processes. SPLide operates in a way that the common SPL Repository where assets are managed is shared by various stakeholders. SPLide consists of sub-tools Domain Engineering tool, Repository & Management Tool and Application Engineering Tool as shown in Fig. 1.

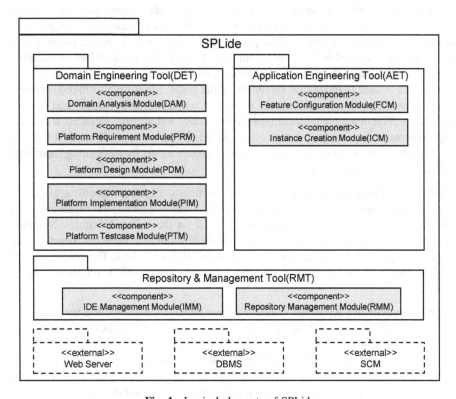

Fig. 1. Logical elements of SPLide

More specifically, two additional elements can be identified. The first is a plug adapter for interfacing with the weapon system software development tool and the second is a platform model library for handling asset data. These two elements are not run independently, but are executable by an interoperable software development tool. For example, IBM Rhapsody's SPLide Plug Adapter has been developed as a plug-in for IBM Rhapsody and can only be run by Rhapsody.

2.2 Weapon System Software Product Line Engineering Process

As described above, existing weapon system software development processes existed only in a single software development process. We define software assets that are constructed to be reusable by separating commonality and variability as 'SPL platform (simply referred to as platform)'. We defined the weapon system SPL process, which is to build SPL platform and to develop software using the platform. The weapon system SPL process is defined based on ISO/IEC 26550 reference model [7] and existing weapon system software development process [5]. The domain engineer and application engineer follow this process to create domain assets and develop SPL platform-based software.

The weapon system software product line engineering process consists of three sub-processes:

Domain Engineering: It consists of the activities to create reusable platform assets to be used in the application engineering process. The commonality and variability of domains are identified using features [8]. In the domain analysis phase, products and features to be included in the product line are derived. The product-feature matrix is created by evaluating the maturity, reusability, and technical feasibility of the feature. This matrix is used to model the variability of the feature. In the platform requirements analysis phase, platform requirements is derived based on feature model and domain knowledge. The domain engineer maps the variability and variable elements within the requirements to the features of the feature model. In the subsequent steps, the developed products can be classified into common/variable assets by associating them with features of the feature model.

Application Engineering: It consists of activities to develop various applications using platform assets. In the software requirements analysis phase, the engineer selects the features to include in the application. Based on the selected features, variation points and variants are determined based on each variability model of development stage, and application artifacts are generated from platform assets. The output of each stage consists of instances derived from platform assets and application specific artifacts.

Asset Management: It consists of activities that manage the change and traceability of assets that will be used in domain engineering processes and application engineering processes.

Figure 2 shows the detailed activities of each engineering process and their relationships. Domain engineering artifacts and application engineering artifacts are stored in an SPL repository. Artifacts include domain models, common domain requirements, architectural design elements, reusable software components, and application specific artifacts. SPLide supports domain engineering, application engineering, and asset management activities efficiently.

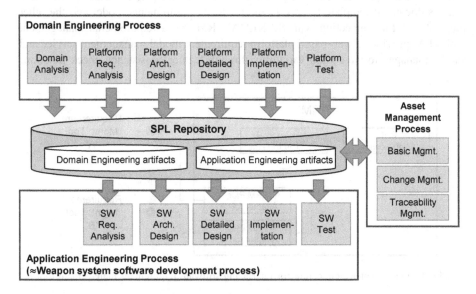

Fig. 2. Weapon system software product line engineering process

2.3 Tools Comprising SPLide

2.3.1 Domain Engineering Tool

The domain engineering tool is a tool that supports the activities of the domain engineering process. It is composed of Domain Analysis Module (DAM), Platform Requirement Module (PRM), Platform Design Module (PDM), Platform Implementation Module (PIM) and Platform Testcase Module (PTM). Each module uses an external tool plug-in for interoperability with software development tools and uses the SPL repository management tool to permanently store and manage platform assets produced through domain engineering activities.

The Domain Analysis Module includes a feature modeling tool to model commonality and variability within a domain. Domain engineers can use feature modeling tools to add/modify/delete features and model relationships between features. It manages the description of features and attributes information of features, manages dependencies between features such as require or mutex through composition rules between features, and examines contradictions that can be caused by composition rules. Feature modeling tools provide feature model check-in/check-out capabilities in the SPL repository.

The Platform Requirement Module (PRM) manages platform requirements. The platform requirements model includes the traceability of the platform requirements specification and the feature model. Engineers use existing requirements management tools to create platform requirements and edit requirements models through plugs provided by SPLide. As shown in Fig. 3, PRM provides the PRM Plug for linking with various requirements tools, and the Plug provides a plug adapter according to the connected tool. Therefore, plug adapters dependent on the associated tools are needed. The PRM Plug provides two plug adapters, one plug adapter for linking with MS-Excel's document template to specify the platform requirements model and the other plug adapter for connecting with SILKLOAD RM [6], a requirements management tool. PRM provides a web-based platform requirement model management service and can be managed to have valid variability through feature consistency check function.

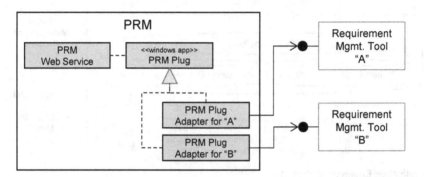

Fig. 3. Plug adapter architecture for interfacing software requirement management tool

The Platform Design Module (PDM) manages the platform design model including variability. The platform design model includes variability information defined by the design information defined by the software design tool and the traceability of the feature model (See Fig. 4).

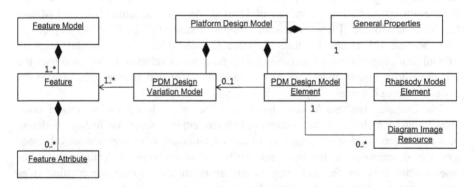

Fig. 4. Conceptual architecture of platform design model

Similar to PRM, PDM provides PDM Plug for linking with various design tools, and Plug provides plug adapter according to the connected tool. The PDM plug provides a plug adapter for IBM Rhapsody. The structure of the plug adapter is similar to that of Fig. 3. Engineers can design software using familiar design tools and establish relationships with features through adapters optimized for design tools. PDM verifies the validity of the variability defined in the platform design model through syntax checking and consistency checking.

The Platform Implementation Module (PIM) manages the platform implementation model. The platform implementation model consists of the management information of the source code created using the software implementation tool and the variability information defined by the traceability establishment of the feature model. That is, the platform implementation model does not include the actual source code file. The PIM plug is integrated into the code development tool to support activities that implement the source code variability. It provides an environment that extends Eclipse CDT for a more convenient implementation. Engineers can implement variability with PIMs plugged into familiar environments and establish relationships with features. PIM traces variable code corresponding to a particular feature and provides consistency checking for the features used in the implementation.

The Platform Test Case Module (PTM) manages the platform test case model. It consists of traceability information between test cases and feature models defined using software testing tool. Like the PRM and PDM, it provides a plug adapter for linking with the testing tool. The PTM plug provides two plug adapters. Controller tester, a unit test tool, and SILKLOAD TestManager, a system level testcase management tool. The engineer can use the adapter to set the variability information through linkage between test cases and features. The PTM checks whether the user-set variability model is consistent.

2.3.2   Application Engineering Tool

Application Engineering Tool supports the activities of the application engineering process. It uses SPL repository management tools to validate feature configurations based on feature selection and to apply the SPL platform for application instantiation. Engineers can use external tool plug-ins for interfacing and linking with software development tools needed for application requirements analysis, application design, application implementation, and application testing.

The Feature Configuration Module (FCM) provides the ability to select features and feature attributes that remove variability from the feature model. The FCM validates the selected feature configuration and stores the results. Validation includes violation of feature composition rule, whether feature attribute value is properly set, and so on. In addition, it provides the ability to identify differences between different feature configurations.

The Instance Creation Module (ICM) selects a feature configuration and creates an application instance from domain artifacts. Engineers can create a requirement model, a design model, a source code model, and a testcase model linked to a feature as application instances. The generated instance is stored in a specific location, and then a consistency check is performed for each instance.

2.3.3   Repository & Management Tool

The SPL Repository & Management tool (RMT) is a tool for the permanent management of development artifacts and SPL process libraries produced by domain engineering tool and application engineering tool. RMT manages variable points, variable elements, and feature traceability information of development artifacts.

3 Pilot Project

We conducted a pilot project to verify the appropriateness of the proposed SPL process and tool functionality. The domain of the pilot project is the Global Control System (GCS), which controls the unmanned aircraft on the ground. In the Pilot project, the extractive approach was applied because there were products developed by applying the single software development method. After developing the GCS SPL platform through the domain engineering process for the GCS domain, applications were created based on the developed SPL platform.

For the GCS software product line scoping, we created feature matrix by deriving the features for five GCS including the existing product. We modified the method of [1] to determine the GCS product line scope. We determine whether product lines are included in the derived features and model commonality and variability using the feature modeler. Figure 5 shows some of the feature models created with the feature modeler. The GCS feature model consists of total 87 features, 38 mandatory features, and 39 optional features.

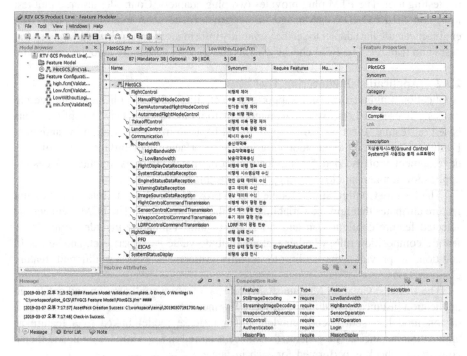

Fig. 5. Feature model of GCS product line

After feature modeling, we analyzed common requirements and variable requirements within the GCS product line. Figure 6 shows the addition of variability to the requirement using the excel adapter. The engineer simply runs the Excel adapter in

Excel and assigns features to requirements. RMM allows multiple engineers involved in the project to check-in/check-out SPL platform artifacts, including variability.

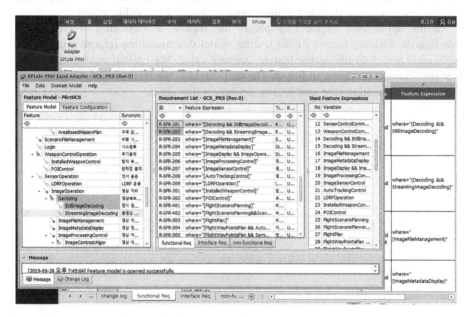

Fig. 6. Platform requirements variability management using excel adapter

Platform design, implementation and test case artifacts are developed in a manner similar to platform requirements. Artifacts were traced to the feature using the adapter of each tool.

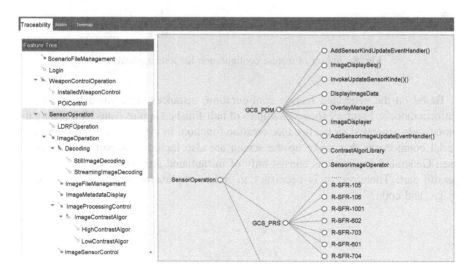

Fig. 7. Feature traceability graph for GCS feature model

Figure 7 shows part of the traceability graph of feature-centered artifacts. When an engineer selects a feature in the feature tree, the tool displays the requirements, design, source code, and test cases associated with the feature. Engineers can easily track domain assets associated with a feature through feature traceability graph.

In the application engineering phase, the feature configuration is created by selecting the variable feature of the feature model that meets the requirements of the application and determining the feature attribute value. We created configurations for four applications, as shown in Fig. 8. The tool validates the feature configuration, such as feature composition rule and feature attribute value check.

▤ Feature Configuration Compare

Index	Feature	High RTVGCS_R13...	Low1 RTVGCS_R13...	Low2 RTVGCS_R13...	Min RTVGCS_R13...
	RTVGCS	☑	☑	☑	☑
1.	FlightControl	☑	☑	☑	☑
1.1.	ManualFlightModeControl	☑	☑	☑	☑
1.2.	SemiAutomatedFlightModeControl	☑	☑	☑	☑
1.3.	AutomatedFlightModeControl	☑	☑	☑	☑
2.	TakeoffControl	☐	☐	☑	☐
3.	LandingControl	☐	☐	☑	☐
4.5.	WarningDataReception	☑	☑	☑	☑
4.6.	ImageSourceDataReception	☐	☑	☑	☐
4.7.	FlightControlCommandTransmission	☑	☑	☑	☑
4.8.	SensorControlCommandTransmission	☐	☑	☑	☐
11.	Login	☑	☑	☐	☑
12.	WeaponControlOperation	☐	☑	☑	☐
12.1.	InstalledWeaponControl	☐	☑	☑	☐

Fig. 8. Subset of feature configuration for four applications

Based on the generated feature configuration, instances are created from various platform models. Figure 9 shows examples of half-finished applications by building the source code generated by the instance creation function. In the case of this pilot project, the UI components that make up the screen are also included as part of the domain asset. Generated applications consist only of instantiated artifacts without application specific part. Therefore, it is necessary to reflect application specific requirements, design, and code.

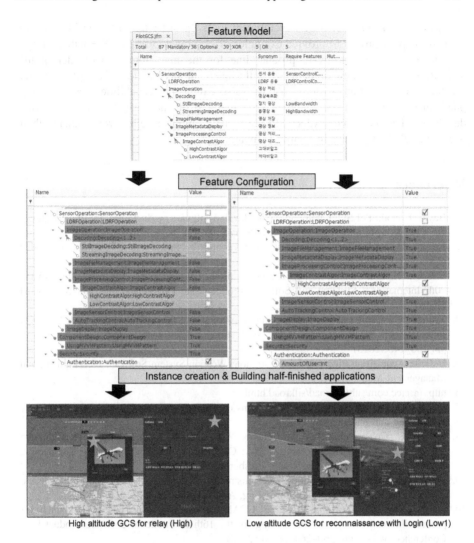

Fig. 9. Building half-finished applications by creating instances from feature configurations

4 Conclusions

In this paper, we introduced SPLide, an integrated development environment that can be used in the entire software development phases for weapon system software product line. SPLide supports the SPL process to efficiently develop high quality weapon system software based on the weapon system SPL platform. SPLide consists of Domain Engineering Tool, Repository Management Tool, and Application Engineering Tool. In this paper, the function of each tool is described. SPLide uses features to distinguish between commonality and variability. SPLide also maintains traceability between artifacts and features at the development phase. In addition, it provides plug adapters to work with software development tools. In order to verify the SPLide, we applied the pilot project to provide examples of step-by-step results. We will soon use SPLide to develop a software product line for the new domain. Considering the characteristics of the new domain, we will implement the function of the plug adapter for each step development tool. We will also extend the capabilities for managing platform evolution and for documentation required by the weapon system software development process. We expect SPLide to help engineers effectively manage their SPLs and efficiently develop quality software.

References

1. Bayer, J., et al.: PuLSE: a methodology to develop software product lines. In: Proceedings of the 1999 Symposium on Software Reusability (1999)
2. Beuche, D.: Variant management with pure: variants. Technical report, Pure-systems GmbH (2003)
3. Beuche, D.: Using pure: variants across the product line lifecycle. In: Proceedings of the 20th International Systems and Software Product Line Conference, pp. 333–336. ACM (2016)
4. Krueger, C., Clements, P.: Systems and software product line engineering with BigLever software gears. In: Proceedings of the 17th International Software Product Line Conference, pp. 136–140 (2013)
5. Defense Acquisition Program Administration: Weapon System Software Development and Management Manual (2018)
6. http://nsetec.com/sub/silkroad/silkroad.html
7. ISO/IEC 26550:2013: Software and systems engineering–reference model for product line engineering and management (2013)
8. Kang, K.C., Cohen, S.G., Hess, J.A., Novak, W.E., Peterson, A.S.: Feature-oriented domain analysis (FODA) feasibility study (No. CMU/SEI-90-TR-21). Software Engineering Institute, Carnegie-Mellon University, Pittsburgh, PA (1990)
9. Kim, J.A., Yang, J.S.: Integration mechanism for software product line development and management workbench. Int. J. Softw. Eng. Appl. 10(11), 39–48 (2016)
10. Lee, H., Yang, J.S., Kang, K.C.: VULCAN: architecture-model-based workbench for product line engineering. In: Proceedings of the 16th International Software Product Line Conference, vol. 2, pp. 260–264. ACM (2012)
11. Thum, T., Kastner, C., Benduhn, F., Meinicke, J., Saake, G., Leich, T.: FeatureIDE: an extensible framework for feature-oriented software development. Sci. Comput. Program. 79, 70–85 (2014)

Analysis of Noise Perturbation on Neural Network Based ECG Classification

Abdoul-Dalibou Abdou[1,3]([⊠]), Ndeye Fatou Ngom[2,3], Oumar Niang[2,3],
and Mohamed Cheikh Ould Guera[4]

[1] Université de Thies, Thiès, Senegal
abdould.abdou@univ-thies.sn
[2] Ecole Polytechnique de Thies, Thiès, Senegal
{fngom,oniang}@ept.sn
[3] Laboratoire Traitement de l'Information et Systémes Intelligents, Thiès, Senegal
[4] Université Gaston berger, Saint-Louis, Senegal
gueramed@gmail.com

Abstract. The heart diseases are diagnosed by analysing the ECG signals. However, during the acquisition process, the ECG signals are affected by different noises. Therefore, it is crucial to realize a pretreatment of the ECG signals before extracting the features. This article aims to study the effects of the Empirical Mode Decomposition filtering and Butterworth filtering on arrhythmia classification based on the convolutional neural network. Five classes of arrhythmia are concerned, including the sino-auricular node dysfunction, the supra-ventricular tachycardia, the ventricular tachycardia, the auricular flutter and the auricular Fibrillation. The proposed approach is evaluated with the MIT-BIH Arrhythmia database.

Keywords: ECG denoising · Arrhythmia classification ·
Convolutional Neural Networks · Empirical Mode Decomposition ·
Butterworth filter

1 Introduction

The arrhythmia diagnosis depends on the analysis of electrocardiogram (ECG) signal properties. Usually real ECG signal faces various types of noises [19]. These noises influence the ECG signals components and lead to false diagnosis. Therefore, all operations of electrocardiograms signals processing must begin with a pretreatment in order to suppress or attenuate noise. The preprocessing allows to filter out signal interference [23] and to remove different types of noise [10]. This paper studies the effects of the four filtering methods on the classification of ECG signals with the convolutional neural network, the Empirical Mode Decomposition filtering, Butterworth filtering and their combination. The proposed CNN consists of the five convolutions, corresponding to five classes of

S. Misra et al. (Eds.): ICCSA 2019, LNCS 11623, pp. 349–358, 2019.
https://doi.org/10.1007/978-3-030-24308-1_29

cardiac arrhythmias: sino-auricular node dysfunction; supra-ventricular tachycardia; ventricular tachycardia; auricular flutter and auricular Fibrillation. The schematic diagram of the processing steps is illustrated by Fig. 1.

The rest of the paper is organized as follows: The ECG signal denoising methods at the Sect. 2; the comparison of the EMD and the Butterworth based on filtering methods at the Sect. 3.1; the classification of cardiac arrhythmias based on CNN at the Sect. 3.2, the data description and the performance indices at the Sect. 3.3; Finally the Sect. 4 presents the results of the approach.

2   Literature Review

Various types of noises [19] such as muscular noise, motion artifacts, baseline drifts changes, are present in an ECG signal. The ECG signals denoising aims to remove different noises of the ECG signals. The noises are originated from various sources:

- Power frequency from 5 Hz to 2 KHz;
- Frequency Interference around 50 Hz;
- Baseline drift from 0.05 to 2 Hz;
- Power line interference around 50 Hz or 60 Hz;
- Baseline wandering with a frequency bellow 0.5 Hz;
- Electrodes motion artifacts from 1 Hz to 10 Hz;
- Electromyographic noise from 25 Hz to 100 Hz.
- Etc.

Many techniques have been implemented to suppress or attenuate noise. Several methods are proposed for noise elimination. The signal are denoised with the empirical mode decomposition [6, 16, 20]. The lower order IMFs represent the high frequency and the upper order IMFs correspond to low frequency. If the ECG is corrupted by baseline wander, it should appear in some higher order IMF. The power frequency noises must be represented in some lower order IMF. Rodriguez [19] has used a 6th order band-pass Butterworth filter for removing high frequencies and baseline wander. Abdou et al. [3] have combined the advantages of EMD filtering and 6th order band-pass Butterworth filter for ECG signal denoising. The high frequency noise is treated by subtracting the first IMF and the signal is smoothed by the Butterworth filter [1, 2]. Many others methods of ECG denoising exist such as:

- Digital filter for the baseline wander;
- Low pass filter for removing power frequency interference;
- PCA-ANN-WT for high frequency noise elimination;
- Butterworth filter for the ECG signal noise smoothing;
- EMD filtering for low and high frequency noise;
- Wavelet threshold shrinkage (WTS);
- Empirical Denoising Algorithm;
- Etc.

The convolutional Neural Networks (CNN) have been used in many domains as computer vision tasks [5, 8, 9], ECG signals processing [4, 17, 18, 22], time series prediction and completing [24], retinal disease diagnosis [5], ureteral stone identification [9], etc.

3   Methodology

The proposed approach is composed of a double denoising method and a CNN Classifier as depicted by the Fig. 1. After the pre-processing steps, the CNN assigns an ECG signal to one of the following arrhythmia classes:

- Class 0: normal, heart rate between 60 and 100 beats per minute.
- Class 1: sino-auricular node dysfunction, heart rate less than 50 beats per minute.
- Class 2: supra-ventricular tachycardia, heart rate between 160 and 200 beats per minute.
- Class 3: ventricular tachycardia, heart rate between 200 and 250 beats per minute.
- Class 4: auricular flutter, heart rate between 250 and 300 beats per minute.
- Class 5: Auricular Fibrillation, heart rate between 300 and 600 beats per minute.

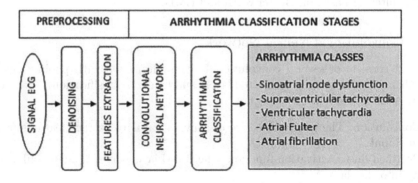

Fig. 1. Chart Flow of the proposed classification system. After, denoising and cardiac frequency computation steps, the CNN classified the ECG signal.

3.1   EMD and Butterworth Denoising

EMD is an auto-adaptive method for decomposing a signal. It decomposes a signal into Intrinsic Mode Functions [6, 14, 16, 20]. The EMD principle is to identify locally the fastest oscillations. The EMD is formulated by Eq. 1. The Fig. 2 illustrated the EMD of the ECG 100 of the MIT-BIH database.

$$s(n) = r_k(n) + \sum_{k=1}^{K} imf_k(n) \tag{1}$$

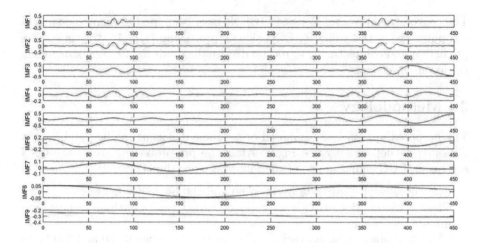

Fig. 2. Empirical mode decomposition of ECG 100

where imf_k is the kth Intrinsic Mode Functions and r_k is the trend residual. The Butterworth filter and empirical mode decomposition are implemented. The two filtering methods are tested and compared. The Fig. 3 shows the Butterworth filter effect and the Fig. 4 presents the EMD filtering effect. The Fig. 5 shows the double filtering based on Butterworth and EMD.

3.2   Convolutional Neural Network

A CNN consists of several convolutional layers alternated with pooling layers and then followed by fully connected layers and finally a classification/regression layer. A CNN has four basics layers:

1. Convolution: The prime objective of convolution is to extract features from the input.
2. Rectified linear activation function: The ReLU layer serves to map nonlinearity into the data.
3. Pooling: This layer reduces the number of parameters and calculations in the network.
4. Fully connected: It returns a vector of size N, where N is the number of classes. Each element of the vector indicates the probability for the image to belong to a class.

The proposed approach is based on the CNN [7,21] and the instantaneous heart rate [12] for arrhythmia classification. The Fig. 6 presents the CNN used for the arrhythmia classification. The convolutions ($conv_{1..5}$) use respectively the reverse of 50, 160, 200, 250 and 300. Then the pooling step reduces the vector size by taking only the frequency corresponding to the arrhythmia class. Finally, the fully connected step compute the probability of the ECG to belong to each

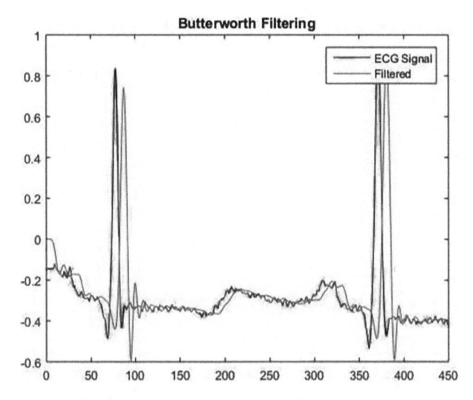

Fig. 3. The Butterworth filter denoises and smooths the ECG Signal 100 of the MIT-BIH Database.

arrhythmia class. That probability is computed with the Eq. 2. The output layer determines the arrhythmia class with the high probability.

$$P = \frac{size(PFV)}{size(CFV)} \tag{2}$$

Where PFV is the frequency vector after the pooling step and CFV is the input vector.

3.3 Performance Measurement

The proposed approach is evaluated with the ECG signals of the MIT-BIH database. The MIT-BIH database is described in many works such as [1–3,13]. It is a set of 48 data files, 48 annotations files and 48 head files.

The Table 1 presents the 48 ECG signals of the MIT-BIH arrhythmia database. Each data has 21600 samples (time), 21600 MLII signals and 21600 V5 signals. The recordings were digitized at 360 samples per second per channel with 11 bit resolution over a 10 mV range.

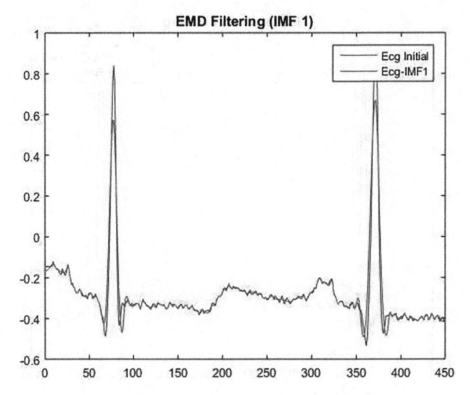

Fig. 4. The EMD Filtering subtracts the upper IMF to denoise the ECG Signal 100 of the MITBIH Database.

Table 1. The ECG signals of the MIT-BIH Arrhythmia database

100	101	102	103	104	105	106	107	108	109	111	112	113	114	115	116
117	118	119	121	122	123	124	200	201	202	203	205	207	208	209	210
212	213	214	215	217	219	220	221	222	223	228	230	231	232	233	234

The CNN is trained with 70% and tested with 30% of the MIT-BIH database ECG signals. After the test, the performance criteria are computed [11,15]:

1. Accuracy $Ac.(\%) = \frac{TP+TN}{TP+TN+FP+FN}$ x 100,
2. Sensitivity $Se.(\%) = \frac{TP}{TP+FN}$ x 100,
3. Specificity $Sp.(\%) = \frac{TN}{TN+FP}$ x 100,
4. Positive Predictivity $Pp.(\%) = \frac{TP}{TP+FP}$ x 100.

Where TP, TN, FP and FN mean:

- TP (True Positive): Abnormal class classifies as abnormal.
- TN (True Negative): Normal class classifies as abnormal.
- FP (False Positive): Normal class classifies as normal.
- FN (False Negative): Abnormal classifies as normal.

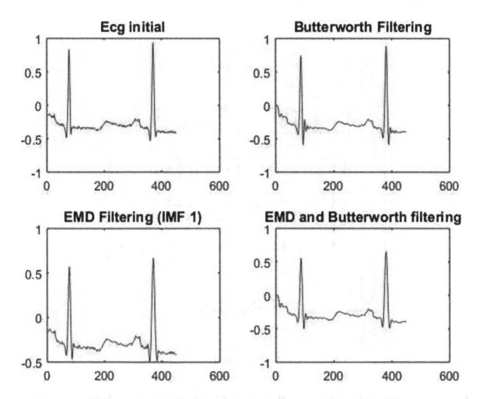

Fig. 5. The two filtering methods are combined to denoise the ECG Signal 100 of the MITBIH Database.

4   Results

The Table 2 shows the performance indices following different denoising method. The first denoising method is the Butterworth filtering. The second is the EMD filtering with the subtracting of the first IMF. The third and the fourth method are the doubles filtering based on the combination of EMD and butterworth filtering. The analysis of the Table 2 contents shows that EMD filtering and Butterworth filtering have the same accuracy of 47%. Butterworth filtering and EMD + Butterworth filtering has more sensitivity (22%) than EMD and Butterworth + EMD filtering, which has 11% sensitivity. In terms of specificity and

Table 2. Performance indices

Performance indices	TP	FP	TN	FN	Ac	Se	Sp	Pp
Butterworth	2	1	5	7	47%	22%	42%	67%
EMD	1	0	6	8	47%	11%	43%	100%
EMD + Butterworth	2	1	5	7	47%	22%	42%	67%
Butterworth + EMD	1	0	6	8	47%	11%	43%	100%

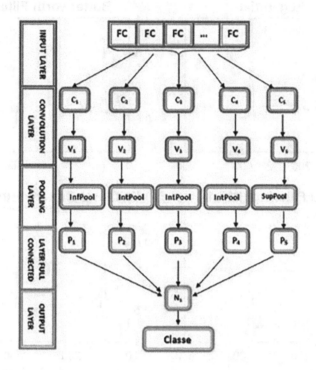

Fig. 6. Convolutional Neural Network for Arrhythmia classification takes input a vector of cardiac frequencies.

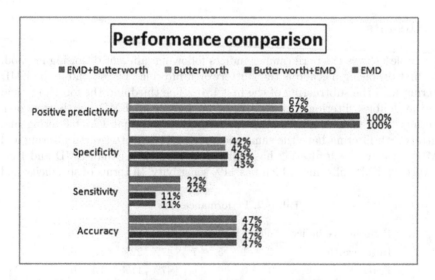

Fig. 7. Performance comparison between EMD and Butterworth based filtering methods.

positive predictivity, EMD filtering and Butterworth + EMD filtering are better than Butterworth filtering and EMD + Butterworth filtering, with respectively 43%, 43%, 42%, 42% for specificity and 100%, 100%, 67%, 67% for the positive predictivity. The Fig. 7 illustrates clearly the performance comparison of the EMD and the Butterworth based filtering methods.

5 Conclusion

This paper investigated the effects of four filtering methods on arrhythmia classification based on the convolutional neural network. It concerns the Butterworth filter, the EMD filtering and their combination. The CNN takes an input a heart rate vector and determines an arrhythmia class. The four pretreatment methods are tested and evaluated with the ECG signals of the MIT-BIH database. The performance comparison shows that the Empirical Mode Decomposition based on filtering methods are better than the Butterworth based on filtering methods. The future work will study the impact of each method on the different types of ECG signal noises.

References

1. Abdou, A.D., Ngom, N.F., Niang, O.: Electrocardiograms patterns analysis using artificial neural network and non-linear regression. In: Nabi, L.G., Eric, B., Watson, B. (eds.) CARI 2018 - Colloque africain sur la recherche en informatique et mathématiques appliquées, Stellenbosch, South Africa, pp. 25–36, October 2018
2. Abdou, A.-D., Ngom, N.F., Niang, O.: Classification and prediction of arrhythmias from electrocardiograms patterns based on empirical mode decomposition and neural network. In: Mendy, G., Ouya, S., Dioum, I., Thiaré, O. (eds.) AFRICOMM 2018. LNICST, vol. 275, pp. 174–184. Springer, Cham (2019). https://doi.org/10.1007/978-3-030-16042-5_17
3. Abdou, A.D., Ngom, N.F., Sidibé, S., Niang, O., Thioune, A., Ndiaye, C.H.T.C.: Neural networks for biomedical signals classification based on empirical mode decomposition and principal component analysis. In: M. F. Kebe, C., Gueye, A., Ndiaye, A. (eds.) InterSol/CNRIA -2017. LNICST, vol. 204, pp. 267–278. Springer, Cham (2018). https://doi.org/10.1007/978-3-319-72965-7_25
4. Pourbabaee, B., Howe-Patterson, M., Reiher, E., Frederic, B.: Deep convolutional neural network for ECG-based human identification. Can. Med. Biol. Eng. Soc. **41** (2018)
5. Al-Bander, B., Al-Nuaimy, W., Williams, B.M., Zheng, Y.: Multiscale sequential convolutional neural networks for simultaneous detection of fovea and optic disc. Biomed. Signal Process. Control **40**, 91–101 (2018)
6. Jin, F., Sugavaneswaran, L., Krishnan, S., Chauhan, V.S.: Quantification of fragmented QRS complex using intrinsic time-scale decomposition. Biomed. Signal Process. Control **31**, 513–523 (2017)
7. Karhe, R.R., Bhagyashri, B.: Arrhythmia detection using one dimensional convolutional neural network. Int. J. Eng. Technol. **5**(8) (2018)
8. Kim, Y.: Convolutional neural networks for sentence classification. In: Conference on Empirical Methods in Natural Language Processing (EMNLP), pp. 1746–1751 (2014)

9. Martin, L., Johan, J., Per, T., Amy, L., Mats, L.: Computer aided detection of ureteral stones in thin slice computed tomography volumes using convolutional neural networks. Comput. Biol. Med. **97**, 153–160 (2018)
10. Hadjem, M., Salem, O., Naït-Abdesselam, F.: An ECG monitoring system for prediction of cardiac anomalies using WBAN. In: IEEE 16th International Conference on e-Health Networking, Applications and Services (Healthcom), pp. 441–446 (2014)
11. Nazarahari, M., Namin, S.G., Markazi, A.H.D., Anaraki, A.K.: A multi-wavelet optimization approach using similarity measures for electrocardiogram signal classification. Biomed. Signal Process. Control **20**, 142–151 (2015)
12. Mitra, M., Chakrabarty, S., Mia, Md.S., Rahman, A.: Identification of arrhythmia in electrocardiogram (ECG) using statistical tools and non-linear analysis. Int. J. Bioinform. Biomed. Eng. **4**(2) (2018)
13. Moody, G.B., Mark, R.G.: The impact of the MIT-BIH arrhythmia database. IEEE Eng. Med. Biol. **20**, 45–50 (2001)
14. Niang, O., Thioune, A., Delechelle, E., Lemoine, J.: Spectral intrinsic decomposition method for adaptive signal representation. ISRN Signal Process. **9**, 3 (2012)
15. Padmavathi, S., Ramanujam, E.: Naïve Bayes classifier for ECG abnormalities using multivariate maximal time series Motif. Procedia Comput. Sci. **47**, 222–228 (2015)
16. Pal, S., Mitra, M.: Empirical mode decomposition based on ECG enhencement and QRS detection. Comput. Biol. Med. **42**, 83–92 (2012)
17. Acharya, U.R., Fujita, H., Oh, S.L., Hagiwara, Y., Tan, J.H., Adam, M.: Application of deep convolutional neural network for automated detection of myocardial infarction using ECG signals. Inf. Sci. **415–416**, 190–198 (2017)
18. Acharya, U.R., Fujita, H., Lih, O.S., Hagiwara, Y., Tan, J.H., Adam, M.: Automated detection of arrhythmias using different intervals of tachycardia ECG segments with convolutional neural network. Inf. Sci. **405**, 81–90 (2017)
19. Rodriguez, R., Mexicano, A., Bila, J., Cervantes, S., Ponce, R.: Feature extraction of electrocardiogram signals by aplying adaptative threshold and principal component analysis. J. Appl. Res. Technol. **13**, 261–269 (2015)
20. Slimane, Z.H., Nait Ali, A.: QRS complex detection using empirical mode decomposition. Digital Signal Process. **20**, 1221–1228 (2010)
21. Subbiah, S., Suresh, S.: Biomedical arrhythmia heart diseases classification based on artificial neural network and machine learning approach. Int. J. Eng. Technol. **7**, 10–14 (2018)
22. Xiang, Y., Lin, Z., Meng, J.: Automatic QRS complex detection using two level convolutional neural network. BioMed. Eng. OnLine **17**, 13 (2018)
23. Zhang, H.: An improved QRS wave group detection algorithm and matlab implementation. Phys. Procedia **25**, 1010–1016 (2012)
24. Ziat, A.Y.: Apprentissage de représentation pour la prédiction et la classification de séries temporelles. Réseau de neurones. PhD thesis, Université Pierre et Marie Curie - Paris VI (2017)

Multi-class Classification of Impulse and Non-impulse Sounds Using Deep Convolutional Neural Network (DCNN)

Adebayo Abayomi-Alli[1]([⊠]), Olusola Abayomi-Alli[2],
Jeffrey Vipperman[3], Modupe Odusami[2], and Sanjay Misra[2]

[1] Department of Computer Science, Federal University of Agriculture,
Abeokuta, Nigeria
abayomiallia@funaab.edu.ng
[2] Department of Electrical and Information Engineering, Covenant University,
Ota, Nigeria
{olusola.abayomi-alli,modupe.odusami,
sanjay.misra}@covenantuniversity.edu.ng
[3] Department of Mechanical Engineering, University of Pittsburgh,
Pittsburgh, USA
jsv@pitt.edu

Abstract. Differentiating between military sounds can be quite tasking with high false detection rate. These sounds can either be impulse sounds (sounds released from the military weapons) or non-impulse sounds (sound released from other sources) thus causing public disturbance and unnecessary panic. This paper utilizes Deep Convolutional Neural Network (DCNN) classifier to detect military impulse and non-impulse sounds and also incorporates Adam algorithm for optimal classification. DCNN was utilized in this study based on its network embedded multiple hidden layers (non-linear) which can learn the very complicated relationship between the input data and require output. The dataset used in this study consist of six sound types with a total number of 37,464 datasets which was partitioned into training (67%) and testing (33%). The performance of the proposed classifier was evaluated based on the following metrics: True Positive (TP), True Negative (TN), False Positive (FP), False Negative (FN), Precision, Matthews Correlation Coefficient (MCC), and Accuracy. The experimental result shows that DCNN classifier gave an optimal accuracy for the Machine gun, Wind, Thunder, Blast, Vehicle, and Aircraft sounds types as 97.43%, 96.98%, 95.16%, 95.13%, 88.83%, and 87% respectively. The average classification error rate for the six sound types was 6.57% which signifies that DCNN is a promising classifier.

Keywords: Military sound · DCNN · Impulse and non-impulse sounds ·
ADAM algorithm

1 Introduction

Impulse noise is generated during military installation and this noise propagates to the surrounding communities thereby resulting in public annoyance [1, 2]. This type of noise can also be characterized by its high-pressure level in a very short duration [3].

© Springer Nature Switzerland AG 2019
S. Misra et al. (Eds.): ICCSA 2019, LNCS 11623, pp. 359–371, 2019.
https://doi.org/10.1007/978-3-030-24308-1_30

Blast noise typically refers to as impulse noise that generated from military bases [4]. Using instrument attack such as weapons and mortal strength to protect and guide everyone interest is the term that described military. The military weapons are machine gun, bomb blast, tank firing, suicide bomber, AK47 assault rifle, double barrel shotgun firing, and so on [5]. The goal of powerful offensive weapons used by the military is to overpower the people fighting against the country by long range and highly accurate mortal strikes. Non-impulse sounds are other sources of sounds that are not from a military weapon such as the cry of a baby, wind, aircraft, and so on. The annoyance caused by impulse and non-impulse noise is important in making a stable task to follow up thus, record sound events to provide additional evidence of any damage claims [6].

Several research works have been done in measuring and analyzing weapon noise such as gunfire noise detection system but there are still problems in classifying military impulse noise and other noise sources such as challenges of severe overlap of Interquartile Range (IQR) between those noises due to wind introduction [7]. Figure 1 shows the diagrammatic representation of a noise classification system.

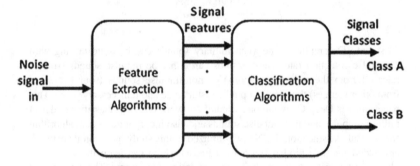

Fig. 1. A diagrammatic representation of a noise classification system.

Military sounds from larger weapons have a much deeper sound than sounds from lighter ones. This suggests that there might be a discernible difference in frequencies which Spectrogram analysis will be able to quantify [8]. False detection mostly occurs when classifying a waveform either impulse noise or non-impulse noise such as wind.

According to [9], it is very useful to have information not only about direction and distance but also about specific weapon category and the sound event it could belong to. Moreover, this can help during an investigation of crime incidents in common life where sound evidence is available.

Several techniques have been used to classify military impulse sounds and non-impulse sound like Bayesian classifier, Multi-Layer Perceptron (MLP), Support Vector Machine (SVM), Fast Random classifier, Artificial Neural Network Classifier. In this study, Deep Convolutional Neural Network classifier was applied to classify both military impulse and non-impulse sounds. The rest of the paper is organized as follows: Sect. 2 gave a detailed literature review and existing methodology deployed in related studies while Sect. 3 describes the proposed methodology. The results and discussion are presented in Sect. 4 and the paper concludes with recommendations in Sect. 5.

2   Literature Review

This section gave a comprehensive review of existing studies based on Machine Learning methods and deep convolutional neural network in sound classification.

Machine Learning is a field emerged from Artificial Intelligence which has gained vast application in several research areas ranging from industry to basic science [10]. Its primary aim is to make machines exhibit or mimic human kind of intelligence for the purpose of decision making, classification, detection, etc. The application of Machine learning varies from supervised learning, unsupervised learning, reinforcement learning, etc. Literature has shown that the majority of the method used in identifying military impulse noise are ML ranging from ANN, SVM, KNN classifier, etc. [11].

Deep Learning is a subarea of Machine learning which is based on algorithms inspired by architectural structure and function of the human brain known as Artificial Neural Network. Convolutional Neural Network (CNN) is a specialized NN used in grid-like topology using multiple filters with fewer connections and parameter thus easier to train [12, 13].

Yang and Chen presented a review of Machine recognition of music emotion in [14]. The study gave a comprehensive study of existing methods and the proposed solutions for recognizing music emotion. [9] identified gunshots sound using spectral characteristics by normalizing the amplitude and the frequency of the sample collected, and converted the signal from time domain to frequency domain through Fourier transform by extracting the features needed. MATLAB was used for the implementation using Neural Network toolbox and C programming language. [15] classified sound of frogs based on their species using three features: signal bandwidth, threshold-crossing rate, and spectral centroid. Frog sound was segmented into syllables before classifying the sound using SVM and Kth Nearest Neighboring (KNN) classifier. [16] however, developed an accurate method for noise classification with event detection of lower peak levels down to 100 dB (decibel) using all the ANN structures and proved that nonlinear capabilities of ANN give an edge over a linear classifier. Time and frequency domain features were used for the classification. [7] developed an ANN based classifier for 330 and 660 military impulse and non-impulse noise, respectively using time domain metrics and custom frequency domain metrics for ANN structure selection. The ANN structures are: SVM with radial basis function, SOM, MLP, and Least Square Classifier. The output of [7] proved that time domain metrics (kurtosis and crest factor) were good in classifying impulse noise. Military aircraft sound was classified by [17] using neural network and compact features vector. ANN method was introduced for aircraft engine signal classification, the ANN technique involved extracting a compact feature from the sound using Frequency Domain Metrics (FDM) as a method of extraction. FDM for the extractions are Spectral Centroid and Signal Bandwidth. [18] employed three architectures: CNN, ANN and Softmax regression. 480 samples of sounds were captured at 240 bmp for two minutes from 13 objects using drum kit and guitar. The three architectures failed to achieve accuracy above 20% on the latter representation after 500 iterations. However, CNN and ANN obtained accuracy above 80% using the frequency-space represented data. Softmax regression failed to successfully classify the data while CNN achieves an accuracy of over 97%. [19] applied different ANN structures, Self Organizing Map (SOM), MLP, image recognition and SVM for sound classification using feature extraction method (time domain and frequency domain metrics). MLP performed most accurate among all the ANN structures.

Cakir applied multilabel Deep Neural Network (DNN) in [20] for real-time detection of multiple recorded sound events. Kumar and Raj applied deep CNN on weakly labeled web data for audio event recognition [21]. The approach emphasized temporal localization was able to train and test recordings of variable length accurately. Piczak proposed a sound event classification using DCNN classifier [22]. All sounds were inputted using Log-scaled Mel-spectrograms as feature extraction technique. The proposed system utilizes DCNN architecture consisting of a convolutional layer, Max-pooling layer, convolutional layer, fully connected layer, dropout layer and two fully connected layers. In conclusion, DCNN gave an accuracy of 73%. Bucci and Vipperman developed an ANN-based classifier for identifying military impulse noise [16]. The study was based on two time-domain and frequency-domain metrics which are kurtosis and crest factors with spectral slope and weighted square error. The study concluded that the system gave up to 100% accuracy during training and testing: The summary of reviewed related works is shown in Table 1.

Table 1. Overall summary of related works.

References	Objectives	Methodology	Contributions
[23]	Recognition of Musical Instrument using Distinctive Characteristics in Artificial Neural Networks	ANN	Effective recognition of musical instrument
[24]	Detection and recognition of gunshot impulsive sound using novel energy formula Recognition	Uses a window sample count and energy formula	MFCC gave better success rate when with High-frequency Amplitude
[25]	Detection of Sound Event in Urban Soundscape using Two-level Classification	Mel-Frequency Cepstral Coefficients (MFCCs) and NB, J48, Random Forest and ANN	Ability to identify/recognize sound events using prominent features
[26]	Development of an efficient acoustic detector for gunshots and glass breaking	Hidden Markov Models (HMMs) and a modified Viterbi decoding process	Easy support detection with low computational requirements
[27]	Improving feature learning for Urban Sound Classification using unsupervised learning	Spherical k-means algorithm	Reduced confusion between car horns, children and street music

(continued)

Table 1. (*continued*)

References	Objectives	Methodology	Contributions
[28]	Audio Signals classification using selected Machine Learning Algorithms	KNN and SVM algorithm using prosodic features	SVM outperforms KNN with reduced time complexity
[29]	Detection of environmental sound using Convolutional Neural Networks	CNN and Mel-Frequency Cepstral Coefficient (MFCC)	Proposed model outperforms other approaches to recognizing some specific classes
[30]	Aircraft classification using radar cross-section of long-range trajectories	Use Bistatic radar (BR) and cross-section (BRCS) profiles	Better classification result
[31]	Classification of aircraft and Estimation of acoustic impact using real-time take-off noise measurements	Two parallel feed-forward neural network combined with a weighted addition	Effective measurement of real-time noise for each take-off
[32]	Analyzing Machine Learning algorithms in music applications	Non-negative matrix factorization (NMF)	Evaluate the performance of LR to NMF in music applications
[33]	Detection of gunshot in a noisy environment	Hidden Markov Models working on LPC and MFCC	Low computational cost and robustness against noise
[34]	Automatic Recognition of Urban Environmental Sounds Events	Uses MPEG-7 audio low-level descriptors spectrum (centroid, spread and flatness)	MPEG-7 features improve the discrimination quality thus outperforming MFCCs

3 Methodology

This study uses a Deep learning technique to classify six different military impulse and non-impulse sounds [35]. The basic step required for military impulse sounds classification are Data collection, Feature extraction, and sounds classification.

3.1 Data Collection

The experiment was conducted on the dataset from six noise type military sound [35]. The dataset consists of six different sounds which we classified as impulse and non-impulse sound. These sound types comprise bomb-blast, wind, machine gun, aircraft, vehicle, and thunder. All sounds were extracted using 25 signal metrics as input with an overall of 37,464 records of sounds. The summary of data collected is depicted in Table 2.

Table 2. Summary of data collected.

S/N	Sound	Sum
1	Vehicle	6829
2	Aircraft	7107
3	Blast	14761
4	Wind	2817
5	Thunder	3991
6	Machine gun	1959

3.2   Feature Extraction

For better human interpretation of military impulse sounds and non-impulse sounds, is important to extract the features needed. This start from the initial set of data in order to derive values (features) intended to be formative with no redundancy. [19] extracting features required the following signal metrics of ANN:

i. Time domain metric: is the variation of amplitude of signals with time.
ii. Frequency domain metric: is how much signal lies in a frequency range.

Both metrics used were successful in the past considering fault check in the direct analysis of the input data [19], which is most likely the similar problem in identifying military impulse noise. Kurtosis and crest factor refer to as time domain metrics while weighted square error and spectral slope refer to frequency domain metrics. To give a good performance of sound classification, the input sounds need to be regularized for the purpose of avoiding overfitting.

Spectral Slope (m): is computed by creating a least-squares fit to a line as depicted in Eq. (1).

$$Y = mx + b. \tag{1}$$

Where:

$y = \log_{10} PSD$ is the base-10 logarithm of the power spectral density (PSD), and $x = \log_{10} fx = \log\_10 \llbracket f \rrbracket$ is the base-10 logarithm of frequency.

Weighted Square Error: This can be expressed as WSE:

$$WSE = \sum_{i=1}^{n} [y_i + y_l]^2 [f_{i+1}] - f_1] \tag{2}$$

$$y_i = \frac{\log_{10} PSD_i - \min[\log_{10} PSD]}{\max[\log_{10} PSD] - \min[\log_{10} PSD]} \tag{3}$$

Where:

y_i is the log10 (PSDi) of the ith frequency of data;
y_i the estimate of y_i from the linear curve fit;
f_i the log base 10 of the ith frequency;
n is the number of the input data.

$[y_i + y_l]^2$ allows WSE to remain positive and also reflects the total magnitude of the error. $[f_{i+1} - f_1]$ is to add greater weight to the error at the lower frequency bins. Distinguishing between military impulse noise and non-impulse noise is best with features which occurs at the lower end of the bandwidth in consideration.

Kurtosis and Crest Factors: When comparing wind noise and military impulse sounds, Crest factor slightly overlaps the IQR. However, Kurtosis has no IQR overlap with comparison of other noise sources and military impulse noise sources. Kurtosis is used for describing or estimating a distribution's peak level and frequency of extreme values, it can be computed as:

$$K = \frac{1}{\delta^4 T} \int_0^T (x - \mu)^4 dt \tag{4}$$

Where:

x refers to the signal;
δ is the variance of the signal;
μ is the mean acoustic pressure;
T is the time frame over which the kurtosis is measured [16].

Crest factor is the peak value of the waveform (PPK) divided by the Root Mean Squared Value (PRMS) of the signal and it is calculated as:

$$Crest\,factor = (peak\,value)/(rms\,value\,of\,currentwaveform) \tag{5}$$

3.3 DCNN Classifier

DCNN is a network embedded classifier with multiple hidden layers (non-linear) which can learn the complicated relationship between the input data and require output. This classifier is inspired by biological variant of MLs for classifying military impulse sound [36]. DCNN consist of three layers: Convolutional layer, pooling layer, and fully connected layer.

  i. Convolutional layer: this layer is the first layer and core building block of DCNN that ensure the equality be-tween the input and output parameters performance. This layer helps the DCNN model to train faster, no matter the number of data. Without a convolutional layer no DCNN model.
 ii. Pooling layer. This is the layer that must follow immediately after convolutional layer output, because the convolutional output is the pooling layer output which helps to simplify the information further.
iii. Fully connected layer. This layer consists of all the input from the beginning of the layer. After each layer, activation function would be applied to give the model power to be more flexible to arbitrary relations. However, there are various activation functions, but Rectified Lineal activation functions (RELu) would be applied with its mathematical expression given in Equations below.

$$y = \frac{1}{(1 + e^{net})} \tag{7}$$

Figure 2 shows the dataflow diagram for the proposed DCNN model..
The hyperbolic target sigmoidal activation function is represented as:

$$y = \frac{e^{net} - e^{-net}}{e^{net} + e^{-net}} \tag{8}$$

Where: y is the output activated, and the net is the sum of the input layer without activation function.

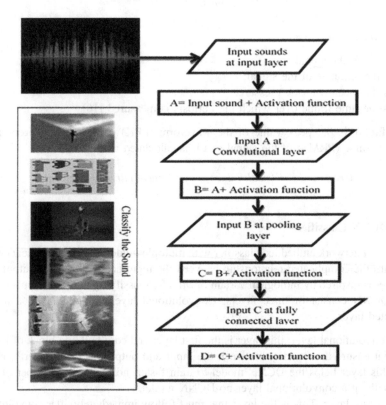

Fig. 2. Flow diagram for the proposed DCNN model.

3.4 ADAM (Adaptive Moment) Algorithm

Adam is an optimizer that can be used to solve problems with larger and noisy parameters in the field of deep learning. The optimizer was implemented using tested default settings for machine learning problems which are $\alpha = 0.002$, $\beta_1 = 0.9$, and

$\beta_2 = 0.999$. With β_1^t denote β_1 to power of t. The learning rate with the bias-correction term for the first moment of ADAM is $\frac{\alpha}{1-\beta_1^t}$. Procedure for the ADAM algorithm is given as:

```
Input: {Stepsize α; Exponential decay ratesβ₁, β₂,
Stochastic objective function f(); Parameter vectorθ₀}
Start;
              For all β₁, β₂ ∈ [0,1]
              Let f(θ): Stochastic objective function with
parameters θ
                  For θ₀ is the initial parameter vector
                  mₒ ← 0 (Initialize 1ˢᵗ-moment vector)
                  u₀ ← 0 (Initialize the exponentially weighted
infinity norm)
                  t ← 0 (Initialize timestamp)
                  While θₜconverged do
                  {
                  t ← t + 1
                  gₜ ← ∇₀fₜ(θₜ₋₁) (Get gradients w.r.t. stochastic
objective at timestep t)
mₜ ← β₁.mₜ₋₁ + (1 − β₁).gₜ (Update biased first moment
estimate)
                      uₜ ← max(β₂.uₜ₋₁),
absolute gₜ (Update the exponentially weighted infinity
norm)
θₜ ← θₜ₋₁ − (α/(1−β₁ᵗ)).mₜ/uₜ (Update parameters)
                      end while
                  }
                  return θₜ(Resulting parameters)
End;
```

4 Results and Discussion

A total record of 37,464 impulse and non-impulse military sounds was used to train and test the developed DCNN classifier. The data was partitioned as training (67%) and testing (33%) datasets consisting of 25,101 and 12,363 sound records, respectively. The results obtained are presented in the sub-sections below.

4.1 Performance Evaluation

The DCNN classifier was evaluated using the confusion matrix containing True Positive (TP), False Positive (FP), True Negative (TN), False Negative (FN), Precision, Matthews Correlation Coefficient (MCC), Accuracy (Acc), Receiver Operating

Characteristics curve (ROC) and the Area Under the ROC Curve (AUC). The order of partitioned for each sound type is depicted in Table 3.

Table 3. Partitioned dataset for each sound type.

Target	Sound	Training	Testing
0	Aircraft	4272	2557
1	Blast	2373	4734
2	Machine gun	14188	573
3	Thunder	1662	1155
4	Vehicle	1456	2535
5	Wind	1150	809
Total		25101	12363

4.2 DCNN Model Performance Result

The experimental result obtained for the performance of DCNN for the six classes of sound types is depicted in Table 4. Table 4 gave an analysis of the number of the predicted results against the actual result. The table shows the true values for the six classes of sound type with vales of TP, TN, FP, and FN.

Table 4. Positives and negative detection in DCNN.

Sound	TP	TN	FP	FN
Aircraft	1625	9132	932	674
Blast	4508	7253	226	376
Machine gun	453	11593	120	197
Thunder	921	10844	234	364
Vehicle	1725	9258	810	570
Wind	693	11297	116	257

The positive and negative detection for DCNN is shown in Table 4 while the overall accuracy of the six classes of sounds based on the precision, MCC and Accuracy is shown in Table 5 with the DCNN classifier returning best accuracy result for Machine gun, Wind and Thunder as 97.43%, 96.98%, and 95.16%, respectively.

Table 5. Positives and negative detection in DCNN.

Sound	Precision	MCC	Acc.	Error rate (%)
Aircraft	63.55	59.00	87.00	12.99
Blast	95.22	89.78	95.13	4.87
Machine gun	79.05	72.89	97.43	2.56
Thunder	79.74	72.94	95.16	4.84
Vehicle	68.04	64.63	88.83	11.16
Wind	85.66	77.47	96.98	3.02

The Table 5 further shows that the classification error rate for Machine gun as the lowest with 2.56% followed by wind with 3.02% thunder with 4.84%. This result depicts that DCNN classifier based on Machine gun, wind, thunder, and blast is quite encouraging as its error rate is still within the acceptable and standard rate.

5   Conclusion

This study was based on a developed DCNN model, a variant of MLP was used to classify six categories of sounds (military impulse and non-military impulse). The experimental result showed that DCNN model gave an optimal accuracy when classifying Machine gun, Wind and Thunder sounds types as 97.43%, 96.98%, and 95.16%, respectively. Classification of Aircraft and Vehicle sound type was lower with 87.0% and 88.83%, respectively. However, the average classification error rate for the six sound types was 6.57% which shows that the detection rate of DCNN signifies a promising classifier. We plan to compare the obtained result with pervious implementations of ANN with varying numbers of inputs features e.g. 4, 8 and 25.

Acknowledgments. The Authors appreciate the Covenant University Centre for Research, Innovation and Discovery for their support. In addition, we appreciate the Sound, Systems and Structures Laboratory, Swanson School of Engineering, University of Pittsburg, Pittsburg for providing the dataset.

References

1. Schomer, P.D., Robert, D.: Neathammer, Community Reaction to Impulsive Noise: A Final 10-Year Research Summary (U.S. Army Construction Engineering Research Laboratories Technical Report, N-167) (1985)
2. Rhudy, M.B.: Real-time implementation of a military impulse noise classifier. Master thesis, Department of Mechanical Engineering, University of Pittsburg, USA (2009)
3. Nakashima, A., Farinaccio, R.: Review of weapon noise measurement and damage risk criteria: considerations for auditory protection and performance. Mil. Med. **180**(4), 402–408 (2015)
4. Bruce, E., Tomasz, R.: High-Level Impulse Sound and Human Hearing, Standard Physiology, Quantization: Army research laboratory (ARL-TR-6017) (2012)
5. Patrick, B., Peter, S.: Noises and Sounds John Hopkin Bloomberg School and Public Health, vol. 6, pp. 1–48 (2006)
6. Zhang, X.T., Meyer, B., Skoie, D.: Anonymous. Office of Economic Adjustment, Office of Assistant Secretary of Defense, and Economic Security. Joint Land Use Study. Office of Economic Adjustment, DUSD(I&E), Suite 200, 400 Army Navy Drive, Arlington, VA 22202-2884 (703), pp. 604–620 (1993)
7. Bucci, B.A.: Development of artificial neural network-based classifiers to identify military impulse noise. Master's thesis, Mechanical Engineering, University of Pittsburgh (2007)
8. Martin, J.: Support vector machine classification of gunshots. Ph.D. Paper, Duke University, pp. 1–9 (2007)

9. Milan, N., VojTech, K., Petr, D.: Neural network classification of gunshots using spectral characteristics. Department of Electronics and Measurement: in proceeding recent researches in automatic control, pp. 262–267 (2011)
10. Das, S., Dey, A., Pal, A., Roy, N.: Applications of artificial intelligence in machine learning: review and prospect. Int. J. Comput. Appl. **115**(9), 31–41 (2015). https://doi.org/10.5120/20182-2402
11. Bucci, B.A., Vipperman, J.S.: Comparison of artificial neural network structures to identify military impulse noise. J. Acoust. Soc. Am. **121**(5), 3112–3113 (2007). https://doi.org/10.1121/1.4782056
12. Goodfellow, I., Bengio, Y., Courville, A., Bengio, Y.: Deep Learning, vol. 1, pp. 326–356. MIT Press, Cambridge (2016)
13. Neural Networks and Deep Learning online book. http://neuralnetworksanddeeplearning.com/
14. Yang, Y.H., Chen, H.H.: Machine recognition of music emotion: a review. ACM Trans. Intell. Syst. Technol. (TIST) **3**(3), 40 (2012). https://doi.org/10.1145/2168752.2168754
15. Chenn-Jung, H., Yang, Y., Dian-Xiu, Y., You-Jia, C.: Frog classification using machine learning techniques. Expert Syst. Appl. **36**, 3737–3743 (2009). https://doi.org/10.1016/j.eswa.2008.02.059
16. Brian, C., Jeffrey, V.: Performance of artificial neural network classifiers to identify military impulse noise. J. Acoust. Soc. Am. **122**(3), 1602–1610 (2007). https://doi.org/10.1121/1.2756969
17. Barbarrosou, M.: Military aircraft's classification based on their sound signature. Aircraft Eng. Aerospace Technol.: Int. J. **88**(1), 66–72 (2016). https://doi.org/10.1108/AEAT-04-2014-0040
18. Authur, J.: Recognizing Sound a Deep Learning as a Case Study. Deep Learning (2016). https://medium.com/.../recognizing-sounds-a-deep-learning-case-study-1bc37444d44
19. Jeffrey, S., Mathew, A., Brian, A.: Development and implementation of metrics to identify military impulse noise. In: 149th Meeting of the Acoustical Society of America, 16–20 May 2010, Vancouver, BC Canada (2010). J. Acoust. Soc. Am. **117**, 1585
20. Cakir, E.: Multilabel sound event classification with neural networks. Master of Science thesis. Tempere University of Technology, Finland (2014)
21. Kumar, A., Raj, B.: Deep CNN framework for audio event recognition using weakly labeled web data (2017). https://doi.org/10.5281/zenodo.27878
22. Piczak, J.: ESC: dataset for environmental sound classification. In: 23rd ACM International Conference on Multimedia, Brisbane, Australia, pp. 1015–1018 (2015). https://doi.org/10.1145/2733373.2806390
23. Toghiani-Rizi, B., Windmark, M.: Musical Instrument Recognition Using Their Distinctive Characteristics in Artificial Neural Networks. arXiv preprint arXiv:1705.04971 (2017)
24. Arslan, Y.: Impulsive Sound Detection by a Novel Energy Formula and its Usage for Gunshot Recognition. arXiv preprint arXiv:1706.08759 (2017)
25. Luitel, B., Murthy, Y.S., Koolagudi, S.G.: Sound event detection in urban soundscape using two-level classification. In: Distributed Computing, VLSI, Electrical Circuits and Robotics (DISCOVER), pp. 259–263. IEEE (2016)https://doi.org/10.1109/discover.2016.7806268
26. Lojka, M., Pleva, M., Kiktová, E., Juhár, J., Čižmár, A.: Efficient acoustic detector of gunshots and glass breaking. Multimedia Tools Appl. **75**(17), 10441–10469 (2016). https://doi.org/10.1007/s11042-015-2903-z
27. Salamon, J., Bello, J.P.: Unsupervised feature learning for urban sound classification. In: International Conference on Acoustics, Speech and Signal Processing (ICASSP), pp. 171–175. IEEE (2015). https://doi.org/10.1109/icassp.2015.7177954

28. Mahana, P., Singh, G.: Comparative analysis of machine learning algorithms for audio signals classification. Int. J. Comput. Sci. Netw. Secur. (IJCSNS) **15**(6), 49–55 (2015)
29. Piczak, K.J.: Environmental sound classification with convolutional neural networks. In: 25th International Workshop on Machine Learning for Signal Processing (MLSP), pp. 1–6. IEEE (2015). https://doi.org/10.1109/mlsp.2015.7324337
30. Ptak, P., Hartikka, J., Ritola, M., Kauranne, T.: Aircraft classification based on radar cross section of long-range trajectories. IEEE Trans. Aerospace Electron. Syst. **51**(4), 3099–3106 (2015). https://doi.org/10.1109/TAES.2015.150139
31. Fernández, L.P.S., Pérez, L.A.S., Hernández, J.J.C., Ruiz, A.R.: Aircraft classification and acoustic impact estimation based on real-time take-off noise measurements. Neural Process. Lett. **38**(2), 239–259 (2013). https://doi.org/10.1007/s11063-012-9258-5
32. Øland, A.: Machine Learning and its Applications to Music. Machine Learning report. e IT University of Copenhagen (ITU) (2011)
33. Freire, I.L., Apolinario, J.A.: Gunshot detection in noisy environments. In: International Telecommunications Symposium (2010)
34. Ntalampiras, S., Potamitis, I., Fakotakis, N.: Automatic recognition of urban environmental sounds events. In: Proceedings of International Association for Pattern Recognition Workshop on Cognitive Information Processing, pp. 110–113 (2008). https://doi.org/10.1007/978-3-540-68127-4_15
35. Shelton, C.M., Vipperman, J.S., Nykaza, E.T., Valente, D.: Six noise type military sound classifiers. In: ASME 2012 Noise Control and Acoustics Division Conference at InterNoise, pp. 127–136 (2012). https://doi.org/10.1115/ncad2012-0326
36. Shelton, C.M.: Six noise type military sound classifier. Master thesis, Department of Mechanical Engineering, University of Pittsburg, USA (2013)

Improving Employability Skills Through a Web-Based Work Integrated Learning Database for Construction Students

Adedeji Afolabi[1]([✉]), Ibukun Afolabi[2], Emmanuel Eshofonie[3], and Faith Akinbo[1]

[1] Department of Building Technology, Covenant University, Ota, Nigeria
adedeji.afolabi@covenantuniversity.edu.ng
[2] Department of Computer and Information Sciences,
Covenant University, Ota, Nigeria
[3] Centre for Systems and Information Services,
Covenant University, Ota, Nigeria

Abstract. Employability and Unemployment continues to be dire issues that Nigerian youth are faced with daily in a saturated employment market. Whereas, the use of work-integrated learning can help bridge the gap by increasing employability skills among students. The study examined the benefits of having a work-integrated learning (WIL) program for students in the construction field. Therefore, the study developed a framework for improving employability skills through a web-based work integrated learning database for construction students. Using a system block diagram, use case diagram and activity diagram, the study illustrated the functional requirement needed for the development of the WIL platform. The WIL platform is a web-based system pooling submission of available WIL positions from employers in construction businesses and former WIL students in order for prospective WIL students to access possible openings where they can learn in a workplace environment. The methodology of this research includes using the combination of HTML, CSS and the C-Sharp programming language for the interface design and server side scripting while MySQL was the database platform used for storing and retrieving the data used for the application. In conclusion, the study designed a WIL platform for construction students. The use of the WIL platform is intended to encourage employability of construction students by ensuring that they are adequately engaged in a work place training.

Keywords: Construction students · Employability · Work-integrated learning

1 Introduction

Employability and unemployment continues to be dire issues that Nigerian youth are faced with daily in a saturated employment market. Despite the high number of higher institution in the country, there are concerns about the quality of graduates that are churned out yearly. The youth unemployment and underemployment rate (15–35 years) for the fourth quarter (Q4) of 2017 were put at 52.65% which is 22.64 million people [1]. There is need to take concerted efforts at reducing these unemployment numbers.

© Springer Nature Switzerland AG 2019
S. Misra et al. (Eds.): ICCSA 2019, LNCS 11623, pp. 372–382, 2019.
https://doi.org/10.1007/978-3-030-24308-1_31

In response to this, institutions of higher learning are trying to emphasize practical experience in academic course [2]. Experts have pointed out that graduates of Nigerian Universities should be creators of new jobs or require little or no training to fit into new employment roles. This means that their employability skills must be adequately sharpened within and outside the four walls of the university.

Some researchers have also argued that employability skills cannot be adequate taught within higher institutions. This notion is emphasized in the study by [3], in that, there is no correlation between the skills acquired in the universities and those required in the place of work. This is the area where industry and higher institutions of learning partnership is very crucial. The Federal Government understanding the importance of employability skills in a formal setting set up the Industrial Training Fund (ITF) in order to achieve the Students' Industrial Work Experience Scheme (SIWES). This skill training usually occurs in a formal setting but most times it is hard for students to get the right placement within the allotted period of 6 months. Using a work-integrated learning, [4] argued that this innovative approach shows the difference between an employable graduate and one that lacks the employability skills.

The case for enhancing construction graduates' employability in a developing economy is built around their relevance in oiling the necessary housing and urban infrastructure needed in developing nations [5]. Nigeria for instance struggles with housing deficit for its over 180 million population and over-pressured infrastructure [6]. Also, a major challenge the construction industry deals with is building collapse. The construction sector is looking for raw talents that are able to assume the required positions within organizations with little or no need of retraining [7]. These employable recruits will be able to fill the skill gap that exists in the construction sector. SME construction businesses are looking for individuals that would enhance the productivity and profit of the firms rather than becoming liabilities and increasing the employment turnover, ones they do not fit.

For employers of labour, [2] noted that a skill deficient graduate will lead to a loss and poor output for the firm. The construction industry is so critical in using graduates that have the required skills because of the nature of the products in terms of housing and other civil infrastructure [7]. It is paramount that the graduates produced in this sector are of utmost quality as mandated by the industry. This is the role work-integrated learning intends to fulfil, by creating a well-rounded graduate for job creation and the world of work. This study posit that with the high level of unemployment, it is difficult for some undergraduate students to find placement in order to experience a work-integrated learning system. It is possible to use information and communication technologies such as web-based systems to track down WIL openings. Therefore the study aims to develop a framework for improving employability skills through a web-based work integrated learning database for construction students.

2 Review of Related Literature

[8] defined work-integrated learning as a learning strategy in a well-designed curriculum that integrates theory with work practice. On the other hand, [9] stated clearly that WIL is the process of creating a linkage between a students' present academic roles

with his/her future professional duties. This means that WIL helps to prepare students that are involved for the future career in their chose career. In the study by [10], WIL is regarded as an inclusive learning framework that integrates practical experiences with their academic courses. These practical experiences can be in form of simulations, problem-based learning in class room settings and investigating real life cases. The study [11] proposed a virtual WIL, whereby students can use virtual reality to experience work place scenarios of their programs. The VWIL comes with the drawback of huge financial investment and inability to portray the reality of physical work place experience for students. Additionally, [11] opined that WIL is a two-way learning process for students. It was recorded in [12] that the major objectives of WIL is that students are able to learn from their employers in a WIL system applied knowledge and transferable skills. WIL empower graduates to be more productive at their workplaces.

WIL can exist as learnship, apprenticeship, internship and traineeships in a work setting [3, 11]. WIL most times expose students to their first work experience. In the study by [4], they measured the overall experience of students in WIL and the graduate attributes that are formed in the process. Further studies in [13] evaluated the impact of WIL on Masters' students in Business Administration in Pakistan. The study [14] measured the impact of WIL on the academic and workplace competencies of 3rd year students in South Africa. In order to design a working framework [15] helped develop a WIL curriculum that takes contribution from the industry in order to build a robust curriculum for the future. The study [4] stated that work-integrated learning (WIL) gives the students in institutions of higher learning the opportunity to mix theory and practice which would help them develop their own personal and professional attributes. By this [16] noted that through WIL, the cognitive skills of students are enhanced through knowledge that helps prepare students for the workplace. Succinctly, [17] reported that WIL helps produced graduates that have enhanced skills for the workplace through competence, experience and employability attributes that are entrenched during the program. An analysis of [15] concluded that the overall benefits of WIL helps students to easily transition from study to work place environment.

3   System Design

There are other systems that have been designed for students' use in previous studies [18, 19]. The study in [18] proposed a web-based system to help secondary school students get the required guidance counselling in the Building profession. The problem identified in this study is the lack of database for students to find placement or positions for the work-integrated learning platform or Students' Industrial Work Experience Scheme (SIWES) in the Building profession. In order to develop the WIL database system, the system block diagram, use case diagram and activity diagram were designed as shown in Figs. 1, 2 and 3 respectively. In Fig. 1, students, employers and former WIL students are able to interact with the WIL database from their devices. The users are able to log into the HTML designed interface and complete the online interaction.

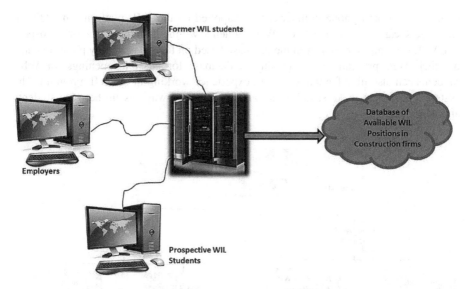

Fig. 1. System block diagram for the WIL system

Figure 2, showed there are majorly two sections of users in the WIL system. The first major component of users involve the employers of labour in construction businesses and former WIL students that had opportunity to work in construction businesses in the WIL program. The second user is the prospective WIL students seeking for placement or positions in a construction business for the WIL program.

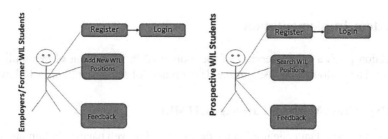

Fig. 2. Use case diagram for the WIL system

Figure 3 showed the activity diagram of the WIL system. The WIL system is designed to have a URL that can be accessed on a web-based platform linked to the university's website. Users of the platform will need to register on the platform and obtain a username and password in order to access the web-based platform. The employers in construction businesses and former WIL students can add new WIL positions available for prospective WIL students to access in the WIL database. Information about the name of the company, location of the company, duration for the WIL, possible start date required, role description for the position and contact details in terms of email and phone number can be supplied on the WIL platform. In addition, Employers can give feedback on WIL students within their organization. Prospective WIL students can pool from the database based on the location they prefer to carry out their WIL program or search all the database for possible openings for WIL. Students can also give feedback of their experience working in the WIL program. The system would help make search faster and create a two-way system between students and employers.

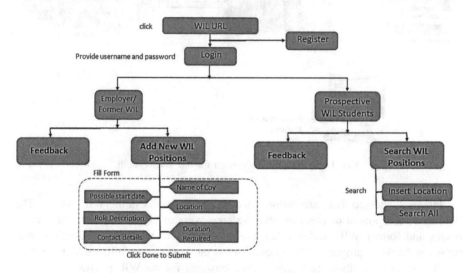

Fig. 3. Activity diagram of the WIL system

4 System Implementation

This section gives a brief overview of the tools used in the coding of the application software. The various tools used in the development of the system are as follows:

4.1 Hyper Text Mark-up Language (HTML)

HTML is a markup language used in the development of web pages. Markup languages are usually written with angled brackets and tags such as <p> which means paragraph, <br> which means break, <body> which means the main contents that will be viewed on the browser and so on. HTML codes can be written with any text editor and are saved using the file extensions ".htm or .html". Once they have been saved any web browser can be used to view it. HTML for this application was written using sublime text as the text editor.

4.2 Cascading Style Sheet (CSS)

CSS is used to add some styling to HTML tags. The particular framework used was Bootstrap. The extension for css file is .css and external style sheets can be added using the html <link> tags. It helped to enforce the behavior of several of the entities of the application.

4.3   MySQL

In order to design the database management system (DBMS) for the work-integrated learning platform, MySQL (Structured Query Language) was used. Using MySQL helped to store the data in separate tables rather than putting each of them in a large warehouse. This is organized for speed, scalability, reliability and easy-to use. A database is a collection of related data. This is a free and open source software and runs on all platforms. MySQL also performs several functions. This was used in this application to store the data.

4.4   C-Sharp(#) Programming Language

The programming language used for controlling the system was C-Sharp (#). A C# program can contain managed or unmanaged parts. The managed code is fussed over by the system which runs it. C# programming language is able to maximize possible performance, and enable direct access to parts of the underlying computer system. C# programming belongs to the family of languages in the visual studio. It can be used for various types of application programming some of which include web programming, windows programing, animation and graphics and so on.

The methodology of this research includes using the combination of HTML, CSS and the C-Sharp programming language for the interface design and server side scripting while MySQL was the database platform used for storing and retrieving the data used for the application.

In the implementation of the work-integrated learning system, Figs. 4, 5, 6, 7, 8, 9 and 10 showed the screenshots of the developed work-integrated learning system. The users of the platforms follows the activity diagram described in Fig. 3. This WIL system is for employers, past SIWES or WIL students to be able to post available SIWES or WIL positions in the construction industry. The requirement include;

a. If you log in as a user, you should be able to do three things (Add New Job, Search for Job, Feedback).
b. If you select Add new Job, you should see a form that contains the following (Name of Company, Location, Duration, Role, Contact email, phone number, Start date, submit).
c. If you select Search for Job, you should see a form that contains the following (Location and search), if you select search, you should be able to see various list of available work learning jobs.
d. If you select feedback you should see a form that contains Name, Email comment and submit.

Figure 4 showed the Login page for the work-integrated learning (WIL) system. Users (students and employers) can access the platform via a link. New users can register on the platform in order to use the WIL system as in Fig. 5.

Fig. 4. Login page for the work-integrated learning system

Fig. 5. Registration page for new users of the work-integrated learning system

Figure 6 showed the Home page of the WIL system. The Home page showed services that can be obtained from the WIL system such as Add Job, Search for Job and Feedback. Figure 7 showed the Add Job interface and the required data for the past SIWES students and employers to provide. By adding the information for the Add Job it helps students to easily search for prospective WIL positions.

Fig. 6. Home page for the work-integrated learning system

Fig. 7. Add WIL job interface in the work-integrated learning system

Figure 8 showed the Search interface based on location input in the WIL job search. Figure 9 presented the Result interface for a prospective WIL student, while the student can select and contact the employer. Figure 10 highlighted the need to provide feedback for the system. The feedback can be provided by the students and the employers.

Fig. 8. Search WIL job interface in the work-integrated learning system

Fig. 9. Result page from WIL job search in the work-integrated learning system

Fig. 10. Feedback page for the work-integrated learning system

5   Conclusion

The study examined the benefits of having a work-integrated learning (WIL) program for students in the construction field. Therefore, the study developed a framework for improving employability skills through a web-based work integrated learning database for construction students. Using a system block diagram, use case diagram and activity diagram, the study illustrated the functional requirement needed for the development of the WIL platform. The WIL platform is a web-based system pooling submission of available WIL positions from employers in construction businesses and former WIL students in order for prospective WIL students to access possible openings. In conclusion using HTML, CSS, MySQL and C-Sharp programming language, the study developed a work-integrated learning platform to add and search for WIL job positions for construction students. The use of the WIL platform is intended to encourage employability of construction students by ensuring that they are adequately engaged in a work place training.

Acknowledgement. The authors appreciate the kind efforts of Covenant University through its Centre for Research, Innovation and Discovery in paying for the article processing charge of this article.

References

1. National Bureau of Statistics, NBS: Labour Force Statistics Vol. 1: Unemployment and Underemployment Report (Q1–Q3 2017), FOS, Nigeria (2017)
2. Jackson, D.: The contribution of work-integrated learning to undergraduate employability skills outcomes. Asia-Pacific J. Coop. Educ. **14**(2), 99–115 (2013)

3. Paadi, K.: Perceptions on employability skills necessary to enhance human resource management graduates prospects of securing a relevant place in the labour market. Eur. Sci. J. Spec. Ed. **10**, 129–143 (2014)

4. Martin, A., Rees, M.: Work Integrated Learning: More than Enhancing Employability and Graduate Attributes. "The Most Beneficial and Rewarding Part of My University Experience", pp. 1–70. Ako Aotearoa, Wellington (2018)

5. Afolabi, A.O., Ojelabi, R.A., Bukola, A., Akinola, A., Afolabi, A.: Statistical exploration of dataset examining key indicators influencing housing and urban infrastructure investments in megacities. Data Brief **18**, 1725–1733 (2018)

6. Afolabi, A., Ojelabi, R., Tunji-Olayeni, P.F., Omuh, I., Afolabi, A.: Quantitative analysis of socio-economic drivers of housing and urban development projects in megacities. Int. J. Civil Eng. Technol. **9**(6), 1096–1106 (2018)

7. Afolabi, A.O., Oyeyipo, O.: The perception of future decision-makers on the building profession. Malays. Constr. Res. J. **21**(1), 55–73 (2017)

8. Patrick, C-J., Peach, D., Pocknee, C., Webb, F., Fletcher, M., Pretto, G.: The WIL [work integrated learning] report: a national scoping study. Australian Learning and Teaching Council (ALTC) Final report. Queensland University of Technology, Brisbane (2008). www.altc.edu.au, www.acen.edu.au

9. Martin, A., Hughes, H.: How to make the most of work-integrated learning. Massey University, Palmerston North (2009)

10. Al-Shehri, W.: Work integrated learning (WIL) in virtual reality (VR). Department of Computing, Macquarie University (2012). https://arxiv.org/ftp/arxiv/papers/1211/1211.2412.pdf

11. Campbell, M., Zegwaard, K.E.: Ethical considerations and values development in work-integrated learning programs. In: Conference Proceedings, New Zealand Association for Cooperative Education, Napier (2011)

12. McLennan, B., Keating, S.: Work-integrated learning (WIL) in Australian universities: the challenges of mainstreaming WIL. In: ALTC NAGCAS National Symposium, Melbourne (2008)

13. Masum, R., Lodhi, M.S.: impact of work-integrated learning on masters of business administration students: employers' perspective, pp. 1–20 (2015). https://www.researchgate.net/publication/320010936_IMPACT_OF_WORK-INTEGRATED_LEARNING_ON_MASTERS_OF_BUSINESS_ADMINISTRATION_STUDENTS_EMPLOYERS'_PERSPECTIVE

14. Rambe, P.: Using work integrated learning programmes as a strategy to broaden academic and workplace competencies. SA J. Hum. Resour. Manag. **16**, 1–19 (2018)

15. Ferns, S., Russell, L., Kay, J., Smith, J.: Responding to industry needs for proactive engagement in work integrated learning (WIL): partnerships for the future, pp. 88–95 (2016). https://eprints.qut.edu.au/105593/2/105593%28paper%29.pdf

16. Bandaranaike, S., Willison, J.: Building capacity for work-readiness: Bridging the cognitive and affective domains. Asia-Pacific J. Coop. Educ. **16**(3), 223–233 (2015)

17. Bates, M.: Preparing Professionals for Autonomy: Workplace-Based Courses in Professional Education. VDM Verlag Dr Muller, Saarbrucken (2008)

18. Afolabi, A., Ojelabi, R., Amusan, L., Adefarati, F.: Development of a web-based building profession career panel as a guidance information system for secondary school students. In: International Conference on Computing Networking and Informatics (ICCNI), IEEE, Lagos, Nigeria, pp. 1–10 (2017)

19. Afolabi, A.O., Ojelabi, R.A., Oyeyipo, O., Tunji-Olayeni, P.F., Omuh, I.O.: Integrating Software development courses in the construction curriculum. Turk. Online J. Educ. Technol. Spec. Issue, 215–225 (2017)

Using Scope Scenarios to Verify Multiple Variability Models

Matias Pol'la, Agustina Buccella$^{(\boxtimes)}$, and Alejandra Cechich

GIISCo Research Group, Faculty of Informatics,
UNComa University, Neuquen, Argentina
agustina.bucella@fi.uncoma.edu.ar

Abstract. Analyzing model variability represents a rapidly evolving discipline with increasing applications in different fields. Several efforts have addressed the analysis of a particular variability model represented, for instance, as feature models (FM). However, due to the proliferation of interrelated models, a major challenge today is detecting inter-model inconsistencies; that is, analyzing inconsistencies among inter-related variability models. In this paper, we introduce a proposal for verifying multiple variability models by using scope scenarios. Our approach is based on the SeVaTax method for building variability through functional datasheets, which are inputs to the process. Preliminary evaluation shows promissory results in terms of detected inconsistencies; however performance rises as a challenging issue for spreading the findings.

Keywords: Variability analysis · Scope scenarios ·
Variability models · Validation

1 Introduction

The product line approach provides a systematic way for reusing software assets. One of its current challenges is to model the variability between the core assets and the applications. Variability is modeled in several ways, such as attached information in UML diagrams [14], variation points that allow a developer to extend components at these points, or inside functional datasheets, as we have proposed previously [5,6]. In this last case, our proposal –SeVaTax– builds variability models upon the work in [15], in order to facilitate automated analysis.

In [3] there is a broader literature review of automatic analysis of feature models (FM), based on a general process that defines a set of tasks for evaluating FM. The process takes as input one FM and translate it into a formal representation, which includes variability in logical terms. Then, a solver is responsible for validating the formal model generated, and also receives an scenario/query

This work is partially supported by the UNComa project 04/F009 "Reuso de Software orientado a Dominios - Parte II" part of the program "Desarrollo de Software Basado en Reuso - Parte II".

© Springer Nature Switzerland AG 2019
S. Misra et al. (Eds.): ICCSA 2019, LNCS 11623, pp. 383–399, 2019.
https://doi.org/10.1007/978-3-030-24308-1_32

set, which determines the results of the analysis process. These queries represent the set of questions that solvers are capable of answer. In this sense, in the literature there exists some common validation scenarios [3,9] such as *valid model*, *valid instantiation*, *all products*, etc. These scenarios are important in order to analyze the capabilities of the solvers.

In [15] we have introduced our SeVaTax process covering all activities of the automated variability analysis as presented in [3]. Our approach towards variability analysis lets the developer/reuser build his/her verification model including diverse types of analysis through the use of scenarios. Particularly, scenarios can address more complex situations, such as managing multiple configurations of the same variability model, or checking consistency of multiple but related variability models. Thus, our contribution in this paper focuses on analyzing variability in multiple models by using scope scenarios. The analysis of this type of scenarios allows us to identify inconsistencies that can emerge from the use of multiple models and variabilities, and to provide a pre-defined set of answers to repair them. At the same time, as the analysis of multiple models generates more resource consumption, we analyze the performance our tool.

This article is organized as follows. Next section describes related work in the literature. Then, we briefly describe our SeVaTax process together with its main components and activities. Following, we focus on the scope operators and the validation scenarios designed for detecting and repairing inconsistencies in multiple models. A performance analysis is also included. Conclusions and future work are discussed afterwards.

2 Related Work

Several literature reviews have been presented analyzing the specific activities involved in a variability analysis process [3,10,20]. For example, in [10] authors analyze domain analysis tools, by considering any modeling approach and evaluating functionalities supported by the tools (according to modeling, derivation and validation). The reviews considering works closer to our proposal are presented by Benavides et al. [3] and Sree-Kumar et al. [20]. They analyze the variability analysis processes taking into account specific techniques, methods and/or resources involved. However, these reviews are only focused on FM, i.e. they do not consider other modeling approaches. This is an important aspect because the modeling approach determines the way the activities of the variability analysis can be applied; for example, the type of inconsistencies that can be generated, the capabilities that reasoners/solvers can provide, etc. Thus, in Table 1 we summarize some proposals in the literature focused on the variability analysis process. We include in the table proposals which vary in the modeling approach in order to show the formal language, the reasoner/solver applied and the scenarios validated. In this case we include three general scenarios, redundancies (R), anomalies (A), and inconsistencies (I) [9].

For example, in the table we can see the FAMA-FM and FAMA-OVM proposals whose variability analysis processes translate FM and OVM models into CSP

Table 1. Summary of automated analysis approaches

Approach	V.M.	F.M.	Solver	Scenarios		
				R	A	I
FAMA-FM [19]	FM	CSP - BDD	SAT4j[a] - JaCoP GPL[b] -	x	x	x
			Choco[c] - JavaBDD[d]			
FAMA-OVM [17]	OVM	DL - PL	Choco - JavaBDD -			x
			Sat4j - JaCoP GPL			
Metzger et al. [13]	OVM - FD	Own	SAT4j			x
Rincon et al. [16]	FM	OWL	JESS[e]		x	x
VariaMos [11]	Independent	Own	SWI-Prolog[f]	x	x	x
S.P.L.O.T. [12]	FM	3-CNF	JavaBDD		x	x
CLAFER [2]	FM	OWL	Alloy Analyzer[g]			x
DOPLER [7]	Own	PL	JBoss Drools[h]	x	x	x
FAMILIAR [1]	Own	PL	JavaBDD - Sat4j			x
Zaid et al [22]	FM	OWL	Pellet[i]			x

[a] http://www.sat4j.org/; [b] http://www.lth.se/jacop/;
[c] www.choco-solver.org; [d] http://javabdd.sourceforge.net/;
[e] https://www.jessrules.com/links/;
[f] http://www.swi-prolog.org/; [g] http://alloytools.org;
[h] https://www.drools.org/; [i] http://pellet.owldl.com/;

and BDD, and DL (Description Login) and PL (Propositional Logic), respectively. In addition they use four reasoners (SAT4j, JaCoP GPL, Choco, and JAvaBDD) in order to find possible redundancies, anomalies and inconsistencies. In the case of FAMA-OVM, authors only define mechanisms for inconsistency detection. Another example is VariaMos that provides its own variability modeling approach to be analyzed by a SWI-Prolog reasoner. It also generate mechanisms for the three scenarios. Finally we can cite the work of Metzger et al. [13] in which authors use two modeling approaches, OVM and FD (feature diagram) for documenting different artifacts, and apply a SAT solver for detecting inconsistencies among them.

There are also other works, more related to the modeling strategies of different variability diagrams during a software product line development, such as [8,18]. Both works propose the use of more than one FM, for documenting or developing multiple product lines, which must be merged or integrated in some stage of the development. However, these proposals do not provide explicit mechanisms for identifying or repairing inconsistencies or anomalies during the process.

The FAMA-OVM proposal is the closest to our work due to OVM is based on the annotation of variability over software artifacts, such as activity or collaboration diagrams of UML. This particularity makes that the variability can be defined in different points, which adds a higher level of complexity when the models must be analyzed together. However, this issue is not addressed in [17]; thus, in this work we propose an extension of our SeVaTax process in order to face to the complexity of analyzing variability belonging to multiple models.

3   Automated Analysis of Variability Models: The SeVaTax Process and Tool

In [15] we describe our SeVaTax tool based on the SeVaTax analysis process. In Fig. 1 we can see the software components and inputs/outputs included in the tool. These components are responsible for performing the following activities:

- The *translator* component (2) takes the variability models (represented as JSON files) and translates them to a formal representation. These models, named functional datasheets [5,6] (1), are described next in Module 1. This component generates two different representations of each variability model, a CNF representation (detailed in Module 2), and a set of underlying structures representing different aspects associated to each service (detailed in Module 2). These structures were developed together with a set of functions (methods) in Angular1, which support the identification of the validation scenarios described in Module 4.
- The *validator* component (3) takes as input the CNF representation and the underlying structures defined in the previous component and performs two main verifications. Firstly, it evaluates each variability model (datasheet) separately; and secondly evaluates the complete set of models (SPL Platform). This validator, also implemented in Java, uses a SAT solver (Sat4j) together with specific functions for supporting the validation scenarios. In Module 3 we describe some of these functions in detail.
- The *configurator* (5) component takes the validated variability models and provides an environment for instantiating the variability (creating a new product of the line). Following, this instantiation is again validated (by the *validator*).
- The *result viewer* (4) component, reports the anomalies or problems found from analyzing the variability models, and performs some corrections (if it is possible). Furthermore, this component allows to modify the variability models in those anomalies without an automatic solution. So, it is an iterative process in which the outputs are the datasheets modified. In Module 4 we describe some of these functions in detail.

The analysis process is divided into five modules, which use the components previously introduced as follows.

3.1   Module 1: The SeVaTax Variability Model

The *SeVaTax variability model* [5,6] is based on variability annotation of collaboration diagrams (of UML). The required variability, according to the functionality to be represented, can be attached to the diagrams by using the OVM

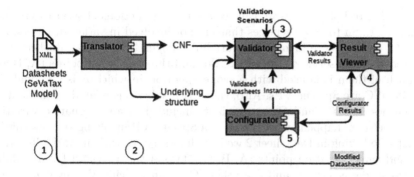

Fig. 1. SeVaTax analysis process according to the general analysis process

notation according to the interactions defined in Table 2. We divide these interactions into *variability types*, for the four first rows; *dependencies* for the fifth,
sixth and seventh rows; and *scope operators* for the two last ones.

Three different interactions, unknown for other proposals, are the *use* dependency and the two *scope operators*. The first one specifies a dependence between
common services, which are not necessarily associated with a variation point.
The other, is related to the *scope* defined for a variation point when it must be
instantiated [4]. A *Global Variation Point* specifies that if the variation point is
instantiated in a specific way, it will be applied in that way for all functionality
including that variation point; and a *Specific Variation Point* specifies that the
instantiation of the variation point is particular for each functionality including
that variation point.

Table 2. Interactions defined for modeling functional datasheets

Dependency	JSON property	Graphical Notation
Mandatory variation point	*MandatoryVP*	———
Optional variation point	*OptionalVP*	··········
Alternative variation point	*AlternativeVP*	⅄
Variant variation point	*VariantVP*	⅄
Use	*use*	⟷
Requires	*requires*	⟶
Excludes	*excludes*	⟶
Global variation point	*GlobalVariationPoint*	GVP
Specific variation point	*SpecificVariationPoint*	SVP

As in this article we are focused on the *scope operators when multiple models
are involved*, in Fig. 2(a) and (c) we show two datasheets with Specific VPs and

Global VPs. In both figures we can see a set of interactions of services in which we name S1...Sn to those services that are not involved in variation points, and A, B, C, etc. to those involved in variability dependencies. In Datasheet 1 we modeled six fixed services (from S1 to S6) and three variation points (A, B and C). Each of them is labeled with a scope operator, in which A is a Global VP, and B and C are Specific VPs. Also, the A-B-F subtree is related by mandatory variabilities, and C1 and C2 are variants included in an alternative variation point. The same happens with E that is a Specific VP involving two alternative variants. Following in Datasheet 2 we have four services without variability (S7–S10) and three variation points (A, B, C). Two of them (A and B) are Global VPs (as in datasheet 1), and the other (C) is an Specific VP involving three alternative variants (C1–C3).

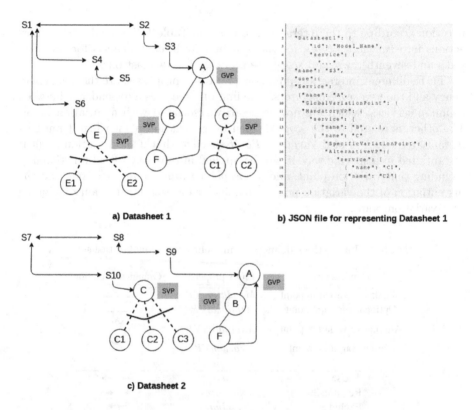

a) Datasheet 1

b) JSON file for representing Datasheet 1

c) Datasheet 2

Fig. 2. (a) Datasheet 1; (b) JSON file for the Datasheet 1; (c) Datasheet 2

Then, these datasheets are translated to JSON files by using the tags defined in Table 2. In Fig. 2(b) we show an extract of the datasheet 1 in which we show the S3 service with a use dependency to the variation point A, which is defined as a GlobalVP. This variation point has the services B and C with a mandatory interaction, and then C defined as a SpecificVP with alternative variants (C1 and C2)[1].

3.2 Module 2: Translator and Formal Representation

The *translator* is responsible for parsing the JSON files (from the datasheets) and generating two outputs, a formal representation (in CNF) and an instantiation of the underlying structures (Module 2 of Fig. 1). The CNF representation was presented in [15] for each interaction defined in Table 2.

Underlying structures are defined for identifying the different scenarios. In Fig. 3(a), we show these structures instantiated according to the datasheet 1 (Fig. 2a). The structure is composed of a set of objects (white boxes) with different attributes, for instance, object lists (gray boxes). Thus, each datasheet is represented by a name and a list of services, and each service by a name. In addition, a service can contain a list of variation points and a list of dependencies. To represent the variation points, we register the variation points scope (which is unique) together with the variation points list. Each variation point contains a variability type and a variant list. Each variant corresponds to a service. Regarding to the dependency list, each dependency is composed of a dependency type (Include, Exclude or Uses) and the target service. Each service belongs to one or more datasheets. In this way, it is possible to represent cross-dependencies.

By following with the datasheet 1 example of Fig. 2, in Fig. 3(b) we can see the CNF translation of the JSON file, in which we have 15 literals (corresponding to the 15 services) composed of 28 clauses. We show 5 of these clauses in which we can see that clause 3 denotes that *S3 requires A*, clause 4 denotes that *A requires B*, clause 5 denotes that *A requires C*, and clauses 6 and 7 specify that the alternative variation point C is represented by two clauses denoting the XOR logic operator (*C requires (C1 XOR C2)*).

3.3 Module 3: Validator

With respect to the *solver*, in [15] we have described the way a set of 17 validation scenarios are defined into five categories. The three main categories are *general*, *scope* and *cross dependency*. The first category is then subdivided into *model error*, *dead service* and *redundancy*.

In the case of the *scope scenarios*, here we extend the categories in a more exhaustive list of possible problems found. Thus, the new list of scenarios to be validated are:

- *False SpecificVP (F-SVP)*: when a Specific VP is related to an only one variant service depending on a Global VP. Then, the scope will be always GlobalVP, because, independently on the way the service is configured, the VP will be always Global. The next variability model denotes a F-SVP:

---

[1] This translation of the datasheets to the JSON file is still manual.

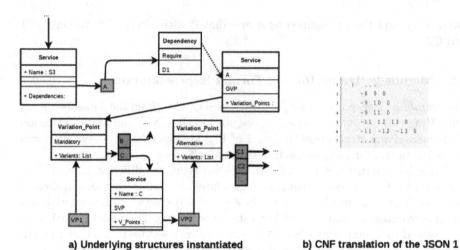

a) Underlying structures instantiated   **b) CNF translation of the JSON 1**

Fig. 3. Translations of datasheet 1

This scenario is validated by using the *Services_Consume_Variation_Point(VP)* function, which given a variation point $'VP'$ returns the number of services that use it; and when this number is one, we have a F-SVP:

```
1       Services_Consume_Variation_Point(VP):
2           For all S in (Dependencies_List U Variant_List)
3               If ( VP==S )Count ++
4               If Count <= 1
5                   return F-SVP
```

– *Mandatory Specific VP (M-SVP)*: when a Specific VP is conformed only by mandatory variant points. Then it can never contain different configurations. The next variability model denotes a M-SVP:

To evaluate this scenario we use the *Mandatories_Childs(VP)* function, which given a variation point $'VP'$ returns true if all its variants are mandatory.

```
1        Mandatories_Childs(VP):
2           For each VP in VariationPoin_List
3              If  VP.VT is mandatory?
4                 Return M-SVP
```

- *Contradictory Scopes (C-S)*: when the same VP with exactly the same variability relationships presents different scopes in different datasheets. The next variability model denotes a C-S:

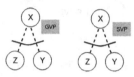

To evaluate this scenario, for each service that represents a variation point, we register its scope into the underlying structure. Therefore, when registering the scope, we check if the service has the same scope. In all other cases, we are in the presence of a scope inconsistency.

```
1        Service_Scope(S):
2           For each S1 in Datasheets_List
3              If  (S1.name == S.name and S1.scope != s.name)
4                 Return C-S
```

- *False GlobalVP (F-GVP)*: when the same VP with different variability relationships is defined as a GlobalVP. Then, this can never be possible because in GlobalVPs the configurations must be the same. The next variability models of different datasheets denote a F-GVP:

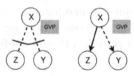

To evaluate this scenario we use the underlying structures analyzing each GlobalVP. Then, we analyze the set of datasheets comparing their variability relationships and detect those situations in which the structures are different.

```
1        Global_analisys(VP):
2           For each VP in VariationPoin_List
3              For each Datasheet
4                 For each VP_D in Datasheet
5                    If VP == VP_D?
6                       If VP.relations != VP_D.relations ?
7                          Return F-GVP
```

Each of these scenarios must be identified within the different datasheets in order to generate corrections. That is, depending on the scenario, we can generate specific results as we will explain in the following module (module 4). For our two datasheets of Fig. 2, we can identify the scenarios described before that are labeled in Fig. 6 (Fig. 4).

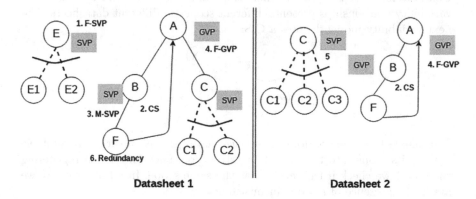

Fig. 4. Identified scenarios in datasheets 1 and 2

For example in (4) we identified a F-GVP because the variation point A is defined with different variability relationships (in datasheet 1, it has two mandatory services; and in datasheet 2, it has only one), so it can be only SpecificVP. It necessarily has different ways to instantiate them. Then, in (2) we identified a C-S scenario because the same variation point has two different scopes in the two datasheets. A different case is (6), in which we add a redundancy only to show that these scenarios, evaluated in [15] are also identified. In this case is redundant because the require dependency is unnecessary. Finally, in (5) the tool does not identify any inconsistency because the two variation points C in both datasheets are correct SpecificVP; and configurations will be different.

3.4   Module 4: Result Viewer

In order to provide more effective solutions when analyzing variability models, the SevTax tool classifies results into a pre-defined set of answer types, such as warnings, identifications, and repairs. In the case of scope scenarios, we can always fix the problem to repair the models. Table 3 shows the action performed once each scenario is detected.

Then, Fig. 7 shows the datasheets with the reparation actions performed. As we can see, scenario (1) was modified to GlobalVP. For the case of (2) and (3) scenarios, involved into the same variation point B, the tool first analyzes the C-S scenario (2) modifying the variation point to SpecificVP. In this point, the variation point B in both datasheets will be SpecificVP. After that, the tools analyzes the M-SVP (3) scenario, modifying B to GlobalVP in both cases.

Table 3. Scope validation scenarios and answer type

Scenario	Answers	Action
False SpecificVP (F-SVP)	R	Modify To GlobalVP
Mandatory SpecificVP (M-SVP)	R	Modify To GlobalVP
Contradictory scopes (C-S)	R	Modify To SpecificVP
False GlobalVP (F-GVP)	R	Modify To SpecificVP

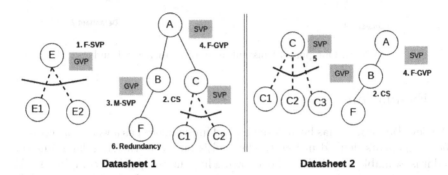

Fig. 5. Datasheets 1 and 2 corrected after validating them

Thus, the final reparation will have this configuration. It is important to highlight that if the process is executed in inverse order, the result will be the same. Finally, in (6), as it is a redundancy, the tool deletes the requires dependency.

3.5 Module 5: Configurator

The *configurator* allows developers to build a specific product by means of instantiating the functional datasheets included into an SPL platform. Therefore, this component presents a user interface (UI) that allows developers to select the different variant services (associated with variation points). To perform that, a developer receives as input the validated functional datasheets (without anomalies), instantiates them, and generates a new set of datasheets without variability. This new set must be again evaluated (by Module 4) due to it can also contain inconsistencies generated by selecting/deselecting variants.

Figure 6 shows the configuration of datasheets 1 and 2 after validating them. So, the configuration is made over the datasheets showed in Fig. 5. In this case, the alternative variation point E contains an inconsistency due to both variants E1 and E2 have been selected. This inconsistency is then detected internally by using the SAT solver of the tool.

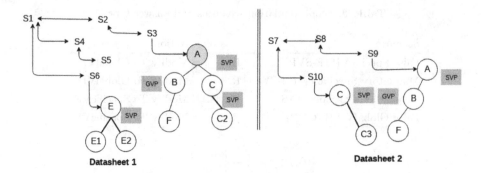

Fig. 6. One possible instantiation of Datasheets 1 and 2

4   Evaluation

The SevaTax process has been designed and implemented as a web tool according the components defined in Fig. 1. The tool is based on the Angular framework and it is available in github at the following link: https://github.com/IngSisFAI/sevataxtool.git. At the same time, a first prototype of the tool is also available at: http://analysis.fi.uncoma.edu.ar. Based on this tool, in [15] we performed a tool analysis, comparing our SeVaTax process to S.P.L.O.T and VariaMos. However, this type of comparison is not useful here due to the scope scenarios are not supported by these tools. This is because most of the tools are based on FM variability models, and those that are based on OVM are not considering this type of problems. At the same time, and considering that the complexity of analyzing multiple model is more resource-consuming, we make a performance analysis according to guidelines from [21]. Following we describe the experiments and the generated results.

A. Selection of Variability Models or Test Cases

We designed and implemented a tool that performs the automatic datasheet generation, taking into account the interactions defined for modeling datasheets presented in Table 3. Thus, the output of the tool is a set of datasheets (or variability models) in compliance with the SeVaTax models in JSON format. That is, this tool uses the model restrictions defined in the SeVaTax Variability Model for generating aleatory models (in datasheets) together with a wide set of validation scenarios included in them. Thus, the tool generated 15 datasheets with 250 services and 85 variation points (each variation point has attached a GlobalVP or SpecificVP).

B. Evaluation Design

For this experiment we define the following hypotheses:

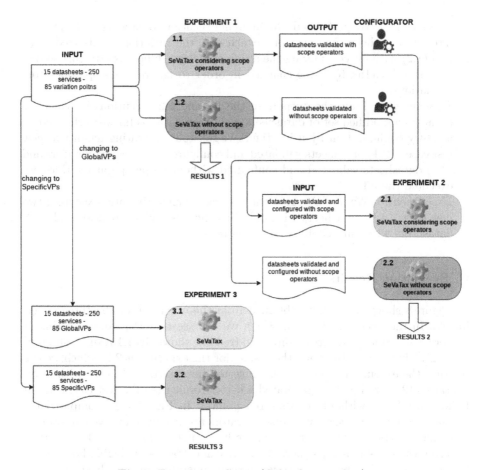

Fig. 7. Experiment design (Color figure online)

Hypothesis 1 (H1): *How does the execution time of the datasheet validation scale-up as the number and type of scope scenarios ?*

Hypothesis 2 (H2): *How does the execution time vary when derived models are involved?*

The hypotheses intent to analyze the way our tool behaves when the number of scenarios and inconsistencies increase, and when the scenarios were or not instantiated. The experiment was executed in a Notebook with an Intel i5 8th Generation and 4 GB DDR2 RAM.

For validating these hypotheses, we used the datasheets generated (as specified in A), but changing the analysis performed over them. Thus we performed three type of experiments (showed in Fig. 7) for analyzing the execution times (in miliseconds):

- *Experiment 1:* We performed two different executions of SeVaTax: (1.1) taking into account the scope operators attached to the variation points (red box), and (1.2) without considering the scope operators (blue box). In this second test, the SeVaTax tool was changed in order to ignore the scope operators validations.
- *Experiment 2:* From the outputs of the 1.1 and 1.2 executions in which we obtained a modified set of datasheets (validated datasheets) we performed an aleatory configuration by using the SeVaTax tool generating again two new test cases: (2.1) datasheets validated and configured with scope operators and (2.2) datasheets validated and configured without scope operators. Here, we executed these two test cases.
- *Experiment 3:* We modify again the test cases generating and executing two new ones: (3.1) datasheets with only SpecificVPs (orange boxes), and (3.2) datasheets with only GlobalVPs (green boxes).

C. Evaluation Results

Figure 8 shows the results obtained from the execution of the three experiments. In the experiment 1 (Fig. 8(a)), we can see that the execution time is higher when scope operators are involved (red line shows the 1.1 results, and blue one 1.2). Then, Fig. 8(b) shows the results for the experiment 2 in which we can see that the execution times are now inverted because the test case with scope operators (2.1 - red points) generated a better result than the test case without them (datasheets without scopes - red points). In Fig. 8(c) we compared the execution times when the two scope operators are involved and we can observe that the execution time is worse when we have only GlobalVPs (3.1 - red line).

From these preliminary experiments, we can extract some highlights. Firstly, the tool has a worse performance when scope operators are involved. Also, the worst performance is obtained when we the number of GlobalVPs increases. This happens because a SAT solver cannot be applied in these cases, making mandatory to use and revise the underlying structures. In the case of GlovalVPs, these structures must be analyzed more than once making the process slower. That is, verifying GlobalVPs requires to analyze each variation point to maintain the same structure.

However, from experiment 1 and 2 we could observe that in spite of the time for validating datasheets with scope operators is longer than without them, after validation and configuration, the execution time decreases in comparison to the datasheets without scope. In Fig. 8(d) we can see that the reduction of found errors after configuration in datasheets with scope operators is lesser because some inconsistencies and redundancies have been already solved, specially when SpecificVPs are involved .

In this way, taking into account the two hypotheses, we evidenced that the execution times increase when scope scenarios are involved (Hypothesis 1) but these times are improved when the models were validated and configured (Hypothesis 2).

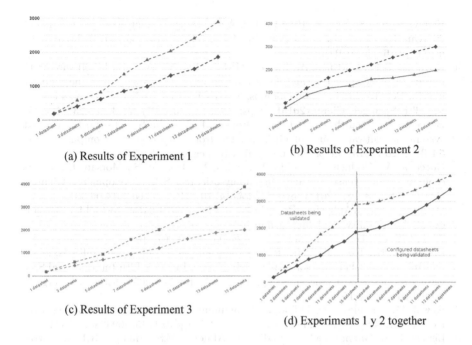

(a) Results of Experiment 1

(b) Results of Experiment 2

(c) Results of Experiment 3

(d) Experiments 1 y 2 together

Fig. 8. Results of the execution of the three experiments (Color figure online)

5   Conclusion and Future Work

In this work we have focused on the analysis of multiple variability models and the inconsistencies that can occur among them.

In particular, we have focused on the fact that each software artifact contains several variability models attached, generating that other types of inconsistencies may be derived from incompatibilities among these models. In this article, our SeVaTax process has been extended with specific operators (called scope operators) together with a classification of the incompatibilities that we can found. Also, we have described the components and activities performed by our supporting tool in order to detect and even repair these inconsistencies.

As future work we are working on evaluating usability in order to analyze our supporting tool interface and compare it to accepted usability principles. Also, we are implementing a graphical interface for managing functional datasheets.

References

1. Acher, M., Collet, P., Lahire, P., France, R.: Familiar: a domain-specific language for large scale management of feature models. Sci. Comput. Program. **78**(6), 657–681 (2013). https://doi.org/10.1016/j.scico.2012.12.004
2. Bak, K., Diskin, Z., Antkiewicz, M., Czarnecki, K., Wkasowski, A.: Clafer: unifying class and feature modeling. Softw. Syst. Model. **15**(3), 811–845 (2016). https://doi.org/10.1007/s10270-014-0441-1

3. Benavides, D., Segura, S., Ruiz-Cortés, A.: Automated analysis of feature models 20 years later: a literature review. Inf. Syst. **35**(6), 615–636 (2010). https://doi.org/10.1016/j.is.2010.01.001

4. Brisaboa, N.R., Cortiñas, A., Luaces, M.R., Pol'la, M.: A reusable software architecture for geographic information systems based on software product line engineering. In: Bellatreche, L., Manolopoulos, Y. (eds.) MEDI 2015. LNCS, vol. 9344, pp. 320–331. Springer, Cham (2015). https://doi.org/10.1007/978-3-319-23781-7_26

5. Buccella, A., Cechich, A., Arias, M., Pol'la, M., Doldan, S., Morsan, E.: Towards systematic software reuse of GIS: insights from a case study. Comput. Geosci. **54**(0), 9–20 (2013). https://doi.org/10.1016/j.cageo.2012.11.014

6. Buccella, A., Cechich, A., Pol'la, M., Arias, M., Doldan, S., Morsan, E.: Marine ecology service reuse through taxonomy-oriented SPL development. Comput. Geosci. **73**, 108–121 (2014). https://doi.org/10.1016/j.cageo.2014.09.004

7. Dhungana, D., GrÃnbacher, P., Rabiser, R.: The DOPLER meta-tool for decision-oriented variability modeling: a multiple case study. Autom. Softw. Eng. **18**(1), 77–114 (2011). https://doi.org/10.1007/s10515-010-0076-6

8. Hartmann, H., Trew, T.: Using feature diagrams with context variability to model multiple product lines for software supply chains. In: 2008 12th International Software Product Line Conference, pp. 12–21, September 2008. https://doi.org/10.1109/SPLC.2008.15

9. Kowal, M., Ananieva, S., Thüm, T.: Explaining anomalies in feature models. SIGPLAN Not. **52**(3), 132–143 (2016). https://doi.org/10.1145/3093335.2993248

10. Lisboa, L.B., Garcia, V.C., Lucrédio, D., Almeida, E.S., Meira, S.R.D.L., Fortes, R.P.M.: A systematic review of domain analysis tools. Inf. Softw. Technol. **52**(1), 1–13 (2010). https://doi.org/10.1016/j.infsof.2009.05.001

11. Mazo, R., Muñoz-Fernández, J., Rincón, L., Salinesi, C., Tamura, G.: VariaMos: an extensible tool for engineering (dynamic) product lines. In: Proceedings of the 19th International Conference on Software Product Line, SPLC 2015, Nashville, TN, USA, 20–24 July 2015, pp. 374–379 (2015). https://doi.org/10.1145/2791060.2791103

12. Mendonca, M., Branco, M., Cowan, D.: SPLOT: software product lines online tools. In: Proceedings of the 24th ACM SIGPLAN Conference Companion on Object Oriented Programming Systems Languages and Applications, OOPSLA 2009, pp. 761–762. ACM, New York (2009). https://doi.org/10.1145/1639950.1640002

13. Metzger, A., Pohl, K., Heymans, P., Schobbens, P., Saval, G.: Disambiguating the documentation of variability in software product lines: a separation of concerns, formalization and automated analysis. In: 15th IEEE International Requirements Engineering Conference (RE 2007), pp. 243–253, October 2007. https://doi.org/10.1109/RE.2007.61

14. Pohl, K., Böckle, G., van Der Linden, F.J.: Software Product Line Engineering: Foundations. Principles and Techniques. Springer, New York (2005)

15. Pol'la, M., Buccella, A., Cechich, A.: Automated analysis of variability models: the SeVaTax process. In: Gervasi, O., et al. (eds.) ICCSA 2018. LNCS, vol. 10963, pp. 365–381. Springer, Cham (2018). https://doi.org/10.1007/978-3-319-95171-3_29

16. Rincón, L., Giraldo, G., Mazo, R., Salinesi, C.: An ontological rule-based approach for analyzing dead and false optional features in feature models. Electron. Notes Theor. Comput. Sci. **302**, 111–132 (2014). https://doi.org/10.1016/j.entcs.2014.01.023

17. Roos-Frantz, F., Galindo, J., Benavides, D., Cortés, A.R.: FaMa-OVM: a tool for the automated analysis of OVMs. In: Proceedings of the 16th International Software Product Line Conference, vol. 2, pp. 250–254. ACM (2012)

18. Rosenmüller, M., Siegmund, N., Thüm, T., Saake, G.: Multi-dimensional variability modeling. In: Proceedings of the 5th Workshop on Variability Modeling of Software-Intensive Systems, VaMoS 2011, pp. 11–20. ACM, New York (2011). https://doi.org/10.1145/1944892.1944894

19. Segura, S., Benavides, D., Cortés, A.R.: Functional testing of feature model analysis tools. A first step. In: 12th International Conference Software Product Lines, Proceedings, Second Volume (Workshops), SPLC 2008, Limerick, Ireland, 8–12 September 2008, p. 179 (2008)

20. Sree-Kumar, A., Planas, E., Clariso, R.: Analysis of feature models using alloy: a survey. In: Proceedings 7th International Workshop on Formal Methods and Analysis in Software Product Line Engineering, FMSPLE@ETAPS 2016, Eindhoven, The Netherlands, 3 April 2016, pp. 46–60 (2016). https://doi.org/10.4204/EPTCS.206.5

21. Wohlin, C., Runeson, P., Hst, M., Ohlsson, M., Regnell, B., Wessln, A.: Experimentation in Software Engineering. Springer, Heidelberg (2012)

22. Zaid, L., Kleinermann, F., Troyer, O.D.: Applying semantic web technology to feature modeling. In: Proceedings of the 2009 ACM Symposium on Applied Computing, SAC 2009, pp. 1252–1256. ACM, New York (2009). https://doi.org/10.1145/1529282.1529563

Service Discovery Based on Social Profiles of Objects in a Social IoT Network

Iury Araújo$^{(\boxtimes)}$, Mikaelly F. Pedrosa, Jessica Castro, Eudisley G. dos Anjos, and Fernando Matos

Informatics Center - Federal University of Paraíba (UFPB),
João Pessoa, PB 58051900, Brazil
{iuryrogerio,jessicamaciel}@ppgi.ci.ufpb.br,
mikaelly.felicio@cc.ci.ufpb.br, {eudisley, fernando}@ci.ufpb.br

Abstract. The service interaction provided by objects in IoT networks enables the creation of advanced services to answer application requests. However, the growing number of objects into the IoT network, besides its ad hoc structure, are disturbing some functionalities, such as service discovery. Therefore, when searching for services, the navigability is impaired because the system needs to sweep a great quantity of objects without a previous organization. Social Internet of Things (SIoT) emerged as an alternative to solve several problems faced by IoT through the concept of social networks. In SIoT each object has its own social profile, which contains its characteristics and information, and are organized by relationships. Thus, this research propose a solution for service discovery in a SIoT network. This solution uses the relationships between objects to improve the discovery scalability and considers their social profiles to meet the requisitions in a more satisfactorily way. Simulated results demonstrates the solution performance to answer service requisitions in an urban SIoT network.

Keywords: Social Internet of Things · Social network · Service discovery

1   Introduction

Urban spaces are each day more crowded, causing a variety of problems related to the quality of life, such as increased pollution, resource shortage, limited access of public services, urban mobility and security [14]. Thereby, intelligent solutions for these problems are always in great demand, which, using technology, are most likely to solve or mitigate problems caused by urban expansion. A large amount of these solutions are developed using the concept of smart environments, defined as a "small world" where different types of smart objects work together to improve the life of its inhabitants [17]. This concept has fomented many research areas, for instance, smart cities, smart healthcare, smart grid, that despite their differences, they have in common the performance of several smart

S. Misra et al. (Eds.): ICCSA 2019, LNCS 11623, pp. 400–414, 2019.
https://doi.org/10.1007/978-3-030-24308-1_33

objects working together to accomplish many tasks. Increasingly, these objects acquire the capacity to connect to the internet, whether to perform actions, gather, send or process data. This capability facilitates collaboration between objects, thus providing greater functionality for applications [16].

The smart environment scenario is possible through the implementation of the Internet of Things (IoT) paradigm. IoT is described as the pervasive presence around us of "things" or objects, which over unique address schemes, are allowed to interact between them and collaborate to achieve a specific goal [3]. These objects are the technological devices of our daily life, such as computers, tablets, smartphones, sensor nodes and so forth. However, the growing number of connected objects is a concern for IoT. According to [9], the number of connected objects is already larger than the world population and will reach fifty billions until 2020. This increase directly affects the network management regarding its scalability, navigability and the heterogeneity of the objects, making it difficult to perform important paradigm tasks [12].

Service management is also hampered by the increase in the number of objects. Because an object can provide one or more services, the total number of services in a network may increase greatly. Such services are abstractions of functionalities offered by objects, without worrying about the technologies or protocols. IoT architecture components that handle services, such as discovery and service composition, suffer directly from these problems. As a solution, a new paradigm was proposed, which uses the concept of social networks to organize the objects and their services, called Social Internet of Things (SIoT) [5].

SIoT introduces the use of a social network for the organization of objects, in which each object has the potential to form "friendships" with others objects through relationships [4]. From the social network generated it is possible to manage the scalability and navigability of the network, the heterogeneity of objects and the transmission of data, as is already done by human social networks [2]. Although SIoT inherits IoT features, most of them need to be adapted to handle with this new paradigm, for instance the service discovery, which is a key feature to attend applications through the discovery of services that can be later can be compound to perform complex activities. Another challenge is to use the social profile of objects as useful information, as a way to improve SIoT network features.

In this paper we propose a service discovery in a SIoT network based on social profiles (Social Profile Search - SPS). In this discovery we use the social network's relationships to improve its navigability and scalability, considering also the information and characteristics contained into social profiles of objects to improve the service requisition satisfaction level. To verify the efficiency of the solution, tests were performed with data from an urban SIoT network, comparing the results between SPS and conventional literature solutions.

This paper is organized as follows. Section 2 exposes a overview of researches in SIoT field, including their approaches to service discovery and the social profile. Section 3 discuss concepts of SIoT and its service discovery. In Sect. 4 is presented this paper proposal for a service discovery based on social profiles.

Section 5 discourse about the proposal implementation, describes the tests carried out and presents and discusses the results achieved. At last, Sect. 6 concludes this paper and discuss future researches.

2 Related Work

Because it is a relatively recent area, most SIoT works focus on conceptual issues of the paradigm, such as, SIoT definitions, applicability, necessary infrastructures and proposed architectures. A small number of researches present paradigm implementations. Nevertheless, some researches focus on the social capacity of objects, using their characteristics, information and the potential of the interactions to provide solutions for the management of objects and services. The works that will be presented, also are concerned with the SIoT network functionalities regarding, explicitly or implicitly, the service discovery.

The SIoTCampus proposed by [1] exemplifies the use of SIoT for the dissemination of academic information among users of a university campus. this work proposes an exclusive smart objects network in which context information, such as location, calendar, user, etc., are used as criteria for establishing relationships between objects. As the social network has dynamic relationships, which can be modified through the acquisition of information from the owner of the object, it is possible to propagate information, events and news through the network to a greater number of users interested on that context.

A possibility proposed by the SIoT is to adopt the objects' social network as a tool to ascertain the trustworthiness of an object. The research performed in [7] attempts to construct a network within a medical environment so that objects can transmit and receive hospital system data securely, identifying the reliability level of objects and blocking attacks. Trustworthiness identified through the creation of a trustworthiness management protocol, which uses the relationships and information of the objects to determine their trustworthiness level. In [18] also is proposed a model that verifies the trustworthiness of objects in SIoT, being based on the collective work of objects that provide computational and storage operations. In this model, tasks are sent to objects and serving them, a reward is given to objects, thus helping to create relationships and establish trustworthiness between objects that cooperate frequently with each other.

The research developed in [15] presents a solution for the implementation of a SIoT architecture service discovery. Using the relationships built by the social network's objects it is possible to create a discovery method that with a small number of hops in a network implemented as graph, find objects which provide the required services. This is accomplished using two properties: the first is intrinsic to the social network, based on object friendships; the second is external to the social network, based on the similarity between the object and the request.

In [8] is proposed the creation of a method for service composition in SIoT using the relationships formed by the objects in the social network. The method encapsulates heterogeneous objects as web. Using the RESTful style, applications may require homogeneous access to objects, allowing collaboration between them to compose more robust processes services. Composition is possible through the modeling of relationships between services over the social network, classifying relationships in three dimensions: location, type and correlation. When requesting a complex process, which needs to be composed of several services, the component performs a search throughout the social network using its three relationships to find the candidate services. These candidates are then evaluated and the best ones are compound into the required process. The work also proposes a service discovery algorithm used to find object services using the breadth-first search for graphs.

Through the works exposed in this section it is possible to notice that there are researches concerned with addressing the social capacity of objects, using its characteristics, information and the potential of their interactions to provide solutions for SIoT applications, especially within the context of smart environment. Likewise, there is a growing concern about creating SIoT functionalities that fit the use of social network, being the service discovery one of them. Therefore, this work presents the proposal of a SIoT service discovery method based on the information and characteristics, from social profiles of objects, to improve its efficiency. Differing from other solutions by restricting the need to sweep the entire network to find the appropriate services required.

3   SIoT Service Discovery

Social Internet of Things (SIoT) is a paradigm derived from the IoT that proposes the use of social networks in conjunction with the well-established IoT infrastructure. The use of the concept of social networks in IoT can lead to great advantages, such as: (i) SIoT structure can be shaped to ensure the navigability of the network, allowing efficient discovery of services and objects; (ii) the trustworthiness of objects can be determined by analyzing the interaction with their "friend" objects and models used to study social networks can be easily applied to address problems related to IoT [5]. The formalized concept of SIoT determines it as a social network where each node is a smart object capable of establishing relationships, autonomously, with other objects, following rules established by its owners [10].

A relationship in SIoT is the representation of a bond that objects can have in the real world, being this representation used for the construction of the social network through the formation of friend objects that are linked by relationships. The researches in SIoT establish five types of relationships that can exist between the objects [4,5,10]: (i) *Parental*: established between objects belonging to the same production batch, are usually homogeneous objects, originated in the same period and by the same manufacturer; (ii) *Co-location*: established between objects that are always used in the same place, in the case of sensors, actuators and objects of augmented reality are considered objects in the same environment as a house or smart city; (iii) *Co-work*: established when objects cooperate to provide certain functionality; (iv) *Ownership*: established between heterogeneous or homogeneous objects that belong to the same user; and (v) *Social*:

established when objects come in contact, continuous or sporadic, because their owners came in contact during some period of their lives.

SIoT objects are organized through a social network of objects, used in several processes of the paradigm, such as service composition and discovery. The social network is composed of representations of the physical existence of objects in the network, called social profiles. Each profile, contains attributes related to the object it represents, such as its identification, the friends formed by its relationships with other objects, the services it offers, its characteristics and information [11]. Characteristics of an object are the data inherent to its constitution and are generally immutable, for example its manufacturer, production batch, number of processing cores and primary and secondary memory, among others. While, the information of an object is data on the object that are constantly changing, such as storage capacity, battery status, object trustworthiness, security settings, among others [13].

The service discovery generally used in the literature, such as Chen et al. [8], uses only the relationships to search the network for objects that have services that satisfy the requests. Due to the peculiarity of such relationships, the search results may be different for the same objects. Figure 1 presents an example of how different relationships affect the discovery in SIoT networks. Each social profile is represented by a node and each edge identifies a relation of friendship between objects. The relationships *Ownership* and *Co-work* (Figs. 1(a) and (b), respectively) are used as examples. When a request is sent to the discovery component, it identifies the object that requested the service (requester) and makes it the initial search object. This is possible because any requester is an object that is part of the social network. In both figures, the requester is the object D. From the requester, the discovery method seeks to know if the services it offers meet the request. Each color represents the set of objects accessed at each search level. In the Fig. 1(a), from D, your friends, which are the objects B, C, D and G, are searched. Search continues on friends of previous objects (A, F, H, I, L and O), thus continuing until the discovery has covered all the objects in the network. Same process occur in Fig. 1(b), where the discovery is performed using a different relationship. In this case, it is possible to visualize that the result will be different, since there is no Co-work relationship between objects (N, M, I) and the rest of the network.

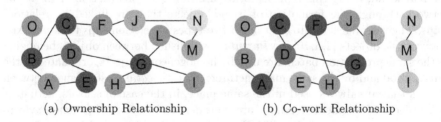

(a) Ownership Relationship   (b) Co-work Relationship

Fig. 1. Graphs representing SIoT network relationships. (Color figure online)

In both cases, the service discovery is performed by the breadth-first search for graphs, which checks all objects in the social network to find the services that best serve the request. This approach returns all the services that can fulfill the request, including several services that perform the same activities or do not meet the requirements of other SIoT network functionalities. Therefore, an additional step to filter services is required. Such step may compromise the performance of the application performing the request.

4   Social Profile Search - SPS

The SPS discovery method proposed in this work uses the characteristics and information contained in the social profiles of the objects as additional comparison criteria to verify if the services of an object, and itself, meet the request requirements. The SPS also introduces a new stopping condition for the breadth-first search, once all requested services are found, regardless of the number of objects visited, the search is interrupted. In addition, as in the breadth-first search, the SPS also ends its execution when all objects in the network have already been searched. Thus, the method ensures that a satisfying response to the request can be found in less time, balancing the quality of the services found and the search time, however leaving open the possibility of the worst case scenario, that happens when it is not possible to find in the network all the services to fulfill such request.

Figure 2 presents the request message that is received by the SPS, which is formed by three attributes: (i) Requester object (RO), containing the identification of the object that requested the search; (ii) Service List (SL), containing the required services that will be searched by SPS; and (iii) Requirements List (RL), containing requirements that will be verified and must be met by the characteristics and information of the objects, for instance, type of transmission technology, amount of memory, trustworthiness of the object, among others.

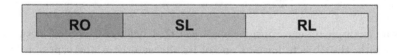

Fig. 2. Service discovery request and their attributes.

In Fig. 3 the SPS process is illustrated in a network with seven objects that receives a service discovery request. As any object that requires a service discovery is also part of the social network of objects, the SPS uses the requester social profile in the network as the initial object of the search. With the other attributes of the request, the SPS begins to verify if the friends of object A have the requested services (Fig. 3(b)). The initial object A is marked as not selected, because it either does not have the services sought or does not meet all imposed requirements, even if it has the required service. When checking the objects B and D, SPS realizes that the two have required services and that they meet all the requirements, so their identifications are added to a list with the possible result. As all required services were not found the search is expanded to the objects F and C (Fig. 3(c)), that having the missing services and meeting the requirements, complete the execution of the search.

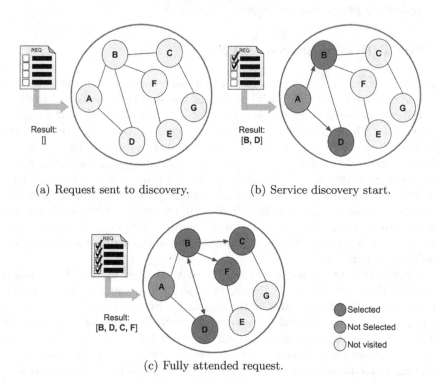

(a) Request sent to discovery.   (b) Service discovery start.

(c) Fully attended request.

Fig. 3. Operation of the SPS method.

As an example we can consider an object that belongs to a SIoT network. In this network, the objects have as one of its characteristic, the types of wireless connections them can perform, such as bluetooth, 3G, GSM and Wi-Fi, being allowed to have any combination of these four connections. This object has only the ability to connect over Wi-Fi, while the discovery request calls for object services that can communicate over Wi-Fi and 3G, even if this object has a service that meets the request, it will not be considered since it does not meet the minimum discovery requirements. This type of approach facilitates the manipulation of the discovery results for other SIoT network functionalities, like the composition of services, since it guarantees that the services found do not have to undergo a new requirement check evaluation.

Algorithm 1 describes the SPS service discovery method considering the profiles of objects. The request is treated as three separate blocks, (i) required service list (*required_service_list*) which represents the list containing the services must be found; (ii) requirement list (*requirement_list*) which contains all the minimum requirements that objects must attend; and requester (iii) (*requester*) which will be used as the starting point of the SIoT network discovery. In addition to the request, the algorithm also receives as input the social network (*social_network*), containing all social profiles of objects in the network.

Algorithm 1. Service Discovery Based on Social Profiles (SPS)

Input: *required_service_list*, *requirement_list*, *requester*, *social_network*
Output: *service_list*

Require: *requester* must be an object belonging to the social network
 1: *search_list*.add(*social_network*.retrieve(*requester*))
 2: **while** search_list is not empty **do**
 3:     *head* ← *search_list*.removeHead()
 4:     **if** *required_service_list* was met **then**
 5:         **break**
 6:     **else**
 7:         **if** *head*.visualized = **true then**
 8:             **continue**
 9:         **else if** *head* met *required_service_list* **and** *head* met *requirement_list* **then**
10:             *service_list*.add(*head*.services())
11:         **end if**
12:     **end if**
13:     *head*.visualized ← **true**
14:     *search_list*.add(*social_network*.retrieveFriends(*head*))
15: **end while**
16: **return** *service_list*

Initially, the SPS adds the social profile of the requesting object to *search_list* and then initiates the loop by searching services over the entire network until the *required_service_list* has been completely met or *search_list* is empty. For each object removed from the list *search_list*, and added to *head*, is verified that the social profile has already been searched (line 7). If so, the next object is checked. If not, it is checked whether one or more of *head* correspond to the services required in *required_service_list* and if that object meets the minimum requirements established in *requirement_list* (line 9). Services that meet both conditions are added to *service_list* (line 10). The SPS then marks the social profile contained in *head* as already seen and add its friends to *search_list* (line 14), starting the process again. When the algorithm finishes its execution by one of the two stopping conditions, the found services are delivered as request response. The end result of the SPS allows three different states, (i) find no service that meets the request, (ii) find only some services, thus partially meeting the request, or (iii) find all services in order to meet the request.

5   Test Environment and Evaluation

The SPS method was implemented in Python and tested using the dataset of an urban SIoT network provided by [6]. which was created in the context of the SmartSantander project and executed in the cities of Belgrade, Guildford, Lübeck and Santander, however, the only available dataset is the one from the city of Santander.

The dataset consists of 16216 devices (objects of the social network) of various technologies. It provides information about social network relationships and the services that each object offers. The services are represented by numbers that indicate some service that the object can provide, and each object can have up to eight different types of services out of a total of sixteen. Because the dataset does not work with the services being unique entities, with their own identification, the SPS was implemented with a minor change, that instead of returning the services encountered, the objects that provide them are returned. The dataset presents object relationships through matrices with Boolean values, that represent the existence, or otherwise, of a friendship between objects. The ownership relationship was used to carry out the tests of this work. Figure 4 illustrates the organization of a relationship matrix where the number one identifies a friendship between two objects. For example, objects (A, C) and (E, F) are friends because the intersection of their columns and rows have one as value.

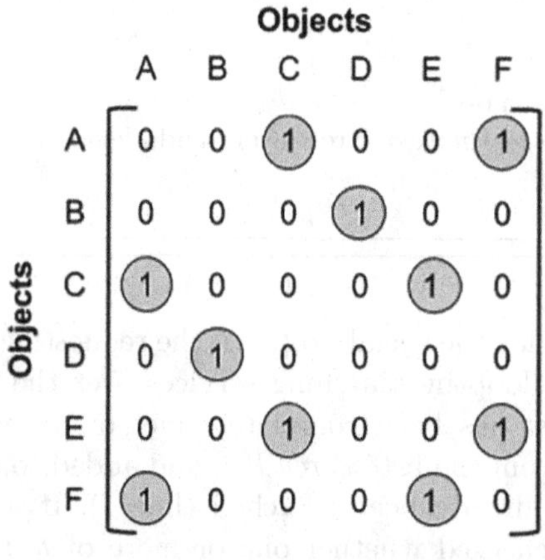

Fig. 4. Dataset relationship matrix.

To verify the efficiency of the SPS, two metrics were used: search time and solution scalability. The search time is the time that the algorithm takes to respond to the request, being calculated from the moment that the algorithm begins to consult the social network to find services until the moment the list of found objects is returned. Scalability evaluates the behavior of the solution as the number of objects in the network increases. The tests were carried out on a machine with a i7-8750H hexa-core of 2666 MHz processor and 16 GB of DDR4 RAM memory.

The SPS was compared with the algorithm proposed by Chen et al. [8], that uses the breadth-first search method. To test the search time, a file was created containing all the requests that were made during the tests. The use of the file guarantees that the requests realized in the method SPS were identical to those realized in Chen. Each line of the file represents a request, containing the following information: the requesting object, the services to be found and the requirements that will be used by the search. This latter information is only used by the SPS method.

Each attribute of the request was generated randomly obeying certain minimum and maximum values. The requesting object is necessarily an object belonging to the network. The desired services are generated from a list of sixteen possible dataset services. Of those, four are chosen to form the desired services of each request, in way that an already chosen service can not be chosen again. To generate the requirements, it was necessary to first create the social profiles for the dataset objects, defining what characteristics and information would be associated with the profile and would become its attributes, these, can be observed in the Table 1. The next step was to fill in the attributes contained in the social profiles, following the allowed values in the Table 1. Finally, the requirements were generated and added to the request, which are based on the social profiles attributes. Random initial values were used for each requirement, respecting certain limits imposed in Table 1. In total, 2380 requisitions were created for the tests.

Table 1. Social profiles attributes and requisition requirements.

Attributes	Minimum value	Maximum value
Primary memory	256 MB	4 GB
Secondary memory	0 MB	512000 MB
Processing cores	1	8
Connectivity	1	5
Storage capacity	15%	75%
Battery status	10%	100%
Trustworthiness	45	95

The scalability test should check how the solution behaves by increasing the number of network objects. To accomplish this, it was necessary to divide the network into several samplings representing networks of varying sizes, consisting of five hundred, a thousand, two thousand, four thousand, twelve thousand and sixteen thousand objects. These samplings must obey the probability distribution of the object types present in the initial dataset. Table 2 displays the percentages for each type of device.

Table 2. Distribution of device types in dataset.

Device type	Percentage
Smartphone	22.45%
Personal computer	20.72%
Car	13.57%
Printer	13.07%
Tablet	9.87%
Smart fitness	5.43%
Parking	4.17%
Home sensors	3.70%
Street light	3.12%
Smartwatch	1.23%
Transportation	0.88%
Environment and weather sensors	0.86%
Point of interest	0.58%
Alarms	0.23%
Indicator	0.06%
Garbage truck	0.04%

Once it was guaranteed that the samplings had the same distribution as the original dataset, it was necessary to deal with another problem caused by the samplings. The randomness choice of objects makes it difficult for objects having relationships to be chosen together, especially for small-sized samplings. This situation impairs the navigability and makes it difficult to perform the search, since it is possible that there are several objects or groups of them isolated in the network. As a solution, it was necessary to manually add new relationships, so that all social profiles have at least one relationship with another object of the same sampling, thus guaranteeing the navigability of the network.

5.1 Results

Ten executions were performed for each network sampling using the SPS and Chen algorithms. For each test the median search time of the 2380 requisitions was calculated, the median was used as a way to prevent outliers from impacting the results. Then, the mean of all the test medians of a sampling were calculated. The Table 3 displays the median of the search time, in seconds, of each sampling. Analyzing the values, it is possible to notice that the SPS algorithm can respond to the requests of all the samplings at a time significantly lower than the algorithm of Chen. This behavior can be seen mainly in sampling 4000 and 8000, where the SPS search time is less 93.98% and 94.32% than Chen, respectively.

Some surprises were observed during the comparison of the search times between the algorithms, being this comparison shown in Fig. 5. Among the 500

Table 3. Search time median, in seconds, for each request in the test samplings.

Samplings (n°of objects)	Chen (s)	SPS (s)
500	0,02594487	0,01072197
1000	0,10345836	0,01405903
2000	0,38549267	0,03829563
4000	1,37108796	0,08257948
8000	4,28259313	0,2434388
12000	0,56687746	0,00898465
16000	0,00587981	0,00399698

to 8000 samplings it is possible to notice that there is a growth in the average time needed for a request to be answered, and this behavior is already expected with the increase of objects in the social network. However, in the 12000 and 16000 samplings we have a totally reverse effect with an abrupt decrease in search time. For example, in the 12000 sampling, the Chen algorithm has a time reduction at the rate of 86.76%, while the SPS has a time reduction of 96.30%.

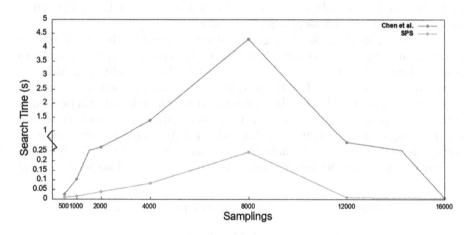

Fig. 5. Comparative graph of search time behavior in algorithms Chen et al. and SPS.

One of the possibilities for this behavior is that adding new objects has created a much more connected network, making it easier for the algorithms to reach objects that previously had few relationships and were more isolated. Another possibility is the randomness used to create relationships and to choose objects from the network have made its operation more complex. A great indication would be the fact that most of the changes made in the network were made in the smaller samplings, from 500 to 8000, while few changes were made at 12000 and even less at 16000. This being the case, these results can be a clear testimony to the efficiency of SIoT solutions, because the smaller the change in the original network, provided by [6], the better its efficiency.

When comparing the algorithms' execution through the analysis of Fig. 5 it is easy to see how the SPS can keep the search time much lower than the algorithm Chen et al., being generally 94.03% faster and taking no more than 0.25 s, on average, to respond to a request. Another important aspect to be observed and analyzed is the algorithms' behavior regarding the network scalability. Obviously 16000 objects are still a very small number to test the scalability of these algorithms in a network that today already bears billions of objects. However, indications that the SPS algorithm is scalable can be observed through the controlled search time increase in relation to the expansion of the number of objects in the network and also of the expressive fall of it in larger samplings.

In contrast to SPS, Chen et al. has a search time increase well accented until the sampling 8000, where it then decrease to values very close to those of the SPS. Although there is a suggestion that Chen et al. is not scalable, the observed results show that it is necessary to verify this algorithm's behavior with an even larger number of objects per sampling to have a final verdict. However, it is possible to affirm that the solution proposed in this work through the SPS algorithm was more scalable than the method proposed by Chen et al. [8]. Other key information indicated by the tests presented in Fig. 5 is the need to verify how the organization of social profiles and their relationships affect service discovery algorithms in a SIoT network.

The Table 4 displays the average of objects returned in the search in each sampling. It is possible to observe that the number of objects returned by Chen is much larger than that of SPS (on average 99.09% more objects). Although Chen's method can always find the best services for each request, an additional step is still required to choose which objects, among those found, will be used to satisfy the requisition, which can impact the performance of the application that is performing such request. In SPS, this additional step is not required, since the method returns, as soon as it finds, the necessary objects to completely satisfy the request. Thus, in addition to a faster search time, the SPS shows that it can

Table 4. Average number of objects returned per request.

Sampling (nº of objects)	Chen	SPS
500	344	3
1000	679	5
2000	1340	8
4000	2459	17
8000	3502	37
12000	3789	42
16000	4102	39

more satisfactorily fulfill service discovery requests by taking into account the network social profiles of objects.

6   Conclusion

This work proposed a solution for a more efficient service discovery in a SIoT network, using the characteristics and information contained in the object social profile to attend the discovery requests more satisfactorily. For this purpose a service search method, called SPS, was proposed from the modification of a breadth-first search for graphs. The SPS adds a new stopping condition to improve discovery efficiency and inserts the use of the characteristics and information of the object social profile to verify the quality of the found services.

Simulated tests using the dataset of an urban SIoT network verified that the SPS algorithm performs a service search, 94.03% on average, faster than the method proposed in the literature. Similarly, the results of these tests also indicate a good adaptability of the SPS to deal not only with the increase in the number of objects in the network, but also with the complexity of its organization. The tests also indicated that there is a need to study how the relationships between objects are being formed in the social network, being one of the points that can lead to improvements in the efficiency and effectiveness of service discovery algorithms in SIoT.

As future works, new tests will be performed to determine the behavior of the SPS with more varied requests, containing a greater number of services required and also a greater variation of the characteristics presented. Another test that should be essentially performed is the verification of the behavior of service discovery algorithms when dealing with the different types of possible relationships in a SIoT network, identifying if there is a specific search order among these relationships that benefits the service discovery. In addition to the tests it is possible to focus efforts on the construction of other functionalities of the SIoT network that depend directly on the service discovery, as methods of social network management and service composition. Other future work can be done by identifying other service discovery strategies used in the Internet of Things and verifying the possibility of adapting them to the SIoT discovery, including methods based on artificial intelligence.

References

1. Alves, T.M., da Costa, C.A., da Rosa Righi, R., Barbosa, J.L.V.: Exploring the social Internet of Things concept in a university campus using NFC. In: 2015 Latin American Computing Conference (CLEI), pp. 1–12. IEEE, October 2015
2. Atzori, L., Carboni, D., Iera, A.: Smart things in the social loop: paradigms, technologies, and potentials. Ad Hoc Netw. **18**, 121–132 (2014)
3. Atzori, L., Iera, A., Morabito, G.: The Internet of Things: a survey. Comput. Netw. **54**(15), 2787–2805 (2010)
4. Atzori, L., Iera, A., Morabito, G.: SIoT: giving a social structure to the Internet of Things. IEEE Commun. Lett. **15**(11), 1193–1195 (2011)

5. Atzori, L., Iera, A., Morabito, G., Nitti, M.: The Social Internet of Things (SIoT)-when social networks meet the Internet of Things: concept, architecture and network characterization. Computer Netw. **56**(16), 3594–3608 (2012)
6. Atzori, L., Nitti, M., Marche, C.: Social Internet of Things (2016). http://www.social-iot.org/index.php?p=downloads. Accessed 28 Mar 2019
7. Brittes, M.P., Schneider Jr., B., Wille, E.C.: Trustworthiness management through social relationships in Internet of medical Things. J. Commun. Inf. Syst. **32**(1) (2017)
8. Chen, G., Huang, J., Cheng, B., Chen, J.: A social network based approach for IoT device management and service composition. In: 2015 IEEE World Congress on Services, pp. 1–8. IEEE, June 2015
9. Evans, D.: The Internet of Things: how the next evolution of the internet is changing everything. CISCO White Pap. **1**(2011), 1–11 (2011)
10. Girau, R., Martis, S., Atzori, L.: Lysis: a platform for IoT distributed applications over socially connected objects. IEEE Internet Things J. **4**(1), 40–51 (2017)
11. Jadhav, B., Patil, S.C.: Wireless home monitoring using social Internet of Things (SIoT). In: 2016 International Conference on Automatic Control and Dynamic Optimization Techniques (ICACDOT), pp. 925–929. IEEE, September 2016
12. Jarwar, M., Kibria, M., Ali, S., Chong, I.: Microservices in web objects enabled iot environment for enhancing reusability. Sensors **18**(2), 352 (2018)
13. Kim, J.E., Fan, X., Mosse, D.: Empowering end users for social Internet of Things. In: Proceedings of the Second International Conference on Internet-of-Things Design and Implementation, pp. 71–82. ACM, April 2017
14. Neves, A.R.D.M., Sarmanho, K.U., Nascimento Jr., F.C., Meiguins, B.S.: Iniciativa Smart Campus: um estudo de caso em progresso na Universidade Federal do Pará. In: Anais do I Workshop de Computação Urbana (COURB 2017), vol. 1, no. 1/2017. SBC, May 2017
15. Nitti, M., Pilloni, V., Giusto, D.D.: Searching the social Internet of Things by exploiting object similarity. In: 2016 IEEE 3rd World Forum on Internet of Things (WF-IoT), pp. 371–376. IEEE, December 2016
16. Santos, B.P., et al.: Internet das coisas: da teoria à prática. Minicursos SBRC-Simpósio Brasileiro de Redes de Computadores e Sistemas Distribuidos (2016)
17. Vodanovich, S., Sundaram, D., Myers, M.: Research commentary–digital natives and ubiquitous information systems. Inf. Syst. Res. **21**(4), 711–723 (2010)
18. Wang, K., Qi, X., Shu, L., Deng, D.J., Rodrigues, J.J.: Toward trustworthy crowdsourcing in the social Internet of Things. IEEE Wirel. Commun. **23**(5), 30–36 (2016)

Guidelines for Architecture Design
of Software Product Line

Jeong Ah Kim[1], DongGi Kim[1(✉)], and JinSeok Yang[2]

[1] Department of Computer Education, Catholic Kwandong University,
Beomll Ro 579 24, Gangneung, Kangwon, Korea
clara@cku.ac.kr, remaindk0@gmail.com
[2] 18F, 145, Gasan digital 1-ro, Geumcheon-gu, Seoul, Korea

Abstract. Product Line Architecture design is a key activity for developing successful Software Product Line projects. But it is difficult and complex task since architecture of software product line should be considered with variability. In this research, we addressed detail guidelines for identifying the component of architecture from the feature model and defining the variability of component in concerns of feature.

Keywords: Software development · Product-line architecture design ·
Logical component modeling · Guidelines

1 Introduction

The objectives of traditional software development are to define, design, and implement the requirements for a single software application to be developed, and to produce defect-free software. Although reuse framework was considered to efficiently conduct this process, only common technical modules or general-purpose algorithm modules, which are not related to the application field, were reusable. In other words, reuse for improving productivity in the developing process for a single application was considered. This type of reuse cannot secure reusable organizational assets in similar application fields for the future. The development that considers only a single software application will not be able to secure general-purpose assets that can be used in a specialized application field, because the diversity of customer, environment, and infrastructure technology cannot be considered in the development phase of a single software application. The construction of a product line is a process that creates the foundation on which one or more applications with diversity can be developed rather than a single application. Product-line engineering aims to create a customized product based on a product line in which the concept of systematic asset management at the organizational level is introduced [1]. From the developer's perspective, the existing development approach appears reproduced by reusing libraries or developing frameworks [2]. Furthermore, managers and developers many not know how to introduce this concept since they thing this is new development methodology. There are few existing researches that are organized into an independent and complete methodology in which the product-line engineering process can be implemented. Most research

© Springer Nature Switzerland AG 2019
S. Misra et al. (Eds.): ICCSA 2019, LNCS 11623, pp. 415–422, 2019.
https://doi.org/10.1007/978-3-030-24308-1_34

works focus on the existing single-system development methodology and the techniques that can be applied to other areas [3–8].

In this study, guidelines for modeling activities of a product-line architecture model included in the product-line architectural design stage are provided. A product-line architecture design model, a design guideline that considers the variabilities and a modeling method that uses a real unified modeling language (UML)-based modeling tool are defined herein to develop a product-line architecture model. Furthermore, a case model to which these models and methods are applied is presented.

2   Proposed Product-Line Architecture Design Model

A design model for the product-line architecture proposed is defined in this section. The model defines three different views, each of which contains information according to the design perspective and share a relationship with one another.

- Conceptual View: This view provides the logical components constituting the product-line architecture, the information of the structure, and the interaction in which the relationship between the logical components are defined.
- Execution View: This view provides the physical components (executable files or libraries) where the identified logical components and their dependency information are executed.
- Deployment View: This view provides information on the relationship between physical computing devices and nodes to which physical components can be deployed. It also provides information on the physical component instances that are deployed and run on the nodes.

2.1   Conceptual View

The model elements of a conceptual view include at least one logical component and an interface of that logical component. In addition, the conceptual view consists of a structural relationship between the logical components and an interaction relationship diagram between the interfaces of the logical components.

This view represents the logical components, which are logical elements necessary to meet the product line requirements including features, and the interfaces that are provided by those components. "Logical" in this context means that the implementation environment for the product line or technology is not considered. A logical component (hereinafter referred to as a component) indicates a software module capable of performing independent functions. It classifies complex software properly so that the relevant software is manageable, and hides the complexity and diversity of methods for the implemented interface. Through this feature, outdated components can be replaced by new components that have different implementation methods.

A component control interface is a set of operations that does not have an implementation body due to the agreement by the developers to allow it to interact with other components or applications. The operations defined in the component control interface are implemented by the component. Therefore, a single component can be a unit that implements multiple interfaces.

The component data interface defines the dataset needed for establishing interaction between components. The data interface defines the dataset that will be used by the logical components and does not define an operation that undertakes the data processing.

A component group logically binds components that are functionally related. However, this is not an essential element in the model. With component groups, an abstract hierarchy between the components can be represented. By using the component group, several components can be logically grouped together to simplify the complexity that can arise from the relationship between the individual components.

The conceptual view provides a component structure diagram that can schematize the relationship between the logical components, a component interaction diagram, and a component interface diagram.

On the one hand, the component structure diagram represents the dependency among the logical components, i.e., the structural association between the components.

On the other hand, the component interaction diagram sequentially represents the interaction between the logical components to meet specific requirements, using the interface implemented by those components.

Moreover, the component interface diagram represents the relationship between the interface implemented by the logical component and the logical component that uses the interface.

2.2 Execution View

An execution view has at least one physical component as a model element. It has a dependency diagram between physical components. The physical components identified in the execution view must be correlated with at least one logical component. More specifically, the physical component is divided into an executable component and a library component. The executable component indicates a component that has the same starting point as the main() function and, thus, can be executed independently, while the library component indicates a component that is called by an executable component during the execution and can be deployed independently. The execution view provides a physical component structure diagram that can be used to schematize the relationship between the declared physical components.

2.3 Deployment View

A deployment view has at least one computing device node as a model element. It also has a phase information diagram between the nodes. The identified node in the deployment view must have at least one physical component instance.

3 Guidelines for Applying Product-Line Architecture Design Model

3.1 Guidelines for Logical Component Modeling

- GUIDELINE1: It is divided into two types of logical components: a logical component with high cohesion and a logical component with low coupling. In other words, one logical component is identified using a unit that has logical cohesion, and it is then verified if the component has low coupling with other logical components. Such a component is identified as an independent unit. Hence, the requirements that have high mutual-functional relevance are grouped together, and the implementation of the function is assigned to one logical component.

- GUIDELINE2: The features having high mutual-functional relevance among the mandatory features are grouped together and the implementation of that function is assigned to one logical component.
- GUIDELINE3: The optional and alternative features are identified as independent logical components by separating them from the logical components that implement the mandatory features.
- GUIDELINE4: If there is a structural relationship between the features, and an optional feature in the child feature, then the logical component for the optional feature is identified independently. Furthermore, an association is established with the logical component that corresponds to the parent feature.
- GUIDELINE5: The logical components for the alternative features are independently identified when a structural relationship between the features and an alternative feature in the child feature is found. Moreover, the inheritance relationship is established with the logical component corresponding to the parent feature.
- GUIDELINE6: When a design is conducted using pattern styles, such as model-view-controller (MVC) and client-server (C/S), it is possible to identify for each element a corresponding logical component.
- GUIDELINE7: A two-level feature without any further sub-features is identified as a logical component. If all the features defined at third-level are mandatory features, then the features defined at two-level can be identified as logical components.
- GUIDELINE8: The logical components that correspond to the features defined at three-level are identified. The mandatory features defined in three-level can be grouped together and identified as one logical component, and the optional features can be grouped together and identified as another logical component.
- GUIDELINE9: The top-level feature of the functional feature is identified as a logical component, but the group feature is not. If there is a strong dependency between the top and bottom features among the functional features, then the bottom feature is not separated into an independent logical component. In this case, only the top functional feature is identified as a logical component.

3.2   Interface Structuring Guidelines

- GUIDELINE10: Among the operations that will be implemented by the logical component, those operations that will be provided to the outside of the product line, or to other components, are defined as control interfaces.
- GUIDELINE11: Among the operations provided by the logical component, those operations with different functions and characteristics are defined as independent interfaces.
- GUIDELINE12: Among data in the logical component, data that will be provided to other components is grouped into a dataset and is defined as a data interface.

- GUIDELINE13: One feature can be identified as a single control interface. However, if features among the mandatory features are grouped into one group, they can be identified as a single interface. In the case where there is an excess number of operations that need to be defined, it is desirable to divide the interface based on the feature. Although a reasonable number of operations included in the interface is academically defined from 7 to 9, it is recommended to define this number as being less than 15.
- GUIDELINE14: The interface corresponding to the variable feature must be identified independently from other interfaces. Inevitably, variable features are matched to the level of operation provided by the interface, but this is not recommended.

3.3 Physical Component Modeling Guidelines

- GUIDELINE15: The logical components with strong dependencies during the execution are grouped together and identified as one physical component, the independently executable logical components are identified as individual physical components, and are identified by considering the distribution units.
- GUIDELINE16: A physical component that executes mandatory features cannot be comprised of logical components that implement the optional feature alone.
- GUIDELINE17: In a real-time system, a task is modeled using executable components. In a general system, an application is modeled using an executable component.
- GUIDELINE18: All the components utilized by an executable component are modeled using library components.
- GUIDELINE19: The logical components that perform similar functions can be grouped together and identified as a single variable library component.
- GUIDELINE20: The name of a physical component can either be the same as the name of the logical component or controller, or can be added to the name.
- The dependency relationships among the identified physical components can be schematized into a structure diagram.

3.4 Node Modeling Guidelines

- GUIDELINE21: Product-line requirement-environment elements for hardware defined in the performance requirements specification are confirmed, and each hardware device is identified as a node.
- GUIDELINE22: An instance of the physical component defined by reviewing the quality requirements such as performance, stability, and reliability is assigned to a node.
- GUIDELINE23: At least one of the physical components to be deployed to the node must be a mandatory component.
- GUIDELINE24: If the cardinality value of the feature executed by the physical component is greater than 1, the physical component instances are assigned to different nodes according to the hardware specification and the number of identified nodes, to check whether the quality requirements such as performance can be satisfied.

4   Example of Application

4.1   An Example of Identifying Logical Components from Feature Models

Table 1 shows a list of identified logical components that have a level of variability similar to that of the first feature model and are functionally identifiable. Among the features with a level of variability similar to that of the first feature model, *Take-offControl*, *LandingControl*, *WeaponControlOperation*, *FlightScenarioPlanning*, *Login*, and *SensorOperation* are the variable features. Among these features, as logical components whose boundaries can be matched with the corresponding feature, *Land-ingController*, *TakeoffController*, *WeaponOperator*, and *LoginManager* are identified as independent logical components. The variability and feature traceability of the logical component groups and the logical components are modeled using Rhapsody's model element tag attributes. The generation of the model for variability and feature trace-ability can be conducted simultaneously by adding a new tag with a VAR name and describing it in a feature expression for the features associated with that value.

Table 1. Identified logical component

Logical component group	Logical component	Feature	Variability
FlightDeviceControlGroup	**LandingController**	LandingControl	OPT
	TakeoffController	TakeoffControl	OPT
	FlightController	FlightControl	MAN
CommunicationGroup	CommunicationInterface	Communication	MAN
SensorGroup	**DisplayViewer**	SensorOperation	OPT
		ImageDisplay	MAN
	ImageOperator	SensorOperation	OPT
		ImageOperation	MAN
	LDRFOperator	SensorOperation	OPT
		LDRFOperation	OPT
	ImageContrastAlgorLibrary	SensorOperation	OPT
		ImageContrastAlgor	ALT
WeaponControlGroup	**WeaponOperator**	WeaponControlOperation	OPT
FlightScenarioGroup	ScenarioFileManager	ScenarioFileManagement	MAN
	MissionPlanEditor	FlightScenarioPlanning	OPT
		MissionPlan	OPT
	FlightPlanEditor	FlightScenarioPlanning	OPT
		FlightPlan	OPT

4.2   Modeling Structural Relationship Between Logical Components

One or more UML class diagrams are used to define the structural relationships among the logical components. In the example, the dependencies among the logical compo-nent groups are modeled before the direct relationship among the logical components is modeled. As shown in the figure below, the relationship between the identified logical component groups is marked as dependency, and the data dependency is described. The generation of model of the structural relationships at the logical component-group level by abstracting the complexities of direct relationships among the logical components can enhance the understanding of the design.

4.3 Variability Modeling of Physical Components

The logical components assigned to the physical components in the example, and the corresponding variability of the physical components, are listed in Table 2. The variability of a physical component depends on the variability of a logical component assigned to that physical component. If one or more mandatory logical components are assigned to it, then the physical component cannot become a variable element. On the other hand, if all assigned logical components are optional design elements, then the physical component must become a variable element.

Table 2. Association between logical component and physical component

Physical component	Assigned logical component	Variability
GCSApplication	GCSApplication InterCoponentGateway ≪VP≫LoginManager	
ContrastAlgorLibrary	≪VP≫ImageContrastAlgorLibrary	≪VP≫
ImageDisplyer	≪VP≫DisplayViewer	≪VP≫
ScenarioEditor	≪VP≫FlightPlanEditor ≪VP≫MissionPlanEditor ScenarioFileManager	
SensorImageOperator	≪VP≫ImageOperator ≪VP≫LDRFOperator	≪VP≫
WeaponController	≪VP≫WeaponOperator	≪VP≫
Communicator	CommunicationInterface	
FlightDeviceController	FlightController ≪VP≫LandingController ≪VP≫TakeoffController	

According to the physical model's variability modeling rules, ContrastAlgorLibrary, ImageDisplayer, ScenarioEditor, SensorImageOperator, and WeaponController physical components could be specified as variable elements.

5 Conclusion

In this paper, three views and models for constructing a product-line architecture and specific construction guidelines are presented. The conceptual view allowed to define the logical units that make up the product-line architecture and the relationships among them. The guidelines for identifying logical units based on feature models are presented. The execution view allowed to define the execution information of the logical unit and suggested guidelines for distinguishing physical components from logical components. In the deployment view, the relationship between the execution device and the physical component could be defined, and, part of the execution device, the criteria for identifying nodes was suggested. In this study, the modeling guidelines are suggested to establish feature-based traceability, which is essential for successful product-line engineering, and the traceability among models was suggested to be defined naturally and by stages. To confirm its effectiveness, the guidelines were applied to a GCS (Ground Control System) example. Although not applied to all examples, a novice engineer who built the product line for the first time proved that it was possible to apply the process more systematically according to the guidelines based on the model, which is a byproduct of the previous stage.

References

1. Bosch, J.: Software product lines and software architecture design. In: Proceedings - International Conference on Software Engineering, January 2001
2. Matinlassi, M.: Comparison of software product line architecture design methods: COPA, FAST, FORM, KobrA and QADA. In: Proceeding ICSE 2004, Proceedings of the 26th International Conference on Software Engineering, pp. 127–136 (2004)
3. Gomaa, H.: Designing Software Product Lines with UML: From Use Cases to Pattern-Based Software Architectures. Addison-Wesley Professional, Boston (2004)
4. Capilla, R., Ali Babar, M.: On the role of architectural design decisions in software product line engineering. In: Morrison, R., Balasubramaniam, D., Falkner, K. (eds.) ECSA 2008. LNCS, vol. 5292, pp. 241–255. Springer, Heidelberg (2008). https://doi.org/10.1007/978-3-540-88030-1_18
5. Tekinerdoganm, B., Cetin, S., Savcı, F.: Exploring architecture design alternatives for global software product line engineering. In: Proceedings of 6th International Conference on Software Engineering Advances, pp. 515–521 (2011)
6. Chaudhary, A., Verma, B.K., Raheja, J.L.: Product line development architectural model. In: Proceedings of the 3rd IEEE International Conference on Computer Science and Information Technology, pp. 749–753 (2010)
7. Gharibi, G., Zheng, Y.: ArchFeature: a modeling environment integrating features into product line architecture. In: Proceedings of 31st Annual ACM Symposium (2016)
8. Lima, C., Chavez, C.: A systematic review on metamodels to support product line architecture design. In: Proceedings of SBES 2016, Proceedings of the 30th Brazilian Symposium on Software Engineering, pp. 12–22 (2016)

HOG Based Facial Recognition Approach Using Viola Jones Algorithm and Extreme Learning Machine

Khushwant Sehra[1], Ankit Rajpal[2($\boxtimes$)], Anurag Mishra[2], and Girija Chetty[3]

[1] University School of Information, Communication and Technology, Guru Gobind Singh Indraprastha University, New Delhi 110078, India
[2] Deen Dayal Upadhyaya College, University of Delhi, New Delhi 110078, India
ankit30sep@gmail.com
[3] Faculty of Science and Technology, University of Canberra, Bruce, ACT 1617, Australia

Abstract. Extreme Learning Machine has attracted widespread attention for its exemplary performance in solving regression and classification problems. It is a type of single layer feed-forward neural machine which relies on randomly allocating the input weights and hidden layer biases. Through this, the ELM has been found to possess running time spans which are within millisecond regime. It does not require complex controlling parameters which makes its implementation elementary. This paper investigates the performance of employing Extreme Learning Machine as a classifier to be used for the face recognition problem. Viola Jones algorithm has been employed to detect and extract the faces from the dataset. Finally, Histogram of Oriented Gradients (HOG) features are extracted which form the basis of classification. The scheme so presented has been tested on standard face recognition datasets from AT&T and YALE. The resulting training/testing time spans of the whole scheme range from milliseconds to seconds, dictating the compatibility of ELM with real-time events.

1 Introduction

The advent of facial recognition in the field of pattern recognition has found a great range of applicability especially for the purpose of cyber investigations. This has been possible due to the progressions made in the analysis and modelling techniques. Increased demand for secured systems has led the researchers to find solutions in terms of accessing control, verifying identities, securing cyber physical systems, internet communications, computer entertainment and establishing surveillance systems that are sturdy and impenetrable [1–3].

Alongside automatic facial recognition systems, automatic processing of digitalized content (like videos and images) has also been achieved due to the low-cost computing systems. As manipulations with identity cards and encroachments into the virtual/ physical areas were creating a nuance, it was realized that there was a dire need to have systems that were reliable and could recognize individuals accurately. A number of

© Springer Nature Switzerland AG 2019
S. Misra et al. (Eds.): ICCSA 2019, LNCS 11623, pp. 423–435, 2019.
https://doi.org/10.1007/978-3-030-24308-1_35

advancements were made including biometric authentication, computer-human inter-actions, machine learning, surveillance etc., thereby leading to a natural discourse of research and development in the field of automatic face recognition.

Identification processes of biometric authentication like iris recognition are highly advanced and individualistic but are intrusive in nature. With the evolution of digital technologies and the challenges offered by human identification and surveillance systems, research in the area of face recognition has become imperative as convenient, natural and non-intrusive in nature [4]. In order to discern facial features correctly, various facial recognition systems are available. However, they do not provide the precision needed for a reliable recognition to be made. Thus, better face detection algorithms form a pre-requisite requirement for pattern recognition and computer vision applications.

Further, issues due to variations in the illumination have greatly reduced the potential of facial recognition systems. This is because there is a marked difference in the facial images of the same individual obtained under different illumination. The existing systems are highly sensitive to light variations [5]. Facial images taken under a condition where illumination was un-controlled suffered a non-uniform illumination. To cope with this, certain adaptive techniques are being used. These normalization techniques emend the illumination and restore the features of an image to its original form. Examples of illumination normalization techniques are: Logarithmic Transform (LT), Gamma correction (GC) and Histogram equalization etc. [5, 6]. Extreme Learning Machine (ELM) and it's kernelized variant K - ELM has been previously employed for facial recognition schemes by Zong et al. [7, 8]. An attempt to enhance the facial classification using ELM based on facial views has been demonstrated by Iosifidis et al. [9]. Rujirakul et al. in [10] demonstrate the use of histogram equalization coupled with principal component analysis (PCA) in hybrid with ELM for facial recognition. Independent Component Analysis (ICA) has also been used in conjunction with hybrid of Standard Particle Swarm Organization (SPSO) and ELM to demonstrate recognition rates upto 93% [11]. Similar schemes employing Linear Discriminant Analysis (LDA) and multi-class support vector machines have also been reported [12–14]. An effort has also been made in using local difference binary (LDB) descriptors and fuzzy logic with histogram of oriented gradients (HOG) for efficient facial recognition systems [15, 16].

In this paper, Viola-Jones algorithm is applied to identify the regions corresponding to the face of a subject which is ultimately used for extraction of Histogram Oriented Gradients (HOG) features. HOG feature selection is used as a pre-processing technique as it corrects the overall brightness of a face image to a pre-defined canonical form which essentially discards the consequence of varying lighting. For each image in the dataset, HOG extracts crucial features which form the basis for training of the neural machine.

The paper is structured as follows. Section 2 describes the basics of ELM. Section 3 gives an outline of Viola-Jones Algorithm. Section 4 gives a brief introduction of HOG. Section 5 gives an insight into the face recognition approach that has been adopted in this paper. The results have been summarized in Sect. 6 and finally, the paper has been concluded in Sect. 7.

2   Extreme Learning Machine

The Extreme Learning Machine (ELM) is a single layer feed forward neural network [17–19]. Unlike traditional neural machines, application of an ELM is simple. It does not require controlling parameters like learning rate, stopping iterations etc. which are technically complex. It works on the basis of random allocations of input weights and hidden layer biases. This necessitates probability distribution functions that are continuous in nature. Using an inverse method i.e. Moore-Penrose generalized pseudo inverse, output weights are determined [18].

2.1   The ELM Model

Let us consider a set of N training samples (x_i, y_i) where $x_i \in \mathbb{R}^n$, $y_i \in \mathbb{R}^m$ and i = 1, 2, ..., N. The number of hidden neurons be denoted as $\widehat{N}$.

If 'g' is the activation function then g: $\mathbb{R} \to \mathbb{R}$. The output of the system [17] can then be given as:

$$\sum_{k=1}^{\widehat{N}} \beta_k g(w_k x_i + b_k) = o_i \, \forall i \in 1, 2, \ldots, N \tag{1}$$

Here w_k is the weighting vector that connects the kth hidden neuron with the input nodes. Similarly, β_k is a weighting vector which connects the kth hidden neuron to the output node. b_k represents the threshold bias of the kth hidden neuron.

As mentioned before, the weighting vectors are chosen randomly as per the continuous probability distribution function. The neural network with $\widehat{N}$ hidden neurons and activation function g:$\mathbb{R} \to \mathbb{R}$ approximates samples with zero error. The Eq. (1) can thus be written as:

$$\sum_{k=1}^{\widehat{N}} \beta_k g(w_k x_i + b_k) = y_i \, \forall i \in 1, 2, \ldots, N \tag{2}$$

Thus, we have,

$$H\beta = Y \tag{3}$$

where,

$$H = \begin{bmatrix} g(w_1 x_1 + b_1) & \cdots & g\left(w_{\widehat{N}} x_1 + b_{\widehat{N}}\right) \\ \vdots & \cdots & \vdots \\ g(w_1 x_N + b_1) & \cdots & g\left(w_{\widehat{N}} x_N + b_{\widehat{N}}\right) \end{bmatrix}_{N \times \widehat{N}} \tag{4}$$

$$\beta = \begin{bmatrix} \beta_1^T \\ \vdots \\ \beta_N^T \end{bmatrix}_{NXm} \quad \text{and} \quad Y = \begin{bmatrix} y_1^T \\ \vdots \\ y_N^T \end{bmatrix}_{NXm} \tag{5}$$

The matrix H represents the hidden layer output matrix. The solution of the above system as given by Huang et al. [13] is:

$$\widehat{\beta} = H^\dagger Y \tag{6}$$

where, $H^\dagger$ is the Moore-Penrose generalized inverse of the hidden-layer output matrix H.

3   Viola Jones Algorithm

Viola Jones algorithm is an object detection framework put forward by Paul Viola and Michael Jones in 2001 [20]. Viola Jones object detector is based on a binary classifier that produces a positive output when the search window consists of the desired object otherwise it returns a negative output. The classifier may be used a number of times as the window slides over the image under test.

The binary classifier used in the algorithm is realized using several layers of hierarchy forming an ensemble classifier [21]. The said classifier operates by classifying images based on value of simple features. This is observed to operate much faster than a system which basis classification on a pixel-based system [20]. The Viola Jones algorithm exercises control over three features as dictated by Viola et al. in [20] viz., Two-Rectangle Feature, Three-Rectangle Feature, and Four-Rectangle Feature. The framework put forward by the group is noted to have following stages: (i) Haar Feature Selection, (ii) Integral Image Generation, (iii) Adaboost Training, and (iv) Cascading Classifiers. This is represented as a flowchart in Fig. 1.

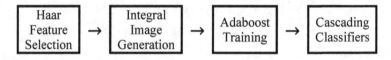

Fig. 1. A depiction of the Viola-Jones Algorithm involving four important stages

The Haar feature selection is computed through Haar basis functions that are based on the three features as listed above and generally include pixel summation of involved adjacent rectangular areas and then calculates the difference between these sums. A depiction of Haar features relative to the corresponding detection window is shown in Fig. 2.

The integral image is then created which is used to evaluate the rectangular features in a constant time. Since the number of features can vary greatly, Adaboost or Adaptive Boosting algorithm is used to select best features and to train the classifiers that use them. This is responsible for creation of a "strong" classifier which is viewed as a linear

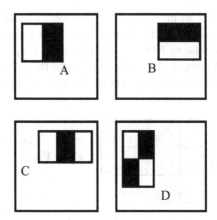

Fig. 2. Depiction of rectangle features shown relative to the detection window.

weighted combination of simple "weak" classifiers. Finally, in cascading, each stage consisting of "strong" classifiers are grouped into several stages. Each stage is responsible for determining whether a sub-window consists of a face or not as depicted in Fig. 3. The algorithm described is implemented using a MATLAB inbuilt routine as described in [22].

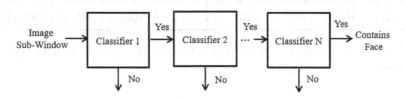

Fig. 3. Depiction of the working flow of classifiers in Viola-Jones algorithm

4 Histograms of Oriented Gradients

Histograms of oriented gradients (HOG) finds applications in object and pattern recognition domain as it is capable of extracting crucial information even from the images that are obtained under garbled environments [23]. It is therefore well suited for tackling the facial recognition problem. The feature extraction process of HOG is based on extracting information about the edges in local regions of a target image [23]. Simply put, HOG feature extraction is primarily the characterization of the orientation and magnitude values of the pixels in an image [24]. That is, it defines an image in terms of groups of local histograms that point to local regions of an image.

The features of HOG can be seen on a grid of rose plots spaced uniformly. The grid dimensions depend upon the size of the cell and image. Thus, every rose plot depicts the gradient orientations distributed in a HOG cell. In a cell histogram, the length of the petals in a rose plot refers to the contribution of every orientation. For the gradient directions, the plot indicates the directions of the edges that are normal. MATLAB inbuilt routine are applied using HOG feature extraction [25].

Thus, in a portion of image with 9 cells (Fig. 4), the HOG feature extraction routine takes input a block of (m × n) cells and arranges them in a vector as depicted in Fig. 5.

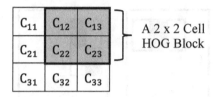

Fig. 4. A portion of image realized using equal sized cells. Each cell consists of pixel values of that portion of the image.

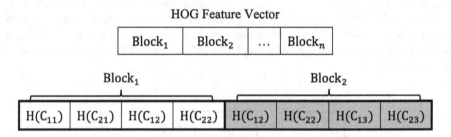

Fig. 5. Depiction of composition of HOG feature vector. $H(C_{ij})$ represents the cell histogram at (i, j) position

5 Algorithmic Description of the Proposed Scheme

The facial recognition methodology adopted in this work is depicted in Fig. 6. Zong et al. in [7] compare the performance of one-against-all (OAA) and one-against-one (OAO) multi-class classification using ELM. Given the multi-label dataset consisting of α different classes, OAA methodology takes into consideration α binary classifiers trained in such a way to distinguish each class and remaining classes. On the other hand, in OAO, one binary classifier is used to distinguish one pair of classes resulting in a total of $(\alpha-1) * \alpha/2$ binary classifiers, α being the number of different classes. As per the results presented in [7, 8] and related work using Linear Discriminant Analysis (LDA) and multiclass Support Vector Machine (SVM) [12–14], OAA has been observed to give better performance as compared to OAO methodology. Hence, for the current work, we adopt OAA ELM methodology for dealing with the facial recognition problem.

The face dataset is first split randomly into training and testing datasets as shown in Fig. 6. To each image in dataset, Viola-Jones algorithm is applied to detect the region

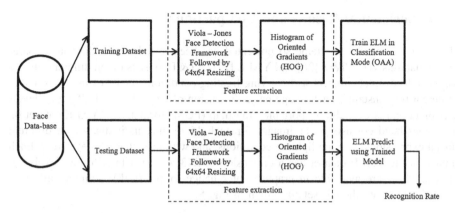

Fig. 6. Block diagram depicting the face recognition approach employing ELM in OAA mode along with Viola Jones object detection framework and HOG feature selection.

which contains useful information pertaining to a subject's facial features. The implementation of Viola-Jones algorithm is as per the MATLAB routine given in [22]. The extracted regions have been resized to a uniform size of 64 by 64. This is done so as to ensure that the number of HOG features extracted in the subsequent stage are similar and so that the processing that follows is uniform for all the subjects under consideration. The HOG features returned by the MATLAB routine [25] is in form of a row vector and consists of 1764 features for the methodology adopted. All such row vectors corresponding to each image in training dataset is stacked one over the other to form the final dataset that would be fed to an ELM for multi-class classification as depicted in Fig. 7. Once the ELM gets trained the images in testing dataset are subjected to same processing and fed to the trained ELM model for classification. The recognition rate is then determined by obtaining the total number of correct hits to the total images under the testing dataset.

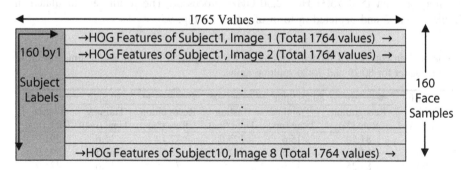

Fig. 7. Depiction of the final dataset that is to be fed to an ELM considering an AT&T database with 80:20 split, giving 160 face images for training dataset. [Note: The images are partitioned randomly into testing and training datasets. The depiction is for understanding purposes.]

6 Experimental Results and Comparisons

The facial recognition scheme so presented has been tested on standard face recognition datasets viz. AT&T [26] and YALE [27]. AT&T consists of ten different images of each 40 distinct subjects with varying lighting conditions, facial expressions and at different time instants. Each image has a dimension of 92 × 112 with 256 grey levels per pixel and is available in portable gray map (PGM) format. The YALE dataset on the other hand consists of 11 images for each 15 distinct individuals with different facial expressions, varying lighting conditions, and with miscellaneous eye wear. Each image in the YALE dataset has a dimension of 243 × 320 with 256 grey levels per pixels. These are available in graphics interchange format (GIF). Some sample face images from both the datasets is shown in Fig. 8.

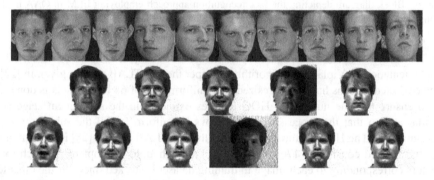

Fig. 8. The first row depicts the face samples of a particular subject from AT&T database, while second and third rows depict face samples of another subject from YALE Dataset

For each dataset, the all images were split into training and testing datasets as per 80:20 and 70:30 splitting ratios. The simulations are carried out using Mathworks MATLAB 9.4 running on the Windows 10 Home Edition with an 8 GB of memory and an i5 0 7300 HQ (2.50 GHz) processor. The results are tabulated in Tables 1 and 2 and depicted in form of curves in Fig. 9.

Table 1. Consequence of hidden neurons on the recognition rate and testing time spans for AT&T dataset for 80:20 and 70:20 splitting ratios.

No. of Hidden Neurons (L)	◄——— 80:20 Split ———►			◄——— 70:30 Split ———►		
	Recognition Rate (%)	Training Time (ms)	Testing Time (ms)	Recognition Rate (%)	Training Time (ms)	Testing Time (ms)
100	81.50	15.6	125.0	77.12	15.6	291.9
150	84.12	15.6	312.5	78.79	62.5	296.9
200	84.25	15.6	62.5	77.25	15.6	421.9
250	79.75	62.5	265.6	63.54	62.5	359.4
500	89.06	140.6	421.9	88.25	140.6	656.3
1000	94.94	171.9	843.8	93.625	140.6	921.9

Table 2. Consequence of hidden neurons on the recognition rate and testing time spans for YALE dataset for 80:20 and 70:20 splitting ratios

No. of Hidden Neurons (L)	◄——— 80:20 Split ———►			◄——— 70:30 Split ———►		
	Recognition Rate (%)	Training Time (ms)	Testing Time (ms)	Recognition Rate (%)	Training Time (ms)	Testing Time (ms)
100	89.16	15.6	109.4	56.44	15.6	187.5
150	76.16	62.5	125.0	62.78	62.5	218.8
200	96.67	625	187.5	82.34	15.6	281.3
250	99.5	15.6	125.0	86.11	15.6	312.5
500	100	15.6	125.0	93.33	31.3	343.8
1000	100	78.1	187.5	96.11	93.8	406.3

The recognition rate mentioned in Tables 1 and 2 and its depiction in Fig. 9 correspond to the average recognition rate so obtained after 20 iterations. This is done to average out the error that emanates due to not so good generalization capabilities of ELM. The ELM may operate in milliseconds regime as dictated by Tables 1 and 2, but lacks in generalization due to random weights being allocated between the input/output and the hidden layers. The results so presented bring forth the fact that as the number of hidden neurons are increased, the recognition rates tend to cross the 90% marker, but the price is paid in terms of the training time spans which although increase but still remain in the scale of few milliseconds.

It is very clear from the results compiled in Tables 1 and 2 that the 80:20 splitting is better placed in comparison to 70:30 splitting ratio. The recognition rate of more than 90% and the training and testing time spans computed thereof is found to be better in case of YALE dataset. Therefore, it is suggested that the images which are captured at different orientations with varying illumination need to be stored in the GIF file format. However, in both these cases, the optimized number of hidden neurons comes out to be slightly more than 250. The recognition rate and the computed testing time first dips prior to $L = 250$ and then maximizes after this value. This is a pattern which is observed in the case of both datasets. The testing time is observed to be inversely varying the recognition rate. At around $L = 250$, the testing times (milliseconds) are maximum which then dip to a lower value in case of both datasets. Therefore, according to us, the optimized value of $L = 250$ for which both recognition rate (%) and testing time (milliseconds) are better placed in YALE dataset in comparison to AT&T dataset.

In order to evaluate the performance of the facial recognition scheme so presented, we compare the results with some state-of-the-art methods for different datasets under Tables 3 and 4.

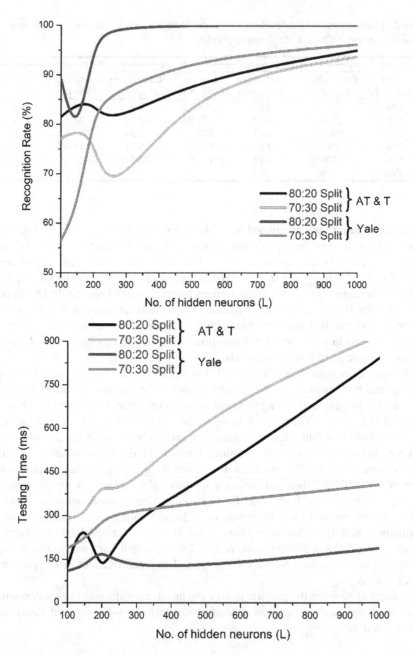

Fig. 9. Curves depicting the effect of hidden neurons on recognition rate, and testing time for the two datasets under 80:20 and 70:30 splitting ratios

Table 3. Comparison of recognition rate and running time spans for some state-of-the art facial recognition techniques for AT&T dataset taking 1000 Hidden Neurons

AT&T Dataset (70:30 Split)		Recognition Rate(%)	Training Time(ms)
PCA – NN [7]		91.67	-
LDA – NN [7]		95.50	-
DLA – NN [7]	32 x 32	97.62	-
PCA – ELM [7]	Resizing	97.11	6380
LDA – ELM [7]		96.46	7680
DLA – ELM [7]		98.44	4540
SPSO – ELM [11]		93.57	102×10^3
Fuzzy – HOG [15]		92.60	-
LDB – HOG [16]		92.00	-
Proposed Work 32 x 32 Resizing		95.00	109.4
Proposed Work 64 x 64 Resizing		93.63	140.6

Table 4. Comparison of recognition rate and running time spans for some state-of-the art facial recognition techniques for YALE dataset taking 1000 hidden neurons

YALE Dataset (70:30 Split)		Recognition Rate (%)	Training Time (ms)
PCA – NN [7]		60.50	-
LDA – NN [7]		83.83	-
DLA – NN [7]		87.25	-
PCA – KELM [8]		85.58	39
LDA – KELM [8]	40 x 40	85.92	23
PCA – ELM [7]	Resizing	82.08	2210
LDA – ELM [7]		83.75	1240
DLA – ELM [7]		89.04	1680
LDB – HOG [16]		92.00	-
Proposed Work 40 x 40 Resizing		93.33	15.6
Proposed Work 64 x 64 Resizing		96.11	93.8

A close observation of the data compiled in Tables 3 and 4 yields a similar pattern. Clearly, our results are better placed than the existing methods presented in this paper particularly for the YALE dataset. This is primarily due to the use of GIF image file format. Additionally, the computed testing time spans are also found to be better than the ones reported by other research groups. We, therefore, conclude that our facial recognition technique not only gives better results in terms of the recognition rate (%), but our testing time span is also measured in milliseconds domain thereby suggesting that all necessary procedures-pre-processing, feature extraction and classification of images is carried out in real-time. This is possible only due to the use of a combination of several existing algorithms in this work. The combination is that of the Viola-Jones Algorithm for object identification, HOG based feature selection and the use of Extreme Learning Machine (ELM) for patter classification. This combination brings in the desirable novelty of the proposed facial recognition technique.

7 Conclusions

A novel facial recognition technique working in real-time domain is proposed in this work. The technique involves the use of existing Viola-Jones algorithm for object identification, the Histogram of Oriented Gradients (HOG) based feature extraction and a single layer feed-forward neural network commonly known as Extreme Learning Machine (ELM). Two different datasets of images are considered for this work. These are AT&T and YALE which have several hundred images in different orientations with varying illumination levels. The ELM is found to carry out successful classification in both the datasets. Our technique, however, gives better results in case of YALE dataset as compared to other similar techniques reported in this paper. We conclude that the better results so obtained are primarily due to the GIF image file format used in YALE and due to the fast processing carried out by Viola-Jones algorithm with HOG feature selection procedures. The extremely fast classification (in milliseconds time domain) carried out by the ELM further supplements it. Overall, we find that a very high recognition rate (%) is achieved in the milliseconds time scale. We therefore conclude that the proposed facial recognition technique outperforms several other similar schemes more particularly for the YALE dataset.

Acknowledgments. The authors would like to thank University School of Information, Communication and Technology, Guru Gobind Singh Indraprastha University and Deen Dayal Upadhyaya College, University of Delhi for providing the necessary software and infrastructure support. The authors also acknowledge Faculty of ESTEM, University of Canberra for providing the necessary financial support.

References

1. Zhao, W., Chellappa, R., Philips, P.J., Rosenfeld, A.: Face recognition: a literature survey. ACM Comput. Surv. (CSUR) **35**(4), 399–458 (2003)
2. Turk, M., Pentland, A.: Eigenfaces for recognition. J. Cogn. Neurosci. **3**(1), 71–86 (1992). Massachusetts Institute of Technology
3. Gumus, E., Kilic, N., Sertbas, A., Ucan, O.N.: Evaluation of face recognition techniques using PCA, wavelets and SVM. Expert Syst. Appl. **37**(9), 6404–6408 (2010)
4. Li, S.Z., Jain, A.K.: Handbook of Face Recognition. Springer, London (2005). https://doi.org/10.1007/978-0-85729-932-1. ISBN 0-387-40595-X
5. Chude-Olisah, C.C., Sulong, G., Chude-Okonkwo, U.A., Hashim, S.Z.: Illumination normalization for edge-based face recognition using the fusion of RGB normalization and gamma correction. In: IEEE International Conference on Signal and Image Processing Applications (ICSIPA), pp. 412–416 (2013)
6. Du, S., Ward, R.: Wavelet-based illumination normalization for face recognition. In: IEEE International Conference on Image Processing (ICIP), vol. 2, pp. 954–956 (2005)
7. Zong, W., Huang, G.B.: Face recognition based on extreme learning machine. Neurocomputing. **74**(16), 2541–2551 (2011)
8. Zong, W., Zhou, H., Huang, G.-B., Lin, Z.: Face recognition based on kernelized extreme learning machine. In: Kamel, M., Karray, F., Gueaieb, W., Khamis, A. (eds.) AIS 2011. LNCS (LNAI), vol. 6752, pp. 263–272. Springer, Heidelberg (2011). https://doi.org/10.1007/978-3-642-21538-4_26

9. Iosifidis, A., Tefas, A., Pitas, I.: Enhancing ELM-based facial image classification by exploiting multiple facial views. In: Procedia Computer Science: International Conference on Computational Science, vol. 51, pp. 2814–2821. Elsevier (2015)

10. Rujirakul, K., So-In, C.: Histogram equalized deep PCA with ELM classification for expressive face recognition. In: IEEE International Workshop on Advanced Image Technology (2018)

11. Wang, Y., Li, H., Guo, Y.: Face recognition based on ICA and SPSO-ELM. In: IEEE Information Technology, Networking, Electronic and Automation Control Conference, pp. 602–606 (2018)

12. Zhang, G.Y., Peng, S.Y., Li, H.M.: Combination of dual-tree complex wavelet and SVM for face recognition. In: Proceedings of International Conference on Machine Learning and Cybernetics, vol. 5, pp. 2815–2819 (2008)

13. Gan, J.Y., He, S.B.: Face recognition based on 2DLDA and support vector machine. In: Proceedings of International Conference on Wavelet Analysis and Pattern Recognition, pp. 211–214 (2009)

14. Zhao, L., Song, Y., Zhu, Y., Zhang, C., Zheng, Y.: Face recognition based on multiclass SVM. In: Proceedings of Chinese Control and Decision Conference, pp. 5871–5873 (2009)

15. Salhi, A.I., Kardouchi, M., Belacel, M.: Histograms of fuzzy oriented gradients for face recognition. In: IEEE International Conference on Computer Applications Technology (2013)

16. Wang, H., Zhang, D., Miao, Z.: Fusion of LDB and HOG for face recognition. In: IEEE 37th Chinese Control Conference, pp. 9192–9196 (2018)

17. Huang, G.B., Zhu, Q.Y., Siew, C.K.: Extreme learning machine: theory and applications. Neurocomputing **70**, 489–501 (2006). Elsevier

18. Huang, G.B., Zhu, Q.Y., Siew, C.K.: Real-time learning capability of neural networks. IEEE Trans. Neural Netw. **17**(4), 863–878 (2006)

19. Huang, G.B.: The MATLAB code for ELM (2004). http://www.ntu.edu.sg/home/egbhuang

20. Viola, P., Jones, M.J.: Robust real-time face detection. Int. J. Comput. Vis. **57**(2), 137–154 (2004)

21. Lo, C., Chow, P.: A high-performance architecture for training Viola-Jones object detectors. In: IEEE International Conference on Field-Programmable Technology, pp. 174–181 (2012)

22. Mathworks MATLAB: Detection objects using the Viola-Jones algorithm. Mathworks MATLAB Documentation R2018b (2012). https://in.mathworks.com/help/vision/ref/vision.cascadeobjectdetector-system-object.html

23. Dalal, N., Triggs, B.: Histogram of oriented gradients for human detection. In: IEEE Computer Society Conference on Computer Vision and Pattern Recognition, vol. 1, pp. 886–893 (2005)

24. Korkmaz, S.A., Akçiçek, A., Bínol H., Korkmaz, M.F.: Recognition of the stomach cancer images with probabilistic HOG feature vector histograms by using HOG features. In: IEEE International Symposium on Intelligent Systems and Informatics (SISY), pp. 339–342 (2017)

25. Mathworks MATLAB: Extract histogram of oriented gradients (HOG) features. Mathworks Matlab Documentation R2018b (2013). https://in.mathworks.com/help/vision/ref/extracthogfeatures.html?s_tid=doc_ta

26. AT&T Laboratories Cambridge: The AT&T Dataset (formerly 'The ORL Dataset of Faces'). http://www.cl.cam.ac.uk/Research/DTG/attarchive:pub/data/att_faces.zip

27. YALE Face Dataset. http://cvc.cs.YALE.edu/cvc/projects/YALEfaces/YALEfaces.html

Automatic Code Generation System for Transactional Web Applications

Hector Florez$^{(\boxtimes)}$ ⓘ, Edwarth Garcia, and Deisy Muñoz

Universidad Distrital Francisco Jose de Caldas, Bogotá, Colombia
haflorezf@udistrital.edu.co, eogt04@gmail.com, deisy.dymo@gmail.com

Abstract. Every day new applications appear, but several of these applications usually share a lot of features. Some applications are based on frameworks; however, most features introduce a lot of source code impacting the performance of an application especially when the application is web-based. Thus, automatic code generators have gained attention in the last years because they provide the required elements to create automatically final applications without introducing a source code that is not part of the application model. In this paper, we present an approach to generate transactional web applications based on a conceptual model as the unique input. Through the conceptual model, modelers can specify the entities, attributes, and relations of the application. Then, the approach is able to generate: (a) the source code separated in UI, business, and persistence layers, (b) the DDL (Data Definition Language) scripts for the corresponding relational database, and a script to create corresponding UML diagrams.

Keywords: Code generation · Conceptual model · Web application

1 Introduction

Nowadays, the amount of web applications developed in the world is increasing rapidly. It might produce several issues in the development process. Since projects are developed by several members of a development group, development processes usually take long time even when the project is not too large. Development time issues have been tackled by several authors and practitioners through several strategies such as code reuse, components development, framework-based development, code generation among others.

Code reuse allows developers to save time; however, usually it requires precise knowledge regarding the requirements solved by the code that is going to be reused. Components development is a great strategy because developers can use available components independently of the language; nevertheless, in most cases such components are domain specific; then, sometimes available components do not match to the desired requirements. Framework-based developments have been used in the last years for web application with good results; nonetheless, the final source code of the application usually includes a lot of instructions that

S. Misra et al. (Eds.): ICCSA 2019, LNCS 11623, pp. 436–451, 2019.
https://doi.org/10.1007/978-3-030-24308-1_36

belong to the framework affecting the performance of the application. Code generation is a strategy that has been used for several purposes because it produces pure source code for final applications; however, such final applications have several but specific services; then, usually developers need to complement the generated source code in order to provide the implementation of all requirements.

In this paper, we present our strategy for developing PHP web applications based on code generation. We designed and developed the code generator project called *DevPHP*, which receives as input a conceptual model written in XML and allows generating PHP projects with a 3-layer architecture based on Bootstrap 4[1] as toolkit for supporting responsive web components and JQuery 3[2] as JavaScript library to support Ajax components. In addition, *DevPHP* generates the DDL (Data Definition Languages) scripts for creating the relational database. Although the script can be used to create the database in any database engine, the generated persistence layer also provides all source code for connections to MySQL[3] databases. Finally, *DevPHP* also generates the UML model that includes component, class, and use case diagrams to be opened and manipulated using UML Designer[4] by Obeo.

In order to validate our approach, we have created various XML conceptual models, which have been run through *DevPHP*. The conceptual models created represents projects in different domains and include different characteristics in order to verify that the generated PHP code corresponds to the modeled project. In addition, we measured the time required to create the model and estimated the time required to create the corresponding PHP source code in order to identify the relevance of this work.

The paper is structured as follows. Section 2 presents the related work. Section 3 illustrates the proposed approach. Section 4 presents the results Finally, Sect. 5 concludes the paper.

2   Related Work

There are some approaches related to automatic code generation of web-based applications. Some of these approaches use XML technologies as the main input for the code generation environment. For example, Li et al. [6] presented an approach using XML, XSLT templates and java language in order to generate automatically the source code of a JSP project, where repetitive patterns in the generated web-based project such as addition, modification, deleting and saving information can be reduced improving the efficiency of developers. Another example is proposed by Turau [16], who presented a framework where its specifications in interfaces for persistence and implementations for the business layer are defined in XML files generating a complete system prototype. Milosavljevic

---

[1] https://www.getbootstrap.com/.

[2] https://www.jquery.com/.

[3] https://www.mysql.com/.

[4] http://www.umldesigner.org/.

et al. [9] present another approach based on a tool that generates a set of standardized database-oriented JSP pages. The JSP pages are generated from the mapping of JavaBeans components to the database. The mapping is specified as an instance of an XML scheme document. These generated pages allow the visualization of a database table or row, as well as provide the possibility to add a new row, update or delete an existing row. Senthil [14] made a code generator implemented in C# which use as an input a model in XML that generates the data access layer code for Microsoft .NET/SQL server platform. Mbarki et al. [7] applied the Model Driven Architecture (MDA) approach in web applications. In this approach two metamodels are made, the first is a meta model to manage the UML source; the second metamodel is responsible to generate an application using MVC2 architecture. Later, mapping rules are used as a transformation algorithm which allows generating an XML file containing all actions, forms, and the JSP pages to generate the necessary code of the application.

Some other approaches use different strategies for the input of the code generator. For instance, Mgheder et al. [8] describe a different approach to generate web user interfaces. In this approach, the web user interface is generated based on metadata hosted in tables of a generic database. To access the database, they use ADOdb, which is a PHP library that generalizes the database connection. By using the ADOdb library, the application can access to the database metadata that contains the information regarding the tables in the database. The flow to get web user interfaces can be summarized in: (a) create a database based on system requirements; (b) get the metadata from Information Schema or directly from the tables of the database; (c) translate the native type data from the database into a generic meta-type table; (d) map the data from the tables obtained in the last step; and (e) get the user interface without behavior or customize properties.

Nadkarni et al. [10] describe WebEAV, which is a generic framework for web development in applications that possess an entity-attribute-value (EAV) component. This database architecture is widely used in clinical data repositories. It addresses the problem of saving data on several thousand potential parameters for a patient across all clinical specialties. The EAV design has a single table that records data as one row per each action. Each row contains the entity, attribute, and value information about the entity. The main objective of the framework consists in the automatic generation of forms based on EAV data. These forms must have different functionalities and need to be responsive according to the business requirement. Furthermore, this framework generates the forms based on metadata attributes in a schema. Besides, all these data are processed through several rules depending on the system complexity. This approach develops Web forms based on metadata extracted from the database. Sanchez et al. [12,13] present a framework to develop PHP web applications based on 3-layer architecture and Model View Controller architectural pattern. Albhbah and Ridley [1] et al., Propose a framework that allows the generation of Web forms from the use of common sense rules and domain specific rules based on a database metadata. RuleML (Rule Markup Language) is the format used to represent the rules taken from the metadata. The implementation begins creating a prototype of database, from which the common rules and the domain specific rules will be created taking its database metadata. Then a PHP script tests which rules have to be implemented depending the database metadata tables to generate its respective Web form.

These approaches are just focused in the automatic code generation on concrete points of a web. However, our approach is centred on creating a complete web application where business, persistence and user interface layers are generated from the input of a XML conceptual model.

Finally, some other approaches are based on the concepts related to Model Driven Engineering (MDE), where conceptual models must conform to desired metamodels. For instance, Sanchez et al. [11] propose an approach based on Model Transformation Chains (MTC) to generate source code for configuring peripherals in mobile applications. Although this approach is very interesting, it demands the creation of a metamodel in order to abstract the features of the domain. In addition, Florez et al. [3] present a MDE approach to generate the required source code to connect unitary reusable components in order to produce a particular web application. Our approach does not need the creation of a metamodel and is able to generate the final source code of a web application.

3 Proposed Approach

We proposed a code generation strategy based on conceptual models written in XML presented in Fig. 1. In this strategy, the modeler is the person who creates the XML model. Later, he runs *DevPHP*, which uses the XML model to generate PHP source files that compose the PHP project.

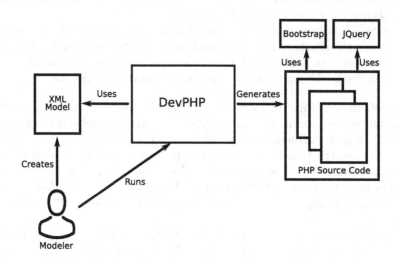

Fig. 1. Code generation strategy.

The XML model follows a specific structure based on the following XML elements:

1. `model`. Is the main XML element that contains the attributes: (a) `name`, which specifies the name of the PHP project; (b) `acronym`; (c) `description` that allows including a short text regarding the project; and (d) `language`, which defines the language of the user interface for the generated PHP project, albeit the source code always is generated in English.
2. `entity`. This element allows modelers to create the concepts involved in the project. It has the attributes: (a) `name`; (b) `actor`, which is boolean and determines whether the entity is an actor; (c) `menuDeploy` that allows excluding an entity from the menu deployed in the user interface; and (d) `delete`, which is also boolean and defines whether the information of this entity in the generated PHP project can be deleted.
3. `attribute`. This element allows including attributes to entities and must be included in the context of the element `entity`. It has the following attributes: (a) `name`; (b) `type` that can be string, text, int, date, email, or password; (c) `mandatory`, which establishes whether the attribute is mandatory in the generated PHP project, when creating or editing information; (d) `length` for setting the length of the attribute; however, when the length is not provided, the attribute will have 45 characters by default; (e) `url`, which is boolean and is used to specify that the attribute contains an url; (f) `visible`, which is boolean and serves to show or hide desired attributes for searching services in the generated PHP project; and (g) `image`, which is boolean and allows including PNG files in the generated PHP project.
4. `relation`. This element must be included in the context of the element `entity` and serves to include one relation to another entity. It has the attributes: `cardinality` that can have the values *1* or * and `entity` that established the target entity of the relation.
5. `service`. This element must be included in the context of the element `entity` only when the attribute `actor` in the element `entity` has the value *true*. This element serves to define which entities can be controlled by a desired actor through the boolean attributes: `create`, `get`, `edit`, and `delete`.

By default, *DevPHP* includes the *entity Administrator*, which is used to provide all required services to manipulate all information related to the generated PHP project. Furthermore, for each entity that is acting as actor, *DevPHP* includes the `entity` Log. For instance, for the entity *Administrator*, it includes the entity *LogAdministrator*. The entities *Log* allows storing the actions made by actors in the generated PHP project. The log includes by default: action, information regarding the action, date, time, operating system, IP address, and browser.

Listing 1.1 presents a fragment of the XML model for a project that we called *RIS (Research Information System)*. *RIS* is intended to manage research information of a research group. Thus, *RIS* has the entities: *Researcher Role, Researcher, Book, Book Chapter, Paper, Software*, and *Project*.

Listing 1.1. Fragment of XML Model

```
1  <model name="Research Information System" acronym="RIS"
       description="Research Information System allows managing the
       research information of a research group" language="en" >
2    <entity name="ResearcherRole" delete="true" >
3      <attribute name="name_en" type="string" mandatory="true" />
4      <attribute name="name_es" type="string" mandatory="true" />
5      <relation cardinality="*" entity="Researcher" />
6    </entity>
7    <entity name="Researcher" actor="true" >
8      <attribute name="name" type="string" mandatory="true" />
9      <attribute name="lastName" type="string" mandatory="true" />
10     <attribute name="email" type="email" />
11     <attribute name="password" type="password" />
12     <attribute name="picture" type="string" image="true" visible="false"
         />
13     <attribute name="isi" type="string" length="200" url="true"
         visible="false" />
14     <attribute name="scopus" type="string" length="200" url="true"
         visible="false" />
15     <relation cardinality="1" entity="ResearcherRole" />
16     <relation cardinality="*" entity="PaperResearcher" />
17     <service entity="Researcher" create="false" get="true" edit="false"
         delete="false" />
18     <service entity="Paper" create="true" get="true" edit="true"
         delete="false" />
19   </entity>
20   <entity name="Paper" delete="true" >
21     <attribute name="title" type="string" mandatory="true" length="200"
         deploy="true" />
22     <attribute name="authors" type="string" mandatory="true"
         length="200" />
23     <attribute name="journal" type="string" length="100" />
24     <attribute name="issn" type="string" nowrap="true" />
25     <attribute name="volume" type="string" visible="false" />
26     <attribute name="pages" type="string" visible="false" />
27     <attribute name="year" type="int" />
28     <attribute name="doi" type="string" length="200" url="true" />
29     <relation cardinality="*" entity="PaperResearcher" />
30   </entity>
31   <entity name="PaperResearcher" delete="true" >
32     <relation cardinality="1" entity="Paper" />
33     <relation cardinality="1" entity="Researcher" />
34   </entity>
35 </model>
```

This fragment of the XML model just describes the entities *ResearcherRole*, *Researcher*, *Paper*, and *PaperResearcher*. The entity *PaperResearcher* is used to make a many-to-many relation between the entities *Paper* and *Researcher*. The fragment of the XML has the following lines:

1. Line 1 includes the element `model` with its corresponding attributes
2. Line 2 has the element `entity` with the concept *ResearcherRole*, which can be deleted by administrators and is intended to classify researchers in the system. In addition, lines 3 and 4 have the attributes *name_en* and *name_es* for including the name of researcher roles in English and Spanish respectively, while line 5 has a relation to the entity *Researcher* with cardinality * in order to represent that one researcher role can have many researchers.
3. Line 7 has the element `entity` with the concept *Researcher*, which is actor. It includes the attributes *name, lastName, email, password, picture, isi,* and *scopus* specified in lines 8 to 14. Moreover, lines 15 and 16 describes relations to *ResearcherRole* with cardinality *1* and *PaperResearcher* with cardinality * indicating that one researcher is related to one researcher role and one researcher can have many papers. Furthermore, lines 17 and 18 have the element `service`. The first one, has the attribute `entity` with the value *Researcher* in order to define that one researcher can consult all researchers, but cannot create, edit, nor delete researcher. The second one, has the attribute `entity` with the value *Paper* in order to define that one researcher can create, consult, and edit papers, but cannot delete any paper.
4. Line 20 has the element `entity` with the concept *Paper*, which can be deleted by administrators. In lines 21 to 28, it has the attributes *title, author, journal, issn, volume, pages, year,* and *doi*. Finally, line 29 has a relation to *Paper-Researcher* with cardinality * indicating that one paper has been written by many researchers.
5. Line 31 has the element `entity` with the concept *PaperResearcher*, which can be deleted by administrators and includes in lines 32 and 33 relations to *Paper* and *Researcher*

3.1 XML Model Validation

In order to generate a suitable project, the XML model that allows generating the project must be properly organized, i.e., the entities, attributes of these entities and relations have to be written with correct syntax and semantic. *DevPHP* has a function that validates the XML model order, syntax, and semantics. The explanation of this validation service is described as follows:

1. As the XML model contains n number of elements, it must have entities, attributes, and relations (between entities) correctly arranged. The approach used to organize the XML model is the use of a XSD file. This file can establish the labels order of the XML model, the required parameters of the corresponding label, the correct data type and the correct name of these parameters.
2. After this arrangement, the validation service evaluates the correct writing of the parameters that have each general label (e.g the entity label has "name" and "delete") and the values of the parameters (e.g "actor" parameter's values must be true or false).
3. Later, it evaluates repetitions of general labels in the XML model.
4. Finally, it validates the correct definitions of the relations between entities.

Listing 1.2 presents a fragment of the XSD file that is used to validate the XML model file.

Listing 1.2. Fragment of XSD validator file

```
1   <xs:schema xmlns:xs = "http://www.w3.org/2001/XMLSchema">
2     <xs:element name="model">
3       <xs:complexType>
4         <xs:sequence>
5           <xs:element name="customize" type="typeCustomize" minOccurs = "1"
                maxOccurs = "1"/>
6           <xs:element name="entity" type="typeEntity" minOccurs = "1"
                maxOccurs = "unbounded"/>
7         </xs:sequence>
8         <xs:attribute name = "name" type = "xs:string" use="required"/>
9         <xs:attribute name = "acronym" type = "xs:string" use="required"/>
10        <xs:attribute name = "description" type = "xs:string"
              use="required"/>
11        <xs:attribute name = "language" type = "xs:string" use="required"/>
12        <xs:attribute name = "br" type = "xs:string" use="optional"/>
13        <xs:attribute name = "text" type = "xs:string" use="optional"/>
14      </xs:complexType>
15    </xs:element>
```

This fragment of the XSD validation file has the following lines:

1. Line 1 indicates the root element of the schema, which defines elements and data types used in the schema based on the definitions stablished in the url http://www.w3.org/2001/XMLSchema.
2. Line 2 defines the root element of the XML model. The *element* tag defines the main definition of the XML model, which in this case is Model.
3. Line 3 defines a complex type, which is an XML that contains other elements or attributes. In this case, the complex type element refers to elements and attributes that the model tag contains in the XML model.
4. Line 4 defines a sequence of elements, in this case, the XML model contains n number of elements and m_n number of attributes per element.
5. Lines 5 and 6 define the correct order of customize and entity in the XML model. Additionally minOccurs and maxOccurs define the number of elements customize and entity that the XML model can contain. Since entity contains n number of attributes and relations, these elements are defined in typeEntity that does not appear in the current fragment.
6. Lines 8 to 13 define attribute elements that represent attributes inside element tags in the XML model. The XSD file defines the element name, data type that contains this element and the required use. Besides, the order of the attributes is the same that must appear in the XML model.

4   Results

We created a full conceptual model for *RIS*, which is a system to manage research information that we have introduced in the previous section. This model includes entities with the concepts: *Researcher Role, Researcher* (as actor), *Book, Book Chapter, Paper, Software*, and *Project*. However, it includes additional concepts that serve to relate the previous concepts. These entities are: *BookResearcher, BookChapterResearcher, PaperResearcher, SoftwareResearcher, ProjectResearcher, BookProject, BookChapterProject, PaperProject*, and *SoftwareProject*.

When running the conceptual model using *DevPHP*, it automatically includes entities with the concepts *Administrator, LogAdministrator*, and *LogResearcher*. The generated PHP project will include three main directories for organizing the project in three layers: UI (user interface), business, and persistence. The UI layer includes all PHP files for the front end of the project. In this layer, *DevPHP* generates one directory for each concept of the conceptual model and inside the folder all PHP files related to the corresponding concept will be created. The business layer includes PHP files for the back end with one class for each concept of the conceptual model. Finally, the persistence layer includes PHP files with one class for each concept; however, a class called *Conection* is generated, which includes services to connect the project to MySQL databases. In addition, an additional file is created with the SQL script of the corresponding relational database.

Moreover, additional folders are created to support the generated project. Those folder are: *css* for Bootstrap cascade style sheet files, *js* for Bootstrap, JQuery, and Validator Javascript files, *img* for images, and *uml* for creating the UML model to be used in UML Designer by Obeo.

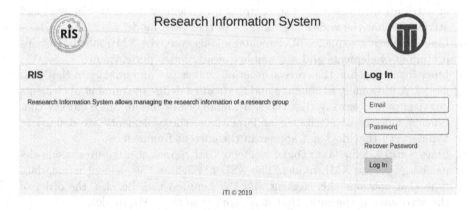

Fig. 2. Index page of *RIS*.

Figure 2 presents the index page of the generated PHP project *RIS*. In this page, actors can log in through their email and password using the card located at the right. It also offers the option to recover password. This option sends

Fig. 3. Session page of administrator.

a new random password to the email registered by the user that is requesting the password recovery. In the card located at the center, it shows the project description that is included in the XML conceptual model. Finally, at the top, it shows the project's name, the project's logo and the logo of our research group. The generated project's logo is a default image that can be replaced in the generated project. Once an actor logs in the system, there is a session page with information of the actor and a menu with the available services included in the XML conceptual model. Figure 3 presents a screenshot of the session page. In particular, the administrator has all services of the project; nevertheless, services for deleting information must be defined in the XML conceptual model. The menu for the administrator includes the following options:

- **Create.** This option allows creating a registry of a desired concept included in the XML conceptual model.
- **Get All.** This option presents all registries of a desired concept included in the XML conceptual model. In this option, for each registry, there are some icons to offer services such as edit, delete, view more information that serves when the concept has a lot of attributes, get all registries of a related concept, and insert a new registry of a related concept.
- **Search.** This option allows finding results that match to one searching word that must have more than 3 characters. These results have the same services presented in the **Get All** option.
- **Log.** This options allows finding the actions made by actors in the systems. Each registry includes the action, data involved in the action, date, time, IP Address, Operating system, and browser.

Another result provided by *DevPHP* is an UML script that contains the corresponding class diagram, use case diagrams, and components diagram. Figure 4 presents a fragment of the generated class diagram for the project *RIS*. It just includes the classes *ResearcherRole*, *Researcher*, *LogResearcher* (not included in the XML conceptual model, but generated because Researcher is an actor),

Paper, and *PaperResearcher*. Every class include all attributes defined through the conceptual model and all methods required to manipulate the corresponding data regarding each concept.

4.1   Results Validation

We have validated our approach by executing five conceptual models of different project contexts. In addition, we analyzed the results of the five generated web applications. The description of the five cases are as follows:

- The first case is a system, which allows managing research information of a research group called *RIS*, which have been introduced in previous sections.
- The second case corresponds to a project for managing information and processes for academic accreditation and self evaluation.
- The third case is a system for managing information of employees fulfillment industrial enterprises.
- The fourth is a document management system specialized for managing thesis documents in a university.
- The fifth is a system for syllabus information of universities academic programs.

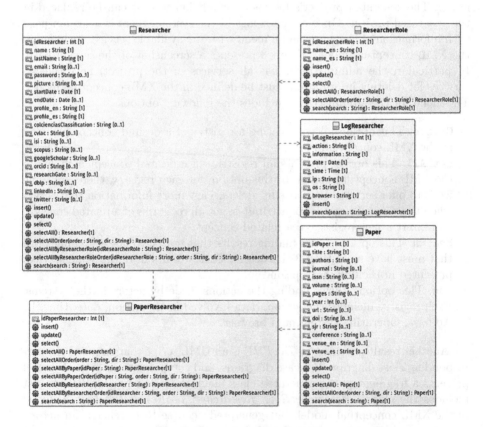

Fig. 4. Generated class diagram.

Table 1 presents the number of entities, attributes, relations and total lines written for the XML model for every case web application, as well as the total number of PHP files and code lines generated by *DevPHP*.

Table 1. Result validation.

Application	Entities	Attributes	Relations	XML lines	PHP Files	Code lines
Web App 1	16	54	18	144	145	16035
Web App 2	15	35	18	117	162	16350
Web App 3	9	32	8	71	94	9791
Web App 4	6	23	5	57	98	9261
Web App 5	6	20	5	49	82	8557

Figure 5 represents the results given in Table 1. Every orange circle represents one of the five web applications generated by *DevPHP*. Inside of each one, there are two light orange circle, where the right one represents the input data included in the XML conceptual model and the left one represents the output data generated by *DevPHP*.

On the one hand, the small yellow circle represents the amount of entities, while the small light purple circle represents the amount of the XML lines. On the other hand, the light green circle represents the generated PHP files, while the big light blue circle represents the total code lines.

We decided to take these values because the PHP files are generated from the different entities features included in the conceptual model. In the same way, we made the comparison with the resulting XML lines and code lines. With this in mind, we can observe how much source code *DevPHP* generates just using the corresponding XML conceptual model in order to offer not only a web application written in PHP, but also SQL, Javascript, CSS and UML scripts.

Also, in order to compare the cost and effort of the previously mentioned web applications, we used the function points model approach to verify the function points of each web application case.

Function Point Analysis (FPA) [15] is a method used for measuring the functional size of a software project. IFPUG [2] is a recognized standard that specifies the use of FPA model. In this model, a software system consists of five components that provide processing information to the user: External Input (EI), External Output (EO), Internal Logical File (ILF), External Logical File (EIF), External Inquiry (EQ). In order to identify these instances, they are classified in complexity levels (Low, Average, High) and the number of each instance is multiplied with the complexity level. For each project, we defined the complexity as Average for every item in the FPA model. Equation 1 is used for calculating the Unadjusted Function Point.

$$UFP = \sum_{i=i}^{5} \sum_{j=1}^{3} x_{ij} \times w_{ij} \qquad (1)$$

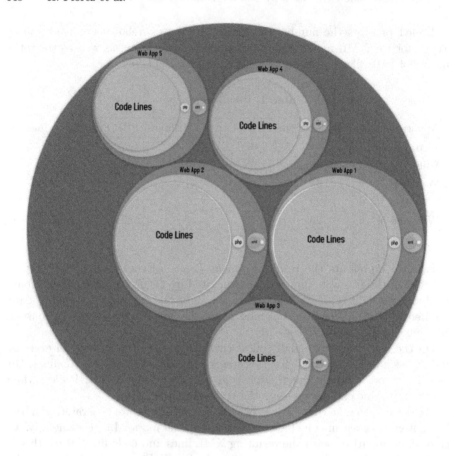

Fig. 5. Result validation

The value for x_{ij} is the number of user function type and w_{ij} is the number of complexity weight. This values can be found in IFPUG table of standard values for the different function type. In this scenario, we define the number of EI, EO and EQ with principals entities for every system with a low complexity.

The calculation of technical complexity adjustment is given by another table that describes features of the operational environment system. This table can be found as well in IFPUG table of Value Adjustment Factors for FPA model, called (VAF) [4]. All web applications cases share similar features related to the environment; consequently, we defined a default number for each of them as the sum of these 14 factors. This number is called TDI (Total degree of influence). Equation 2 calculates the Technical Complexity Adjustment, while Eq. 3 calculates the function points.

$$TCA = 0.65 + 0.01 \times TDI \tag{2}$$

$$FP = UFP \times TCA \tag{3}$$

Finally, using the macro-estimate technique Ball-park or Indicative Estimate [5], which estimates the effort by using function points values, we used the Eq. 4 to establish the effort of every web application.

$$Ef = \frac{FP}{150} \times FP^{0.4} \tag{4}$$

Where Ef is the effort measured in staff month. This measure indicates that 1 staff month is equivalent to 174 h.

The relation between function points and effort for each web application is presented in Table 2. The second column designates the function points value calculated through the Eq. 3. The third column shows the effort measured in staff month determined through the Eq. 4. The last column describes the person hours effort through the month staff value.

Since *DevPHP* works based on a XML file that represents a conceptual model of a system, the required time to make a complete project is given by the requirements analysis, the abstract representation of the system, as well as the constructions of every entity, attributes, and relation between entities. Activity for creating entities spend around ten minutes including the definition of its attributes. The time to evaluate and define the relations can spend around ten minutes considering many to many or many to one relations. Thus, the development effort for the web application cases using *DevPHP* are shown in Table 3.

From the estimation of function points and the month staff value shown in Table 2, we determine that the time to develop the current web application cases described in Table 1 can vary between 239.3 and 516 person-hours. This value is given by the complexity of the web application and it can increase depending of the business requirement. In addition, the time spent to develop these web application cases using *DevPHP* was between 2.1 and 5.6 person-hours.

With this in mind, the time to develop some of these web applications using *DevPHP* or pure development can vary between 200 and 500 h (e.g., the time using *DevPHP* to develop the Web Application 1 was 5.6 h; nevertheless, based on the estimated function points, the time to develop the same web application is 516.9 h), which is an important effort saving and clearly a huge cost saving.

Table 2. Development effort estimation.

Application	Function points	Staff month effort	Person-hours
Web App 1	78	3	516.9
Web App 2	62	2.1	370.6
Web App 3	53	1.7	302.9
Web App 4	45	1.4	239.3
Web App 5	45	1.4	239.3

Table 3. Development effort estimation using *DevPHP*.

Application	Person-hours
Web App 1	5.6
Web App 2	5.5
Web App 3	2.8
Web App 4	2.2
Web App 5	2.1

5   Conclusions

DevPHP is a tool that allows the minimization of time and effort in the development of web applications built using PHP. In such a way, from the construction of a consistent conceptual model *DevPHP* can generate a web application that achieves the majority of requirements that a transactional web application could have.

Projects generated by *DevPHP* are scalable and flexible considering that *DevPHP* has been developed to generate projects with a 3-layer architecture; therefore, the project can be edited by the developer depending on specific requirements, either for creating new services or editing and deleting generated project elements.

In order to make the best use of *DevPHP* it is necessary to create a consistent conceptual model. For this the modeler requires to know how to abstract the system requirements in entities, attributes, and relations. Once the web application is generated by *DevPHP*, it might be upgraded using the generated components.

References

1. Albhbah, A.M., Ridley, M.J.: A rule framework for automatic generation of web forms. Int. J. Comput. Theor. Eng. 4(4), 584 (2012)
2. Cuadrado-Gallego, J.J., Rodríguez, D., Machado, F., Abran, A.: Convertibility between IFPUG and COSMIC functional size measurements. In: Münch, J., Abrahamsson, P. (eds.) PROFES 2007. LNCS, vol. 4589, pp. 273–283. Springer, Heidelberg (2007). https://doi.org/10.1007/978-3-540-73460-4_25
3. Florez, H., Leon, M.: Model driven engineering approach to configure software reusable components. In: Florez, H., Diaz, C., Chavarriaga, J. (eds.) ICAI 2018. CCIS, vol. 942, pp. 352–363. Springer, Cham (2018). https://doi.org/10.1007/978-3-030-01535-0_26
4. Jones, C.: Applied Software Measurement: Global Analysis of Productivity and Quality. McGraw-Hill Education Group, New York City (2008)
5. Lawrie, R.: Using functional sizing in software projects estimating. Charismatek Software Metrics (2002)
6. Li, L., Yang, J., Liu, Z., Bao, L.: The research and application of web page code automatic generation technology. In: 2011 2nd International Conference on Artificial Intelligence, Management Science and Electronic Commerce (AIMSEC), pp. 5246–5249. IEEE (2011)

7. Mbarki, S., Erramdani, M.: Toward automatic generation of mvc2 web applications. INFOCOMP **7**(4), 84–91 (2008)
8. Mgheder, M.A., Ridley, M.J.: Automatic generation of web user interfaces in PHP using database metadata. In: 2008 Third International Conference on Internet and Web Applications and Services, ICIW 2008, pp. 426–430. IEEE (2008)
9. Milosavljević, B., Vidaković, M., Konjović, Z.: Automatic code generation for database-oriented web applications. In: Proceedings of the Inaugural Conference on the Principles and Practice of Programming, 2002 and Proceedings of the Second Workshop on Intermediate Representation Engineering for Virtual Machines, 2002, pp. 59–64. National University of Ireland (2002)
10. Nadkarni, P.M., Brandt, C.M., Marenco, L.: WebEAV: automatic metadata-driven generation of web interfaces to entity-attribute-value databases. J. Am. Med. Inf. Assoc. **7**(4), 343–356 (2000)
11. Sanchez, D., Florez, H.: Model driven engineering approach to manage peripherals in mobile devices. In: Gervasi, O., et al. (eds.) ICCSA 2018. LNCS, vol. 10963, pp. 353–364. Springer, Cham (2018). https://doi.org/10.1007/978-3-319-95171-3_28
12. Sanchez, D., Mendez, O., Florez, H.: Applying the 3-layer model in the construction of a framework to create web applications. In: IMCIC 2017–8th International Multi-Conference on Complexity, Informatics and Cybernetics, Proceedings, vol. 2017-March, pp. 364–369 (2017)
13. Sanchez, D., Mendez, O., Florez, H.: An approach of a framework to create web applications. In: Gervasi, O., et al. (eds.) ICCSA 2018. LNCS, vol. 10963, pp. 341–352. Springer, Cham (2018). https://doi.org/10.1007/978-3-319-95171-3_27
14. Senthil, J., Arumugam, S., Kapoor, S.M.A.A.: Automatic code generation for recurring code patterns in web based applications and increasing efficiency of data access code. Int. J. Comput. Sci. **9**(3), 473–476 (2012)
15. Symons, C.R.: Function point analysis: difficulties and improvements. IEEE Trans. Softw. Eng. **14**(1), 2–11 (1988)
16. Turau, V.: A framework for automatic generation of web-based data entry applications based on XML. In: Proceedings of the 2002 ACM Symposium on Applied Computing, pp. 1121–1126. ACM (2002)

Computed Tomography of Polymer Composites Reinforced with Natural Short Fiber

César Paltán[1], Josep Costa[2], and Jorge Fajardo[1](✉) (iD)

[1] Universidad Politécnica Salesiana, Cuenca, Ecuador
jfajardo@ups.edu.ec
[2] AMADE, Polytechnic School, University of Girona, Girona, Spain

Abstract. X-ray computed tomography is a technique that provides a high level of detail in three-dimensional (3D) inspections of composite materials, but the acquisition of phase contrast together with absorption contrast in traditional tomography makes it difficult to obtain information in some composite materials reinforced with natural fibers. In this work, X-ray computed tomography has been used to evaluate an image reconstruction process using the phase-contrast method with three different algorithms (MBA, BAC, PPR). The results of the image reconstructions were compared to traditional methods. Additionally, details of the variation of parameters in each reconstruction method are presented. The phase-contrast image capture technique did not provide an adequate reconstruction of images that showed similar contrast. Finally, the absorption contrast was applied to analyze morphological properties of a bio-based composite showing a significant decrease of fiber length distribution during the manufacturing process.

Keywords: X-ray tomography · Phase contrast · Phase retrieval · Absorption phase · Modified Bronnikov Algorithm (MBA) · Paganin Phase Retrieval (PPR) · Bronnikov Aided Correction (BAC) · Bio-based composite

1 Introduction

In X-ray computed tomography (CT), a sample is inspected by taking a series of X-ray transmission images at different angles, since X-ray can be transmitted thought large composite components [1, 2]. These projection images hold data about the X-ray absorption coefficients of the different materials in the sample, and are used to obtain a 2D or 3D representation of the sample [2–4]. This technique is non-destructive [5], and is used to determine the internal structure of the materials (with a post process, the fiber length distribution (FLD) and the fiber orientation distribution (FOD) are measured, two critical parameters for the behavior of composite materials reinforced with short fiber) [6–8]. A typical X-ray computed tomography (CT) imaging procedure is composed of two steps: data acquisition and image reconstruction [9, 10].

It is known that there three different ways of doing an X-ray tomography. The absorption mode is presented by the variation between the linear attenuation

© Springer Nature Switzerland AG 2019
S. Misra et al. (Eds.): ICCSA 2019, LNCS 11623, pp. 452–467, 2019.
https://doi.org/10.1007/978-3-030-24308-1_37

coefficients, the greater the difference, the better the contrast and the easier the subsequent analysis of image [2, 11–13]. The phase contrast mode is observed when the distance between the detector and the sample increases in comparison with the absorption mode. The interference after the propagation between the wave on each side of an interface, generates the contrast because it has undergone a different phase delay [11, 13, 14]. This contrast is superimposed onto the conventional absorption contrast, especially when absorption only leads to weak contrast [12] and is important when edge detection is necessary. The increased distance between the detector and the sample extends the Fresnel Zone that covers the image, and this results in stronger edges in the material [11]. This zone is the space between the transmitter of a wave and a receiver [15, 16]. Holotomography mode uses images taken at various distances from the sample to the detector. By using a specific algorithm, the quantitative distribution of the optical phase can be recovered. With this mode, quantitative 3D analysis of the density in the material is feasible [11, 12].

When X-ray computed tomography is performed on a very low absorbing or low attenuation sample, the X-rays that pass through the sample undergo a phase shift [17–19]. This attenuation is a function of the density and thickness of the sample along with the X-ray wavelength [5, 12]. Low attenuation is results from the reduction of the intensity of an X-ray beam as it passes through the material. This is caused by absorption and can be affected by different factors, such as the energy of the beam and the atomic number of the sample [16]. Then, the contrast of the image depends on the attenuation of the X-ray beam due to the sample [5] and also on the Fresnel Zone that is affected by the variation of the distance from the sample to the receiver [15]. With these conditions, the projection images obtained contain not only absorption contrast but also phase contrast, such as in plastics and composites [5]. While images without a phase signal can be reconstructed very well, such mixed phase images complicate slice reconstruction.

For these cases, the phase contrast imaging technique is used since this method takes the phase shift as an image signal and provides a better contrast in different samples such as soft tissues and samples with a low atomic number. This results in an improvement of the edge in the projection images, which can be analyzed as a positive peak in the intensity next to a negative one (relative to the intensity of absorption) [3, 19]. Phase contrast imaging techniques have two advantages: first, light elements, which show poor contrast in absorption radiography, can be easily detected and second, phase contrast radiography helps to reduce the dose of radiation deposited on the object under investigation [4]. Phase contrast can be measured with different methods, such as interferometric techniques [20].

The best modality of image capture in the phase contrast method is cone beam computed tomography (CBCT), which efficiently scans three-dimensional isotropic high-resolution images [10]. Within the CBCT technique, there are four ways to analyze the passage of X-rays [2]. Propagation Based Imaging (PBI) is the simplest because an optical element in the beam is not required and the restriction on the spectral width is relaxed [18, 21]. PBI depends on the interference fringes that arise in the propagation of free space in the Fresnel Zone. This method is particularly good at improving the edge in the image and, therefore, is very suitable for fiber samples, foams and for locating non-homogeneities in metals [21].

After image capture, phase contrast reconstruction has three methods that use mixed projections containing absorption contrast and phase contrast, the Modified Bronnikov algorithm (MBA), the Bronnikov aided correction (BAC) and the Paganin phase retrieval (PPR). Although the presence of the phase signal makes the projections (and even the reconstruction) look sharper, the phase signal is highly unwanted since it causes serious artifices in the reconstructed slices and introduces edges which are not physically present in the scanned object [22, 23].

The aim of this work is to explore reconstruction algorithms that transform the 2D projections acquired into 3D stacks specifically designed to improve the contrast in samples where all the constituents have a similar absorption of X-ray (as is the case of natural fiber composites). In particular, there will be an in-depth analysis of phase contrast algorithms. The document begins with a brief theoretical introduction, highlighting the basic concepts of reconstruction algorithms. Secondly, the methodology used to perform the analysis of the algorithms with variation of parameters is described. Finally, the absorption contrast method is applied to analyze morphological properties of a bio-based composite after the process manufacturing.

2 Background

2.1 Material Parameters

This section describes the main properties with respect to the X-ray CT imaging of composites.

Linear Attenuation Coefficient (μ)
One of the parameters for the detection of contrast between the different constituents within the volume of interest, in this specific case between matrix and fibers. It is a constant that describes the incident attenuation fraction (interaction of radiation with matter [24, 25]) per unit of thickness of material. It is expressed numerically in units of cm^{-1} [12, 16, 26, 27]. It is necessary to know the attenuation coefficient of a sample to correct the auto-attenuation. The attenuation coefficient is usually determined using the ratio of transmitted gamma-ray intensities and incidents with well-collimated sources and detectors [28, 29]. If the chemical composition of a sample is known, it can be calculated using simple data [28, 30].

$$\mu(x, y, z) = K\rho \frac{Z^4}{E^3} \tag{1}$$

Where K is a constant, ρ is the material density, Z is the material atomic number and E the energy of the incident photons.

Calculating μ for the intensity of the beam at distance x (cm) within a material using the following equation [12, 26].

$$I_x = I_0 e^{-\mu x} \tag{2}$$

Where I_x is the intensity at depth of x (cm), I_0 is the original intensity, and μ is the linear attenuation coefficient [27]. Rearrange and take the log of both sides gives the equation for μ.

$$\mu = \frac{Ln\left(\frac{I_0}{I_x}\right)}{x} \tag{3}$$

The mass attenuation coefficient is a normalization of the linear attenuation coefficient per unit density of the material that produces a value that is constant for a given element or compound [27].

Refractive Index Decrement (δ)

The Refraction Index Decrement is calculated from the atomic scattering factors and the cross-sections of Compton and Rayleigh. The atomic scattering factors are based on experimental measurements of atomic photo-absorption. The measurements provide values for the imaginary part of the atomic scattering factor and the real part, which describes the scattering of the radiation when it interacts with the matter, is calculated from the absorption measurements using the integral Kramers-Kronig relationships [31].

The refractive index n, describes the interaction of X-rays with matter, this depends on the material and the X-ray energy [1].

$$n = 1 - \delta + i\beta \tag{4}$$

Where the imaginary part β describes the attenuation (absorption) and the real part δ the phase shift. For polymer composites, the range of X-ray energies generally used are 15–20 keV for synchrotron sources, with δ higher than β by orders of magnitude [1, 13].

2.2 Algorithms

This section briefly describes the main algorithms with respect to the Phase contrast mode.

MBA (Modified Bronnikov Algorithm)

This method describes a correction application to these mixed projections to eliminate the phase signal [3]. The algorithm extracts and converts the phase signal from the mixed projection image, which allow reconstructing the phase signal as an absorption signal [19].

The algorithm is based on the transport of intensity equation [32]. The intensity distribution $I_{\theta,z}(x,y)$ at a distance z from the sample and angle of rotation θ, for samples with weak absorption and distances d in the nearby Fresnel zone, is expressed as [3, 19, 25]:

$$I_{\theta,d}(x,y) = I_{\theta,0}(x,y)\left[1 - \frac{\lambda d}{2\pi}\nabla^2 \phi_\theta(x,y)\right] \tag{5}$$

Where $I_{\theta,0}(x, y)$ is the absorption-contrast intensity measured at $z = 0$, λ is the X-ray wavelength and $\phi_\theta(x, y)$ is the phase function of the sample.

Based on the Eq. (5) a filter is derived which is applied to the original projection data. This problem can be partially corrected by adding a correction parameter to the filter [3, 19].

In this filter, a correction factor is added that allows the algorithm to be used without knowledge of the intensity distribution at a distance d from the object near the Fresnel zone $(I_{\theta,d}(x, y, \lambda))$, therefore not requiring an additional scan. The two-dimensional Fourier transform of this filter has the following form [3, 4, 19].

$$p(\xi, \eta) = Q_{cor} = \frac{1}{\xi^2 + \eta^2 + \alpha} \tag{6}$$

Where ξ and η are the spatial frequencies and α is a correction parameter dependent on absorption; the constant α is an MBA correction. Very small values of the constant leads to fuzzy results because it eliminates the phase edges. Higher values maintain the sharpness of the projection but cannot eliminate the phase edges in their entirety. The use of large constant values eliminates the filter.

Applying Eq. (6) to the original projection images, the phase signal is eliminated and the absorption signal is converted into a set of line integrals $\phi_\theta(x, y)$ that contain information about the phase coefficients φ of the sample:

$$\phi_\theta(x, y) = \int \varphi dL \tag{7}$$

BAC (Bronnikov Aided Correction)
This method reduces the phase signal in the mixed projection, resulting in an almost pure absorption contrast projection, which can be reconstructed without introducing phase contrast artifices. The phase signal is used to correct original projection images and obtain a pure absorption image from which the attenuation coefficients μ of the object can be reconstructed [33]. According to Eq. (5), it is possible to obtain the pure absorption image $I_{\theta,0}(x, y)$ of the mixed projection $I_{\theta,d}(x, y)$ when the function $\phi_\theta(x, y)$ is known:

$$I_{\theta,0}(x, y) = \frac{I_{\theta,d}(x, y)}{1 - \frac{\lambda d}{2\pi} \nabla^2 \phi_\theta(x, y)} \tag{8}$$

For the proposed BAC algorithm, the original projection images are first filtered using the modified Bronnikov filter, which results in the approximate phase function $\tilde{\phi}_\theta(x, y, \lambda)$. Then the correction function $C_\theta(x, y, \lambda)$ is calculated as [3]:

$$C_\theta(x, y, \lambda) = 1 - \gamma \cdot \nabla^2 \tilde{\phi}_\theta(x, y, \lambda) \tag{9}$$

Where the parameter γ allows to control the amplitude of the correction. The parameter (BAC correction) controls the amplitude of the phase correction that is performed. Finally, the original projections $I_{\theta,d}(x, y, \lambda)$ are divided by the correction function $C_\theta(x, y, \lambda)$ to obtain the corrected projection $I^a_{\theta,d}(x, y, \lambda)$ that should now contain only the absorption signal [3].

PPR (Paganin Phase Retrieval)
The algorithm is based on the transport of intensity equation [17, 32] and assumes that the object under study is composed of a single material, that the object is homogeneous.

It uses parameters that are geometrical, such as Source Detector Distance (SDD), Source Object Distance (SOD) and pixel size. The parameters μ and δ represent the linear attenuation coefficient and the refractive index decrement of the sample [4, 26, 34], assumed to be homogeneous [35]. For non-homogeneous samples and samples with an unknown composition, these parameters can be derived by visual comparison. By using the fast Fourier transform in the numerical implementation, a fast-deterministic method is obtained for phase extraction from a single defocused image of a homogeneous object.

$$T(r_\perp) = -\frac{1}{\mu}\log_e\left(\mathfrak{F}^{-1}\left\{\mu\frac{\mathfrak{F}\{M^2 I(Mr_\perp, z = R_2)\}/I^{in}}{R_2\delta|k_\perp|^2/M + \mu}\right\}\right) \tag{10}$$

Here, $T(r_\perp)$ is the projected thickness of homogeneous object in the plane in which the image is taken, I^{in} is the uniform intensity of the incident radiation. The inverse Fourier transform is denoted $\mathfrak{F}^{-1}$, $M = (R_1 + R_2)/R_1$ is the magnification of the image resulting from the illumination of point source.

3 Materials and Methodology

3.1 Materials

The base composite material of this work was developed by the GiMaT group, which is a PP/bamboo fiber at different compositions. Polypropylene with flow index (MFI) of 12 g/10 min, was used as a polymeric matrix. Bamboo fibers belongs to mesh number 60 according to ASTM E 11–95 were employed as natural reinforcement. They were previously dried at 110 °C for 2 h [36–38].

3.2 Experimental Tests of X-ray Micro-tomography

The inspection equipment consisted of an X-ray source (20 W and 5 μm maximum power and focal spot) and a 2400 × 2400-pixel detector. Both were manufactured by HAMAMATSU and assembled by Novadep Scientific Instruments. The energy used was 30 keV, the effective pixel size was 6 μm and 1100 projections were taken (1 integration per projection). The distance between the sample and the camera (SOD) was 98,560 mm.

3.3   Reconstruction by Phase Contrast Mode

Three methods were used for reconstruction. The first method (Modified Bronnikov Algorithm) uses Eq. (6) with variation in the MBA attenuation parameters $(\xi^2 + \eta^2)$ between 0.25 to 2. At each different attenuation, it has a sub variation between 0.25 to 1.25 of the MBA correction parameters (α).

The second method (Bronnikov Aided Correction) uses Eq. (9) with variation in the BAC correction (γ) between 0.0025 to 1.

The third method (Paganin Phase Retrieval) uses Eq. (10) with a Source Detector Distance (SDD) of 821.33 mm, Source Object Distance (SOD) of 98.560 mm and pixel size 0.05.

The linear attenuation coefficient (μ), with a mass attenuation coefficient of $\mu_m = 0.2707 \frac{cm^2}{g}$ and a density of $\rho = 0.2707 \frac{cm^2}{g}$, has a value of $\mu = \mu_m \cdot \rho = 0.251 \, cm^{-1}$ for polypropylene [30].

The refractive index decrement (δ) with values of $\delta = 2.48897e^{-7}$ and $\beta = 7.3776e^{-11}$ for polypropylene [39], behaves as shown in Fig. 1.

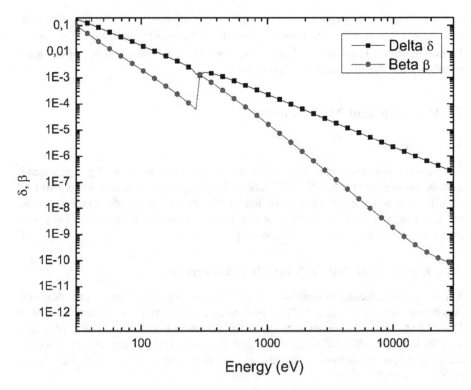

Fig. 1. Index refraction for polypropylene [39].

4 Results and Discussion

4.1 MBA (Modified Bronnikov Algorithm)

The first analysis shows the effect of the MBA algorithm with the variation of different parameters. The profile shows the transition between the edge of the fiber and the PP matrix shown in Fig. 2. As can be seen, the slices are different from each other. The slice image in Fig. 2(b) is very sharp with respect to the slice image in Fig. 2(a), but the reconstruction suffers from phase artifices. Because of these, the fiber, which is rather homogeneous, has a very dense edge and an internal region with a very high density that differs from the matrix.

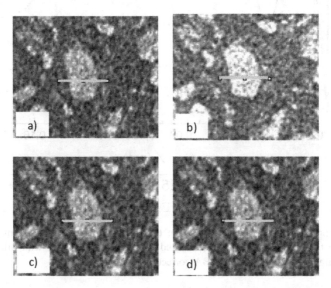

Fig. 2. (a) Original projection image. (b) Projection image after applying MBA (Modified Bronnikov Algorithm). (c) BAC (Bronnikov aided correction). (d) PPR (Paganin Phase retrieval).

Figure 3 shows a comparison of the line profiles for the original projection images and the MBA attenuation images at different values of this parameter. The profile shows the transition between the edge of the fiber and the PP matrix.

If the parameter is low (0.25 to 2), the peaks become smaller but do not disappear completely. If the parameters increase (>2), the peaks are similar to a normal reconstruction. For values that are lower (<0.25), the image loses a high amount of contrast and the edge is undetectable.

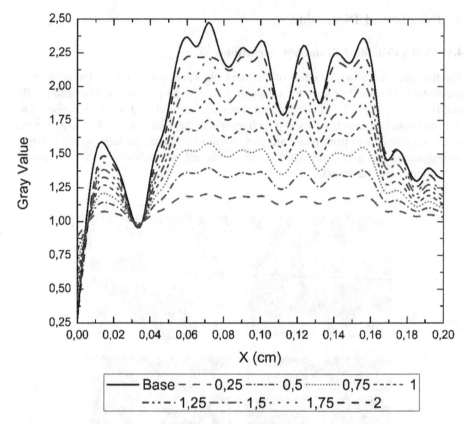

Fig. 3. Line profiles of the transition between the edge of the fiber with PP matrix for the original projection and for the MBA (Modified Bronnikov Algorithm) with different MBA attenuation parameter values and an MBA correction equal to 1.

Similarly, in Fig. 4, the line profiles of the original projection image and the MBA correction images are compared for different values of the MBA Correction parameter. The profile shows the transition between the edge of the fiber and the PP matrix.

With this parameter variation, no large changes are shown. If the parameter is low (0.25), the peaks are slightly reduced. If the parameter increases (>0.5), the peaks are similar to a normal reconstruction but remain under the original curve. As the parameter increases, there are no large-scale changes seen, with the curves of the parameter variation staying more or less the same. For values which are lower (<0.25), the image becomes blurred and the edge is not perceptible.

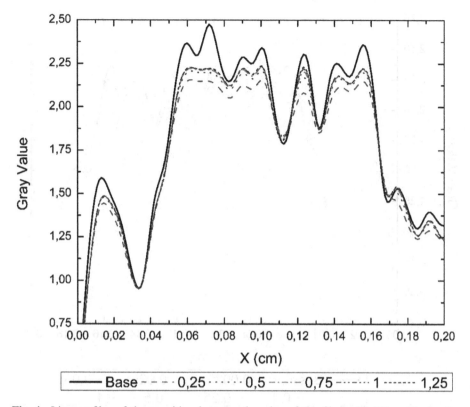

Fig. 4. Line profiles of the transition between the edge of the fiber with PP matrix for the original projection and for the MBA (Modified Bronnikov Algorithm) with different MBA correction parameter values and an MBA attenuation equal 1.

4.2 BAC (Bronnikov Aided Correction)

In the second analysis, the BAC slice, shown in Fig. 2(c), has little blurring as compared to the normal reconstruction shown in Fig. 2(a). The profile shows the transition between the edge of the fiber and the PP matrix.

In Fig. 5, the line profiles of the original projection and the BAC correction images are compared for different values of the parameter as it pertains to the behavior the BAC algorithm. If the parameter is very low (<0.0025), the peaks do not have significant changes (similar curves). As the parameter increases from (0.025 to 0.25), the peaks decreases with respect to normal reconstruction; the edge fades but not in its entirety. For lower values (>0.5), the image loses a high amount of contrast and the edge is undetectable.

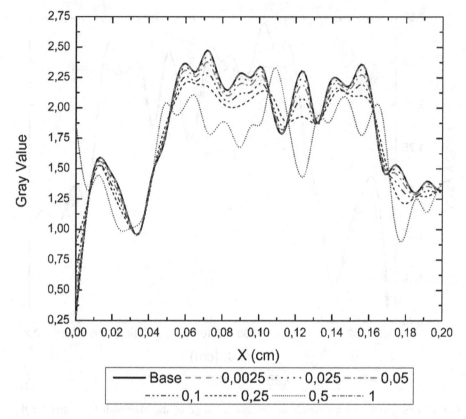

Fig. 5. Line profiles of the transition between the edge of the fiber and PP matrix for the original projection and for the BAC (Bronnikov Aided Correction) with different values for the BAC correction parameter.

4.3 PPR (Paganin Phase Retrieval)

Finally, the last analysis shows the effect of the PPR algorithm with the values of the properties of the PP Matrix. It is necessary to point out that in this reconstruction, the imaginary part of the refractive index parameter is used, the β factor, with results shown in Fig. 6. As can be observed, the peaks are similar to a normal reconstruction but under the original curve. When the real part of the refractive index parameter, the δ factor, is applied, the reconstruction that obtained is very blurred, with the edge is undetectable.

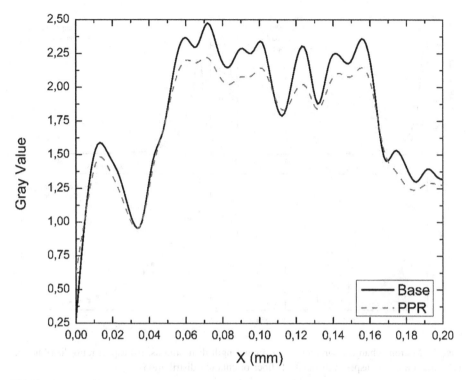

Fig. 6. Line profiles of the transition between the edge of the fiber with PP matrix for the original projection and for the PPR (Paganin Phase retrieval)

5 Case Study with Bio-Based Composite

In order to evaluate the method, a bio-based composite was developed from a thermoplastic matrix reinforced with natural fibers. Bamboo fibers with length 0.5 ± 0.1 mm, diameter 98.15 ± 0.1 μm, were used as reinforcement. Polypropylene homopolymer (PP), was used as a polymeric matrix. Composite materials at different formulations of bamboo (30 to 40 wt%) were manufactured. For the microstructural analysis of the bio-based composite, the X (μ-CT) was employed. With this technique it was possible to recreate images of the internal structure of the composite material and evaluate their microstructure (fiber length, diameter and orientation distribution). The images were acquired with a resolution of 6.5 μm using a voltage of 45 kV and current of 160 μA, by means of a Novadep micro-tomograph. The aspect ratio, diameter and length of the fibers were determined from 100 000 cross-sectional samples through the method developed by Miettinen et al. [40].

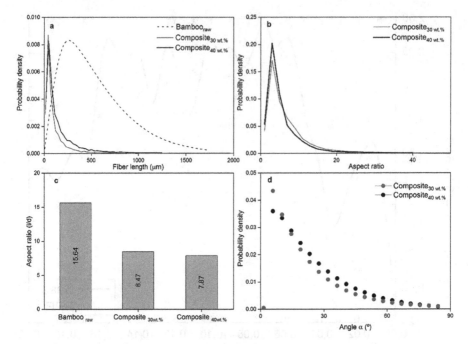

Fig. 7. Micromechanical parameters: (a) fiber length distributions, (b) aspect ratio distribution, (c) variation of the aspect ratio and (d) fiber orientation distributions.

Figure 7(a), shows a significant reduction of fiber length during processing. The fiber length distribution has been shifted towards the shorter fibers. The average fiber length before processing was ~500 μm and after processing (extrusion + injection) it was reduced to 241 μm and 165 μm in the composite at 30 wt% and 40 wt% of bamboo fiber respectively. The aspect ratio of bamboo fiber was reduced by approximately half, due to the size reduction (Fig. 7b–c). The average fiber diameter before processing was found to be 33 μm, reduced to 28 μm and 21 μm at 30 wt% and 40 wt% of bamboo fiber respectively. Despite this effect, the average aspect ratio showed similar values in both compositions after processing (Fig. 7c). Figure 7(d), shows the fiber orientation distributions obtained from the weighted and averaged orientation distributions through the thickness of the specimens. The micromechanical information obtained from X (μ-CT) could be used together with micromechanical models to predict the mechanical behavior of these new materials.

6 Conclusions

The phase-contrast image capture technique proved not to offer a better method for the reconstruction of images, since the X-ray source does not have enough spatial coherence to increase the distance from the sample to the receiver and thus is not able to vary the Fresnel Zone. The captured images show only the absorption phase, which is why the reconstruction algorithms (MBA, BAC, PPR) do not work in these cases. Normal reconstruction better maintains the detectability of the details showing a positive peak in the intensity next to a negative one. The BAC method is a technique for reconstructing mixed phase and absorption projections, since the method requires no additional combinations of parameters, projection data or prior information. The PPR method is a tool for analysis if the phase contrast is in the sample.

Acknowledgements. A grateful acknowledgement to the AMADE research group from the Universitat de Girona - Spain and the GiMaT research group from the Universidad Politécnica Salesiana – Cuenca, Ecuador for their support.

References

1. Garcea, S.C., Wang, Y., Withers, P.J.: X-ray computed tomography of polymer composites. Compos. Sci. Technol. **156**, 305–319 (2017)
2. du Plessis, A., le Roux, S.G., Tshibalanganda, M.: Advancing X-ray micro computed tomography in Africa: going far, together. Sci. Afr. **3**, e00061 (2019)
3. De Witte, Y., Boone, M., Vlassenbroeck, J., Dierick, M., Van Hoorebeke, L.: Bronnikov-aided correction for X-ray computed tomography. JOSA A **26**(4), 890–894 (2009)
4. Groso, A., Abela, R., Stampanoni, M.: Implementation of a fast method for high resolution phase contrast tomography. Opt. Express OE **14**(18), 8103–8110 (2006)
5. Stolidi, A.: High resolution X-ray phase contrast imaging for dynamic non-destructive testing of composite material. Paris-Saclay Ondes et Matière, Saclay
6. Shen, H., Nutt, S., Hull, D.: Direct observation and measurement of fiber architecture in short fiber-polymer composite foam through micro-CT imaging. Compos. Sci. Technol. **64**(13), 2113–2120 (2004)
7. Scott, A.E., Mavrogordato, M., Wright, P., Sinclair, I., Spearing, S.M.: In situ fibre fracture measurement in carbon–epoxy laminates using high resolution computed tomography. Compos. Sci. Technol. **71**(12), 1471–1477 (2011)
8. Wagner, P., Schwarzhaupt, O., May, M.: In-situ X-ray computed tomography of composites subjected to fatigue loading. Mater. Lett. **236**, 128–130 (2019)
9. Cai, W.: Feasibility study of phase-contrast cone beam CT imaging systems. Department of Physics and Astronomy, University of Rochester (2009)
10. Nasseh, I., Al-Rawi, W.: Cone beam computed tomography. Dent. Clin. North Am. **62**(3), 361–391 (2018)
11. Salvo, L., et al.: X-ray micro-tomography an attractive characterisation technique in materials science. Nucl. Instrum. Methods Phys. Res. Sect. B: Beam Interact. Mater. Atoms **200**, 273–286 (2003)
12. Barigou, M., Douaire, M.: 9 - X-ray micro-computed tomography for resolving food microstructures. In: Morris, V.J., Groves, K. (eds.) Food Microstructures, pp. 246–272. Woodhead Publishing, Sawston (2013)
13. Endrizzi, M.: X-ray phase-contrast imaging. Nucl. Instrum. Methods Phys. Res. Sect. A: Accelerators Spectrometers Detectors Assoc. Equip. **878**, 88–98 (2018)
14. Busse, G., Hemelrijck, D.V., Solodov, I., Anastasopoulos, A.: Emerging Technologies in NDT. CRC Press, Boca Raton (2008)
15. Chu, Y.S., et al.: Hard-X-ray microscopy with Fresnel zone plates reaches 40 nm Rayleigh resolution. Appl. Phys. Lett. **92**(10), 103119 (2008)

16. McKetty, M.H.: The AAPM/RSNA physics tutorial for residents. X-ray attenuation. RadioGraphics **18**(1), 151–163 (1998)
17. Paganin, D., Mayo, S.C., Gureyev, T.E., Miller, P.R., Wilkins, S.W.: Simultaneous phase and amplitude extraction from a single defocused image of a homogeneous object. J. Microscopy **206**(1), 33–40 (2002)
18. Taba, S.T., et al.: Toward improving breast cancer imaging: radiological assessment of propagation-based phase-contrast CT technology. Acad. Radiol. **26**, e79–e89 (2018)
19. Boone, M., De Witte, Y., Dierick, M., Van den Bulcke, J., Vlassenbroeck, J., Van Hoorebeke, L.: Practical use of the modified Bronnikov algorithm in micro-CT. Nucl. Instrum. Methods Phys. Res. Sect. B: Beam Interact. Mater. Atoms **267**(7), 1182–1186 (2009)
20. Momose, A., Takeda, T., Itai, Y., Hirano, K.: Phase–contrast X-ray computed tomography for observing biological soft tissues. Nat. Med. **2**(4), 473–475 (1996)
21. Jian, F.: Phase contrast computed tomography. In: Computed Tomography-Clinical Applications. InTech (2012)
22. Inside Matters, Octopus Reconstruction User Manual, 8.9.2 (2016)
23. Fu, J., Hu, X., Li, C.: X-ray differential phase-contrast tomographic reconstruction with a phase line integral retrieval filter. Nucl. Instrum. Methods Phys. Res. Sect. A: Accelerators Spectrometers Detectors Assoc. Equip. **778**, 14–19 (2015)
24. Gupta, M.K., Sidhu, B.S., Mann, K.S., Dhaliwal, A.S., Kahlon, K.S.: Advanced two media (ATM) method for measurement of linear attenuation coefficient. Ann. Nucl. Energy **56**, 251–254 (2013)
25. Bronnikov, A.V.: Theory of quantitative phase-contrast computed tomography. J. Opt. Soc. Am. A (JOSAA) **19**(3), 472–480 (2002)
26. Biswas, R., Sahadath, H., Mollah, A.S., Huq, M.F.: Calculation of gamma-ray attenuation parameters for locally developed shielding material: Polyboron. J. Radiat. Res. Appl. Sci. **9**(1), 26–34 (2016)
27. Priamo, J.M.F.: Linear attenuation coefficient—radiology reference article—Radiopaedia. org. Radiopaedia. https://radiopaedia.org/articles/linear-attenuation-coefficient. Consultado 01 June 2018
28. Byun, J.-I., Yun, J.-Y.: A calibration transmission method to determine the gamma-ray linear attenuation coefficient without a collimator. Appl. Radiat. Isotopes **102**, 70–73 (2015)
29. Midgley, S.M.: Measurements of the X-ray linear attenuation coefficient for low atomic number materials at energies 32–66 and 140 keV. Radiat. Phys. Chem. **72**(4), 525–535 (2005)
30. Suplee, C.: XCOM: Photon cross sections database. In: NIST, 17 September 2009. https://www.nist.gov/pml/xcom-photon-cross-sections-database. Consultado 13 June 2018
31. Kuznetsov, S.: X-ray optics calculator. http://purple.ipmt-hpm.ac.ru/xcalc/xcalc_mysql/refractive.php. Consultado 09 July 2018
32. Teague, M.R.: Image formation in terms of the transport equation. J. Opt. Soc. Am. A (JOSAA) **2**(11), 2019–2026 (1985)
33. Abramovitch, K., Rice, D.D.: Basic principles of cone beam computed tomography. Dent. Clin. North Am. **58**(3), 463–484 (2014)
34. Wilkins, S.W., Gureyev, T.E., Gao, D., Pogany, A., Stevenson, A.W.: Phase-contrast imaging using polychromatic hard X-rays. Nature **384**(6607), 335–338 (1996)
35. Yu, R.P., Kennedy, S.M., Paganin, D.M., Jesson, D.E.: Phase retrieval low energy electron microscopy. Micron **41**(3), 232–238 (2010)
36. Fajardo, J.I., Santos, J., Garzón, L., Cruz, L.J.: Factorial study of process parameters on the orientation state of injected bamboo fibre/polypropylene composite parts, Ottawa (2015)

37. Fajardo, J., Lasso, D., Paltán, C., López, L., Perguachi, D., Cruz, L.: Improving the processing and rheological properties of natural fibre/polypropylene composites (2015)
38. Mera-Moya, V., Fajardo, J.I., de Paula Junior, I.C., Bustamante, L., Cruz, L.J., Barros, T.: Semi-automatic determination of geometrical properties of short natural fibers in biocomposites by digital image processing. In: International Conference on Information Theoretic Security, pp. 387–396 (2018)
39. Index of Refraction. http://henke.lbl.gov/optical_constants/getdb2.html. Consultado 01 June 2018
40. Miettinen, A., et al.: Non-destructive automatic determination of aspect ratio and cross-sectional properties of fibres. Compos. Part A: Appl. Sci. Manuf. **77**, 188–194 (2015)

Discrete Optimization Based Rail Passengers Safety and Comfort Communication System Configuration Design

Adam Galuszka[1]([⊠]) [iD], Tomasz Grzejszczak[1] [iD],
Carmen Lungoci[2] [iD], Ewa Gilner[1] [iD], and Tomasz Hejczyk[3] [iD]

[1] Institute of Automatic Control, Silesian University of Technology,
Akademicka 16, 44-100 Gliwice, Poland
{adam.galuszka,tomasz.grzejszczak,
ewa.gilner}@polsl.pl
[2] Transilvania University, Politehnicii 1, 500019 Brasov, Romania
lungoci@unitbv.ro
[3] ENTE Sp. z. o.o., Gaudiego 7, 44-100 Gliwice, Poland
t.hejczyk@ente.com.pl

Abstract. This paper presents rail passengers safety and comfort communication system configuration design proposal. The objective is to integrate four communication modules in the vehicle: general communication, wireless technology relevant to project implementation, data transmission to the Control Centre and passenger access point module. For each module three or four available solutions were proposed and analyzed. Then, each solution has been evaluated by experts under different criteria: functionality, upgradeability and implementation costs. Basing on obtained results, we propose to present configuration design of the system as multi-objectives discrete optimization process. Proposed solution leads to optimal system configuration.

Keywords: Communications systems · Multi-criteria optimization ·
Optimal system configuration design · Configuration management

1 Introduction

Passenger safety is the most important objective for operators and providers of railway services, manufacturers and carriers. It is therefore a basic factor for assessing its performance and determines its efficiency, as well as the broader criterion of transport service quality [1–5, 16, 18]. Monitoring the state of rail safety in Poland is maintained by the Office of Rail Transport, Chalubinskiego Street 4, 00-928 Warsaw. Within the framework of the statutory tasks the office prepares quarterly reports summarizing the state of rail safety. Last analysis show that the number of three types of events is growing [6]: collisions of trains, the derailment of trains and fires of railway vehicles. These conditions justify starting work on a system which helps to reduce the negative effects of railway incidents. Design experiences of ENTE company indicates that it is possible to develop an integrated system in terms of on the following aspects:

© Springer Nature Switzerland AG 2019
S. Misra et al. (Eds.): ICCSA 2019, LNCS 11623, pp. 468–481, 2019.
https://doi.org/10.1007/978-3-030-24308-1_38

1. trains collision detection,
2. driver monitoring,
3. fire and potential causes of fire detection

Within the project the concept of a prototype of Integrated System Supporting Information Management of Railway Passenger Traffic has been proposed [7]. The concept is presented in Fig. 1 and consists:

1. the traffic data taken from a railway vehicle,
2. warnings of possible dangers during the journey,
3. transmission the data in case of disasters.

The prototype is based on multilayer distributed architecture, which provides the expected scalability of the whole solution. The integration of modules within information management system under different assumptions (excluding communication configuration) has been considered earlier in our works [8, 13, 14]. In this paper the goal is to configure four communication modules optimally considering the below factors:

1. general communication architecture to be used in a vehicle,
2. wireless technologies relevant to project implementation,
3. links implementing for data transmission to the Control Centre,
4. passenger - access point module in a vehicle.

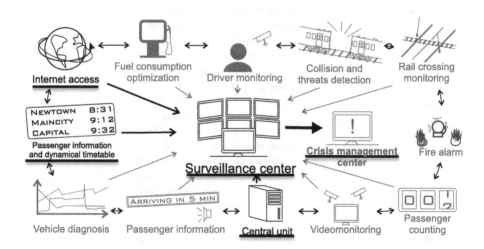

Fig. 1. The concept of integrated system supporting information management of railway passenger traffic. Analyzed items highlighted

1.1   Motivation and Contribution

Basing on expert assessments we propose to present configuration design of the communication system as discrete optimization problem. In Sect. 2 the basic features and functionality of the recommended solutions for each communication module in the system are presented. In Sect. 3 problem of configuration design of the system as two-objectives discrete static optimization problem is formulated and solved. In Sect. 4 optimal system configuration is presented. Finally, results are concluded.

2   Basic Features and Functionality of the Recommended Solutions for Each Communication Module

As a part of the work associated with the development of the conceptual framework for each module, three or four different methods of its implementation has been analyzed, taking into account their architecture, technology, functionality and implementation costs. Each of these methods has been evaluated by independent experts under two evaluation criteria: criterion 1 - functionality, criterion 2 - costs.

Table 1. Passenger - access point module in a vehicle

Method	Architecture	Technology	Functionality	Other	Costs	Functionality
1	IrDa	Wireless	Small range of up to 3 m/low optical power, point-to-point communication	Used for short distances, need for direct vision	1	1
2	Bluetooth	Wireless	The relatively small range point-to-multipoint	Use for approx. 5 m, low signal strength	2	3
3	Wi-Fi	Wireless	Acceptable range point-to-multipoint	Good coverage of rooms and other spaces	3	4

Assessments used the following rating: 1 - very low, 2 - average, 3 - high, 4 - very high. The optimal choice of module implementation method based on analysis result is summarized in presented tables. In Table 1 three methods with corresponding ratings of Passenger - access point module in a vehicle implementations are presented.

In Table 2 four methods with corresponding ratings of general communication architecture to be used in a vehicle are presented. In Table 3 three methods with corresponding ratings of wireless technologies relevant to project implementation are presented. Finally, in Table 4 four methods with corresponding ratings of links implementing for data transmission to the Control Centre are presented.

Table 2. General communication architecture to be used in a vehicle

Method	Architecture	Technology	Functionality	Other	Costs	Functionality
1	RS-232	Wire	Low range	Up to 15 m	4	1
2	RS-485	Wire	Long range, noise resistance	High cost of converters, limited bandwidth	3	2
3	Optical fiber	Wire	Long range	Complexity of the arrangement, the high cost of converters	4	3
4	Ethernet	Wire	Open standard, no interference	Simplicity, standard accessibility, large and sufficient bandwidth	1	4

Table 3. Wireless technologies relevant to project implementation

Method	Architecture	Technology	Functionality	Other	Costs
1	WiMax	Wireless	The network under development	No cover the whole area, the system under development	1
2	GSM-R	Wireless	Standard dedicated for use only in railways	Large organizational costs, not widespread network	2
3	GSM	Wireless	Standard	General availability, drop-down, gradual increase system capacity	4

Table 4. Methods of links implementing for data transmission to the Control Centre

Method	Architecture	Technology	Functionality	Other	Costs
1	Leased lines/Frame relay	Wire	Network operating phase	High costs	1
2	Polish telecommunication	Wire	Standard	High costs, general availability	2
3	Internet	Wire/wireless		Costs depend on operator	3
4	GPRS	Wireless	Standard	Low costs	4

3   Problem of Configuration Design of the System as Discrete Optimization Problem

In this section multi-objective optimization problem is presented. The concern is the minimization of a vector of objectives F(x) that can be the subject of a number of constraints or bounds [9–15, 17]. Denoting that n is a number of decision variables, k is a number of criteria, m is a number of inequality constraints and p is a number of equality constraints, we have $x = [x_1, x_2, \ldots, x_n]^T$, and:

$$F(x) = [f_1(x), f_2(x), \ldots, f_k(x)]^T, \tag{1}$$

$$g_i(x) \leq 0, \text{ for } i = 1, 2, \ldots m, \tag{2}$$

$$h_i(\mathrm{x}) = 0, \text{ for } i = 1, 2, \ldots p. \tag{3}$$

Due to the fact that $F(x)$ is a vector, if any of the components of $F(x)$ are competing, there is no unique solution to this problem. Then the concept of non-inferiority (also called Pareto optimality) must be used to characterize the objectives. It is assumed that non-inferior solution (Pareto optimal solution) is one in which an improvement in one objective requires a degradation of another. To describe the concept of non-inferior solutions, introduce the set of all possible solutions that satisfy constraints, such as the project budget, available technologies, etc. It is called set of feasible solutions that satisfies constraints (2) and (3). This allows to find all values of different objectives included in the objectives vector. If, for example, one takes two objectives minimization problem, for each feasible solution one can determine values for the two objectives and illustrate them in two-dimensional space, as shown in Fig. 2.

There are many methods of selecting a particular solution from the set of Pareto solutions (e.g. [12]). This weighted sum method is based on transformation of the multiple criteria problem to the problem of single-criteria, where each component of objectives vector describes the impact of this criterion for the final solution. The impact depends of the weight value w_i, $i = 1, 2\ldots k$. This leads to the following problem objective formulation:

$$\operatorname*{Min}_{x \in \Omega} F(x) = \sum_{i=1}^{k} w_i f_i(x) \tag{4}$$

It is assumed that solving multi-objective maximization problem result indicates each module implementation method. The problem is built on the basis on values in Table 5 that summarizes data from Tables 1, 2, 3 and 4. Assume:

- i – module index, $i = 1, 2, \ldots 4$;
- j – criterion index, $j = 1, 2$;
- k – method index, $k = 1, 2, 3$;

then $x_{i,j,k}$ – denotes value taken from Table 5, e.g. $x_{4,2,2} = 2$.

Table 5. Data for optimization

Method	Costs	Functionality
I. Passenger - access point module in a vehicle		
1	1	1
2	2	3
3	3	4
II. General communication architecture to be used in a vehicle		
1	4	1
2	3	2
3	4	3
4	1	4
III. Wireless technologies relevant to project implementation		
1	4	1
2	3	2
3	1	4
IV. Methods of links implementing for data transmission to the Control Centre		
1	4	1
2	4	2
3	3	3
4	1	4

Set of all $x_{i,j,k}$ forms the space of feasible solutions $\Omega = \{x_{i,j,k} \in \mathbb{Z}^n : 1,2,3,4,5\}$ for all admissible i, j, k. Objectives of the problem to be maximized are overall evaluation of criteria, i.e.:

$f_1(x)$ – is the first objective defined as a sum of all modules criterion 1 values depending on the method, i.e.:

$$f_1(x) = \sum_{i=1}^{4} x_{i,1,k}; \quad i = 1, 2, \ldots 4; \quad k = 1, 2, 3, (4); \tag{5}$$

$f_2(x)$ - is the second objective defined as a sum of all modules criterion 2 values depending on the method, i.e.:

$$f_2(x) = \sum_{i=1}^{4} x_{i,2,k}; \quad i = 1, 2, \ldots 4; \quad k = 1, 2, 3, (4); \tag{6}$$

Optimization the two-component vector of objective functions would give the solution for the problem given:

$$F(x) = (f_1(x), f_2(x)). \tag{7}$$

Admissible solutions are presented in Fig. 2, where Pareto solutions are indicated by red circles. The number of possible variants (L), i.e. set of admissible solutions, based on the number of modules built and possible system configurations can be easily determined:

$$L = 3 * 4 * 3 * 4 = 144. \tag{8}$$

Two-criteria optimization problem was formulated as a minimization problem, so if: Max $F(x) = -$ (Min $(- F(x))$ and the goal is to maximize functionality (criterion 1) and minimize the cost (criterion 2), one can assume following objective function:

$$\text{Min} \leftarrow F'(x) = (-f_1(x), \ f_2(x)). \tag{9}$$

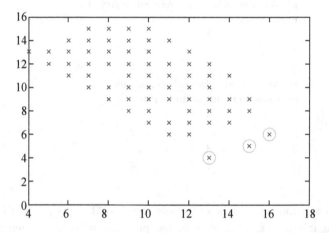

Fig. 2. Set of admissible solutions and Pareto solutions (in circles). Vertical axis denotes variant costs, horizontal axis denotes variant functionality

Basing on formula (9) objective function is transformed to one-objective optimization problem:

$$\text{Min} \leftarrow F''(x) = -w_1 * f_1(x) + w_2 * f_2(x). \tag{10}$$

Example. Let No. 1 of possible variant (admissible) solution will be the choice of method 1 for each of the built modules. Therefore, on the basis of the Table 5, one can built Table 6 with exemplary admissible solutions and corresponding values of objective functions. The values of each objective function for admissible solution No. 1 (first row in Table 6) data from Table 6 are presented below:

$$f_1(x) = 1 + 4 + 4 + 4 = 13,$$
$$f_2(x) = 1 + 1 + 1 + 1 = 4.$$

Optimal configuration design problem has been solved in three cases:

Case 1: $w_1 = 1$, $w_2 = 1$. Each criterion is equally important. The optimal solution is a variant of No. 144, the minimum value of $F''(144) = -10$.

Case 2: $w_1 = 0$, $w_2 = 1$. Border case, where optimization problem is reduced to costs. The optimal solution is a variant of No. 48, the minimal value of F'' $(48) = 4$.

Case 3: $w_1 = 1$, $w_2 = 0$. Border case, where optimization problem is reduced to functionalities. The optimal solution is a variant of No. 144, the minimal value of $F''(144) = -9$.

Table 6. Exemplary admissible solutions and corresponding values of objective functions

Module	I			II			III			IV			$f_2(x)$	$f_1(x)$
No	method	costs	Functionality	Method	costs	Functionality	method	Costs	functionality	Method	Costs	functionality	Sum fo costs	Sum of functionalities
1	1	1	1	1	4	1	1	4	1	1	4	1	13	4
2	1	1	1	1	4	1	1	4	1	2	4	2	13	5
etc.														
144	1	1	1	1	4	1	1	4	1	4	1	4	10	7

Optimal modules configurations are presented in Table 7.

Table 7. Optimal modules configurations

Module	I			II			III			IV			$f_2(x)$	$f_1(x)$
No	method	costs	Functionality	Method	costs	functionality	Method	Costs	functionality	Method	Costs	functionality	Sum fo costs	Sum of functionalities
Case 1 = Case 3	3	3	4	4	1	4	3	1	4	4	1	4	6	16
Case 2	1	1	1	4	1	4	3	1	4	4	1	4	4	13

4 Optimal System Configuration

The scheme resulting from the multi-criteria optimization for passenger communication analysis - the access point in the vehicle is shown in Fig. 3.

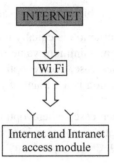

Fig. 3. Architecture recommendation according to variant I after passenger communication analysis - access point in the vehicle (source in Polish: project documentation)

Based on the analysis from the previous chapter of multicriterial optimization, a solution based on an Ethernet network in the context of architecture for use in a vehicle was chosen. The architecture resulting from the optimization will be implemented using UTP cat. 5 and UTP cat. 7 for the backbone of the network. Critical points will be the transitions between vehicle combinations in case of more than one composition. All connections between individual modules in the wired area will be made as shown in Fig. 4.

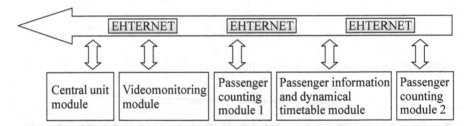

Fig. 4. Architecture recommendation according to variant II after the analysis of architecture for use in the vehicle (source in Polish: project documentation)

Considering the choice of the variant resulting from the analysis of wireless technologies relevant from the point of view of the project implementation, the GSM network was chosen, which allows the functionality of the central unit modules to be implemented. It will be equipped with a GSM module and enable communication and data transfer via the GSM/UMTS network. If the GSM/UMTS network coverage is missing, the data will be saved in the "black box" and transmitted to the server after receiving the coverage. The functionality of the Supervision Center module, such as displaying on the maps in the dispatch center, the current position of each vehicle will be implemented via the GSM network. The functionality of the vehicle diagnostics module will also be implemented through the GSM network, based on reading the controller's operating parameters and sending them, via the GSM network, to the Supervisory Center on an ongoing basis (Fig. 5).

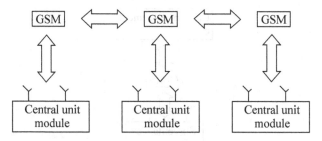

Fig. 5. Recommendation of wireless technologies important from the point of view of project implementation (source in Polish: project documentation)

A data link based on GPRS packet data transmission will be used for data transmission (Fig. 6). It results from the bi-objective optimization in the aspect of the analysis of links in terms of transmission to the Supervisory Center. This link will enable the functionality of the fire signaling module consisting in sending information about alarms occurring in the vehicle to the Supervisory Center module. Then, activation of the fire alarm sensor will automatically change the monitoring system monitoring in the vehicle's cabin and send the information and photos of the threatened area to the Monitoring Center module without delay. In terms of the basic functionality of the collision and threat detection module, a packet-based data transmission link will enable sending important information to the Crisis Management Center (i.e. immediate delivery of information on the geographical location and size of the disaster to the appropriate services). The signal will first reach the Surveillance Center and then to the Crisis Management Center. Information and photographs of the threatened area will also be sent to the Surveillance Center without delay. The content of information sent in the GPRS packet will be: data on the speed of the vehicle at the time of the disaster, data on the number of passengers at the time of the disaster, exact geographical location of the vehicle at the time of the disaster, recording of camera images and conversations in the driver's cab just before the disaster. This amount of data will be enabled by a packet-based GPRS data transmission connection, where access to the APN of the mobile operator will be a prerequisite. APN is the IP address of the backbone network element that allows routing of packets between the operator's network and the external packet network.

The collision and accident detection module after collision detection and determination of the impact force and bank angle will enable immediate transmission of information to the Supervisory Center (Fig. 7).

The level crossing monitoring module will allow automatic detection of cases of improper behavior driving motor vehicles on level crossings through continuous analysis of the area and registration of incorrect situations. The GPRS connection selected as a result of the optimization of variant No. IV will allow sending information about the event (i.e. the intrusion of the vehicle on the railway crossing with closed tall boots or active traffic lights) to the Supervision Center. A photo material will be sent to the registration of the registration number of the vehicle which entered passing. The general architecture of the recommended solution are presented in Figs. 8 and 9.

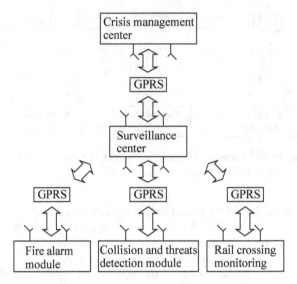

Fig. 6. Recommendation of links in terms of transmission to the Supervision Center - option IV (source in Polish: project documentation)

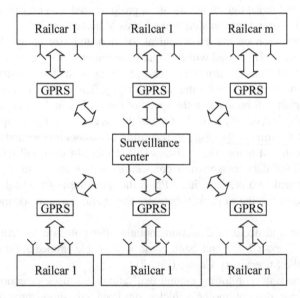

Fig. 7. Mutual communication between vehicles after the area analysis stage (source in Polish: project documentation)

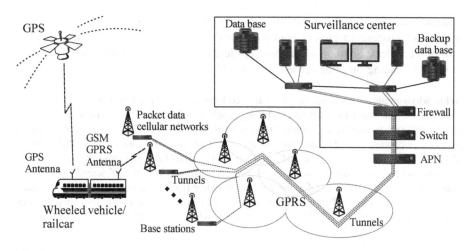

Fig. 8. Diagram of individual system components (source in Polish: project documentation)

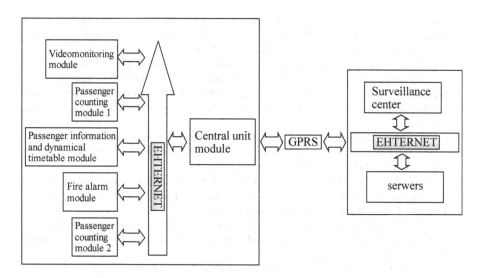

Fig. 9. System topology (source in Polish: project documentation)

5   Conclusion

The paper presents the design of rail passengers safety and comfort communication system as multi-objective optimization problem The system is an integration of four modules: general communication architecture to be used in a vehicle, wireless technologies relevant to project implementation, links implementing for data transmission to the Control Centre and Passenger - access point module in a vehicle into one coherent solution. For each module three or four different construction methods were proposed and considered. Then, each method has been evaluated under different criteria: functionality, upgradeability and implementation costs. Basing on obtained results, we propose to present configuration design problem of the system as optimization problem. Solution of the problem leads to different optimal system configurations, depending on priorities assigned to objectives.

Acknowledgments. This article is the result of collaboration between ENTE Sp. z o.o. company with and the Silesian University of Technology, which jointly operate the project No UOD-DEM-1-243/001 funded by the National Research and Development Centre. This work has been partially supported by Institute of Automatic Control BK Grant 02/010/BK18/0102 (BK/200/Rau1/2018) in the year 2019 for the first (Adam Galuszka) and second (Tomasz Grzejszczak) author. This work was supported by the National Ministry of Science and Higher Education funds 10/DW/2017/01/1 for the fourth author (Ewa Gilner). The analysis has been performed with the use of IT infrastructure of GeCONiI Upper Silesian Centre for Computational Science and Engineering (NCBiR grant no. POIG.02.03.01-24-099/13).

References

1. Młyńczak, J.: Analysis of intelligent transport systems (ITS) in public transport of Upper Silesia. In: Mikulski, J. (ed.) TST 2011. CCIS, vol. 239, pp. 164–171. Springer, Heidelberg (2011). https://doi.org/10.1007/978-3-642-24660-9_19
2. Krystek, R.: (ed.): Integrated Safety Transportation System [Zintegrowany system bezpieczeństwa transportu]. Tomy I-III, WKiŁ Gdańsk 2009–2010 (2010). (in polish)
3. Wilson, J.R., Mills, A., Clarke, T., Rajan, J., Dadashi, N. (eds.): Rail Human Factors Around the World: Impacts on and of People for Successful Rail Operations. CRC Press, Croydon (2012)
4. Hu, Z., Cui, J., Zhang, J., Zhang, L., Chang, L.: Railway safety monitoring system based on CAPS. In: Fifth International Conference on Measuring Technology and Mechatronics Automation (ICMTMA) (2013). ISBN 978-1-4673-5652-7
5. Popescu, T.: Proiectul Feroviar Romanesc. Editura Simetria (2014). (in romanian)
6. Summary of the State of Rail Safety: Report for the Third Quarter of 2013. Railway Transport Office, Warsaw, November 2013 (2013)
7. Hejczyk, T., Wszołek, B., Galuszka, A., Mlynczak, J., Burdzik, R.: Application of safety and communication modules as an integrated intelligent system in rail vehicles. Vibroeng. Procedia **4**, 105–110 (2014)
8. Galuszka, A., Krystek, J., Swierniak, A., Lungoci, C., Grzejszczak, T.: Information management in passenger traffic supporting system design as a multi-criteria discrete optimization task. Arch. Control Sci. **2017**(2), 229–238 (2017)
9. Bukowiecki, B., Galuszka, A., Szweda, S.: Optimization of the geometrical features of the powered roof support unit kinematic chain due to the criterion of minimizing the weight. Przeglad Elektrotechniczny **88**(3A), 131–138 (2012)
10. Belazzoug, M., Boudour, M., Sebaa, K.: FACTS location and size for reactive power system compensation through the multi-objective optimization. Arch. Control Sci. **20**, 473–489 (2010)
11. Cacciabue, P.C.: Guide to Applying Human Factors Methods, Human Error and Accident Management in Safety Critical Systems, p. 2004. Springer, London (2004). https://doi.org/10.1007/978-1-4471-3812-9
12. Emmerich, M.: MATLAB help optimization toolbox. In: Multiobjective Optimization (2005)

13. Galuszka, A., Swierniak, A., Hejczyk, T., Wszołek, B., Mlynczak, J.: Design of rail passengers safety and comfort system as three-objective discrete static optimization problem. In: Enrique, C., Salvador, P. (eds.) ISC 2015, 13th Annual Industrial Simulation Conference, Valencia, Spain, 1–3 June 2015, pp. 89–94 (2015). ISBN 978-90-77381-89-2
14. Galuszka, A., Swierniak, A., Hejczyk, T., Mlynczak, J.: Hybrid optimization method for design of rail passengers safety and comfort system. In: The 9th International Conference INTER-ENG 2015 Interdisciplinarity in Engineering, "Petru Maior" University of Tîrgu - Mures Faculty of Engineering, Romania, 8–9 October 2015 (2015a)
15. Jarosław, B., Sara, A., Jolanta, K., Magdalena, T.: Availability analysis of selected mining machinery. Arch. Control Sci. 27(2), 197–209 (2017)
16. Bertini, R.L., El-Geneidy, A.M.: Advanced traffic management system data. In: Gillen, D., Levinson, D. (eds.) Assessing the Benefits and Costs of ITS, pp. 287–314. Springer, Boston (2004). https://doi.org/10.1007/1-4020-7874-9_15
17. Pedersen, Ch.R.: Multicriteria discrete optimization – and related topics. Ph.D. dissertation, Department of mathematics, Aarhus University (2006)
18. Gorev, A., Solodkiy, A., Enokaev, V.: Improving efficiency of traffic management and safety based on integration of local ATMS. Transp. Res. Procedia 36(2018), 207–212 (2018)

VIoT – A Step Towards Easing the Interoperability of IoT-Based Applications

Dannylo J. B. Egídio$^{(\boxtimes)}$ and Gibeon S. de Aquino Jr.

Department of Informatics and Applied Mathematic,
Federal University of Rio Grande do Norte, Natal, Brazil
dannylojohnathan@gmail.com, gibeon@dimap.ufrn.br

Abstract. The growing improvement in embedded computing, sensing technologies, and connected devices has enabled the advancement of innovative paradigms, such as the Internet of Things (IoT). However, the considerable diversity of devices and, consequently, of protocols that have emerged have made this process difficult. Numerous challenges emerged, such as heterogeneity, interoperability, multiplicity of data representation and services, etc. These challenges have made the development of IoT applications somewhat complex and costly since the capabilities of these devices, protocols, and standards have become device-specific, forcing the developer to come up with complex integration strategies to address these specifications. In this sense, this work proposes a framework, called VIoT, that seeks to facilitate the process of developing IoT applications for heterogeneous environments through device virtualization. The strategy will attempt to abstract the heterogeneous aspects related to the physical devices, which will be represented by a virtualized model, encapsulating the operations common to its protocols and providing a common interface between the real device and the virtualized one, thus reducing, from the developer's point of view, the effort in implementing applications for these environments.

Keywords: Internet of Things · Framework · Virtualization · Easing · Application

1 Introduction

The recent years have been marked by a growing advance in embedded computing, sensing technologies, and smart devices. Some predictions state that about 29 billion devices will be connected by 2022 [7]. This strong emergence of intelligent and connected devices has led to the development of a series of services that are both useful and important to people. These services seek to base themselves on innovative computational paradigms such as the Internet of Things (IoT).

The Internet of Things is a concept based on smart objects, considered as "thing", that cooperate with each other through the internet to reach a common

S. Misra et al. (Eds.): ICCSA 2019, LNCS 11623, pp. 482–496, 2019.
https://doi.org/10.1007/978-3-030-24308-1_39

goal [10]. This concept has provoked the interest of both the industry and the market in basing their new services and applications on the IoT principles [3]. This way, smart ecosystems have been suggested for many contexts, such as smart homes, smart cities, smart farms, smart factories, among others [14].

However, many challenges still need to be overcome to achieve the IoT concepts. Among these challenges, it is possible to highlight the heterogeneity and interoperability of devices and standards, which are considered by Tayur [13] as one of the most significant limitations of IoT. Also, issues related to the devices' resource restrictions [2], the variety of forms of data representation, and multiple communication protocols [1,9,11] are also considered critical challenges of the IoT paradigm. Finally, all of these challenges consequently end up making the development of IoT applications complex and costly.

Considering these challenges, standards have been suggested by many suppliers consortia to deal with many of the limitations mentioned. These standards seek to provide mechanisms for the registration, discovery, and communication for the devices involved, as well as strategies for security, identification, and management of resources. However, they only reach a very specific and restricted set of devices. Besides, these patterns are usually incompatible with each other, requiring developers to formulate generally complex integration strategies [13].

In this sense, this work's goal is the development of the VIoT framework. Furthermore, VIoT aims to facilitate the development of IoT-based applications by abstracting the heterogeneous capabilities of the communication protocols. This approach will seek to treat the application devices uniformly, providing resources for their virtual representation. This way, it will be possible to reduce the effort needed to implement these applications, since the devices involved will be interoperable, even if they are heterogeneous.

This paper is organized into seven sections. Section 2 will delimit, in a detailed way, the problem addressed by this work. Section 3 will describe the works related to this research. Section 4, in its turn, will provide details on the implementation of the proposed framework's architecture, its components and the details related to instantiation and use. Section 5 will describe a proof of concept using VIoT and the evaluation of the proposal considering how easy it was to use. The Sect. 6 deals with conclusions and future works and the Sect. 7 will describe the acknowledgements.

2   The Problem

To illustrate VIoT's utility, we will use a typical scenario of a room with temperature control. The room would consist of a temperature sensor that would measure the temperature and a thermostat that would regulate the environment's temperature. Both would have separate communication protocols: the sensor would use UPnP, while the thermostat would work with Bluetooth.

In addition to the communication protocols, the devices also have different capabilities, which makes it difficult for the application to manipulate them. To handle the UPnP sensor, it is necessary to discover it on the network, know its services and actions and send messages to its status variables. For the Blue-tooth, however, it will be necessary to consult the network, pair with the chosen device and, after obtaining the connection, transmit the data required, finally terminating the connection.

To perform such an operation, two logic modules will be needed to deal with each of the protocols and their specificities. In this case, each module will contain the code (which must be written by the developer) needed to meet the characteristics and architecture of each protocol. The developer will need to handle each protocol individually for the application to be effective.

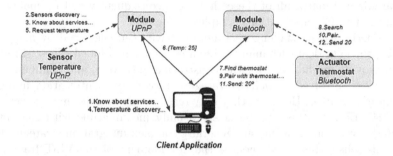

Fig. 1. Temperature control scenario with heterogeneous devices.

The Fig. 1 illustrates the scenario mentioned above: the application requests the available services from the UPnP module (1) which, in turn, sends its discovery commands to the UPnP stack (2) and receives information about the services available to inform the client application. Once it has the services in its hand, the application can discover the temperature (4) and receive, from the module, a JSON format containing its value (6).

After verifying the temperature's value, the application was able to identify that it is higher than desired, thus initiating its communication with the Bluetooth module (actuator protocol) to modify the temperature's state. For this, it is necessary to follow the steps required by the protocol: search for the thermostat (7) on the Bluetooth stack; when it is found on the network, pair with it (9) so that the protocol grants us a valid connection with the device for the communication; only then, send information about the appropriate temperature (11) which, in the example mentioned, is 20 °C.

The infrastructure considered in this scenario demonstrates the need to understand how each device operates and what are its service capabilities, how they are implemented and how they can be accessed and configured remotely. These questions have very different answers considering each device.

Our proposal, which aims to treat the heterogeneous devices in a unified and homogeneous way, will seek to promote the integration of these heterogeneous devices, thus reducing the effort needed to develop the application. The application's components will be abstracted as virtual devices in the application logic, with properties and behaviors defined in a single virtualized model. Its capabilities will be abstracted from drivers that will be included in the VIoT. These drivers, when added, become proxies that know how to handle the individual capabilities of each protocol and consequently make VIoT capable of performing the operations needed on the devices.

3   Related Works

The proposal of [3] introduces a framework called DataTweet, which focuses on multiple domains and uses the Machine-to-Machine Measurement (M3) Framework to solve heterogeneity issues. The author's proposal is a two-part project division: the components of the application logic (AL) and the Common Service Entities (CSE). The first part abstracts all of the application's mechanisms in which the users are interested in, such as user interface, query mechanisms, and resources discovery, among others, while the second part abstracts the available services offered by the application in this module. The whole dynamics of registration, management, and interoperability is handled in the CSE, and the application-oriented functions belong to AL. These modules are intermediated by a common interface.

The proposal explained above is based on the work of [10] which, in turn, seeks to develop a conceptual framework based on the division of skills found in an IoT infrastructure. Their approach features descriptive languages called "Srijan Vocabulary" which will model existing devices and generate executable codes for the applications.

The work of [5] stands out for providing a framework that aims to treat the heterogeneity of protocols of an IoT application. The IoTDelegate abstracts the application in three layers: Plug-In, Collaboration, and Service Management. The first layer will remove any protocol-related dependency from the smart objects, while the others will create abstractions that allow the communication and collaboration of the constituent devices. The proposal of [6] reports a framework that is different from the ones previously mentioned, because it aims to simplify the development through a user-centered approach, reducing or eliminating the use of programming in levels closer to the hardware. The approach is based on models and uses Task Script for this purpose.

A proposal focused on abstraction that was considered in this work was the one made by [8], which proposes an API for accessing IoT-based services through REST and SOAP protocols. The approach seeks to provide means to facilitate the complexity inherent to the diversity of devices found in IoT applications. Basically, the proposal will present a framework that will provide uniform access to resources and operations through structured messages in SOAP and REST. The author used UPnP as the guiding standard for his experiment and evaluated aspects related to performance, discarding the use of SOAP due to results below expectations.

The work of [4] also raised the need to have a model that can uniformly represent the devices. The author proposed in his work a configuration platform infrastructure (IoT-PIC) trying to consider the many layers found in an IoT infrastructure. Simplification occurs through a model-based approach for the development of new IoT-based applications and services. For this purpose, the author used XMPP in the entity communication process and Resource Application Interface (RAI) to handle the virtualization. However, the solution virtualizes according to the driver available in the RAI layer and returns a virtualized instance specific to each driver.

The approaches mentioned above relate to this work because they use ways of abstracting objects through model proposals. However, most of the proposals omit details of how the devices will relate to the models in the application. Although some evidence the need for network discovery mechanisms, such as [3], they do not report clearly when this operation occurs. Some proposals seek solutions through specialized virtualizations for specific protocols, such as [4], so that the specialized knowledge of each protocol is still necessary. Our proposal believes that globalized and unique virtualization would reduce the complexity inherent to the development of IoT applications, facilitating coding in the treatment of the several existing devices.

4   VIoT: Proposed Architecture

The proposed architecture is illustrated in Fig. 2 and considers common operations in IoT-based applications to enable a harmonic interaction between the VIoT and the physical devices present in the solution's infrastructure. The operations considered in the architecture were those related to registry, status update, and device discovery, which will be explained next.

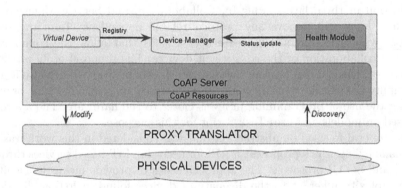

Fig. 2. Framework's architecture.

The registry operation is responsible for making the device known to VIoT by registering it in the Device Manager to considerer it, from the moment it is registered, a virtualized entity to be used in the application logic. The status update operation occurs periodically to prevent an inoperable device from being available in VIoT. In the case of an inoperability happening, it will be removed from the Device Manager and disregarded by the device discovery operation.

The device discovery operation occurs in two different moments. The first moment is during the Proxy Translator discovery process, which will encapsulate each device discovered in a Virtual Device instance. The second moment occurs when the client application invokes it through the Device Manager's discovery methods. In this second moment, the devices returned in the discovery process will already be virtualized.

As for the architecture layers, as shown in Fig. 2, they are arranged as follows: the Physical Devices layer concentrates all the real devices found in the solution's infrastructure and their processing and communication capabilities. The Proxy Translator layer provides the communication protocol drivers inherent to the devices existing in the solution's infrastructure; each driver implements a common interface that will represent it as a valid Proxy for the framework. This layer is responsible for making the devices communicable and recognizable in VIoT.

Finally, the highest layer of the architecture concentrates VIoT's main idea. It is the layer responsible for the abstraction of the physical devices and the communication processes that form it. This layer is divided into four components: Virtual Devices, CoAP Server, Device Manager, and Health Module, which will be described in more details below.

4.1 Proxy Translator

The Proxy Translator's workflow is basically geared to the mechanisms that are particular to each proxy added, so that functions that are typical of the discovery of devices in the network and of sending and querying data for each device are necessarily implemented and available. This way, the process of discovering the devices of this layer implies in each proxy performing its own discovery processes and therefore encapsulating the devices found in Virtual Devices, thus registering in their own instances the proxy instance responsible for the operation, its resources and the actions it can perform.

Proxies are addable in this layer of the architecture. In this case, it is essential to consider that some communication protocols do not have high-level features such as automatic device discovery included in their structure. Therefore, for the proxy to be in accordance with VIoT's architecture, the developer will need to implement these additional features based on what the protocol can provide.

4.2 Virtual Device

A Virtual Device is a virtualized representation of the physical device present in the infrastructure of the IoT solution. It encapsulates the capabilities of the physical device so that they can be delivered to the client application through standardized methods. Virtualizing a device ensures that it will be handled uniformly during the process of developing the application's logic, since all of the devices, regardless of their individual characteristics, will be represented through virtualization.

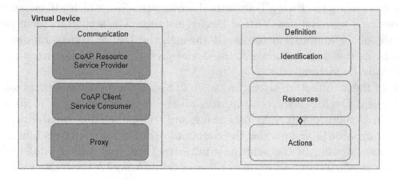

Fig. 3. Virtual Device's structure.

The internal structure of a Virtual Device is illustrated in Fig. 3. It is composed of two groups of components: the first group, called the communication group, represents the components that are essential for the communication between the Virtual Device and its real Device. The second group, called the definition group, represents the attributes that identify the Virtual Device in the VIoT. The definition group consists of the following components:

- **Identification:** stores, in the Virtual Device, the information that identifies it exclusively in the VIoT. The information that can be considered part of the identification of a device includes a unique ID, the type of device, the device's nominal description, its supplier, its version, etc.;
- **Resources:** represent a nominal description of a group of tasks that can be performed by a device, such as control the temperature, control the energy, etc. A Resource can be made up of one or more actions.
- **Actions:** represent a nominal description of each task that can be performed by the device, such as turning on or off the lights, checking the temperature status, etc. Each action belongs to a Resource.

The communication group, in its turn, consists of the following components:

- **CoAP Resource:** it is a representation of an Action through a URL in the standards required by the CoAP Protocol. For example: if we have an action named Check Temperature Status, we will have a CoAP Resource named coap://0.0.0.0/01/CheckTemperatureStatus, where 01 is the discovered device's identifier.
- **CoAP Client:** a CoAP Client represents an instance that can communicate with the valid CoAP Resources in the CoAP Server. This way, when the device wants to request an action, it will use the CoAP Client, informing it of the desired CoAP Resource.

– **Proxy:** represents an instance of the Proxy that discovered the physical device in the discovery process performed by the Proxy Translator.

The Coap Server managed by the VIoT will be responsible for mediating the communication between the proxies and their virtualized devices. This way, each call to its interaction methods will initiate the endpoints responsible for each Resource in the CoAP Server. An endpoint is a CoAP Resource represented through its URL. The interaction methods, in their turn, represent procedures capable of performing the communication between the virtual device and the physical device.

4.3 CoAP Server

The CoAP Server is an internal structure that will manage all of the resources and actions of the discovered devices, which have been converted into CoAP Resources. These resources have their own URL defined at the moment of virtualization and ensure that all communication with the device's resources happens through the CoAP Protocol, thus avoiding unexpected situations when dealing with devices and restricted networks.

The features of the CoAP Server, which represent the features and actions of the IoT solution's Devices, can also be accessed through the endpoints provided at the time of the VIoT's execution. These endpoints are the URLs mentioned above and can either return information from the devices or modify their state variables.

The use of the CoAP Protocol is justified by the need to deal with networks and devices with computational restrictions, as well as to enable other client applications to use the services of the IoT solution. These other applications will not necessarily need the VIoT if they know the endpoints it will make available.

4.4 Device Manager

The Device Manager is a component responsible for registering and storing all of the devices discovered and virtualized by the Proxy Translator layer. It is the access point of the client application to all of the devices that are virtualized and has dynamic discovery mechanisms that will enable the use of more comprehensive search semantics, such as search by the device's name or part of the name, by its identifier, by its type, etc. Any device that is not registered in the Manager is disregarded by the VIoT.

4.5 Health Module

The Health Module is a module that will periodically check the "health" status of the application's devices. It is essential because the physical devices involved in the IoT solution's infrastructure need to be always available and in full operation so that the application's logic will not fail due to the lack of availability of a device. This way, the module is responsible for monitoring all of the devices that are registered, thus canceling the registration of those that, by chance, do not present viable conditions or fail to respond to a request made by the Health Module.

The monitoring starts from the first discovery of Devices performed by the Proxy Translator. This monitoring occurs through the status update operation, which will periodically request the discovery of the devices in the network, waiting to obtain a response from them. In cases of repeated denials, its registration is canceled in the Application Manager, and it consequently becomes unavailable in the discovery operations. For the proposed architecture, we defined three consecutive requests as the maximum tolerance. If the device exceeds this limit, it is considered unavailable by the Health Module. By default, the status update operation is repeated every 30 s after the first verification.

4.6   Device Communication

The communication between the devices is represented in Fig. 4 and illustrates how the VIoT will handle Virtual Devices in the process of executing the client application. The communication will only use methods of the Virtual Devices that were specifically defined for the interaction with the Physical Devices, which are *getDataEvent(action)* and *sendEvent(action, params)*.

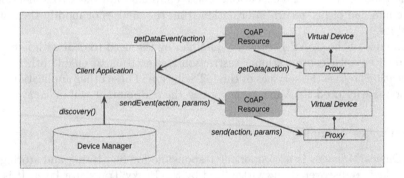

Fig. 4. Process of communication between virtual and physical devices.

The *getDataEvent(action)* method is responsible for requesting information from a particular action of the device that invoked it. The action represents what the device can perform. The *sendEvent(action, params)* method, in its turn, sends data to the device through well-defined parameters (*params*). The actions defined in this case modify the state of the devices that invoked them. In other words, invoking this method will not return any value, but will modify the state variables of the device that invoked it.

The Virtual Devices involved in the communication process need to be discovered by the Client Application through the *Device Manager*. If any requested device is not returned by the discovery method, it means that it is not operable.

In other words, it is not available for use by the Application or has not been identified by the *Proxy Translator* during the execution of that layer's discovery methods.

For the Virtual Devices to communicate with their physical devices, CoAP Resources are used as intermediaries. This way, when the application invokes any of the Devices' method of interaction (*getDataEvent* or *sendEvent*), the method is directed to the CoAP Resource that represents the desired action which, in turn, directs the method call to its Proxy, which also has a similar method of interaction (*getData* or *send*) for the action to be performed on the physical Device.

4.7   Framework Instanciation

The VIoT will be made available through a Java (.jar) compiled file that must be added to the IoT application's classpath. The whole instantiation process will occur through the Core class, which is responsible for methods that solve the dependencies necessary for VIoT's operation. The dependencies mentioned above are basically limited to searching for the existing proxies in the Proxy Translator layer and checking if there are any proxies defined by the client application. The base method for solving these dependencies is called *start()*.

A file called *config.properties* must be created in the root directory of the client application, and the VIoT will process it to define its execution guidelines. These guidelines are defined from two properties: *application.proxy.package* and *ignore.defaul.* The first property is responsible for indicating the package that will contain the additional proxies that were defined outside the VIoT. The second property can only assume two values: yes or no. This property will inform the framework if it should ignore its default proxies or should consider them during the client application's execution process. This routine has been defined for occasions when the device that will run the client application shows incompatibility with the proxies already natively defined by the VIoT.

```
1  Core.start ();
2  VirtuaDevice sensor = DeviceManager.discovery ("Sensor")
3  .get (0);
```

Fig. 5. Code responsible for the instantiation and discovery of devices in the VIoT.

After the proxies' dependency resolution process, which is triggered by the invocation of the *start()* method (Line 1), the devices can be searched using the DeviceManager and its discovery methods. Figure 5 shows the code snippet required for this process. Also, the example shown in the Figure demonstrates how to search for a device using its name.

It is possible to interact with virtualized devices through their interaction methods. Figure 6 demonstrates how to retrieve data captured by the virtualized

```
1 String rawData = sensor.getDataEvent(ResourceManager
2 .SensorService
3 .GET_DATA_SENSOR);
```

Fig. 6. Code required to obtain data from a sensor.

sensor. The *ResourceManager* is the class that maps all of the resources and actions defined by the proxies in the Proxy Translator's discovery process. In the case that was used as an example, the *getDataEvent* method shown in the Figure requests from the sensor the SensorService's *GET_DATA_SENSOR* action and stores its data in the *rawData* variable. The data is returned in the JSON format.

```
5  newValues.put(ResourceManager.ActuatorServices
6  .NEW_VALUE, "OFF");
7
8  actuator.sendEvent(ResourceManager
9  .ActuatorServices
10 .POWER_ACTION, newValues);
```

Fig. 7. Code required to send data to the actuator.

The use of the *sendEvent* method (see Fig. 7) is similar to the one shown in Fig. 6. However, among the mandatory parameters of this method, there is a mapping of the values that will represent the device's state variables and its new values. It is important to consider that these variables are also mapped by the *ResourceManager* in the Proxy Translator's discovery process. All of the code illustrated represents the basics of a client application that uses the VIoT as a facilitator resource for the devices' interoperability.

5   Evaluation

To evaluate the VIoT, a proof of concept was built based on an environment with temperature control. The scenario was chosen due to the simplicity of its structure; however, the main focus is the diversity of devices with heterogeneous capabilities. For this, a client application was implemented using the VIoT for the manipulation of the devices present in the IoT infrastructure. The client application can read the data captured by the temperature sensors and send a status change command to the thermostat, when necessary.

The implementation of the client application took place in an Android 4.1 device, the Samsung Galaxy Note, with Quad Core 1.9 GHz and 3 GB of RAM. A similar application with the same objective was developed in the same environment, without the aid of the VIoT. This was done to assist in the evaluation of aspects related to the facility of the developers in dealing with the interoperability of heterogeneous devices.

It is important to consider that the projects had similar coding structures (same number of classes) and used a simulated sensor and a thermostat each (which we will call Implementation 1). The number of devices involved represents a minimally heterogeneous environment since each device has a different communication protocol. The metrics used for the analysis were Lines of Code (LOC) and Cyclomatic Complexity (CC). The first one aims at measuring an application by the number of lines of code implemented, while the second metric focuses on verifying the project's level of complexity through the generation of a flow graph [12].

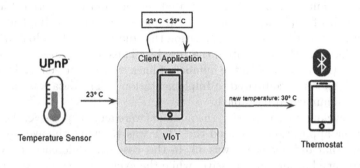

Fig. 8. Proof of concept of the proposed framework (VIoT).

The application developed used two distinct protocols, the Bluetooth and the UPnP. To make the development of the application viable, the Android platform was used, since it has a rich API focused on the manipulation of Bluetooth adapters. This way, an Android application was created to simulate a thermostat. The Bluetooth API was used for the definition of the application's routines, allowing the temperature to be set either from the application itself or through a remote command sent by a Bluetooth communication channel. The temperature sensors involved used the UPnP protocol and were programmatically simulated using Cling. The fact that the devices are simulated does not threaten the validity of the experiment since the protocols used in the simulations are identical to those used in real devices.

Thus, as shown in Fig. 8, the application recovered the virtualized sensors and thermostat and started its logic, verifying if the temperature captured by the sensors was equal to or greater than 25 °C. In cases of temperatures over 25 °C, the application would terminate its execution. In different cases, in which the temperatures were lower than 25 °C, the application would invoke the VirtualDevice's *sendEvent()* method, which represents the thermostat, sending parameters capable of modifying its state to 30 °C.

The lines of code from Implementation 1 were extracted and compared. The application that did not use the VIoT totaled 285 lines of code, while the one that used it revealed a total of 118 lines of code, thus making it possible to attest an approximate reduction of 58,60% of lines of code in the application that used the VIoT.

Additionally, the analysis of the cyclomatic complexity also resulted in meaningful data. The application that used the VIoT had an average cyclomatic complexity of 12; for the application that did not use the VIoT, this value increased to 36. Thus, in terms of complexity and risk of development, the application that used the VIoT also demonstrated substantial evidence of a reduction in this aspect.

As another objective of the evaluation, it was also verified if the insertion of devices involved in the applications would impact the metrics that were found for the VIoT. For this, another pair of applications was developed, similar to the previous one, but containing ten simulated sensors and two thermostats each. This new pair of applications was called Implementation 2. In Implementation 2, 306 lines were counted in the application that did not use the VIoT, while 132 lines were found in the application that used it. Thus, it was possible to observe a total reduction of 56.90% in the number of lines, which represents a little more than 1% of difference compared to Implementation 1. The data referring to this metric was summarized in Table 1.

For the cyclomatic complexity, the numbers were more expressive: the general mean for the application that used the VIoT was 13, while the average for the application that did not use it was 43. In this case, the difference in LOC was considered very low and inexpressive, while the cyclomatic complexity revealed that there is a considerable increase in the risk for the application that does not use the VIoT when there are many devices involved. The other metrics considered and collected from implementations which also demonstrate advantages in using VIoT can be read in Table 2.

Table 1. LOCs of the proof of concept.

Projects	LOCs (with VIoT)	LOCs (without VIoT)
Implementation 1	118	285
Implementation 2	132	306

Table 2. Metrics collected from implementations.

Metrics	Implementation 1		Implementation 2	
	With VIoT	Without VIoT	With VIoT	Without VIoT
Number of methods	5	7	5	7
Lines of Code by Methods	11.41	15.86	7.34	10.52
Number of attributes	10	20	10	20
Lines of Code by Classes	59.1	142.5	66.0	153.5

This way, the numbers found showed that the use of the VIoT in the proposed proof of concept presents relevant indications for the reduction of coding effort and cyclomatic complexity in the process developing environments with heterogeneous devices.

6 Conclusions

IoT applications are permeated with critical challenges that need to be overcome. These challenges range from the variety of capabilities of communication devices and protocols to their computational and storage constraints. Consequently, these challenges make the development complex and costly.

In this context, our work presented the VIoT, a framework that can facilitate the development of IoT-based applications through a device virtualization approach. The approach aims to smooth out the heterogeneous aspects from the developer's point of view by reducing the coding effort needed to make the devices interoperable. It was possible to define and present an architecture that favors this approach, showing the components that form it and the means of instantiating it and extending it into IoT application projects.

Through a proof of concept that used a temperature control environment composed of devices with heterogeneous capacities, it was possible to test the proposed VIoT to obtain information necessary to validate it in aspects related to the reduction of coding, specifically focused on facilitating the development of IoT applications. This way, metrics (LOC and CC) were used to verify these aspects, thus obtaining, through this analysis, relevant results that attested a considerable decrease in the implementation effort.

As proposed future works we intend to create a Description Service Language (DSL) for the communication of IoT devices. The language will use the VIoT to accomplish its objectives. It will provide a simple syntax suitable for the definition of the devices' communication mechanisms, as well as for the execution of routines involving these devices and for the development of decision mechanisms, among other resources that are necessary for an IoT context. All of these resources must obey the architectural model defined in this work. We also believe that the evolution of the Health Module found in the VIoT's architecture would be essential for implementing more advanced fault tolerance strategies, guaranteeing greater reliability of the VIoT-based applications.

Acknowledgements. This work was financed in part by the Coordenação de Aperfeiçoamento de Pessoal de Nível Superior – Brasil (CAPES) – Finance Code 001.

References

1. Ashraf, Q.M., Habaebi, M.H., Islam, M.R., Khan, S.: Device discovery and configuration scheme for Internet of Things. In: 2016 International Conference on Intelligent Systems Engineering (ICISE), pp. 38–43. IEEE (2016)
2. Carranza-García, F., Rodríguez-Domínguez, C., Garrido, J.L., Guerrero-Contreras, G.: BaaS-4US: a framework to develop standard backends as a service for ubiquitous applications. In: International Conference on Ubiquitous Computing and Communications and 2016 International Symposium on Cyberspace and Security (IUCC-CSS), pp. 23–30. IEEE (2016)
3. Datta, S.K., Bonnet, C.: Easing IoT application development through datatweet framework. In: 2016 IEEE 3rd World Forum on Internet of Things (WF-IoT), pp. 430–435. IEEE (2016)
4. Ferrera, E., et al.: XMPP-based infrastructure for IoT network management and rapid services and applications development. Ann. Telecommun. **72**(7–8), 443–457 (2017)
5. Kum, S.W., Kang, M., Park, J.I.: Iot delegate: Smart home framework for heterogeneous IoT service collaboration. KSII Trans. Internet Inf. Syst. **10**(8) (2016)
6. Manione, R.: User centered integration of Internet of Things devices. In: Smart Sensors, Actuators, and MEMS VIII, vol. 10246, p. 102461K. International Society for Optics and Photonics (2017)
7. Mehta, A., Baddour, R., Svensson, F., Gustafsson, H., Elmroth, E.: Calvin constrained a framework for IoT applications in heterogeneous environments. In: 2017 IEEE 37th International Conference on Distributed Computing Systems (ICDCS), pp. 1063–1073. IEEE (2017)
8. de Melo Silva, C.C., Ferreira, H.G.C., de Sousa Júnior, R.T., Buiati, F., Villalba, L.J.G.: Design and evaluation of a services interface for the Internet of Things. Wirel. Pers. Commun. **91**(4), 1711–1748 (2016)
9. Pal, A., Mukherjee, A., Balamuralidhar, P.: Model-driven development for Internet of Things: towards easing the concerns of application developers. In: Giaffreda, R., et al. (eds.) IoT360 2014. LNICST, vol. 150, pp. 339–346. Springer, Cham (2015). https://doi.org/10.1007/978-3-319-19656-5_46
10. Patel, P., Cassou, D.: Enabling high-level application development for the Internet of Things. J. Syst. Softw. **103**, 62–84 (2015)
11. Sasirekha, S., Swamynathan, S.: Collaboration of IoT devices using semantically enabled resource oriented middleware. In: Proceedings of the Third International Symposium on Computer Vision and the Internet, pp. 98–105. ACM (2016)
12. Sharma, M., Singh, G., Arora, A., Kaur, P.: A comparative study of static object oriented metrics. Int. J. Advancements Technol. **3**(1), 25–34 (2012)
13. Tayur, V.M., Suchithra, R.: Review of interoperability approaches in application layer of Internet of Things. In: 2017 International Conference on Innovative Mechanisms for Industry Applications (ICIMIA), pp. 322–326. IEEE (2017)
14. Yen, I.L., Zhang, S., Bastani, F., Zhang, Y.: A framework for IoT-based monitoring and diagnosis of manufacturing systems. In: 2017 IEEE Symposium on Service-Oriented System Engineering (SOSE), pp. 1–8. IEEE (2017)

Adaptive Channel Borrowing Scheme for Capacity Enhancement in Cellular Wireless Networks

Onyinyechi F. Steve-Essi[1], Francis F. Idachaba[1],
Segun I. Popoola[1,2(✉)] ⓘ, Aderemi A. Atayero[1] ⓘ,
Bamidele Adebisi[2] ⓘ, and Craig Nitzsche[3]

[1] IoT-Enabled Smart and Connected Communities (SmartCU) Research Cluster,
Department of Electrical and Information Engineering,
Covenant University, Ota, Nigeria
{onyinyechi.steve-essi,francis.idachaba,
atayero}@covenantuniversity.edu.ng,
[2] Department of Engineering, Manchester Metropolitan University,
Manchester M1 5GD, UK
segun.i.popoola@stu.mmu.ac.uk, b.adebisi@mmu.ac.uk
[3] Department of Mechanical and Aeronautical Engineering,
University of Pretoria, Pretoria, South Africa

Abstract. The very limited nature of the GSM spectrum, coupled with the increasing demand by an extending number of subscribers place a strain on the network capacity. This leads to an equally raised number of calls that dropped and hence, subscriber dissatisfaction. Several strategies have been implemented in order to minimize these occurrences, with the most prominent being channel borrowing. Channel borrowing process is a scheme whereby frequencies allocated to other cells are temporarily assigned to cells with higher traffic loading so as to reduce the rate of dropped calls in the busy location, hence improving the grade of service of the entire network. This concept is implemented in such a manner as to ensure that the call quality in the original cell is not jeopardized by the borrowing process and the borrowed frequency is returned as soon as possible. The goal of channel borrowing is to ensure maximal utilization of the available spectrum to an operator in such a manner that the owner cell is not disadvantaged. This article presents a detailed review of various Channel Borrowing Schemes and proposes an Adaptive Channel Borrowing Scheme that efficiently borrows free Channels from nearby Cells deploying features in MATLAB R2012a. The ACB algorithm has suitable characteristics for a novel hybrid channel borrowing algorithm and it is based on real time call statistics using random number generators. It is measured with parameters such as Lending Potentials (LP), Borrowing Potentials (BP) and Borrowing Need (BN). These are traffic driven frequency borrowing parameters adopted in the investigation. From the result, an efficient and reliable means of borrowing additional Channels for temporary use without giving the entire system huge workload, was arrived at. The ACB algorithm has the capacity to maximally utilize the system resources hence, reducing the cost or need for the purchase of additional resources.

© Springer Nature Switzerland AG 2019
S. Misra et al. (Eds.): ICCSA 2019, LNCS 11623, pp. 497–511, 2019.
https://doi.org/10.1007/978-3-030-24308-1_40

498   O. F. Steve-Essi et al.

Keywords: Channel efficiency · Spectrum · Cell capacity · Cellular traffic · Wireless networks

1 Introduction

The ever-growing number of mobile network subscribers and the limited available radio frequency spectrum is of major concern and therefore, requires very urgent attention and action. This problem can easily be linked to the fact that there are rapid technological advancements, coupled with tremendous shift of different applications to multimedia and mobile platforms with the aim of making information more accessible.

It is becoming difficult to see any web-based application that does not have a mobile friendly version hence, further reduction in the limited radio spectrum. Considering these factors, lots of techniques have been deployed in [1], in a bid to enhance the capacity of a cellular network.

According to Kahwa and Georganas [2], some of these techniques include but not limited to Frequency reuse, Cell splitting, Sectoring, Microcell zoning and frequency borrowing. While frequency reuse has to do with deploying same radio frequencies on the transmitter sites within a given geographic area that are separated by enough distance to prevent or minimize interference, Cell splitting is the process of subdividing large cells into smaller ones with their corresponding BTSs (Base Transceiver Stations), with reduced antenna height and transmission power. Sectoring increases cell capacity by reducing the number of cells in a given cluster and thereby increasing frequency reuse. The existing sectoring angles include angles 60°, 120° and 360°. Microcell zoning, on the other hand, deals with dividing cells into micro (smaller) cells or zones with each connecting with the same base station. Each zone uses a directional antenna while the Base Station Controller (BSC) keeps switching calls to the nearest zone when on transit. Frequency borrowing on the other hand is a scheme whereby frequencies allocated to other cells are temporarily assigned to cells with higher traffic loading so as to minimize the rate of dropped calls, hence improving the efficiency of the entire network.

Channel borrowing schemes are the various methods adopted in order to reduce the call dropping or blocking rates of a cell in a mobile cellular network. The major aim of frequency borrowing is to improve cell capacity utilization and also reduce blocking probability of a cellular network. In this process, cells (the acceptors) whose nominal channel sets are exhausted; borrow free channels from the neighboring cells (the donors) for temporary use in order to accommodate new or handoff calls. This process is successful once conditions for co-channel interference and other related challenges are handled properly. Channel borrowing can be Simple borrowing or Hybrid channel borrowing strategies. In Simple Channel Borrowing, nominal channel sets in a cell can be borrowed by neighboring cells for use but in Hybrid Borrowing, channel sets are divided into A (standard, local non-borrowable channels) and B (nonstandard and borrowable channels). While Set A channels are only usable in the assigned cell, set B channels can be lent to neighboring cells for temporary usage [1].

In Simple Borrowing Scheme (SBS) [2], a nominal channel set is assigned particularly to a cell as it is in the case of Fixed Channel Assignment and when the assigned channels are completely used, more channels are borrowed from the neighboring cell. This borrowing strategy is only possible if the channel does not interfere with or completely disrupt any calls in progress. This borrowing strategy can as well, reduce call blocking rate but also causes interference in the lending cell, hence preventing the completion of other ongoing calls. As demonstrated in [3], this SBS presents improved lower call blocking probability when compared to FCA despite the fact that the channel assignment schemes are similar to each other. Quite a reasonable number of SBS were proposed in [4] for channels to be borrowed only from non-adjacent cells. They include; Borrow from the Richest (SBR), Basic Algorithm (BA), Basic Algorithm with Reassignment (BAR) and Borrow First Available (BFA).

2   The Erlang Traffic Model

An *Erlang* is the basic unit of telecommunications traffic measurement which represents the continuous use of one voice path or a single circuit [5].

The Erlang is mathematically dimensionless and it is used to describe the total traffic volume of one hour. In practice, one voice path (single circuit) used continuously carries 60 min of calling in an hour therefore, one erlang is usually defined as 60 min of traffic. When someone receives 200 two-minute calls in an hour, it implies the person received 400 min, or 6.7 erlangs of traffic in that hour. Similarly, if another person makes one call and occupies one channel for one hour (60 min), it is said that the system under consideration has just 1 Erlang of traffic on it at that time [6].

The traffic in Erlang is usually represented by the letter A and the formula is given as

$$\mathbf{A} = \lambda \times \mathbf{T} \tag{1}$$

Where:

λ = the mean arrival rate of new calls
T = the mean call length or holding time
A = the offered traffic in Erlangs.

Using this simple Erlang function or Erlang formula, the traffic can easily be calculated.

In terms of total number of calls, the offered traffic in erlang A is given as

$$A = \frac{QT}{60} Erlangs \tag{2}$$

Where;

A is the offered traffic in Erlang
Q is the total number of calls in busy hour
T is the mean call length or holding time

The total number of calls in the busy hour Q is given as

$$Q = ncW \tag{3}$$

Where;

Q is the total number of calls in busy hour
nc is the total number of subscribers and
W represents a given number of subscribers

Erlang calculations are further broken down into Erlang B and c depending on the respective use of each of them. While Erlang B model is applied in determining the number of lines required from the knowledge of the traffic figure during the busiest hour and with the assumption that blocked calls are immediately cleared, the Extended Erlang B model is used to determine how many calls are blocked and are tried again immediately. It is the most commonly used figure for any telecommunications capacity calculations and a sample of the Erlang B table with its associated readings can be seen at [7]. This work took certain readings from the Erlang B.

How many channels per cell are needed in a cellular system to ensure a reasonably low probability that a call will be blocked or dropped as the case may be? In order to provide the answer to this question, we determined the number of subscribers and subsequently the capacity of a given network. Some other factors under consideration include the call blocking probability (probability that a call will not go through), the offered traffic, A (in Erlang), the total number of calls at busy hour Q in that given location, the number of Channels, N and the duration of each call, T (in secs). To determine the number of subscribers the system can accommodate at busy hour, there is need to assign values to the above parameters. This will be done based on the frequency allocation dataset provided by the Nigerian Communications Commission (NCC). Table 1 shows the frequency band allocation to Network operators in Nigeria on the 1800 MHz GSM Band by NCC.

Table 1. NCC frequency allocation to GSM Network operators in Nigeria

Network	Airtel	Etisalat	GLO	MTEL	MTN
Tx	1850–1865	1865–1880	1820–1835	1805–1820	1835–1850
Rx	1755–1770	1770–1785	1725–1740	1710–1725	1740–1755

From Table 1, the following parameters are seen

Total allocated bandwidth for a duplex wireless cellular system for each operator, A = 30 MHz

The networks are allocated 30 MHz of spectrum with a full *duplex channel bandwidth* of 200 kHz.

This implies that Channel bandwidth for each duplex channel, B = 200 kHz

Hence to determine the number of Channels, it is given to be $= \frac{A}{B}$ (Dunlop and Smith 1994).

Therefore, number of available Channels

$$= \frac{(30 * 10^6)}{200 * 10^3} = 150 \qquad (4)$$

Number of Duplex channels in a cluster

$$= \frac{150}{2} = 75 \qquad (5)$$

Hence, the number of Channels per Cell

$$= \frac{75}{7} \approx 11 \text{ Channels per Cell} \qquad (6)$$

It is necessary to find the total offered traffic during heavy traffic (busy hour). From [7], we extracted the formulas, Eqs. (4)–(6).

If we assume W subscribers per cell and that during busy hour a fraction nc of these makes or receives a call of duration T minutes.

From Eq. (3), the total number of calls in the busy hour is $Q = ncW$ and Eq. (2) showed the offered traffic to be

$$A = \frac{QT}{60} Erlangs$$

In Nigeria, the blocking probability for calls is placed at 2% by the Nigerian Communications commission (NCC). This implies that only two (2) out of every hundred (100) calls placed will be dropped. Although there is improvement in call drop rate according to recent research reports during uniform traffic, this 2% standard blocking probability is still not achieved in cellular network services in Nigeria during heavy traffic.

Working with the 2% blocking probability, the Erlang B table has the relationship between offered traffic, blocking probability and number of channels as shown in a typical Erlang B table.

From any Erlang B table, 21 channels will support an offered traffic of 14.04 Erlangs with a blocking probability of 2%. Therefore, from Eq. (2),

Offered traffic A is given as

$$14.04 = \frac{QT}{60}$$

Substituting Eq. (1) into Eq. (2) gives

$$14.04 = \frac{QT}{60} = ncWT/60$$

Hence the number of subscribers, W is given as

$$W = \frac{14.04 \times 60}{(ncT)} \tag{7}$$

Where nc refers to the total subscribers in the network and T, the average call duration of calls.

Typical value of T = 1.76 min. Assuming 80% of the total subscribers nc make a call during the busy hour, substituting into Eq. (7) gives;

$$W = \frac{14.04 \times 60}{0.8 \times 1.76} = 598.3$$

Therefore, the number of subscribers that can be accommodated at busy hour is **598**.

Taking similar assumption from [7], a user density of $1.74 \times 10^{-3}/m^2$

$$User\ density = \frac{W}{\pi R^2} = \frac{598.3}{\pi R^2} = 1.74 \times 10^{-3} \tag{8}$$

Therefore, $R = 330.75\,m$ and the approximate cell diameter is **662** m.

Where R is the Cell Radius in meters.

With the above analysis, we discover that the major reason behind increased call drops in cellular networks is due to limited available resources. Quite a large number of subscribers are demanding access to this limited number of network resources thereby leading to increased call drops.

In order to tackle the issue of Call drops, we consider the spacing distance between Cells. The formula for the spacing distance between interfering Cells is given as;

$$D = R\sqrt{(3N)} \tag{9}$$

Where:

D is the spacing distance between interfering Cells
R is the radius of the Cell and N is the cluster size.

For the study of our interest where R is given as 330.75 m and N = 7, the frequency reuse distance D is therefore obtained as shown;

Substituting into Eq. (9);

$$= 330\sqrt{21}$$
$$= 330 * 4.583$$
$$= 1515\,m$$

This implies that the distance between interfering Cells, D (that is the closest or minimum distance between two cells using the same frequency) in this case is 1.515 km. If the above condition is not met, it leads to co channel interference and increase in call dropping rates due to excessive closeness of clusters to each other [8]. But if using a channel causes no interference in a cell, then the channel is said to be available for use in such cell(s).

3 System Design

The reason behind the choice of this specific layout is that our algorithm will consider the first tier of neighboring cells only. This helps in dealing with the effects of co-channel interference which occurs when channels are reused incessantly. Considering the diagram of Fig. 1, the cluster is divided into three sub regions of Hot, Warm and Cold regions. This subdivision is done to aid simulation. For this work only, Cells A, B and C are in the Hot Region, Cells D and E are in the warm Region while Cells F and G are in the Cold Region. These regions were categorized due to the level of call traffic they have per time. Cell A is an acceptor cell and is surrounded by one tier of six (6) cells. It can borrow free Channels from any of its other surrounding neighbor cells (with priority from the Cold Region) to service any new calls. It must fill up the other two members of the Hot region (Cells B and C) to maximum capacity, before proceeding to borrow more Channels from Cells in the Cold region (F and G). When these Channels are used up to maximum capacity, the ones from Cells in the Warm region are further borrowed for use by the acceptor Cell A in the Hot region. The number of call simulations in each Cell determines the region it belongs to. The same factor forms the parameters from which the Capacity Utilization (CU) table is built as shown in Table 2.

Fig. 1. A 7 cell cluster

This table contains entries of various characteristics of each Cell and the cumulative represents that of the regions they belong to. Furthermore, the acceptor Cell A can borrow channels from one and only one neighboring Cell in a region at a time. The algorithm does not allow for multiple donations in order not to increase the system calculation time and bring about overhead. Also, until a Cell gets above 15 simulated calls (call activity rate); it cannot be in the Hot region. The system threshold is set at 60%. Having reviewed quite a number of works done in this field of study, the choice of having the threshold placed at 60% was made considering some works already done in literature such as that by Rappaport [1].

Cells with less than 60% threshold are not permitted to borrow Channels from neighboring Cells. In this arrangement, a particular channel cannot be busy in two different Cell locations at the same time except if their geographical distance apart exceeds the minimum reuse distance value also known as the spacing distance between interfering Cells (D) [9]. This condition of having a channel locked up in other Cells when in use in one Cell is known as Channel locking and is more prevalent with fixed channel allocations. Our algorithm tackles this problem by returning every borrowed Channel after each use.

4 The Proposed Algorithm

The Adaptive Channel Borrowing Scheme (ACBS) is the proposed algorithm in this work. Each Cell has six other neighboring cells. Each of the seven (7) Cells in the cluster has a total of 21 Channels allocated to each of them as against eleven (11) calculated Channels. This is the minimum number of Channels that can be allocated to a GSM network. This is because; a Telecommunication Service Provider in practice can decide to assign more Channels to a particular area depending on the traffic demand of the area under consideration. These seven Cells are further subdivided into three regions of Hot, Warm and Cold. Normally, every Cell in each region is able to manage its call allocations without having issues. At busy hour with increased traffic density, the rate of Call arrival increases tremendously. This triggers the BSC to check for the level of traffic for each region by computing the Capacity Utilization (CU), using the Call activity rate of each Cell. These Call activity rates were obtained using MATLAB random number generation. A threshold of 60% is set as a standard to determine the various levels of Hotness, Warmness or Coldness of a particular region. The state of a Cell or any region depends on the Call activity rate of the region. The first three (3) Cells with activity rates above 15 calls are classified as Hot region Cells. Their cumulative Capacity Utilization value is more than the set 60% threshold. As this value is being calculated, the BSC also executes the channel borrowing process simultaneously and subsequently reallocates a channel, if need be. This it does by looking through the computed values in the Capacity Utilization table for the Cell with the greatest number of free Cells which is inadvertently the Cells and region with the least cumulative Capacity Utilization threshold values, to borrow Channels from.

Normally all the Cells in the Cluster are not busy; they have varying levels of simulated call activity rates going on in each of them in the Cluster. The region with the highest call activity rate is termed the Hot region (C1). The total call activity rate (total number of simulated channels in use) in the Hot region is 49 out of 63 Channels allocated to the entire region (21 Channels per Cell for the three Cells in the Hot region). This results in 77% of the region's total capacity. This automatically qualifies this region for borrowing since its calculated CU value is above the threshold of 60%. The Warm region (Cells F4 and F5) is next with a cumulative value of 15 Call activity rate and a cumulative capacity utilization value of 40%. This value is still less than the threshold value and therefore does not meet the conditions for borrowing Channels.

Once this region exceeds the 40% capacity and meets the 60% threshold value, it will qualify to borrow. The Cold region has very low Call activity rate of 8 with a CU value of less than 20% of the entire region's capacity. Each Cell can in any point in time migrate from one region to the other depending on the level of traffic or the amount of call activity taking place in such Cells. For the purpose of the simulation, it was necessary to assign the Cells to regions for more clarity and perform the CU calculations as shown in expression below.

Capacity Utilization is given as $\left(\frac{Ci}{CT} * \frac{100}{1}\right)$.

Where Ci is the individual or Cumulative (in case of a region) call activity rate, CT is the total number of Channels in the individual Cell or the entire region.

Using the above formula to derive the results of Table 1, it will have the region as;

$$C3 = \left(\frac{8}{42} * \frac{100}{1}\right) = 19.04\%$$

$$C2 = \left(\frac{17}{42} * \frac{100}{1}\right) = 40.47\%$$

$$C1 = \left(\frac{49}{63} * \frac{100}{1}\right) = 77.77\%$$

As the cellular traffic at the location of Cells F1, F2 and F3 increases, the Base Station Controller (BSC) gets to work by looking through the Capacity Utilization Table (CUT), to determine the freest Cell to switch new calls to, in order to prevent possible call block or drop due to lack of sufficient resources. A threshold of 60% is set and once a Cell in any region gets to this threshold, it attains a high Borrowing Affinity (BA) to borrow Channels from neighboring Cells. The neighboring Cells are often characterized with equally high Lending Potentials (LP) and a low Borrowing Need (BN). In order to generate the values for Borrowing Potential (BP), Borrowing Need (BN) and Borrowing Ability (BA) for each of the Cells (A, B... G), we need to determine the individual CU values for each of the seven Cells in the cluster.

The table below is a summary of the regions and their levels of activities.

Table 2. Cumulative CUT Values for each region

Regions in the cluster	Cells in each zone	Capacity utilization $(\frac{Ci}{CT} * 100)$ (%)	Cumulative Call activity rate (x)
Hot Region (C1)	Cells A, B, C	>60% to 100%	49
Warm Region (C2)	Cells D and E	30% to 59%	15
Cold Region (C3)	Cells F and G	0% to 29%	8

5   Results and Discussion

Lending Potential/Ability (LP) is the factor that determines the possibility of a Cell to lend Channels to neighboring Cells in need. It is obtained by subtracting a Cell's capacity utilization value from the capacity utilization threshold which is set at 60%. A cell with a high lending potential will have a low borrowing affinity and borrowing need.

$$LP = CU(i) - CUT \tag{10}$$

Borrowing Need (BN) is the factor that determines the claim for a Cell or region to borrow channels from neighbor Cells. It is obtained by assigning priority to each Cell based on the value of its CU and that of the LP. Cells whose CU values are less than the threshold cannot borrow but can lend Channels to Cells in need of them. Priorities are set with 1 being the highest priority and 5 the least. A Cell with high LP will have a low BN and vice versa.

Borrowing Potential/Ability (BP) considers the capability of a cell to borrow cells even when the LP value is low. Cells with their CU values above the threshold are able to borrow and are assigned numbers one (1) while those with CU values less than 60% is such that they have very minimal borrowing ability hence, they have BA values of zero (0). There is need to calculate the various capacity utilization values for each Cell in order to set up the values of the capacity utilization table (CUT).

The range of CU values for each region is 60–100% for the Hot Region, 30–59% for the Warm Region and 0–29% for Cold Region.

For Cell A, we have the CU value calculated thus:

$$A = \left(\frac{18}{21} * \frac{100}{1}\right) = 85.7\% \quad \text{Hot Region}$$

$$B = \left(\frac{15}{21} * \frac{100}{1}\right) = 71.4\% \quad \text{Hot Region}$$

$$C = \left(\frac{17}{21} * \frac{100}{1}\right) = 76.2 \quad \text{Hot Region}$$

$$D = \left(\frac{7}{21} * \frac{100}{1}\right) = 33.3 \quad \text{Warm Region}$$

$$E = \left(\frac{9}{21} * \frac{100}{1}\right) = 42.8 \quad \text{Warm Region}$$

$$F = \left(\frac{5}{21} * \frac{100}{1}\right) = 23.8 \quad \text{Cold Region}$$

$$G = \left(\frac{3}{21} * \frac{100}{1}\right) = 14.3 \quad \text{Cold Region}$$

The borrowing decision will depend on the values of a CU table. The table amongst other information, will reveal the Cell with the highest potential to lend Channels, this is inadvertently the Cell with the highest value of LP (in this case is Cell G) with the value of 45.7 which is approximately equal to 46. This will be directly followed by Cell F with LP value of 36.2. This implies that Cells F6 and G have approximately 36 and 46 free Channels' capacity respectively to lend to any neighbor in need. The table also shows that these two Cells have higher potentials or ability (in this case 1, where 1 is the maximum) to lend out free Channels when compared to other Cells in the Network. It is worthy to note that both Cells F and G are members of the Cold Region hence; they are in the right state to lend to demanding neighbors from any region but in this case, most likely the Hot Region.

Table 3. Cell capacity utilization

Cells	Call activity rate	Capacity Utilization (%)	Lending Potential/Ability (LP) (60 – CU)	Borrowing Need (BN)	Borrowing Potential/Ability (BP)
F1	18	85.7	−25.7	1	1 Can Borrow
F2	15	71.4	−11.4	2	1 Can Borrow
F3	16	76.2	−16.2	3	1 Can Borrow
F4	7	33.3	26.7	4	0 Can't Borrow
F5	9	42.8	17.2	5	0 Can't Borrow
F6	5	23.8	36.2	6	0 Can't Borrow
F7	3	14.3	45.7	7	0 Can't Borrow

Adaptive Channel Borrowing Scheme (ACBS) has the following processes to its algorithm execution:

1. The arrival of a new call triggers the Base Station controller (BSC) to calculate the Capacity Utilization (CU) values for each of the three specified regions, Hot, Warm or Cold.
2. If the calculated CU value is above the set threshold of 60% in any of the Regions;
   (i) More new incoming Calls should be assigned to this Region until it reaches a maximum capacity of 100% utilization.
   (ii) Else, the CU table should be updated accordingly and the next step initiated.
3. When the Region is filled up to its maximum capacity, the CU table is used to determine the Region where the borrowing process is to be initiated. This is the Region with the least Capacity Utilization (CU), Borrowing Potential (BP) and threshold value less than 30% but with the highest Lending Potential value of 6 on the average as seen in Tables 2 and 3.

4. Process number three is repeated until the entire system is at its maximum capacity before new calls can be blocked. This is a very rare occurrence since calls always drop at its completion (Figs. 2, 3, 4, 5 and 6).

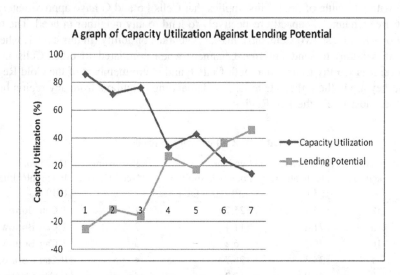

Fig. 2. A graph of Capacity Utilization against Lending Potential

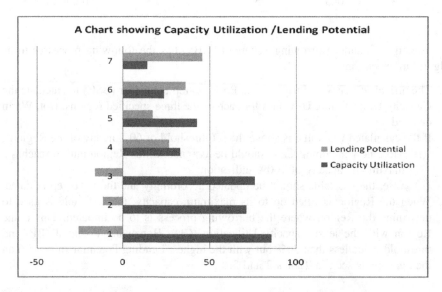

Fig. 3. A bar chart showing the relationship between Capacity Utilization and the Lending Potential of the system

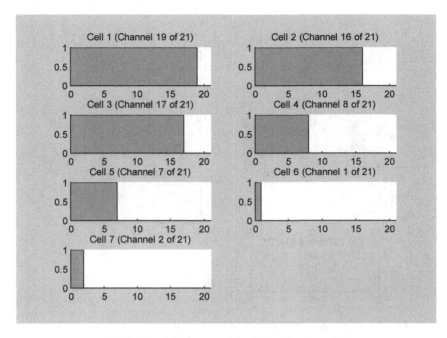

Fig. 4. The initial state of the Cells when launched

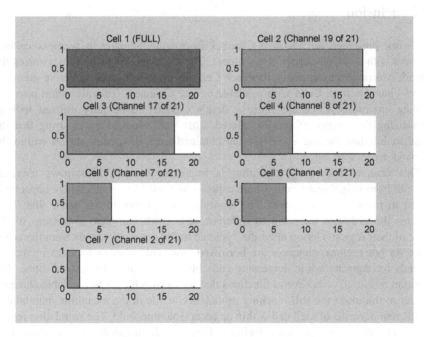

Fig. 5. Cell 1 completely filled and more Channels borrowed from free Channels in the Region

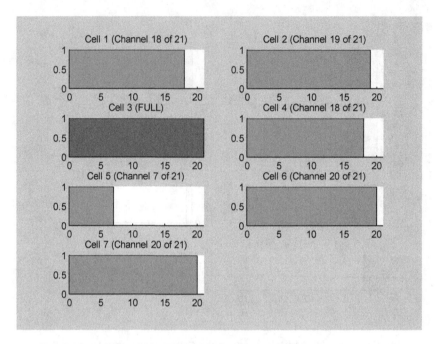

Fig. 6. Calls that ended can be dropped from any of the initially busy Cells

6 Conclusion

This work presented an adaptive Channel Borrowing Scheme in wireless cellular networks with a 7-Cell cluster arrangement. The developed algorithm maximizes the network's resources by ensuring that each Cell fills up to full capacity before it is fit to borrow channels from Cells with available or free Channels. This algorithm provides enabling environment for the entire system's capacity to be fully utilized without jeopardizing the quality of service offered. This was achieved by ensuring that the Signal to Interference Ratio (SIR) value obtained from this study stayed within the approved acceptable range.

This channel borrowing algorithm is important because it borrows channels available from neighboring cells where capacity is available to cells where capacity is needed to meet traffic demands. The algorithm is adaptive in the sense that it re-allocates the channels allocated to different cells (with complete awareness of the nature of their regions) based upon the dynamic traffic pattern demands from the users. Hence, in hot regions, channels are borrowed from cold regions to meet increasing demands for capacity while decreasing calls blocking or dropping probabilities. The algorithm essentially has several functions that try to switch calls to available channels in order to minimize the call blocking probability, while in the meantime maintaining the SIR requirements of each call within an acceptable threshold. The simulation results show some importance of this algorithm. This include the increase in network efficiency as more calls can be accepted for the same amount of resources, the quality of service provided by the network is enhanced as SIR did not exceed the set threshold.

Acknowledgement. This work was carried out under the IoT-Enabled Smart and Connected Communities (*SmartCU*) research cluster of the Department of Electrical and Information Engineering, Covenant University, Ota, Nigeria. The research was fully sponsored by Covenant University Centre for Research, Innovation and Development (CUCRID), Covenant University, Ota, Nigeria.

References

1. Rappaport, T.S.: Wireless Communications: Principles and Practice, vol. 2. Prentice Hall PTR, Upper Saddle River (1996)
2. Kahwa, T., Georganas, N.: A hybrid channel assignment scheme in large-scale, cellular-structured mobile communication systems. IEEE Trans. Commun. **26**(4), 432–438 (1978)
3. Elnoubi, S.M., Singh, R., Gupta, S.C.: A new frequency channel assignment algorithm in high capacity mobile communication systems. IEEE Trans. Veh. Technol. **31**(3), 125–131 (1982)
4. Zhang, M., Yum, T.-S.: Comparisons of channel-assignment strategies in cellular mobile telephone systems. IEEE Trans. Veh. Technol. **38**(4), 211–215 (1989)
5. Lindsey, W.C., Simon, M.K.: Telecommunication Systems Engineering. Courier Corporation, Chelmsford (1991)
6. Angus, I.: An introduction to Erlang B and Erlang C. Telemanagement **187**, 6–8 (2001)
7. Dunlop, J.: Telecommunications Engineering. Routledge, Abingdon (2017)
8. Baiocchi, A., et al.: The geometric dynamic channel allocation as a practical strategy in mobile networks with bursty user mobility. IEEE Trans. Veh. Technol. **44**(1), 14–23 (1995)
9. Nesargi, S., Prakash, R.: Distributed wireless channel allocation in networks with mobile base stations. IEEE Trans. Veh. Technol. **51**(6), 1407–1421 (2002)

Data Analytics: Global Contributions of World Continents to Computer Science Research

Segun I. Popoola[1,2](✉) ⓘ, Aderemi A. Atayero[2]ⓘ, Onyinyechi F. Steve-Essi[2], and Sanjay Misra[2]ⓘ

[1] Department of Engineering, Manchester Metropolitan University, Manchester M1 5GD, UK
segun.i.popoola@stu.mmu.ac.uk
[2] IoT-Enabled Smart and Connected Communities (SmartCU) Research Cluster, Covenant University, Ota, Nigeria
{atayero,onyinyechi.steve-essi,sanjay.misra}@covenantuniversity.edu.ng

Abstract. In this paper, we present and analyze comprehensive data about scholarly contributions that were indexed in Scopus database between 2012 and 2017. The datasets are categorized (based on the country where the research was carried out) into: Africa; Asia Pacific; Europe; Middle East; North America; and South America. Scholarly contributions of each region are measured based on fifteen Scival metrics namely: grant award volume (count); grant award volume (value); international collaboration; academic-corporate collaboration; scholarly output; citations; field-weighted citation impact; outputs in top citation percentiles; publications in top journal percentiles; citations per publications; publication views; citing-patents count; patent-cited scholarly output; patent-citations count; and the number of authors. Frequency distributions and trends across the six-year study period are presented in graphs and plots. The analyses provided in this paper are made easy to facilitate further inferential studies towards a more objective and better decision making by research institutions.

Keywords: Data analytics · Computer science · Research · Data mining

1 Introduction

Computer science is one of the fastest growing field of research due to its multidisciplinary application in diverse aspects of human endeavour. Computer science re-search seeks to develop simplified and efficient approach to computation and its applications. The global research community is actively working towards achieving greater feats in computer science. However, empirical evidence and statistical analyses of scholarly contributions of each region of the world to this discipline is not publicly available yet.

© Springer Nature Switzerland AG 2019
S. Misra et al. (Eds.): ICCSA 2019, LNCS 11623, pp. 512–524, 2019.
https://doi.org/10.1007/978-3-030-24308-1_41

In this paper, we present and analyze comprehensive data about scholarly contributions that were indexed in Scopus database between 2012 and 2017. Understanding the scholarly contributions of world regions to computer science research will help funding bodies to make right decisions in the administration of limited resources [1–3]. The volume of data and the depth of statistical analyses presented in this paper will encourage more empirical research in the emerging field of ranking analytics that seeks to objectively assess scholarly contributions to academic research [4]. The results presented in plots and graphs will make further exploratory studies much easier for useful insights and logical conclusions [5–8]. In addition, the information provided in this paper will help researchers in computer science to explore new research collaborations [9,10]. Data presentations in this paper are made easy to facilitate data reuse, data interpretations, and further inferential studies towards a more objective ranking and better decision making.

2 Research Methodology

Research areas that are covered in this dataset include: artificial intelligence; computational theory and mathematics; computer graphics and computer-aided design; computer networks and communications; computer science applications; computer vision and pattern recognition; general computer science; hardware and architecture; human-computer interaction; information systems; signal processing; and software. Only publications indexed in Scopus that fall under the "Computer Science" category using Elsevier classification as at 8th December 2017 are included in this data article.

Scientific contributions are categorized (based on the country where the research was carried out) into: Africa; Asia Pacific; Europe; Middle East; North America; and South America. Of the 57 countries in Africa, 56 have publications focused on Computer Science within the six-year study period. On the other hand, 48 of the 56 countries in Asia Pacific have publications focused on Computer Science within the study period. Also, out of the 49, 32, and 18 countries in Europe, North America, and South America, only 48, 29, and 15 have publications in Computer Science from 2012 to 2017. Middle East, North America, and South America. All of the 17 countries in Middle East have at least one publication in Computer Science within 2012–2017.

3 Results

Figures 1, 2, 3, 4, 5 and 6 illustrate the distributions of awarded grant count, awarded grant value, international collaboration, academic-corporate collaboration, scholarly output, and scholarly output growth by world regions (2012–2017). The quotas of Africa, Asia Pacific, Europe, Middle East, North America, and South America in global citations, overall citations, field-weighted citation impact, outputs in top citation percentiles, publications in top journal percentiles, and citations per publication are shown in Figs. 7, 8, 9, 10, 11 and 12.

The trends in publication views, overall publications views, citing-patents count, patent-cited scholarly output, patent-citations count, number of authors, and author growth rate can be clearly seen in Figs. 13, 14, 15, 16, 17, 18 and 19.

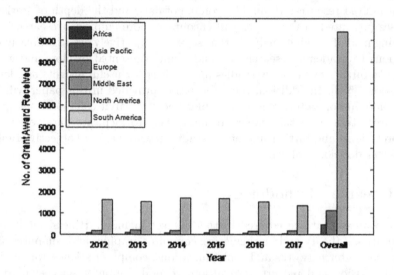

Fig. 1. Bar chart of awarded grants received by world regions

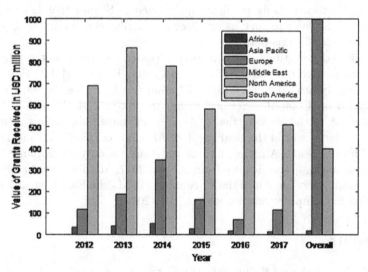

Fig. 2. Bar chart of awarded grants value received by world regions

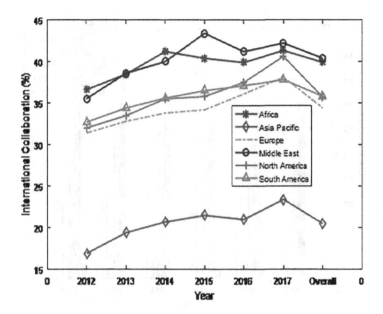

Fig. 3. Plot of international collaboration by world regions

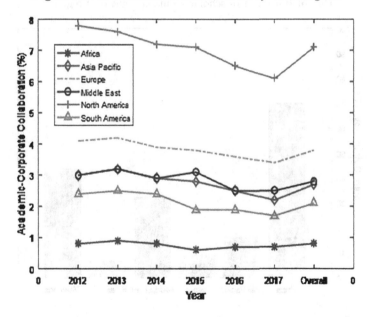

Fig. 4. Plot of academic-corporate collaboration by world regions

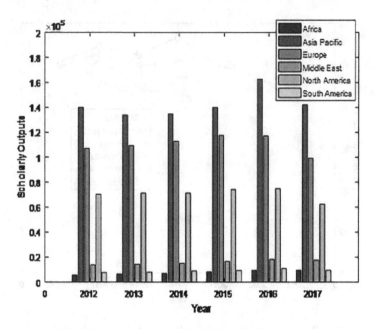

Fig. 5. Bar chart of scholarly outputs by world regions

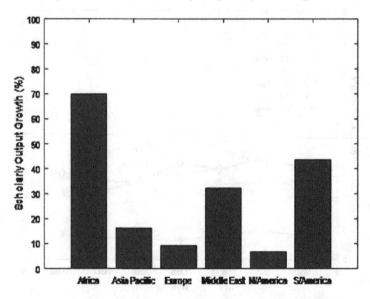

Fig. 6. Bar chart of scholarly output growth by world regions

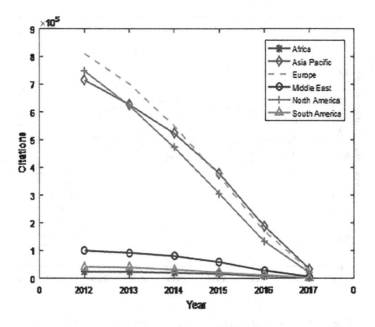

Fig. 7. Plot of citation by world regions

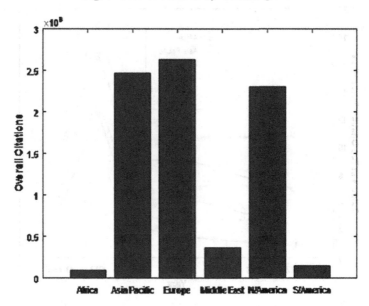

Fig. 8. Bar chart of overall citation by world regions

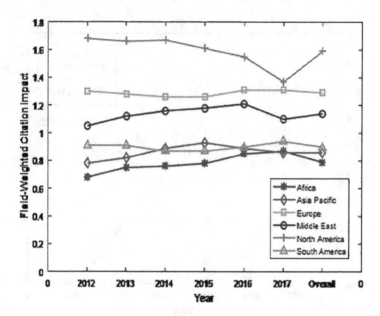

Fig. 9. Plot of field-weighted citation impact by world regions

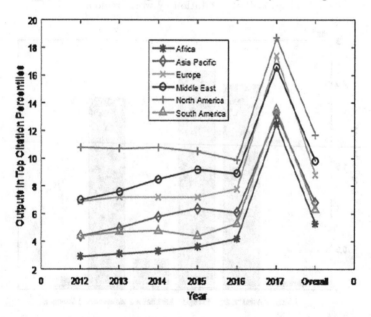

Fig. 10. Plot of outputs in top citation percentiles by world regions

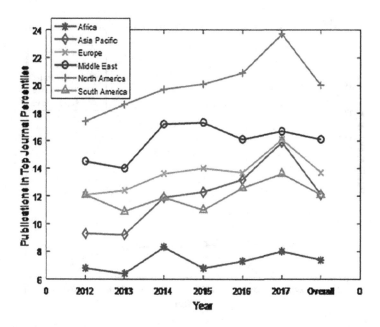

Fig. 11. Plot of outputs in publications in top journal percentiles by world regions

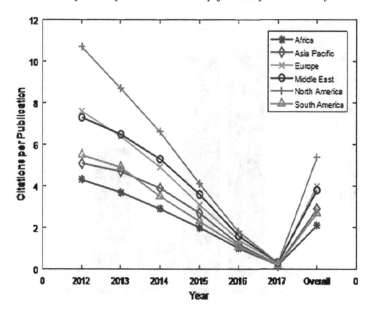

Fig. 12. Plot of citations per publication by world regions

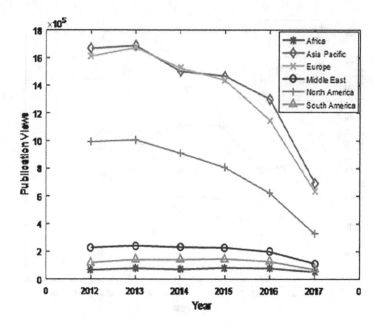

Fig. 13. Plot of publication views by world regions

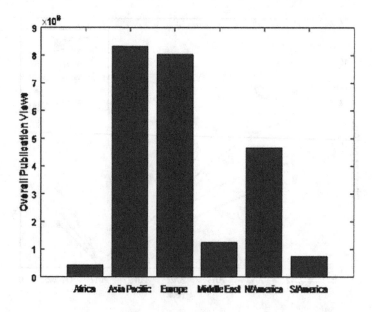

Fig. 14. Bar chart of overall publication views by world regions

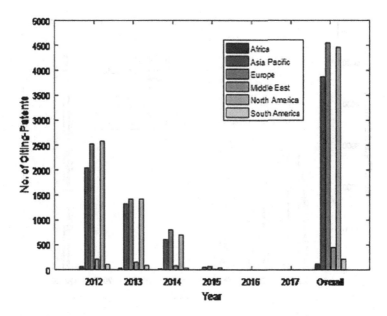

Fig. 15. Bar chart of citing-patents by world regions

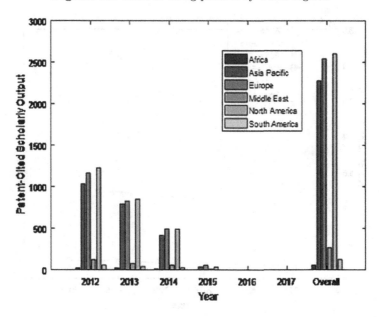

Fig. 16. Bar chart of patent-cited scholarly output by world regions

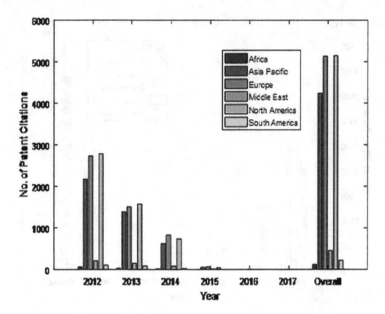

Fig. 17. Bar chart of patent citations by world regions

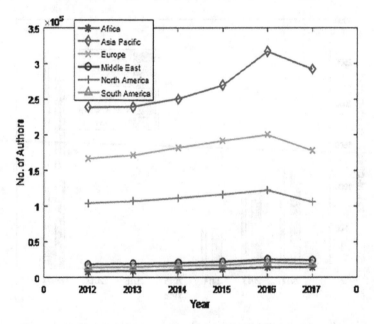

Fig. 18. Plot of number of authors by world regions

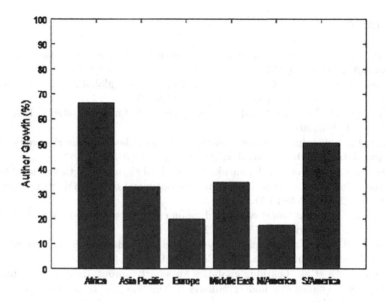

Fig. 19. Bar chart of author growth by world regions

4   Conclusion

In this paper, we presented and analyzed comprehensive data about scholarly contributions that were indexed in Scopus database between 2012 and 2017. Frequency distributions and trends across the six-year study period were presented in tables, graphs, and plots. The data showed that there is paucity of awarded grants for certain regions due to the fact that only a limited number of grant awarding bodies are considered in Scopus database. Understanding the scholarly contributions of world regions to computer science research will help funding bodies to make right decisions in the administration of limited resources. The volume of data and the depth of statistical analyses presented in this paper will encourage more empirical research in the emerging field of ranking analytics that seeks to objectively assess scholarly contributions to academic research. In short, the Information provided in this paper will help researchers in computer science to explore new research collaborations.

Acknowledgement. This work was carried out under the IoT-Enabled Smart and Connected Communities (*SmartCU*) research cluster of the Department of Electrical and Information Engineering, Covenant University, Ota, Nigeria. The research was fully sponsored by Covenant University Centre for Research, Innovation and Development (CUCRID), Covenant University, Ota, Nigeria.

References

1. Suresh, S.: Research funding: global challenges need global solutions. Nature **490**(7420), 337–338 (2012)
2. Eckhouse, S., Lewison, G., Sullivan, R.: Trends in the global funding and activity of cancer research. Mol. Oncol. **2**(1), 20–32 (2008)
3. Hicks, D.: Performance-based university research funding systems. Res. Policy **41**(2), 251–261 (2012)
4. Jacsó, P.: The h-index, h-core citation rate and the bibliometric profile of the Scopus database. Online Inf. Rev. **35**(3), 492–501 (2011)
5. Popoola, S.I., Atayero, A.A., Faruk, N.: Received signal strength and local terrain profile data for radio network planning and optimization at GSM frequency bands. Data Brief **16**, 972–981 (2018)
6. Popoola, S.I., et al.: Smart campus: data on energy consumption in an ICT-driven university. Data Brief **16**, 780–793 (2018)
7. Popoola, S.I., et al.: Data on the key performance indicators for quality of service of GSM networks in Nigeria. Data Brief **16**, 914–928 (2018)
8. Popoola, S.I., et al.: Learning analytics for smart campus: data on academic performances of engineering undergraduates in Nigerian private university. Data Brief **17**, 76–94 (2018)
9. Lee, S., Bozeman, B.: The impact of research collaboration on scientific productivity. Soc. Stud. Sci. **35**(5), 673–702 (2005)
10. Katz, J.S., Martin, B.R.: What is research collaboration? Res. Policy **26**(1), 1–18 (1997)

Bridges Reinforcement Through Conversion of Tied-Arch Using Crow Search Algorithm

Sergio Valdivia[1,2], Broderick Crawford[1], Ricardo Soto[1],
José Lemus-Romani[1(✉)], Gino Astorga[2], Sanjay Misra[3],
Agustín Salas-Fernández[1], and José-Miguel Rubio[4]

[1] Pontificia Universidad Católica de Valparaíso, Valparaíso, Chile
{broderick.crawford,ricardo.soto}@pucv.cl,
{jose.lemus.r,juan.salas.f}@mail.pucv.cl
[2] Universidad de Valparaíso, Valparaíso, Chile
{sergio.valdivia,gino.astorga}@uv.cl
[3] Covenant University, Ota, Nigeria
sanjay.misra@covenantuniversity.edu.ng
[4] Universidad Tecnológica de Chile INACAP, Santiago, Chile
jrubiol@inacap.cl

Abstract. The bridges reinforcement is an expensive activity. In this line, new cheap ways to fix bridges have been developed. One of them is the bridges reinforcement through conversion of the cable-stayed arch. The main aim is minimizing the distances between the tensions of each lengthwise position between the original bridge and the bridge with the reinforcement by the cable-stayed arch. For that, it is necessary to know the order that the tension must be applied. In this paper, we resolve this problem by using a recent metaheuristic called Crow Search Algorithm which is based on the intelligent behavior of crows, this approach is inspired by the feature of crows to hide their excess food. The obtained results are compared other approximate techniques by using a well-known statistical test. Promising results reveal that this new algorithm is competitive to solve the proposed problem.

Keywords: Crow Search Algorithm · Metaheuristic optimization · Bridges reinforcement

1 Introduction

In this paper, we will talk about bridges that cross rivers, because that kind of bridges has a very specific problem, the water. It is well know that corrosion [4] and erosion [12] are a big trouble. Also scours can collapse them by the hydraulic action.

Build bridges is an expensive activity [15] and can take years depending on the size. Also, in order to extend the useful life of the structure, this one can be

© Springer Nature Switzerland AG 2019
S. Misra et al. (Eds.): ICCSA 2019, LNCS 11623, pp. 525–535, 2019.
https://doi.org/10.1007/978-3-030-24308-1_42

damaged it is not fixed in the right way. A support plan that allows minimizing expenses is crucial.

Nowadays, new affordable ways to fix bridges structures have been developed by engineering. One of them is the bridges reinforcement through conversion of the cable-stayed arch, the main aim is to install an arch over the bridge and applied tension over hangers that support them, then remove the piers.

Our goal is optimizing those solutions for this new technique can be applied. In order to succeed, we have to minimize the distances between the tensions of each lengthwise position. Besides, we indicate the order that the tension must be applied, because the tension of the cables cannot be performed simultaneously, an excessive tearing can make the bridge collapse (Fig. 1).

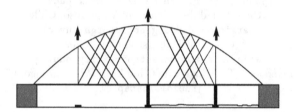

Fig. 1. Bridge reinforcement technique

Finding the best solution for the order of the straps and their magnitude is a complex task that must be supported by some optimization technique. Within the optimization techniques there are complete and approximate ones (Fig. 2) being the metaheuristics an approximate technique that we will use for the solution of the best order and magnitude that we will use.

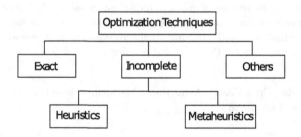

Fig. 2. Optimization techniques

This paper contemplates 5 sections, Sect. 1 is an introduction, Sect. 2 is an explanation of the present problematical, Sect. 3 describes how the new algorithm works, Sect. 4 indicates how we implement the algorithm, also describes the computational results obtained and a statistical test show us comparisons. Finally, Sect. 6 exposes the conclusions of this paper.

2 Problem

Bridges decks are reusable [15]. The concrete of bridges is supported by 3 beams side to side [16]. Beams has finite cuts along lengthwise position that is associated with a tension, we assume work with just 2 beams in order to satisfy the problems because outside beams are similar. Also, the upper and lower tensions of the deck are different, so we must study them because if the maximum or minimum capacity of tension is exceeded, the bridges can collapse. To avoid the collapse is crucial to minimize the distances between the tensions of each lengthwise position [17].

To solve this problem, the metaheuristics will indicate the order and the tensions that must be applied. Subsequently, these solutions are evaluated by the SAP2000 software that makes it possible to design, analyze and build a structure of virtual form and whose communication is realized by means of APIs [1].

2.1 Objective Function

The objective function is defined as the summation of the difference tense of both top and low, for each one of K cuts and each one of the 2 beams, as described by Eq. 1:

$$min \sum_{i=1}^{2} \sum_{k=1}^{k} |\sigma o_{i,k} - \sigma m_{i,k}| \tag{1}$$

Where: $\sigma oi, k$ is the tension of the original bridge in the beam i and in the cut k.
$\sigma m_{i,k}$ is the tension of the bridge modified in the beam i and in the cut k.
This function is evaluated for the low tensions as upper to those of the deck, and the objective is to minimize the differences.

2.2 Constraints

The problem have constraints that must be met to satisfy the objective function

– The hangers cannot be jacking simultaneously.

$$ord_1, ord_2, \ldots, ord_n \in \{1, 2, \ldots, n\} \tag{2}$$

$$ord_w \neq ord_j \; ; \; \forall w, j \quad con \; w \neq j \quad w, j \in \{1, 2, \ldots, n\} \tag{3}$$

– The effort of the modified bridge deck should not pass the limits of the Band Admissible Modified (BAM):

$$\sigma m \geqslant \sigma o \tag{4}$$

$$\sigma m \geqslant fct \tag{5}$$

$$\sigma m \leqslant fcmax2 \; (in \; intermediate \; stages) \tag{6}$$

$$\sigma m \leqslant fcmax \; (in \; final \; stages) \tag{7}$$

Where:

σm is the tension (top or bottom) of the modified bridge.

σo is the tension (top or bottom) of the original bridge.

fct is the maximum tension to traction admissible for the concrete.

fcmax is the maximum tension to admissible compression for the concrete.

fcmax2 is the maximum tension to compression for the concrete, extended.

fct, fcmax and fcmax2 are information obtained by SAP2000.

Any tension on the modified bridge deck that is not inside the BAM described from the original model is discarded because can generate damage to the bridge.

3   Algorithm

Engineering and Construction areas are close to optimizations problems, indeed some problems have been solved by heuristics, like Design of reinforced concrete bridge frames [10] or the Infrastructure Asset Management [13]. Additionally, we have antecedents about problems solved by metaheuristics, like Optimal sizing, geometrical and topological design [5] and Discrete optimization of structures [11]. But reinforcement through conversion of cable-stayed arch is almost new in the optimization area. we only have 2 related works the first is proposed by Valenzuela [14] and the second one by Matus [9]. That is the purpose why we are suggesting to test this new algorithm. This type being techniques not only used in problems of this nature [2,8].

3.1   Crow Search Algorithm

Crows are considered like the world's most intelligent animals, some features of this birds are: memorize faces, use tools, communicate in sophisticated ways and hide their excess food in certain positions of the environment and retrieve the stored food when it is needed, Also they have been known to watch other birds, observe where the other birds hide their food, and steal it once the owner leaves.

Assume that at iteration $iter$, crow j wants to visit its hiding place, $m^{j,iter}$. At this iteration, crow i decides to follow crow j to approach to the hiding place of crow j. In this case, two states may happen:

- State 1: Crow j does not know that crow i is following it. As a result, crow i will approach to the hiding place of crow j.
- State 2: Crow j knows that crow i is following it. As a result, in order to protect its hidden place from being stolen, crow j will fool crow i by going to another position of the search space. The new position of crow i is obtained as follows:

$$x^{i,iter+1} = \begin{cases} x^{i,iter} + r_i fl(m^{j,iter} - x^{i,iter}) & r_j \geqslant AP \\ a\, random\, position & otherwise \end{cases} \qquad (8)$$

Where: r_i and r_j are random numbers with uniform distribution between 0 and 1 and fl denotes the flight length of crow i and AP denotes the awareness probability of crow j. Being the movement is applied to each variable.

In Crow Search Algorithm (CSA) [3], intensification and diversification are controlled by the parameter of awareness probability (AP), small values of AP, increases intensification (local search) and large values of AP increases diversification (explore).

Algorithm 1. CSA pseudo code

---

1 N crows are randomly initialized
2 Evaluate the position of the crows.
3 For each crow its memory is initialized.
4 **while** $iter < iter_{max}$ **do**
5   **for** $i = 1$ to N **do**
6   A random crow is selected
7   **for** $j = 1$ to D **do**
8   **if** $r_j \geqslant AP$ **then**
9                  $x^{i,iter+1} = x^{i,iter} + r_i\, fl\, (m^{j,iter} - x^{i,iter})$
10   **else**
11                 $x^{i,iter+1} = $ a random position of the search space
12   **end**
13   **end**
14   **end**
15   Check the feasibility of new positions
16   The new position of the crows must be evaluated
17   The memory of the crows must be updated
18 **end**

---

4 Experimental Results

The first step is take de CSA and make a clear implementation to try to solve this problem, because is very important to prove algorithms in its natural state to verify how they can mutate in time to get better results later.

This problem was proposed by Valenzuela [14] by using Genetic Algorithm (GA) [7] and was compared against Black Hole (BH) [6] by Matus [9]. BH got better results than GA so our experiment will be to compare CSA against BH.

At first we said that the solution vector has the positions of hangers (discrete variables) and the magnitude of tights that must be applied (continues variables), Table 1 show us an example how to represent a solution vector.

Table 1. Example of solution vector

Position 1	Position 2	Position 3	Magnitude 1	Magnitude 2	Magnitude 3
2	1	3	0.78	0.41	0.999

The first hanger that must be tense is position 2 and will have a tension of 41%, then the hanger in position 1 will be tense by 78% and so on, remember that if we have N hangers we will have N magnitudes, for this example we choose a N = 3. As the algorithm explain at the pseudo code the positions of crows that represent a feasible solution is randomly initialize.

4.1 Parameter Settings Used in Experiments

It is necessary to clarify that all instances where executed with the same settings that show us Table 2 for CSA. The values of this configuration were obtained through the parametric scanning technique [8].

Table 2. CSA parameters

Population	Awareness probability	Flight length	Iterations
50	0,4	1e−05	1000

4.2 Computational Results

CSA for Bridges reinforcement was implemented in Python 3.6 and executed in a Personal Computer running Windows 10 on Intel core i7-6700 CPU (3.4 GHz), 16 GB of RAM. The problem has 11 instances, which were executed 15 times.

4.3 Comparison

Now that we have the CSA results we will proceed to compare Fitness against BH proposed by Matus [9].

As we can see at Table 3 the fitness of BHA are compared with CSA in their 15 executions of the instances PV-TCV, HW-TCV, PT-TCV and AB-TCV, at first look we can notice at this moment that BHA is getting better results.

Table 3. Fitness comparation of PV-TCV, HW-TCV, PT-TCV and AB-TC

#	PV-TCV		HW-TC		PT-TCV		AB-TC	
	BH	CSA	BH	CSA	BH	CSA	BH	CSA
1	521950,827	531882,606	518227,336	528989,406	526676,105	530594,126	517068,779	530594,126
2	523427,989	533085,557	518554,722	529211,843	519411,917	531386,203	524023,770	531386,203
3	523381,036	530664,013	521443,876	529494,654	525110,874	530729,813	524821,681	530729,813
4	524362,167	530634,237	518566,592	529751,772	520610,728	530720,987	520848,212	530720,987
5	520927,571	532416,806	516990,684	529558,764	524252,033	530951,184	520622,784	530951,184
6	525788,701	532820,292	522992,527	527809,505	520560,471	531957,290	520152,444	531957,290
7	518788,669	532698,100	522006,562	528984,055	523880,059	532288,375	517564,071	532288,375
8	521114,467	531465,878	519225,675	528889,737	525204,201	530651,000	523623,834	530651,000
9	523983,245	532956,003	520271,778	528398,840	523880,059	531459,352	519373,561	531459,352
10	522809,147	531667,503	523204,076	528122,659	520863,041	533030,705	524246,509	533030,705
11	522648,276	530980,392	520515,557	528762,658	522029,399	530274,053	523785,395	530274,053
12	521351,709	532952,753	519526,112	528202,239	522617,218	531388,957	520203,824	531388,957
13	523941,247	530695,516	517752,373	527747,883	518340,350	530697,510	520872,273	530697,510
14	517407,410	532615,396	521967,482	528308,692	517173,901	530926,098	518973,967	530926,098
15	520202,016	530923,334	521974,260	528870,514	518891,310	531526,666	522447,219	531526,666
Best	517407,410	530664,013	516990,684	527747,883	517173,901	530274,053	517068,779	528454,356

Table 4. Fitness comparation of WR-TCV, VC-TCV, CC-TCV and TC-TCV

#	WR-TCV		VC-TCV		CC-TCV		TC-TCV	
	BH	CSA	BH	CSA	BH	CSA	BH	CSA
1	521210,450	529929,365	517454,836	529169,091	520682,197	527510,958	519824,404	536471,118
2	519448,379	529276,267	516764,747	527600,827	520212,174	527069,873	519571,134	537469,853
3	519880,227	529309,294	526420,203	528470,513	520538,000	526748,922	524103,151	536933,420
4	519204,810	528565,399	523586,259	527963,379	524706,864	527761,352	521301,708	537202,956
5	526646,976	530174,589	517878,923	527091,654	522918,409	528221,432	522386,876	537202,956
6	523896,152	528415,258	521676,411	526987,972	518616,048	527155,806	522834,907	537202,956
7	519162,739	530171,474	515963,267	528123,404	519413,560	528607,198	522191,193	538781,779
8	522611,368	528930,193	524091,123	528572,943	524143,332	527828,843	519926,614	537017,178
9	522236,031	528760,534	520710,801	528714,816	522562,147	527210,139	522591,311	536763,476
10	518685,865	529449,539	520958,228	528606,885	515930,442	528043,516	521634,820	537925,269
11	521471,347	529303,607	522523,255	529405,439	520447,927	527872,354	523052,417	536413,910
12	523417,258	529440,568	521104,325	528034,057	523472,335	527963,324	524988,999	537612,494
13	525384,947	528606,536	521939,460	528436,253	517694,832	526767,144	525268,020	537169,334
14	520876,224	529781,300	521888,839	527493,676	519115,906	527412,494	520641,954	537039,754
15	522051,315	528851,927	520548,389	528610,744	515608,056	529284,467	519598,167	536488,893
Best	518685,865	528415,258	515963,267	526987,972	515608,056	526767,144	519571,134	536413,910

The next step is evaluate instances WR-TCV, VC-TCV, CC-TCV and TC-TCV and again as we see in Table 4 BHA still is getting better results as CSA.

Finally instances RD-AA10, RC-AA10 and CR-AA10 are compared and once again BH got better results as CSA (Table 5).

Table 5. Fitness comparation of RD-AA10, RC-AA10, and CR-AA10

#	RD-AA10		RC-AA10		CR-AA10	
	BH	CSA	BH	CSA	BH	CSA
1	517038,968	523412,188	514019,852	520941,35	517761,806	522137,908
2	519226,401	523972,103	514605,633	522305,13	514470,308	521515,493
3	513572,503	523358,836	517856,008	520951,095	517102,869	521477,768
4	512678,644	522658,448	517790,493	522591,275	517088,897	521148,122
5	511665,241	523982,924	514457,070	520932,178	514502,449	520147,613
6	517200,649	522906,100	514508,111	522357,696	511024,809	520526,858
7	515799,785	523106,237	510072,744	520279,079	516154,932	522624,078
8	516494,402	523035,493	514272,046	521204,525	512943,624	520729,088
9	511107,489	523992,084	515619,911	522056,966	515740,371	520516,490
10	514930,924	521828,964	513847,138	519474,345	512584,970	520488,382
11	509176,298	521545,011	514603,894	519999,895	517126,961	520174,824
12	512632,111	521870,639	513776,522	521028,367	516430,949	521935,361
13	508556,024	522661,916	514564,776	520875,930	514210,370	520867,278
14	520999,995	523603,099	511927,536	522660,726	513743,602	521560,786
15	513408,64	523524,378	513593,241	521046,366	512808,821	520427,006
Best	508556,024	521828,964	510072,744	519474,345	511024,809	520174,824

The Table 6 describe us each instance with the minimum value of fitness of CSA and BH. Also we can see the Relative Change and Difference (RPD) and the difference between the results of the algorithms.

Table 6. Fitness differences and RPD

Instance	Min. CSA	Min. BH	RPD	Difference
PV-TCV	530664,013	517407,410	2,56	13256,603
HW-TCV	527747,883	516990,684	2,08	10757,199
PT-TCV	530274,053	517173,901	2,53	13100,152
AB-TCV	528454,356	517068,779	2,20	11385,577
WR-TCV	528415,258	518685,865	1,88	9729,393
VC-TCV	526987,972	515963,267	2,14	11024,705
CC-TCV	526767,144	515608,056	2,16	11159,088
TC-TCV	536413,910	519571,134	3,24	16842,776
RD-AA10	521828,964	508556,024	2,61	13272,94
RC-AA10	519474,345	510072,744	1,84	9401,601
CR-AA10	520174,824	511024,809	1,79	9150,015

4.4   Instance Distribution

Now that we have all results of both algorithms, we will compare the distribution of the samples of each instance through a violin plot that shows the full distribution of the data Fig. 3.

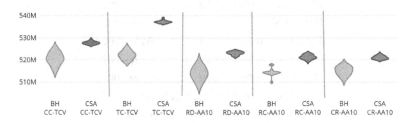

Fig. 3. Instances distribution

After study all the instances we can conclude that all the plots are showing us the same, CSA is caught in a local optimum, do not converge as well as BH.

5   Statistical Tests

It is very important to show how significant difference have BH over CSA in this type of problem, and that is the reason why we perform a contrast statistical test for each instance through the *Kolmogorov-Smirnov-Lilliefors* test to determine the independence of samples and the *Mann-Whitney-Wilcoxon* test to compare the results statistically.

Kolmogorov-Smirnov-Lilliefors test, allow us to analyze the independence of the samples by determining the Z_{min} obtained from the 15 executions of each instance. To determinate independence, we propose the following hypotheses:

- H_0: states that Z_{min} follows a normal distribution.
- H_1: states the opposite.

The test performed has yielded *p_value* lower than 0.05; therefore, H_0 cannot be assumed. Now that we know that the samples are independent and it cannot be assumed that they follow a normal distribution, it is not feasible to use the central limit theorem. Therefore, for evaluating the heterogeneity of samples we use a non-parametric test call *Mann-Whitney-Wilcoxon* test to compare all the results of each instances we propose the following hypotheses:

- H_0: CSA is better than BH
- H_1: states the opposite.

As we can see at Table 7 BH got better results than CSA in all instances.

Table 7. p-value *Mann-Whitney-Wilcoxon* test

Instance	CSA vs BH	BH vs CSA
PV-TCV	0.999999679	3.21470612e−007
HW-TCV	0.999999679	3.21470612e−007
PT-TCV	0.999999679	3.20839521e−007
AB-TCV	0.999999679	3.21470612e−007
WR-TCV	0.999999679	3.21470612e−007
VC-TCV	0.999999679	3.21470612e−007
CC-TCV	0.999999679	3.21470612e−007
TC-TCV	0.999999681	3.18952541e−007
RD-AA10	0.999999679	3.21470612e−007
RC-AA10	0.999999679	3.21470612e−007
CR-AA10	0.999999679	3.21470612e−007

6   Conclusion

In this paper, bridges reinforcement through conversion of cable-stayed arch by using Crow Search Algorithm, we use a new algorithm to solve the problem of bridges reinforcement, but was very clear after all the tests that CSA is not better than BH solving this problem in its natural state, when we see the graphs of instances distribution we can observe that CSA is trapped in a optimum local. BH always got better results. In order to improve results of CSA it will be necessary to make some modification in the perturbation operator for example or change the way of penalization for the feasible solutions, this options or more will be discuses in a future work, meanwhile Matus et al. [9] still have the best results.

Acknowledgements. Broderick Crawford is supported by Grant CONICYT/ FONDECYT/REGULAR/1171243, Ricardo Soto is supported by Grant CONICYT /FONDECYT /REGULAR/1190129, Gino Astorga is supported by Postgraduate Grant Pontificia Universidad Católica de Valparaíso 2015, José Lemus is Beneficiario Beca Postgrado PUCV 2018. This work was funded by the CONICYT PFCHA/DOCTORADO BECAS NACIONAL/2019 - 21191692.

References

1. Sap2000. http://www.csiespana.com/software/2/sap2000
2. Almonacid, B.: Simulation of a dynamic prey-predator spatial model based on cellular automata using the behavior of the metaheuristic African Buffalo optimization. In: Ferrández Vicente, J.M., Álvarez-Sánchez, J.R., de la Paz López, F., Toledo Moreo, J., Adeli, H. (eds.) IWINAC 2017. LNCS, vol. 10337, pp. 170–180. Springer, Cham (2017). https://doi.org/10.1007/978-3-319-59740-9_17
3. Askarzadeh, A.: A novel metaheuristic method for solving constrained engineering optimization problems: crow search algorithm. Comput. Struct. **169**, 1–12 (2016)
4. Benin, A.V., Semenov, A.S., Semenov, S.: Fracture analysis of reinforced concrete bridge structures with account of concrete cracking under steel corrosion. Adv. Mater. Res. **831**, 364–369 (2013)
5. Grierson, D.E., Pak, W.H.: Optimal sizing, geometrical and topological design using a genetic algorithm. Struct. Optim. **6**(3), 151–159 (1993)
6. Hatamlou, A.: Black hole: a new heuristic optimization approach for data clustering. Inf. Sci. **222**, 175–184 (2013)
7. Holland, J.H.: Adaptation in Natural and Artificial Systems: An Introductory Analysis with Applications to Biology, Control, and Artificial Intelligence. MIT Press, Cambridge (1975)
8. Lanza-Gutierrez, J.M., Crawford, B., Soto, R., Berrios, N., Gomez-Pulido, J.A., Paredes, F.: Analyzing the effects of binarization techniques when solving the set covering problem through swarm optimization. Expert Syst. Appl. **70**, 67–82 (2017)
9. Matus, S., Soto, R., Crawford, B.: Optimización del refuerzo de puentes mediante arco atirantado con black hole algorithm. Master's thesis, Escuela de Ingeniería Informática, Pontificia Universidad Católica de Valparaíso, Valparaíso, Chile (2018)
10. Perea, C., Alcala, J., Yepes, V., Gonzalez-Vidosa, F., Hospitaler, A.: Design of reinforced concrete bridge frames by heuristic optimization. Adv. Eng. Softw. **39**(8), 676–688 (2008)
11. Rajeev, S., Krishnamoorthy, C.S.: Discrete optimization of structures using genetic algorithms. J. Struct. Eng. **118**(5), 1233–1250 (1992)
12. Swann, C., Mullen, C.: Predicting erosion impact on highway and railway bridge substructures. Technical report, Mississippi Mineral Resources Institute University of Mississippi and Department of Civil Engineering University of Mississippi, 111 Brevard Hall, Mississippi, June 2016
13. Torres-Machí, C., Pellicer, E., Yepes, V., Chamorro, A.: Heuristic optimization model for infrastructure asset management. In: Bielza, C., et al. (eds.) CAEPIA 2013. LNCS (LNAI), vol. 8109, pp. 300–309. Springer, Heidelberg (2013). https://doi.org/10.1007/978-3-642-40643-0_31
14. Valenzuela, M.: Refuerzo de puentes de luces medias por conversion en arco atirantado tipo network. Ph.D. thesis, Universitat Politècnica de Catalunya, Barcelona, España, February 2012
15. Valenzuela, M., Casas, J.: Bridge strengthening by conversion to network arch: design criteria and economic validation. Struct. Infrastruct. Eng. **12**(10), 1310–1322 (2015)
16. Valenzuela, M.A., Casas Rius, J.R.: Bridge strengthening by structural change: optimization via genetic algorithm. In: IABSE-IASS 2011 Symposium (2011)
17. Valenzuela, M.A., Casas Rius, J.R., et al.: Structural behavior and design criteria for bridge strengthening by tied arch. comparison with network arch bridges. In: ARCH 2013, Proceedings of the 7th International Conference on Arch Bridges, pp. 829–836 (2013)

Software Architecture Enabling Effective Control of Selected Quality Aspects

Michal Žemlička[1,2]([⊠]) [iD] and Jaroslav Král[3] [iD]

[1] Faculty of Mathematics and Physics, Charles University,
Malostranské nám. 25, 118 00 Prague 1, Czech Republic
`zemlicka@sisal.mff.cuni.cz`
[2] AŽD Praha, Závod Technika,
Žirovnická 3146/2, Záběhlice, 106 00 Prague 10, Czech Republic
`zemlicka.michal@azd.cz`
[3] Faculty of Informatics, Masaryk University,
Botanická 68a, 602 00 Brno, Czech Republic
`kralq@seznam.cz`

Abstract. The number of requirements on information and control systems features grows. They often contain flexibility, safety, reliability, and security. Balancing all these features is not easy. We propose architectural turn enabling to control flexibility and security (and to some extent also reliability/availability). The proposed solution enables agile involvement of people into processes. It simplifies solution of rare cases or emergency situations. It can be used during system development and maintenance. We discuss some implementation details.

Keywords: Software quality aspects control ·
Software confederations · System flexibility

1 Introduction

There is a strong tendency to digitalize a growing part of human society as well as its autonomous subsystems like industry, social processes, ecology, education, artificial intelligence, robotics, or e-government.

Achieved solutions are enhanced and extended very quickly due to changing needs, aims, and advances in technical domain. The result is dynamic computerization of human society. Many human activities are computerized already now. It can be surprising that the importance of human involvement into the processes grows. Human must be able to formulate aims, implement systems, maintain them, and control (supervise) them. It implies that the system must be understandable for involved people and must be structured as a network of collaborating autonomous components having properties of services.

We propose in the area of information and control systems a solution enabling all human-oriented rules. The proposed solution is advantageous for all human-oriented roles (front-end users, IT specialists, customers, managers, experts, etc.) needed during system development, maintenance, and use.

© Springer Nature Switzerland AG 2019
S. Misra et al. (Eds.): ICCSA 2019, LNCS 11623, pp. 536–550, 2019.
https://doi.org/10.1007/978-3-030-24308-1_43

Current trends towards Industry 5.0 [20] and Society 5.0 [19] increase the importance of human involvement in software system development and use. Human involvement increases the necessity to use specific types of service-oriented architecture. The service orientation with emphasized human involvement must be designed/structured as a complex of cooperating autonomous entities (services).

They must have understandable interface and function and must communicate in the way understandable to the involved people (e.g. domain experts) – typically using messages having easily understandable semantics. To achieve it, the messages must be of textual nature and the services should not be too complex. In order to keep the system structure understandable to people, the system granularity should be adequate to human limits mentioned e.g. in [14] (there should be cooperation of a limited number of partners at any level).

The systems grow. It is they consist from increasing number of services, the services become more complex and their communication becomes also more complex. The system becomes less understandable and more difficult to be maintained and properly used.

With respect to 7 ± 2 rule [14] it makes sense to limit the number of interfacing services. As we need to handle many services at the same time, solution of this issue can be to build the systems having hierarchical or very similar architecture. We propose a specific variant of service-oriented architecture (SOA) having combinable services. Their combinations can be treated again as combinable services. It also enables reuse of existing services.

With the increasing number of requirements being often the requirements on quality aspects [10, 26] there is an increasing chance that the requirements can be contradictory and must be orchestrated. With the growing number of requirements it grows also the chance that some of the requirements could be at least to some extent contradictory. Example of such "contradictory" requirements are security and flexibility or openness. Flexibility and openness require that data and functions should be easily available. From security point of view it is like opening a door to attacks.

We discuss design and implementation principles enabling effective orchestration of requirements and develop systems and having many further advantages [12]. We introduce a turn simplifying balancing between various requirements as well as between quality aspects of the final product. Our goal is creation of systems that are able to work (at least partially) also under emergency or unexpected conditions.

It is advantageous for users that the communication between services is understandable and they can therefore take part in debugging and maintenance. It is surprisingly advantageous also for managers and developers. The solution brings some security advantages. It also simplifies analysis of incidents. It is advantageous for both users and developers.

Communication between services must be textual to allow involved people to understand them. Properly chosen message format and processing it has many technical as well as other advantages.

Textual messages can have various formats and application rules and there are several procedures how to achieve it. Different formats as well as different forms of transformations could fit to various situations. Individual variants are discussed below.

2   Selected Quality Aspects

We focus on selected software quality attributes. We describe them and show how they influence each other.

Architectures discussed here allow improvement of many characteristics of quality according ISO 25010:2011 [10], ISO 9126-x [7–9] (compare also [26, Table 2]). They enable easier balancing e.g. between flexibility and security or between easiness of programming and user understandability of interfaces. Some issues could appear with efficiency but this issue is for many reasons weakening now.

This architecture significantly improves development and maintenance processes. It weakens the danger of failures. Surprisingly, it could be important that the system could be built and deployed stepwise and protecting proven existing interfaces – inter-human relations inclusive.

Importance of understandability and learnability of service interfaces grows. Proper design and use of service interfaces positively influences technical aspects of system – including stability, maintainability, and many others. It moreover enables to design systems providing interfaces easily usable for real-world business processes. Another advantage is that such systems could be built incrementally and some of their parts could be temporarily or forever based on human involvement or even human processing.

It leads to growing similarity between development and maintenance processes. It allows easier implementation of support of modern business processes and their management.

Modern information and control systems often integrate Internet of Things (IoT, see e.g. [3]). It is crucial that they use implementation and design principles and rules used by IoT systems. Crucial point is that IoT use messages in structured (tagged) text. The text format encodes structure understandable by human beings either directly or after simple transformations. It is possible to use results from theory of formal languges and linguistcs. It enables collaboration of different professions during system life cycle. Proper use of message formats is a precodition of high quality of the system.

It is also quite popular to connect services through middleware. Then it is virtually possible to let cooperate any service with any of the others. It is advantageous in an environment under single supervision. When there are multiple companies or organizations working together, there could be a problem with setting access rights for the shared middleware.

From various service-oriented approaches the one recommended by Thomas Erl and his team e.g. in [5] appears to be the most popular now. Moreover, service orientation as a whole loses its popularity toward cloud and edge computing.

Clouds are difficult to be integrated in a secure way. We propose a solution encapsulating cloud systems to be standard services. It enables e.g support of humans in the form supposed by Industry 5.0.

3   Real-World and Software Services

Many of software services are built as a support for real-world services or real-world agendas. Some of the real-world processes are used the same way for years, some for decades, some even for centuries. It is, the processes and agendas had enough time to be deeply studied and optimized. Their business processes could be polished to be optimal. The optimality of the processes is in their level of abstraction (they are as precise as necessary and as general as possible) in their granularity, in their procedurality (they are as procedural as necessary and as declarative as possible), etc. Similarly, there have been developed language dialects specific for given tasks. These dialects are for stable processes to some sense also optimal.

The dialects could be based on different languages – there are specific dialects covering the same purpose in all languages where the agenda makes sense (and is used for long time and within the same or similar legal framework).

When software services are created using knowledge and structure of corresponding real-world services, it is possible to consult non-software issues (system extensions and modifications inclusive) with problem domain experts: they, in such situation, understand system structure, system communication and individual processes. They can therefore recognize anything improper in the system and have better chance to find solution of the issues and challenges.

The necessary level of similarity between real-world communication and its software counterpart is still open. For programmers it is easier to use languages closer to machine processing (XML [21], JSON [11], or another language well supported by development tools). For domain experts it is easier if the language is easy to read and write – it is, if it is closer to used real-world languages. Such languages are usually simple and slightly redundant (to avoid situation when it has not been said or heard properly).

For taking full advantages of service orientation, support for human involvement is crucial – compare the differences between Industry 4.0 and 5.0 [20]. Human involvement must be supported at various levels and for various tasks. Let us mention at least some of them:

- coordination of business processes,
- system orchestration and supervision,
- processing of business processes and their individual steps.

Such involvement is a very strong tool: It must be therefore used with respect and evidence.

4   From Software System to Software Service

Complex software support for real-world services and agendas usually does not start from scratch. There are usually various applications and system covering part of the work. The questions are how to interconnect them to cooperate and whether they fulfil our expectations about interfaces (and what to do if they do not fulfil them).

We will show the creation of a complex system step by step in the bottom-up manner. We start with ensuring connectivity of the existing software, then converting the interface to problem-oriented and user understandable one, ensuring access control, creation of a hierarchy, etc. It is possible to modify classical design turns for use in our systems, see below.

4.1   Ensuring Connectivity

Existing applications are typically equipped with interface to human users. For interconnecting applications we need them to be equipped by interface reachable by other applications – ideally by a network interface supporting sending and receiving messages. The basic question is whether the yet not connected application is intended for single user or multi user use and whether it is single process or multi-process one. These features imply some basic limits like availability of concurrent use of the applications by people and computers or possible security settings and functions.

The existing user interface is usually possible to wrap by a new code to provide message connectivity. According to [25] such piece of code is called *primary gate* (PG) as it provides primary access (from the integration point of view) to the integrated (legacy, third-party, or newly-developed one) application/system (software artefact) *A*. Its purpose is to provide access to all functionality of *A*.

Technically we can use existing interfaces if they match our needs or we can accommodate the existing interface. At first, we must ensure that we can consume its outputs and provide its inputs. For such task wrapping suits well.

Textual interfaces, menus, and dialogs could be wrapped. The wrapper could be provided as an integrated part of the system (but then source codes of the wrapped system must be available) or the wrapper can work on top of the application – e.g. as its host. It can catch creation of the input and use the presented data for generating output for partners of the system. Similarly, it can capture any input opportunity and fill in the data prepared and sent by partners.

For such purpose suit better systems with textual input and output than the GUI (graphical user interface) ones – it is just simple to wrap them. The resulting situation could look like in Fig. 1 or in Fig. 2.

4.2   Providing Understandable Interface

The communication in real world is optimized for human users. It uses structured or simplified natural language. Such language is understandable and intuitive

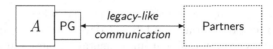

Fig. 1. Very simple application wrapped for network cooperation

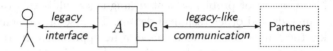

Fig. 2. Wrapped application with preserved legacy user interface

for the problem domain experts (at least the ones using the same basic natural language).

According our experience the communication languages are usually so simple that they can be parsable by LL-techniques[1]. For such languages there are tools, parser generators (like bison [1], ANTLR [18], or KindCons [22]), that can generate very efficient decoders of such languages using their formal description (LL or LR (attribute) grammars).

The programmer usually like communication using means that are well supported by available libraries – it is sending data using XML, JSON or other machine-oriented format. It is easier to let generate the serializer from record/object definition than to think about matching the stored data with existing problem-oriented language. In practice it could be reasonable to think about balancing between problem orientation and easiness of programming.

Now we can expect that the integrated application or system is in principle reachable from other applications. The issue is that the logic and interface of the integrated system could significantly differ from the logic and interfaces of its prospective partners. Accidentally, it is often the case – compare service-oriented architectures recommended by OASIS [15], Open Group [16], or Progress Software.

The interface based on existing user interface is usually revealing too much from the implementation details of A. It makes the interface dependent on the implementation of A. It can be source of change propagation of it is necessary to change some implementation details (e.g. to correct some errors). When also the cooperating partners use implementation revealing interfaces, the change propagation could hit significant part of the system.

Implementation techniques evolve in time quite quickly: every several years there are significant changes and every about ten – fifteen years there are changes also of the used programming paradigm. Updating entire system at once (to keep compatibility between parts) is usually not possible – technically it is too complex and moreover Big Bang (replacement of a big system by another one

---

[1] LL parsing techniques are discussed in literature on formal languages and automata theory as well as in literature on parsing and compiler construction literature – compare e.g. any of [2,6,23,24].

at once) is known as a frequent problem source [4]. Coupling systems using implementation-oriented interface and being developed using different implementation techniques or even different implementation paradigms is a very hard (if not solvable) task.

The defence against it is known – information hiding as proposed by Parnas e.g. in [17]. The use of problem-oriented languages fulfils this task well – it hides all commands and other technical details. The use of problem-oriented language makes the connection between cooperating applications more stable as the problem-oriented language is stable in time and can hide changes of implementation of any of the partner.

It is necessary to convert the available interface following the existing interface logic (typically detailed procedural and often also implementation-oriented one) to the one used in real world (usually declarative and problem-oriented one). Such conversion can be provided by special convertors (services providing the interface conversion) first described in [13] and called *front-end gate* (FEG). Generally it could convert sequences of messages from the partner to sequences of other messages to the integrated application/system (Fig. 3).

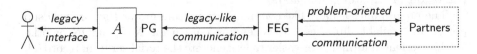

Fig. 3. Service with a front-end gate

If there are partners with different requirements on the interface, it is possible to construct for each partner group specific front-end gate (Fig. 4).

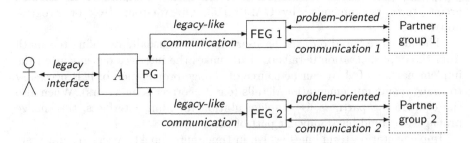

Fig. 4. Service with multiple front-end gates

Such construction rises the chance that implementational changes in any of the partners will not affect A or that implementational changes of A will not affect its partners. It increases stability of the system and reduces maintenance costs.

Let us note that the problem-oriented communication could be based on simple commands, event notifications or even forms containing complex applications as well as entire documents. The message-based communication is more common in control systems and at lower levels of information systems, whereas the document-based communication suits better higher levels of information system (e.g. for communication between cooperating institutions).

4.3   Birth of a Service

The service is expected to transparently serve multiple partners that do not need not know (and usually do not know) the requests of the other service partners, respective the other partners themselves. As the partners access outer interface of service front-end gate(s), such behaviour is expected at last at this border.

Where the border should be, depends also on the application from which the service is created: If it is already a multi-user information system, then it is easy to reach all advantages of service at the primary gate interface. If it is a single-user (and single-thread) application, it depends on number of attached front-end gates: When there is just one, primary gate can be simple – just converts existing user interface to network-reachable interface. Such interface must be at least able to be locked for a single front-end gate at a moment. The serialization of the requests can be done either by extending such simple primary gate by request queue or the request queue(s) can be in the front-end gate(s). In all cases at the outer interface of the front-end gates the expected service behaviour should be provided. In the case when PG has features of a service, front-end gates are full-featured services themselves.

4.4   Access Control

One of the most popular cyber attacks are denial of service (DoS) ones. It is, the service is blocked by enormous load that it is not able to fulfil. The correct users than have no chance that their requests could be solved.

We decided to separate the channels to individual partners and put a control on them. There could be services playing the role of access point for given partner. It authenticates the partner. When something goes wrong, the access point can be simply made inactive what closes access to the system. When the situation restores, the access point can be restored too.

As the partner has only access to its access point, it cannot access other access points easily (they can be e.g. on proprietary connections). It is, when e.g. erroneously some of the partners produce more load than can be processed, the connection can be quickly closed and the other partners can therefore work without any interruption.

It could work also as a protection against DoS attacks (or, more precisely, reduction of their impact) led through connections over Internet. If necessary, access point could be used also for further restriction of the interface provided by front-end gate: it could limit applicable values to given range (i.e. given partner could not ask for arbitrary number of products, but only within agreed range).

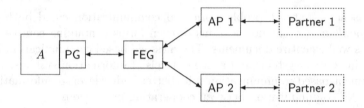

Fig. 5. Service with front-end gate and access points

It is reasonable especially if the limits are not set by supporter company limits but by agreements or legal settings (Fig. 5).

Although it is technically feasible to connect both sides of the access point to the same communication mean (like LAN, Internet, or some middleware products), for security reasons it is not good to do so. Separation of various levels of a system by the use of various separated communication means gives the system a higher overall system resistance to attacks and other network security issues.

4.5 Building Hierarchy/System Composition

Single service is usually not enough – we need to create more complex systems. One possible way is to compose multiple services into a more complex one – into a *composite service*.

Such group should be from outside visible as a sole service: For this purpose there should be created a special service *head of composite service* concentrating communication of any service in the group (incoming and outgoing) with any partner being outside the group (Fig. 6). The composite service can be built from simple service as well as from other composite services or from a mixture of simple and composite services (Fig. 7).

Any request for the composite service must be sent to its head. It decides which service should handle the request and passes the request to the selected service. The responses are usually passed back along the same path. Real composite service could have more complex structure where front-end gates and probably also access points take place – compare Fig. 8.

Sometimes the language of requests from outside do not match the language used by the services in the composite service C. In such case the service of a front-end gate that will provide the request and response transformation could be used. The composite service could be composed from simple services or other composite services. It is possible to build entire hierarchy of composite services forming a complex system.

4.6 Smart Access (Portals)

Larger organizations have dedicated entry points where it is possible to request their service. Incoming requests are evaluated and assigned to some internal service (department) that will process it.

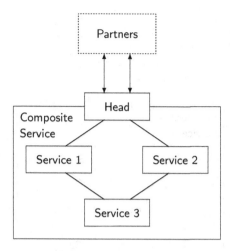

Fig. 6. Simplified composite service

We can build software service behaving like this. It will receive requests from outer world (digital or real), register them, and forward them (probably after some transformation) to the proper target (service that is or should be able to handle it). From the system point of view portal behaves similarly as head of composite service: both services concentrate communication to themselves. The difference is that portals designed to handle human-computer interaction, whereas heads are designed to serve primarily for fully computerized communication.

Many systems have multiple portals: one for inner service (intranet), one for outer service (extranet), and others for special service like supervision of business processes by their owners.

4.7 Service Type Summary

Integrated service/application with its primary gate, front-end gates and access points form a *logical service*. Logical service can have specific interfaces for different partner groups provided by the front-end gates, and managed access regulated by access points.

All the presented services that must be developed (like front-end gates, access points, heads or portals) determine architecture of the system (especially its structure). They play the role of *architectural services*. Architectural services could be equipped with supervising interface allowing responsible people to influence their behaviour and make, if necessary, the decision on their own. Such extension could make sense e.g. when documents are communicated and the service handles its assignment.

In some cases it makes sense to let the request handle manually. Then it could be supported by simple shell allowing receiving requests and sending

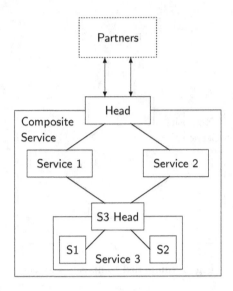

Fig. 7. Simplified hierarchical composite service

replies – *screen prototype*. It could also check correctness of the outgoing messages/documents. It is possible to arrange such tools for handling situation that were not expected or were considered to be too rare to be implemented.

5   Communication Means

Generally there can be used any communication means able to transfer messages or documents between the cooperating services. In practice, there are some aspects that should be taken into account (there are more of them but let us remember just sample of them):

1. Security,
2. Understandability,
3. Usability.

The security aspect is primarily addressed by services called access point. Their proper functionality is conditioned by the fact whether their both ends are connected to the same or different communication mean. If they are connected on the both ends to the same mean, they can be easily bypassed by direct connection on the given mean. There can be established virtual subnetworks or circuits what could improve the situation. When high security is required, the separated communication means appear to be a necessity.

The communication language and format depends on priority setting between understandability and usability (ease of use – here form the programmers' point of view): When communication should be easily understandable to domain experts and if it should be easy to generate by the users, it appears that the

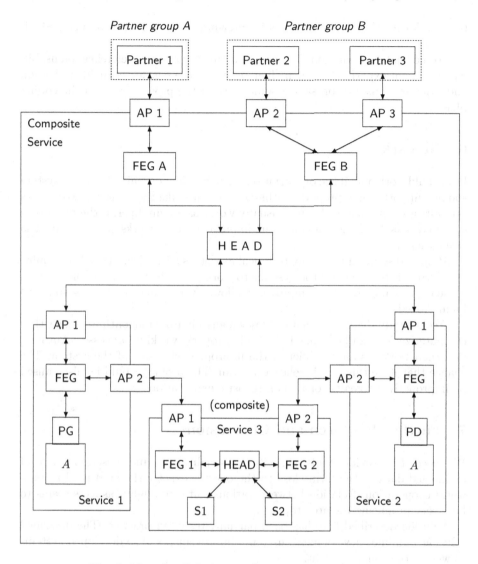

Fig. 8. More detailed view on the same composite service

communication language should be close to programming language – plain text with predefined syntax. For example LL(1) languages can be easy to read by human readers as well as by the computer ones (LL parsers and transducers are very efficient and easy to develop).

Last years communication in many systems is based on semi-structured languages like XML or JSON. They are text-based, there are many tools able to generate and analyse them (for programmers it means minimal work) but their readability for non-programmers are limited. Moreover, data exchange could result in longer messages that require for processing by domain experts additional tools or longer time than messages in inter-human-communication-inspired LL languages.

So the final decision is on the system architect and their preferences on usability of domain experts (and then their potential use e.g. for error identification and emergency use) or on saving some work of the programmers in the coding phase.

6   Remarks

It all could work only if the organization (or network of organizations) the system should support works properly. Otherwise it can make the situation worse – as the software designed in this way usually works as an amplifier: if the real-world system works fine, the software can improve it; if it works poor it can also strengthen it.

Proposed solution has many technical as well as user advantages. Philosophy, on which it is built, allows the systems to work properly, to be available in time, to be easy to maintain and improve. It allows overall quality of the systems to be improved.

Accidentally there are situations known already from monolithic systems that computerization can be applied also to improperly working processes. Automation then works as an amplifier of the improper behaviour of the system. The chance that it be this way is relatively small. The problem could be also caused by improperly set goal(s) or by non-realistic expectations.

7   Further Research and Conclusions

We need to provide tools simplifying serialization and deserialization of exchanged data to the form close to the one (or exactly the one) used in real-world cooperation. Relation between various software quality aspects seems to be a very promising research topic.

Solution described here has been partially tested in practice. The described solution simplifies development, use, and improvements of so developed systems as well as their management.

Turns described here proven themselves in practice and could be significantly extended using services that could be used as extended middleware. It could be used for building e-government. It enables useful application of information technology at global level. It also allows relatively safe use of open systems.

Systems having described architecture could be developed and deployed by smaller IT companies. It concerns also quite big systems. It has many other technical advantages, e.g. broader spectrum of testing and building prototypes.

References

1. Bison (1998). http://www.gnu.org/software/bison/bison.html
2. Aho, A.V., Ullman, J.D.: The Theory of Parsing, Translation and Compiling: Parsing, vol. I. Prentice-Hall, Englewood Cliffs (1972)
3. Atzori, L., Iera, A., Morabito, G.: Understanding the internet of things: definition, potentials, and societal role of a fast evolving paradigm. Ad Hoc Netw. **56**, 122–140 (2017). https://doi.org/10.1016/j.adhoc.2016.12.004. http://www.sciencedirect.com/science/article/pii/S1570870516303316
4. Clark, P.: Big bang rarely works. https://projectone.com/big-bang-rarely-works/
5. Erl, T.: Service-Oriented Architecture: Concepts, Technology, and Design. Prentice Hall PTR, Upper Saddle River (2005)
6. Grune, D., van Reeuwijk, K., Bal, H.E., Jacobs, C.J.H., Langendoen, K.: Modern Compiler Design, 2nd edn. Springer, New York (2012). https://doi.org/10.1007/978-1-4614-4699-6
7. International Organization for Standardization: ISO/IEC 9126–1:2001 software engineering - product quality - part 1: quality model (2001). https://www.iso.org/standard/22749.html
8. International Organization for Standardization: ISO/IEC 9126–2:2003 software engineering - product quality - part 2: external metrics (2003)
9. International Organization for Standardization: ISO/IEC 9126–3:2003 software engineering - product quality - part 3: internal metrics (2003). https://www.iso.org/standard/22891.html
10. International Organization for Standardization, International Electrotechnical Commission: ISO/IEC 25010:2011 systems and software engineering - systems and software quality requirements and evaluation (SQuaRE) - system and software quality models (2011). https://www.iso.org/obp/ui/#iso:std:iso-iec:25010:ed-1:v1:en
11. Internet Engineering Task Force (IETF): The Javascript object notation (JSON) data interchange format, December 2017. https://tools.ietf.org/html/rfc8259
12. Král, J., Pitner, T., Žemlička, M.: Document-oriented middleware: the way to high-quality software. In: Gervasi, O., et al. (eds.) ICCSA 2017. LNCS, vol. 10408, pp. 607–619. Springer, Cham (2017). https://doi.org/10.1007/978-3-319-62404-4_45
13. Král, J., Žemlička, M.: Component types in software confederations. In: Hamza, M.H. (ed.) Applied Informatics, pp. 125–130. ACTA Press, Anaheim (2002)
14. Miller, G.A.: The magical number seven, plus or minus two: some limits on our capacity for processing information. Psychol. Rev. **63**, 81–97 (1956). https://doi.org/10.1037/h0043158
15. OASIS: Reference architecture foundation for service oriented architecture version 1.0, committee specification 01, December 2012. http://docs.oasis-open.org/soa-rm/soa-ra/v1.0/
16. Open Group: Open Group standard SOA reference architecture, November 2011. https://www2.opengroup.org/ogsys/jsp/publications/PublicationDetails.jsp?publicationid=12490
17. Parnas, D.L.: Designing software for ease of extension and contraction. IEEE Trans. Softw. Eng. **5**(2), 128–138 (1979). https://doi.org/10.1109/TSE.1979.234169
18. Parr, T.J., Quong, R.W.: ANTLR: a predicated-LL(k) parser generator. Softw. Pract. Exp. **25**(7), 789–810 (1995). https://doi.org/10.1002/spe.4380250705
19. Shiroishi, Y., Uchiyama, K., Suzuki, N.: Society 5.0: for human security and well-being. Computer **51**(7), 91–95 (2018). https://doi.org/10.1109/MC.2018.3011041

20. Skobelev, P.O., Borovik, S.Y.: On the way from industry 4.0 to industry 5.0: from digital manufacturing to digital society. Industry 4.0 **II**, 307–311 (2017). https://stumejournals.com/journals/i4/2017/6/307/pdf
21. W3 Consortium: Extensible Markup Language (XML) 1.0, 5th edn, November 2008. https://www.w3.org/TR/xml/
22. Žemlička, M.: Kind constructor (2002). http://www.ms.mff.cuni.cz/~zemlicka/KindCons/
23. Žemlička, M.: Principles of kind parsing. Ph.D. thesis, Faculty of Mathematics and Physics, Charles University, Prague, Czech Republic, July 2006
24. Žemlička, M., Král, J.: Run-time extensible (semi-)top-down parser. In: Matousek, V., Mautner, P., Ocelíková, J., Sojka, P. (eds.) TSD 1999. LNCS (LNAI), vol. 1692, pp. 121–126. Springer, Heidelberg (1999). https://doi.org/10.1007/3-540-48239-3_22
25. Žemlička, M., Král, J.: Legacy systems as kernel of web services. Technical report 2004/1, Faculty of Mathematics and Physics, Department of Software Engineering, Charles University, Prague, Czech Republic, January 2004
26. Žemlička, M., Král, J.: Software architecture and software quality. In: Gervasi, O., et al. (eds.) ICCSA 2016. LNCS, vol. 9790, pp. 139–155. Springer, Cham (2016). https://doi.org/10.1007/978-3-319-42092-9_12

Automation of Workflow Design in an Industrial Enterprise

Nikolay Voit[ID], Sergey Kirillov[(✉)][ID], and Dmitry Kanev

Ulyanovsk State Technical University, Ulyanovsk, Russia
n.voit@ulstu.ru, kirillovsyu@gmail.com,
dima.kanev@gmail.com

Abstract. The fundamental scientific problem of the business process management theory is to increase the efficiency of automated systems workflow synthesis and processing in order to reduce the time spent on their development, increasing the success of processing diagram models, namely the implementation of the requirements for resource constraints, functionality, financial component and deadlines, as well as improving the diagram models quality in terms of error control, narrowing the semantic gap between business process analysis and execution. The article proposes an approach to the analysis of workflow diagram models on the basis of temporal automatic grammar with linear analysis time. The approach allows to control and analyze structural-semantic and temporal errors. The results of the research represent that the approach has significant advantages over similar methods of analysis. The effectiveness of this analytical approach is proved by concrete real and relevant examples.

Keywords: Workflow · Business-process · Grammar · Visual language

1 Introduction

The industrial enterprises success in the market depends on many factors: the range of offered services, market saturation, marketing policy, etc. In order to maintain competitiveness, modern, focused on continuous development, industrial enterprises are forced to constantly improve their activities, which requires the development of new technologies and business techniques, as well as the introduction of more effective management methods and activities organization. That is why, among other activities, it is necessary to be able to choose and use the methodology of design, modeling and analysis (processing) of business processes. Today, methodologies and tools for processing business processes are both a serious area of research and a thriving sector of the software market. The range of processing methods used to describe business processes is very wide: from the simplest graphical notations used to construct flowcharts of algorithms, and such strict mathematical devices as Petri nets, to object-oriented modeling languages such as UML (Unified Modeling Language), and specially designed to describe business systems methodologies, such as XPDL (XML Process Definition Language) and BPEL (Business Process Execution Language).

Analysis methods are used to research the qualitative and quantitative characteristics of workflows. Qualitative characteristics are understood as logical and algebraic

© Springer Nature Switzerland AG 2019
S. Misra et al. (Eds.): ICCSA 2019, LNCS 11623, pp. 551–561, 2019.
https://doi.org/10.1007/978-3-030-24308-1_44

correctness of workflows, formalized with the graph theory, workflow networks, matching matrices, graphical modeling languages, including UML, BPMN, IDEF0 and eEPC, etc., as well as evolutionary approach, logic of statements, etc. Quantitative characteristics represent the effectiveness of the workflows execution in the parameters, such as average service time, the utilization rate of production capacity (downtime), etc. Evaluation of the workflows effectiveness is done using simulation modelling (Petri nets), Markov chains and Queuing theory (Queuing systems). The use of a time machine in the workflows design, specification, control and analysis in the development of complex technical systems in an industrial enterprise is a well-known practice [1]. Time and hybrid automata are used for workflows analysis and management [2] in solving problems of access to resources, blocking, limitation of liveliness (vitality, reversibility, boundedness, reachability, dead transitions, deadlocks, home states). For example, it can be tasks such nuclear reactor temperature control, barrier control at the railway crossing [3], in which time context-free grammars are successfully applied. The large number presence of interacting complex automated systems poses the problem of formal control and analysis that can be performed by various methods. Currently π-calculus is a promising, but still very young and developing theory, it has many open questions and unsolved problems. Widely used Petri nets do not have a universal framework for workflows modeling and analysis. In order to analyze various properties (liveliness, reachability, safety) of workflows are modeled in different types of Petri nets. The model checking method is widely used for the workflows analysis in the development of error-free systems at the conceptual design stage. However, it is intended for experienced scientists and engineers, as it is difficult to understand and use [2]. Workflows are also specified by managers who are not trained in formal models and Informatics, and formal analysis requires a detailed representation of the process model in a formal language that is difficult for managers to construct and understand.

Thus, the problem of the workflows analysis and management mechanisms researching is relevant and has great practical importance. The authors propose a mathematical apparatus based on the development of temporal automatic RVTI-grammar. The work is focused on the automation of workflows qualitative structural, semantic and temporal errors identification. The work contains an Introduction, Related Work, the theoretical statements and Conclusion.

2 Related Work

The theory of business process management engaged in both business practice and science. There are areas of business processes design, analysis, modeling, implementation and control [4–19]. In the modern theory of business processes represented with graphic visual languages, the logical model (behavioral model) is used [20, 21], which contain graphic objects and connections between them. The following graphic languages are widely used at large enterprises: UML [22], BPMN [23], AMBER [19], IDEF [24], eEPC [25], PERT [26]. The paper [19] describes the AMBER language, which has a simple data structure (there are no arrays, records and classes), so the implementation of complex business process structures is impossible. The structural approach, laid down in the methodology IDEF [24], was developed in the languages

UML, BPMN, eEPC and specialized language Pilot Workflow ASCON (Russian developer of workflow management systems, firm ASCON [27]) in terms of the object-oriented paradigm inheritance and the introduction of the "time" concept in the diagram workflow models [2]. However, in the most common tools for creating and processing diagram models, such as Microsoft Visio [28], Visual paradigm for UML [29], Aris Toolset [25], IBM Rational Software Architect (RSA) [30], the Pilot workflow ASCON analysis of diagram models is performed by direct methods, requires several "passes" depending on the type of error being controlled, no analysis of integrated diagrammatically models structural peculiarities and operating semantic analysis attached software modules diagrammatically models of dynamic workflows.

Promising approach for treatment diagrammatically workflow is syntactically oriented and based on formal grammars. The most well-known are Web grammar [31], Positional grammar [32], Relational grammar [33], multilevel graph grammar [34] and preserving graph grammar [35]. Positional grammars are the simplest. Developing on the basis of Plex structures [34], they inherited their shortcomings. These grammars do not involve the use of join regions. They cannot be used for graphic languages whose graphical objects have a dynamically changing number of inputs/outputs and cannot be used to control the syntax of graphical languages that contain parallelism. The advantage of relational grammars is the ability to handle errors, but they do not have a mechanism to neutralize such errors. Multilevel and preserving graph grammars are able to provide the graphic languages analysis with "deep" context dependence, which is necessary in the languages, allowing to specify synchronization of the performed actions. Examples of such languages are the languages of process flow diagrams and graphical message sequence Charts. Common shortcomings [36–39] of these grammars are:

1. Increasing the number of products in the construction of grammar for unstructured graphic languages, i.e., with a constant number of graphic language primitives, there is a significant increase in the number of products, because it is necessary to determine all possible variants of unstructured.
2. The grammar construction complexity (increasing the complexity of products and their number), and for some formalisms the impossibility of grammar construction, for graph-schemes with unstructured parallelism.
3. High time complexity. The analyzers built on the basis of the considered grammars offer polynomial or exponential analysis time of graphic languages diagrams.

The main limitation of the above-mentioned methods is that they do not work in the presence of different types (temporal, multi-level, etc.) of diagrams simultaneously, which means that in some cases the input diagrams cannot be analyzed.

3 Workflow Analysis on the Example of the Design and Approval Process of Engineering Documentation

The main approach is to use special RV-grammar family for analyzing, translating, synthesis and control of business processes.

Table 1 presents a mathematical description of the author's RVTI-grammar for graphic language BPMN, proposed in [40–42].

Table 1. Grammar for basic BPMN

Prev. state	Quasi termin	Next state	Memory operations
r0	A0	r1	$W_1(t^{1m^{(n-1)}})$
r1	rel	r2	Θ
r2	E	r1	$W_1(1^{t(1)},\ 1^{t(4)},\ (ts_{max} + tc)_j^{t(15)})/W_3(e^{t(1)})$
	Em	r1	$W_1(1^{t(2)},\ 1^{t(5)},\ (ts_{max} + tc)_j^{t(15)}))/W_3(e^{t(5)})$
	Et	r1	$W_1(1^{t(3)},\ 1^{t(6)},\ (ts_{max} + tc)_j^{t(15)})/W_3(e^{t(6)})$
	Ak	r3	Θ
	A	r4	$W_1(1^{t(16)},\ k^{t(17)},\ t^{1m^n},\ (ts_{max} + tc)_j^{t(15)})/W_3(e^{t(17)})$
	_A	r4	$W_1(inc(m^{t(16)}),\ comp(ts_{max} + tc)^{t(15)})/W_3(m^{t(16)} < n^{t(17)})$
	EG	r5	$W_1(1^{t(9)}, k^{t(10)},\ t^{1m^n},\ (ts_{max} + tc)_j^{t(15)})/W_3(e^{t(10)})$
	_EG	r5	$W_1(inc(m^{t(9)}),\ comp(ts_{max} + tc)^{t(15)})/W_3(m^{t(9)} < n^{t(10)})$
	EBG	r6	$W_1(1^{t(11)},\ k^{t(12)},\ t^{1m^n},\ (ts_{max} + tc)_j^{t(15)})/W_3(e^{t(12)})$
	_EBG	r6	$W_1(inc(m^{t(11)}),\ comp(ts_{max} + tc)^{t(15)})/W_3(m^{t(11)} < n^{t(12)})$
	PG	r7	$W_1(1^{t(13)}, k^{t(14)},\ t^{1m^n},\ (ts_{max} + tc)_j^{t(15)})/W_3(e^{t(14)})$
	_PG	r7	$W_1(inc(m^{t(13)}),\ comp(ts_{max} + tc)^{t(15)})/W_3(m^{t(13)} < n^{t(14)})$
r3	labelA0	r2	$W_2(b^{1m},\ tc^{t(15)})$
	labelA	r2	$W_2(b^{2m},\ tc^{t(15)})$
	labelEG	r2	$W_2(b^{3m},\ tc^{t(15)})$
	labelEBG	r8	$W_2(b^{4m},\ tc^{t(15)})$
	labelPG	r2	$W_2(b^{5m},\ tc^{t(15)})/W_3(m^{t(13)} = n^{t(14)})$
	no_label	r9	*
r4	labelA0	r2	$W_2(b^{1m},\ tc^{t(15)})$
	labelA	r2	$W_2(b^{2m},\ tc^{t(15)})$
	labelEG	r2	$W_2(b^{3m},\ tc^{t(15)})$
	labelEBG	r8	$W_2(b^{4m},\ tc^{t(15)})$
	Et	r1	$W_1(1^{t(3)},\ 1^{t(6)},\ (ts_{max} + tc)_j^{t(15)})/W_3(e^{t(6)})$
r5	labelA0	r2	$W_2(b^{1m},\ tc^{t(15)})$
	labelEG	r2	$W_2(b^{3m},\ tc^{t(15)})$
	labelEBG	r8	$W_2(b^{4m},\ tc^{t(15)})$
r6	labelA0	r2	$W_2(b^{1m},\ tc^{t(15)})$
	labelEG	r2	$W_2(b^{3m},\ tc^{t(15)})$
	labelEBG	r8	$W_2(b^{4m},\ tc^{t(15)})$
	relEBG	r8	Θ
r7	labelA	r2	$W_2(b^{2m},\ tc^{t(15)})$
	labelPG	r2	$W_2(b^{5m},\ tc^{t(15)})/W_3(m^{t(13)} = n^{t(14)})$
r8	Em	r1	$W_1(1^{t(2)},\ 1^{t(5)},\ (ts_{max} + tc)_j^{t(15)}))/W_3(e^{t(5)})$
r9			

In Table 1, "n" is the number of outgoing links; "k" is the number of incoming links; "m" is the number of analyzed incoming links; "t" is the number of the current graphic primitive from the number of primitives of this type; "b" is the number of the graphic primitive from which the "control signal" comes (applies only to links); "e" is the sign of emptiness; "tsmax" is the maximum time characteristic of the operation, "tc" is the current time characteristic; "inc()" is the operation of the value increment for the current element; "comp()" is the operation returns a larger value between the current value and what is already written in the tape for the current element.

For example, the operation "W1(1t(1), kt(2), $t^{1m^{(n-1)}}$)/W3(et(2))" can be described as follows: provided that the tape number "2" value for the current element is not set, the number "1" is recorded in the tape number "1" for the current element, the total number of incoming links k in the tape number "2" for the current element and the number of element t in the store number "1" in quantity $(n - 1)$.

Symbol "*" implies the following operations: * = W2(e1 m) ... && W3(mai (7) == nai(8)) ... && W3(mai(8) > 1) ... && W3(mai(15) < td)..., where «td» is the time characteristic of the deadline.

An operation of the form "W2(e1 m)" means that all stores must be empty (i.e. there are no return points)."W2(1ai(1))" is operation of reading units from all cells of tape #1 to check elements with 1 fixed link; "W3(mai(1) = nai(2))" is operation of checking whether the number of analyzed links corresponds to the total number of corresponding element inputs; "W3(mai(8) > 1)" is operation of checking the number of incoming links that they are greater than one; "W3(mai(15) < td)" is operation of checking the output of time characteristics for a certain period of time;

The automaton of temporal automata-based RVTI grammar [43, 44] of visual BPM language is presented as a graph in Fig. 1.

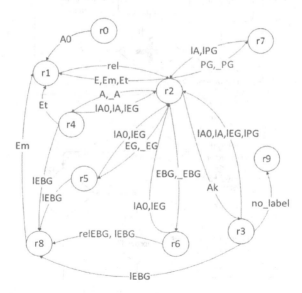

Fig. 1. Temporal automata-based RVTI grammar of the visual language BPMN presented as a graph

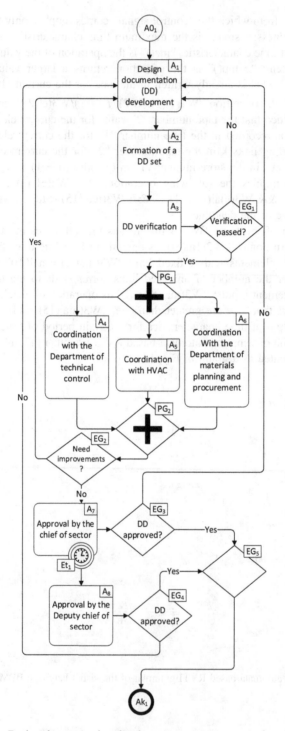

Fig. 2. Design documentation development process, presented on BPMN

We decided to test the developed mathematical apparatus and methods on the real business process of a large industrial enterprise. The process of design documentation development is shown in Fig. 2. It should be borne in mind that in the business process there are cycles, so in the most "sad" situation, he can strive for endless implementation. The exact value can only be obtained when the real process is started. In a situation where the process has a certain completion date and the analysis is static, the maximum time limit is assumed. If the process does not have time to complete in the absence of design documentation (DD) revision, it will not be able to complete if they are available, so the calculation is carried out for the first option. Therefore, it is necessary to pre-build a business process in advance in a more optimal way, to reduce the amount of execution of certain tasks or to postpone the deadlines forcibly.

To demonstrate the grammar's ability to control semantic errors, the correct example was changed to erroneous by reassigning the endpoint to PG1 connections from EG3 to A1. This change will result in a logical error called a "deadlock". At the moment, the memory stores only one continuator, and the link is coming from element 1 PG. However, the retrieval of a continuation is impossible because it fails the necessary condition $(1 = 2)$ analysis of all incoming links (Table 2).

Table 2. State of machine memory at the time of the "deadlock" error

Step	Quasi termin	Memory operations	State of machine memory			Errors
11.	labelPG	$W_2(b^{1m})/W_3(m^{t(1)} == n^{t(2)})$	1 m	t(1)	t(2)	Deadlock
			PG_1	1_{PG1}	2_{PG1}	

The developed software that implements the described methods successfully catches structural, semantic and temporal types of errors [45, 46]. The screenshot of the error message of the computer program for the analysis of the diagram model of the visual language BPM is shown in Fig. 3.

An experiment was conducted to confirm the linear velocity of the method. To create a test base of diagram models, students were involved, as well as a special software tool that allows you to generate voluminous business processes. For the purity of the experiment, analysis and control were performed in several iterations for each diagram. The generation mechanisms allowed to take into account the main criteria that most significantly affect the final measurement time, namely the number of elements and errors, their complexity and the maxima of the "fork" (Fig. 4).

With various combinations of these criteria values, a General trend is observed on the chart, which confirms the theoretical calculations about the linear nature of the speed of the method [43].

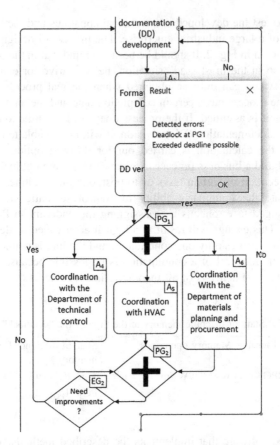

Fig. 3. Error screenshot, found by the developed computer program

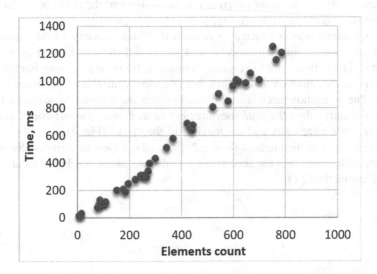

Fig. 4. A dependence graph of the analysis time by the automatic RVTI grammar on the number of elements

4   Conclusion and Future Works

Developed automata-based temporal grammar for visual language BPMN. A special feature is the linear characteristic of the time of the algorithm. The initial experiment showed practical confirmation of this. In future works, it is expected to attract more test data, both through automatic generation and manual generation business processes diagrams, to conduct a more detailed experiment, including comparison with the analogues. Work is also underway to expand the possibility of semantic analysis with respect to the textual matching of the diagrams attributes of the same processes in different visual languages between themselves and the project documentation.

Acknowledgements. The reported study was funded by RFBR according to the research project № 17-07-01417 and Russian Foundation for Basic Research and the government of the region of the Russian Federation, grant № 18-47-730032.

References

1. Lee, E.A.: Cyber physical systems: design challenges. In: 2008 11th IEEE International Symposium on Object and Component-Oriented Real-Time Distributed Computing (ISORC) (2008)
2. Wang,Y., Fan, Y.: Using temporal logics for modeling and analysis of workflows. In: IEEE International Conference on E-Commerce Technology for Dynamic E-Business (2004)
3. Heitmeyer, C., Lynch, N.: The generalized railroad crossing: a case study in formal verification of real-time systems. In: Proceedings Real-Time Systems Symposium REAL-94 (1994)
4. Schael, T.: Workflow Management Systems for Process Organisations. LNCS, vol. 1096. Springer, Heidelberg (1998). https://doi.org/10.1007/3-540-49450-2
5. Van Der Aalst, W.M.P., et al.: ExSpect 6.4 an executable specification tool for hierarchical colored petri nets. In: Nielsen, M., Simpson, D. (eds.) ICATPN 2000. LNCS, vol. 1825, pp. 455–464. Springer, Heidelberg (2000). https://doi.org/10.1007/3-540-44988-4_26
6. Dellarocas, C., Klein, M.: A knowledge-based approach for designing robust business processes. In: van der Aalst, W., Desel, J., Oberweis, A. (eds.) Business Process Management. LNCS, vol. 1806, pp. 50–65. Springer, Heidelberg (2000). https://doi.org/10.1007/3-540-45594-9_4
7. Sharp, A., McDermott, P.: Workflow Modeling: Tools for Process Improvement and Applications Development. Artech House, Norwood (2009)
8. Bock, C.: Introduction to business process and definition metamodel. US National Institute of Standard and Technology. Manufacturing Engineering (2008)
9. Poizat, P., Salaün, G., Krishna, A.: Checking business process evolution. In: Kouchnarenko, O., Khosravi, R. (eds.) FACS 2016. LNCS, vol. 10231, pp. 36–53. Springer, Cham (2017). https://doi.org/10.1007/978-3-319-57666-4_4
10. Martens, A.: Analyzing web service based business processes. In: Cerioli, M. (ed.) FASE 2005. LNCS, vol. 3442, pp. 19–33. Springer, Heidelberg (2005). https://doi.org/10.1007/978-3-540-31984-9_3
11. Raedts, I., Petkovic, M., Usenko, Y.S., van der Werf, J.M.E., Groote, J.F., Somers, L.J.: Transformation of BPMN models for behaviour analysis. In: Proceedings of the 5th International Workshop on Modelling, Simulation, Verification and Validation of Enterprise Information Systems (2007)

12. Dijkman, R.M., Dumas, M., Ouyang, C.: Semantics and analysis of business process models in BPMN. Inf. Softw. Technol. **50**(12), 1281–1294 (2008)
13. Wong, P.Y.H., Gibbons, J.: A process semantics for BPMN. In: Liu, S., Maibaum, T., Araki, K. (eds.) ICFEM 2008. LNCS, vol. 5256, pp. 355–374. Springer, Heidelberg (2008). https://doi.org/10.1007/978-3-540-88194-0_22
14. Decker, G., Weske, M.: Interaction-centric modeling of process choreographies. Inf. Syst. **36** (2), 292–312 (2011)
15. Decker, G., Weske, M.: Local enforceability in interaction petri nets. In: Alonso, G., Dadam, P., Rosemann, M. (eds.) BPM 2007. LNCS, vol. 4714, pp. 305–319. Springer, Heidelberg (2007). https://doi.org/10.1007/978-3-540-75183-0_22
16. Güdemann, M., Poizat, P., Salaün, G., Dumont, A.: VerChor: a framework for verifying choreographies. In: Cortellessa, V., Varró, D. (eds.) FASE 2013. LNCS, vol. 7793, pp. 226–230. Springer, Heidelberg (2013). https://doi.org/10.1007/978-3-642-37057-1_16
17. Kossak, F., et al.: A rigorous semantics for BPMN 2.0 process diagrams. In: Kossak, F., et al. (eds.) A rigorous semantics for BPMN 2.0 process diagrams, pp. 29–152. Springer, Cham (2014). https://doi.org/10.1007/978-3-319-09931-6_4
18. Janssen, W., Mateescu, R., Mauw, S., Springintveld, J.: Verifying business processes using SPIN. In: Proceedings of the 4th International SPIN Workshop, November, pp. 21–36 (1998)
19. Van Der Aalst, W., Van Hee, K.M., van Hee, K.: Workflow Management: Models, Methods, and Systems. MIT press, Cambridge (2004)
20. Fischer, L. (ed.): Workflow Handbook 2005. Workflow Management Coalition (2005)
21. Booch, G., Jacobson, I., Rumbaugh, J.: The unified modeling language reference manual (1999)
22. Business Process Model and Notation (BPMN), v. 2.0. OMG (2011). http://www.omg.org/spec/BPMN/2.0
23. Mayer, R.J., Painter, M.K., de Witte, P.S.: IDEF Family of Methods for Concurrent Engineering and Business Re-Engineering Applications. Knowledge Based Systems, College Station (1994)
24. Santos, P.S., Almeida, J.P.A., Pianissolla, T.L.: Uncovering the organisational modelling and business process modelling languages in the ARIS method. Int. J. Bus. Process Integr. Manag. **5**(2), 130 (2011)
25. Pozewaunig, H., Eder, J., Liebhart, W.: ePERT: extending PERT for workflow management systems. In: ADBIS, September, pp. 217–224 (1997)
26. https://ascon.ru
27. Roth, C.: Using Microsoft Visio 2010. Pearson Education, London (2011)
28. Visual Paradigm: Visual Paradigm for UML. Visual Paradigm International, Hong Kong (2010)
29. Hoffmann, H.-P.: Deploying model-based systems engineering with IBM® rational® solutions for systems and software engineering. In: 2012 IEEE/AIAA 31st Digital Avionics Systems Conference (DASC) (2012)
30. Suppes, P.: Syntactic methods in pattern recognition (K. S. Fu). SIAM Rev. **19**(4), 746 (1977)
31. Costagliola, G., De Lucia, A., Orefice, S., Tortora, G.: Positional grammars: a formalism for LR-like parsing of visual languages. In: Marriott, K., Meyer, B. (eds.) Visual Language Theory, pp. 171–191. Springer, New York (1998). https://doi.org/10.1007/978-1-4612-1676-6_5
32. Zhang, D.-Q., Zhang, K.: Reserved graph grammar: a specification tool for diagrammatic VPLs. In: Proceedings of the 1997 IEEE Symposium on Visual Languages (1997). (Cat. No. 97TB100180)

33. Rekers, J., Schürr, A.: Defining and parsing visual languages with layered graph grammars. J. Vis. Lang. Comput. **8**(1), 27–55 (1997)
34. Zhang, D.-Q.: A context-sensitive graph grammar formalism for the specification of visual languages. Comput. J. **44**(3), 186–200 (2001)
35. Sharov, O.G., Afanas'ev, A.N.: Syntax-directed implementation of visual languages based on automaton graphical grammars. Program. Comput. Softw. **31**(6), 332–339 (2005)
36. Sharov, O.G., Afanas'ev, A.N.: Methods and tools for translation of graphical diagrams. Program. Comput. Softw. **37**(3), 171–179 (2011)
37. Aho, A.V.: Compilers: Principles, Techniques and Tools (for Anna University), 2nd edn. Pearson Education, Noida (2003)
38. Sharov, O.G., Afanasiev, A.N.: Syntax error recovery in graphical languages. Program. Comput. Softw. **34**(1), 44–48 (2008)
39. Afanasyev, A., Voit, N.: Grammar-algebraic approach to analyze workflows. In: Gervasi, O., et al. (eds.) ICCSA 2018. LNCS, vol. 10963, pp. 499–510. Springer, Cham (2018). https://doi.org/10.1007/978-3-319-95171-3_39
40. Afanasyev, A., Voit, N., Timofeeva, O., Epifanov, V.: Analysis and control of hybrid diagrammatical workflows. In: Abraham, A., Kovalev, S., Tarassov, V., Snasel, V., Vasileva, M., Sukhanov, A. (eds.) IITI 2017. AISC, vol. 679, pp. 124–133. Springer, Cham (2018). https://doi.org/10.1007/978-3-319-68321-8_13
41. Afanasyev, A., Ukhanova, M., Ionova, I., Voit, N.: Processing of design and manufacturing workflows in a large enterprise. In: Gervasi, O., et al. (eds.) ICCSA 2018. LNCS, vol. 10963, pp. 565–576. Springer, Cham (2018). https://doi.org/10.1007/978-3-319-95171-3_44
42. Voit, N.N.: Development of timed RT-grammars for analysis of business process at manufacturing and in cyber-physical systems. In: 2017 International Conference on Computing Networking and Informatics (ICCNI) (2017)
43. Afanasyev, A.N., Voit, N.N., Kirillov, S.Y.: Development of RYT-grammar for analysis and control dynamic workflows. In: 2017 International Conference on Computing Networking and Informatics (ICCNI) (2017)
44. Afanasyev, A., Voit, N., Gaynullin, R.: The analysis of diagrammatic models of workflows in design of the complex automated systems. In: Abraham, A., Kovalev, S., Tarassov, V., Snášel, V. (eds.) Proceedings of the First International Scientific Conference "Intelligent Information Technologies for Industry" (IITI'16). AISC, vol. 450, pp. 227–236. Springer, Cham (2016). https://doi.org/10.1007/978-3-319-33609-1_20
45. Afanasyev, A., Voit, N., Gaynullin, R.: The analysis of diagrammatic of workflows in design of the automated systems. In: Uncertainty Modelling in Knowledge Engineering and Decision Making (2016)
46. Afanasyev, A.N., Voit, N.N., Voevodin, E.Y., Gainullin, R.F.: Control of UML diagrams in designing automated systems software. In: 2015 9th International Conference on Application of Information and Communication Technologies (AICT) (2015)

The Method of Translation
of the Diagram with One Type Directed
Links into the Inhibitor Petri Net

Nikolay Voit⬡, Dmitry Kanev, Sergey Kirillov(✉),
and Maria Ukhanova

Ulyanovsk State Technical University, Ulyanovsk, Russia
n.voit@ulstu.ru, dima.kanev@gmail.com,
kirillovsyu@gmail.com, mari-u@inbox.ru

Abstract. The fundamental scientific problem of the business process management theory is to increase the efficiency of automated systems workflow
synthesis and processing in order to reduce the time spent on their development,
increasing the success of processing diagram models, namely the implementation of the requirements for resource constraints, functionality, financial component and deadlines, as well as improving the diagram models quality in terms
of error control, narrowing the semantic gap between business process analysis
and execution. The article proposes a method of translation of the diagram with
one type of directed communication into the Petri inhibitor network. The results
of the research represent that the approach has significant advantages over
similar methods of analysis. The effectiveness of this analytical approach is
proved by concrete real and relevant examples.

Keywords: Business processes · Graphical language analysis · EPC ·
Petri net component

1 Introduction

In modern practice of organizational management, graphical models of business processes have become widespread. However, graphical models research, even carried out
in accordance with the rules of the structural approach (limited context, limiting the
number of elements at each level of decomposition, etc.), presents considerable complexity. Therefore, a mandatory step in the modeling of business processes of enterprises is the automatic verification of the models obtained. The issues of analysis of
defect-free completion are relevant, since the complexity of models is constantly
increasing, and the test tools built into the simulation environment are far from perfect.

The main goal of this work is to reduce the time to develop graphical models of
business processes and improve their quality by expanding the class of diagnosed
errors.

Petri net is one of the approaches for it. Since its inception in 1962, Petri nets have
been used in a wide variety of applications. Although Petri nets are graphical and easy
to understand, they have formal semantics and allow analysis methods from model

© Springer Nature Switzerland AG 2019
S. Misra et al. (Eds.): ICCSA 2019, LNCS 11623, pp. 562–572, 2019.
https://doi.org/10.1007/978-3-030-24308-1_45

checking and structural analysis to process and performance analysis. Over time, Petri nets have become a solid foundation for research in the field of business process management. Petri nets allow semantic and syntactic models analysis. In particular, to obtain all possible scenarios for the business process execution, to determine never-executing functions and system deadlocks, which is especially important when analyzing cyclic processes.

At the same time, the existing methods for translating graphical diagrams of business process management into the Petri net are specialized and aimed at working with one or two graphical languages.

2 Analysis of Existing Approaches

In article [1], the rules for the transformation of UML activity diagrams in the Petri net are considered and an algorithm for their implementation is proposed. The waiting state is transformed into a position, the action state is transformed into a transition. The separation and merging of control, branch and condition flows is converted into the corresponding Petri net; constraint conditions are represented using transition constraint conditions.

Practically in each developed system one can meet the sequence and condition, branching and merging. Consequently, one of the advantages of the described rules seto is that it contains recommendations for the mutual obtaining of the more frequently encountered elements in the UML activity diagrams and Petri nets algorithms. Algorithmic rules presentation contributes to their formalization.

In the article [2] the technique of software design using UML-diagram and Petri net consisting of 7 stages is considered:

1. Compilation of a case diagram with the identification of all entities in the form of actors and use cases.
2. Drawing a class diagram and highlighting the class methods.
3. Selection based on the class diagram of objects that are involved in the system and will help determine the initial values for marking all the vertices of the Petri net.
4. Construction of activity diagrams to describe the dynamic properties of the system.
5. Translation of the constructed activity diagram into the Petri net using formal transformation rules.
6. Analysis of properties using automated software packages for working with Petri nets, which allow identifying logical errors in modeling activity diagrams: finding unused work scenarios, identifying dead-end branches of algorithms, etc. For classes or objects that need detailed elaboration of their logic, a separate activity diagram should be drawn up and analyzed using Petri nets. If necessary, the dynamics of work should be tracked on the state of the system. This is possible using Petri nets apparatus, whose analysis results will be the basis of the state space construction and exploration.
7. In case of successful analysis and set of diagrams that do not need to be improved, the simulated diagrams are ready for automatic code generation.

In [3], the converting UML diagrams into Petri nets rules are given. These are the following.

1. The waiting state is transformed into a position, and the action state is transformed into a transition that starts the action. It is possible that two states of the action are arranged in series, then the end of the first and the beginning of the second action are combined and shown by one transition.
2. Separation and merging of parallel control flows of UML diagrams is converted to the corresponding Petri net equivalent.
3. The branch in the activity diagram, denoted by the decision symbol, is converted to the corresponding Petri net equivalent.
4. Restriction conditions are shown with transition restriction conditions.
5. The critical section (access to the critical resource realized by the critical section) is converted to a position with one mark in the initial marking. When a critical section is executed, the label is removed from the position and returns upon completion of the critical Sect.
6. The semaphore used to simulate the employment of a specific resource from the resource pool is converted to a position with the same number of labels that differ from each other in colors in the initial labeling. A label with an arbitrary index should be removed from the site and returned when it is no more used. In a simple semaphore, labels of the same type must be used, and their number in the initial marking is equal to the number of resources.
7. It is necessary to add a counter-position to the sections that are critical in terms of execution time. To check the maximum execution time of the transitions of the critical section, you must add protective conditions. The counter must be provided with a transition with the opposite protective condition.
8. In case of mutual transition from or to the hierarchical Petri net, it is necessary to add empty spaces and corresponding transitions, which are connected in series.

The goal of [4] is to describe the method of (H)MSC diagrams into the Petri net translation and apply the method for formal analysis and verification of the properties of such diagrams. The algorithm result is the Petri net in a format compatible with the CPN Tools system. This net will be hierarchical if the source specification is specified using the HMSC diagram, or if the input MSC contains reference expressions.

Message sequence diagrams (MSC diagrams) are popular scripting language designed to formalize and analyze system requirements during the software design phase. In this paper, the syntax of the SDL-2010 language is used to describe declarations and expressions with data.

General description of the translation algorithm is considered. At the first stage, the input (H)MSC-diagram builds its internal representation, which will be called the partial order graph (H)MSC. For each event in the diagram, a node is created in the partial order graph, which stores information about the set of adjacent nodes, the process identifier and the structural structure to which the event belongs.

In stage 2, the partial order graph is processed. During processing, such actions as auxiliary graph nodes creation (input and output nodes for MSC embedded expressions), links unfolding (constructing partial order graphs for referential MSC), searching and processing alternatives with non-local choice occur.

At stage 3, the processed graph of partial order is transmitted to the Petri net (CPN). Each node of the graph corresponds to the transition to CPN. Each arc connecting two nodes in a partial order graph corresponds to a position and two oriented arcs connecting two transitions in the CPN. The orientation of the constructed network arcs coincides with the orientation of the arcs of the partial order graph. The event execution in MSC corresponds to the triggering of the corresponding transition in the resulting CPN. The start events of the MSC-diagrams correspond to transitions with input start sites with an initial marking of 1'(). The MSC-diagrams correspond to eventual transitions with output end places that do not contain outgoing arcs. All data types and variables declared in the MSC document are converted to the corresponding data types and CPN ML variables.

Each event from the base set of MSC elements is modeled by a single CPN transition. According to the MSC standard, the event of receiving a message is preceded by the event of its sending. Each message is modeled by two transitions in CPN. The order of transitions corresponding to the events of sending and receiving a message is observed with the help of a place that connects these transitions and ensures the correct sequence between their operations.

Predicative (guarding) conditions are used to check in the process of executing the truth diagram of a predicate specified in the MSC data language. Such conditions can be placed at the beginning of an inline expression or MSC diagram.

If the test condition is false, then the execution of chart events that follow the protection condition is terminated. In the process of translation, each predicate condition is transformed into a single transition of a network with a trigger function that calculates the value of the established predicate.

The article describes the translation of the basic elements of the MSC, MSC elements with data, structural elements. The resulting CPN size estimation is also proposed.

The article [5] proposes formal semantics for mapping the business process modeling (BPMN) notation to color Petri nets. The choice of CPN is due to the presence of formal verification methods, analysis of the space of states and invariants. And the concept of colored markers allows you to model the process data.

The elements analyzed are limited to the core BPMN, and include the following types. Common elements that are used in several types of diagrams (for example, "Process", "Interaction", "Choreography"). Common elements provide model developers with the ability to display additional information about the process, such as operations, error detection, and resources. The CPN ML declaration, corresponding to the standard BPMN 2.0 structure diagram, is considered. These declarations allow converting BPMN elements and their attributes one-on-one to Petri Net. Gateways are used to control the actions flows. The article uses the matrix display of various types of gateways to the corresponding Petri nets. BPMN tasks are matched with CPN ML ads. The CPN ML color set is created for each type of BPMN task in order to cover all of its optional attributes. In BPMN, an action can have attributes that define its optional behavior, such as looping and parallel loops on objects. The article proposes replacing them with a flow control construct using various types of gateways. A hierarchical CPN is used to represent the BPMN sub process. Each subprocess is represented as an embedded Petri net. A reusable task is a task definition that can be invoked from any process using a call operation. In CPN, a reusable task and its challenge is modeled using nested Petri nets.

The article [6] considers only a limited subset of the BPMN notation used to model orchestration processes. The nodes of the diagram are the control flow objects, including: operations, logical operators, and events. The difference of the proposed approach in the rejection of behavioral equivalence, which will simplify the display method.

The proposed approach distinguishes between nodes that produce a change in the management object, leading to a change in its state and nodes that do not change it, but route it. Operations transform the process object, they are associated with transitions. The arcs define the order in which the process operations are executed.

Logical branching and merging operators, such as AND, OR, are modeled by an equivalent Petri net. The BPMN notation allows for an "abbreviated" notation when one graphic element combines an operation and a logical operator at the same time. For analysis, such elements are expanded into a separate operation and a logical operator. Cyclic execution of the operation is modeled by a pair of transitions. The first is responsible for carrying out the work, and the second is for checking the condition.

Start, end and intermediate events placed in the stream are modeled by the Petri Net transition. Events attached to the boundaries of operations are modeled by the logical operators "OR"/"AND" depending on whether the event stops the flow of control or not.

Based on the review, we can conclude that a single approach is used to translate various types of diagrams into the Petri net: sequential transformation of the elements of the diagrams into equivalent subsets of the Petri nets. At the same time, the existing methods of translating graphic diagrams are specialized and aimed at working with one/two graphic languages.

3   Diagram to Inhibitory Petri Net Translation

Consider the task of translating some diagram into the inhibitor Petri net. The input parameter is a diagram, the diagram model has the form [7–12]:

$$G = (V, E, TV, TE),$$

Where

V is vertices set,
E is connections set, $E \subset (V \times V)$
TV is vertices types set,
TE is connections types set.

Restriction on the input data is assumed that the diagram may contain only one type of directional communication, which corresponds to an edge in Petri nets.

At the output, an inhibitor Petri net is obtained, the model of which has the form:

$N = (P, T, F)$, где
P is positions set,
T is transitions set,
F is arcs set, $F \subset (P \times T \times ING) \cup (T \times P \times ING)$, $ING = \{0, 1\}$ is an inhibitory arc attribute.

The input diagram vertices are translated on the Petri nets that implement the equivalent function. Inhibitor Petri net is Turing complete, which allows to implement any computable function on it. The unidirectional communication diagram is translated into the corresponding arc of the Petri net.

Displaying algorithm is the following.

Step 1. Defining the function of translating the top of the diagram into the extended Petri net.

For each type of diagram, it is necessary to define the function of translating the top of the diagram into the extended Petri net model (*Ftrans* : $V \rightarrow VN$). Extended Petri net model has the following view:

$$VN = (V, N, PIN, TOUT),$$

where

V is a diagram vertex,
N is Petri net,
PIN is input positions tuple,
$TOUT$ is output positions tuple.

For each incoming connection v there must be an input position in the Petri net $vn[N]$ and for each outgoing connection there must be a transition.

Step 2. Formation of a set of extended Petri nets.

For each vertex $v \in V$ of the diagram $g \in G$ translation to the extended Petri net $vn \in VN$ is formed and AVN set is formed:

$$AVN = \{Ftrans(v) \mid v \in V\}$$

Step 3. Consolidation of multiple extended Petri nets into the output Petri nets.

Let *pn* be the empty Petri net $(\emptyset, \emptyset, \emptyset)$. Copy all the arcs, positions and transitions of all extended Petri nets into pn:

$$pn[P] = \{p | \exists a \in AVN, p \in a[N][P]\},$$
$$pn[T] = \{t | \exists a \in AVN, t \in a[N][T]\},$$
$$pn[F] = \{f | \exists a \in AVN, f \in a[N][F]\}$$

Step 4. Translation of diagram connections.

Based on each connection of the $e \in E$ of the diagrams, we connect the positions and transitions of the output Petri net. For each connection, the initial and final vertices and the corresponding extended Petri nets $vn1 \in VN$, $vn2 \in VN$ are found. From the output transitions tuple for $v1$ the transition corresponding to the chosen connection is found, from the input positions tuple for $v2$ the position corresponding to the selected connection is found. Selected output transition and input position are connected with an arc:

$$pn[F] = pn[F] \cup \{(vn\_in[TOUT][e], vn\_out[PIN][e], 0) \mid \forall e \in E,$$
$$\exists vn\_in \in AVN, \exists vn\_out \in AVN, vn\_in[V] = e1, \quad vn\_out[V] = e2\}.$$

Figure 1 shows diagram translation example. Petri nets $P1$, $P2$, $P3$, $P4$ match vertices $V1$, $V2$, $V3$, $V4$. They are interconnected with arcs $A1$, $A2$, $A3$, $A4$, $A5$ corresponding connections $E1$, $E2$, $E3$, $E4$, $E5$. For $V1$ and $V2$ connection the arc is created, outgoing from the transition $t1$ of the network $P1$ and entering the position $p1$ of the network $P2$.

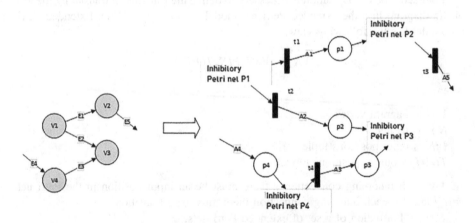

Fig. 1. Diagram to Petri net translation

4 EPC-Diagram Management Stream to Petri Net Translation

Event Chain Process (EPC) is type of diagrams used for modeling, analysis and reorganization of business processes. At the same time, EPC-diagrams can be used to simulate the behavior of individual parts of the system when implementing functions and serve as a replacement for traditional flowcharts (behavioral modeling). The EPC method was developed by Augusto-Wilhelm Scheer in the early 1990s.

Consider broadcasting EPC charts. The model for the EPC notation consists of many types of vertices TV = {Event, Function, Information, Document, File, Cluster, Object Set, Message, Product, Organizational Unit, Position, Artist, Location, Application, Module, AND, OR, XOR, Purpose, Term}, and many types of connections TE = {Control flow, Organizational flow, Resource flow, Information flow, Information service flow, Inventory flow}. The following types of vertices are directly responsible for the control flow: Event, Function, AND, OR, XOR; and communication type: Control flow. Thus, the flow of control of the EPC-diagram fits the limitations of one type of communication. We define the function of translating the top of the diagram into the extended Petri net model (see Table 1).

Table 1. EPC-diagrams elements to extended Petri nets translation

Element	Graphical symbol	Extended Petri net
Function		PIN = (P1) TOUT= (T2)
OR operator (merging)		PIN = (P5, P6) TOUT= (T13)
XOR operator (merging)		PIN = (P7, P6) TOUT= (T10)

For each diagram element, Petri nets are built in accordance with Table 1, and interconnected.

Since this approach uses semantic formalization of semi-formal languages due to the specialization of these languages, there are limitations.

It is necessary to abandon some of the features of the translated language, simplify it, give it new features, etc., which will have a positive impact on the formalization. Bring the language to a state where ambiguity disappears.

5 Implementation

The proposed method is implemented on the.NET Framework 4.5 platform for translating EPC diagrams from Microsoft Visio 2017 to the Petri network for the Platform Independent Petri Net Editor.

The algorithm of the program consists of the following steps.

- connect to a running copy of Microsoft Visio;
- read the EPC-diagrams elements and relationships between them;
- consistently convert each element of the EPC-diagrams into an equivalent extended Petri net in accordance with the translation function of the diagram vertices;
- connect extended Petri nets into a single Petri net based on the original EPC diagram links;
- save the received Petri net in the Platform Independent Petri Net Editor format;
- show the received Petri net on the screen.

The developed tool has the following features: translation of EPC-diagrams built in Microsoft Visio, including the highlighted part of the diagram; output of the received Petri net to the screen with support for saving the image to a file, automatic positioning of elements, scaling and printing; save the Petri file in Platform Independent Petri Net Editor format.

The Fig. 2 shows the diagram in the visual language EPC, taken for translation example. In the Fig. 3 you can see the resulting equivalent of the original EPC diagrams in Petri.

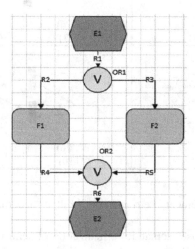

Fig. 2. The source EPC diagram in MS Visio

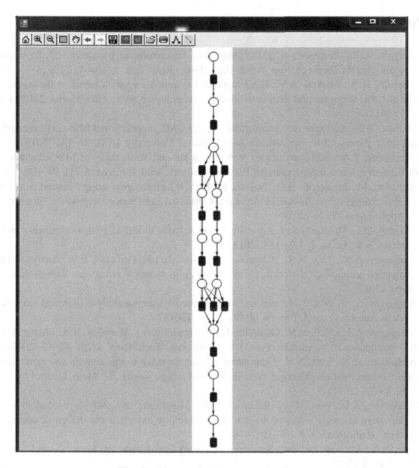

Fig. 3. The result diagram on Petri net

6 Conclusion

The article deals with the task of translating various types of diagrams into the inhibitor-Petri nets. A universal method of translation of a diagram with one type of directional communication is described, the models of a diagram, an inhibitor Petri net, and a translation algorithm are described. The application of the method for translating the flow of control of an EPC diagram consisting of 8 types of elements into a Petri net is shown, and examples of the translation of various diagrams are given. As an experiment, the algorithm was tested in other most well-known visual languages of business processes, such as BPMN, IDEF3, and successfully achieved its goal.

Acknowledgements. The study was supported by the Russian Foundation for Basic Research No. 17-07-01417 and the regional support of the Russian Foundation for Basic Research, grant No. 18-47-730032.

References

1. Markov, A.V., Romannikov, D.O.: Algorithm for automatic translation of the activity diagram into the Petri net. Rep. Acad. High. Educ. Russ. Fed. **1**, 104–112 (2014)
2. Voevoda, A.A., Markov, A.V.: CAD methods for complex systems based on the combined use of UML-diagrams and Petri nets. Modern technologies. Syst. Anal. Model. **2**(42), 110–115 (2014)
3. Markov, A.V.: Software development by sharing UML diagrams and Petri nets (overview). Scientific papers oft he Novosibirsk Stet Technical University **1**(71), 96–131 (2013)
4. Chernenok, S.A., Nepomnyaschiy, V.A.: Analysis and verification of MSC-diagrams of distributed systems using expanded Petri nets. Model. Anal. Inf. Syst. **6**(21), 94–106 (2014)
5. Ramadan, M., Elmongui, H.G., Hassan, R.: BPMN formalisation using coloured petri nets. In: Proceedings of the 2nd GSTF Annual International Conference on Software Engineering & Applications (SEA) (2011)
6. Fedorov, I.G.: The method of displaying the executable model of a business process on the Petri net. Stat. Econ. **4**, 179–183 (2013)
7. Afanasyev, A.N., Voit, N.N., Ukhanova, M.E., Ionova, I.S., Epifanov, V.V.: Analysis of the design and technological workflows in a large radio-technical enterprise. Radiotechnics **6**, 49–58 (2017)
8. Afanasyev, A.N., Voit, N.N.: Intelligent agent-based system for analysis of design work flow models. Autom. Control. Process. **4**(42), 52–61 (2015)
9. Afanasyev, A.N., Voit, N.N., Gainullin, R.F., Brigadnov, S.I., Horodov, V.S., Sharov, O.G.: RV grammatics metacompiler. Proc. Ulyanovsk State Tech. Univ. **4**(76), 48–52 (2016)
10. Afanasyev, A.N., Voit, N.N.: Grammar-algebraic approach to the analysis and synthesis of diagrammatic models of hybrid dynamic flows of design works. Inf. Meas. Control Syst. **12** (15), 69–78 (2017)
11. Afanasyev, A.N., Voit, N.N., Ukhanova, M.E.: Monitoring and analysis of denotative and significative semantic errors of diagrammatic workflow models in the design of automated systems. Radiotechnics **6**, 84–92 (2018)
12. Voit, N.N.: Methods and tools for automating workflow design. Inf. Meas. Control Syst. **11** (14), 84–89 (2018)

Software Development Activities
for Secure Microservices

Peter Nkomo[⊠] and Marijke Coetzee[⊠] [iD]

University of Johannesburg, Auckland Park 2006, South Africa
ptnkomo@gmail.com, marijkec@uj.ac.za

Abstract. The decomposition of an application into a set of distributed and collaborating microservices using microservices architecture principles, increases an application's attack surface. A preliminary risk analysis can provide an understanding of security threats from a hypothetical attacker's point of view. Identified security threats equip software engineers of microservices compositions with knowledge of assets most likely to be targeted, the most likely attack vectors, and the potential attacker's profile. The knowledge is useful to ensure that microservices compositions are designed to avoid vulnerabilities and to withstand any attack, and in the event of an attack to ensure that adverse consequences of an attack are minimized. In this regard, this paper aims to identify security threats that could arise as a result of flaws in the design of microservices compositions and harm that may arise from misuse of a microservices composition by malicious users. The preliminary risk analysis leads to a list of security requirements to be met by this research to be able to develop secure microservices compositions. The contribution of this review is a list of development activities for secure microservices.

Keywords: Microservices architecture · Security threats ·
Security requirements · Software development activities

1 Introduction

In the quest to compete in a fast-paced business environment, the complexity of maintaining and enhancing traditional SOA applications has presented significant challenges to many enterprises [1]. These challenges have led to the emergence of a new architectural style called the microservices architecture [1, 2]. The microservices architecture uses a collection of small, loosely coupled software components called microservices that collaborate to automate business functionality, and are ideally developed within fast software release cycles [3]. The microservices architecture promises to provide agility by allowing each microservice to be quickly built, modified, tested and deployed in isolation [4].

Over the past few years, a new trend called DevOps has emerged that aims to unify agile software development, continuous integration, continuous delivery, continuous deployment with software operations [5]. DevOps aims to shorten software development cycles, increase the frequency of deployments and create more dependable software releases that are closely aligned with business objectives. The goals of

© Springer Nature Switzerland AG 2019
S. Misra et al. (Eds.): ICCSA 2019, LNCS 11623, pp. 573–585, 2019.
https://doi.org/10.1007/978-3-030-24308-1_46

DevOps are achieved using automation at all steps of software development from integration, testing, releasing software to production and also the management of servers. A common set of DevOps and continuous delivery ideologies at companies such as Amazon [6], Netflix [7], SoundCloud [8], Facebook [9] and several others has been instrumental in the adoption of the microservices architecture. Microservices architecture is seen as a natural fit to enable continuous delivery and has become a prelude of a new form of concrete implementation of SOA. The adoption of microservices architecture as part of DevOps practices introduces complications when implementing security controls. As development teams continue to deliver software in short and agile sprints cycles, usually one to two weeks in length, often little attention is given to the security of the application.

The research question to be addressed by this paper is *How can software engineers build microservices in a systematic way so that security is an integral part of the entire microservices lifecycle?* This requires an understanding of the underlying architecture that software engineers should address as there may exist new security weaknesses [10]. Once potential security challenges are identified, appropriate security guidelines can be identified to assist software engineers to avoid subtle architecture-level security weaknesses.

The main contribution of this paper is a list of software development activities to be applied in agile approaches when developing secure microservices. Such a list of guidelines can be useful and convenient for software engineers who are generally not trained in software security. To address this research question, Sect. 2 identifies the architectural design features of the microservices architectural style using an example application. Section 3 describes five security challenges of the microservices architectural style. Section 4 pinpoints the security threats due to the identified security challenges. Section 5 gives relevant security requirements that are identified from the list of security threats. Finally, a list of software development activities is given that can guide software engineers when developing secure microservices and finally the paper is concluded.

2   The Microservices Architectural Style

A *microservice* is defined as a self-contained, autonomous, lightweight unit of logic running in its own process [3]. Microservices communicate using lightweight mechanisms over hypertext transfer protocol [2], using the RESTful architectural style as a means of communication. A *microservice* provides a narrowly-focused standardized application programming interfaces to its consumers. The *microservices architectural style* is an approach that structures an application as a set of loosely coupled collaborating microservices. There are no set of rules when choosing between various frameworks or protocols to use in a *microservices architecture*. However, the protocol should be lightweight, keeping in mind that the microservices architecture relies heavily on messaging between collaborating microservices. Using this architecture style, an enterprise can structure development teams as a collection of small autonomous teams, usually at most nine members, who focus on one or more microservices [11].

In a microservice architecture, choreography is preferred when creating a microservices composition, unlike traditional SOA that employs orchestration. No central microservice is thus used as a composition controller to control communication with other microservices [12]. Microservices communicate using point-to-point exchanges or by listening to events on their environment [13]. The inter-communication mechanisms can either be synchronous or asynchronous.

Consider an imaginary on-demand taxi application such as Uber [14] that is implemented as an SOA-based application as shown in Fig. 1.

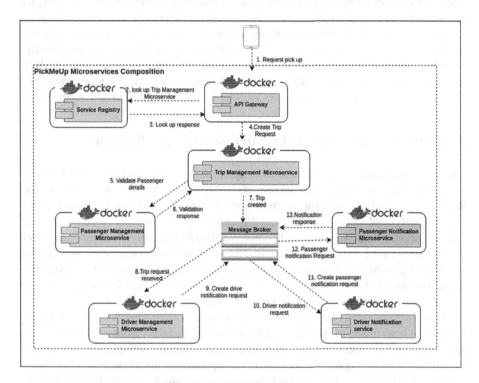

Fig. 1. PickMeUp application

The application is referred to as the PickMeUp application. Registered passengers request taxi rides using mobiles phone or desktop computers. As soon as the request is made, a notification about location and passenger details is sent to the nearest driver. The driver either accepts or rejects a request for a ride. In case the ride is rejected, a notification is sent to drivers in the area. If the driver accepts the ride, driver details are sent to the customer along with the estimated arrival time. The passenger can track the drivers and drivers can track the exact location of the passenger to reach their exact location. The payment procedure between the passenger and the driver is either cash or credit card. The various architectural components of the microservices composition for the PickMeUp application are shown in Fig. 1 namely the API gateway, a service registry, and message broker. The deployment strategy adopted for the application is to deploy components of the application on separate Docker containers that run on a single host. Access to the composition is given via the API gateway. The API gateway locates the instance of a trip management microservices using the service registry. The trip management microservices communicate either directly by calling other microservices' REST interface or by sending a message to the message broker. Each microservice is deployed in its Docker container.

Security challenges arise from the manner in which microservices are deployed as the microservices architecture provides an attacker with more avenues to attack the microservices compositions. In general, a set of distributed microservices are designed to trust each other completely where a compromise of a single microservice could affect an entire application. Furthermore, many of the most popular tools used for ensuring continuous integration, continuous delivery and continuous deployment and DevOps are often new to the market or are open-sourced. The relative immaturity leads to concerns about the degree to which secure development standards are being adhered to.

The manner in which microservices security can be implemented is described next.

3 Security Challenges of the Microservices Architecture

The development of secure microservices applications is not a problem that has been solved yet. However, the core security principles that apply to SOAP-based, and RESTful web services hold for microservices as well. WS-Security [15] specifies the way integrity and confidentiality can be enforced, and security tokens used for authentication. Middleware is used to enforce distributed security via components such as interceptors [16]. In contrast, the RESTful style of web services does not provide any formal guidance on how security mechanisms should be applied and leaves their implementation to the discretion of software engineers. Such services mainly rely on ad-hoc security mechanisms or transport layer security.

With microservices, security becomes more of a challenge because no middleware component is available to manage security-based functionality. Instead, each service is required to manage security on its own, or in other cases, an API gateway is given the responsibility of managing the security of the application. REST web services lack a specific security model, unlike SOAP-based services which rely on the WS-Security standard. Most REST web services rely on transport-layer security and custom message protection mechanism. Transport-layer security offers secure point-to-point communication channels. REST web services can use JSON Web Tokens (JWT) [17] as the format for security tokens for authentication and ensuring message integrity. API keys and JWT does not solve the problem of confidentiality therefore custom mechanisms need to be used to ensure data confidentiality and non-repudiation.

Microservices are changing the assumptions about how SOA-based applications are created and consequently how SOA applications should be secured. The adoption of microservices architecture presents the following five security challenges.

(a) *Increased surface attack:* When microservices are considered from a networking perspective, the instance of a microservice is a unique network endpoint with an open network port exposing an application programming interface. When a new instance of microservice is created, a new application programming interface is exposed. An attack on the microservices-based application can be made directly on each microservice [2]. This gives the attacker an increased attack surface due to the spread of microservices instances exposed across the network. Security of microservices consequentially become a distributed security challenge.

(b) Indefinable security perimeters: Many microservices are deployed in containers [18]. The challenge of deploying microservices on containers is that containers can be set up quickly from anywhere within the network without any consideration for the traditional notion of demilitarised security perimeters. Containers allow port mapping functionality to masquerade standard microservices application programming service ports to dynamically allocated ones. The use of dynamic addressing and scaling of microservices makes it a challenge to statically configure internet protocol addresses or steer network traffic to traditional perimeter security appliances.

(c) Security monitoring is complex: Containers present a security monitoring challenge. Containers on a host machine can use network address translation (NAT) which makes them invisible to the outside world. Network address translation is the process where a network device, usually a firewall, assigns a public address to a computer inside a private network. Network traffic from containers using NAT is challenging to identify. When containers use NAT, a definition of security policies becomes complicated because it becomes difficult to know which microservices is running in each container. Containers may also bundle applications with a lot of software libraries and files that software engineers may not be aware of. This may increase the security risk due to vulnerabilities that may be hidden inside the software libraries.

(d) Authentication is centralized: Microservices deployed in containers interact remotely, mostly over HTTP. The challenge of this approach is how users of microservices are authenticated and how user credentials are passed between microservices in a symmetric manner. Another challenge when ensuring inter-microservices communication between a large number of microservices is that when microservices use transport layer security, certificate revocation becomes a harder problem. The microservices that initiate the handshake may get a list of revoked certificates from the corresponding certificate authority which can grow bigger.

(e) Threat modeling and risk assessment is localized: The emphasis on team autonomy makes it challenging to ensure that threat modeling, and risk assessment is done before new versions of microservices are released. Continuous delivery can mean that new vulnerabilities are delivered with every new microservices deployment.

The five security challenges above provide an answer to the research question formulated in the introduction of this paper. Considering the five challenges listed above, the adoption of microservices, therefore, require new ways of ensuring security. To this end, the next section discusses a preliminary risk analysis of the microservices architecture to provide an understanding of security threats. This knowledge is useful to ensure that microservices-based applications are designed to avoid vulnerabilities and to withstand any attack.

4 Microservices Composition Threat Modeling

Various security weaknesses or vulnerabilities may exist on microservices and their runtime infrastructure that an attacker can exploit. To be able to understand the security of microservices compositions, it needs to be analysed from the perspective of a potential attacker. There are various approaches to threat modeling, where the architecture-centric threat modeling approach is found to be more suitable as it provides a means to step through the components of a microservices composition to identify potential types of attacks against each component. The architecture-centric threat modeling approach, also called system-centric, or design-centric approach focuses on the design of a system and attempts to identify the potential types of attacks against each component of the system [19]. The architecture-centric threat modeling steps from the Microsoft threat modeling process is followed, as shown in Fig. 2 [20]. Each of the four steps are followed by analyzing the PickMeup application.

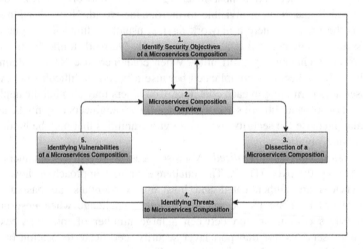

Fig. 2. Architecture-centric threat modeling

Step 1: Identify microservices composition security objectives. Each microservice is an open system similar to any web service, and therefore needs to address security services as prescribed by ISO 7498-2 [21] namely authentication, access control, data confidentiality, data integrity and non-repudiation.

Step 2: Microservices composition overview. The essential components that any microservices architecture application generally consist of is as follows:

- *The API gateway* - a lightweight entry point into an application.
- *A set of microservices* - components that automate business functionality.
- *Service registry* - a database of instances and locations of all active microservices in a microservices composition.

- *Message broker* - used by microservices in composition to publish and receive messages.
- *Containers or virtual machine* - provide the runtime environment to microservices.

Step 3 and 4: Decomposition of a microservices composition: Steps 1 to 13 in Fig. 1 shows the flow of information from when a request for a trip is received from a passenger using a mobile device until the final response is sent. For the sake of brevity, information flow for payment is not shown. The deployment strategy adopted for the application is to deploy components of the application on separate Docker containers. The containers run on a single host. The following architectural components provide potential entry points to maliciously access and compromise the PickMeUp microservices composition:

- *The API gateway and the microservices API* - the attacker may use the gateway and microservices API to perform various types of injection attacks.
- *The service registry* - the attacker may control the service registry to compromise the microservices composition or to shut the microservices composition down by ensuring that collaborating microservices cannot locate one another.
- *Message broker* - the attacker may gain access to messages exchanged by microservices or to bring the message broker down so that the composition cease to function.
- *Container or virtual machine* - the attacker may gain control of the runtime environment where the application is running and control or shut down the microservices composition.

  The four entry points listed above can in general form the attack surface of any microservices composition. Considering the technical design and implementation choices made during the development of the API gateway, service registry, message broker, containers or virtual machines the following five security threats are derived from the four entry points listed above:

1. Insecure application programming interfaces
2. Unauthorized access
3. Insecure microservice discovery
4. Insecure runtime infrastructure
5. Insecure message broker

Step 5: Identifying vulnerabilities for a microservices compositions: Conceptually, threat modeling is performed by applying a methodology. For this research, STRIDE [22] is chosen as it offers a very systematic approach to analyse threats against each of the microservices architectural components. STRIDE supports a comprehensive review of security services such as authentication, authorization, confidentiality, integrity, nonrepudiation, and availability. STRIDE is an acronym that stands for spoofing, tampering, repudiation, information disclosure, denial of service and elevation of privilege.

Due to space considerations, only the first of the five threats is discussed as an example of how such vulnerabilities are identified.

Insecure Application Programming Interfaces: A weak set of APIs exposes microservices to a variety of security attacks that may result in tampering with data, information disclosure, denial of service and elevation of privileges. Table 1 below list the applicable attack methods and weaknesses on the composition that can make the attack possible.

Table 1. STRIDE analysis of insecure application programming interfaces

Security threats	Attack methods	Exploitable weaknesses or known vulnerabilities
Tampering with data	• Intercept and modify messages sent to a microservices API when communication channels used is not secured • Exploit vulnerability in mechanisms used for transport-layer security • Perform all forms of injection attacks on the API	• Insecure communication channel • Lack of mechanisms to protect against injections of all forms on the APIs • Weak access control schemes on the microservices API • Vulnerability CVE-2014-3566 [23] that allows an attacker to obtain clear text when Secure Socket Layer (SSL) v3.0 is used
Information disclosure	• Perform all forms of injection attacks on the microservices API • Exploit weak access control schemes used to protects APIs	• Lack of mechanisms to protect against injections of all forms on the APIs • Weak access control schemes on the API. For example, the United States of America Internal Revenue Service (IRS) exposed over three hundred thousand (300 000) customer records using a vulnerable web API [24] • Vulnerability CVE-2017-9805 in the REST plugin of a web application framework called Struts. The vulnerability resulted in the Equifax data breach were an attacker gained access to consumer credit reports of about one hundred and forty-three (143) million United States citizens [25]
Denial of service	• Craft a request to API gateway that fans out into multiple computationally expensive requests to microservices behind the gateway so that microservices slow down and impact all legitimate users [26]	• Failure to prioritize authenticated traffic over unauthenticated one traffic • Lack of reasonable microservices requests time-outs • Lack of fallback options when microservices does not respond on time • Lack of fault isolation mechanisms
Elevation of privileges.	• Exploit a parser of messages used on the API that allow deserialization of hostile or tampered objects by changing the serialized object to gain administrative privileges	• Insecure message deserialization

5   Microservices Composition Security Requirements

Security requirements for a microservices composition describe more concretely the conditions and capabilities that must be met or be possessed by the microservice composition to assure the security of assets. Security requirements of interest for this research are secure functional requirements, functional security requirements and secure development requirements. Using the five security threats listed in the tables above, the security requirements for a secure microservices composition are now documented. Satisfying the security requirements should lead to more secure microservices compositions (Table 2).

Table 2. Security requirements

Security threats	Security requirements	Suggested protection measures
Insecure application programming interfaces	• Only authenticated users should access the API • Keys, tokens, and password should be rotated periodically • The API should validate all requests • The communication channel between microservices should be secure	• Use keys or security tokens or passwords to protect API • Perform input validations on the microservices API • The API should white-list permitted HTTP methods • Ensure secure management of keys, password, and tokens • Use transport-layer security • Monitor the microservices API at all times
Unauthorized access	• Access to microservices should be denied by default • The microservices composition should use multi-factor authentication at all entry points • Any credentials used in the microservices composition should be rotated periodically	• Use keys, security tokens, and password to protect API • Use transport-layer security • Automate management of keys, password, and tokens
Insecure microservice discovery	• The service registry should authenticate all requests for registration • Communication between microservices and service registry should use a secure channel • Messages for registration and de-registration should be protected for integrity	• Ensure the host on which the registry run is securely configured • The service registry should use certificates and certificates should be distributed securely • Use the transport-layer security • Monitor the service registry at all times

(continued)

Table 2. (*continued*)

Security threats	Security requirements	Suggested protection measures
Insecure runtime infrastructure	• Containers and virtual machines should only use verified operating system platforms or container-specific operating system • The outbound network traffic sent by container should be monitored and controlled • The configuration of containers and virtual machines should comply with the configuration standards	• Create secure configurations of infrastructure • Validate the configurations of infrastructure • Scan container images before deployment • Grouped containers by relative sensitivity and only run containers of a single sensitivity level on a single host • Monitor infrastructure at all times
Insecure message broker	• The message broker should authenticate all requests • No client should be able to subscribe to data on the broker • A secure channel should be used for communications • The client should protect the message it sends for integrity • A redundancy mechanism should be configured to guarantee the delivery of the messages	• User transport-layer security • Use authentication plugins or write a custom filter to authenticate a message • Set up read and write permissions on the message broker • Monitor the service registry at all times

The list of security requirements and the protection measures above points to the need to integrate security in different phases of the software development lifecycle such as requirements gathering, design, implementation, and testing. To achieve this, various security-focused activities are required during the different development phases of microservices to assure that the microservice composition is not subject to security vulnerabilities. The Open Security Alliance refer to such security-focused activities as secure development activities [27].

6 Software Development Activities for Secure Microservices Compositions

Using the security requirements and suggested protection measures, a list of six software development activities is now derived that can be used to ensure that microservices are adequately protected.

1. *Document security requirements of microservices compositions.* Documentation is vital to provide a security strategy to secure various assets of the microservices.
2. *Adopt secure programming best practices.* A vital activity is to ensure that engineers adopt identified guidelines to ensure that microservices are designed and

implemented to avoid vulnerabilities. Examples of such documented instructions include validating inputs, ensuring that the application executes with the least set of privileges required for the job and sanitizing any data sent to other application to avoid injection attacks.

3. *Validate security requirements and secure programming best practices.* Validating the implementation of a microservices composition against a set of security requirements and security coding standards at various stages of the microservices' build, test and deployment is vital to ensure that end-to-end security.

4. *Secure configuration of runtime infrastructure.* A vital security activity is to ensure that containers and the virtual machine are securely configured in an automated manner. Such configuration eliminated human errors that may result in misconfiguration.

5. *Continuously monitor the behavior of components of the microservices composition.* Ensuring continuous security of microservices composition requires engineers to have a view of the behavior of the various components at runtime. Given the potential for harm that can arise from persistent attacks by hostile entities at runtime, there is a need to monitor microservices and their runtime environments. Monitoring allows identification, detection, and even ability to foresee critical events and situations that occur during runtime.

6. *Securely respond to attacks using adaptation mechanisms.* A microservices composition should be built to withstand failures of individual components. Mechanisms that ensure that the application responds adequately to changes at runtime to maintain an appropriate security posture are referred to as secure adaptation mechanisms.

7 Conclusion

Building secure microservices compositions is a complicated exercise. This paper has laid the foundation towards understanding the microservices architecture's security threats using an attacker's point of view and identified security requirements common to most implementation of the microservice architecture. Suitable protection measures have also been identified. Even when security requirements and protection measures are identified early during the development process, there is still the challenge of validating if the implementation of various components of the architecture is safe. Furthermore, there is a need to ensure that the runtime environment does not provide attackers with the means to control or compromise the microservices composition. To this end, this paper identified security-focused activities that ensure that the suitable protection measures are implemented. The next research will identify various tools, techniques, and methods that can be used to support software engineers in incorporating the six secure development activities to become part of their daily development task.

References

1. Zimmermann, O.: Do microservices pass the same old architecture test? Or: SOA is not dead-long live (micro-)services. In: Microservices Workshop at SATURN Conference, SEI (2015)
2. Dragoni, N., et al.: Microservices: yesterday, today, and tomorrow. In: Present and Ulterior Software Engineering, pp. 195–216 (2017)
3. Nadareishvili, I., Mitra, R., McLarty, M., Amundsen, M.: Microservice Architecture: Aligning Principles, Practices, and Culture. O'Reilly Media Inc., Newton (2016)
4. Bossert, O.: A two-speed architecture for the digital enterprise. In: El-Sheikh, E., Zimmermann, A., Jain, L.C. (eds.) Emerging Trends in the Evolution of Service-Oriented and Enterprise Architectures. ISRL, vol. 111, pp. 139–150. Springer, Cham (2016). https://doi.org/10.1007/978-3-319-40564-3_8
5. Bass, L., Weber, I., Zhu, L.: DevOps: A Software Architect's Perspective. Addison-Wesley Professional, Boston (2015)
6. Bernstein, D.: Is Amazon becoming the new cool software company for developers? IEEE Cloud Comput. 2(1), 69–71 (2015)
7. Ravichandran, A., Taylor, K., Waterhouse, P.: DevOps foundations. In: DevOps for Digital Leaders, pp. 27–47. Apress, New York (2016)
8. Baresi, L., Filgueira Mendonça, D., Garriga, M.: Empowering low-latency applications through a serverless edge computing architecture. In: De Paoli, F., Schulte, S., Broch Johnsen, E. (eds.) ESOCC 2017. LNCS, vol. 10465, pp. 196–210. Springer, Cham (2017). https://doi.org/10.1007/978-3-319-67262-5_15
9. Feitelson, D.G., Frachtenberg, E., Beck, K.L.: Development and deployment at facebook. IEEE Internet Comput. 17(4), 8–17 (2013)
10. Feng, Q., Kazman, R., Cai, Y., Mo, R., Xiao, L.: Towards an architecture-centric approach to security analysis. In: 2016 13th Working IEEE/IFIP Conference on Software Architecture (WICSA), pp. 221–230. IEEE, April 2016
11. Lalsing, V., Kishnah, S., Pudaruth, S.: People factors in agile software development and project management. Int. J. Softw. Eng. Appl. 3(1), 117 (2012)
12. Butzin, B., Golatowski, F., Timmermann, D.: Microservices approach for the internet of things. In: 2016 IEEE 21st International Conference on Emerging Technologies and Factory Automation (ETFA), pp. 1–6. IEEE, September 2016
13. Sheng, Q.Z., Qiao, X., Vasilakos, A.V., Szabo, C., Bourne, S., Xu, X.: Web services composition: a decade's overview. Inf. Sci. 280, 218–238 (2014)
14. Rogers, B.: The social costs of Uber. U. Chi. L. Rev. Dialogue 82, 85 (2015)
15. Nadalin, A., Kaler, C., Monzillo, R., Hallam-Baker, P.: Web services security: SOAP message security 1.1 (WS-Security 2004). Oasis Standard, 200401 (2006)
16. Shah, D., Patel, D.: Dynamic and ubiquitous security architecture for global SOA. In: The Second International Conference on Mobile Ubiquitous Computing, Systems, Services and Technologies, UBICOMM 2008, pp. 482–487. IEEE, September 2008
17. Jones, M., Bradley, J., Sakimura, N.: JSON web token (JWT) (No. RFC 7519) (2015)
18. Merkel, D.: Docker: lightweight Linux containers for consistent development and deployment. Linux J. 2014(239), 2 (2014)
19. Martins, G., Bhatia, S., Koutsoukos, X., Stouffer, K., Tang, C., Candell, R.: Towards a systematic threat modeling approach for cyberphysical systems. In: Resilience Week (RWS), pp. 1–6. IEEE, August 2015
20. Priya, S.S., Arya, S.S.: Threat modeling for a secured software development. Int. J. Adv. Res. Comput. Sci. 7(1), 40–48 (2016)

21. IEC/ISO 7498-2: Information Processing Systems - Open Systems Interconnection, 7498-2 (1989)
22. Shostack, A.: Threat Modeling: Designing for Security. Wiley, Hoboken (2014)
23. Sheffer, Y., Holz, R., Saint-Andre, P.: Summarizing known attacks on transport layer security (TLS) and datagram TLS (DTLS) (No. RFC 7457) (2015)
24. Borazjani, P.N.: Security issues in cloud computing. In: Au, M.H.A., Castiglione, A., Choo, K.-K.R., Palmieri, F., Li, K.-C. (eds.) GPC 2017. LNCS, vol. 10232, pp. 800–811. Springer, Cham (2017). https://doi.org/10.1007/978-3-319-57186-7_58
25. Gressin, S.: The Equifax Data Breach: What to Do (2017)
26. Behrens, S., Heffner J.: The avalanche application DoS in microservice architectures (2017). https://medium.com/signal-sciences-labs/starting-the-avalanche-application-dos-in-microservice-architectures-4f5eb4730a60. Accessed 20 Jan 2019
27. Open Security Alliance: IT Security Requirements (2017). http://www.opensecurity architecture.org/cms/definitions/it_security_requirements. Accessed 15 Jan 2018

A Students' Perspective of Native and Cross-Platform Approaches for Mobile Application Development

Paulo Meirelles[1]($\boxtimes$), Carla S. R. Aguiar[2], Felipe Assis[2], Rodrigo Siqueira[3], and Alfredo Goldman[3]

[1] Federal University of São Paulo (UNIFESP), São Paulo, Brazil
`paulo.meirelles@unifesp.br`
[2] University of Brasília (UnB), Brasilia, Brazil
`caguiar@unb.br, fel.cesar@gmail.com`
[3] University of São Paulo (USP), São Paulo, Brazil
`{siqueira,gold}@ime.usp.br`

Abstract. One of the software industries with the most significant growth nowadays is the mobile application industry. In this paper, we study the differences between two mobile development approaches: (i) native (the development that's specific for each platform) and (ii) cross-platform (when a standard code is shared among different platforms). Inexperienced teams, students, and all newcomers in mobile development might find difficulties in choosing among approaches and frameworks. Our goal is to provide a comparison of these approaches from 3 different surveys with 166 participants, from students to experts perspectives, and study the factors that might influence the choice between them. We focus not only on quantitative aspects but also on qualitative and practical considerations that may also affect this decision (e.g., project requirements, final product category, and platform support). The results can aid students and inexperienced teams to obtain a more unobstructed view of the most recommended mobile development approach in a specific context and guide them to systematize their choice. Through our research, we observed that even when the quantitative aspects point towards a hybrid approach, it may not be the best decision due to other qualitative and practical factors. We found two nontechnical characteristics that may impact the selection of the best approach: previous team experiences with the chosen technology; and how well established and consolidated the technology is. With that in mind, we propose a mapping between project requirements and the benefits/drawbacks of each approach.

1 Introduction

In 2017, Stack Overflow, a popular and respected website among the developers, released the results of a global Developer Survey with $64,000$ developers from all around the world. The survey revealed that 23% of the interviewees were mobile

© Springer Nature Switzerland AG 2019
S. Misra et al. (Eds.): ICCSA 2019, LNCS 11623, pp. 586–601, 2019.
https://doi.org/10.1007/978-3-030-24308-1_47

developers. From this group, 64% worked with Android, 57% with iOS, 4.3% with Windows Phone and 0.7% with the Blackberry platform [22]. This data reflects the number of worldwide smartphone sales to end users, where 325 394.4 of units use Android, 71 525.9 use iOS, 4 395.0 use Windows, and 906.9 use Blackberry platform [24]. Therefore, developers and companies that wish their applications to reach a higher number of users will focus mainly on Android and iOS environments.

Applications that need to run on multiple platforms have distinct source codes per platform [4]. An application for a specific platform which has direct access to the device resources is known as a native app [11]. Developing a native app for multiple platforms is complicated and consumes a considerable amount of resources, since the source code must be duplicated for different platforms, possibly increasing project costs [19]. In response, tools that allow developers to implement a single application and export it to multiple platforms emerged. This sort of app is known as a cross-platform app and has the main advantage of simplifying the app life-cycle by centralizing development in a single code-base [4]. Despite this advantage, cross-platform approaches can also have their downsides, e.g., access to device resources and high memory usage [15].

The game development industry is one example where software development must be, as a requirement, multi-platform. The most used and mature game engines, such as Unity and Unreal, allow cross-platform development not only between mobile platforms, but even between consoles, desktop operating systems, smart TVs, and web browsers. In 2016, approximately 59% of the mobile games used cross-platform technologies as their game engine [23].

Native and cross-platform approaches have different trade-offs, and it is necessary to consider them before selecting the most appropriate. Among different contexts, technologies and requirements, it can be difficult to determine which is the best approach for a given project. Evidence of these factors, considering both technical and non-technical aspects of each strategy and technology, is necessary. We aim to provide such evidence through surveys, where we gathered the main qualitative and non-technical aspects when deciding among technologies.

Previous studies have compared both qualitative and quantitative aspects of adopting one of the approaches [14,15]. We compare native and cross-platform development from students' perspectives. We also validated these perspectives with professional developers point of view. We conducted surveys, separating our target into three categories: beginner (undergraduate students with different levels of practice), intermediate (advanced students from graduate courses) and advanced (professionals from different communities of mobile software development). After analyzing the results of our surveys, we inferred that quantitative characteristics might not be the primary factor to consider when selecting between native or cross-platform.

The remainder of this paper is organized as follows. Section 2 discusses the background of mobile development approaches and technologies. Section 3 presents some related works to position our contribution. Section 4 presents the research design of this study, discussing our research questions and methodology.

In the sequence, Sect. 5 summarizes our results, in particular, based on surveys conducted with students and mobile software development professionals. Finally, Sect. 6 concludes the paper, highlighting its main contributions and providing paths for future work.

2   Background

Mobile applications have particularities in their development due to hardware features, software distributions, and release cycles. Developers have to handle issues related to storage capacity, mobile specifications, mobility, user experience, security, and privacy [11]. Mobile applications are commonly dynamically developed, released in small cycles, and they require small storage and have a low cost to the final user [9].

Native applications are designed for a particular Operating System (OS), e.g., iOS or Android, which means there is no portability between platforms. Commonly, these apps are available at digital stores (e.g., App Store for iOS and Play Store for Android), responsible for downloading the app in the devices and make it available to the end user [18]. Native apps tend to follow the interface (look and feel) and the technical patterns supported by the specific platform. This sort of app has direct access to device resources such as sensors, cameras, GPS (Global Positioning System) [11]. This approach delivers both high performance and specialized UI/UX for users [18]. However, it requires a specific framework and SDK [15].

An alternative to developing an app for multiple platforms is the use of cross-platform technologies. This strategy produces a single code base that enables app distribution for various platforms. Two different cross-platform technologies are being considered: Web apps and Hybrid apps. **Web apps** are applications developed using web technologies customized for mobile restrictions. The device needs to access these apps through a browser (e.g., Firefox, Safari, Chrome). They provide a uniform experience across different mobile platforms [18]. This technique follows the client-server model, in which the source code runs in a remote server. However, it uses modified front-end technologies that can detect mobile device restrictions and adapt the UI. A vast number of frameworks exist to support this approach, as illustrated in Table 1, and most of them use well-known front-end technologies for the web.

Hybrid applications combine native and Web App approaches. This approach enables developers to use web technologies to target multiple mobile platforms from a single code base and produce an app that works similarly as a native app. Hybrid apps installed in the device, internally use the WebKit rendering engine, an engine that depends on the browser of the OS, and is available in Safari, Mail, App Store, and many other apps on macOS, iOS, and Linux [2]. It shows web content inside the application while using native components to improve the user experience [1]. In this paper, we define a hybrid app as a web app, primarily built using HTML5 and Javascript. A native container wraps the web app providing access to native platform features [20].

Table 1. Examples of cross-platform technologies.

Platform	Languages
Alpha Anywhere	C++, C#, Javascript, VisualBasic
Cocos 2D	C++, C#, JS, Swift, Objective-C
Corona	Lua
Ionic	Javascript, HTML, CSS
PhoneGap	Javascript, HTML, CSS
Qt	C++
Sencha	Javascript, HTML, CSS
Titanium	Javascript
Unity	C#, UnityScript
Unreal	C++
Xamarin	C#, ruby

According to Ciman [8], the battery consumption is significantly increased when using hybrid technologies, in some cases exceeding 250% when compared with an equivalent native app. Also, according to Rakesh [20], compared to the native approach, hybrid apps usually consume a significantly more significant amount of RAM, they handle animations with less fluidity and often appear sluggish during page and state transitions.

Deciding among native, web app, and hybrid approaches require a careful analysis of the technical and nontechnical characteristics of the project. However, they are not equally weighted, since they depend on a variety of external factors such as development experience on the target OS, project schedule, software requirements, and the number of platforms to be released.

3   Related Work

We examined related works on mobile development. We observed in the past 13 years a significant discussion, research, and development of new approaches to improve mobile development [13]. We were looking for alternatives that could lower the costs and development time with the least possible impact on other aspects such as app performance, UI/UX, and security. Some of these studies have goals and methodologies similar to ours. We compared some approaches adopted by other researchers with ours.

Charland et al. [7] present a theoretical comparison of cross-platform and native application development on aspects like UI coding, performance on each platform and compliance with conventions. They concluded that hybrid solutions have several advantages over native ones when dealing with cross-platform development. Following the same motivation, we also considered non-quantitative factors in our research, in particular, empirical (e.g., project requirements).

Prezotto [21] makes a distinction between native, web app, and hybrid approaches. The author made proof of concept by building a hybrid app. After the implementation of the solution, Prezotto noticed different behavior between platforms that executed the application. We note that there is a concern in verifying the capacity of the hybrid apps in front of the Native approach. In our surveys, we aimed to highlight those differences to beginner and advanced developers, analyzing their perspectives.

Dalmasso [10] presented several hybrid app development tools available in the market (e.g., PhoneGap, Titanium, Rhomobile, and JQuery Mobile) and made a comparison through a survey. Dalmasso's work discussed a qualitative study of these frameworks to provide a quick overview to mobile developers. Our research intends to cover not only the cross-platform approaches but also put it in a more empirical comparison against the native approach.

Majchrzak and Grønli [16] discussed how to choose between different hybrid technologies. The author adopted Ionic, React, and Fuse as the objects of his study, considering purely technical and mostly quantitative aspects. Most recently, Biørn-Hansen et al. [5] defined an overview of core concepts and domain terminology regarding cross-platform app development, establishing a taxonomy. The authors argue that the developers face many cross-platform development options to choose and there is no one technology fits all. Other works of Biørn-Hansen and Majchrzak [6,17] suggested Progressive web apps as the final approach to cross-platform development. In our research, we discussed nontechnical issues when determining the ideal strategy for a project. We also discussed how to select a mobile development approach, but we did not consider individual technologies for this decision.

Latif [15] made a case study of how various hybrid technologies work (i.e., language, architecture, and performance) and highlighted their benefits and their challenges. Gaouar [14] conducted a similar work, where the author mapped the technical requirements for cross-platform into six categories: support platforms, documentation, security, access to native resources, look and feel, and resource consumption. Different from those authors, we did not focus on mapping the characteristics of each approach or technology, but to take those already highlighted and mapped topics from the students perspective. In our study, we also compare cross-platform and native development of each Operating System, not only related to the multi-platform SDKs itself.

Carlström [3] conducted a study closer to our goal, a practical experiment that separated results for each predefined use cases defined. In general, the time spent in the development of cross-platform applications were smaller than native development separately. Jiang [12] considered technical, empirical, and practical aspects of the different solutions. The author concluded that there is no universal solution, once there is no extreme difference regarding development processes and products to name a final approach to mobile app development.

4   Research Design

We aim to investigate native, hybrid, and web app approaches regarding mobile applications development for inexperient teams. In the context, we guide this study to answer the principal research question:

#RQ: *What should be considered when choosing the best approach (Native, hybrid, or Web App) to develop a mobile app?*

The following questions emerged to investigate this scenario when respecting the qualitative context:

#Q1: *What are the technical advantages (technical features) of cross-platform (hybrid) frameworks from the perspective of inexperienced mobile developers and experts?* We hypothesized that inexperienced mobile developers would suggest that the strongest technical advantage will be the cross-platform (hybrid) "cost per platform". In counterpart, we expect that experts will not corroborate on all cases. Even with all these considerations, analyzing other practical factors is required, and it led us to the second research question.

#Q2: *What non-technical factors influence decision making regarding the approach and framework used for developing a mobile application?* We hypothesized that several subjective aspects like "project requirements", "technology learning curve" and "previous practice with technology" will not only influence but be decisive in the choice of an approach. We expected that developers would classify nontechnical aspects to be more relevant to decide between approaches than technical ones.

We conducted three questionnaires to collect data to answer these research questions. From the data collected and analyzed from these questionnaires, we elaborated a guideline that guides students with little or no mobile development experience to make the best decision on mobile application development. Also, it could be used as guidelines in mobile development courses with a project-oriented approach.

4.1   Students' Perceptions on Implementing Using Native and Cross-Platform Mobile Solutions

The first questionnaire collected the perception from advanced Computer Science undergraduate and graduate students at the University of São Paulo (USP). Previous to questionnaire application, students developed, through 4 months course, simple features with both Native and Hybrid mobile frameworks. This survey intended to evaluate the main advantages and difficulties faced by intermediate developers when implementing a mobile application in both approaches, and if these challenges are perceived differently in hybrid and native strategies. Also, we could evaluate the learning curve in both technologies and this way answer the #Q1 and #RQ.

The questionnaire was composed of four sections:

- **Section 1 - Participants Profile:** age, gender, prior knowledge of programming languages (such as C, C++, Python, PHP, and Ruby). Ex: "Have you ever developed some software that is being used by other users?";

- **Section 2 - Previous experiences on mobile development:** familiarity level with programming languages and technologies such as Java to Android, Android Studio, HTML, Javascript, Angular 2, and Ionic. Ex: "How many other development platforms have you ever used?";
- **Sections 3 and 4 - Perceptions on Android Studio and Ionic development:** difficulty to install Web Services to implement the login, development of student registration feature. Implementation of Bluetooth and Wifi communications, camera image capture, QR-Code reading, and finally the upload of files using Web Services.

All responses were based on the Likert's scale with the following levels: (1) Strongly disagree; (2) Disagree; (3) Not agree or disagree; (4) Agree; (5) Strongly agree. Finally, the student had two open questions to write open comments on the development using Android Studio and using Ionic.

4.2   Students and Developers' Perspectives on Selecting Mobile Technology

The following two questionnaires intended to answer the #Q2 and #RQ. We conducted surveys in two distinct contexts. First, we wanted to understand the factors developers with little experience or utterly inexperienced in mobile development take into account on their first mobile projects. Second, we validated this set of factors with advanced and experts mobile developers.

The second questionnaire collected the point of view of undergraduate students of the Software Engineering course from the Federal University of Brasília. In this context, we collected data from students that enrolled in a based-project course, where students are expected to choose the technologies they are going to use (there are no restrictions) and to justify their choice. Differently, from students evaluated in the first survey, these students developed an entire mobile application with only the selected approach (native or cross-platform).

The third questionnaire collected the point of view from experienced mobile developers. We provided an anonymous online and shared to developers enrolled in mobile online communities. We consider specialists those who fit into the following requirements:

- 3 or more years of professional experience in software development.
- Worked at least on two published software for mobile.
- Worked on at mobile development with recent technologies (2015 onward).

Both questionnaires collected data about the current knowledge of the participant and also to determine the primary factors when selecting between different approaches, frameworks, and platforms. The questionnaire was composed of four sections:

- **Section 1 - Participants Profile and previous experience:** age, gender, prior knowledge of programming languages (such as C, C++, Java, Javascript, Python, Objective-C, and Swift). Ex: "How many projects were published, how many are still in production?"

Table 2. Nontechnical factors that interfere with the choice mobile approach.

1 - Previous knowledge regarding the platform
2 - Learning Curve
3 - Development project requirements
4 - Stakeholders preferences
5 - Code reuse
6 - Quality of support (Documentation, API, Community, Wiki)
7 - Recommendations of specialists
8 - Google research trend
9 - Final product performance (Battery consumption, response time, graphical performance)
10 - I can't tell. (In this case, do not consider all of the above options)

- **Sections 2 and 3 - arbitrary preferences regarding mobile application development:** cover the currently most used languages and frameworks in mobile development. For example, Xcode (Objective-C and Swift) and Android Studio (Java) for native development, and Ionic framework and ReactNative for hybrid approaches;
- **Section 4 - Factors that interfere with the selection of mobile technology:** the list of the factors evaluated are depicted in Table 2.

When asked about each of those factors, the respondents have different options. They could select the priority level they attribute to each of them when starting a software project. All response options followed a scale from 1 to 5: (1) "I do not know or can not answer"; (2) "little interest or value"; (3) "moderate interest or value"; (4) "big interest or value"; (5) "maximum priority, interest, and value for the solution over the others".

5   Exploratory Data Analysis

This section presents the data collected from the respondents to the questionnaires described in Sect. 4. First, we analyze the learning curve of both approaches, where 40 computer science undergraduate and master students implement, for the first time, simple features in both native Android and Ionic. We evaluate their perceptions and difficulties while configuring the development environment, using IDEs, programming language, testing and deploying a mobile application in both approaches.

In a different University, we analyze which factors 96 undergraduate software engineering students take into account to choose between native and hybrid approaches when developing their first mobile application. Finally, we evaluate if the same factors guide more advanced practitioners when choosing an adequate approach to develop a mobile app. Table 3 gives an overview of the results

Table 3. Overview of the surveys' participants.

Survey	Nr of participants	Profile interviewee	Survey intent
1	40	Undergraduate and Master Students in Computer Science	Evaluate technical comparison between both native (Android) and hybrid (Ionic)
2	96	Undergraduates in Software Engineering	Evaluate the factors an inexperienced developers consider when choosing technology for a mobile project
3	30	Experienced mobile developers	Evaluate the factors experienced developers/experts consider when choosing technology for a mobile project

obtained from these three surveys with 136 students and 30 professionals. From the acquired data, we derived both non-technical and technical aspects to define between native and hybrid approaches when students begin a new mobile project.

5.1   First Survey

We conducted experiments related to Android (Native) and Ionic (hybrid) throughout the Mobile Computing course at the University of São Paulo. Most of the 40 students had a good background in C, Java, and Python programming languages. On C language, 80% declared that they have "good" or "excellent" skills. For Python, 42% reported having the "medium" knowledge. 32.5% of the respondents have "good" to "excellent" domain over the language. More than 65% declared to have "zero" or "minimum" knowledge of Javascript (mostly used by Ionic), PHP, and Ruby programming languages.

Regarding the IDE/Framework, 87.5% of the respondents answered that they did not have any previous experience with Android Studio and 80% claimed the same for Ionic. After developing in both technologies (Android and Ionic), they were asked the question "How easy is to set up the development environment?". 67.5% of the participants said that it is easy to configure Android Studio and only 35% had the same opinion about the Ionic environment. More than half of students (55%) claimed the Ionic environment is unintuitive to set up.

In general, the results show some pieces of evidence that developing simple tasks, both Android and Ionic are quite similar. We were also interested in investigating the differences between Android and Ionic environments when using particular hardware resources.

We verified the use of Bluetooth, Wifi, and a camera device on both platforms. Our results indicated that developers found more complicated to access the hardware in Ionic than in Android Studio.

There were two questions about their perception of the advantages and disadvantages of Android Studio, and the second one, on the aspects of Ionic. Most comments were favorable toward Android IDE like: "very useful IDE", "excellent debugger" and "good log terminal and refactoring tool". However, many of them complained about the quite steep learning curve, the difficulties when manually configuring the development environment and with deprecated methods.

Concerning Ionic, students were quite unanimous in its use for straightforward applications. There were comments as "Easy to do HTML interfaces and to navigate among pages" and "Easy for developers with knowledge on HTML and Javascript". However, there were lot more critics related to several topics as: "Not good to use the smartphone resources", "hard to find the correct libraries", "large dependence on third-party plug-ins". Students also complained about the framework being quite recent with not enough documentation, the "Lack of comprehensive documentation and lack of support", "hard to configure it", "sensation of adopting a'Frankenstein like' application with different functional parts", "the final application ran slower than the native correspondent", "hard to debug", and "It is frustrating to make HTTPS requests work".

5.2 Second Survey

We conducted experiments related to native, hybrid, and web app mobile development throughout the Software Development Methods course at the University of Brasília. The survey intended to understand how the 96 students enrolled in this course chose the development techniques and tools for their first mobile projects. The students evaluated are mostly men (85%) and have an age range between 18 and 25 years old. Most of them (77.1%) have 0 to 1 year of practice in mobile software development.

When asked about their current knowledge regarding programming languages, students declared a medium to a good experience in C/C++ (74%), Java (58.4%), and Python (52.1%). Opposing to that, the iOS platform languages, Swift and Objective-C, where the most uncovered among all students, presenting 88.5% of the answers as "zero knowledge". We observed the Javascript had well-distributed sample space with 29.2% of respondents with "low or zero knowledge", 44% with "medium knowledge" and 26.1% with "high knowledge".

We asked them about specific frameworks, platforms, and IDEs that they use during hybrid development. 42.7% of the students have practice at least in Ionic, React Native, PhoneGap, Xamarin, or Rails. As for the native approaches, Android was the most used native platform among the students with 49% of the responses. According to this data, we can observe that the students have practice with cross-platform technologies.

We also asked the students to select three factors (from a predefined list showed in Table 2) that would be decisive when choosing what platform, framework, technology, or approach to decide when developing a mobile project. 67.7% of the respondents indicated the "quality of support (wiki, community, documentation, API)" and the "project requirements" as the factors with the highest score. The second most selected factors were "previous knowledge" and "learning curve" (both nontechnical topics), with 53.1% and 44.8% of responses, respectively. It is evident that, for beginners, technical and community support available are crucial for their framework evaluation. It means that inexperience mobile developers are unlikely to be early adopters of mobile emerging technologies since it increases the risks. Equally vital to beginners are project requirements and previous experience in technology. However, when it comes to projects requirements, they tend to choose the hybrid approach when it is required availability in multiple platforms. This fact is due to rigid deadlines, limited budgets, and risk management. Consequently, if the project requirement is to have the application available on only one platform, inexperienced developers tend to choose the native approach.

5.3   Third Survey

We conducted a third survey to collect data from 30 advanced developers who actively participate in the developers' community to verify our founds from the two previous questionnaires. The participants are mostly men, and they have an age range from 22 to 35 years old (80%).

When asked about their current knowledge regarding programming languages, the majority 50% declared from medium to good experience in Objective-C/Swift (56,7%), Java (66,6%), Javascript (53,5%); other languages were also mentioned, such as PHP, Ruby, C# e Python, C++. More specifically when argued about their empirical preferences for each technology (outside of any specific use case), we can observe that between cross-platform development technologies, the most significant community of developers are Xamarin and React Native, and Web Apps, all with just over 30% of any level of acceptance between low and maximum. The preference for native alternatives (iOS and Android) remain at 90% of any level of choice.

As in the previous questionnaire, among a list of factors, the developers had to choose up to 3 factors that influence the choice of the framework/technology when starting a software development project mobile. Just like the students, "quality of the support" (documentation, Wiki, APIs) with 46.7% was the most relevant aspect for choosing a technology, but also the "Performance of the final product" aspect also 46.7% in contrast to previous research. "Learning curve" (36.7%) and "prior knowledge of technology" (33.7%) were also considered again resembling the result of previous questionnaires.

In the questionnaire, we presented to the participants with mobile applications hypothetically developed with the iOS and Android platforms. In each option, they should choose which technology (Native, Hybrid, Web App) would have the preference for software development. The types of applications were: (1) "Electronic game", (2) "CRUD based application", (3) "Application with complex UI/UX elements and animations", (4) "Application that relies heavily on device features (GPS, Accelerometer, Gyroscope, iCloud, Native Login, Touch ID, Push Notifications, etc.)". For alternatives (3) and (4), a significant preference over the native approach was evident (90%); for CRUD-based applications, the majority had a choice for cross-platform approaches, with 40% hybrid and 13.13% Web-App. Finally, for electronic games, there was a preference of just over 50% for the native approach and 3% for hybrid approaches (Unity, Unreal Engine, and Game Engine).

6   Discussion

In this section, we discuss some of the insights and results obtained from the collected data. Our results show that the most critical factor to be considered when choosing a mobile development approach is "how well established and consolidated the technology is". It means that developers, in general, should check how good or how extensive is the technical documentation (e.g., code documentation, wiki, forums) and how active is their support and community in a project context. This factor is directly linked to the stability and consolidation of mobile technology in the developer community in general. The previous practice and learning curve of the development team regarding the candidate technology also influence this decision. The surveys evidence that students intuitively prioritize, with a slightly different priority, some of the same factors of experts.

We hoped that, contrary to what literature and recent studies point to, hybrid approaches are not the best choice for most cases. This statement seems to be true even if several hybrid technologies are already well consolidated. The adoption tends towards native approaches as the application requires UI/UX features and non-standard animations. The same choice is preferable as more native resources (not common to other devices) are needed.

We observed from the collected data that there is no optimal choice for all situations, where each project and each kind of software has its particularities. From the results obtained from data analysis, we proposed a general set of recommendations depicted in Table 4 and described as follows.

Native approach presents the best UI/UX graphical performance, easier to implement complex animations. It has maximum conformity with the selected platform (Android or iOS) design guidelines and standards. The most used native Operating Systems excels in providing extensive documentation, technical support for bug fixes and extensive community of developers already with ongoing projects. For the native approaches, the vendors offer a variety of well-established development tools. With the proper implementation of the features, optimization for low battery consumption, RAM usage, video memory, and latency are viable. We recommend the native development approach for:

- Projects that need high performance;
- Projects that require technical support from the technology providers;
- Projects that need a faster learning curve for inexperienced developers.

Hybrid approach presents an acceptable UI and UX compliance for each platform for the basic native graphical elements. However, it imposes a higher difficulty in implementing new (non-standard) or more complex animations and graphical elements. This approach excels in the cost-benefit regarding the budget and the schedule in front of the number of platforms that can be implemented. It happens due to its main advantage concerning code reuse among different platforms. Even though a specific platform code is still needed for features that use specific resources. Not all of the hybrid technologies provide a well-established development environment (e.g., IDEs, SDKs, CLIs). The current

Table 4. Recommended criteria to choose between different approaches in mobile application development.

	Native	Hybrid	Web App
UI/UX performance	High	Low	Low
UI/UX customization	High	Medium to Low	Relative to web technology adopted.
UI/UX platform guideline compliance	Maximum	Medium to High	None
Documentation, support, community	High	Low to Medium (relative to the selected hybrid technology)	Relative to web technology adopted. But low in the context of web app
Hardware stress (battery consumption, RAM, GPU, response time)	Low	Medium to High, (Very perceptive in some cases)	High to Maximum
Optimized product output (binary or generated source)	Can be very optimized (relative to developer)	Not optimized	Not optimized
Relative cost per number of platform.	Maximum cost per platform.	medium or low (relative to the selected hybrid technology)	Minimum cost per platform
Other comments	Easy to set up the working environment, a high number of developer tools; maximum optimization for game software.	Usually longer to set up the working environment (with exceptions);	Limited access to the device resources
Recommended for	For projects with a lower priority in the budget, projects that do not need to be deployed on multiple platforms, apps that need high or maximum performance are required as well as a need for proper support from the technology providers and needs a faster learning curve in the development team.	For projects targets, two or more platforms, require access to primary device resources, projects that do not require excellence in graphical performance or compliance and have a high priority of a lower budget.	For apps that have simple UI/UX requirements do not need to be stored in the device, apps that need to run in an undetermined number of devices and applications that do not require device-specific features (camera, accelerometer, touch-id, gyroscope, compass, proximity, microphone).

most used hybrid approaches also provide good and extensive documentation, wiki, and support from their communities. The final output code or binary application is not optimized for an individual platform, leading to higher hardware stress compared to its native equivalent. We recommend the hybrid approach for:

- Projects targeting two or more platforms;
- Projects that require access to essential device resources;
- Projects that do not require excellence in graphical performance or compliance;
- Projects that have budget restrictions.

Web App approach presents the lowest UI/UX compliance, as its frameworks do not comply with the specific platform guidelines. This approach excels for use cases that have already a production environment and have simple end-user features (e.g., CRUD-based applications). This approach has the best level of code reuse. In counterpart of its higher compatibility, the access to the device resources is very limited. We recommend this approach for:

- Projects that have simple UI/UX requirements;
- Projects that do not need to be completely stored in the device;
- Projects that need to run in an undetermined number of devices;
- Projects that do not require specific device features (e.g., camera, accelerometer, touch-id, gyroscope, compass, proximity, microphone).

7 Conclusion

In this paper, we studied the considered factors to choose a better approach, either a native or cross-platform, to develop a mobile application. Our findings can support students and professors to systematize the choice of the most suitable framework in a mobile project during an undergraduate or graduate course related to the software engineering field as well. To answer the principal research question, we conducted surveys with 166 participants from three groups: inexperienced, intermediate, and expert mobile developers. From the data analysis, we concluded that practitioners, no matter their experience, regard both technical and nontechnical requirements such as the support offered by the technology (documentation, wiki, and community), the performance of the final product, project requirements, and learning curve.

When it comes to technical aspects, we studied the advantages and challenges of the native, hybrid, and web app mobile approach. We performed an experiment with intermediate developers where they implemented features in both native Java Android and Ionic and later, compared their experience. Students came to similar conclusions of experts, where we concluded that practitioners are strongly inclined to choose a native approach when it comes to achieving high performance (i.e., low battery consumption, low latency, high graphical performance, animations, low memory usage). However, if performance is not obligatory, and there are few hardware/device access, hybrid solutions are considered a better approach to develop mobile apps for multiple platforms.

Based on these results, we recommended a set of technical and nontechnical aspects to help newcomers of mobile development to systematize the choice of the mobile software development strategy for their projects. We should stress that we found no evidence that there is an optimal mobile approach choice, and it is strongly influenced by both technical and nontechnical factors presented in this papers, and also by the context of the application.

7.1 Threats to Valid and Future Work

As threats to validity, all of the surveyed students are from Brazil as well as most of the expert participants are from the Brazilian industry and communities. We developed the questionnaires from our experiences in software engineering and software mobile development and teaching. Thereby we did not formally evaluate the reliability of the surveys.

Regarding the related work, we conducted a systematic literature review during the first phase of this study in 2017. After the analysis of the questionnaires, we complete our review with a few related papers from 2018.

As future work, we need to complete our analysis collecting data of developers in other countries to confirm our findings from different perspectives. Another study should perform a quantitative analysis comparing both native and cross-platform mobile approaches to validate the results. We also suggest using the profiling tools to have a clear understanding of the performance difference between implementations of the same feature in native and cross-platform applications.

Acknowledgements. The authors are indebted to the students from USP and UnB, as well as, the professionals for answering the questionnaires providing valuable data for this study.

References

1. Ahti, V., Hyrynsalmi, S., Nevalainen, O.: An evaluation framework for cross-platform mobile app development tools: a case analysis of adobe phonegap framework. In: Proceedings of the 17th International Conference on Computer Systems and Technologies, CompSysTech 2016, Palermo, Italy, 23–24 June 2016, pp. 41–48 (2016)
2. Webkit: Webkit is a trademark of Apple Inc. (2017). https://webkit.org
3. Axelsson, O., Carlström, F.: Evaluation targeting react native in comparison to native mobile development (2016). Student Paper
4. Bernardes, T.F., Miyake, M.Y.: Cross-platform mobile development approaches: a systematic review. IEEE Lat. Am. Trans. **14**(4), 1892–1898 (2016)
5. Biørn-Hansen, A., Grønli, T.M., Ghinea, G.: A survey and taxonomy of core concepts and research challenges in cross-platform mobile development. ACM Comput. Surv. **51**(5), 108:1–108:34 (2018). https://doi.org/10.1145/3241739. http://doi.acm.org/10.1145/3241739
6. Biørn-Hansen, A., Majchrzak, T.A., Grønli, T.-M.: Progressive web apps for the unified development of mobile applications. In: Majchrzak, T.A., Traverso, P., Krempels, K.-H., Monfort, V. (eds.) WEBIST 2017. LNBIP, vol. 322, pp. 64–86. Springer, Cham (2018). https://doi.org/10.1007/978-3-319-93527-0_4
7. Charland, A., Leroux, B.: Mobile application development: web vs. native. Commun. ACM **54**(5), 49–53 (2011)
8. Ciman, M., Gaggi, O.: An empirical analysis of energy consumption of cross-platform frameworks for mobile development. Pervasive Mob. Comput. **39**, 214–230 (2017)
9. Corral, L., Janes, A., Remencius, T.: Potential advantages and disadvantages of multiplatform development frameworks - a vision on mobile environments. Procedia Comput. Sci. **10**, 1202–1207 (2012)
10. Dalmasso, I., Datta, S.K., Bonnet, C., Nikaein, N.: Survey, comparison and evaluation of cross platform mobile application development tools. In: 2013 9th International Wireless Communications and Mobile Computing Conference (IWCMC), pp. 323–328, July 2013

11. El-Kassas, W.S., Abdullah, B.A., Yousef, A.H., Wahba, A.M.: Taxonomy of cross-platform mobile applications development approaches. Ain Shams Eng. J. (2015). http://www.sciencedirect.com/science/article/pii/S2090447915001276

12. Jiang, S.: Comparison of native, cross-platform and hyper mobile development tools approaches for iOS and Android mobile applications. University of Gothenburg (2016)

13. Johnson, H., et al.: Methods and systems for providing platform-independent shared software components for mobile devices. US Patent 6,986,148, 10 January 2006. https://www.google.com/patents/US6986148

14. Gaouar, L., Benamar, A., Bendimerad, F.T.: Desirable requirements of cross platform mobile development tools. Electron. Devices **5**, 14–22 (2016)

15. Latif, M., Lakhrissi, Y., Nfaoui, E.H., Es-Sbai, N.: Cross platform approach for mobile application development: a survey. In: 2016 International Conference on Information Technology for Organizations Development (IT4OD), pp. 1–5, March 2016

16. Majchrzak, T., Grønli, T.M.: Comprehensive analysis of innovative cross-platform app development frameworks. In: Proceedings of the 50th Hawaii International Conference on System Sciences (2017)

17. Majchrzak, T.A., Biørn-Hansen, A., Grønli, T.M.: Progressive web apps: the definite approach to cross-platform development? In: Proceedings of the 51st Hawaii International Conference on System Sciences (2018)

18. Malavolta, I.: Beyond native apps: web technologies to the rescue! (keynote). In: Proceedings of the 1st International Workshop on Mobile Development, Mobile!SPLASH 2016, Amsterdam, Netherlands, 31 October 2016, pp. 1–2 (2016)

19. Martinez, M., Lecomte, S.: Towards the quality improvement of cross-platform mobile applications. In: 2017 IEEE/ACM 4th International Conference on Mobile Software Engineering and Systems (MOBILESoft), pp. 184–188, May 2017

20. Rakesh, P.K., Kannan, M.: Online mobile application development using ionic framework for educational institutions. Int. J. Adv. Res. Methodol. Eng. Technol. **1** (2017)

21. Prezotto, E.D., Boniati, B.B.: Estudo de frameworks multiplataforma para desenvolvimento de aplicações mobile híbridas. Universidade Federal de Santa Maria, Trabalho de Conclusão de Curso (2014)

22. StackOverflow: Developer survey results 2017 (2017). https://insights.stackoverflow.com/survey/2017

23. Unity: Cross-platform game engines (2018). https://unity3d.com/public-relations

24. Woods, V., van der Meulen, R.: Gartner says worldwide smartphone sales grew 9.7 percent in fourth quarter of 2015 (2016). http://www.gartner.com/newsroom/id/3215217

Integration Strategies of Cross-Platform Microarray Data Sets in Multiclass Classification Problem

Sebastian Student[1(✉)], Alicja Płuciennik[1,2], Krzysztof Łakomiec[1], Agata Wilk[1], Wojciech Bensz[1], and Krzysztof Fujarewicz[1]

[1] Institute of Automatic Control, Silesian University of Technology, Gliwice, Poland
sebastian.student@polsl.pl
[2] Wasko S.A., Gliwice, Poland

Abstract. Despite the increasing amount of available gene expression data, integrative analysis is still hindered by its high susceptibility to microenvironment fluctuations, resulting in inter-experiment variability known as batch effects. Therefore the development of data integration strategy is now more necessary than ever. Although several normalization algorithms have already been proposed, we believe that an effective model must rely on data migration between schemes. In this paper we apply this approach to a set of microarray data from core needle biopsy of breast cancers spanning different microarray platforms, and demonstrate its effectiveness in data preparation for unsupervised analysis and multiclass classification tasks. We propose a custom tool dedicated to defining the model structure. Additionally, we compare several pipelines of data processing, combining data normalization with different batch effect correction methods.

Keywords: Data integration · Batch effect · Multiclass classification

1 Introduction

Batch effects due to sample preparation or array variation are commonly observed across multiple series of microarray experiments. They are artifacts not related to the biological variation of scientific interest. The batch effects can influence the whole analysis, especially meta-analysis across studies. In high throughput gene expression experiments one of the biggest challenges is the data integration of different microarray platforms.

From the very beginning of microarray era the considerable impact of experiment microenvironment, such as position of the sample, time of day when the assay is performed [1] or the atmospheric composition [2], has been recognized. In large-scale studies, owing to the limitations concerning both the microarray scanner capacity and the prolonged time period of specimen acquisition, the readings cannot be conducted simultaneously. This induces further variability

© Springer Nature Switzerland AG 2019
S. Misra et al. (Eds.): ICCSA 2019, LNCS 11623, pp. 602–612, 2019.
https://doi.org/10.1007/978-3-030-24308-1_48

related to experiment conditions including, but not limited to the utilized hardware, reagents, or the responsible technician [3,4,8]. Furthermore, technological advances over the experiment timeline often result in microarray type or platform change mid-study [9].

While batch effect bias is inevitable even under the most rigorous experiment protocols, integrative analysis is not unfeasible. In particular, when analyzing data originating from several experiments, the two possible approaches are meta-analysis and merging. In the first one, each sub-experiment is evaluated independently, and the integration of obtained results (for instance in the form of accuracy measures) only occurs subsequently [10]. In the second strategy the available data is combined into a larger dataset, which is, after certain processing countering batch effect, used in further analysis.

Over the years since the problem identification, several computational methods have been proposed addressing inter-experimental variability. In 2000, the singular value decomposition (SVD) method based on linear space transformations and eigenarrays was introduced [5,6,11]. Later developed was an algorithm of Distance Weighted Discrimination (DWD) based on support vector machines [7], replacing the minimal distance criterion with a sum of inverse distances [9]. Other methods include batch mean-centering [13] and Surrogate Variable Analysis [12]. Finally, the Empirical Bayes method (also referred to as ComBat) in a parametric and non-parametric version, is now commonly used, which can be attributed to its applicability even for small sample sizes [16–18]. The rest of the paper is organized as follows: First, we give an overview of the methodology used, system architecture and data description. Then we describe the numerical experiment assumption. We describe the numerical experiment results in details. Finally, we summarize and discuss the obtained results.

2 Methodology

2.1 Data Normalization Schemes

We used three different strategies to combine data from two different microarrays platforms. First, in all used strategies we normalize each of microarray platform using FRMA algorithm [15]. The FRMA is quantile based microarray normalization method which is considered as robust and platform independent method. To normalize the input microarrays we used the custom (Entrez v19) chip definition file downloaded from Brainarray website [14]. Next we merge the normalized data by choosing the common genes in both platforms. And after that we used different algorithms to remove the batch effect. Used strategies are depicted in Fig. 1.

2.2 Classification System Description

The system described in this work is built around Spicy, an R language library (ver. 3.5.1), originally developed as a part of remote platform for hypothesis

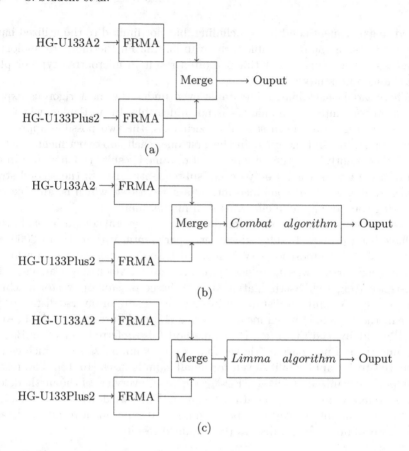

Fig. 1. Different strategies used to combine data from two different microarray platforms: (A) Without additional batch effect removing step, (B) Scheme with remove the batch effect using *Combat* algorithm, (C) Scheme with remove the batch effect using *Limma* algorithm.

testing and analysis of multiclass biomedical data [19] described in [20,21]. The instance of Spicy central to the described system is installed on high performance computing cluster Ziemowit. We used R environment and a Galaxy server tool with additional custom visual interface that constitutes a convenient alternative to the standard, form based method of defining model structure. Galaxy Server was installed on CentOS 7 virtual machine. The system is available up on request.

3   Numerical Experiment

We performed a numerical experiment using Principal Component Analysis (PCA) to check if different array platforms will cause batch effect. As a result, we made scatterplots for the first two PC and we marked the spots from different platforms with distinct colors.

For validation of investigated data combining strategies we performed both, an unsupervised and a supervised methods. For the unsupervised analysis we used hierarchical clustering (with euclidean distances) for both, samples and preselected features. We chose the features with the highest mean variance (the threshold was the 0.75 quantile). We annotated samples with the proper microarray platform. We also checked the classification accuracy for a multi-class problem. We used a popular genomic feature selection method—fold change(FC) and SVM classifier with bootstrap validation (500 iterations). The classifier was used in one versus rest (OvR) mode to manage multiple cancer types. We computed the mean quality for models in the range from 2 up to 20 features with step equal to 2. We calculated the classification error with a confidence interval for all tested variants.

3.1   Data Description

Our data set contains 241 microarrays with samples form core needle biopsy of breast cancers. Samples belong to 5 cancer types - luminal A (LumA), luminal B (LumB), basal-like (Basal), HER2-enriched (Her2) and normal-like (Normal) breast cancer. The microarrays were made using two microarray types - 200 microarrays were performed on Affymetrix HG-U133 Plus 2 arrays and 41 microarrays were performed with Affymetrix HG-U133 A2 arrays.

3.2   Results

In this section we present the influence of data migration strategies selection on microarray data unsupervised analysis and data classification. To explore the variability in analysed data and show the integration strategies differences we have used Principal Component Analysis methodology. The biggest difference we have observed between the simple integration variant A and the other variants (B and C). The platform difference variability is represented by the first principal component and the variability is much higher in the first variant A (Figs. 2, 3 and 4). As Fig. 5 indicates in the simplest integration scheme A the probe platform type groups are distinguishable in contrast to the other two methods (see Figs. 6 and 7). The results of the hierarchical clustering analysis confirm that the main variability source of 2998 most variable genes in the data integrated with strategy A is related with microarray platform group and not with the biological classes (see Figs. 8, 9 and 10).

Results of cancer type multiclass classification obtained using model built in Spicy tool are presented in Table 1. The best bootstrap based accuracy rate is obtained using the integration based on Combat algorithm (scheme B). Lowest accuracy is for the simplest integration variant based on scheme A. We denote significant difference between scheme A and the other two methods based on

Limma and Combat algorithm integration scheme (p-value < 0.05). Independently of gene number chose the data integration is necessary to obtain the best classification rate in multiplatform microarray data analysis (see Fig. 11).

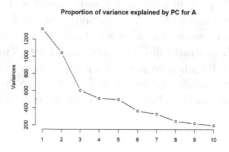

Fig. 2. The variability retained by each principal components in PCA analysis for data merging scheme A

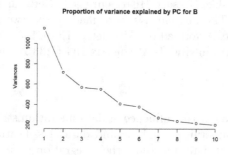

Fig. 3. The variability retained by each principal components in PCA analysis for data merging scheme B

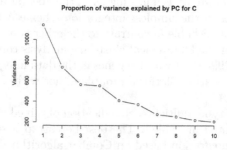

Fig. 4. The variability retained by each principal components in PCA analysis for data merging scheme C

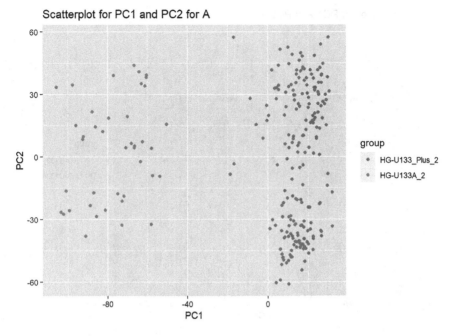

Fig. 5. PCA based probe groups analysis for data merging scheme A (Color figure online)

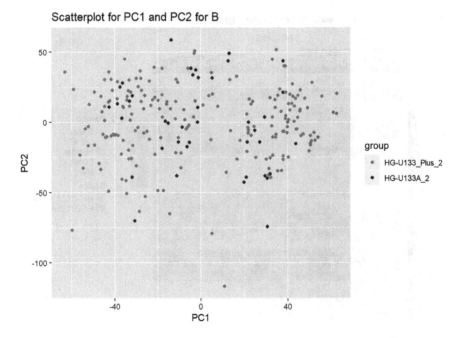

Fig. 6. PCA based probe groups analysis for data merging scheme B (Color figure online)

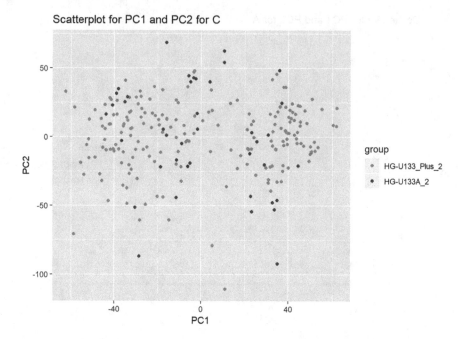

Fig. 7. PCA based probe groups analysis for data merging scheme C (Color figure online)

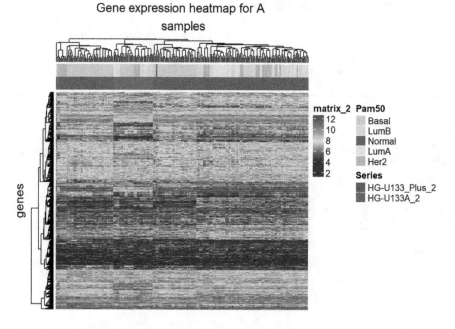

Fig. 8. Heatmap with 2998 most important features for data merging scheme A

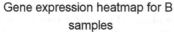

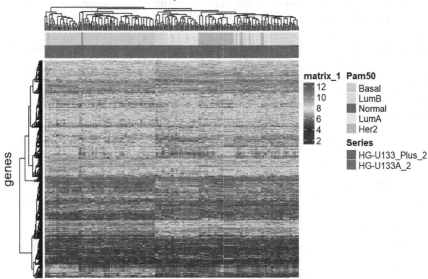

Fig. 9. Heatmap with 2998 most important features for data merging scheme B

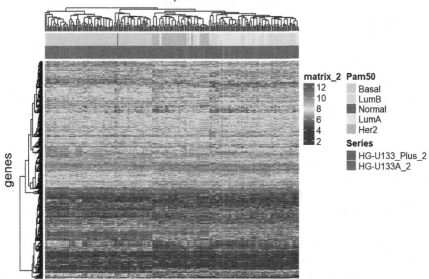

Fig. 10. Heatmap with 2998 most important features for data merging scheme C

Table 1. Bootstrap based classification accuracies with 95% confidence intervals and t-test statistics based p-values of data obtained using different combine strategies from two different microarray platforms. Strategy A - simple data merging, Strategy B - Combat algorithm, Strategy C - Limma algorithm

Algorithm	Number of features	acc	accL	accH	p-values A	p-values B	p-values C
Scheme A	20	80.93	80.59	81.28	–	0.021	0.029
Scheme B	20	81.46	81.11	81.81	0.021	–	0.903
Scheme C	20	81.39	81.04	81.75	0.029	0.903	–

on

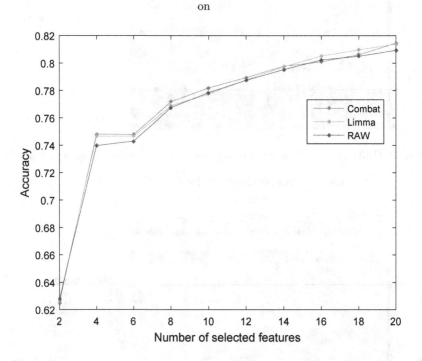

Fig. 11. Accuracy obtained for different number of selected features.

4   Conclusion

Our results show that for combining data from two different microarray platforms one need to take care about the batch effect. The general conclusion is that in case of multi-platform microarray analysis the standard data normalization is insufficient to remove the differences between compatible Affymetrix HG-U133 Plus 2 and Affymetrix HG-U133 A2 platforms. In our case the Combat algorithm was slightly better in the terms of multi-class classification problem.

Acknowledgement. This work was supported by Polish National Centre for Research and Development under Grant Strategmed2/267398/4/NCBR/2015 and Silesian University of Technology Grant 02/010/BK_18/0102 and by Polish Ministry of Science and Higher Education as part of the Implementation Doctorate program at the Silesian University of Technology, Gliwice, Poland (contract No 10/DW/2017/01/1) (AP). Data analysis was partially carried out using the Biotest Platform developed within Project n. PBS3/B3/32/2015 financed by the Polish National Centre of Research and Development (NCBiR). Calculations were performed using the infrastructure supported by the computer cluster Ziemowit (www.ziemowit.hpc.polsl.pl) funded by the Silesian BIO-FARMA project No. POIG.02.01.00-00-166/08 and expanded in the POIG.02.03.01-00-040/13 in the Computational Biology and Bioinformatics Laboratory of the Biotechnology Centre at the Silesian University of Technology. This work was partially supported by the Polish Ministry of Science and Higher Education as part of the Implementation Doctorate program at the Silesian University of Technology, Gliwice, Poland (contract No 10/DW/2017/01/1).

References

1. Lander, E.S.: Array of hope. Nat. Genet. **21**, 3–4 (1999)
2. Fare, T.L., et al.: Effects of atmospheric ozone on microarray data quality. Anal. Chem. **75**(17), 4672–4675 (2003)
3. Luo, J., et al.: A comparison of batch effect removal methods for enhancement of prediction performance using MAQC-II microarray gene expression data. Pharmacogenomics J. **10**, 278–291 (2010)
4. Leek, J.T., et al.: Tackling the widespread and critical impact of batch effects in high-throughput data. Nat. Rev. Genet. **11**, 733–739 (2010)
5. Simek, K., et al.: Using SVD and SVM methods for selection, classification, clustering and modeling of DNA microarray data. Eng. Appl. Artif. Intell. **17**(4), 417–427 (2004)
6. Lisowska, K., et al.: Unsupervised analysis reveals two molecular subgroups of serous ovarian cancer with distinct gene expression profiles and survival. J. Cancer Res. Clin. Oncol. **142**, 1239–1252 (2016)
7. Fujarewicz, K., Kimmel, M., Rzeszowska-Wolny, J., Swierniak, A.: A note on classification of gene expression data using support vector machines. J. Biol. Syst. **11**(1), 43–56 (2003)
8. Chen, C., et al.: Removing batch effects in analysis of expression microarray data: an evaluation of six batch adjustment methods. PLoS One **6**(2), e17238 (2011)
9. Perou, C.M., et al.: Adjustment of systematic microarray data biases. Bioinformatics **20**(1), 105–114 (2004)
10. Coletta, A., et al.: Batch effect removal methods for microarray gene expression data integration: a survey. Brief. Bioinform. **14**(4), 469–490 (2012)
11. Alter, O., Brown, P.O., Botstein, D.: Singular value decomposition for genome-wide expression data processing and modeling. Proc. Nat. Acad. Sci. **97**(18), 10101–10106 (2000)
12. Leek, J.T., Storey, J.D.: Capturing heterogeneity in gene expression studies by surrogate variable analysis. PLoS Genet. **3**(9), 1724–1735 (2007)
13. Sims, A.H., et al.: The removal of multiplicative, systematic bias allows integration of breast cancer gene expression datasets–improving meta-analysis and prediction of prognosis. BMC Med. Genomics **1**, 42 (2008)

14. Sandberg, R., Larsson, O.: Improved precision and accuracy for microarrays using updated probe set definitions. BMC Bioinform. **8**, 48 (2007)
15. McCall, M.N., Bolstad, B.M., Irizarry, R.A.: Frozen robust multiarray analysis (fRMA). Biostatistics (Oxford, England) **11**(2), 242–253 (2010)
16. Li, C., Johnson, W.E., Rabinovic, A.: Adjusting batch effects in microarray expression data using empirical Bayes methods. Biostatistics **8**(1), 118–127 (2006)
17. Müller, C., et al.: Removing batch effects from longitudinal gene expression - quantile normalization plus combat as best approach for microarray transcriptome data. PLoS One **11**, e0156594 (2016)
18. Cai, H., et al.: Identifying differentially expressed genes from cross-site integrated data based on relative expression orderings. Int. J. Biol. Sci. **14**, 892–900 (2018)
19. Student, S., Fujarewicz, K.: Stable feature selection and classification algorithms for multiclass microarray data. Biol. Direct **7**(33), 1–20 (2012)
20. Fujarewicz, K., et al.: Large-scale data classification system based on galaxy server and protected from information leak. In: Nguyen, N.T., Tojo, S., Nguyen, L.M., Trawiński, B. (eds.) ACIIDS 2017. LNCS (LNAI), vol. 10192, pp. 765–773. Springer, Cham (2017). https://doi.org/10.1007/978-3-319-54430-4_73
21. Pojda, K., Jakubczak, M., Student, S., Świerniak, A., Fujarewicz, K.: Comparing different data fusion strategies for cancer classification. In: Rocha, Á., Guarda, T. (eds.) ICITS 2018. AISC, vol. 721, pp. 417–426. Springer, Cham (2018). https://doi.org/10.1007/978-3-319-73450-7_40

Forensic Analysis of Mobile Banking Apps

Oluwafemi Osho[1] , Uthman L. Mohammed[1], Nanfa N. Nimzing[1],
Andrew A. Uduimoh[1] , and Sanjay Misra[2(✉)]

[1] Federal University of Technology, Minna, Nigeria
{femi.osho,a.uduimoh}@futminna.edu.ng
[2] Covenant University, Ota, Nigeria
sanjay.misra@covenantuniversity.edu.ng

Abstract. Over the years, the proliferation of mobile banking applications has been on the increase. Financial institutions are taking advantage of mobile technology to provide accessible, ubiquitous, user-friendly, convenient, and cost-effective services to their customers. The mobile banking applications access and process sensitive user data. As such, they are required to manage such data in a high secure manner and run in secure environment. This study conducts a forensic investigation of twelve popular Android m-banking apps in Nigeria to determine if the generated backups by the mobile OS do not save sensitive data; the application removes sensitive data from view when backgrounded; sensitive data are not held longer than necessary in the memory, with the memory cleared after use; minimum device access security policies are enforced by the app, and users are educated by the app about the type of PII processed and security best practices in using the app. Our findings revealed that while none of the apps saved sensitive data in generated backup, all except one held data of sensitive value in the memory of the test device and did not enforce any device access security policy. Also, none of the apps removed sensitive data when backgrounded. In addition to serving as a source of information for forensic investigators, we believe our study could assist mobile banking app developers in identifying aspects of the development process that need attention, which would lead to better secured apps.

Keywords: m-banking · Forensic · UFED · FRED

1 Introduction

Globally, there has been a constant increase in the adoption of mobile devices [1]. A forecast by Statista [2] estimated a growth in the number of smartphone users from 2.1 billion in 2016 to 2.5 billion in 2019.

With improvement in the processing power of smartphones, relatively at par with computers, and array of functionalities provided, more banks continue to take advantage of mobile technology in their quest to offer personalized and customer-oriented financial and non-financial services to their customers, in ways that are more ubiquitous, accessible, user-friendly, convenient, and cost-effective [3–8].

© Springer Nature Switzerland AG 2019
S. Misra et al. (Eds.): ICCSA 2019, LNCS 11623, pp. 613–626, 2019.
https://doi.org/10.1007/978-3-030-24308-1_49

Mobile banking, also known as m-banking, is growing in popularity. In the US, m-banking apps are one of the top three most used apps [9]. It has been reported that by 2021, over 2 billion people will have used their mobile devices for banking [10]. Reports have also shown that more bank customers are choosing it over e-banking [10, 11]. While the common activity is checking account balance, users also engage m-banking apps for paying bills and transferring money to other people.

The situation in Nigeria is no different from those in most of the other countries. There has been dramatic increase in mobile usage [12, 13]. From around 110 million mobile subscribers in 2012, the number of mobile users by December 2018 had grown by more than 120% to above 250 million [14]. This has resulted in the proliferation of mobile banking services in the country, which has contributed significantly towards the implementation of cashless economy in the country [15].

However the benefits that mobile banking offers, studies have identified security risk as one of the main factors that negatively impact its adoption [7, 16]. At the core of any m-banking app is security [3]. The fact is, attackers are less likely to gain physical access to web servers than to mobile devices. The implication is that data on memory of mobile devices could be more susceptible to unauthorized access by attackers than those on web servers [17]. Regrettably, compared to other devices, one disadvantage associated with mobile devices is increased likelihood of being stolen or lost. An attacker who lays hold of such device could gain access to sensitive data. It has been reported that attacks against mobile devices have grown in number and sophistication [18]. This underscores a need for security of these data.

The OWASP's Mobile AppSec Verification Standard (MASVS) stipulates two security verification levels: L1 and L2 [19]. The MASVS-L1 defines some sets of mobile app security best practices. On the other hand, the MASVS-L2 consists of advanced security controls beyond the standard requirements. Mobile banking apps were categorized under MASVS-L2. With regards to data storage and privacy, seven security verification requirements are stipulated for L1. For a mobile app to achieve MASVS-L2, five additional requirements must be satisfied. These include: (1) Generated backups by the mobile OS do not save sensitive data, (2) When backgrounded, the application removes sensitive data from view, (3) Sensitive data are not held longer than necessary in the memory, with the memory cleared after use, (4) Minimum device access security policies are enforced by the app, and (5) Users are educated by the app about the type of PII processed and security best practices in using the app.

Very few studies have focused on forensic analysis of mobile banking apps [20]. Fewer works have investigated Nigerian mobile banking apps. Our study therefore seeks to investigate twelve of the most popular mobile banking apps in Nigeria based on the five MASVS-L2 additional requirements.

The findings in this research will serve as a source of information for forensic investigators. It will assist mobile banking app developers in identifying aspects of the development process that need attention, which would lead to better secured apps. For users of m-banking apps, the study will not only serve as an awareness tool, but also could incentivize them to take the security of their mobile devices more seriously. For instance, being aware that PII are stored in memory for long should naturally motivate a user to be more security-conscious.

The rest of the study is organized as follows: section two summarizes related studies. In section three, the experiment setup is discussed. The findings are presented in section four. The study concludes in section five.

2 Related Studies

Many studies have been conducted in the area of forensic extraction of evidentiary artifacts in mobile devices. While many have focused on Android-based devices, some considered other operating systems, such as Windows and iOS. While some studies analyzed the devices, without focusing on any particular app, e.g. [18], in most literature, specific apps were considered.

One of the mostly covered were social networking apps. In the work of Al Mutawa et al. [21], three social networking apps: Facebook, Twitter, and MySpace were analyzed. Each was installed on Android, Blackberry, and iPhone devices. Analysis of acquired logical images revealed substantial amount of evidentiary data extracted from the Android and iPhone devices, while none was retrievable from the Blackberry device. Another study by Alyahya and Kausar [22] investigated data stored by Snapchat application on an Android device, Samsung Galaxy Note GT-N7000, using Autopsy and AXIOM Examine. Both forensic tools extracted different amount of data. However, one of the issues with AXIOM, the authors reported, was that deleted snaps could not be presented. Autopsy, on the other hand, could not preview databases and indicate senders and receivers of snaps.

Another category of apps were instant messaging apps. Walnycky et al. [23] analyzed 20 popular instant messaging apps for evidentiary data. In most of the apps, data such as passwords, pictures, audios, videos, and more were either intercepted or reconstructed. In [24], a forensic analysis of Kik messenger on Android devices was performed. Artefacts extracted included deleted contacts, messages from deleted contacts, deleted chats and exchanged files. Ovens and Morison [25] also analyzed the Kik messenger app, however on iOS device. They were able to extract deleted images, not only from the device, but also downloaded from the kik servers.

Some literature experimented on multiple apps. For instance, Azfar et al. [26] logically analyzed Android phone images on 30 instant messaging (IM), Voice-over IP (VoIP), and Argumentative and Alternative Communication (AAC) apps using XRY. Based on their findings, they proposed a forensic taxonomy for existing communication apps.

Another study that proposed a taxonomy based on evidentiary artifacts extracted from examined apps is [27]. Focusing on mobile health applications, the authors analyzed 40 mHealth apps. Data extracted include user credentials (e.g. login password and PIN), email addresses, and sequence of user locations and food habits.

A thorough search through literatures revealed very few works have been devoted to mobile banking apps. Three of the studies we found actually focused on identifying vulnerabilities on and potential attacks against m-banking apps. Jung et al. [28], in their study, forged seven m-banking apps in Korea, to explore the possibility of exploiting repackaging attack to transfer money to unintended recipients. They found that existing security measures to mitigate this were not effective. Bojjagani and Sastry [29] proposed STAMBA, a security testing framework for Android-based mobile banking apps. The framework was tested on several m-banking apps using four testing mechanisms: static and dynamic analyses, web app server security, and device forensic. These were considered on three levels of security testing: app, communication, and device levels. Their findings revealed 356 vulnerabilities that could be exploited. Another study by Chen et al. [30] performed automated security risk assessment to identify security weaknesses in mobile banking apps. Their research considered the most number of apps examined in any related studies. Proposing an assessment system that combines static program analysis of data and control flows and natural language processing, they tested 693 m-banking apps from more than 80 countries. They found, among other things, a total of 2,157 weaknesses exploitable by attackers.

One of the studies, however, similar in scope to ours, that focused on forensic examination of apps, is that of Chanajitt et al. [20]. The study focused on seven Android mobile banking apps in Thailand. Using two acquisition tools: DD and JTAG, it was discovered that several of the apps did not encrypt user data. Consequently, the authors were able to extract personally identifiable information (PII) such as users' date of birth, PIN code, account number, account type, and account balance.

So far, the only related study that considered m-banking apps in Nigeria is [31]. The authors used UFED Touch and FRED to forensically analyze five m-banking apps. Their investigation focused on identifying sensitive data held in the memory longer than usual and if the data could be used to deduce users' interactions with the apps. Similar to results in other studies, they found PII, such as user login and transaction details, were retained by the apps in the memory of the devices.

Currently in Nigeria, there are up to nineteen banks that provide mobile banking services. It is therefore pertinent to analyze other apps, to ascertain if they manage securely users' sensitive data. Our study, in addition to considering more mobile banking apps, expands the scope of investigation.

3   Experimental Setup

Materials Used
For the test device, we used a Samsung Galaxy SIII SGH-i747 device. The phone runs Android KitKat 4.4.2. Twelve popular mobile banking apps (Table 1) in Nigeria were downloaded and installed. We created user account on each. The registration, authentication, and transaction requirement for each mobile banking application are presented in Table 2. A total of 10 SIM cards were utilized, two of which were used to provide Internet connection. The remaining eight (SIM 1–8) were used in the course of transactions performed. We undertook some transactions, from July 27–August 7,

2017, such as transfer of funds, payment of bills, and recharge of mobile airtime. Table 3 presents transactions performed on the twelve m-banking apps. For acquisition of data from the mobile device, we used the Cellebrite Universal Forensic Evidence Device (UFED) Touch 4.0. To analyze acquired data, we employed the Forensic Recovery Evidence Device (FRED). To ensure that extracted data were handled in a forensically sound manner, we used a removable drive for dumping the memory.

Methods
Data Acquisition Procedures
To extract data from our test device, two acquisition methods were used: manual and physical acquisition.

Manual Acquisition
This method allows us to manually interact with the device [32]. We employed this method to ascertain if data were retained in the internal memory and cache of the mobile device after transactions were performed. To access the device memory, we opened the application manager via Setting > Application manager > All apps. This allows us to confirm any changes in the data size of the internal memory and cache of the device.

Physical Acquisition
Next, we performed a bit-by-bit imaging of the internal memory of our test device using UFED. This was to ensure that access to the lower file systems to extract all necessary data, including deleted ones. The steps followed to physically acquire the memory are presented in Table 4.

Table 1. m-banking apps version and functions

App name	Application functions							
	App version	Fund transfer	Bill payment	Airtime top-up	Open account	ATM/Branch locator	Account statement	Get help
Bank 1	v0.1.3	Yes	Yes	Yes	No	No	Yes	No
Bank 2	v1.4.0.0	Yes	Yes	Yes	No	Yes	No	No
Bank 3	v3.0.0	Yes	Yes	Yes	Yes	Yes	Yes	Yes
Bank 4	v2.3.2	Yes	Yes	Yes	No	Yes	Yes	Yes
Bank 5	v1.4.0.0	Yes	Yes	Yes	No	Yes	Yes	Yes
Bank 6	v2.2	Yes	Yes	Yes	Yes	Yes	Yes	Yes
Bank 7	v5.0.0.0	Yes	Yes	Yes	No	Yes	Yes	Yes
Bank 8	v1.6.0.0	Yes	Yes	Yes	No	Yes	Yes	Yes
Bank 9	v2.3	Yes	Yes	Yes	No	Yes	Yes	Yes
Bank 10	v3.0	Yes	Yes	Yes	No	Yes	Yes	No
Bank 11	v5.1.6	Yes	Yes	Yes	No	Yes	Yes	Yes
Bank 12	v2.4.3.22	Yes	Yes	Yes	No	Yes	Yes	Yes

Table 2. m-banking apps registration, authentication and transaction requirement

Source	Registration requirements	Authentication requirements	Transaction requirement
Bank 1	Username, Acct. No, 4-digit PIN, OTP, Password	Username, Password	4-digit PIN
Bank 2	Username, Acct. No, 4-digit PIN, OTP, Password	Username, Password	4-digit PIN
Bank 3	Phone No, Acct. No, 4-digit PIN, OTP, Password	Phone No, Password	4-digit PIN
Bank 4	Phone No, Acct. No., Email address, OTP, Password, Security Question, 4-digit PIN	Phone No, Password	4-digit PIN
Bank 5	Internet banking ID, Acct. No, 4-digit PIN, OTP, Password	Acct. No, Password	OTP
Bank 6	Phone No, Acct. No, 6-digit PIN, OTP ATM card/pin	6-digit PIN	6-digit PIN
Bank 7	Acct. No, Phone number, Internet Banking ID, Password	Username, Password	4-digit PIN
Bank 8	ATM card, Acct. No, Username, Password	Username, Password	4-digit PIN
Bank 9	Phone No, Acct. No, Username, Password, Security Question	Phone No, Password	4-digit PIN
Bank 10	Acct. No, Phone No, Username, Password	Phone No, Password	4-digit PIN
Bank 11	Internet Banking ID, Phone No, Acct. No, Password, Security Question	Username, Password	4-digit PIN
Bank 12	Acct. No, Phone No, Password, Soft token	Acct. No, Password	4-digit PIN

Analysis of Acquired Data

After manual and physical acquisition of the mobile device, we perform both manual and physical analysis of acquired data. The following process, guided by the OWASP Mobile Security Testing Guide (MSTG) [17], were followed to determine how each of the m-banking apps satisfied the five additional MASVS-L2 requirements.

Generated Backups by the Mobile OS Do Not Save Sensitive Data

The FRED was used to analyze the dumped memory of our test device, generated during physical acquisition, to check if sensitive data were present in the auto-back copies of data and settings for the m-banking apps. We followed the process presented in Table 5.

Table 3. Activities performed on the 12 m-banking apps

Transaction date (mm/dd/yy)	Transaction type	Description
07/27/17	Fund transfer	₦3,000 from Bank 4 to Bank 6
		₦5,000 from Bank 2 to Bank 3
		₦4,000 from Bank 6 to Bank 4
		₦6,000 from Bank 1 to Bank 2
		₦5,000 from Bank 3 to Bank 5
		₦5,000 from Stanbic IBTC to Bank 1
07/29/17	Fund transfer	₦3,900 from Keystone to Bank 7
		₦3,140 from Bank 9 to Bank 10
		₦17, 000 from Bank 12 to Bank 7
		₦1,050 from Bank 11 to Bank 12
	Mobile airtime recharge	₦100 on SIM 4 from Bank 10
07/31/17	Fund transfer	₦2,000 from Bank 4 to Bank 12
		₦2000 from Bank 2 to Bank 6
	Mobile airtime recharge	₦200 on SIM 1 from Bank 3
		₦100 on SIM 2 from Bank 5
		₦100 on SIM 2 from Bank 1
		₦100 on SIM 2 from Bank 6
08/03/17	Fund transfer	₦1000 from Bank 1 to Bank 6
		₦1000 from Bank 5 to Bank 2
		₦2000 from Bank 3 to Bank 6
		₦500 from Bank 6 to Bank 4
		₦2000 from Bank 4 to Bank 3
	Mobile airtime recharge	₦200 on SIM 2 from Bank 2
		₦200 on SIM 2 from Bank 4
		₦200 on SIM 2 from Bank 4
08/04/17	Fund transfer	₦1000 from Bank 12 to Access Bank
		₦3,500 from Bank 7 to Bank 9
		₦1,500 from Bank 10 to Bank 11
	Mobile airtime recharge	₦80 on SIM 4 from Bank 8
		₦50 on SIM 4 from Bank 12
		₦150 on SIM 4 from Bank 11
08/05/17	Fund Transfer	₦16,000 from Bank 10 to Bank 12
	Mobile airtime recharge	₦50 on SIM 4 from Bank 7
		₦1000 on SIM 6 from Bank 9
		₦70 on SIM 4 from Bank 11
		₦50 on SIM 4 from Bank 8
		₦100 on SIM 4 from Bank 12

(continued)

Table 3. (*continued*)

Transaction date (mm/dd/yy)	Transaction type	Description
08/06/17	Mobile airtime recharge	₦100 on SIM 7 from Bank 7
		₦100 on SIM 4 from Bank 10
		₦100 on SIM 4 from Bank 9
		₦100 on SIM 4 from Bank 11
		₦30 on SIM 4 from Bank 8
		₦20 on SIM 4 from Bank 12
08/07/17	Fund Transfer	₦2000 from Bank 5 to Bank 3
	Mobile airtime recharge	₦200 on SIM 3 from Bank 6
		₦100 on SIM 3 from Bank 3
		₦100 on SIM 2 from Bank 5
		₦100 on SIM 2 from Bank 1
		₦80 on SIM 5 from Bank 7
		₦150 on SIM 4 from Bank 12
		₦120 on SIM 8 from Bank 8
		₦30 on SIM 4 from Bank 11
		₦50 on SIM 4 from Bank 9
		₦65 on SIM 4 from Bank 10
	Bill payment	₦400 electricity bill to PHCN from Bank 4
		₦200 electricity bill to PHCN from Bank 2

Table 4. Physical acquisition procedure

1:	**START** UFED
2:	**BROWSE** to select Samsung GSM SGH-i747 Galaxy SIII
3:	**SELECT** Physical extraction
4:	**SELECT** bootloader option
5:	**SELECT** removable drive, as the destination of the extracted data
6:	**INSERT** removable drive into the USB port of the UFED
7:	**CLICK** continue
8:	**REMOVE** phone battery and reinsert (the phone should remain unpowered)
9:	**CONNECT** Cellebrite extension cable A, with T-133 yellow head, to the phone
10:	**CONNECT** the USB end of the extension cable A to the USB port of the UFED
11:	**CLICK** continue, to initialize the extraction process
12:	**DISCONNECT** phone, once extraction process is completed
13:	**REMOVE** removable drive

Table 5. Physical analysis procedure

1:	**START** FRED
2:	**INSERT** removable drive into FRED workstation
3:	**OPEN** Physical Analyser
4:	**SELECT** Samsung GSM SGH-i747 Galaxy SIII. (The memory dump in.bin format is loaded into the computer memory in clear text)
5:	**OPEN** Analysis page
6:	**OPEN** No_backup folder, for each m-banking app
7:	**ANALYSE** folder contents using Database, Hex View and File Info Format

Application Removes Sensitive Data from View when Backgrounded
Device manufacturers may provide screenshot-saving feature that is used when an application is backgrounded. While an application is displaying sensitive data, these data could be exposed if the application is screenshot. For each app, on a screen that contained sensitive information, such as login page containing login details, we clicked the home button to background the app. We then press the app switcher button to restore the app to the foreground. We observed if the app was screenshot when backgrounded by checking if the screen still contained the sensitive data.

Sensitive Data Are Not Held Longer than Necessary in the Memory, with the Memory Cleared After Use
To determine if sensitive data were only held as briefly as possible in the memory, we followed the same procedure in Table 5, however, instead of the No_backup folder, we checked for the presence of PII, registration- and transaction-related data in the Databases, Cache, Files, Logical storage, Shares_Pref, GPUCache, and APP_Webview folders under each m-banking app.

Minimum Device Access Security Policies Are Enforced by the App
Applications that process and manage sensitive data, to enforce some measure of device access security, can require users to activate some security measures, including setting a device passcode. During registration of each app, after installation, we observed if the app requested us to set a password for the test device.

Users Are Educated by the App About the Type of PII Processed and Security Best Practices in Using the App
During app registration, information on security best practices, such as advising user not to reveal their PIN to any third party, could be displayed. Also, during login for transaction, similar information could pop up. We observed each app for such measure during registration and transactions.

4   Findings

After analysis of acquired data from our test device, investigation revealed that none of the twelve m-banking apps saved sensitive data in the generated backup. Also, the entire apps often educated their users on security best practices. However, with the

Table 6. Summary of analysis of m-banking apps

m-banking apps	Sensitive data			App enforces device access security policies	App educates users
	Not saved in generated backup	Not held in memory	Removed when backgrounded		
Bank 1	Yes	No	No	No	Yes
Bank 2	Yes	No	No	No	Yes
Bank 3	Yes	No	No	No	Yes
Bank 4	Yes	No	No	No	Yes
Bank 5	Yes	No	No	No	Yes
Bank 6	Yes	No	No	No	Yes
Bank 7	Yes	No	No	No	Yes
Bank 8	Yes	No	No	No	Yes
Bank 9	Yes	No	No	No	Yes
Bank 10	Yes	No	No	No	Yes
Bank 11	Yes	No	No	Yes	Yes
Bank 12	Yes	Yes	No	No	Yes

Table 7. User information stored on mobile banking application after registration

Mobile applications	Username	Password	Transaction PIN	Security questions	Registered email address	Phone number	ATM card number/ type	Account number	Account name	Account type	OTP
Bank 1	Yes	Yes	Yes	No	No	Yes	No	Yes	Yes	Yes	No
Bank 2	Yes	No	Yes	No	No	No	Yes	Yes	Yes	Yes	No
Bank 3	Yes	Yes	No	No	Yes	Yes	No	Yes	Yes	Yes	No
Bank 4	Yes	No	No	Yes	Yes	Yes	No	Yes	Yes	No	Yes
Bank 5	Yes	No	No	No	No	Yes	No	Yes	Yes	No	No
Bank 6	Yes	No	No	No	No	Yes	No	Yes	Yes	No	No
Bank 7	Yes	No	No	No	No	No	Yes	Yes	Yes	Yes	No
Bank 8	Yes	No	No	No	No	No	No	Yes	No	No	No
Bank 9	Yes	No	No	Yes	No	Yes	No	Yes	No	No	No
Bank 10	Yes	Yes	No	No	Yes	Yes	No	Yes	Yes	No	No
Bank 11	Yes	No	No	No	No	No	No	No	Yes	Yes	No
Bank 12	No	No	No	No	No	No	No	No	No	No	No

Table 8. User- and application-generated data after transaction

Mobile applications	Account balance	Amount transferred	Beneficiary details	Date of transaction	Transaction time
Bank 1	Yes	Yes	Yes	Yes	Yes
Bank 2	Yes	Yes	Yes	Yes	Yes
Bank 3	Yes	Yes	Yes	Yes	Yes
Bank 4	Yes	Yes	Yes	Yes	Yes
Bank 5	Yes	Yes	Yes	Yes	Yes
Bank 6	Yes	Yes	Yes	No	No
Bank 7	Yes	Yes	Yes	Yes	Yes
Bank 8	No	Yes	No	Yes	Yes
Bank 9	Yes	No	No	No	No
Bank 10	No	Yes	Yes	Yes	Yes
Bank 11	No	No	No	No	No
Bank 12	No	No	No	No	No

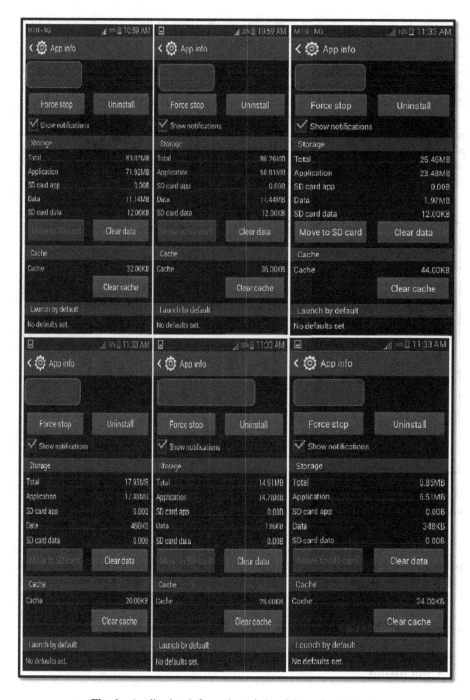

Fig. 1. Application information of six of the m-banking apps

exception of Bank 12, the apps held sensitive user data in their memory longer than necessary in the memory. Evidence of increase in the size of data in the internal memory and cache of the mobile device, after transactions, for six of the apps are presented in Fig. 1. Our findings also revealed that none of the apps removed sensitive data when backgrounded. Regrettably, it was discovered, only Bank 11 enforced any device access security policy. A summary of the findings are presented in Table 6.

Regarding sensitive data being held in the memory, data such as username, phone number, account number, and account name were displayed by most of the apps. In few of them, we were able to retrieve password, transaction PINs, security question, registered email address, ATM card number/type, account type, and OTP. Table 7 contains the user registration information retrieved from the apps.

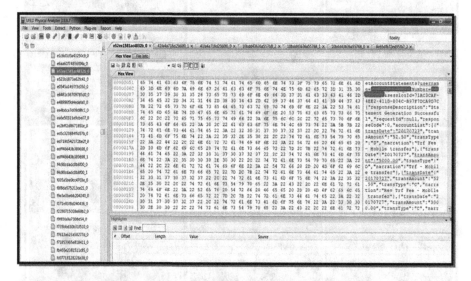

Fig. 2. Screenshot of memory dump showing user name, account number, beneficiary details, transferred amount and transaction timestamp for one of the m-banking apps

Other sensitive data generated after transaction were found. A summary of the performance of each app in this regard is presented in Table 8. We retrieved account balance, amount transferred, details of beneficiary, and date and time of transaction from Banks 1–5 and 7. Banks 6, 8–10 stored some of the data. We did not retrieve any of such data from Banks 11 and 12. Figure 2 shows the transaction-related information extracted from one of the m-banking apps.

5   Conclusion

In this study, we conducted forensic examination of twelve popular Android m-banking apps in Nigeria and assessed their performance based on five OWASP MASVS-L2 requirements. From our findings, while all of the apps performed well in two of the requirements: not saving sensitive data in backup generated by the mobile OS and educating users on security best practices, all except one of the apps held data of sensitive value, such as PII and transaction-generated data, in the memory of the test device and did not enforce any device access security policy. All the m-banking apps failed the requirement of removing sensitive data when backgrounded.

Our findings corroborate those in [20] and [31]. We also align with their recommendations on the need for app developers to consider security as a critical necessity right from the design phase and incorporate the guidelines stipulated in standard documents, such as the OWASP Mobile Security Testing Guide [17] and Mobile AppSec Verification Standard [19].

References

1. Ntantogian, C., Apostolopoulos, D., Marinakis, G., Xenakis, C.: Evaluating the privacy of Android mobile applications under forensic analysis. Comput. Secur. **42**, 66–76 (2014)
2. Statista: Number of smartphone users worldwide from 2014 to 2020 (in billions), 29 March 2019
3. Nie, J., Hu, X.: Mobile banking information security and protection methods. In: 2008 International Conference on Computer Science and Software Engineering Mobile, pp. 587–590 (2008)
4. Odumeru, J.A.: Going cashless: adoption of mobile banking in Nigeria. Arab. J. Bus. Manag. Rev. (Niger. Chapter) **1**(2), 9–17 (2013)
5. Shaikh, A.A., Karjaluoto, H.: Telematics and informatics mobile banking adoption: a literature review. Telematics Inform. **32**(1), 129–142 (2015)
6. Bankole, F.O., Bankole, O.O., Brown, I.: Mobile banking adoption in Nigeria. Electron. J. Inf. Syst. Dev. Ctries. **47**(2), 1–23 (2011)
7. Bankole, O., Cloete, E.: Mobile banking: a comparative study of South Africa and Nigeria. In: IEEE Africon 2011, Livingstone, Zambia, pp. 1–6. IEEE (2011)
8. Fenu, G., Pau, P.L.: An analysis of features and tendencies in mobile banking apps. Procedia Comput. Sci. **56**, 26–33 (2015). Elsevier Masson SAS
9. Citi: Mobile Banking One of Top Three Most Used Apps by Americans, 2018 Citi Mobile Banking Study Reveals (2018). (30 Mar 2019)
10. Juniper Research: Mobile Banking Users to Reach 2 Billion by 2020, Representing More than 1 in 3 of Global Adult Population, 30 Mar 2019
11. Elkhodr, M., Shahrestani, S., Kourouche, K.: A proposal to improve the security of mobile banking applications. In: 2012 Tenth International Conference on ICT and Knowledge Engineering A, pp. 260–265 (2012)
12. Osho, O., Yisa, V.L., Ogunleke, O.Y., Abdulhamid, S.M.: Mobile spamming in Nigeria: an empirical survey. In: 2015 International Conference on Cyberspace Governance, pp. 150–159 (2015)
13. Agwu, E.M., Carter, A.: Mobile phone banking in Nigeria: benefits, problems and prospects. Int. J. Bus. Commer. **3**(6), 50–70 (2014)
14. NCC: Monthly Subscriber Technology Data. Subscriber Statistics, 29 Mar 2019
15. Osho, O., Ajisola, T.H., Onoja, A.D., Ugwu, J.N.: Were we ready in the first place?: an analysis of cashless policy implementation in Nigeria. In: CEUR Workshop Proceedings, pp. 70–78 (2016)

16. Islam, M.S.: Systematic literature review: security challenges of mobile banking and payments system. Int. J. u- e-Serv. Sci. Technol. **7**(6), 107–116 (2014)
17. Mueller, B., Scheier, S., Willemsen, J.: Mobile Security Testing Guide (MSTG). Open Web Application Security Project (OWASP), pp. 1–412 (2019)
18. Osho, O., Ohida, S.O.: Comparative evaluation of mobile forensic tools. IJ Inf. Technol. Comput. Sci. **1**(January), 74–83 (2016)
19. Scheier, S., Willemsen, J.: OWASP Mobile Application Security Verification Standard (MASVS) version 1.1.3. Open Web Application Security Project (OWASP), 99. 1–32 (2019)
20. Chanajitt, R., Viriyasitavat, W., Choo, K.R.: Forensic analysis and security assessment of Android m-banking apps. Aust. J. Forensic Sci. **50**(1), 3–19 (2018)
21. Al Mutawa, N., Baggili, I., Marrington, A.: Forensic analysis of social networking applications on mobile devices. Digit. Invest **9**(Suppl), S24–S33 (2012)
22. Alyahya, T., Kausar, F.: Snapchat analysis to discover digital forensic artifacts on Android smartphone. Procedia Comput. Sci. **109**, 1035–1040 (2017)
23. Walnycky, D., Baggili, I., Marrington, A., Moore, J., Breitinger, F.: Network and device forensic analysis of Android social-messaging applications. Digit. Invest. **14**, S77–S84 (2015)
24. Adebayo, O.S., Sulaimon, S.A., Osho, O., Abdulhamid, S.M., Alhassan, J.K.: Forensic analysis of Kik messenger on Android devices. In: 2nd International Engineering Conference (IEC 2017), Minna, Nigeria (2017)
25. Ovens, K.M., Morison, G.: Forensic analysis of Kik messenger on iOS devices. Digit. Invest. **17**, 40–52 (2016)
26. Azfar, A., Choo, K.R., Liu, L.: An Android communication app forensic taxonomy. J. Forensic Sci. **61**(5), 1337–1350 (2016)
27. Azfar, A., Choo, K.R., Liu, L.: Forensic taxonomy of popular Android mHealth apps. In: 21st Americas Conference on Information Systems, pp. 1–19 (2015)
28. Jung, J.H., Kim, J.Y., Lee, H.C., Yi, J.H.: Repackaging attack on android banking applications and its countermeasures. Wirel. Pers. Commun. **73**, 1421–1437 (2013)
29. Bojjagani, S., Sastry, V.N.: STAMBA: security testing for Android mobile banking apps. In: Thampi, S., Bandyopadhyay, S., Krishnan, S., Li, K.C., Mosin, S., Ma, M. (eds.) Advances in Signal Processing and Intelligent Recognition Systems. AISC, vol. 425, pp. 671–683. Springer, Cham (2016). https://doi.org/10.1007/978-3-319-28658-7_57
30. Chen, S., Meng, G., Su, T., Fan, L., Xue, M., Xue, Y., et al.: AUSERA: large-scale automated security risk assessment of global mobile banking apps. arXiv:180505236, pp. 1–14 (2018)
31. Uduimoh, A.A., Ismaila, I., Osho, O., Abdulhamid, S.M.: Forensic analysis of mobile banking applications in Nigeria. i-manager's. J. Mobile Appl. Technol. **6**(1), 9–20 (2018)
32. Srivastava, H., Tapaswi, S.: Logical acquisition and analysis of data from android mobile devices. Inf. Comput. Secur. **23**(5), 450–475 (2015)

Investigating Enterprise Resource Planning (ERP) Effect on Work Environment

Quoc Trung Pham[1], Sanjay Misra[2(✉)], Le Ngoc Huyen Huynh[1], and Ravin Ahuja[1,2,3]

[1] School of Industrial Management, Ho Chi Minh City University of Technology (VNU-HCM), HCMC, Ho Chi Minh City, Vietnam
pqtrung@hcmut.edu.vn, ngochuyen.huynh@gmail.com,
ravinahujadce@gmail.com
[2] Covenant University, Ota, Nigeria
sanjay.misra@covenantuniversity.edu.ng
[3] Viswakarma Skill University, Gurugram, India

Abstract. This study aims to identify the effect of ERP system on the work environment of end users, in regarding of problem-solving support, job discretion, management visibility and cross-functionality, authority and decision rights and overall impact on the organization. This research used the survey methodology to collect data from the end-users who work for enterprises with an ERP system in Ho Chi Minh City, Vietnam. SPSS and Amos were used to test hypotheses through the Structural Equation Modeling (SEM). The study reports the impact of ERP system product performance in term of problem-solving support, job discretion, management visibility and cross-functionality, authority and decision rights and overall impact on the organization in the period of post-ERP implementation in the viewpoint of end-user in Vietnam. Based on this result, some managerial implications have been suggested.

Keywords: ERP · Work performance · Problem-solving · Job discretion · Product performance · Cross-functionality · Vietnam

1 Introduction

Overall observation the demand of an organization to implement an Enterprise Resources Planning (ERP) has been extensively recognized to reduce the errors caused by users manually input, promptitude the flow of streamline of information, and expectantly improve the comprehended decision making during of the whole process in organizations. As current, the ERP system is not required anymore in the introduction phase. For business, heretofore the beginning of startup stage, the consideration looking for a good operating system is the once necessity investment. This system has been an element of the information system which will be maintained and running during the whole business life of an organization.

Even this is an expensive and extremely a complicated system as the cost of ERP is not only for licensing fee or an implementation fee but also for training, development of customization, process redesign, maintenance, upgrade and support [13] and ERP

© Springer Nature Switzerland AG 2019
S. Misra et al. (Eds.): ICCSA 2019, LNCS 11623, pp. 627–644, 2019.
https://doi.org/10.1007/978-3-030-24308-1_50

will be the core system, this means no permissive for failure thus high expectation for the guarantee reliability and security required. Moreover, the business process that should be coded or configured which are incredibly complex base on per business operation or per location for customization follow their practice or local regulation [9]. But being the reason behind these investments is the firm looking for the enables to reduce the transaction costs of the business and improve organizational efficiency, effectiveness which basically help for its productivity and profitability [2]. Once it is the way to help users who are increased process efficiency, can connect easily with cross function and possibly assess data without any affair of its accuracy. And the ERP is defined as the developing common system which applying in business operation process and data integrated from all users from all functions areas. Follow the finding from Fryer [10] that the list of ERP implementation's tangible benefits is the optimization of inventory, reduction of personnel, enhancement of productivity. It's also given other intangible benefit to the organization are the perceptibility of information, process improvement, the quickest to react of customer and reduction of cost.

In the early 2000s, ERP solutions were the first to enter into Vietnam market, which can be considered is a proof for confirmation that ERP solution is the prospecting way in helping their business more efficiency and effectiveness. However, reported from the Vietnam Chamber of Commerce and Industry in the middle of 2006 that the successful implementation of the ERP of the Vietnam enterprise is only 1.1%. In 2013, the local vendor reported that the sales of business software such as ERP were rumbustious increases in demand in various industries and likely to be expansion area and account for a large portion of software budgets in data analysis and database software. But only 17% is the rate of the enterprise using the ERP packages [24]. This is the lowest rate when doing the comparative to many developing countries since most enterprises is still not aware of the importance of the ERP solution. Besides, the barrier from the limitation of their technical and financial resource, and the low of the number expert who has to fulfill experience and practices in the ERP implementation solution field in Vietnam.

Notwithstanding with the fact was shared above for situation in Vietnam context, the of huge of investment required for implementation and maintenance an ERP system, but the success rate is quite low which means the benefit is not highly guaranteed for an organization even the ERP system performance as an effective tool that enhances the performance and extended complete advantage. Additional the limitation of number research which studies the application ERP in Vietnam while an early testing focus on identifying which determinants of ERP system impact on the firms' performance in case of Small and Medium Enterprises [19, 20]. And current no investigation has been found to have examined on the impact of ERP usage on the end users level of Vietnam's companies to acquire an exceeding insight of this area.

For current the understanding of how the individual and organization are affected in post-implementation and how the benefit is significant and critical which have received very little consideration [1, 12].

With the novelty of this system applied to Vietnam, in which different employee culture, education level, the management need more information to understand the user perspective of usage the ERP post-implementation in Vietnam to develop and perfect ERP and improve processes for an organization which lead improve performance for an individual as well as an organization. And how the organization utilizes of these applications for contributing to their user performance efficiency and effectiveness. For that reason, this study aims to provide an investigation on how the impact of ERP system usage on end-user levels in Vietnam specifically at Ho Chi Minh City.

This research has the focal point on the impact of ERP usage to end-user level and starting for these purposes: (1) Measuring the impact of ERP implementation on user performance; (2) Suggesting the managerial implications to leverage and promote the positive impact of ERP on user performance for finding the way to leverage its benefit in improving the performance for end users and for the organization.

The structure of this paper is organized as follows: (2) concepts & literature review, (3) hypotheses and research model, (4) research process, (5) analysis results, (6) discussion and implications, and finally (7) conclusion.

2 Concepts and Literature Review

2.1 ERP System Performance

There are many ways of presenting and there are many different interpretations of Enterprise Resource Planning (ERP) concepts. In this context, ERP is a software solution which can install on the computer or using via a cloud platform. It can be used in different functions and department (Finance, Production, Supply Chain, Human Resource...). ERP data were stored centralize in the data pool, that support all information in the enterprise is managed by the ERP. From theory, ERP system has been one of the most significant systems in recent times and play a large supporting role in the most of major industries including airline, telecommunication, transportation, education, etc. [11].

There are several available methods for measuring ERP system performance. Some of the methods are played in the financial return on investment calculation. Wei, Liou and Lee [26] identified that has three performance measurements, including the performance indicator (PI) structure construction, fuzzy group ERP performance measurement and result from analysis and system improvement.

Since the ERP system is an enterprise level system so that the performance will be a complexity of measurement. Another approach based on the flow network model is used by Chen and Lin [4]. It mentions an ERP system performance depending upon the result of the ERP examination of the user involved.

However, difference researcher refers to different dimensions to assess the IS system which leads the comparison becomes more challenging. To overwhelm this barrier, DeLone [5] updated the successful model to the combination of three dimensions "information quality", "system quality", and "service quality" for identifying the IS system. Measurement the system quality via some characteristics such as usability, adaptability, reliability, the response time (e.g. downtime), easy for use, easy for learning are examples of qualities that valued by users. For information, quality characteristics are captured via completeness, easy for understanding, personalization, relevance, security or conciseness. Some characteristics of service quality are quality of roles in supporting users in term of the empathy, accuracy, technical competency and responsiveness of staffs [5, 6, 21]. These researches also provided extensive other elements to measure user satisfaction via time-saving, accuracy, precision, and format. In this study, the most focusing will under the "ERP system performance".

2.2 Work and Work-Life in an Organization

Correlation end-user satisfaction and their constructive perception about a new ERP are commonly used to measure of system success [6]. And Calisir [3] found that user's perception of usefulness is a significant determinant of end-user satisfaction, which assists in the maximum utilization of the ERP system while following the critical success factor of the studies from Zhang, Lee and Banerjee [27], user involvement was determined the ERP system implementation. For this study, "work and work-life in an organization" refers to the post-implementation impact of an ERP system for end users in term of problem-solving support, job discretion, and management visibility and cross-functionality, authority and decision rights, and overall impact on the organization which was summarized by Wickramasinghe [25].

2.3 ERP Adoption

ERP implementation issues are not only just technical but also compound wider behaviors factors. The management needs to realize the system adoption from the user's point of view to ready arrange for their employee to overcome the new challenge to learn how to make better utilization of the technology to bring in intangible benefits. Moreover, the implementation of an ERP system provides for extending to the point of change in the organization and its processes. Hence, the management of the organization must understand that the support from an organization is significant for the successful adoption of an ERP system. The installment may require short term and more focus on designation, but the post implements of the system required more change in execution, structure, working process and coordination across functions.

3 Hypotheses and Research Model

3.1 Research Hypothesis

Impact of ERP on Problem-Solving

DeLone and McLean [6] used the level of the individual impact term to clarify the effect of information on the receiver. At the level of an end user, the system provided richness information that was unknown in previous, but it is relevant to solving problems and making decisions [7]. Overall, the last studied literature review above suggests that ERP product performance positively impacts on problem-solving support. Therefore, hypothesis 1 could be stated as follows:

H1. ERP system performance positively impact on problem-solving.

Impact of ERP on Job Discretion, Management Visibility, and Cross-Functionality
With ERP systems, the firms can form a specific resource that guides both internal and external collaboration. According to Ruivo and Neto [23], ERP system helps users to collaborate, up, down and cross their department, company, and industry. On the other hand, the process of the software will be integrated for cross functions. This design of ERP support gives more job discretion. Besides, the integrated information from front end to back end givens for the expansion opportunity for the user can access the information easily with greater support for flexibility in doing their jobs and in exchanges their work priorities. Therefore, hypothesis 2 could be stated as follows:

H2. ERP system performance positively impact on job discretions, management visibility, and cross-functionality.

Impact of ERP on Authority and Decision Rights
Due to the visibility of information provided by the ERP, there is an increase in both control and empower through the usage of ERP. The greater visibility of information makes employees more visible to others in the organization, who can then easily exercise process and outcome control [8]. Additionally, in studies of Ellis [7] and Jasperson et al. [16], an enterprise system leads to greater equality of participation in decision making for low-status participants. Hence, the end-user enjoys the reduction of power, authority and decision rights. Therefore, it is hypothesized:

H3. ERP system performance negatively impact on authority and decision right.

Impact of ERP on the Organizational Performance
In the studies of DeLone [5], the organizational impact is used to explain the effect of IS on organization performance. In other research of Mason [18], the hierarchy of influence levels in an organization was proposed. However, Petter, Delone and McLean [21] have used another term that is "net benefits" for explaining the extent to which the system is contributing to the success of individuals, groups, organizations, industries, and nations. All of the above researches fully supports that ERP performance positively impacts on the organizational performance. Therefore, it is hypothesized:

H4. ERP system performance positively impact on organizational performance.

3.2 Research Model

From the above discussion, the research model could be summarized as follows (See Fig. 1):

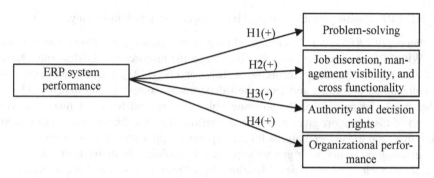

Fig. 1. The proposed research model

4   Research Process

The scales will support measurement the impact on work and work life of ERP and the Likert scales with five points where from 1 – Strongly disagree, 2 – Disagree, 3 – Neutral, 4 – Agree and 5 – Strongly agree. There are 5 items measure for ERP system product performance and 17 items measure for impacts of ERP on the work environment. Besides that, some demographic factors were added to the survey questionnaire such as company size, type, year of experience, position… for more detail findings.

This research was conducted in 2 steps: primary qualitative research for finalizing the questionnaire, and quantitative research for evaluating the research model. The primary qualitative research was used to adjust and to supplement of measurement scales. The interviews were arranged to involve 20 respondents. The questionnaire was translated into Vietnamese for support interviewer easy to understand. The quantitative research was used to evaluate measurement scales and model. In this phase, the survey was implemented by directly send to respondents who are currently using ERP for their work or work for the company which has completed an ERP project.

The sample size for this research base on experience principal, number of items is 22, but the minimum sample size should be 5×1 for each observed variable follow the conduct of Hair et al. [14]. So that minimum sample size should be $5 \times 22 = 110$. In order to support the hypothesis test, this research tries to collect ≥ 150 samples. And data was collected by convenience sampling which is non-probability sampling type for simply. And data will be consolidation from the online source and manual typing from hardcopy after gathering the return of hardcopy survey result.

Then, the collected data will be tested by SPSS & AMOS software. Some techniques for data analysis include Descriptive statistics, Cronbach's Alpha, Exploratory factor analysis (EFA), Confirmatory factor analysis (CFA), Structural equation model (SEM) analysis for the hypothesis test, etc.

5   Analysis Results

5.1   Sample Description

The main research was conduct by a survey of the ERP end user from all departments who are working at any company that is using ERP for their operation. The industrial is no limitation but the boundary of selection only within Ho Chi Minh city. To have a correct result, the respondent should have to confirm they are using an ERP. Detail of total survey collected for the pilot was not be used for main research due to the changes in the questionnaire. In the main phase, the detailed survey was collected by off-line hardcopy and online via google form as detail given in Table 1:

Table 1. Description of data collection

Sample	Received	Valid verify	Rate
Online	89	70	79%
Offline	150	112	75%
Total	239	182	76%

The 182 samples were coded for prepared input data for analysis with using the SPSS version 24.0. The analysis result was delivered via the list in Table 2. The matching criteria and no missing and duplicate to drive the reliability result, the first input was removed all duplicate and missing the required information.

Table 2. Descriptive statistics of sample data

	Frequency	Percentage
Respondent level		
Professional	112	61.5
Manager	55	30.2
Senior manager	10	5.5
Non-declare and other	5	2.7
Respondent year of using ERP experience		
Less than 03 years	60	33.0
From 03 years to 05 years	36	19.8
Above 05 years	83	45.6
Non-declare	3	1.6
ERP use duration by the firm		
Less than 03 years	15	8.2
From 03 years to 05 years	13	7.1
Above 05 years	151	83.0
Non-declare	3	1.6
Total employee (Company size)		
Less than 500 employees	34	18.7
From 500 to 1,000 employees	12	6.6
Above 1,000 employees	131	72.0
Non-declare	5	2.7
Industrial		
Consumers	123	67.6
Services	23	12.6
Financial	14	7.7
Other and non-declare	22	12.1

The above sample description expressed the sample characteristics are usable and appropriate for the study of ERP impact on work and work-life of end users.

5.2 Descriptive Statistics on Main Variables

Table 3 summarized the descriptive statistics of all variables.

Table 3. Descriptive statistics of main variables

Item		Minimum	Maximum	Mean	Stdev.
ERP1	ERP system performance	2	5	4.27	.706
ERP2		2	5	3.90	.787
ERP3		2	5	3.95	.707
ERP4		2	5	3.97	.837
ERP5		2	5	4.05	.741
ERP6		2	5	4.22	.755
PRS7	Problem-solving	2	5	3.87	.713
PRS8		2	5	3.69	.784
PRS9		2	5	3.63	.775
PRS10		1	5	3.84	.797
JMC11	Job discretion, Management	2	5	3.76	.784
JMC12	visibility, and Cross-functionality	2	5	3.75	.816
JMC13		2	5	3.88	.775
JMC14		2	5	3.85	.786
JMC15		2	5	3.85	.797
ADR16	Authority and Decision rights	1	5	2.85	.937
ADR17		1	4	2.37	.855
ADR18		1	5	3.14	1.078
ADR19		1	5	2.87	1.041
ORG20	Organizational performance	1	5	4.09	.738
ORG21		1	5	4.15	.701
ORG22		1	5	3.90	.804

5.3 Reliability Analysis Cronbach's Alpha Test for Each of Scales

The reliability of the scale was figured out by the internal consistency method using the Cronbach's Alpha coefficient. Using Cronbach's Alpha coefficient of dependence method to testing and remove the dummy factors. Purpose of using the calculation of corrected item-total correlation will help to exclude those variables that do not contribute much to the description of the concept for measurement investigation [15]. The result is summaries in Table 4.

Table 4. Cronbach Alpha analysis results

Scales/Item	Factors	Scale mean if item deleted	Scale variance if item deleted	Corrected item-total correlation	Cronbach's Alpha if item deleted
ERP1	ERP system	20.10	7.427	.551	.755
ERP2	performance	20.47	6.880	.617	.738
ERP3		20.42	7.439	.546	.756
ERP4		20.40	7.048	.517	.764
ERP5		20.32	7.544	.480	.771
ERP6		20.15	7.291	.536	.758
Cronbach's Alpha		.789			
PRS7	Problem-solving	11.15	3.873	.671	.784
PRS8		11.34	3.683	.654	.789
PRS9		11.40	3.655	.679	.778
PRS10		11.19	3.678	.638	.797
Cronbach's Alpha		.831			
JMC11	Job discretion,	15.33	6.653	.632	.829
JMC12	Management	15.34	6.104	.759	.794
JMC13	visibility, and Cross-	15.20	6.594	.662	.821
JMC14	functionality	15.24	6.626	.639	.827
JMC15		15.24	6.634	.623	.831
Cronbach's Alpha		.852			
ADR16	Authority and	8.38	4.824	.616	.574
ADR17	Decision rights	8.87	5.728	.434	.682
ADR18		8.09	4.726	.501	.645
ADR19		8.36	5.050	.450	.677
Cronbach's Alpha		.709			
ORG20	Organizational	8.04	1.954	.789	.835
ORG21	performance	7.98	1.961	.852	.785
ORG22		8.24	1.894	.716	.906
Cronbach's Alpha		.888			

In summary, all 22 observed variables are accepted and will be used in the next running steps of discriminant validity.

5.4   Uni-Dimensionality Analysis Test for Each of Scales

Follow Hair et al. [14], the uni-dimensional test is to evaluate even if items, on each scale, which have significantly correlated with each other and illustrated that a single concept. Hence, the high loading item on a single factor of every scales should be contained. When analysis, the researcher normally will focus on some of the standardization scores (0.5 < Kaiser-Meyer-Olkin (MKO) < 1; Bartlett's Test of Sphericity with Sig. < 0.05; Cumulative factor loading > 50%).

All the factors were run only 1 time and the result was matched with the requirement, however only the factor ERP system performance which takes two times in running for refinement. Because of the result of the first run with KMO lower than 50% which was reached 48.9% for the first run even Sig.: .000. The refinement result of this factor which has one change with eliminating ERP6 which contribute only 0.473 in extraction, lead the percentage of cumulative increased to 52.7% (>50%).

And the result for all factor after running the uni-dimensional analysis could be summarized as follows: 5 factors were extracted with explained above 50% (the lowest at 52.722% and the highest at 82.322%) of total variance after refinement. The KMO result was from the lowest at 0.677 to highest at 0.784 which were match with condition requirements of for KMO index 0.5 < KMO < 1. Besides that, the factor loadings of 21 items were various from 0.643 to 0.941 and which were satisfied with the threshold criteria 0.5. So that we can conclude that factor analysis is suitable with research data (KMO > 0.5), moreover, this data is adequate for factor analysis and can explain more than 50% of the variations.

5.5   Confirmatory Factor Analysis (CFA)

After tested the reliability Cronbach's Alpha scales and dimensionality, researchers can use the Confirmatory Factor Analysis (CFA) to clear hypotheses about the number of factors and dimension contain it items and additional present the links between specific items and specific elements or between the elements. The CFA method also helps analyze to confirm whether the measurement model is satisfied with research data or not, if the measurement model is appropriated with the research data, CFA also assess the theoretical value of measurement model [14]. And the result of CFA can provide compulsory evidence of the convergent and discriminant validity of theoretical constructs. The CFA approach allows analysts to determine the convergent validity of each observation variable of the concept of the measure and the discriminant validity between concepts in the research model.

Moreover, according to Hair et al. [14], the researcher confirmed that it could not show the validity and reliability of the standard input data, the research will able to utilize SEM's outcome unstandardized characteristics. Current there are having distinct kind of useful measuring for building the validity and reliability which such as Composite Reliability (CR) and Average Variance Extract (AVE).

5.6   Composite Reliability (CR) Testing

According to Hair et al. [14], the latent variable's composite reliability evaluation was recommended should be greater than the default limit of 0.70 to have better reliability and internal consistency. The CR is calculated for each factor which like the Cronbach's Alpha implementation, that will run separately for each factor.

Follow Hair et al. [14], with the Standardized Regression Weights of all observed variable were above 0.5 (from 0.518 to 0.94), the Average Variances Extracted (AVE) were from 0.5 to 0.7, combined with the Composite Reliability (CR) were higher than 0.7, all scales could be confirmed to be unidimensional and convergent (Table 5).

Table 5. Summary of CR and AVE values

Code	Factor	CR	AVE	Assessment
ERP_F	ERP system product performance	76%	51%	Accepted
PRS_F	Problem-solving support	80%	57%	
JMC_F	Job discretion, management visibility & cross-functionality	82%	61%	
ADR_F	Authority and decision rights	72%	49%	
ORG_F	Impact on organization	90%	75%	

5.7 Discriminant Validity Testing

Correlation coefficients between factors show that all correlation coefficients are <1 statistically significant. Thus, the above concepts achieve distinct values. Can be able to verify the discriminant validity of the concepts in the Saturate model, in that model, the concepts can be able to be correlated together. That could be processed to test correlation in the total range of all concept whether having the different or not. If it is different, the scales are reached the discriminant validity. In the analysis result, the P is 0.000, <0.05, the scales are valuable for discriminant.

5.8 Test the Model Fit

To test the suitability of the model with data, analysts often depend on multiple indicators. Follow Hair et al. [14], the indicator of the model fit is specific default threshold can be summarized in Table 6.

Table 6. Indicators of the model fit of CFA

Indicator	Threshold
Absolute Fit Indices	
Chi-Square/degree of freedom (df): X2/df	<2 (In some cases, ~3 is acceptable)
The goodness of Fit Index (GFI)	≥ 0.9
Root Mean Square Error Approximation (RMSEA)	≤ 0.08
Incremental Fit Indices	
Tucker Lewis Index (TLI)	≥ 0.9
Comparative Fit Index (CFI)	≥ 0.9

The CFA analysis result could be summarized in Fig. 2.

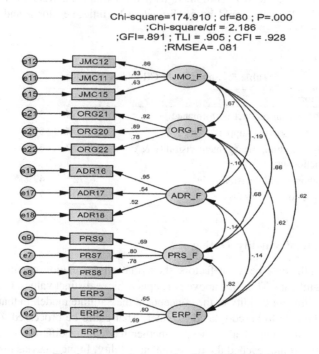

Fig. 2. The analysis result of the CFA model

Follow more than 4 round time to run the analysis, 06 more items (ERP4, ERP6, PRS10, JMC13, JMC14, ADR19) were deleted due to not achieving the standard criteria. After complete last time with 15 observation variable, the result after calculating CFA from AMOS tool, the CFA result showed that the model achieved high rate in market data compatibility TLI = 0.905 and CFI = 0.928 matching the arrange of the better rate from 0.9 to 1. The above data shows that the survey data is quite consistent with market data in the case study. At the same, Chi-square/df adjusted to 2.186 (less than 3), combine with RMSEA approximation 0.08 presented that the data matched the case study. Conclusion: the measurement model is a good fit.

5.9   Structural Equation Modeling Hypothesis Testing

Structural equation modeling hypothesis-testing measurement indicated an adequate fit between the observed covariance matrix and theoretic covariance matrix. Similarly, to the CFA model, the SEM used to estimate the parameter of the model. SEM analysis will continue to develop base on the result of refined scales measurement that had been done in the CFA analysis step. In the CFA step, the analysis starting by evaluation the proposal structure model via scan through the indicator of the Model fit, this support to ensure that the collected data is based on the model fit. And the SEM step, these indicators were used to assess the model's reliability for the actual data. Here is the SEM analysis result in detail (Fig. 3):

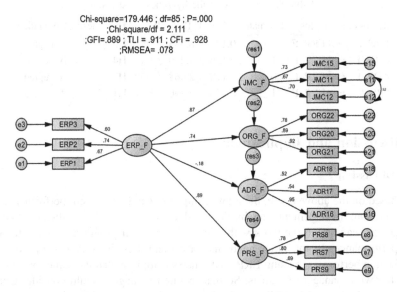

Fig. 3. The analysis result of the SEM model

All these outcome indicators were satisfying the standard requirement follow Hair et al. [14] and meet with the Goodness of Fit Indices. Thus, it can be concluded that the theoretical model is suitable and can be used to test the expected and hypothesized relationship in the hypothesis model. The detail result shown in Table 7.

Table 7. Summary result of the SEM model

Indicator	Result	Assessment
Absolute Fit Indices		Accepted
Chi-Square/degree of freedom (df): X2/df	2.111	
The goodness of Fit Index (GFI)	Approximal 0.9	
Root Mean Square Error Approximation (RMSEA)	0.078	
Incremental Fit Indices		Accepted
Tucker Lewis Index (TLI)	0.911	
Comparative Fit Index (CFI)	0.928	

Thus, it can be concluded that the theoretical model is suitable and can be used to test the research model. The result of the estimate of parameters in the linear model (SEM) to test the relationship in the model are shown in the table. The hypotheses H1,

H2, H3, H4 in the research model, through Table 8 of normalized regression coefficients are determined to be accepted.

Table 8. Summary of the hypothesis test result

Regression weights			Estimate	S.E.	C.R.	P	Hypothesis	Concluded
JMC_F	←	ERP_F	1.165	0.177	6.595	***	H2	Accepted
ORG_F	←	ERP_F	1.132	0.156	7.259	***	H4	Accepted
ADR_F	←	ERP_F	−0.368	0.178	−2.068	0.039	H3	Accepted
PRS_F	←	ERP_F	1.128	0.166	6.796	***	H1	Accepted

6 Discussion and Implications

6.1 Discussion

First, based on the above result, the relationship between ERP system performance and job discretion, management capabilities, and cross-functionality indicated that the management can assign the work with a team, follow their progress, and self-tracking their performance. In the other hand, the best control is the way can optimize the organization performance using ERP. With the system, it treated the same for all users, no matter who manager or staff is. So that required manager should consider using a clear task with clear responsibility for each user to support smoothly in the long run and may increase user performance with frequently keep track subordinate closely.

Second, there is a significant link between ERP system performance and problem-solving support. In practice, ERP can provide their solution for operational issues by supporting automatic processes and integrating separate functional information system. The integration data center is the key feature of an ERP. When all information is in one place and they are updated automatically, they will be used for decision-making process and to increase the quality of managerial decisions. Finally, it will help the managers and employees to solve their problems more effectively.

Third, the negative impact of ERP performance on authority and decision rights implies that individual authorization seems recognition reduces in decision making by the ERP system. Usage ERP, the system utilizes systematic in setting up the power into the system, was not required more involvement from the user after implementation. Besides that, the challenge of control resource by ERP usage that also one term in the data controller. Data is the outcome of ERP, with eliminating the separate owner mean more security. And there is no motivation for an employee must own the data without contribution to business development. Follow the current trend of data insight which indicated that for keeping the raw data without the insight that data is usefulness action. So, management should share the ton of the top refreshment for the end user understand that better ERP, support reduce their daily task for more time focal in business insight rather than keep data.

Finally, the positive impact of ERP system performance on organizational performance implies that using the ERP has improved the organization working process.

This has consistence researcher acknowledge that the benefit that ERP has given to organizations that can be precise at the improvement of the business process level. The better of organization process lead business process is also improved which should gain more benefit for business performance measurement such improve productivity as well. And it is interesting to agree that invested that have significant links between ERP and user performance, and user performance will be indicated for organizational performance. Besides that, the user performance has a relationship with user satisfaction. In summary, the ERP system is also impacting operate effectively and manager should focus improve the working process and user satisfaction.

6.2 Managerial Implications

In summary, the finding of this research would extend to improve the understanding of the ERP end-user approached for the practitioners regarding ERP system performance and its impact on work and work-life of employees, such as problem-solving, job discretion, management visibility, and cross-functionality, authority and decision rights, and organizational performance. This study becomes important and empirically important to address the human problems in these areas that are still lacking. Therefore, the managers should improve the positive impact of ERP system, such as problem-solving, job discretion, management visibility, cross-functionality, and organizational performance, and they should reduce the negative effect of ERP system, such as: authority and decision rights. Besides, sharing the change communication to all user about the benefit from ERP and which change needs to adapt will be helpful.

Designation the progress of changing, make them understand that the reducing their authority in routing work, which reduces their spending on work lead support in their work have more time on other tasks to improve other functional skill, and balance work and life with maximizing productivities. Another the benefit of pre-design approval workflow for operation transaction which not only supports for user reduce time as above but also creates the consistent business process which ensures high compliance follow every time in huge transactions. Moreover, it also supports eliminating the errors, time spending for chasing approval or getting their signature.

Some detail recommendations for managers could be summarized as follows:

- Working with ERP, the people may change the ways of doing things because the core of ERP is once data source and this required the cross-functional data integrated. Because of that changing, working together with other people will apply to modify their working practices to adjust to different conditions of using ERP. So that the teamwork has become much essential in the role and skill of users and it became more critical and complexity as the role of leader or manager.
- As the management role, who in charge of change communication and change agents to support for user understand the benefit of ERP usage. The level of control the subordinate or peers must be a balance between the management and operational users. This revealed that managers should start to dialog away control which is used and anticipated. For example, a significant amount of autonomy should be accepted so that users feel reliant on and trust by the organization that leads to more

empowerment, while weekly inspection or report from the ERP system. That could be sufficient controllable but also engage in the self-discipline of users [22].

– At different levels of management, the concern and focus are not the same. Nowadays, the trend for digital industry 4.0 development under the management visibility base, such as by knowing what is occurring on your production real-time, issues can be resolved much faster. With the level of the middle manager and supervisor – who involve much more in detail of the daily operation, the benefits of visibility management can go further simple improvement via the ERP support, it can enhance and output better for employees and better service for your customer. Additional, with the job of a rider in daily business, visibility management is also important and can be productive in identifying the problem before they erupt into larger issues.

7   Conclusion and Future Research

The study found the link of significant predicts from "ERP system performance" positive impact to "problem-solving support", "job discretion, management visibility and cross-functionality", "organizational performance", but the negative impact to "authority and decision rights" for end users.

It was found the positive effect between ERP system product performance on organizational performance, this finding was consistent with results from previous studies from [5, 17].

Follow the finding, the managerial still consideration the action plan, whether the support for the user to understand the benefit of ERP which applies the standard business rules for approval hierarchy through the system which reduce human mistake and release time-consuming for other development opportunities of end users. That is also support business can adapt to digital trend with the competitor.

There are a few limitations of this study which need to highlight for future research continue investigating as follows:

– Cross-sectional study and convenience sampling method limit the possibility to generalize the findings. Hence, longitudinal study and other sampling methods should be used in future research.
– The sample size is small and limited in Ho Chi Minh City. It should be a future investigation to respond from other locations to access a fair insight picture.
– This study does not address the character of the user in the current framework. So, future research should evaluate the effect of users' demographic factors.

References

1. Arnold, V.: Behavioral research opportunities: understanding the impact of enterprise systems. Int. J. Acc. Inf. Syst. 7, 7–17 (2006)
2. Beheshti, H., Beheshti, C.: Improving productivity and firm performance with enterprise resource planning. Enterp. Inf. Syst. 4, 445–472 (2010)

3. Calisir, F., Calisir, F.: The relation of interface usability characteristics, perceived usefulness, and perceived ease of use to end-user satisfaction with enterprise resource planning (ERP) systems. Comput. Hum. Behav. **20**, 505–515 (2004)

4. Chen, S., Lin, Y.: An evaluation method for enterprise resource planning systems. J. Oper. Res. Soc. Jpn. **51**, 299–309 (2008)

5. Delone, W.H., McLean, E.R.: The DeLone and McLean model of information system success: a ten-year update. J. Manag. Inf. Syst. **19**, 9–30 (2003)

6. DeLone, W., McLean, E.: Information systems success: the quest for the dependent variable. Inf. Syst. Res. **3**(1), 60–95 (1992)

7. Ellis, P.: Office planning and design: the impact of organization change due to advanced information technology. Behav. Inf. Technol. **3**(3), 221–233 (1984)

8. Elmes, M., Strong, D., Volkoff, O.: Panotic empowerment and reflective conformity in enterprise system-enable organizations. Inf. Organ. **15**, 1–37 (2005)

9. Ezra, O.: Blog: Why Are ERP Systems So Hard to Configure? Panaya Ltd. (2014). http://www.panaya.com

10. Fryer, B.: The ROI challenge: can you produce a positive return on investment from ERP?, pp. 85–90. CFO (1999)

11. García-Sanchez, N., Pérez-Bernal, L.E.: Determination of critical success factors in implementing an ERP system: a field study in Mexican enterprises. Inf. Technol. Dev. **13**, 293–309 (2007)

12. Gattiker, T., Goodhue, D.: What happens after ERP implementation: understanding the impact of interdependence and differentiation on plant-level outcomes. MIS Q. **29**, 559–585 (2005)

13. Glenn, T.: Buyer's guide: The balance. The balance Website (2017). https://www.thebalance.com

14. Hair Jr., J., Black, W., Babin, B., Anderson, R., Tatham, R.: Multivariate Data Analysis, 6th edn. Pearson Education, New Delhi (2006)

15. Hoang, T., Chu, N.M.N.: Data Analysis with SPSS. Hong Duc Publishing House, Hanoi (2008)

16. Jasperson, J., Carte, T., Saunders, C.S., Butler, B., Croes, H., Zheng, W.: Review: power and information technology research: a metatriangulation review. MIS Q. **26**, 397–459 (2002)

17. Knox, H., O'Doherty, D., Vurdubakis, T., Westrup, C.: Transformative capacity information technology, and the making of business experts. Sociol. Rev. **55**, 22–41 (2007)

18. Mason, R.: Measuring information output: a communication systems approach. Inf. Manag. **1**, 219–234 (1978)

19. Minh, D.L., Han, K.S.: Understanding the impact of ERP system implementation on firm performance – focused on Vietnamese SMEs. Int. J. Softw. Eng. Appl. **10**, 87–104 (2016)

20. Nguy, T.H., Pham, Q.T.: Critical success factors of ERP projects in Vietnam. Sci. Technol. Dev. J. **16**(2), 57–66 (2013)

21. Petter, S., Delone, W., McLean, E.: Measuring information systems success: models, dimensions, measures, and interrelationships. Eur. J. Inf. Syst. **17**(3), 236–263 (2008)

22. Pham, Q.T.: A Knowledge Management Approach for Ensuring the Success of IT Industries in Vietnam. Nova Science Publishers, New York (2017)

23. Ruivo, P., Oliveira, T., Neto, M.: ERP use and value: Portuguese and Spanish SMEs. Ind. Manag. Data Syst. **112**, 1008–1025 (2012)

24. VECITA: National e-commerce development program 2014–2020. Vietnam eCommerce and Digital Economy Agency (2014). http://www.vecita.gov.vn/

25. Wickramasinghe, V.M.K.: Impact of ERP systems on work and work-life. Ind. Manag. Data Syst. **112**, 982–1004 (2012)

26. Wei, C., Liou, T., Lee, K.: An ERP performance measurement framework using a fuzzy integral approach. J. Manuf. Technol. Manag. **19**, 607–626 (2008)
27. Zhang, L., Lee, M., Banerjee, P.: Critical success factors of enterprise resource planning systems implementation success in China. In: IEEE Proceedings of the 36th Hawaii International Conference on System Sciences, pp. 1–10 (2002)

Using Policy Refinement to Assist IoT Device Management in Smart Hospitals

Jessica M. de Castro$^{(\boxtimes)}$, Luiz Fernando F. P. de Lima$^{(\boxtimes)}$, Iury Araújo$^{(\boxtimes)}$,
Eudisley G. dos Anjos$^{(\boxtimes)}$, and Fernando M. Matos$^{(\boxtimes)}$

Federal University of Paraiba, João Pessoa, Brazil
luizfernando@cc.ci.ufpb.br,
{jessicamaciel,iuryrogerio}@ppgi.ci.ufpb.br,
{eudisley,fernando}@ci.ufpb.br

Abstract. The implementation of the Internet of Things paradigm in the most diverse environments is already a reality. One of these environments is the smart hospital that uses several devices to improve patient care and streamline the internal processes of hospitals. However, an obstacle in the use of IoT systems is the difficulty encountered by their user to change devices behaviours as their needs changes. When the users can not update, the system may be outdated. This leads to problems in the hospital which is a critical environment and needs everything to be working properly every time. A way to customize the behavior of IoT devices is the use of police that can be described in high-level programming language. For this reason, this paper proposes a solution that uses policy refinement to assist IoT device management in smart hospitals. The proposed solution was implemented and tested, achieving favorable results for the hospital scenario.

Keywords: Internet of Things · Smart hospital · Policy management

1 Introduction

The Internet of Things (IoT) presents a set of devices connected to a network and interaction with each other. Those devices can be sensors, actuators, everyday objects, as refrigerators, smartphones, and so on. They have the ability to interconnect without human intervention and to obey pre-defined rules [1]. The IoT paradigm can be implemented in several domains seeking to improve the lives of its users. Some examples of environments are smart houses, smart offices and smart hospitals [2,3]. The smart environments are being implemented with a variety of functionalities, such as monitoring, recognition and smart management. The health care area can benefit from the implementation of IoT using the smart services that integrate the function of diagnosis, decision, management and treatment [4]. For this, sensors can be embedded in patients, employees, devices, environments in order to monitor, act and alert [5].

© Springer Nature Switzerland AG 2019
S. Misra et al. (Eds.): ICCSA 2019, LNCS 11623, pp. 645–657, 2019.
https://doi.org/10.1007/978-3-030-24308-1_51

For the smart environment deliver the functionality for its users, its devices need to be configured to act as the context requires. In addition, if there are changes, it is necessary to reconfigure the devices so they can act according to the new rules of the environment. However, reconfiguring these devices can be a difficult task to lay people without programming experience [6]. Since users can not make the changes, it is necessary to request the assistance of a technician. This may lead to delays and/or disruptions in environmental services. Another problem caused by the dependence in specialized professionals to configure and reconfigure the devices is the hesitation to adopt the technology. Users are afraid to adopt a technology they do not fully understand or dominate [7].

Hospitals are critical environments. Thus, it is important that all systems work with the minimum of complications, including IoT systems [8]. Thereby, it is necessary to provide tools that facilitate the redefinitions of IoT devices behavior by users. One approach used to address this need is the use of policies. A policy is the representation of one or more rules that determine an action from an event. They are commonly represented in Event-Condition-Action (ECA) format [9] and can be used to dictate the behavior of IoT devices. The use of policy allows users to create and manage their own policies with more facilities instead of having to program each device in the environment [11]. And it brings more flexibility to the system and ensures that the behavior of the devices can be changed whenever necessary [9]. With this approach it is possible to provide tools so that users can create their own policies in a high level programming language. It can provide tools such as applications and users to create their policies [11]. As well as platforms across the most diverse visual language types to make it easier for the user to manage IoT systems and their devices [6].

However, to provide the creation of high level programming language policies it is necessary to refine the policy created by the user from a high to a low level of abstraction, so it can be enforced in IoT devices. It is important to ensure the consistency throughout the process. That is, it is necessary realize the translation as well as others requirements, such as policy validation according to the used resources [10]. Furthermore, in a smart hospital it is important to ensure that the policy follows the standards set by hospital and national and international health regulatory agencies. The standards can establish the temperature and humidity conditions inside the hospital rooms [17], medicine refrigerator temperature [18], illumination [19], among others.

This paper presents a solution to assist in the management of IoT devices using policy refinement in smart hospitals. It aims to provide to the IoT systems users with the autonomy they need to manage devices according to context changes. For this, it performs the policy translation from XML into a configuration file that can be executed by Middleware (MW). So, the Middleware uses the file to configure the behavior of IoT Devices. The solution also ensures policy validation in terms of hospitals standards and existing resources. The solution was implemented and validated with efficiency tests.

The rest of this article is organized as follows. Section 2 presents the related works. Section 3 describes the proposed solution and its operation. The Sect. 4

details the implementation and results achieved. Finally, Sect. 5 presents the final considerations of the article.

2 Background

In [11] the authors present about a IoT device programmable language for home automation. They show the architecture developed for this as well as the tests that were performed. Although they do not use the term policy refinement, they do the translation and validation of the policy, verifying that the devices used are available and can perform the required tasks. As it is a proposal to be deployed in a residence, they use a centralized architecture. In [7] a flow language for assisted monitoring is presented in order to facilitate the programming of the devices in houses. However, the presented language is not accessible for lay users, which makes it impossible to be used in more complex scenarios, such as a hospital. As the papers in the literature are generally focused on IoT system applications for residential environments, and in this context it is not necessary to obey standards, they do not present validation of standards.

In work [12] is presented a performance management model for IoT as a service for e-health caregivers. The model is based on low complexity policies, they are implemented as a program code that runs on the gateway and are inspired by an approach that is constructed as event-condition-action. The work is focused on constructing policies to manage the performances of devices and not on customizing their behavior.

The paper [10] presents a Survey on methods of policy refinement for sustainable networks. Even though the work focuses on refinement for the scenario of computer networks, it served as the basis for defining the necessary requirements in a refinement method that could be implemented in the IoT devices scenario. From the requirements presented by the authors, we consider relevant for the scenario of this work the following: Translation, Resource, Verification/Coverage and Conflict. Besides these, with the survey of requirements the need for a new

Table 1. Requirements summary.

Requirements	Summary
Translation	Should have the steps that ensures the translation of a high level policy to a low level
Resource	During the transformation process it is necessary to ensure that the resources in the IoT system environment are taken into account
Coverage	Verify if the refined policies meet the requirements of the original policy
Conflict	Deal with conflicts, detecting and resolving them
Standard	During the transformation process it is necessary to ensure that the hospital standards are taken into account

requirement for hospital application was identified. The new requirement is Standards. The explanation of all these requirements can be found in the Table 1. The Fig. 1 shows the requirement and those that are circled are those that were considered in the development of this work (Standard, Translate and Resource).

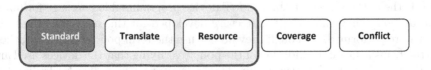

Fig. 1. Refinement requirements

3   Solution Proposed

The proposed solution aims to assist in the management of IoT devices using policy refinement in smart hospitals. So, the Fig. 2 presents the solution architecture integrated to a IoT Framework. The Policy Refiner and Data Manager modules are part of the proposal and Front-end, Middleware and IoT Devices of

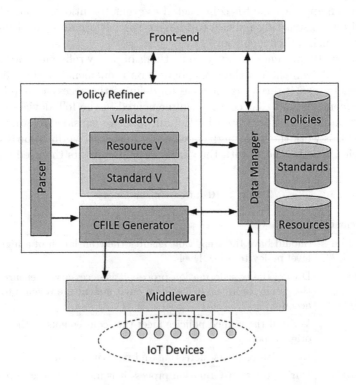

Fig. 2. Solution architecture

the framework. The Front-end module is responsible for presenting the platform to the user. He will use it to create, edit and view existing policies. The fronteend will perform the transformation of the policy from a visual language to an XML file.

The Policy Refiner module is responsible for performing the refinement process of the policy described in XML for a configuration file that will be used to customize the behavior of the devices. The Parser module receives the file and parse of all the information using a object-oriented programming language. Moreover, the parse tree is created and contains the condition defined in the policy. Such elements will be used by the validator and the Configuration File (CFILE) Generator. Validator is responsible for the validation of resources and standards. The Resource Validator is responsible for ensuring that the IoT devices, which are being used to perform the event capture or the resulting action, exist and are available for use. So, the role of the Policy Validator is to verify that the policy complies with the hospital standards. The CFILE Generator uses the information generated by the Parser to create the configuration in a language that can be executed by the Middleware.

The Data Manager is in charge of managing the data that is inserted or requested to the databases (DBs). There are three DBs: Policies, Standards and Resources. The first one stores the policies that have been submitted by the users and have already been validated and accepted. The policies are stored in XML format because if users need to view or change them, they can be easily converted to the visual programming language that the users uses to create the policies. The second maintains the hospital standards. For example: which category of patient can enter what room or what is the minimum and maximum temperature allowed in the hospital rooms. The third one is used to store the information of all the IoT resources. Such as which devices are available at the hospital, their location, and what services they offer. Furthermore, the Data manager is also responsible for organizing and inserting into the database the new resources discovered by the Middleware.

And last, there is the MW. It has the function to coordinate the existing IoT devices in the hospital. So, its receive the policies configuration file and when an event happens the MW interprets the corresponding policy and define the behavior of the responsible devices, as the one presented in [9]. And the IoT devices are the sensors and actuators that act in the hospital environment, such as lights, sensors of vital signs, luminosity, temperature, among others.

So, the policy refinement consists of the entire policy transformation process presented in this section, from its defined form in XML file to the configuration file that will be used by the MW configure the devices. It is guaranteed that the policy can dictate the behavior of the hospital's IoT devices by ensuring that the translation is performed correctly, maintaining all its initial characteristics. As well as ensuring that it complies with all hospital standards and that the policy will be executed without error by ensuring that all IoT devices required for its implementation exist.

3.1 Solution Operation

The solution uses refinement to from high level policies generate low level policies. For this, it is necessary to ensure that the policy can be translated correctly,
assuring that all its initial characteristic. Also, during the refinement process
it is important to take into consideration the hospital standards and existing
resources in the environment. Figure 3 shows the operating scheme of the solution. Demonstrating the process since the submission of the policy by the user
to the configuration of the IoT system and its devices.

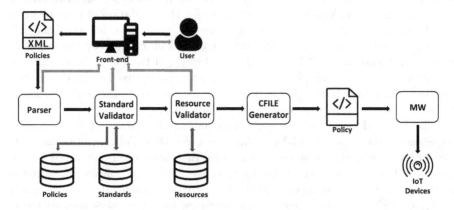

Fig. 3. Solution operation

When the user creates a new policy or edited an existing one, the policy
in visual programming language is submitted and the front-end translates it
to a XML file. The XML contains all the policy information and also of the
user that submitted it. This file is the input artifact for the beginning of the
policy refinement process. So, the Parser parses the policy in XML format for a
programming language object and creates the parser tree. The parser tree will
be used for the validation process and creating the configuration file. If any error
is found, the information is returned to the user.

When the parser is completed successfully, the process of validating the policy
is initiated. First, it is verified that the policy is in accordance with the hospital
standards. To do this, the Standard Validator requests the Data Manager the
current standards of the hospital. It is then checked if the submitted policy is
in accordance with the standards. If it is, the process continues. If not, an error
message is returned to the user. After this, the resource validation is done. So, it
is necessary to check whether the services and devices used to capture the event,
check the condition and perform the action exist in the hospital and have the
ability to perform what was required. Therefore, the Resource Validator requests
information from the Data Manager about the services and devices available in
the hospital and their location in the hospital. The Data Manager returns the
requested information to the Resource Validator. Then it is checked if there are

the resources for performing the event and the action in the room defined in the policy. If it does not exist, an error message is sent to the user.

Once the policy validation is successfully completed, the XML file is saved in the Policy DB. Now it is necessary to complete the translation process for a language that will be easier to be processed by MW. Therefore, the Configuration File Generator uses the policy object and also the parser tree to construct the file in a programming language that can be interpreted by the MW to determine the behavior of the devices. This file contains the information of the sensors and actuators used to execute the policy, such as the event and the condition and action. The file is then sent to the MW so that it can manage and order the behavior of the devices contained in the hospital network.

4 Prototyping and Results

The policy refinement process was implemented to prove that the proposed solution can be applied in the scenario of a smart hospital. This section presents the implementation process, the tests and results obtained from the execution and simulation of the proposal. For this, the programming language Python, version 3.x was used. The choice of the use of this language was due to some advantages that it provides, such as rapid development, easy integration with new modules, even other languages and also because it is an interpreted language that has portability for several operating systems (Windows, Linux and Windows). Moreover, Python has been used as a programming language for projects in the context of IoT [13–15]. The use of Python as a programming language influenced how the data was represented in the solution. The DBs were implemented using CSV files, because the Pandas library was created for manipulation and data processing in Python and is a very intuitive tool for this purpose [16].

The first step was to define the XML policy file. This is, what information the file would contain and how they would be arranged. An example of the file can be seen in Fig. 4. The XML file is organized as follows: Line 3 to 6 presents general information about the policy. In line 3 has the policy identification number (ID) and name. Lines 4 and 5 are about the author and present the author ID and the id of author's department, respectively. The policy event is described between line 7 and 10. The type of the event is shown in Line 7. Lines 8 and 9 bring the local that the policy will be applied, the department and room, respectively. Line 10 describes if any medical equipment, such as ECG, it is necessary in policy implementation. Lines 12 to 17 present the condition for applying the policy. It condition element can have a several operation elements where is described in 'op' what type of operation it has to perform and inside it have the two value that will be applied the operation. Lastly, the action is defined between lines 18 and 20. Line 18 shows the action that will be performed if the condition is positive. The file presented in Fig. 4 represents a policy that by identifying that there is a new person with a patient band (Line 7) on the door of a specific room (Line 9), that band is read and the category of that patient is checked. If it is orange or red (lines 14 and 15), the door will open for him (Line 19).

```
1    <?xml version="1.0" encoding="UTF-8"?>
2    <policy>
3        <info id="1" name="Porta 100">
4            <id_author>15</id_author>
5            <id_dep>1</id_dep>
6        </info>
7        <event type="new_band">
8            <at_dep>1</at_dep>
9            <at>100</at>
10           <equip>None</equip>
11       </event>
12       <condition>
13           <operation op="or">
14               <operation op="equal">band;orange</operation>
15               <operation op="equal">band;red</operation>
16           </operation>
17       </condition>
18       <action>
19           <do>open_door</do>
20       </action>
21   </policy>
```

Fig. 4. Policy in XML example

With the policies xml template ready, the Parser was implemented. The cElementTree library was used to read the XML file. It creates a tree with all elements of the document. The parser is then responsible for finding and mapping all the data contained in the XML to its corresponding variable in the policy class. Furthermore, there is also the creation of the parser tree, in this step the operations contained in the condition (for example: Fig. 4, lines 12–16), as well as the values, are identified and the parser tree is built.

Once the file has been parsed, it is necessary to validate the policy. Before checking the standards and resources, it is important to check the user information contained in the policy. So, the existence of the room defined in the policy is checked and it is checked if the employee can create a policy for that location.

Then, it made the validation of standards. It is verified what type of event, condition and action is described in the policy. After this is checked if there is any current standard that applies in politics. If there is, it is necessary to check the condition of the policy to verify that the policy can be applied. These information checks and norms are sequential, so if the policy is not validated in any of them, the process is interrupted and an error message that describes the reason for the validation failure is sent to the user. One example of standard is that the temperature of the medicine refrigerator should remain between $2\,°C$ and $8\,°C$ [18]. Therefore, if a policy is created for this equipment, the validator checks if this standard is met, that is, if the user attempts to implement a temperature outside that range for that equipment, the policy will not be validated and an error message will be displayed.

So, it is need to ensure that the resources used exist in the defined location. There are two steps to do this. The first is to verify that the event defined in the policy can be performed at the desired location and the second is whether the action can be performed or not. To do this, it is verified which services are required to perform the event and the defined action. Having the service information, a search is performed on the resources DB to check if there is any device that performs such events on the site. If it is found, then it follows the process to the data manager, but if not, a message is returned to the user stating the error. For example, for an event that identifies the presence of a new band (bracelet), it is necessary to have a sensor that can read the patient band. Or, to perform an action that opens the door, you must have an automatic door that can perform the action.

After verifying that the policy does not violate any hospital standard and that all resources used exist, a configuration file as shown in Fig. 5 is generated. It shows the information about the sensor identifier number (line 1) and actuator (line 2) that are used to execute the policy. Line 4 shows when this policy will be verified, then when the described event occurs. Line 5 presents the condition and Line 6 the action that will be performed if the condition is positive. These last two lines are written in the Python language and can be easily executed.

```
1    SENSOR_ID: 3
2    ACTUATOR_ID: 2
3
4    when new_band
5    if (( band equal orange ) or ( band equal red )):
6        answer = 'open_door'
```

Fig. 5. Configuration file example

4.1 Results

Based on the work of [11] two experiments were performed: (i) validation of the policy refinement process; (ii) performance test focused on the response time of the proposal. The tests were performed on a Desktop computer with an Intel i5 processor and 8 GB RAM, as it is a machine with processing power that a hospital can easily have. To test the translation, validation of resources and standards, the implemented solution was executed and the output was analyzed. All the policies and situations that were envisaged during the proposal for an intelligent hospital were described in a XML file and later translated into the configuration file that contains the executable code, succeeding in policy coverage and in all implemented translation steps.

To test the standards and resource validation, situations where the submitted policy violated hospital standards were tested. During the execution of these policies, the solution successfully identified the violations and returned the error by showing which standard was infringed. The situations in which the resource

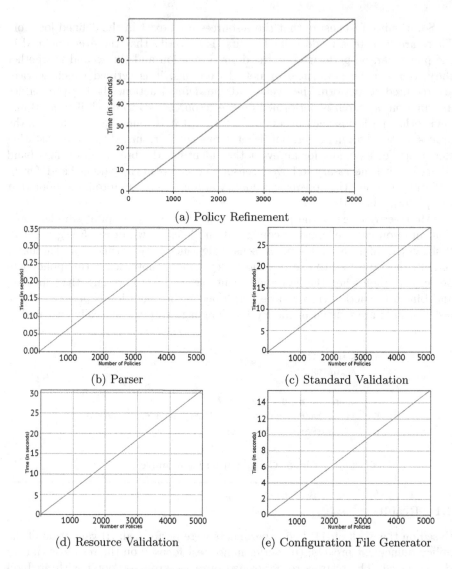

(a) Policy Refinement

(b) Parser

(c) Standard Validation

(d) Resource Validation

(e) Configuration File Generator

Fig. 6. Policy refinement test graphics

described in the policy was not existing was also tested. And, just as validation of standards, the solution was able to correctly identify all policies that use non-existent resources and returned the error message pointed out which was the resource that was unavailable.

Moreover, the time needed for policy refinement was verified as well as for each separate step. For this, the policies were executed 30 times to calculate the average time used and to have a fair result. The policy refinement was performed with 1 policy to 5000 policies to ensure the scalability of the proposal. The Fig. 6

shows the graphs of the test results. The first one, Fig. 6a show the time required to run the policy refinement from the input of the XML file to the output of the configuration file. The other figures are from each step of the refinement process: Parser (Fig. 6b), Standard Validation (Fig. 6c), Resource Validation (Fig. 6d) and Configuration File Generator (Fig. 6e). The total time for policy refinement was 5000 policies was 79.15 s, that is, the time required for a policy was only 0.0158 s. Analyzing the total time of the process, it is possible to verify that the time used by the parser is only 0.44% of the whole process. While standards and resources validation spend 37.04% and 38.77%, respectively. This is due to access to standards and resources databases. Lastly, the file generation process consumes 19.63% of the process, as it is also necessary to access databases, writing and reading.

Therefore, the results obtained in the tests of 0.0158 s to perform the entire refinement process for a policy are satisfactory. We can notice that the return time of success or error message to the user will not be time consuming and the policies can be modified as soon as the user needs. Based on the results, the solution proposed in this article can be implemented in a critical environment, such as the hospital. These results ensure that the hospital is always functioning properly without major problems. In addition to the low execution time, we have the guarantee of the successful refinement process. This allows the user to perform policy creation at a more abstract level, such as in a visual programming language. And by doing this, it ensures that users are able to create policies that will be used to reconfigure the IoT devices in the hospital. This ensures that the hospital is always functioning perfectly and that the system is not out of date.

5   Conclusion

With the evolution of technology and the implantation of the IoT paradigm and smart environments, it is important to develop tools that allow users to customize their IoT devices. Providing these tools to users, they will be more confident and will be easier to them to adopt the technologies. Aiming it, This article presented a solution that facilitates the customization of IoT devices in smart hospitals. For this, we used policy refinement to ensure a user-created policy will be translated correctly and validated according to existing resources and hospital standards. With the implementation of the proposal it was possible to verify that it works and can accomplish what was proposed. The results were satisfactory and showed that the solution can be implemented in a hospital. Thus, it is expected that in conjunction with the front-end application, hospital employees can manage their own policies without the need to request a technician, ensuring that the system is always functioning correctly and as expected. As future work, we hope to develop Front End and a visual programming language so that users can create their policies. We also want to implement a hospital scenario in which tests with real devices can be performed.

References

1. Atzori, L., Iera, A., Morabito, G.: The internet of things: a survey. Comput. Netw. **54**(15), 2787–2805 (2010)
2. Kafle, V.P., Fukushima, Y., Harai, H.: Internet of things standardization in ITU and prospective networking technologies. IEEE Commun. Mag. **54**(9), 43–49 (2016)
3. Ahmed, E., Yaqoob, I., Gani, A., Imran, M., Guizani, M.: Internet-of-things-based smart environments: state of the art, taxonomy, and open research challenges. IEEE Wirel. Commun. **23**(5), 10–16 (2016)
4. Dhariwal, K., Mehta, A.: Architecture and plan of smart hospital based on Internet of Things (IOT). Int. Res. J. Eng. Technol. **4**, 1976–1980 (2017). e-ISSN 2395-0056
5. Barroca Filho, I.M., de Aquino Junior, G.S.: Proposing an IoT-based healthcare platform to integrate patients, physicians and ambulance services. In: Gervasi, O., et al. (eds.) ICCSA 2017. LNCS, vol. 10409, pp. 188–202. Springer, Cham (2017). https://doi.org/10.1007/978-3-319-62407-5_13
6. Reisinger, M.R., Schrammel, J., Fröhlich, P.: Visual languages for smart spaces : end-user programming between data-flow and form-filling, pp. 165–169 (2017)
7. Edgcomb, A.D., Vahid, F.: MNFL: the monitoring and notification flow language for assistive monitoring. In: Proceedings of the 2nd ACM SIGHIT Symposium International Health Informatics, IHI 2012, pp. 191–200 (2012). https://doi.org/10.1145/2110363.2110387
8. Ullah, M., Fiedler, M., Wac, K.: On the ambiguity of quality of service and quality of experience requirements for eHealth services. In: 2012 6th International Symposium Medical Information and Communication Technology, pp. 1–4 (2012). https://doi.org/10.1109/ISMICT.2012.6203030
9. Singh, J., Bacon, J.M.: On middleware for emerging health services. J. Internet Serv. Appl. **5**, 1–19 (2014). https://doi.org/10.1186/1869-0238-5-6
10. Riekstin, A.C., Januario, G.C., Rodrigues, B.B., Nascimento, V.T., de Brito Carvalho, T.C.M., Meirosu, C.: A survey of policy refinement methods as a support for sustainable networks. IEEE Commun. Surv. Tutorials. **18**, 222–235 (2016). https://doi.org/10.1109/COMST.2015.2463811
11. Ponte, F.R.P., Gomes, R.L.: IoT device programmable language customization for home automation. In: IEEE Symposium on Computers and Communications, pp. 168–173 (2018)
12. Ha, M., Lindh, T.: Distributed performance management of Internet of Things as a service for caregivers. In: 2017 IEEE 19th International Conference e-Health Networking, Applications and Services, pp. 1–6 (2017). https://doi.org/10.1109/HealthCom.2017.8210765
13. Patchava, V., Kandala, H.B., and Babu, P.R.: A smart home automation technique with Raspberry PI using IoT. In: International Conference on Smart Sensors and Systems. IEEE (2015)
14. Shete, R., Agrawal, S.: IoT based urban climate monitoring using Raspberry PI. In: International Conference on Communication and Signal Processing. IEEE (2016)
15. Quadri, S.A.I., Sathish, P.: IoT based home automation and surveillance system. In: International Conference on Intelligent Computing and Control Systems. IEEE (2017)
16. McKinney, W.: Python for Data Analysis: Data Wrangling with Pandas, Numpy, and Ipython, 1st edn. O'Reilly, Sebastopol (2012)

17. Anvisa: RESOLUTION-RE N° 9. http://portal.anvisa.gov.br/documents/33880/2568070/RE_09_2003.pdf
18. Ebserh: Controle de Temperatura da Geladeira de Medicamento. http://www2.ebserh.gov.br/documents/147715/0/ROP_controle_temp_geladeira.pdf
19. ABNT: Iluminancia de interiores. http://ftp.demec.ufpr.br/disciplinas/TM802/NBR5413.pdf

Parallel Symbiotic Organisms Search Algorithm

Absalom E. Ezugwu$^{(\boxtimes)}$, Rosanne Els, Jean V. Fonou-Dombeu,
Duane Naidoo, and Kimone Pillay

School of Computer Science, University of KwaZulu-Natal, King Edward Road,
Pietermaritzburg Campus, Pietermaritzburg 3201, KwaZulu-Natal, South Africa
{ezugwua, rosanne, fonoudombeuj,
214550818, 214553962}@stu.ukzn.ac.za

Abstract. Symbiotic organisms search algorithm is a population-based evolutionary optimization technique that is motivated by the simulation of social behaviour that emanates from the symbiosis relationship amongst organisms in an ecosystem. It is a popular global search swarm intelligence metaheuristic that is widely being used in conjunction with several other algorithms in different fields of study. Fascinatingly, the algorithm has also been shown to have the capability of optimizing several NP-hard problems in both continuous and binary search spaces. More so, because most of the modern day real-world computational problems requires machines with high processing power and improved optimization techniques, it is important to find ways to improve the speedup of the optimization process of this algorithm, as the complexity of the problems increase. Therefore, this paper explores the possibility of improving the optimization speedup and performance of the symbiotic organisms search algorithm through parallelization methods. The proposed parallelization procedure is implemented using OpenMP on a shared memory architecture and evaluated on a set of twenty mathematical test problems. The computational results of the parallel symbiotic organisms search algorithm was compared to its serial counterpart using a measure of run-time complexity.

Keywords: Symbiotic organisms search ·
Parallel symbiotic organisms search · OpenMP

1 Introduction

The symbiotic organisms search (SOS) algorithm is a simple yet effective population-based metaheuristic technique that has been applied widely to solve problems in both continuous and combinatorial domains [1–9]. As SOS is relatively new in the literature compared to other related state-of-the-art swarm intelligence and population based optimization metaheuristic algorithms such as the Particle Swarm Optimization (PSO), Genetic Algorithm (GA), Ant Colony Optimization (ACO), Firefly Algorithm (FA), Flower Pollination Algorithm (FPA) and Differential Evolution (DE), its development as a standard optimization tool is still in its early stage. Although several aspects of improvement for the SOS algorithm have been proposed [2–4], nonetheless others

S. Misra et al. (Eds.): ICCSA 2019, LNCS 11623, pp. 658–672, 2019.
https://doi.org/10.1007/978-3-030-24308-1_52

require considerable research effort. Performance efficiency in terms of computational speedups with regards to using the SOS algorithm to solve complex and large scale real-world problems has not been investigated and therefore can be considered as a serious bottleneck to the algorithm's development.

The advent of parallel programming has in so many ways been useful in solving compute intensive problems, which require the use of high computational resources. Parallelization has likewise been used to improve the efficiency of other similar population-based algorithms, which is the case for PSO [10], ACO [11], GA [12], FA [13], and DE [14]. This paper proposes a parallelization strategy for the standard SOS algorithm and describes the application of the parallel SOS (PSOS) to solve a set of continuous optimization problems, which the algorithm was originally designed to solve. This paper is the first to parallelize the SOS algorithm, which makes this the main motivation of the current study.

The rest of the paper is organized as follows: Sect. 2 presents detailed discussion of some related works on other population-based metaheuristic algorithms. Section 3 gives a brief overview of the SOS algorithm and subsequently describes the parallelization model used to implement the PSOS version of the serial code. Section 4 describes the experimentation, parallel implementation strategy for the PSOS, results and discussion. Finally, Sect. 5 gives the concluding remarks and future directions.

2 Related Work

In the field of parallelizing population-based metaheuristics, Zhou et al. [15] parallelized the ACO algorithm on a multi-core Single Instruction Multiple Data (SIMD) CPU architecture. In this model, each ant was mapped with a CPU core and the construction of a solution, for each ant, was accelerated through vector instructions. However, it was found that this simple vectorization strategy was not suited to the SIMD CPUs. An alternative approach was proposed which involved the algorithm distinguishing between branch codes and data-intensive codes and all codes were then executed on scalar and vector units. A wide range of traveling salesman problem cases, which varied from 198 to 4461 cities, was used to assess the algorithm. The speedup achieved was 57.8 times faster than its serial counterpart. This approach was then verified by comparing it with GPU-based ACO algorithms as it proved to be highly competitive with respect to its performance.

Shonkwiler [16] parallelized the GA by executing identical copies of the algorithm on independent processors. The only communication that took place between the processes is that one process collected the final result from each of the other processes and reported it to the user. This is called identical, independent processing – IIP parallel. The theoretical analysis from this investigation showed that this particular technique achieved a speedup using m processors given by $m.s^{m-1}$ where s, the acceleration factor, is a parameter that depends on the specifications of the GA. Usually s > 1. Shonkwiler showed that super-linear speedup is possible with the Genetic Algorithm and algorithms similar to it.

Differential Evolution algorithms possess special attributes which enable it to be used to build asynchronous parallel versions. These parallel versions make more sufficient use of the available computational power. Ntipteni, *et al.* [17] developed a parallel DE that made use of computer clusters. This parallelization was performed using an asynchronous implementation of the master-slave approach. The procedure was then tested with two airfoil optimization problems and the parallel version was compared to its serial counterpart. It was found that for optimization problems of low dimensions, the parallel DE algorithm behaved well, in terms of its convergence rate and the speedup of the computational procedure. For larger populations, this procedure became unstable.

Chang *et al.* [18] parallelized the PSO algorithm with three communication strategies, each of which can be used according to the data independency. The first strategy was designed for independent or loosely correlated solution parameters (Rosenbrock and Rastrigin functions). The second strategy was designed for more strongly correlated solution parameters (Griewank function), while the last strategy was a hybrid communication strategy which can be used when the properties of the parameters are unknown. The parallel PSO algorithm was effective in speeding up the algorithm with the first communication strategy. With the second strategy, performance could be improved by up to 66%. Lastly, the hybrid strategy was effective for all three functions (Rosenbrock, Rastrigin and Griewank).

In Koh *et al.* [19] a parallel asynchronous PSO (PAPSO) algorithm was introduced with the aims of enhancing its efficiency. The proposed parallel algorithm dynamically adjusts the workload allocated to each processor. Hence, all available processors, in a heterogeneous cluster, are efficiently used. This implementation was compared to a parallel synchronous implementation of PSO (PSPSO) in computing environments of both a heterogeneous and homogenous nature. Small and medium analytical test problems, as well as a biomechanical test problem, were used in order to make this comparison. The results showed that the asynchronous parallel implementation was notably more effective than its synchronous counterpart. In the case of the biomechanical test problem, PAPSO proved to be 3.5 times faster than PSPSO, which was executed on a heterogeneous cluster with 20 processors.

3 Symbiotic Organisms Search Algorithm

The SOS algorithm is inspired by the interactive behaviour between different organisms in nature. Organisms normally live with and rely on each other for survival and feeding. This kind of relationship is called symbiosis [1, 2]. There are two kinds of symbiotic relationships, namely: obligate relationships and facultative relationships [20]. Obligate relationship refers to relationship where two organisms live with each other and depend on each other for survival, while facultative relationships refer to relationships where two organisms live with each other, but do not depend on each other for survival.

The SOS algorithm was designed to handle problems in a continuous space, and the algorithmic process starts with an initial population, also known as the ecosystem. First, different organisms are randomly generated in the ecosystem, where each organism refers to the problem at hand. Each organism is attached to a specific fitness value, which mirrors the amount of change to the defined objective function.

Furthermore, new sets of solutions are generated based on the interactive behaviour between two organisms in the population or ecosystem. There are different kinds of symbiotic relationships found in nature, but the most popular relationships include: mutualism, commensalism, and parasitism. Also, there are three major phases in SOS and these phases are designed to mimic parasitism, mutualism and commensalism. In the parasitic phase, interactions between organisms benefit one party but the other is disadvantaged or harmed. Also, in mutualism phase, interaction benefit both parties, while in commensalism, interactions benefit only one party but does not harm or affect the other party. Each organism randomly interacts with the other organisms in the ecosystem through all the afore-mentioned phases. These phases are briefly explained next.

As aforementioned, mutualism describes the interaction between two different organisms that benefits both organisms. The two organisms $(x_i \, and \, x_j)$ interact with each other with the goal of increasing their chances of survival within the ecosystem [2]. As shown in Eqs. (1) and (2), new solutions for the two organisms $(x_i \, and \, x_j)$ are calculated based on their interactions.

$$X_{inew} = X_i + rand(0, 1) * (X_{best} - MV * BF_1) \tag{1}$$

$$X_{jnew} = X_j + rand(0, 1) * (X_{best} - MV * BF_2) \tag{2}$$

$$MV = \frac{X_i + X_j}{2} \tag{3}$$

where $rand(0, 1)$ refers to random numbers between 0 and 1, $BF_1 \, and \, BF_2$ represent benefit factors for the two interacting organisms. The benefit factor represents the level of benefit for each organism – partial or full. The term MV refers to the mutual vector obtained using Eq. (3), which represents the relationship features between the two interacting organisms.

Commensalism describes the relationship between two organisms, where one of the organisms benefits and the other is not harmed or affected. During interaction, a new solution for the benefitting candidate (X_i) is calculated using Eq. (4).

$$X_{inew} = X_i + rand(-1, 1) * (X_{best} - X_J) \tag{4}$$

where $rand(-1, 1)$ refers to random numbers between −1 and 1, X_{best} refers to the best organism in the ecosystem.

Parasitism describes the relationship between two organisms, where one of the organisms' benefits and the other is disadvantaged. In this relationship, the parasite organism (X_i) is given a role, by creating a parasite vector. The parasite vector is created in the ecosystem by duplicating the parasite organism (X_i), and then modifying a randomly selected dimension with the aid of a random number. Further, the host organism (X_j) is randomly selected, which serves as the host to the parasite organism (X_i). The fitness value for the host and parasite organisms are both calculated, and if the fitness value of the host organism is better, then the parasite organism will be eliminated from the ecosystem, otherwise, the host organism will be eliminated. Pseudocode for the classical SOS algorithm is presented in Algorithm 1 [1].

Algorithm 1: Standard SOS pseudocode

1: Begin SOS
2: Randomly Initialize population
3: Evaluate the fitness of initial population
4: Retain the best solution
5:   While (termination point is not reached)
6:       Mutualism phase
7:       Commensalism phase
8:       Parasitism phase
9:       Evaluate fitness of the population
10:      Update the best solution
11: End While
12: Return best solution
13: End SOS

3.1 Open Multiprocessor

Open multiprocessor or OpenMP as its often called is a simple application program-ming interface which is used to write multithreaded applications. It consists of a set of compiler directives and library routines which makes parallelizing applications in C, C ++ and Fortran straightforward to implement [21]. Most OpenMP constructs are applied to a "structured block" which is a block of one or more statements with one point of entry at the beginning of the block and one exit point at the end of the block, with each thread executing a copy of the code in the block. OpenMP is a multi-threading, shared address model, in essence the threads communicate by the use of shared variables [22]. It provides a fork-join type of parallelism which consists of a master thread that spawns a team of threads at parallel regions of the code. An illus-tration of the fork–join model is shown in Fig. 1, in which the parallelizable regions are identified using various coloured blocks. The sequential program execution is pre-sented at the top of the diagram, while the fork–join program execution section is displayed on the bottom part.

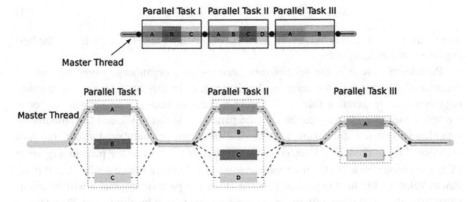

Fig. 1. OpenMP fork-join parallelism model [23]

The basic approach, when using OpenMP, is to find in a program, the specific sections with compute intensive loops and then modify them so that the iterations are independently implemented by adding the OpenMP directives. The following code snippet illustrates an OpenMP loop construct which splits the iterations among the threads.

```
#pragma omp for
for (int i = 0; i < dim; i++) {
        array_rand[i]=randon (-1, 1);
        new_x_i[i]=pop[index_i] [i] + (array_rand[i]×(best[i]-pop[index_j] [i]));
        if(new_x_i[i]<lb)new_x_i[i]=lb;
        if(new_x_i[i]>ub)new_x_i[i]=ub;
}

#pragma omp for
for (int i = 0; i < dim; i++) {
        parasite[i] = pop[index_i] [i];
}
```

The other more complex approach of parallelizing a for-loop is to write a program that shares the loop iterations among the threads instead of using the OpenMP for-loop construct. The OpenMP for-loop construct is a simplified and time-efficient way of parallelizing "for" loops. This is because just by simply adding one line of code above the "for" loop, the iterations are split among the threads that are spawned from the master thread. It is worth noting that when the number of threads is not specified, the default number of threads will be used which is equal to the number of cores on the machine that is running the program.

3.2   Test Functions

Standard mathematical test functions are used to evaluate certain attributes of an optimization algorithms. These attributes include convergence rate, precision, robustness and general performance. Since the SOS algorithm was proposed to solve single-objective optimization problems, single-objective optimization test functions were used to also investigate the performance of the proposed PSOS. In this paper, a collection of twenty different test functions is presented and used as benchmark functions to evaluate the PSOS implementation. Each benchmark function is identified by its own unique properties that are described in terms of continuity, differentiability, convexity, modality and separability properties. A comprehensive list of the selected test functions is shown in Table 1.

Table 1. Twenty mathematical test functions (D: dimension, M: multimodal, N: non-separable, U: unimodal, S: separable)

S/n	Test function	Search space range	D	Type	Min
1	Ackley	[32, 32]	30	MN	0
2	Beale	[−4.5, 4.5]	2	MN	0
3	Boachevsky1	[−100, 100]	2	US	0
4	Bohachevsky2	[−100, 100]	2	UN	0
5	Bohachevsky3	[−100, 100]	2	MN	0
6	Booth	[−10, 10]	2	US	0
7	Colville	[−10, 10]	4	MN	0
8	Dixon-Price	[10, 10]	30	UN	0
9	Griewank	[−600, 600]	30	UN	0
10	Michalewicz10	[0, π]	30	MS	−9.6602
11	Michalewicz2	[0, π]	2	MS	−1.8013
12	Michalewicz5	[0, π]	5	MS	−4.6877
13	Quartic	[−1.28, 1.28]	30	US	0
14	Rastrigin	[−5.12, 5.12]	30	MS	0
15	Rosenbrock	[−30, 30]	30	UN	0
16	Schaffer	[−100, 100]	2	UN	0
17	Sphere	[−100, 100]	30	US	0
18	Step	[−5.12, 5.12]	30	US	0
19	SumSquares	[100, 100]	30	US	0
20	Zakharov	[−5, 10]	30	UN	0

4 Experimentation

The C programming language was used for the implementation of the serial SOS algorithm on a Linux platform. Furthermore, OpenMP was used to implement the parallel programs on a multicore architecture. The experiments were conducted on a personal computer desktop with the following specifications: Processor- Intel Core i7 CPU 870 @ 2.93 GHz x 8, RAM- 4 GB, Operating system – Linux Fedora 25, Graphics card- NVIDIA GeForce GTX 470. The SOS serial code was obtained from open-source material available online in [24]. Twenty different test functions were selected, and the SOS algorithm was then executed with each of the test functions in order to obtain the serial processing time of the algorithm. The parameter setting used for the algorithm implementation were set as follows: number of iterations: 10, population size: 50, number of problem variables: 50, number of replication runs: 20, the number of dimensions varied for each of the test functions, and similarly for the upper and lower bounds. A Gprof profiler, which is a performance analysis tool for Unix applications was used to observe the implemented PSOS algorithm execution time [25].

4.1   Parallel Algorithm Methodology

Thereafter, OpenMP was applied to the serial implementation of the SOS algorithm to parallelize it. This was done differently for each test function. The reason for this was that a maximum speedup was only obtained for each test function when an OpenMP was applied to different search phases of the SOS algorithm. That is, OpenMP had to be applied to each of the SOS's algorithm phases namely, mutualism, commensalism, and parasitism respectively to achieve a speedup when using a particular test function. For example, for a particular test function, when an OpenMP call function was implemented in the mutualism phase, the computational time usually slowed down, whereas when OpenMP call function was implemented in the commensalism phase alone, a speedup in the computation time was observed. In Table 2 below, it can be seen where the OpenMP parallel model was executed for each of the different test functions in order to obtain the fastest execution time in parallel.

Table 2. OpenMP application in SOS for each test function

Fn	Test function	Objective function	Mutualism	Commensalism	Parasitism
F1	Ackley		√	√	√
F2	Beale			√	√
F3	Bohachevsky1			√	
F4	Bohachevsky2			√	√
F3	Bohachevsky3			√	√
F6	Booth			√	√
F7	Colville			√	
F8	Dixon-Price			√	
F9	Griewank		√	√	√
F10	Michalewicz2			√	
F11	Michalewicz5	√		√	√
F12	Michalewicz10		√	√	√
F13	Quartic	√	√	√	√
F14	Rastrigin	√	√	√	√
F15	Rosenbrock		√	√	√
F16	Schaffer	√		√	√
F17	Sphere		√	√	√
F18	Step			√	
F19	SumSquares			√	√
F20	Zakharov			√	√

It was found that in most cases, parallelizing the mutualism phase of the SOS algorithm actually incurred additional computational cost, while parallelizing the commensalism phase mostly reduced the execution time. For the parallel algorithm implementation, different sets of threads were employed namely, two, four and eight threads. Finally, the computational results were recorded, analysed and compared with the serial times. It is noteworthy to mention here that only the computational time complexity was used as a measure of merit in determining the performance superiority of the proposed PSOS algorithm. This is because there were no observed significant differences in the solution qualities obtained by both the serial and parallel codes. The evaluation process is further characterized by the identified differences or gaps in computational time between the serial and the parallel implementation. Furthermore, each algorithm speedup was computed using the formula represented in Eq. (5).

$$speedup = \frac{T_{serial}}{T_{parallel}} \tag{5}$$

Where T_{serial} denotes the computational time to solve a test function with the fastest serial code on a specific parallel computer, while $T_{parallel}$ is the computational time to solve the same problem with the parallel code using P processors (or thread) on the same computer.

4.2   Results and Discussion

The results obtained from the serial executions of the SOS algorithm, with the various test functions, are shown below in Table 3. The table also presents the ranges (upper and lower bounds), dimensions used, formulations, the average solutions and the standard deviations, for each test function. The averages were calculated over 20 runs. Considering the results presented in Tables 3 and 4, for the Ackley test function, when SOS was parallelized with all thread variations (two, four, and eight threads), there was a noticeable reduction in execution time mostly for two and four threads. However, the average solution and standard deviation for each of the implementations, remained consistent. A similar observation where speedup was recorded in favour of the parallel implementation as compared to their serial counterparts, includes those test functions with high dimension between ten and thirty, while the serial implementation seemed to have outperformed the parallel approach in those test functions with smaller dimensions. It can also be seen that the execution time increases as the number of threads increases.

Table 3. Serial execution times (in seconds) for the serial SOS algorithm (Avg.: average solution for 20 runs, s.dev.: standard deviation)

Fn	Function	Range	D	Avg.	s.dev.	CPU time
F1	Ackley	[−32, 32]	30	0	0	0.033878
F2	Beale	[−4.5, 4.5]	2	0	0	0.005961
F3	Bohachevsky1	[−100, 100]	2	0	0	0.005580
F4	Bohachevsky2	[−100, 100]	2	0	0	0.005515
F5	Bohachevsky3	[−100, 100]	2	0	0	0.005299
F6	Booth	[−10, 10]	2	0	0	0.004399
F7	Colville	[−10, 10]	4	−131.619	28.2474	0.006420
F8	Dixon-Price	[−10, 10]	30	0.2959	0.5911	0.027063
F9	Griewank	[−600, 600]	30	0	0	0.042255
F10	Michalewicz2	[0, π]	2	−1.8013	0	0.008939
F11	Michalewicz5	[0, π]	5	−4.6877	0	0.018634
F12	Michalewicz10	[0, π]	10	−9.3681	0.1576	0.036714
F13	Quartic	[−1.28, 1.28]	30	0.0021	0.0008	0.067570
F14	Rastrigin	[−5.12, 5.12]	30	0	0	0.037385
F15	Rosenbrock	[−30, 30]	30	24.8821	0.3386	0.031379
F16	Schaffer	[−100, 100]	2	0	0	0.008314
F17	Sphere	[−100, 100]	30	0	0	0.021405
F18	Step	[−5.12, 5.12]	30	0	0	0.023198
F19	SumSquares	[−10, 10]	30	0	0	0.021615
F20	Zakharov	[−5, 10]	10	0	0	0.013108
	Average					0.021232

In Table 4 below, the parallel results for two and four threads, are presented along with the corresponding average solutions and standard deviations. Again, the averages were calculated over 20 runs. With regard to the parallel versions of SOS with the Bohachevsky1 test function, using two threads achieved a computational time of 0.000179 s which was faster than the serial time, using four threads achieved an execution time that was 0.000033 s faster, whilst using eight threads slowed down the execution time. The least execution time was achieved with just two threads and as the thread number increased, so did the execution time. When the Bohachevsky2 test function was used, using two threads achieved a time that was 0.000082 s faster than the serial, using four threads achieved a time that was 0.000024 s faster and using eight threads slowed down the time. Again, it can be seen that the execution time increases proportionately with an increase in the number of threads. For the Bohachevsky3 test function, two threads achieved a slight decrease in execution time of 0.00020 s, four threads achieved a better execution time of 0.0000129 s, while eight threads witnessed an increase in execution time. With this particular test function, it can be seen that initially, increasing the thread number increased the speed of the execution time, but when the thread number got too large (eight threads), the execution time deteriorated. For all the three Bohachevsky functions, the average solutions and standard deviations (when compared to that of the serial SOS) remained unchanged.

Table 4. Parallel SOS algorithm results with two and four threads for each test function

Function	CPU time	Avg.	s.dev.	CPU time	Avg.	s.dev.	CPU time	Avg.	s.dev.
F1	0.031994	0	0	0.032092	0	0	0.033058	0	0
F2	0.00507	0	0	0.005141	0	0	0.006035	0	0
F3	0.005401	0	0	0.005547	0	0	0.00559	0	0
F4	0.005433	0	0	0.005491	0	0	0.00552	0	0
F5	0.005097	0	0	0.00517	0	0	0.005464	0	0
F6	0.004472	0	0	0.004323	0	0	0.004667	0	0
F7	0.006179	−130.372	28.2159	0.006186	−125.155	38.8878	0.006459	−131.633	28.2505
F8	0.025908	1.0991	2.7537	0.026	0.9075	2.673	0.027028	2.3903	6.0451
F9	0.041157	0	0	0.041252	0	0	0.042116	0	0
F10	0.009102	−1.8013	0	0.009109	−1.8013	0	0.009242	−1.8013	0
F11	0.018772	−4.6877	0	0.019441	−4.6877	0	0.018884	−4.6877	0
F12	0.035273	−9.3091	0.1867	0.036675	−9.3505	0.1916	0.037106	−9.4740	0.1514
F13	0.054024	0.0018	0.0006	0.05705	0.0023	0.0010	0.066896	0.0022	0.0011
F14	0.03042	0	0	0.031309	0	0	0.040076	0	0
F15	0.030851	24.8821	0.2451	0.0311	24.9423	0.3891	0.030557	24.9482	0.2116
F16	0.007656	0	0	0.007802	0	0	0.008011	0	0
F17	0.020077	0	0	0.020756	0	0	0.022487	0	0
F18	0.021006	0	0	0.022383	0	0	0.023545	0	0
F19	0.01159	0	0	0.021464	0	0	0.022469	0	0
F20	0.011017	0	0	0.011463	0	0	0.01301	0	0
Average	0.019025			0.019988			0.021411		

The results shown in Tables 2 and 3 also revealed that the serial SOS algorithm solved the Booth function more efficiently with less computational time when compared to the parallel version of the algorithm. Furthermore, the parallelized versions of the SOS resulted in slower execution times than that of the serial SOS when used to solve Michalewicz2 and Michalewicz5 test functions respectively. The results also show that as the number of threads increased, so did the execution time. Using the Colville function to analyse both algorithms, shows that with a parallel SOS, two threads lead to an execution time that was 0.000241 s faster than its serial counterpart. Using four threads also lead to an increase in the speed of execution, which was 0.000234 s faster than the serial time, but eight threads lead to a slower time than that of the serial implementation. However, the average solutions and standard deviations increased as SOS was parallelized using more threads.

When a parallelized SOS was run with the Dixon-Price function, using two threads produced a better execution speed which was 0.00155 s faster than the serial time, while using four threads resulted in a speed that was 0.001063 s and eight threads produced a better execution speed of 0.000035 s above the serial time. However, two and four threads obtained average solutions and standard deviations that were much higher than that of the serial time. When running the Griewank function with a parallel SOS, two threads obtained a better execution speed, four and eight threads obtained execution speeds that were 0.001003 and 0.00039 s better than the serial program. The average solutions and standard deviations remained unchanged. The average computation cost difference (denoted as Gap) between SOS serial code and its parallel code versions is shown in Fig. 2 below.

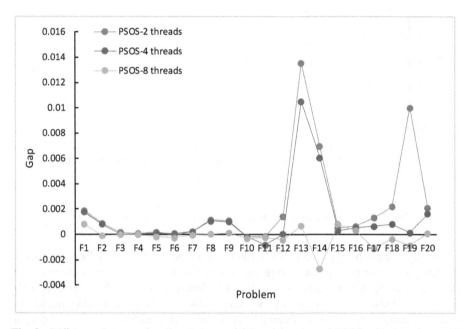

Fig. 2. Difference in execution time between SOS serial code and PSOS with two, four, and eight threads

In Fig. 3, the speedup obtained by the parallel SOS or PSOS using two, four, and eight threads is presented. Although by many measures the speedup appears to be rather poor, the illustrated results in Fig. 3 shows that in most cases speedup >1 is achieved for all the test functions, except for test function F7, F11, and F12 using two threads and F11 and F12 using four threads. However, in the case of eight threads, speed >1 were only achieved for test functions F1, F9, F10, F14, F16, F17, and F20. In general, the speedup increase as the test function problem dimension increases concurrently. Therefore, the proposed parallelization strategy could be used to decrease the amount of computational cost required to accomplish real-world problems with complex large graph sizes.

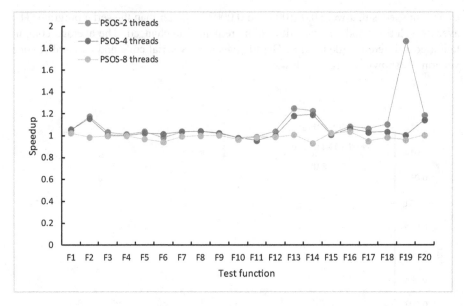

Fig. 3. Speedup on each test function using two, four and eight threads.

To summarize the entire analyses, it can be observed that the parallelization process yielded productive effort, considering the fact that reasonable execution speeds were attained in using the parallel SOS to solve test functions with high dimension. This somewhat appears to attain one of the main goals of parallel computing model. In several instances, it was also observed that using two threads for any test function produced a better speedup for the parallel SOS algorithm than its serial counterpart, and that the execution times increased as the number of threads increased. This characteristic can be attributed to the fact that the communication taking place between the threads actually creates additional computational cost overhead to the program making it less efficient. However, if using eight threads was somehow more efficient than when using four threads, this can be explained by the fact that randomness is present in the program (SOS being a population based metaheuristic) or by the fact that a particular execution time may have been an outlier when compared to the other times.

5   Conclusion and Future Work

This paper experimented the first parallel implementation techniques for the symbiotic organisms search algorithm on a multicore computing system using the well-known Open multiprocessor parallel programming model or OpenMP. The computational results obtained from the experiments showed that the SOS algorithm does possess some potential for parallelism. For example, an overall average of 0.021232 s was recorded in the case of using the serial SOS to solve the twenty test functions, while overall averages of 0.019025, 0.019988, and 0.021411 s were recorded for the PSOS respectively. However, using OpenMP may not be the best parallel programming technique to do so because it is mostly used for loop parallelization. This work can be extended by investigating the use of either a different parallel communication strategy such as Message Passing Interface (MPI) or on a Graphic Processor Unit (GPU) to parallelize the SOS algorithm. Using test functions with higher dimensions can also be investigated to determine whether better execution times will arise due to the fact that parallelization thrives on more compute intensive operations.

References

1. Cheng, M.Y., Prayogo, D.: Symbiotic organisms search: a new metaheuristic optimization algorithm. Comput. Struct. **139**, 98–112 (2014)
2. Ezugwu, A.E., Prayogo, D.: Symbiotic Organisms Search Algorithm: theory, recent advances and applications. Expert Syst. Appl. **119**(2019), 184–209 (2018)
3. Ezugwu, A.E.S., Adewumi, A.O., Frîncu, M.E.: Simulated annealing based symbiotic organisms search optimization algorithm for traveling salesman problem. Expert Syst. Appl. **77**, 189–210 (2017)
4. Ezugwu, A.E.S., Adewumi, A.O.: Discrete symbiotic organisms search algorithm for travelling salesman problem. Expert Syst. Appl. **87**, 70–78 (2017)
5. Ezugwu, A.E., Adeleke, O.J., Viriri, S.: Symbiotic organisms search algorithm for the unrelated parallel machines scheduling with sequence-dependent setup times. PLoS ONE **13** (7), e0200030 (2018)
6. Ezugwu, A.E.: Enhanced symbiotic organisms search algorithm for unrelated parallel machines manufacturing scheduling with setup times. Knowl.-Based Syst. **172**, 15–32 (2019)
7. Govender, P., Ezugwu, A.E.: A symbiotic organisms search algorithm for optimal allocation of blood products. IEEE Access **7**, 2567–2588 (2019)
8. Govender, P., Ezugwu, A.E.: A symbiotic organisms search algorithm for blood assignment problem. In: Blesa Aguilera, M.J., Blum, C., Gambini Santos, H., Pinacho-Davidson, P., Godoy del Campo, J. (eds.) HM 2019. LNCS, vol. 11299, pp. 200–208. Springer, Cham (2019). https://doi.org/10.1007/978-3-030-05983-5_16
9. Ezugwu, A.E., Adeleke, O.J., Akinyelu, A.A., et al.: A conceptual comparison of severalmetaheuristic algorithms on continuous optimisation problems. Neural Comput. Appl. (2019). https://doi.org/10.1007/s00521-019-04132-w
10. Lalwani, S., Sharma, H., Satapathy, S.C., et al.: A survey on parallelparticle swarm optimization algorithms. Arab. J. Sci. Eng. **44**, 2899 (2019). https://doi.org/10.1007/s13369-018-03713-6
11. Randall, M., Lewis, A.: A parallel implementation of ant colony optimization. J. Parallel Distrib. Comput. **62**(9), 1421–1432 (2002)
12. Mühlenbein, H., Schomisch, M., Born, J.: The parallel genetic algorithm as function optimizer. Parallel Comput. **17**(6–7), 619–632 (1991)
13. Husselmann, A.V., Hawick, K.A.: Parallel parametric optimisation with firefly algorithms on graphical processing units. In: Proceedings of the International Conference on Genetic and Evolutionary Methods (GEM12), Number CSTN-141. CSREA, Las Vegas, USA, 16–19 July 2012 pp. 77–83, July 2012
14. Tasoulis, D.K., Pavlidis, N.G., Plagianakos, V.P., Vrahatis, M.N.: Parallel differential evolution. In: Congress on Evolutionary Computation 2004, CEC2004, vol. 2, pp. 2023–2029. IEEE, June 2004

15. Zhou, Y., He, F., Hou, N., Qiu, Y.: Parallel ant colony optimization on multi-core SIMD CPUs. Future Gener. Comput. Syst. **79**(2018), 473–487 (2017)
16. Shonkwiler, R.: Parallel genetic algorithms. In: ICGA, pp. 199–205, June 1993
17. Ntipteni, M.S., Valakos, I.M., Nikolos, I.K.: An asynchronous parallel differential evolution algorithm. In: Proceedings of the ERCOFTAC Conference on Design Optimisation: Methods and Application (2006)
18. Chang, J.F., Roddick, J.F., Pan, J.S., Chu, S.C.: A parallel particle swarm optimization algorithm with communication strategies. J. Inf. Sci. Eng. **21**(2018), 809–818 (2005)
19. Koh, B., George, A., Haftka, R., Fregly, B.: Parallel asynchronous particle swarm optimization. Int. J. Numer. Meth. Eng. **67**(4), 578–595 (2006)
20. Nama, S., Saha, A., Ghosh, S.: Improved symbiotic organisms search algorithm for solving unconstrained function optimization. Decis. Sci. Lett. **5**(3), 361–380 (2016)
21. Silberschatz, A., Gagne, G., Galvin, P.B.: Operating System Concepts. Wiley, Hoboken (2018)
22. Chapman, B., Jost, G., Van Der Pas, R.: Using OpenMP: Portable Shared Memory Parallel Programming, vol. 10. MIT Press, Cambridge (2008)
23. OpenMP: Admin Magazine. http://www.admin-magazine.com/HPC/Articles/Programming-with-OpenMP. Accessed 23 Nov 2018
24. SOS source code. http://140.118.5.112:85/SOS/MOSOS.html. Accessed 23 Nov 2018
25. https://www.howtoforge.com/tutorial/how-to-install-and-use-profiling-tool-gprof/. Accessed 28 Nov 2018

Stock Price Forecasting Using Symbiotic Organisms Search Trained Neural Networks

Bradley J. Pillay[1] and Absalom E. Ezugwu[2(✉)]

[1] School of Mathematics, Statistics and Computer Science,
University of KwaZulu-Natal, Westville Campus, Private Bag X54001,
Durban 4000, South Africa
215031687@stu.ukzn.ac.za
[2] School of Computer Science, University of KwaZulu-Natal,
King Edward Road, Pietermaritzburg Campus, Pietermaritzburg 3201,
KwaZulu-Natal, South Africa
EzugwuA@ukzn.ac.za

Abstract. The prediction of stock prices is an important task in economics, investment and financial decision-making. This has for decades, spurred the interest of many researchers through their focused research in designing stock price predictive models. In this paper, the symbiotic organisms search algorithm, a new metaheuristic algorithm is employed as an efficient method for training feedforward neural networks. The training process is used to build a better stock price predictive model. The Straits Times Index, Russell 2,000, NASDAQ Composite and Dow Jones Industrial Average indices are utilized as time series dataset for training and testing the new system. Three evaluation methods namely, Root Mean Squared Error, Mean Absolute Percentage Error and Mean Absolute Deviation are used to compare the results of the implemented model. The results obtained revealed that the hybrid model exhibited outstanding predictive performance compared to the hybrid Particle Swarm Optimization, Genetic Algorithm, and Auto Regressive Integrated Moving Average based models. The new model is a promising predictive technique for solving high dimensional nonlinear time series data that are difficult to capture by traditional models.

Keywords: Stock price prediction · Symbiotic organisms search algorithm · Particle Swarm Optimization · Artificial Neural Networks

1 Introduction

Stock market prediction is the act of trying to determine the future value of a company stock or other financial instruments traded on an exchange. The successful prediction of a stock's future price serves as a guide for investors to be cautious of their investments. The efficient-market hypothesis suggests that stock prices reflect all currently available information and any price changes that are not based on newly revealed information thus are inherently unpredictable [1]. Other schools of thoughts disagree and these individuals rely on various methods and technologies to gain insight on future price information [2].

© Springer Nature Switzerland AG 2019
S. Misra et al. (Eds.): ICCSA 2019, LNCS 11623, pp. 673–688, 2019.
https://doi.org/10.1007/978-3-030-24308-1_53

The value of a stock price is influenced by the earnings per share, firm's book value, price earnings ratio and dividends per share. Although these factors are the fundamental units influencing the base stock price, the market also reflects a power over a specific stock price at any point in time. This is due to the constant pull and push of demand and supply within the market, this fluctuation may be due to trader's personal preference, events portrayed by the news, strategic approaches to stock exchange or perceptions based on other traders behaviour. These fluctuations may be estimated based on past behavioural patterns of a particular stock to an extent, however random events that force the stock to behave out of its norm are very difficult to predict. These occurrences are what experienced traders look for in maximising their profits. As such, any insight on these anomalies prove to be highly valuable to any trader within the market [3].

Traditionally, stock price forecasting has been carried out using time series analysis [4]. With the emergence of Artificial Neural Networks (ANNs), this form of analysis could be effectively performed at scale with higher levels of accuracy and accountability for unconceived variables [5–7]. Furthermore, non-hybridized time series models are outperformed by ANNs and Auto Regressive Integrated Moving Average (ARIMA) hybrids [2]. Evaluation of the prediction accuracy of these approaches are undertaken through the computation of the Root Mean-Squared Error (RMSE) and the Mean Absolute Percentage Error (MAPE). However, this evaluation should represent how much financial value each possesses, as such performance is measured by profitability, consistency and robustness [8].

In this paper, an efficient hybrid symbiotic organisms search (SOS) algorithm, which is combined with a Feed-forward Neural Networks (FFNNs) is developed to solve the stock price prediction problem. The goals of this paper is therefore, to demonstrate the applicability of the SOS algorithm an ANNs and to also show that the new hybrid method is able to obtain better predications when compared with other existing methods that have been applied to solve the same problem. The ARIMA based model, Particle Swarm Optimization (PSO) algorithm, and Genetic Algorithm (GA), of which the last two are well-known global optimization metaheuristics are implemented and evaluated in order to demonstrate the outperformance of the proposed hybrid SOS algorithm.

The rest of the paper is organized as follows: Sect. 2 presents related work, which involves using FFNNs and hybrid models that consist of both metaheuristic algorithms. The motivation and methodology of the proposed prediction approach and three other implementation models are discussed in Sect. 3. Section 4 presents the experimental results using recent time-series datasets. Finally, the concluding remarks is given in Sect. 5.

2 Related Work

In the past decade, the application of artificial intelligence and machine learning techniques such the ANNs have been used for the forecasting of Straits Time Indices (STI). Several literatures tend to focus on portfolio optimisation which is the act of selecting which stocks to invest your money in, given a finite capital and finite set of available stocks [9, 10]. This however is not the focus of this study, although it is a main focus point when considering utilising machine learning techniques for optimising return on investment.

In [8], the use of multiple methods for the prediction of stock prices was investigated. The authors used the stock prices of five different companies which were obtained from Yahoo Finance. The four different forecasting methods investigated were: ARIMA model, ANNs, Holt's Winters (a statistical forecasting method for seasonal time-series data) and time-series linear model (TSLM). It was found that the Holt's Winters method produced the best overall forecasting accuracy compared to the other methods [8]. In [11], the SOS algorithm was proposed for training a FFNNs. The computational results from the training with SOS were compared to other results obtained from similar training of FFNNs using other metaheuristic search algorithms, such as the culture search (CS), genetic algorithm (GA), particle swarm optimisation (PSO), mean-variance optimisation (MVO), gravitational search algorithm (GSA), and biogeography-based optimisation (BBO). The results showed that the SOS trained the FFNNs the best for the task at hand [11].

The study conducted in [12] used both the PSO and backpropagation algorithm to train a FFNNs for time-series forecasting. There were four types of time-series data used, these are sunspots (number of sunspots observed over a period of time), exchange-rate (the USD to INR exchange rate), earthquake (seismogram readings over time) and airline (the number of airline passengers). The results obtained were compared to results from other methods used to predict time-series data, such as the PSO-only trained FFNNs, backpropagation trained ANNs, and the Box-Jenkins models (which are statistically based models for predicting time-series data). Experimentation from the study showed that the PSO-only models were notably better than the backpropagation only models and that the hybrid approach (PSO + backpropagation) was better than the Box-Jenkins models [12].

The FFNNs variants proposed in [13] were used for stock market data (NAV of SBI mutual fund) prediction and evaluation of the performances of three different methods for adjusting the network weights during training: the resilient backpropagation method, the Levenberg-Marquardt (also referred to as Bayesian regularisation) method and the scaled conjugate gradient method. It was observed that the Bayesian regularisation method was the best at being able to generalise on the given data compared to the other training methods [13]. The study in [14] used the PSO algorithm to optimise the weights of an artificial neural network, which was used to forecast the exchange rate of the Straits Times Index (STI) time series data. The results obtained were very promising and interesting.

Therefore, building on the identified gap from the above related literature, the current study tries to replicate the earlier proposal made in [14] where the PSO algorithm was utilised for training neural networks. The current study, however, considers the employment of a more recent metaheuristic algorithm for the training of FFNNs with the main goal of building a more robust and efficient stock price predictive model.

In the next section, two of the main algorithms that inspired the current work, namely SOS and PSO are briefly discussed. Thereafter, the implementations of four hybrid models including SOS + FFNN, PSO + FFNN, GA + FFNN, and ARIMA model are explained.

3 Motivation and Methodology

The symbiotic organisms search algorithm is a new metaheuristic optimization algorithm that in recent time, attracted the attention of the research community because of the simplicity of its implementation and success records [15, 16]. The SOS algorithm has been widely used in many applications, such as parallel machine scheduling problem [17, 18], optimal allocation blood products [19, 20], and traveling salesman problem [21, 22]. The algorithm simulates the symbiotic interactions within a paired organism relationship that are used to search for the fittest organism [16]. The SOS iteratively uses a population of candidate solutions to promising areas in the search space in the process of seeking the optimal global solution. In the initial ecosystem, a group of organisms is generated randomly for the search space. Each organism represents one candidate solution and is associated with a certain fitness value, which reflects the degree of adaptation to the desired objective. The generation of new solutions is governed by three phases: the mutualism phase, commensalism phase, and parasitism phase. The nature of the interaction defines the main principle of each phase. Interactions benefit both sides in the mutualism phase; interactions benefit one side and do not impact the other in the commensalism phase; interactions benefit one side and actively harm the other in the parasitism phase. Each organism interacts with the other organism randomly through all phases. The process is repeated until termination criteria are met. The reader may refer to the work presented in [16] for an in-depth understanding of the fundamental design concept and computational representation of the three SOS global optimization search phases.

The SOS algorithm was chosen because of its successful implementations in related researches [16], the SOS algorithm is perceived to have the capability of yielding good results and performance when applied to stock price. Another reason for choosing SOS is that its operations require no specific control parameter. There are many advantages of SOS that also factored into the decision to consider this algorithm for the training of FFNNs. The algorithm avoids the risk of compromised performance due to improper parameter tuning. This is the case since the only parameters that need to be set are the size of the population/ecosystem and the maximum number of evaluations. Other algorithms such as the Genetic Algorithm (GA), Differential Evolution (DE), PSO, Mine Blast Algorithm (MBA), and Cuckoo Search (CS) require the tuning of at least more than one specific algorithm control parameters in addition to these two parameters. The SOS algorithm uses three interaction strategies, mutualism, commensalism, and parasitism, to gradually improve candidate solutions. This makes the algorithm simpler and quicker to implement since no time needs to be spent on the choice of operators. An organism (candidate solution) in this algorithm is represented by a vector of size 2, where the values are the open and close stock values for a company. This representation was chosen since it is the most efficient way to represent all the necessary data and to be able to manipulate the data to get the best solutions.

The PSO algorithm used is the global best PSO hybridized with a neural network. In this algorithm, the neighborhood of each particle is the entire swarm. A swarm consists of a collection of particles, where each particle is a candidate solution. The particles are then evolved where each particle's position and velocity are changed according to its own experience and that of its neighbors. Each particle can communicate with every other particle, and each particle is attracted to the best particle found by any member in the swarm. Each particle is a point in an n-dimensional space and contains the set of all the weights in the neural network and the bias. The algorithm stops when the maximum number of iterations has been reached. The position of the ith particle is represented as $x_i = (x_{i1}, x_{i2}, \ldots, x_{in})$ and these components of position represent the individual weights and bias. The velocity of the ith particle is represented as $v_i = (v_{i1}, v_{i2}, \ldots, v_{in})$. There are no selection or evolutionary operators that are used. Instead, it uses a fitness function with updates of positions and velocities to find near optimal solutions.

The PSO algorithm has been chosen as a candidate competitive algorithm for the proposed SOS algorithm because it is a common algorithm used for stock price predictions. It is a good algorithm to compare SOS with since the results for the PSO implementation with neural networks has produced notable results for stock price prediction. It does not use operators such as mutation and crossover which makes it simpler and easier to implement. The search can be carried out by the speed of the particle. During the development of several generations, only the most optimist particle can transmit information onto the other particles, and the speed of the researching is very fast. The global best PSO model has been chosen since it converges faster than the l-best or the local best PSO models. This is due to the larger particle interconnectivity of the global best PSO model. However, global best PSO can easily be trapped in local minima, so more focus has to be given to exploration rather than exploitation during training. This is done by changing the PSO parameters such as higher values for the maximum velocity and inertia weight.

3.1 Modelling and Program Design

The model implementation for this study was coded in C# using Microsoft Visual Studio 2017 as the IDE. The program has a GUI interface where each of the three hybrid algorithms and ARIMA model can be run and the results displayed upon completion of the program run. The dataset used for training and testing contains data from 24 August 2017 to 1 November 2018 [24–27]. All the algorithms used the same dataset so that the performance comparisons between the algorithms would be more meaningful. All the algorithms were run on the same computer for 1000 iterations with a population size of 30. The details of the SOS, PSO, and GA with neural network algorithms and the ARIMA model are presented next.

3.2   Hybrid Symbiotic Organisms Search with Neural Networks

In order to improve the SOS algorithm, it is hybridized with a FFNNs. The idea of hybridizing SOS with a neural network was motivated by similar implementation method presented in [14], in which the PSO was hybridized with a neural network. Therefore, since hybridizing PSO with a neural network seemed to be a very common experience in the literature, it spurred interest on how SOS would perform if it was hybridized with a neural network. When it comes to stock price prediction there can be many companies involved and neural networks have good scalability to large datasets and work well with high dimensions. Neural networks also have the ability to model non-linear complex relationships and real-world stock market prediction is complex, so the application of neural networks will be beneficial. This hybridization works by using the SOS algorithm to train the neural network by finding the optimal weights and bias for the network in a similar way the PSO algorithm was used to train FFNNs in [14]. The network comprises of a single input layer with 2 nodes, a hidden layer with 8 nodes and an output layer with 2 nodes. A vector represents each organism or candidate solution, which contains the weights from the input layer to the hidden layer, the weights from the hidden layer to the output layer and the bias value for the network. This vector has a length of 34. The representation of the vector is illustrated as shown in Fig. 1.

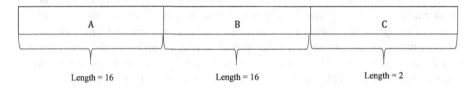

Fig. 1. Structure (Design) of candidate solution

A – weights linking the input layer nodes to the hidden layer nodes
B – weights linking the hidden layer nodes to the output layer nodes
C – the values for the bias.

The algorithm is trained using 240 instances which formed the training set. The testing set contains 60 instances since the dataset was split 80% for training and 20% for testing. The training and testing set was normalized independently after the train-test split. A population size of 30 is used and the algorithm is run over 1000 iterations. The algorithm takes two inputs: the open value and the close value for a stock and then predicts these two values for the next day. The RMSE is used as the fitness function in this algorithm since the goal is to minimize the error of the prediction, so an error formula is an appropriate fitness function.

Algorithm 1: Hybrid SOS with a Feed-forward Neural Networks

1	Initialize a population of size 30, composing of individuals described in Figure 1 (above). Each cell of the individuals is randomly initialized to values that are between 0 and 1.
2	REPEAT for each individual in the population
3	Initialize the weights of the neural network with the corresponding weights contained by the individual
4	REPEAT for each training instance
5	Input the instance in the FFNNs to obtain an output
6	Calculate RMSE for the output and the expected output
7	END
8	Calculate the Average of RMSE values which will serve as the fitness value of the individual
9	END
10	REPEAT
11	Increase number of iterations by 1
12	REPEAT for each individual X_i in the population
13	Set the best individual X_{best} to the individual with the lowest fitness value
14	MUTUALISM PHASE

15	Select an individual X_j randomly
	            Determine a mutual relationship vector
	            Mutual_Vector $= (X_i + X_j) / 2$

16	Determine the benefit factors BF1 and BF2, where the benefit factors are either 1 or 2

17	Modify X_{i_new} and X_{j_new} based on their mutual relationship
	            $X_{i\_new} = X_i + rand(0,1) * (X_{best} - \text{Mutual\_Vector} * BF1)$
	            $X_{j\_new} = X_j + rand(0,1) * (X_{best} - \text{Mutual\_Vector} * BF2)$

18	Calculate the fitness of X_{i_new} and X_{j_new} by using lines 3 to 8
19	IF X_{i_new} fitness value is less than X_i
20	Replace X_i with X_{i_new}
21	END
22	IF X_{j_new} fitness value is less than X_j
23	Replace X_j with X_{j_new}
24	END
25	END
26	COMMENSALISM PHASE
27	Select an individual X_j randomly
28	$X_{new} \leftarrow X_i + rand(-1,1) * (X_{best} - X_j)$
29	Calculate the fitness of X_{new}
30	IF X_{i_new} fitness value is less than X_i
31	Replace X_i with X_{new}
32	END
33	END
34	PARASITISM PHASE
35	Select an individual X_j randomly
36	Create a parasite ($X_{parasite}$) from X_i
37	Calculate the fitness of $X_{parasite\text{-}+}$
38	IF $X_{parasite}$ fitness value is less than X_j
39	Replace X_j with $X_{parasite}$
40	END
41	END
42	END
43	UNTIL number of iterations are equal to 1000

3.3   Hybrid Particle Swarm Optimization with Neural Networks

The second model implementation is the employment of the PSO hybridized with a FFNNs. The neural network consists of an input layer that has 2 nodes, a hidden layer that has 8 nodes and an output layer that has 2 nodes. The inputs are opening value for a stock and a closing value for a stock for a day. The network outputs the predicted opening and closing values for the stock for the next day. In this algorithm a swarm is initialized with 30 particles where each particle is represented by a vector of size 34 that holds all the weights for the network as well as the bias value. The swarm is also initialized with random velocities. The $minX$ and $maxX$ values are set to -1 and 1. The fitness function used is RMSE so that the error between the predicted values and the actual values can be minimized. The positions and velocities are updated for every iteration. The inertia value is set at 0.9, the two constants c_1 and c_2 are both set at 2 and the probability of death is 0.01. The algorithm runs until the maximum number of 1000 iterations are reached. The best positions after the PSO is run provides the optimal weights for the neural network to be able to predict the output values.

3.4   Hybrid Genetic Algorithm with Neural Networks

The third model implementation is the Genetic Algorithm hybridized with a FFNNs. The operators used includes the Roulette Selection, Uniform Crossover with a cross-over rate set to 0.5, and Uniform Mutation with a mutation rate set to 1/(Length of individual) = 1/34. The population comprised of 30 individuals that were randomly initialized, and each individual is a vector of size 34. Elitism was used in selection for the population for the next generation, where the best individual is kept for the next generation. The fitness function used for this algorithm is the RMSE because we aim to minimize the error between the actual and predicted values. This algorithm was allowed to run for a maximum of 1000 iterations, and the best individual served as the optimal weights for the neural network to predict the output values.

3.5   Auto Regressive Integrated Moving Average

The fourth model is an Autoregressive Integrated Moving Average model. This implementation was done with an assistance of using the Extreme Optimization Numerical Libraries for .NET [23]. This library was built to assist developers to program financial, engineering and scientific applications. The auto regressive order was set to 0, the degree of differencing was set to 0 and the moving average was set to 2. These parameters yielded the best result compared to other combination of parameters settings tested on these datasets. Two ARIMA models were used, one to forecast the Open Stock Values for each day and the other was to forecast the Close Stock Values for each day.

3.6   Evaluation Metrics

A testing strategy that is used is the Mean Absolute Percentage Error (MAPE), which is a measure of the prediction accuracy of a forecasting method in statistics, for example in trend estimation. It is a very common testing strategy for stock price prediction algorithms and many organizations focus primarily on MAPE when assessing forecast accuracy. Most people are also more comfortable when dealing with percentage terms which makes this error easy to interpret. The formula is given in Eq. 1.

$$MAPE = \frac{100\%}{n} \sum_{t=1}^{n} \left| \frac{A_t - F_t}{A_t} \right| \tag{1}$$

where A_t is the actual value of the stock price and F_t is the forecast value from the algorithm. The absolute value in this calculation is summed for every forecasted point in time and divided by the number of fitted points n. Multiplying by 100% makes it a percentage error. A drawback of this method is that it cannot be used for data that has zero values since this could result in a division be zero error. This model is used nonetheless because it is highly unlikely that the price of a stock will be zero. Due to the pitfalls in MAPE, it is used in conjunction with other evaluation techniques like the Mean Absolute Deviation (MAD). With MAPE the lower the percentage error the better.

Another common evaluation metric to test forecasting accuracy is the Root Mean Squared Error (RMSE). The RMSE is frequently used measure of the differences between values predicted by a model or an estimator and the values observed. This technique is used mainly when there is variance in the data, and it makes use of standard deviation which is good when it comes to mathematical operations. RMSE is the square root of the average of squared differences between prediction and actual observation. It expresses the average model prediction error in units of the variable of interest. The metric can range from 0 to infinity and is indifferent to the direction of error. The formula for RMSE is given in Eq. 2.

$$RMSE = \sqrt{\frac{1}{n} \sum_{j=1}^{n} (y_j - \hat{y}_J)^2} \tag{2}$$

where n is the number of values, y_j is the forecast and the variable $\hat{y}_J$ is the mean error. Since the errors are squared before they are averaged, the RMSE gives a relatively high weight to large errors. This means that the RMSE should be more useful when large errors are particularly undesirable. RMSE avoids the use of taking the absolute value, which is not wanted in many mathematical calculations. It is a negatively-oriented score, which means lower values are better.

The last testing metric discussed is the MAD. Other than MAPE, MAD is the most popular metric for evaluating forecast accuracy. The mean absolute deviation of a dataset is the average distance between each data point and the mean. This strategy measures variance just like MSE but lacks the strong statistical relationship MSE has. MAD has the advantage of being easier to understand among people who are not specialists in the field, and this is partly due to the fact that the error has the same dimension as the forecast. The formula for calculating MAD is represented in Eq. 3.

$$MAD = \frac{1}{T}\sum_{t=1}^{T}|e_t - \hat{e}_t| \tag{3}$$

where T is the number of time periods, e_t is the forecast error in period t and the last term denoted by $\hat{e}_t$ is the mean error for period t. The metric MAD is used in conjunction with MAPE to help overcome the pitfalls of MAPE and give a better overall view of the results. The three testing metrics are used to ensure that the error of the forecast can be seen using different evaluations to make it easier to determine which forecasting algorithm produces the best results. This combined evaluation technique allows for a better comparison between the algorithms, so that a more informed decision can be made.

4 Experimental Results

All the algorithms were run on the same Micro-Star International (MSI) computer to allow for better comparison of the results. The computer specifications are indicated as follows: Processor: Intel® Core™ i7-7700HQ, CPU @ 2.80 GHz, Installed Memory (RAM): 12.0 GB, GPU: Nvidia GTX1050, System Type: 64-bit Operating System, x64-based processor Operating System: Windows 10 Home. Each algorithm was run 20 times and the average of the results was recorded. All the simulation results presented in this paper was generated using the stock price prediction GUI simulator shown in Figs. 2 and 3.

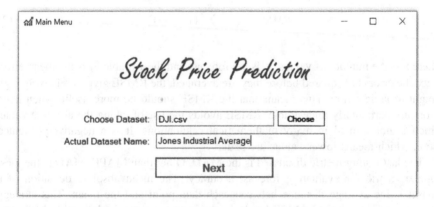

Fig. 2. Stock price prediction user interface with datasets file selection phase

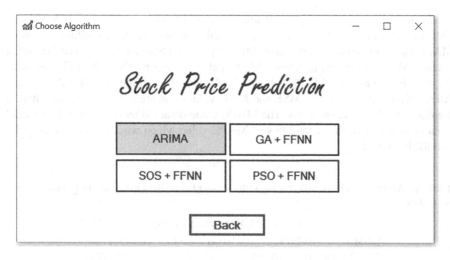

Fig. 3. Stock price prediction user interface with algorithm selection phase

4.1 Results and Discussion

The dataset used in this research are the Straits Times Index [24], NASDAQ Composite [25], Russel 2000 [26], and Dow Jones Industrial Average [27] financial stock data. The three hybrid algorithms were executed 20 times for each dataset and compared to the ARIMA model using parameters specified in Sect. 3.5. The results for each execution were evaluated using RMSE, MAD and MAPE. These evaluation metrics was applied to the open and close stock values independently. Thereafter, the final RMSE, MAD and MAPE values were calculated by taking the average evaluations obtained for the open and close stock values for each execution. Table 1 below displays the average results obtained by making use of the Straits Times Index (STI) dataset [24]. The algorithms that predicts values that are higher than the actual values obtain MAPE scores that are higher than 100%. All algorithms except the hybrid SOS model obtained MAPE values are significantly greater than 100%, as shown in Table 1 below. The ARIMA model obtained the highest average MAPE value. The hybridized PSO obtained the second highest average MAPE value, while the hybrid GA obtained the third highest average MAPE value. The SOS hybridized model achieved the lowest average MAPE value, together with the lowest MAD and RMSE values. All the MAD and RMSE values obtained by the four algorithms are close to zero indicating a small prediction error.

Table 1. Average results of different algorithms executed on Straits Times Index (STI) dataset

	Average RMSE	Average MAPE	Average MAD
ARIMA	0.27061	602.45719	0.22998
GA + FFNN	0.158544925	247.2920749	0.136108794
PSO + FFNN	0.178063764	287.124298	0.148943577
SOS + FFNN	**0.117305261**	**95.01212301**	**0.094189188**

Table 2 displays the average results obtained by making use of the Dow Jones Industrial Average (DJI) dataset [24]. For this dataset, all the algorithms obtained MAPE values extremely greater than 100%. The hybrid SOS model received the lowest average MAPE value, with hybrid PSO model following it. The hybrid GA obtained the third lowest average MAPE value and ARIMA achieved the highest MAPE value. All the algorithms received RMSE and MAD values that are very close to zero, hence, there are small prediction errors. The MAPE value obtained by the hybrid SOS model is more than half of the second lowest MAPE value which was achieved by the PSO hybridized model.

Table 2. Average results of different algorithms executed on the Dow Jones Industrial Average (DJI) dataset

	Average RMSE	Average MAPE	Average MAD
ARIMA	0.29781	4141.64874	0.24341
GA + FFNN	0.169998799	1958.530227	0.141143727
PSO + FFNN	0.191264126	1704.068111	0.157681562
SOS + FFNN	**0.144319287**	**841.839545**	**0.118860402**

Table 3 below displays the average results obtained by making use of the NAS-DAQ Composite dataset [25]. All four algorithms received MAPE values greater than 100%. However, the ARIMA model produced an average MAPE value that is the highest. The GA hybridized algorithm obtained the second highest MAPE value and PSO hybridized received the third highest. SOS hybridized proved again to obtain the lowest MAPE value and receiving MAD and RMSE values that are the closest to zero. The other algorithms also achieved MAD and RMSE values close to zero, showing a low prediction error, as shown in Table 3.

Table 3. Average results of different algorithms executed on the NASDAQ Composite dataset

	Average RMSE	Average MAPE	Average MAD
ARIMA	0.28175	2195.20135	0.23301
GA + FFNN	0.171553204	1654.548538	0.146370212
PSO + FFNN	0.168955706	933.3688597	0.140076609
SOS + FFNN	**0.123727032**	**785.8357967**	**0.102633434**

Table 4 displays the average results obtained by making use of the Russel 2000 (RUT) dataset [26]. All algorithms obtained MAPE values higher than 100%. The SOS hybridized obtained the lowest average MAPE, RMSE and MAD values. The highest MAPE value was obtained by ARIMA followed by hybrid GA and tagged behind is the hybrid PSO algorithm. However, the RMSE and MAD values follow a different trend. The highest RMSE and MAD values was obtained by ARIMA followed by the hybrid PSO and then the hybrid GA. The hybrid SOS algorithm obtained values that are small and close to zero.

Table 4. Average results of different algorithms executed on the Russel 2000 dataset

	Average RMSE	Average MAPE	Average MAD
ARIMA	0.30676	832.86160	0.27815
GA + FFNN	0.169451308	459.2586704	0.145671891
PSO + FFNN	0.171527905	359.3365194	0.144370396
SOS + FFNN	**0.110566035**	**237.4466027**	**0.090007681**

Overall, it can clearly be seen that the hybrid SOS with a FFNNs outperforms the hybrid PSO, hybrid GA and ARIMA model for all the three evaluation techniques. Analyzing the results closely it can be seen that the hybrid SOS has lower scores for both RMSE and MAD values than the other three algorithms, which means that there is less variability in the data. Hence, the results are much more clustered around a line of best fit. Therefore, the findings of the current study reveals that the proposed hybrid SOS can be used as an alternative robust stock prices prediction algorithm.

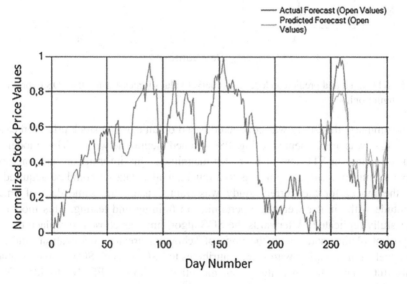

Fig. 4. STI actual and predicted open stock market values forecast using the SOS hybrid model (Color figure online)

Figure 4 above illustrates the forecast for the open stock values, while Fig. 5 shows the forecast for the close stock values for an execution of the SOS hybrid model on the STI dataset. The horizontal axis represents the days in chronological order, and the vertical axis represents the normalized stock values. The blue line graph in figure Figs. 4 and 5 depict the actual forecast for the given time period. Whilst, the orange line is the predicted forecast which starts around the 240th day mark. Comparing the actual and predicted forecast we can see that the predicted forecast is able to follow the same trend as the actual forecast. Majority of the predictions are really close to the actual values. However, when the actual stock values are greater than 0.8 for the open stock value forecast graphs, the predicted stock values do not come as close to the actual stock values, but the underestimation is a difference approximately below 0.2.

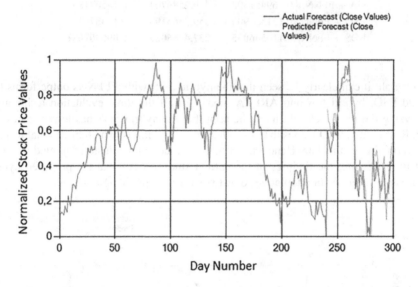

Fig. 5. STI actual and predicted close stock market values forecast using the SOS hybrid model (Color figure online)

In summary, this study was conducted based on an existing stock price-forecasting model that was implemented using PSO-trained neural networks. This model was initially trained on STI data of a greater magnitude, this information has since been removed from the source and access to a much smaller data set could be acquired. As such the model for the current study was trained using the same data of smaller magnitude with similar weighting pertaining to training and testing. This model was successfully replicated. Afterwards the SOS algorithm was chosen to replace the PSO component of the model with the hope of achieving greater optimization efficiency. SOS excels in many areas with similar attributes to PSO, as such SOS seemed viable as a substitute. The implementation was modelled without a FFNNs to identify the relationship between the algorithm and the problem without overlapping influence from the FFNNs. This model continued to show promise as the results experienced surpassed that of the PSO, GA, algorithms with a FFNNs. This inspired a further adaptation of the model to include a FFNNs to not only gain insight on this relationship but also in hopes of achieving better results.

5 Conclusion

The SOS with FFNNs model was developed and tested based on the existing combination of PSO and FFNNs study. Additional comparison that involves the implementation of hybrid GA with FFNNs and ARIMA model were carried out to further validate the superior performance of the hybrid SOS algorithm. The hybrid SOS with FFNNs outperformed hybrid PSO, GA with FFNNs and ARIMA models by noticeable margins. The shortcomings of SOS with FFNNs has been identified and attributed to the increased implementation complexity given by the combination of two already complex algorithms. Future improvements of SOS with FFNNs could include training on a much larger data set or data sets with much higher complexity levels. This could then be adapted to incorporate multi-objective parameters between relative stock prices that may influence another stock's price. Finally, a model consisting of a FFNNs with a hybridization that utilizes the SOS optimization algorithm shows promise in the area of stock price prediction and supersedes that of the PSO, GA, ARIMA models implementation. However, the added complexity of a FFNNs may prove to be an area that requires greater fine-tuning to achieve a better predictive accuracy.

References

1. Pownall, G., Wasley, C., Waymire, G.: The stock price effects of alternative types of management earnings forecasts. Acc. Rev. **68**, 896–912 (1993)
2. Pai, P.-F., Lin, C.-S.: A hybrid ARIMA and support vector machines model in stock price forecasting. Omega **33**(6), 497–505 (2005)
3. Seetharaman, A., Niranjan, I., Patwa, N., Kejriwal, A.: A study of the factors affecting the choice of investment portfolio by individual investors in Singapore. Acc. Financ. Res. **6**(3), 153 (2017)
4. Montgomery, D.C., Johnson, L.A., Gardiner, J.S.: Forecasting and Time Series Analysis. McGraw-Hill, New York etc. (1990)
5. Refenes, A.N., Zapranis, A., Francis, G.: Stock performance modeling using neural networks: a comparative study with regression models. Neural Netw. **7**(2), 375–388 (1994)
6. Schöneburg, E.: Stock price prediction using neural networks: a project report. Neurocomputing **2**(1), 17–27 (1990)
7. White, H.: Economic Prediction using Neural Networks: The Case of IBM Daily Stock Returns, pp. 451–458. University of California, Oakland (1988)
8. Ponnam, L.T., Rao, V.S., Srinivas, K., Raavi, V.: A comparative study on techniques used for prediction of stock market. In: International Conference on Automatic Control and Dynamic Optimization Techniques (ICACDOT), pp. 1–6. IEEE (2016)
9. Konno, H., Yamazaki, H.: Mean-absolute deviation portfolio optimization model and its applications to Tokyo stock market. Manag. Sci. **37**(5), 519–531 (1991)
10. Trippi, R.R., By-Lee, P., Jae, K.: Artificial Intelligence in Finance and Investing: State-of-the-Art Technologies for Securities Selection and Portfolio Management. McGraw-Hill Inc., New York (1995)
11. Wu, H., Zhou, Y., Luo, Q., Basset, M.A.: Training feedforward neural networks using symbiotic organisms search algorithm. Comput. Intell. Neurosci. **2016**, 14 (2016)
12. Adhikari, R., Agrawal, R.K.: Hybridization of artificial neural network and Particle Swarm Optimization methods for time series forecasting. Int. J. Appl. Evol. Comput. (IJAEC) **4**(3), 75–90 (2013)
13. Jabin, S.: Stock market prediction using feed-forward artificial neural network. Int. J. Comput. Appl. **99**(9), 4–8 (2014)
14. Junyou, B.: Stock price forecasting using PSO-trained neural networks. In: IEEE Congress on Evolutionary Computation 2007, CEC 2007, pp. 2879–2885. IEEE (2007)

15. Ezugwu, A.E., Adeleke, O.J., Akinyelu, A.A., Viriri, S.: A conceptual comparison of several metaheuristic algorithms on continuous optimisation problems. Neural Comput. Appl. 1–45 (2019)
16. Ezugwu, A.E., Prayogo, D.: Symbiotic organisms search algorithm: theory, recent advances and applications. Expert Syst. Appl. **119**, 184–209 (2019)
17. Ezugwu, A.E., Adeleke, O.J., Viriri, S.: Symbiotic organisms search algorithm for the unrelated parallel machines scheduling with sequence-dependent setup times. PLoS ONE **13** (7), e0200030 (2018). https://doi.org/10.1371/journal.pone.0200030
18. Ezugwu, A.E.: Enhanced symbiotic organisms search algorithm for unrelated parallel machines manufacturing scheduling with setup times. Knowl.-Based Syst. **172**, 15–32 (2019)
19. Govender, P., Ezugwu, A.E.: A symbiotic organisms search algorithm for optimal allocation of blood products. IEEE Access **7**, 2567–2588 (2019)
20. Govender, P., Ezugwu, A.E.: A symbiotic organisms search algorithm for blood assignment problem. In: Blesa Aguilera, M.J., Blum, C., Gambini Santos, H., Pinacho-Davidson, P., Godoy del Campo, J. (eds.) HM 2019. LNCS, vol. 11299, pp. 200–208. Springer, Cham (2019). https://doi.org/10.1007/978-3-030-05983-5_16
21. Ezugwu, A.E., Adewumi, A.O., Frîncu, M.E.: Simulated annealing based symbiotic organisms search optimization algorithm for traveling salesman problem. Expert Syst. Appl. **77**, 189–210 (2017)
22. Ezugwu, A.E., Adewumi, A.O.: Discrete symbiotic organisms search algorithm for travelling salesman problem. Expert Syst. Appl. **87**, 70–78 (2017)
23. https://www.extremeoptimization.com/Default.aspx. Accessed 12 Dec 2018
24. https://finance.yahoo.com/quote/%5ESTI%3FP%3D%5ESTI/history/. Accessed 02 Dec 2018
25. NASDAQ Composite dataset. https://finance.yahoo.com/quote/%5EIXIC/history?period1=1511987617&period2=1543523617&interval=1d&filter=history&frequency=1d. Accessed 29 Nov 2018
26. Russel 2000 (RUT) dataset. https://finance.yahoo.com/quote/%5ERUT/history?period1=1511987909&period2=1543523909&interval=1d&filter=history&frequency=1d. Accessed 29 Nov 2018
27. Dow Jones Industrial Average. https://finance.yahoo.com/quote/%5EDJI/history?period1=1511987909&period2=1543523909&interval=1d&filter=history&frequency=1d. Accessed 29 Nov 2018

A Comparative Analysis of Temporal Changes in Urban Land Use Resorting to Advanced Remote Sensing and GIS in Karaj, Iran and Luxor, Egypt

Abdelaziz Elfadaly[1,2,3], Beniamino Murgante[4],
Mohamad Molaei Qelichi[5(✉)], Rosa Lasaponara[1], and Ali Hosseini[5]

[1] Italian National Research Council, C.da Santa Loja, Potenza, Tito Scalo, Italy
[2] National Authority for Remote Sensing and Space Sciences, Cairo, Egypt
[3] Department of European and Mediterranean Cultures, University of Basilicata, Matera, Italy
[4] School of Engineering, University of Basilicata, Potenza, Italy
beniamino.murgante@unibas.it
[5] Faculty of Geography, University of Tehran, Tehran, Iran
Molaeil@ut.ac.ir

Abstract. As many developing countries, Iranian and Egyptian cities are growing in population and physically expanding at a high rate. The uncontrolled scattered construction causes loss of orchards, agricultural lands as well as spatial chaos, traffic congestion and increasing costs of municipal services. As a consequence, this also induces a loss of identity and social characteristics of neighborhoods, poor quality of life and degradation of natural landscapes, etc. To face with these issues, it is important to quantify trend and the rate of land cover conversion in order to support plan for a rational land use policy. The main purpose of this research is to set up low cost and reliable tools useful for the monitoring of the urban growth. In this paper, multi-temporal satellite data (Landsat TM 1984, Landsat TM 1998 and L8 2016) have been analyzed for investigating and assessing the effects of the urban expansion in Karaj (Iran) and Luxor (Egypt). According to the results obtained from change detection analysis, both of the investigated sites clearly exhibit an increasing trend in urban expansion much more evident in the case of Luxor than Karaj area. The integration between remote sensing and GIS and the joint use of analytical methods for quantitative-qualitative assessment enable the identification of changes and the mapping of new planned and unplanned urban construction. The availability of timely information free available from NASA web site and the data processing herein adopted provide useful information for supporting planning and sustainable developing policies.

Keywords: Urban distribution · Land use changes · Urban growth ·
Karaj (Iran) · Luxor (Egypt)

© Springer Nature Switzerland AG 2019
S. Misra et al. (Eds.): ICCSA 2019, LNCS 11623, pp. 689–703, 2019.
https://doi.org/10.1007/978-3-030-24308-1_54

1 Introduction

The urbanization is recognized as one of the most irreversible human impacts on environment causing loss of soil, altering hydrological and biogeochemical cycles, modifying energy demand, changing precipitation patterns at scales of hundreds of square kilometers [1] therefore, altering the climate. Moreover, unplanned human settlement consumes land at an alarming rate, fragments habitats reduces biodiversity and produces unsustainable and unlivable city with the lack of open space and arterial grids. This poses serious threats to high-value of urban ecosystems and makes the need for sustainable urban planning and monitoring an urgent priority [2–4]. As in other parts of the world, also in Iran and Egypt, the rapid development of urbanization has been causing critical environmental problems in different areas.

Actually, in Egypt uninhabited lands represent about 95% of the total area. However, the majority of the population is concentrated around the Nile River. This unbalanced distribution causes serious social and economic problems. In particular, the current fast growing of Luxor region is expected to further increase over the next twenty years with at least a doubling in population. The recent completion of a Luxor Bridge and the nearby expansion of a port for the cruise at the south of Luxor City, will favor informal, unplanned development in the southern part of the area. Unplanned urban sprawl will result in negative consequences for the future prosperity of the whole area that is actually one of the biggest and most famous tourist attractions also due to the discovery of the Tutankhamen tomb in 1922. Timely actions to stem this undesirable growth are essential. To this aim, some authors as [5] suggest that a new attractive town can become a magnet for a new planned development in the Luxor region.

Similar critical situations are also present in Iran, as for example in Karaj metropolis whose periphery is involved in an extensive urban expansion and needs to face the relative critical challenges as currently occurring for the whole national territory [6]. This is due to interrelate economic, social and political factors, which induce diffuse changes in lifestyles and drive the evolution of the city so that urban suburbs moved into rural lands involving the conversion of open space into built-up areas.

This current situation and the expected future scenarios impose the need of planning and monitoring. To this aim, the availability of reliable information on the past and current conditions is a critical point for defining and planning potential future scenarios. In this context, satellite data (today also available free of charge) can provide both (i) historical time-series data set and (ii) timely updated information related to the current urban spatial structure and city edges as well as parameters to assess urban effects.

The main purpose of this research is the use of satellite Landsat data for the assessment of urban distribution in both Karaj and Luxor city, respectively in Iran and Egypt, as a comparative analysis. The study is addressed to the investigation of urban growth pattern process for the detection and analysis of changes in urban areas at Karaj and Luxor occurred over the same time period spanning from 1984 to 2016.

2 Study Area

Luxor city is located 600 km (DMS Long 32° 38′ 22.6932″ E, DMS Lat 25° 41′ 14.0748″ N) south of Cairo on the west and east bank of the River Nile [7]. On the Nile's west bank, across from Luxor, is Thebes, the capital of Egypt from around 2000 to 1075 B.C.E. (Middle and New Kingdoms). The area is one of richest in antiquity treasures and attractive, but today threatened by urban sprawl and many parts of the Luxor city is lacking infrastructure (Fig. 1).

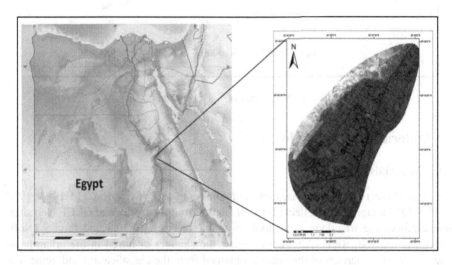

Fig. 1. Study area of Luxor city, Egypt

Karaj is capital of Alborz province in Iran, spanning between latitudes 35° 67′–36° 14 ′N and longitudes 50° 56′–51° 42 ′E and covers a total area of about 141 km^2. [8]. Over the last three decades, Karaj has been experiencing a significantly growing mostly due to its socioeconomic attractions. Past developments and current challenges have led to some instability in various aspects of environmental, socio-cultural, political-security, economic, spatial and etc. [9] (Fig. 2).

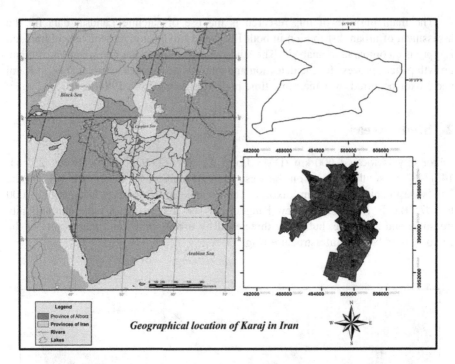

Fig. 2. Study area of Karaj city, Iran [10]

3 Material and Methodology

3.1 Materials

For both of the two study areas, multi-temporal data sets of Landsat TM 1984, 1998 and L8 2016 images were collected free of charge from the USGS and GLCF web sites. Image processing was done using tools available in Arc GIS 10.3 and Envi 5.1 software. The analyses were addressed to detect the changes occurred in the urban areas based on the comparison of the outputs obtained from the classification and geospatial analysis of the past and present data (Table 1).

Table 1. Data collection properties of the study areas (Luxor and Karaj).

Satellite	Sensor	Resolution (M)	Acquisition date
Landsat	TM	30 m	Sep 1984
Landsat	TM	30 m	Oct 1998
Landsat	L8	30 m	Sep 2016

3.2   Methodology

The selected images were geometrically and atmospherically corrected, in order to remove the effect of the atmosphere and make the images of 1984, 1998 and 2016 comparable. To this aim, the dark object subtraction was applied. After the pre-processing, the change detection was made by comparing the results from the classification.

Classification enables the clusterization of similar targets on the basis of the measured reflection values which depend on the local characteristics of the earth surface. In other words, there is a relationship between land cover and measured reflection values using several spectral bands (multi-spectral classification). Land cover types were identified on the basis of their spectral properties, classified and mapped for each study area and each time data set using both unsupervised, supervised classifications, and post supervised classification in order to capture the statistical patterns of the urban distribution.

Unsupervised Classification of Images
Normally there are two types of the algorithm (K-means and ISODATA) to perform the unsupervised classification [11]. In unsupervised classification method, clustering is obtained according to the number of classes required and the digital number exhibited by the processed pixels. Result from un-supervised classified is useful adopted as a reference/preliminary step for understanding the distribution of pixel values. In this research the ISODATA unsupervised classification was used for extracting the urban layer and carry on a preliminary analysis of the statistical distribution pattern.

Supervised Classification of Images
The classification of multi-temporal data set can inform us about the changes occurred over time i.e. quantify the area Involved in land cover change as for example variation from vegetation cover to urban. In supervised classification method, There are different image algorithms such as Parallelepiped, Minimum Distance, Maximum Likelihood, Binary Encoding, etc. [12, 13]. The categorization is done using the training sets (signatures) provided by the user on the basis of field knowledge. In this research, Maximum Likelihood Classification was applied to the spectral bands of each date.

Post Classification of Images
The accuracy of supervised image classification is a function of the consistency between the algorithms and input data [14]. The overall accuracy and Kappa coefficient was calculated for each study area on the basis of the Confusion Matrix (Table 2) which generates random subset of the training sets. The accuracy is generally quite high due to the fact that having an excellent knowledge of the both study areas we can provide reliable training sets related both to urban cover and other areas.

Table 2. Kappa coefficient of ROIs for each period

Year	Luxor		Karaj	
	Kappa coefficient	Overall accuracy	Kappa coefficient	Overall accuracy
1984	0.9974	99.8387%	0.9909	99.4142%
1998	0.9967	99.7976%	0.9938	99.5652%
2016	0.9925	99.5290%	0.9949	99.6606%

Getis-Ord and Hot Spot for Analyzing Spatial Distribution

Spatial autocorrelation in GIS helps understand the degree to which one object is similar to other nearby objects [15]. The process of urban growth associated with the study areas of Karaj and Luxor has analyzed also using spatial autocorrelation analysis to assess the spatial pattern of urban land use [16, 17]. Data derived from satellite images (using ENVI software) have been further processed and analyzed by using Getis-Ord (General G) statistic (in ArcGIS) to assess the degree of clustering by the identification of both "hot spots" and "cold spots". Getis-Ord Gi* statistic is denoted as Eq. 1 [18–22]:

$$Getis - Ord\ G_i^* = \frac{\sum_{j=1}^n w_{ij}x_j - \bar{X}\sum_{j=1}^n w_{ij}}{S\sqrt{\frac{\left[n\sum_{j=1}^n w_{ij}^2 - \left(\sum_{j=1}^n w_{ij}\right)\right]}{n-1}}} \tag{1}$$

In formula 1, X_j represents the value of attributes to features J. Wij is spatial weight between i and j features and (n) is the number of features: G_i is kind of Z score, so no more calculations are required (Table 3).

Table 3. Classification of Z-Score and P-value in analysing of spatial patterns

Z-Score	p-value	Type of spatial distribution
<−2.58	0.01	High-Clusters
−2.58 – 1.96	0.05	–
−1.96 – 1.65	0.10	Low-Clusters
−1.65 – 1.65	–	Random
1.65 – 1.96	0.10	Low-Clusters
1.96 – 2.58	0.05	–
>2.58	0.01	High-Clusters

NDVI Index

The Normalized Difference Vegetation Index (NDVI) is a numerical indicator that uses the red and near-infrared bands of the electromagnetic spectrum [23] and is one of the most commonly used vegetation index [24]. The NDVI algorithm subtracts the red reflectance values from the near-infrared and divides it by the sum of near-infrared and red bands, as in Eq. 2.

$$[NDVI = (NIR - RED)/(NIR + RED)] \tag{2}$$

4 Results

In this study, satellite images, free downloaded from the NASA web site, have been analyzed in order to detect and quantify urban expansion from 1984 to 2016 in Luxor (Egypt) and Karaj (Iran) area both involved in a rapid urbanization process. The changes have been captured by the differences revealed from supervised classification applied to the scenes acquired at different times for both Luxor and Karaj area. The results obtained from the classification images of the three dates are used to calculate the area of change related to different land covers. In particular, the analysis of Landsat TM and L8 imagery in Luxor revealed that the urban area increased about 955 km^2 from 1984 to 1998; about 2.739 km^2 from 1998 to 2016. In another hand, the urban area in Karaj increased about 13.695 km^2 from 1984 to 1998, and about 5.56 km^2 from 1998 to 2016. (Table 4) (Figs. 3 and 4). As a whole, over time between (1984 to 2016), the urban area clearly increased for both of the two investigated areas (Figs. 5 and 6).

Table 4. Total changes in the urban area by Km^2 in (Luxor and Karaj).

Study area	1984-9	Change detection ($\pm$Km^2)	1998-10	Change detection ($\pm$Km^2)	2016-9
Luxor	10.873 km^2	.955 km^2	11.828 km^2	2.739 km^2	14.567 km^2
Karaj	43.420 km^2	13.695 km^2	57.115 km^2	5.56 km^2	62.675 km^2

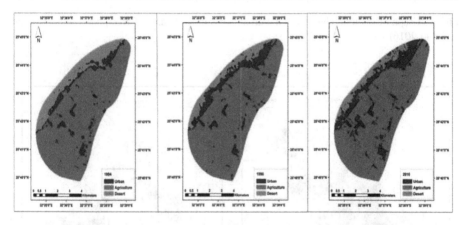

Fig. 3. Supervised classification in study area of Luxor between (1984 to 2016)

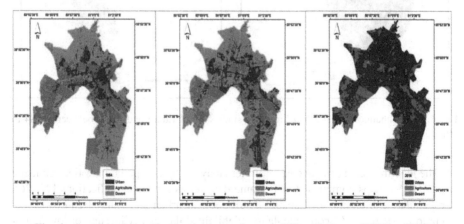

Fig. 4. Supervised classification in the study area of Karaj between (1984 to 2016)

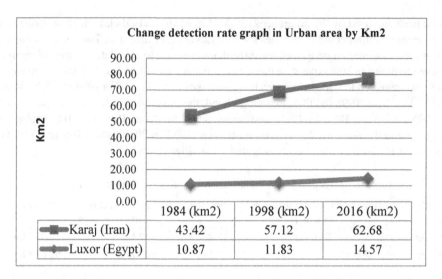

Fig. 5. Graph of the total changes in the urban areas in study area of Karaj and Luxor between (1984 to 2016)

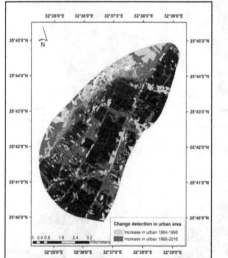

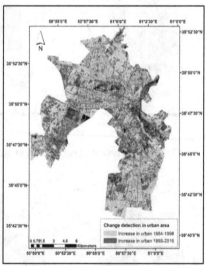

Fig. 6. Total changes in the urban Layers in study area of Luxor and Karaj between (1984 to 2016)

The identified changes have been further analyzed by geospatial investigation made on the NDVI maps computed for the same data set as for the classifications [25, 26]. For calculating the pattern of spatial distribution in urban areas the High/Low Clustering tool was used. Z-Score calculation highlighted the areas with high or low values that are clustered accordingly. The General G in the first period Luxor city at 1984 (Fig. 7) is 0.000258 and statistic Z is approximate −0.293. However, the statistics for the 2nd period 1998 (Fig. 8) is 0.000054 and statistic Z is approximate −1.480. Although the intensity of this concentration is reduced, the changes are minimal. Finally, in the 2016 year (Fig. 9) the G statistic is 0.000040 and Z-Score is −0.0843. In all periods the Z-Score value is negative, this means that low values cluster together. On the other hand, in the case study of Karaj, results show that in the first year 1984 (Fig. 10), the General G is 0.000024 and statistic Z is approximate −1.628. Also, statistics for the 2nd period 1998 (Fig. 11) is 0.000067 and statistic Z is −0.907. Finally, in the 2016 year, the G statistic is 0.000006 and Z-Score are −2.729 (Fig. 12).

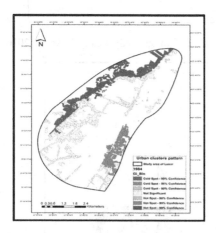
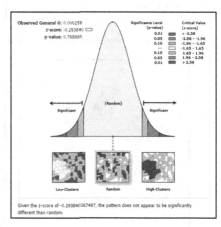

Fig. 7. Spatial Autocorrelation changes in urban clusters in the study area of Luxor in 1984

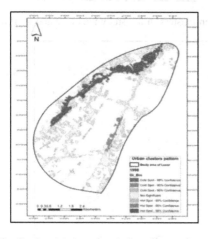
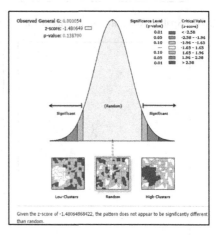

Fig. 8. Spatial Autocorrelation changes in urban clusters in the study area of Luxor in 1998

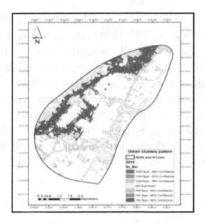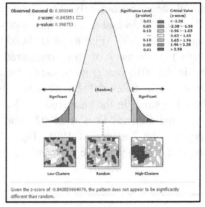

Fig. 9. Spatial Autocorrelation changes in urban clusters in the study area of Luxor in 2016

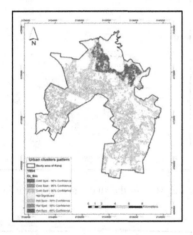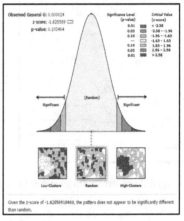

Fig. 10. Spatial Autocorrelation changes in urban clusters in the study area of Karaj in 1984

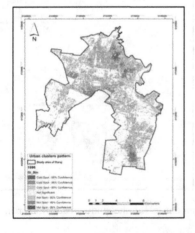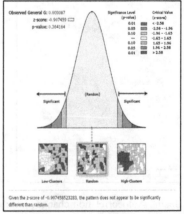

Fig. 11. Spatial Autocorrelation changes in urban clusters in the study area of Karaj in 1998

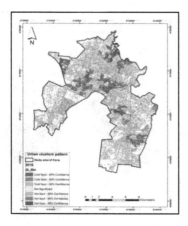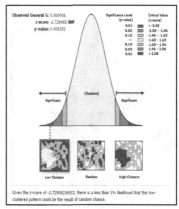

Fig. 12. Spatial Autocorrelation changes in urban clusters in the study area of Karaj in 2016

NDVI analysis was taking place in both of the study areas in order to measure the effects of urban sprawling in the vegetated areas [27]. In Luxor area, the NDVI value highlighted and identified that the change in the vegetation value from 1984 to 2016 was enormous [28]. These effects are very clear in the agricultural land around the urban area in 2016. For Karaj area in the study made during the same period as for Luxor, vegetated areas were "invaded" by urban but less than in Luxor area (Figs. 13 and 14).

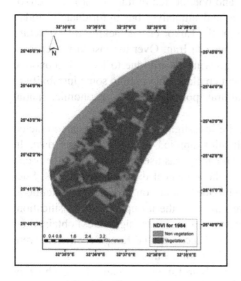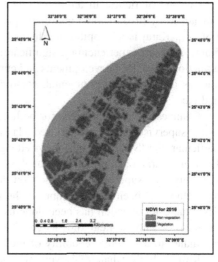

Fig. 13. Changes in vegetation index of NDVI in study area of Luxor

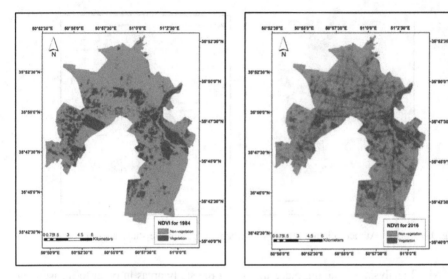

Fig. 14. Changes in vegetation index of NDVI in study area of Karaj

5   Discussions

In this research, Maximum Likelihood Classification was used along with geospatial analysis in order to capture the change from 1984 to 2016 in urban areas and characterize their statistical patterns. Two study areas were selected for a comparative investigation, one located in Egypt (Luxor) and one located in Iran (Karaj). The Luxor area is one of richest in antiquity treasures and attractive, but unfortunately, today threatened by urban sprawl and many parts of the Luxor city is lacking infrastructure [29, 30]. Karaj is the capital of Alborz Province in Iran. Over the last three decades, Karaj has been experiencing a significantly growing mostly due to its socioeconomic attractions [10]. Past developments and current challenge have led to some instability in various aspects of environmental, socio-cultural, political-security, economic, spatial and etc.

Changes in the urban areas for both of the investigated sites have been conducted using supervised and unsupervised classification applied to multi-temporal data. In particular; the ISODATA unsupervised classification was used for extracting the urban layer and carry on a preliminary analysis of the statistical distribution patterns. Successively the supervised classification technique, based on maximum Likelihood algorithm, has been used to improve the results from the unsupervised classification. The final categorization has been done using the training sets (signatures) obtained on the basis of authors' field knowledge. The overall accuracy and Kappa coefficient were calculated to assess the reliability of the classification results.

Results, higher than 99%, were obtained for both Luxor and Karaj. For each study area, the maps of changes were obtained by comparison (subtraction) of the multi-date supervised classification. The change detection analysis revealed that, over time between (1984 to 2016), the urban area clearly increased for both of the two investigated areas (see Figs. 5 and 6). To better characterize these changes captured from the comparison of multi-date and multi-spectral classification we focalized on the multi-temporal pattern variation of NDVI maps. The high clustered pattern in the urban area in Luxor was related by the high numbers of Temples like Medinet Habu, Ramesseum temple, Set I, Hatshepsut temple, and the Valley of the Kings. Many of the people there are depended on the tourism activities, so they prefer to live near to the historical places. In the fact to prevent further urban sprawl and the deleterious effects of unplanned development on the cultural heritage as well as on the population's living conditions, new opportunities for the citizens of the region should be favoured and created also working at the development of the plan for the City of Luxor.

On another hand, also the study area of Karaj has shown similar trends. Its physical development is one of the main critical challenges and caused the loss of orchards and agricultural lands, low level quality in some parts of suburbs and increased the cost of municipal services. Other problems include the scattered construction, traffic congestion, loss of identity and social characteristics of neighborhoods, pollution, loss of natural landscapes, poor quality of life and etc.

NDVI index was used to capture the urban vegetation health, both in urban and non-urban areas because degradation of ecosystem vegetation, or a decrease in green, would be reflected in a decrease in NDVI value. Generally, we can see that the loss of vegetation caused by the urban sprawl in Luxor area is quite high with negative effects, but these effects were less in the area of Karaj which appears in the results of NDVI maps. These effects in Luxor area are a result of population growth in the urban area which included many of archaeological temples. The effects of urban sprawling in Karaj seem to have been a positive phenomenon unlike Luxor area as evident by the development of the trees and parks around the transportation networks.

6 Conclusion

The paper aims to set up low cost and reliable tools useful for the monitoring of the urban growth using multi-temporal satellite data. In this paper, multi-temporal satellite data (Landsat TM 1984, Landsat TM 1998 and L8 2016) have been analyzed for investigating and assessing the effects of the urban expansion in Karaj (Iran) and Luxor (Egypt). According to the results obtained from the multi-spectral and multi-temporal classifications of all the analyzed periods (shown Figs. 3 to 6); both of the investigated areas clearly exhibited an increasing trend in urban expansion actually much more evident in the case of Luxor than Karaj area.

In Luxor, land uses in the north and west regions had a high clustered pattern in the urban layer, but the majority of the areas are characterized by random pattern between 1984 to 2016. Another high clustered area was located at south side of Luxor, but from 1998 to 2016 this clusterization appeared lower.

In the case of Karaj; results showed that in 1984, urban had high clustered areas at the north side of the city, whereas other areas did not show a significant pattern but appeared quite randomly distributed. According to the NDVI index, the vegetation value decreased in both of the two areas from 1984 to 2016 because of urban growth, but different behaviors were observed for the two sites. In the Luxor area most of the "vegetated pixels" were related to agricultural activities. Whereas, in the study area of Karaj most of the "vegetated pixels" were parks and trees around the roads. It means that the urban growth in Karaj has had positive effects unlike in Luxor.

There is a need to suggest areas for further studies. Firstly, it is aimed to develop a research study on the effectiveness of image classification techniques in urban sprawl analysis and modeling. Secondly, it is aimed to gather the satellite data from Sentinel 2 with additional improvement.

References

1. Kaufmann, R.K., Seto, K.C., Schneider, A., Liu, Z., Zhou, L., Wang, W.: Climate response to rapid urban growth: evidence of a human-induced precipitation deficit. J. Clim. **20**(10), 2299–2306 (2007)
2. Amato, F., Maimone, B.A., Martellozzo, F., Nolè, G., Murgante, B.: The effects of urban policies on the development of urban areas. Sustainability **8**, 297 (2016)
3. Romano, B., Zullo, F.: The urban transformation of Italy's Adriatic coastal strip: fifty years of unsustainability. J. Land Use Policy **38**, 26–36 (2014)
4. Romano, B., Zullo, F., Fiorini, L., Ciabò, S., Marucci, A.: Sprinkling: an approach to describe urbanization dynamics in Italy. Sustainability **9**(97), 1–17 (2017)
5. Abraham, G., Bakr, A., Lane, J.: Comprehensive Development Plan for the City of Luxor, Egypt – Investment Project #6, Investment Portfolio for the Creation of an Open Museum and Heritage District in Luxor City, Egypt, December 1999, p. 18 (1999)
6. Darvishi, Y., Masoumi, D.: Role of government in the rapid urban growth in Iran (the Ardebil city instance study). Int. Res. J. Appl. Basic Sci. **7**, 201 (2013)
7. McLane, J., Wust, R.A.J., Porter, B., Rutherford, J.: Flash-flood impacts and protection measure in the valley of the kings, Luxor, Egypt. JSTOR Terms Cond. **34**, 37 (2003)
8. Iranian Statistics Center: Karaj Statistical Yearbook 2012. Tehran, Iran (2012)
9. Sakieh, Y., Amiri, B.J., Danekar, A., Feghhi, J., Dezhkam, S.: Simulating urban expansion and scenario prediction using a cellular automata urban growth model, SLEUTH, through a case study of Karaj City, Iran. J. Hous. Built Environ. **30**(4), 591–611 (2014)
10. Molaei Qelichi, M., Murgante, B., Farhoudi, R., Zanganeh Shahraki, S., Ziari, K., Pourahmad, A.: Analyzing effective factors on urban growth management focusing on remote sensing indices in Karaj, Iran. In: Gervasi, O., et al. (eds.) ICCSA 2017. LNCS, vol. 10407, pp. 469–484. Springer, Cham (2017). https://doi.org/10.1007/978-3-319-62401-3_34
11. Lasaponara, R., Elfadaly, A., Attia, W.: Low cost space technologies for operational change detection monitoring around the archaeological area of Esna-Egypt. In: Gervasi, O., et al. (eds.) ICCSA 2016. LNCS, vol. 9787, pp. 611–621. Springer, Cham (2016). https://doi.org/10.1007/978-3-319-42108-7_48
12. Oruc, M., Marangoz, M., Buyuksalih, G.: Comparison of pixel-based and object-oriented classification approaches using Landsat-7 ETM spectral bands. In: Society for Photogrammetry and Remote Sensing XXXV:1118–22 (2004)
13. Platt, R.V., Lauren, R.: An evaluation of an object-oriented paradigm for land use/land cover classification. Prof. Geogr. **60**(1), 87–100 (2008)
14. Lasaponara, R., Leuccz, G., Masini, N., Persico, R., Scardozzi, G.: Towards an operative use of remote sensing for exploring the past using satellite data: the case study of Hierapolis (Turkey). Remote Sens. Environ. **174**, 148–164 (2016)

15. Balyani, S., Rointan, S., Qelichi, M.M., Halimi, M., Mohamadi, C.: Evaluating spatial structure of annual rainfall in relation to local factors in Iran. Spat. Inf. Res. **25**(3), 411–420 (2017). https://doi.org/10.1007/s41324-017-0106-6

16. Nolè, G., Lasaponara, R., Lanorte, A., Murgante, B.: Quantifying urban sprawl with spatial autocorrelation techniques using multi-temporal satellite data. Int. J. Agric. Environ. Inf. Syst. (IJAEIS) **5**(2), 19–37 (2014)

17. Lanorte, A., Danese, M., Lasaponara, R., Murgante, B.: Multiscale mapping of burn area and severity using multisensor satellite data and spatial autocorrelation analysis. Int. J. Appl. Earth Obs. Geoinf. **20**, 42–51 (2013)

18. Getis, A., Ord, J.K.: The analysis of spatial association by use of distance statistics. Geogr. Anal. **24**(3), 189–206 (2010)

19. Getis, A., Ord, J.K.: Local spatial autocorrelation statistics: distributional issues and an applications. Geogr. Anal. **27**(4), 189–206 (1995)

20. Getis, A., Ord, J.K.: The analysis of spatial association by use of distance statistics. Geogr. Anal. **24**(3), 189–206 (1992)

21. Ord, J.K., Getis, A.: Testing for local spatial autocorrelation in the presence of global autocorrelation. J. Reg. Sci. **41**, 411–432 (2001)

22. Qelichi, M.M., Murgante, B., Feshki, M.Y., Zarghamfard, M.: Urbanization patterns in Iran visualized through spatial auto-correlation analysis. Spat. Inf. Res. **25**(5), 627–633 (2017). https://doi.org/10.1007/s41324-017-0128-0

23. Holm, A.M., Burnside, D.G., Mitchell, A.A.: The development of a system for monitoring trend in range condition in the arid shrublands of Western Australia. Rangel. J. **9**(1), 14 (1987)

24. Kumari, M., Sarma, K.: Changing trends of land surface temperature in relation to landuse/cover around thermal power plant in Singrauli district, Madhya Pradesh. India. Spat. Inf. Res. **25**(6), 769–777 (2017). https://doi.org/10.1007/s41324-017-0142-2

25. Elfadaly, A., Attia, W., Qelichi, M.M., Murgante, B., Lasaponara, R.: Management of cultural heritage sites using remote sensing indices and spatial analysis techniques. Surv. Geophys. **39**(6), 1347–1377 (2018)

26. Elfadaly, A., Lasaponara, R.: On the use of satellite imagery and GIS tools to detect and characterize the urbanization around heritage sites: the case studies of the Catacombs of Mustafa Kamel in Alexandria, Egypt and the Aragonese Castle in Baia, Italy. Sustainability **11**(7), 2110 (2019)

27. Lasaponara, R., et al.: Spatial open data for monitoring risks and preserving archaeological areas and landscape: case studies at Kom el Shoqafa, Egypt and Shush, Iran. Sustainability **9**(4), 572 (2017)

28. Elfadaly, A., Lasaponara, R., Murgante, B., Qelichi, M.M.: Cultural Heritage management using analysis of satellite images and advanced GIS techniques at East Luxor, Egypt and Kangavar, Iran (A Comparison Case Study). In: Gervasi, O., et al. (eds.) ICCSA 2017. LNCS, vol. 10407, pp. 152–168. Springer, Cham (2017). https://doi.org/10.1007/978-3-319-62401-3_12

29. Elfadaly, A., Wafa, O., Abouarab, M., Guida, A., Spanu, P., Lasaponara, R.: Geo-environmental estimation of land use changes and its effects on Egyptian Temples at Luxor City. ISPRS Int. J. Geo-Inf. **6**(11), 378 (2017)

30. Elfadaly, A., Attia, W., Lasaponara, R.: Monitoring the environmental risks around Medinet Habu and Ramesseum Temple at West Luxor, Egypt, using remote sensing and GIS techniques. J. Archaeol. Meth. Theory **25**(2), 587–610 (2018)

Experimental Comparison of Stochastic Optimizers in Deep Learning

Emmanuel Okewu[1(✉)], Philip Adewole[2], and Oladipupo Sennaike[2]

[1] Centre for Information Technology and Systems,
University of Lagos, Lagos, Nigeria
eokewu@unilag.edu.ng
[2] Department of Computer Sciences, University of Lagos, Lagos, Nigeria
{padewole, osennaike}@unilag.edu.ng

Abstract. The stochastic optimization problem in deep learning involves finding optimal values of loss function and neural network parameters using a meta-heuristic search algorithm. The fact that these values cannot be reasonably obtained by using a deterministic optimization technique underscores the need for an iterative method that randomly picks data segments, arbitrarily determines initial values of optimization (network) parameters and steadily computes series of error functions until a tolerable error is attained. The typical stochastic optimization algorithm for training deep neural networks as a non-convex optimization problem is gradient descent. It has existing extensions like Stochastic Gradient Descent, Adagrad, Adadelta, RMSProp and Adam. In terms of accuracy, convergence rate and training time, each of these stochastic optimizers represents an improvement. However, there is room for further improvement. This paper presents outcomes of series of experiments conducted with a view to providing empirical evidences of successes made so far. We used Python deep learning libaries (Tensorflow and Keras API) for our experiments. Each algorithm is executed, results collated, and a case made for further research in deep learning to improve training time and convergence rate of deep neural network, as well as accuracy of outcomes. This is in response to the growing demands for deep learning in mission-critical and highly sophisticated decision making processes across industry verticals.

Keywords: Deep learning · Deep neural networks · Error function ·
Neural network parameters · Stochastic optimization

1 Introduction

The training of deep learning models remains a challenge despite many feats in recent memory [1]. The training is a stochastic optimization problem that is non-convex (i.e. global minimum differs from local minimum), high-dimensional, and complex. Presently, the most solicited approach is the use of stochastic gradient descent and its variants [2]. In a bid to handle specific issues in the training of deep learning models, several extensions to the basic (standard) gradient descent algorithm have been proposed. In Sect. 2, some of these methods are reviewed.

© Springer Nature Switzerland AG 2019
S. Misra et al. (Eds.): ICCSA 2019, LNCS 11623, pp. 704–715, 2019.
https://doi.org/10.1007/978-3-030-24308-1_55

Despite the fact that variants and extensions of stochastic gradient descent perform well empirically, further improvement is possible [3]. This is evidenced by the emergence of several methods that simplify the optimization problem such as backpropagation of error, weight updating, normalization methods and weight initialization techniques.

Pattern recognition (classification) using deep neural networks commences with an activation function that introduces non-linearity into the linear data as follows:

$$\text{Neuron output } (\hat{y}) \;=\; x_1.w_1 + \; x_2.w_2 + x_3.w_3 + \ldots + \; x_n.w_n + \; b \qquad (1)$$

where $x_1, x_2, \ldots, x_n$ are input variables
$w_1, w_2, \ldots w_n$ are network parameters
b is a network constant called bias.

This neural network learning process continues with the computation of an objective (cost) function as follows:

$$\delta = y_{\text{target}} - \hat{y}$$

Since it is unlikely that the network (neuron) output $(\hat{y})$ will equal target output (y_{target}), it means $\delta \neq 0$. It implies an error in the network and attempt is made to exactly match the real-world data. The neural network then starts an iterative stochastic process that progressively reduces the error until it is within acceptable limit. This process is a non-deterministic optimization process that requires a search algorithm otherwise referred to as a stochastic optimization algorithm. At the end of the iterative process, the deep neural network is assumed to have learnt sufficiently the patterns in the historical data.

SGD decides which direction to move each network parameter and by how much to move each parameter [4]. This is achieved by computing the gradient of the loss (error) with respect to each parameter. Each gradient is scaled by the learning rate. Parameter update is performed using the gradient step:

$$w = w - \eta \cdot \nabla F(w;x(i);y(i)) \qquad (2)$$

where $\{x(i), y(i)\}$ are training examples, η is learning rate, ∇F is gradient.

Each update is referred to as a gradient step and the process is known as gradient descent. As indicated in Eq. 2, step size (learning rate) is set by estimating curvature (gradient) from first order information. Given m passes over sample data and n neural network parameters $(w_1, w_2, \ldots, w_n)$ with cost functions $(f_1, f_2, \ldots f_m)$, the gradient is a matrix of first order partial derivatives $(\partial f / \partial w)$ given as:

$$\frac{\partial f}{\partial w} = \begin{bmatrix} \frac{\partial f1}{\partial w1} & \frac{\partial f1}{\partial w2} & \cdots & \frac{\partial f1}{\partial wn} \\ \frac{\partial f2}{\partial w1} & \frac{\partial f2}{\partial w2} & \cdots & \frac{\partial f2}{\partial wn} \\ & & \cdot & \\ & & \cdot & \\ & & \cdot & \\ \frac{\partial fn}{\partial w1} & \frac{\partial fn}{\partial w2} & \cdots & \frac{\partial fn}{\partial wn} \end{bmatrix}$$

At the point where $\partial f / \partial w = 0$, the deep neural network has sufficiently learnt patterns in the data.

The manner in which data is fetched from the training dataset and learning conducted has given rise to three variants of gradient descent – standard (batch) gradient descent, stochastic gradient descent, and mini-batch gradient descent as discussed in Sect. 2. The generic version is stochastic gradient descent (SGD) [5].

The term stochastic refers to the process of random selection of training instances {x(i); y(i)} and random initialization of network parameters [4]. Since the error is computed based on randomly selected data and randomly initialized network parameters, the error function is a stochastic objective function.

Stochastic optimization involves taking a number of gradient steps such that the model secures very low loss on training data as a condition for generalization [6].

2   Background and Related Work

2.1   Deep Learning

Deep learning is a subset of machine learning that makes use of deep neural networks. It is based on a set of algorithms used to model high level abstractions in data [7]. It can also be seen as a computational software that imitates the network of neurons in a brain. Deep learning models are constructed with connected layers which include input layer, output layer and hidden layers [1]. Each hidden layer is composed of neurons. The connected neurons process and propagate the input signal they receive to the next layer. The determinants of the strength of the signal are the weight, bias and activation function. The network takes in large amounts of input data, process them through multiple layers as it learns increasingly complex features of the data at each layer. From object detection to speech recognition, deep neural networks offer accuracy as they learn from data directly without coding of any predefined knowledge by programmers. The machine (deep) learning process involves understanding the problem, identifying data, selecting appropriate deep learning model, training of model, and finally, testing of the model.

Each layer in a neural network represents a deeper level of knowledge which suggests the presence of a hierarchy of knowledge. Hence, a neural network with four layers learns more complex and complicated features than one with two layers. The learning process takes place in two phases: the first phase involves the application of a nonlinear transformation of the input so as to create a statistical model as output. The second phase targets the improvement of the model using a mathematical method called derivative. These two phases are repeated many times until a tolerable level of accuracy is reached. This repetition is called an iteration. Typical deep neural networks are convolutional neural networks and recurrent neural networks [8].

The popular algorithm for training deep neural networks is the first order method called gradient descent [9]. The use of second order methods like Newton's method for deep neural networks (DNN) is discouraged in that they are computationally intensive. Moreover, DNN problems are non-convex high dimensional problems for which second order methods are unsuitable. Non-convex problems are problems whose local minimum differs from global minimum [10].

The optimization focus of DNN is to minimize the objective function with respect to (w.r.t) the network parameters and SGD algorithm is used. SGD is a stochastic approximation of gradient descent optimization [11]. It is an iterative method that optimizes the differentiable objective function. It is called stochastic for two reasons: training samples are chosen randomly or in a shuffled manner and network parameters are randomly determined or initialized. In a nutshell, it means involving chance or probability.

2.2 Gradient Descent Algorithm and Optimization in Deep Neural Networks

Gradient descent algorithm is an optimization algorithm that helps to refine machine learning operations. In artificial neural networks generally and deep learning in particular, its focus is to adjust the input weights of neurons towards finding local minima or global minima in order to optimize a problem. In deep neural networks, the algorithm minimizes the objective function parameterized by the network parameters. It searches for the values of the parameters (coefficients) of a function (f) that minimize the cost function (cost). This search algorithm is best used when it is difficult to calculate the parameters using analytical tools like linear algebra. The strategy of the search and optimization algorithm is to try different coefficient (parameter) values, evaluate their cost, and select new coefficients with better (lower) cost. The repetition of this process for a number of times will lead to the local minimum as shown in Fig. 1 and the values of the coefficients that culminated in this minimum cost would be ascertained. Deep learning problems are non-convex in that local minimum differs from global minimum [10, 11].

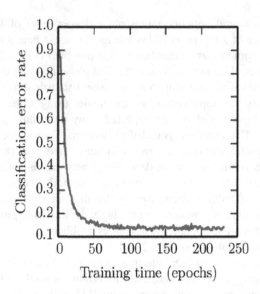

Fig. 1. Length of time to reach local minimum measured in epochs (Source: Dabura 2017)

The length of time it takes an algorithm to reach the local minimum in deep neural networks is a measure of the efficacy of the gradient descent algorithm. As a result, various improvements on the basic gradient descent algorithm had focused on tackling one impediment or the other that tends to impede on convergence. In this section, related works covered are optimizers, all of which modify learning rates by estimating curvature (gradient) from first order information. The works underscore efforts by various researchers to make efficient and effective use of gradient descent in deep neural networks and are analyzed under four titles: parameter updates using simple decay rate; adapting parameter updates to slope error function; per-parameter update using individual learning rate; and per-parameter updates using individual momentum changes.

2.3   Related Works

Previous works on stochastic optimizers in deep learning are as follows.

In the work of [5], first-order iterative methods were discussed, with particular focus on standard (batch) gradient descent. Though first order methods can evade saddle points by following directions of negative curvature (gradient), these saddle points are surrounded by plateaus otherwise referred to as regions of small curvature. This accounts for the slowness of first order methods near saddle points which creates illusion of a local minimum.

First order gradient descent is an algorithm suitable for non-convex optimization models like deep neural networks [13, 14]. In training and optimizing such intelligent systems, gradient descent is the most popular algorithm [15]. However, the limitation of the standard (batch) gradient descent is that it computes the gradient of the entire dataset before performing an update. This makes it to be very slow as well as difficult to control for very large datasets and don't fit in the memory. The size of an update (big or small) is determined by the learning rate (η). For convex error surfaces, it is guaranteed to converge to the global minimum while it converges to local minimum for non-convex problems like deep neural networks. Another drawback of standard batch gradient descent is that it calculates redundant updates for huge datasets.

[16] credited [17] for developing stochastic gradient descent (SGD) to tackle the problem of prolonged training time associated with standard gradient descent. Standard gradient descent calculates gradient for all training instances before performing parameter update. SGD is also called incremental gradient descent and it is an iterative method that optimizes differentiable objective function which is seen as stochastic approximation of gradient descent optimization. It is called stochastic in that data instances are selected randomly or shuffled unlike in standard gradient descent where samples are chosen as a single group or better still, in the order they appear in the training set. It performs parameter update for every training example. It is a faster technique than standard gradient descent as it executes one update at a time.

The frequent updates have high variance and stimulate the loss function to fluctuate to different intensities. This is a positive development on one hand, as it aids the discovery of new and possibly better local minima, whereas standard gradient descent only converges to the minimum of the basin. Nevertheless, the setback of SGD is that it complicates convergence to exact minimum and can overshoot the local minimum owing to frequent updates and fluctuations (oscillations). Studies, have however, shown that as the learning rate (η) slowly decreases, SGD exhibits the same convergence paradigm as standard gradient descent.

Mini-batch gradient descent was developed to address the limitations of SGD [5]. When using SGD, the updates for each training dataset instance can give rise to a noisy plot of cost over time. In a bid to rectify these challenges of high variance parameter updates and unstable convergence associated with SGD, mini-batch gradient descent (MGD) emerged as a response and an improvement. It circumvents the issues with standard batch gradient descent and SGD by combining the best of both techniques. MGD breaks down dataset into mini-batches and executes an update for each mini-batch with n training instances. MGD is credited with ability to reduce the variance in the parameter updates which results in much better and stable convergence. It also uses highly optimized matrix optimizations commonly found in state-of-the-art deep learning libraries which makes computation of the gradient w.r.t. a mini-batch very efficient. The flexibility of MGD as mini-batch sizes can range from 50 to 256. Additional credit is that these batch sizes vary as per the application and problem being tackled. It is therefore a good algorithm for training a neural network.

In [18] and [19], proposals for the use of momentum as an optimization algorithm were made. Momentum was designed to tackle the problem posed by high variance oscillations in SGD which mini-batch gradient descent could not handle comprehensively. These oscillations impede SGD from converging on time. The Momentum technique accelerates SGD by navigating along the relevant direction while softening oscillations in irrelevant directions.

[20] developed Nesterov accelerated gradient (NAG) to solve a problem associated with the Momentum technique: as the minima (the lowest point on the curve) is reached, the momentum is very high and the convergence may not slow down at that point owing to high momentum. This potentially could cause the loss function to miss the minima completely and rather continue to move up. To address this problem, NAG algorithm computes the gradient after making a big jump premised on previous momentum. Then after, it makes a correction which culminates in a parameter update. This strategy of anticipatory update prevents the loss function from decreasing too fast so that it does not miss the minima. It equally makes the convergence process to be more responsive to changes.

In [4], a new SGD algorithm called Adagrad that improved on Momentum and Nesterov Accelerated Gradient (NAG) was proposed. Adagrad means adaptive gradient. Sparse gradients constitute a key issue in training deep learning models. To solve this problem, Adagrad algorithm was developed. The algorithm adaptively tunes learning rate for each parameter and in the process performing larger updates for rarely updated parameters. Nevertheless, Adagrad's update rule results in a vanishing (decaying) rate which forces the learning rate to monotonically decrease to a very small amount. A very small learning rate stalls the algorithm.

[21] introduced Adadelta to address the problem of decaying learning rate associated with Adagrad. The algorithm is an extension of Adagrad aimed at eliminating its decaying learning rate problem. Rather than accumulate all previous squared gradients, Adadelta limits the number of accumulated previous gradients to certain constant size w. Since the storage of w previously squared gradients could be inefficiently done, there is a recursive definition of the sum of gradients as a decaying mean of past squared gradients. Hence, the running average at time step t only depends on previous average and current gradient. A further enhancement in Adadelta is the fact that setting a default learning rate is not necessary.

In furtherance of efforts to solve the problem of vanishing learning rates, [22] developed Root Mean Square Propagation (RMSProp). The technique maintains per-parameter learning rates and it is an extension of stochastic gradient descent algorithm that attempts to fix the issue of vanishing (decaying) learning rate. A version of RMSProp optimization algorithm uses momentum [23]. RMSProp with momentum computes parameter updates using momentum on rescaled gradient Bias-correction term is missing in RMSProp.

[11] proposed Adam stochastic optimization algorithm. The method rides on the philosophy that in as much as it is useful to calculate learning rate for each parameter as demonstrated in previous algorithms, then computing individual momentum changes for each parameter and storing them separately would likewise be beneficial. Hence, the emergence of a new modified technique and improvement called Adam. Adam means Adaptive Moment Estimation. It is a popular algorithm for training deep neural

networks and integrates the benefits of Adagrad and RMSProp. It leverages on the moving average of past gradients to ascertain the direction of descent just as it uses the running average of past squared gradients to scale (modify) the learning rate. Adam offers a remarkable improvement on stochastic gradient descent in that it performs well in practice. It converges fast and enhances the learning speed of neural network models. Generally, it favourably compares with other adaptive learning-method algorithms. Nevertheless, there is room for further improvement [3].

3 Methodology

Overtime, research efforts towards improving deep neural networks via stochastic optimization algorithms have yielded some results that are well documented. This study attempts to validate the reported improvement by experimentally evaluating established optimizers like Adam, RMSProp, Adadelta, Adagrad and SGD using Python deep learning environment. High dimensional data suitable for deep learning as well as a suitable deep neural network model were carefully chosen for experiments. The details of the series of experiments and analysis of outcomes are outlined as follows:

To empirically validate the performances of the deep learning optimizers and justify research efforts committed to improving stochastic optimization in deep neural network with respect to accuracy and training time, select optimizers were executed using Python deep learning libraries [12]. The libraries include Tensorflow and Keras API. The data used is the MNIST (Modified National Institute of Standards and Technology) database, a dataset of handwritten digits images [24]. Convolutional Neural Network was used as the deep neural network model [25].

MNIST dataset is partitioned into training data and testing data. The training data comprises 60,000 images while the testing data is made up of 10,000 data. The linear structure of the database is further analyzed as follows:

Training Data
Total examples (images) = 60,000 (images of handwritten digits)
Pixels per image = 28 x 28 = 784
Size (shape) of training (image) data = [60000,784]

Testing Data
Total instances (images) = 10,000
Pixels per image = 28 x 28 = 784
Size (shape) of training data = [10000, 784]

Label Data
Total examples (images) = 60,000
Total values in label = 60,000
Size (shape) of label data = [60,000]

The Python code implemented in turn for each of the select optimizers (Adam, Adagrad, Adadelta, RMSProp, and SGD) is outlined as follows:

```
# Program for image classification using deep learning (convolutional neural
# network) and MNIST database
import tensorflow as tf
(x_train, y_train), (x_test, y_test) = tf.keras.datasets.mnist.load_data()
x_train.shape
x_train = x_train.reshape(x_train.shape[0], 28, 28, 1)
x_test = x_test.reshape(x_test.shape[0], 28, 28, 1)
input_shape = (28, 28, 1)
x_train = x_train.astype('float32')
x_test = x_test.astype('float32')
x_train /= 255
x_test /= 255
print('x_train shape:', x_train.shape)
print('Number of images in x_train', x_train.shape[0])
print('Number of images in x_test', x_test.shape[0])
from keras.models import Sequential
from keras.layers import Dense, Conv2D, Dropout, Flatten, MaxPooling2D
model = Sequential()
model.add(Conv2D(28, kernel_size=(3,3), input_shape=input_shape))
model.add(MaxPooling2D(pool_size=(2, 2)))
model.add(Flatten()) # Flattening the 2D arrays for fully connected layers
model.add(Dense(128, activation=tf.nn.relu))
model.add(Dropout(0.2))
model.add(Dense(10, activation=tf.nn.softmax))
model.compile(optimizer='adam',
loss='sparse_categorical_crossentropy',
metrics=['accuracy'])
model.fit(x=x_train, y=y_train, epochs=20)
model.evaluate(x_test, y_test)
image_index = 4444
plt.imshow(x_test[image_index].reshape(28, 28), cmap='Greys')
pred = model.predict(x_test[image_index].reshape(1, img_rows, img_cols, 1))
print(pred.argmax())
```

4   Results and Interpretations

The above Python code was implemented for each of the five deep learning optimizers (Adam, RMPProp, Adadelta, Adagrad and Stochastic Gradient Decent), one after the other using 20 iterations. However, due to space constraint in this report, we show the output for only 15 iterations. The three categories of outcome are training time, loss function, and accuracy as shown in Tables 1, 2 and 3 below.

Table 1. Training time

Optimizer	1st iteration	2nd iteration	3rd iteration	4th iteration	5th iteration	6th iteration	7th iteration	8th iteration	9th iteration	10th iteration	11th iteration	12th iteration	13th iteration	14th iteration	15th iteration
SGD	83 s	78 s	95 s	95 s	94 s	94 s	94 s	87 s	87 s	86 s	88 s	103 s	98 s	91 s	88 s
Adagrad	86 s	82 s	103 s	114 s	104 s	104 s	104 s	102 s	113 s	109 s	109 s	110 s	106 s	105 s	106 s
Adadelta	127 s	121 s	145 s	145 s	152 s	138 s	131 s	139 s	135 s	129 s	130 s	133 s	135 s	145 s	139 s
RMSProp	95 s	88 s	109 s	107 s	108 s	107 s	106 s	116 s	115 s	109 s	106 s	108 s	107 s	108 s	110 s
Adam	110 s	106 s	125 s	125 s	125 s	127 s	125 s	125 s	127 s	126 s	123 s	121 s	121 s	115 s	119 s

Table 2. Loss function

Optimizer	1st iteration	2nd iteration	3rd iteration	4th iteration	5th iteration	6th iteration	7th iteration	8th iteration	9th iteration	10th iteration	11th iteration	12th iteration	13th iteration	14th iteration	15th iteration
SGD	0.5094	0.2330	0.1814	0.1534	0.1380	0.1231	0.1144	0.1058	0.0979	0.0929	0.0891	0.0823	0.0799	0.0766	0.0736
Adagrad	0.1858	0.0906	0.0696	0.0576	0.0499	0.0451	0.0403	0.0364	0.0338	0.0308	0.0281	0.0261	0.0249	0.0232	0.0220
Adadelta	0.1998	0.0806	0.0575	0.0436	0.0368	0.0302	0.0253	0.0232	0.0185	0.0171	0.0137	0.0125	0.0119	0.0104	0.0095
RMSProp	0.2057	0.0882	0.0664	0.0586	0.0507	0.0455	0.0426	0.0349	0.0340	0.0302	0.0267	0.0259	0.0247	0.0217	0.0223
Adam	0.2183	0.0891	0.0635	0.0504	0.0389	0.0328	0.0278	0.0248	0.0216	0.0190	0.0181	0.0178	0.0155	0.0141	0.0152

Table 3. Accuracy

Optimizer	1st iteration	2nd iteration	3rd iteration	4th iteration	5th iteration	6th iteration	7th iteration	8th iteration	9th iteration	10th iteration	11th iteration	12th iteration	13th iteration	14th iteration	15th iteration
SGD	0.8565	0.9305	0.9464	0.9544	0.9586	0.9625	0.9658	0.9689	0.9700	0.9713	0.9721	0.9746	0.9756	0.9762	0.9772
Adagrad	0.9448	0.9738	0.9793	0.9830	0.9853	0.9863	0.9881	0.9896	0.9901	0.9912	0.9921	0.9924	0.9930	0.9935	0.9938
Adadelta	0.9408	0.9760	0.9828	0.9863	0.9890	0.9909	0.9924	0.9928	0.9940	0.9948	0.9958	0.9958	0.9964	0.9963	0.9970
RMSProp	0.9378	0.9739	0.9806	0.9835	0.9860	0.9870	0.9887	0.9898	0.9902	0.9915	0.9925	0.9933	0.9936	0.9943	0.9946
Adam	0.9353	0.9726	0.9803	0.9842	0.9875	0.9894	0.9906	0.9913	0.9928	0.9937	0.9940	0.9939	0.9949	0.9952	0.9947

In terms of training time, Table 1 shows that SGD has the best time (with the lowest training time) followed by Adagrad, RMSProp, Adam and Adadelta in that order. However, Table 2 indicates that the lowest value of the loss function at the 15th iteration was obtained by Adadelta (0.0095) followed by Adam (0.0152), Adagrad (0.0220), RMSProp (0.0223), and SGD (0.0736). With respect to accuracy, Table 3 shows that at the 15th iteration, Adadelta has the best accuracy Fig. (0.9970) followed by Adam (0.9947), RMSProp (0.9946), Adagrad (0.9938), and SGD (0.9772).

These experimental outcomes confirm that research efforts to improve on gradient descent algorithms for training deep neural networks have paid off in terms of convergence rate and accuracy. The results also show why Adam is considered in the literature as one of the best optimizers for training deep neural networks [3, 11]. Overall, the figures indicate that Adam is the most consistent in terms of performance across the three metrics: training time, loss function, and accuracy.

Though it is difficult to say that any particular algorithm outperformed others across board (across the three metrics), the outcome gives a ray of hope that future research aimed at improving performance of deep learning models could make deep learning more attractive to various industries as a tool for generating useful and timely information for informed decision making.

5   Conclusion and Future Work

The series of experiments in this study were conducted using select deep neural network optimizers like stochastic gradient descent, Adagrad, Adadelta, RMSProp and Adam. We used the MNIST database of images of handwritten digits with a total of 60,000 training data and 10,000 testing data on a Python platform, using Python deep learning libraries (Tensorflow and Keras API). The outcome showed remarkable improvement in both accuracy of output and convergence rate of loss function. In any case, as observed by [3], there is room for further improvement. Researchers are therefore encouraged to invest more time and efforts in deep learning. This is particularly so given the increasing relevance of deep learning in various industry verticals. Therefore, in future research work, further efforts should be made towards resolving open issues of deep learning. These challenges include sparse gradient, variance (oscillations) in parameter updates, vanishing (decaying) learning rate, and presence of poor local optima.

References

1. Glorot, X., Bengio, Y.: Understanding the difficulty of training deep feedforward neural networks. DIRO, Université de Montréal, Montréal (2010)
2. Bengio, Y., LeCun, Y., Hinton, G.: Deep learning. Nature 521(7553), 436–444 (2015). https://doi.org/10.1038/nature14539. Bibcode:2015Natur.521..436L. PMID 26017442
3. Koushik, J., Hayashi, H.: Improving stochastic gradient descent with feedback. In: Conference Paper at ICLR 2017

4. Duchi, J., Hazan, E., Singer, Y.: Adaptive subgradient methods for online learning and stochastic optimization. J. Mach. Learn. Res. **12**(Jul), 2121–2159 (2011)
5. Kim, D., Fessler, J.A.: Optimized first-order methods for smooth convex minimization. Math. Prog. **151**, 8–107 (2016)
6. Walia, A.S.: Types of Optimization Algorithms used in Neural Networks and Ways to Optimize Gradient Descent (2017)
7. Shridhar, K.: A Beginners Guide to Deep Learning (2017)
8. Tran, D.T., Iosifidis, A., Gabbouj, M.: Improving efficiency in convolutional neural networks with multilinear filters. Neural Netw. **105**, 328–339 (2018)
9. Li, J., Zhou, T., Wang, C.: On global convergence of gradient descent algorithms for generalized phase retrieval problem. J. Comput. Appl. Math. **329**, 202–222 (2018)
10. Anandkumar, A.: Nonconvex optimization: challenges and recent successes. In: ICML 2016 Tutorial
11. Kingma, D., Ba, J.: Adam: a method for stochastic optimization. In: Published as a Conference Paper at ICLR 2015
12. Brownlee, J.: How to setup a python environment for machine learning and deep learning with anaconda. In: Python Machine Learning (2017)
13. Li, G., et al.: Training deep neural networks with discrete state transition. Neurocomputing **272**, 154–162 (2018)
14. Schmidhuber, J.: Deep learning in neural networks: an overview. Neural Netw. **61**, 85–117 (2015). arXiv:1404.7828 . https://doi.org/10.1016/j.neunet.2014.09.003. PMID 25462637
15. Sutskever, I.: Training recurrent neural networks (PDF). Ph.D., University of Toronto, p. 74 (2013)
16. Mei, S.: A mean field view of the landscape of two-layer neural networks. In: Proceedings of the National Academy of Sciences (2018)
17. Robbins, H., Monro, S.: For developing SGD in their 1951 article titled "A Stochastic Approximation Method" (1951)
18. Sutskever, I., Martens, J., Dahl, G., Hinton, G.E.: On the importance of initialization and momentum in deep learning'(PDF). In: Dasgupta, S., Mcallester, D. (eds.) Proceedings of the 30th International Conference on Machine Learning (ICML-13), Atlanta, GA, vol. 28, pp. 1139–1147. Accessed 14 Jan 2016
19. Rumelhart, D.E., Hinton, G.E., Williams, R.J.: Learning representations by back-propagating errors. Nature **323**(6088), 533–536 (1986)
20. Nesterov (1983)
21. Zeiler, M.D.: Adadelta: an adaptive learning rate method. arXiv preprint arXiv:1212.5701 (2012)
22. Tieleman, T., Hinton, G.: Lecture 6.5-rmsprop: divide the gradient by a running average of its recent magnitude. COURSERA: Neural Netw. Mach. Learn. **4**(2), 26–31 (2012)
23. Graves, A.: Generating Sequences with Recurrent Neural Networks (2014)
24. Yalçın, O.G.: Image Classification in 10 Minutes with MNIST Dataset (2018)
25. Torres, J.: Convolutional Neural Networks for Beginners. Practical Guide with Python and Keras (2018)

Application of Data Mining Algorithms for Feature Selection and Prediction of Diabetic Retinopathy

Tinuke O. Oladele[1], Roseline Oluwaseun Ogundokun[2(✉)],
Aderonke Anthonia Kayode[2], Adekanmi Adeyinka Adegun[3],
and Marion Oluwabunmi Adebiyi[2]

[1] Department of Computer Science, University of Ilorin,
Ilorin, Kwara State, Nigeria
[2] Department of Computer Science, Landmark University,
Omu Aran, Kwara State, Nigeria
ogundokun.roseline@lmu.edu.ng
[3] Discipline of Computer Science, University of KwaZulu-Natal,
Durban, South Africa

Abstract. Diabetes Retinopathy is a disease which results from a prolonged case of diabetes mellitus and it is the most common cause of loss of vision in man. Data mining algorithms are used in medical and computer fields to find effective ways of forecasting a particular disease. This research was aimed at determining the effect of using feature selection in predicting Diabetes Retinopathy. The dataset used for this study was gotten from diabetes retinopathy Debrecen dataset from the University of California in a form suitable for mining. Feature selection was executed on diabetes retinopathy data then the Implementation of k-Nearest Neighbour, C4.5 decision tree, Multi-layer Perceptron (MLP) and Support Vector Machines was conducted on diabetes retinopathy data with and without feature selection. There was access to the algorithms in terms of accuracy and sensitivity. It is observed from the results that, making use of feature selection on algorithms increases the accuracy as well as the sensitivity of the algorithms considered and it is mostly reflected in the support vector machine algorithm. Making use of feature selection for classification also increases the time taken for the prediction of diabetes retinopathy.

Keywords: Data mining · Feature selection · Diabetic retinopathy ·
Prediction · Classification

1 Introduction

Diabetic Retinopathy is a disease that is common in adults and it occurs when diabetes is not treated for a long period of time. The dataset used in this research is the Diabetes Retinopathy Debrecen dataset from the University of California, Irvine (UCI) repository of machine learning databases. The dataset was provided by some researchers from the University of Debrecen, Hungary containing features extracted from the Messidor image set to predict whether an eye image contains signs of diabetic retinopathy or not.

© Springer Nature Switzerland AG 2019
S. Misra et al. (Eds.): ICCSA 2019, LNCS 11623, pp. 716–730, 2019.
https://doi.org/10.1007/978-3-030-24308-1_56

The research paper on the work done which generated the dataset is (Antal and Hajdu 2014). The dataset contains 1151 instances with 19 attributes each and a binary outcome feature as to whether the instance has signs of diabetic retinopathy or not.

This study is poised to help in the automatic prediction of diabetes retinopathy so as to help diagnose it quickly and to protect those having it from becoming totally blind. It also seeks to discover the effect of using the same algorithm for both feature selection and classification with a view to understanding whether it will reduce the size while maintaining accuracy. The feature selection technique used is the wrapper feature selectors such that the algorithms to be used in the classification are the same one used in feature selection. The algorithms will be compared in terms of their accuracy and sensitivity.

2 Literature Review

2.1 Related Work

Rathi and Sharma (2017) performed a review on the prediction of Diabetes Retinopathy using data mining techniques, Algorithms, techniques and approaches used in literature were compared and it was discovered that SVM and kNN performed best on Diabetes Retinopathy data. Ramesh and Padmini (2017) conducted a study on risk level prediction of diabetes retinopathy using classification algorithms. They collected data from patients in different hospitals through questionnaires. The information in the questionnaires was organized and mined using Naïve Bayes, Multilayer perceptron, Random forest, Bayesian networks and decision stump. Multi-layer perceptron was found most suitable in predicting risk level as it has the highest accuracy.

Elibol and Ergin (2016) extracted time domain features from retina images and those features are used to classify the stage of diabetic retinopathy in which an image is in. The algorithms used are Fisher's linear discriminant analysis, Linear Bayes Normal classifier, Decision tree and k-Nearest Neighbour. The classification accuracies show that when all the extracted features were used in the classification, kNN gives the highest average accuracy of 92.22% while when 7 features were carefully selected, Linear Bayes Normal classifier gave the highest average accuracy. The dataset used in this research is the publicly available retina images DIARETDB1.

Bhaisare et al. (2016) proposed a model for a web-based system for the diagnosis of diabetic retinopathy using eye images, such that people can upload their eye images and the system will mine the images for signs of diabetic retinopathy. This system has the potential of saving time and money for patients.

Mankar and Rout (2016) presented a method for automatic detection of diabetic retinopathy; SVM was used to classify the retina data into normal, having non-proliferative diabetic retinopathy or having proliferative diabetic retinopathy. The presence and amount of Hemorrhages and Exudates in the retina data was used as the classifying feature. The source of the dataset used in the research was not reported.

Jalan and Tayade (2015) proposed a method for diagnosing diabetic retinopathy by combining kNN and SVM algorithms together. The method is to detect the presence or absence of diabetic retinopathy and the severity of the disease.

Sujatha and Divya (2015) proposed a method for identifying people with Diabetes Mellitus and non-proliferative diabetes retinopathy samples from images of the tongue of individuals. The images were pre-processed using a median filter and classified using the proximal support vector machine. The results were said to achieve high performance and can handle a large number of data. The tongue images used in this research were captured by the researchers.

Antal and Hajdu (2014) presented a method for the screening of images to investigate the presence or absence of diabetic retinopathy. Several features were extracted from retinal images using image processing algorithms. The extracted features are based on three components which are Image level components (quality assessment, pre-screening and multi-scale Amplitude-Modulation Frequency-Modulation), lesion-specific components (microaneurysms, exudates) and anatomical components (macula, optic disc). The anatomical components were introduced by the researchers as components to be considered in the determination of the presence of diabetic retinopathy. The extracted features were then classified using ensembles of machine learning classifiers; eight machine learning classifiers were stated as potential members of the ensemble and were combined in different ways. Using an ensemble of a lot algorithm can be time-consuming and have very high complexity in real life scenarios and some algorithms might not contribute to an increase in accuracy when the algorithms are much. Aravind et al. (2013) presented a method for automatic detection of microaneurysms and classification of diabetic retinopathy images by removing the optic disk and similar blood vessels from the eye image so as to reduce the size and the memory space, the eye images take. The pre-processed image was used for feature selection and the features selected were used for classification. Support vector machine was reported to have an average accuracy of 90%. The retina data used in this research were gotten from patients in an eye care hospital.

Evirgen and Çerkezi (2004) presented a model for the prediction of diabetes retinopathy using Naïve Bayes using a dataset obtained from a hospital and reported that Naïve Bayes gave an accuracy of 89%.

3   Methodology

3.1   The Approach

The proposed system is to determine the effectiveness of using the same algorithm for feature selection and classification at the same time. The data mining algorithms considered are k-nearest neighbor, J48 (decision tree algorithm), support vector machines and multilayer perceptron. The algorithms are applied individually on the dataset as classifiers without feature selection and then each algorithm is applied on the dataset first as a feature selector and then as a classifier. The algorithms will be compared in terms of their accuracy and sensitivity. The data mining software to be used for carrying out this research is "WEKA" – (Waikato Environment for Knowledge Analysis) tool.

3.2 Data Collection

The dataset used in this research is the Diabetes Retinopathy Debrecen dataset from the University of California, Irvine (UCI) repository of machine learning databases. The dataset was provided by some researchers from the University of Debrecen, Hungary containing features extracted from the Messidor image set to predict whether an eye image contains signs of diabetic retinopathy or not. The research paper on the work done which generated the dataset is (Antal and Hajdu 2014). The dataset contains 1151 instances with 19 attributes each and a binary outcome feature as to whether the instance has signs of diabetic retinopathy or not.

3.3 Dataset Pre-processing

The dataset is already in arff format which is one of the required formats for dataset used with WEKA. No pre-processing was done for the application of the same algorithm with and without feature selection.

3.4 System Architecture

In Fig. 1, the dataset of diabetes retinopathy is classified with and without feature selection on each algorithm namely k-nearest neighbor, J48 (decision tree algorithm), support vector machines and multilayer perceptron. The labels with feature selection using NN, feature selection using J48, feature selection using SVM, feature selection using MLP connote, applying feature selection on those algorithms before classifying each, to predict the presence of diabetes retinopathy. The label with applying classifiers (J48, KNN, MLP, SVM) denote performing classification on each algorithm without feature selection.

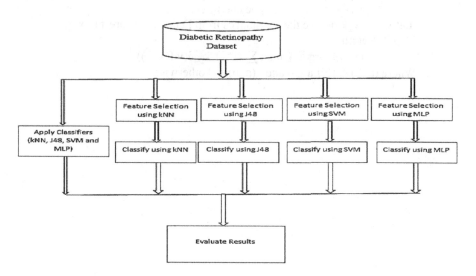

Fig. 1. System architecture

3.5   System Pseudocode

Step 1: Collect dataset
Step 2: Classify using kNN algorithm and record the result
Step 3: Classify using J48 algorithm and record the result
Step 4: Classify using SVM algorithm and record the result
Step 5: Classify using MLP algorithm and record the result
Step 6: Select features and classify using KNN algorithm and record the result
Step 7: Select features and classify using J48 algorithm and record the result
Step 8: Select features and classify using SVM algorithm and record the result
Step 9: Select features and classify using MLP algorithm and record the result
Step 10: Evaluate and compare results.

In step 1, the data are collected from diabetes retinopathy debrecen dataset from the University of California which contain features extracted from the Messidor image set to predict whether an eye image contains signs of diabetes retinopathy or not. The dataset contains 1151 instances with 19 attributes each.

In step 2, 3, 4, 5 involve the use of J48, kNN, SVM, MLP algorithms respectively to classify he 1151 instances without feature selection and the results are recorded. In step 6, 7, 8, 9 involve the use of feature selection to classify the 1151 instances using J48, kNN, SVM, MLP algorithms respectively and the result of each is recorded. In step 10, the results obtained from classification without feature selection are compared with their respective classification with feature selection using the same algorithm.

KNN Algorithm
Training
Step 1: Build the set of training examples D.
Classification
Given a query instance x_q to be classified,
  Let x_1…x_k denote the k instances from D that are nearest to x_q
Step 2: Return

$$F(x\_q) = \arg_{v} \left[\max \sum_{(i=1)}^{k} \delta(v, f(x\_i)) \right]$$

Where (a, b) = 1, if a = b and –(a, b) = 0 otherwise

Decision Tree Algorithm

Training
DecisionTreeTrain(data, remaining features)
guess ← most frequent answer in data
If the labels in data are unambiguous then
    return LEAF(guess)
else if remaining features is empty then
    return LEAF(guess)
else
for all f ϵ remaining features do
NO ← the subset of data on which f=no
YES ← the subset of data on which f=yes
Score[f] ← # of majority vote answers in NO
            # of the majority answers in YES
end for
f ← the feature with maximal score(f)
NO ← the subset of data on which f=no
YES ← the subset of data on which f=yes
left ← DecisionTreeTrain(NO, remaining features \ {f})
right ← DecisionTreeTrain(NO, remaining features \ {f})
return NODE(f, left, right)
   end if

Testing
DecisionTreeTest(tree, test point)
If tree is of the form LEAF(guess) then
Return guess
else if tree is of the form NODE(f, left, right) then
    if f = yes in test point then
        return DecisionTreeTest(left, test point)
    else
        return DecisionTreeTest(right, test point)
   end if
end if

SVM Algorithm

Let $(x^{(i)}, y^i)$ be training data points
Step 1: Compute matrix $H = [H_{i,j}]$ where $H_{i,j} = y^{(i)}y^{(j)}(x^{(i)}.x^{(j)})$
Step 2: Select value β that controls misclassification.
Step 3: Obtain $\alpha = (\alpha_1, \alpha_2, ..., \alpha_n)$ by solving the following quadratic optimization problem

Maximize $(\sum_i \alpha_i + \frac{1}{2}\alpha^T H\alpha)$ subject to the constraints $\sum_i \alpha_i y^i = 0, 0 \leq \alpha_i \leq \beta$

Step 4: Calculate $\alpha = \sum_i \alpha_i y^{(i)} x^{(i)}$
Step 5: Identify the supporting vectors. These are all the points for which $0 < \alpha_i \leq \beta$
Step 6: Compute $b = \frac{1}{n_s}\sum_{s'}(y^s - \sum_s a_i y^{(i)} x^{(i)}.x^{(s)})$
Step 7: Compute $sign(\alpha^T x' + b)$ for the classification of the given point x'.

MLP Algorithm

Algorithm (forward pass)

Require: pattern $\vec{x}$MLP, enumeration of all neurons in topological order

Ensure: Calculate output of MLP

1: **for all** input neurons i **do**

2: set $a_i \leftarrow x_i$

3: **end for**

4: **for all** hidden and output neurons i in topological order **do**

5: set $net_i \leftarrow w_{i0} + \sum_{j\in} Pred(i)^{W_{ij}} a_j$

6: set $a_i \leftarrow f_{log}(net_i)$

7: **end for**

8: **for all** output neurons i **do**

9: assemble in output vector $\vec{y}$

10: **end for**

11: return $\vec{y}$

3.6   Parameters Used for Evaluation

1. Correctly and Incorrectly Classified instances: The correctly and incorrectly classified instances show the percentage of test instances that were correctly and incorrectly classified while the unclassified instances show the percentage of test instances incorrectly classified. The percentage of correctly classified instances are often called accuracy and the percentage of incorrectly classified instances are gotten by subtracting the correctly classified instances from 100.

 f TP = True positive
 FP = False positive
 TN = True negative
 FN = False negative

$$Accuracy = \frac{TP + TN}{TP + FP + TN + FN} \times 100\% \qquad (2)$$

2. Sensitivity: This is the proportion of people who have the disease and was rightly classified as having the disease. It is also known as recall or true positive rate.

$$Sensitivity = \frac{TP}{TP + FN} \times 100\% \qquad (2)$$

3. Time taken to build model: This is the time taken by the classifier to build the model to be used for classification.

4   Results and Discussions

Simulations were done by applying the four classification algorithms namely KNN, C4.5, SVM and MLP on diabetes retinopathy dataset, the same algorithms were also used in evaluating features using wrapper feature selection method and then used to classify after feature selection. The results are evaluated and presented as follows.

4.1   Experimental Results

Figure 2 shows how to load the data set into WEKA application. The data set is already in arff format, no pre – processing was carried out.

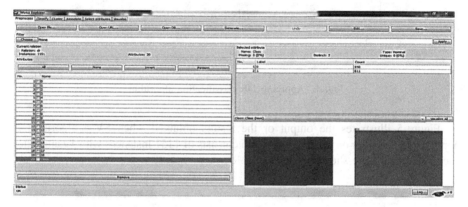

Fig. 2. Loading the data into WEKA

Figure 3 illustrates the output or the results obtained when KNN algorithm is applied as a classifier on the data set which consists of 1151 instances with 19 attributes each. The results are shown in the Table 1.

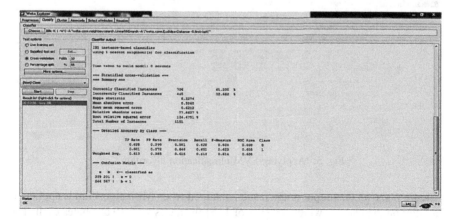

Fig. 3. Applying KNN classification algorithm

Figure 4 illustrates the output or the results obtained when J48 algorithm is applied as a classifier on the data set which consists of 1151 instances with 19 attributes each. The results are shown in the Table 1.

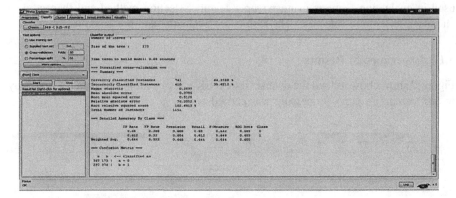

Fig. 4. Applying J48 classification algorithm

Figure 5 illustrates the output or the results obtained when SVM algorithm is applied as a classifier on the data set which consists of 1151 instances with 19 attributes each. The results are shown in the Table 1.

Fig. 5. Applying SVM classification algorithm

Figure 6 shows the output or the results obtained when MLP algorithm is applied as a classifier on the data set which consists of 1151 instances with 19 attributes each. The results are shown in the Table 1.

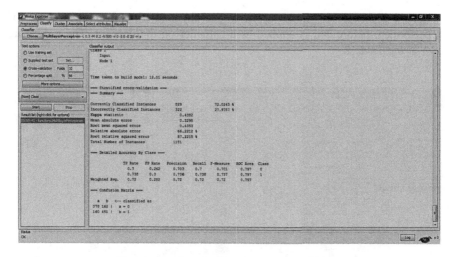

Fig. 6. Applying MLP classification algorithm

Table 1. Summary of confusion matrix for classification algorithms

Algorithms	True positive	False negative	False positive	True negative	Accuracy	Sensitivity
KNN	339	201	244	367	61.32%	62.78%
J48	367	173	237	374	64.38%	67.96%
SVM	142	398	83	528	58.21%	26.3%
MLP	378	162	160	451	72.02%	70%

Figure 7 illustrates the output or the results obtained when feature selection was first performed before KNN is applied as a classifier on the data set. The results are shown in the Table 2.

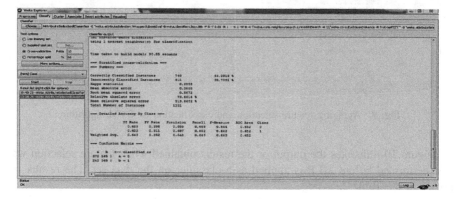

Fig. 7. Applying feature selection and classification on KNN algorithm

Figure 8 illustrates the output or the results obtained when feature selection was first performed, before J48 is applied as a classifier on the data set. The results are shown in the Table 2.

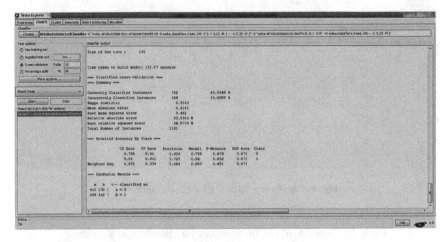

Fig. 8. Applying feature selection and classification on J48 algorithm

Figure 9 illustrates the output or the results obtained when feature selection was first performed before SVM is applied as a classifier on the data set. The results are shown in Table 2.

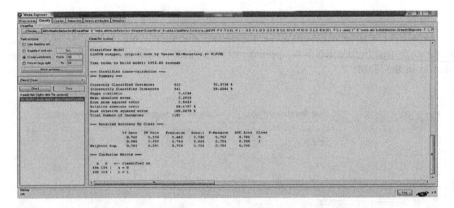

Fig. 9. Applying feature selection and classification on SVM algorithm

Figure 10 illustrates the output or the results obtained when feature selection was first performed before MLP is applied as a classifier on the data set. The results are shown in the Table 2.

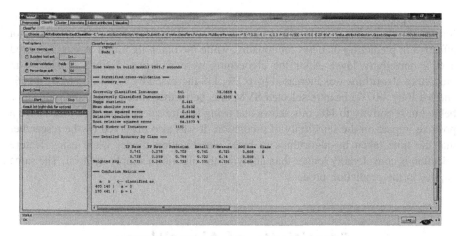

Fig. 10. Applying feature selection and classification on MLP algorithm

Table 2. Summary of confusion matrix for feature selection and classification on the algorithms

Algorithms	True positive	False negative	False positive	True negative	Accuracy	Sensitivity
KNN	372	168	243	368	64.29%	68.8%
J48	410	130	269	342	65.33%	75.90%
SVM	404	136	205	406	70.37%	74.8%
MLP	400	140	170	442	73.7%	74.07%

As depicted in Fig. 11, Comparing the accuracy of each algorithm with its feature selected version, it was discovered that the feature selected version achieves a better accuracy, while the difference is just about 1% in J48 and MLP, and about 3% in KNN, the effect of feature selected SVM was highly pronounced in SVM of which it's accuracy at predicting the presence of diabetes retinopathy was increased by 12.16%. This shows that while using the same algorithms for feature selection and classification have a positive influence in the accuracy of prediction, its influence is emphasized more on some algorithms than others.

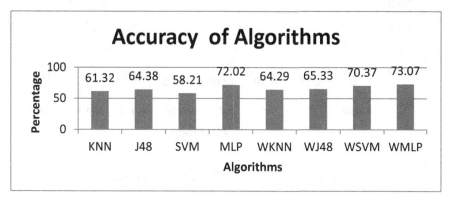

Fig. 11. Accuracy of algorithms in predicting diabetes retinopathy

As depicted in Fig. 12, when the individual algorithms were applied, SVM performed poorly as it was only able to achieve a sensitivity level of 26%, which is not effective in predicting diabetes retinopathy, while the other algorithm at least achieved a 62% sensitivity level. After the algorithms were wrapped, KNN's sensitivity in predicting algorithms was increased by 6.1%, J48 increased by 7.96%, SVM by 48.5% and MLP by 4.07%. Feature selected SVM thus performed much better and only came behind in sensitivity to J48, this shows that using feature selected for algorithms have a positive impact on the sensitivity of prediction. It was also observed by the researcher that the time taken by algorithms to build classification model when using feature selection is considerably longer than applying the algorithm simply by itself. The same applies in the prediction process

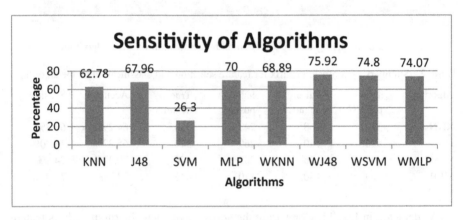

Fig. 12. Sensitivity of algorithms in predicting diabetes retinopathy

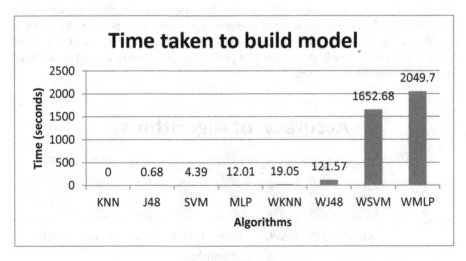

Fig. 13. Time taken to build classification model

As depicted in Fig. 13, the time taken to build the classification model was quite small, the highest time taken was by MLP which is 12 s, but for the use of feature selection for classification model, the time taken increased drastically with KNN that built its classification model initially now taking as much as 19 s. The models that took the longest time to build were wrapped SVM and wrapped MLP. It is worthy to note that the researcher observed that both the time it takes to build classification model and the time taken to classify are directly proportional, thus feature selected MLP took the longest time to classify.

5 Conclusion

Using the same algorithm for feature selection in predicting diabetes retinopathy disease has been shown to positively influence the accuracy and sensitivity of prediction having greater effect on support vector machines in comparison with other algorithms considered, but was also discovered to increase the time taken to build and apply classification model considerably. Thus apart from SVM in which it increases performance considerably, the time-performance trade off in other algorithms might not be worth it except in areas where it is not applied real time and any little increase in the accuracy of prediction is of great importance. This study shows that while using the same algorithm for feature selection and classification improved the performance of algorithms than using the same algorithm for classification without feature selection. In most algorithms considered, the improvement was most pronounced for support vector machines.

6 Recommendations

The results obtained from this research work, show vividly that the use of the same algorithm for feature selection and classification, improve the accuracy and sensitivity in predicting diabetes retinopathy. Therefore, the use of the same algorithm for feature selection and classification should be encouraged.

7 Future Work

Further research can be carried out in order to ascertain the effects; the use of the same algorithm will have in the classification in term of accuracy and sensitivity on other diseases. The use of feature selection and classification can also be applied on other data mining algorithms apart from the algorithms used in this research work, so as to discover those ones that it will enhance their performance greatly.

References

Aravind, C., PonniBala, M., Vijaychitra, S.: Automatic detection of microaneurysms and classification of diabetic retinopathy images using SVM Technique. In: International Conference on Innovations in Intelligent Instrumentation, Optimization and Signal Processing, pp. 18–22 (2013)

Antal, B., Hajdu, A.: An ensemble-based system for automatic screening of diabetic retinopathy. Knowl.-Based Syst. **60**, 20–27 (2014)

Bhaisare, A., Lachure, S., Bhagat, A., Lachure, J.: Diabetic retinopathy diagnosis using image mining. Int. Res. J. Eng. Technol. **3**(10), 858–861 (2016)

Elibol, G., Ergin, S.: The assessment of time-domain features for detecting symptoms of diabetic retinopathy. Int. J. Intell. Syst. Appl. Eng. **4**(Special Issue), 136–140 (2016)

Evirgen, H., Çerkezi, M.: Prediction and diagnosis of diabetic retinopathy using data mining technique. Online J. Sci. Technol. **4**(3), 32–37 (2004)

Jalan, S., Tayade, A.A.: Review paper on diagnosis of diabetic retinopathy using KNN and SVM algorithms. Int. J. Adv. Res. Comput. Sci. Manag. Stud. **3**(1), 128–131 (2015)

Mankar, B.S., Rout, N.: Automatic detection of diabetic retinopathy using morphological operation and machine learning. ABHIYANTRIKI Int. J. Eng. Technol. **3**(5), 12–19 (2016)

Ramesh, V., Padmini, R.: Risk level prediction system of diabetic retinopathy using classification algorithms. Int. J. Sci. Dev. Res. **2**(6), 430–435 (2017)

Rathi, P., Sharma, A.: A review paper on prediction of diabetic retinopathy using data mining techniques. Int. J. Innov. Res. Technol. **4**(1), 292–297 (2017)

Sujatha, S., Divya, D.: A narrative approach for analyzing diabetes mellitus and non proliferative diabetic retinopathy using PSVM classifier. Int. J. Adv. Res. COmput. Eng. Technol. **4**(8), 3341–3345 (2015)

Author Index

Printed in the United States
By Bookmasters